MODERN LANGUAGE TEACHING

The Reform Movement

MODERN LANGUAGE TEACHING

The Reform Movement

Selection and new introduction by
A. P. R. Howatt and Richard C. Smith

Volume IV

Britain and Scandinavia

London and New York

First published 2002
by Routledge
2 Park Square, Milton Park, Abingdon, Oxon, OX14 4RN

Simultaneously published in the USA and Canada
by Routledge
270 Madison Ave, New York, NY 10016

Routledge is an imprint of the Taylor & Francis Group

Transferred to Digital Printing 2006

Typeset in Times by RefineCatch Limited, Bungay, Suffolk

British Library Cataloguing in Publication Data
A catalogue record for this book is available from the British Library

Library of Congress Cataloging in Publication Data
Modern language teaching : the Reform Movement / selection and new
introductions by A. P. R. Howatt and Richard C. Smith.
p. cm.
Includes bibliographical references and indexes.
Contents: v. 1. Linguistic foundations – v. 2. Early years of reform
– v. 3. Germany and France – v. 4. Britain and Scandinavia
– v. 5. Bibliographies and overviews.
ISBN 0–415–25194–X (set) – ISBN 0–415–25195–8 (v. 1) –
ISBN 0–415–25196–6 (v. 2) – ISBN 0–415–25197–4 (v. 3) –
ISBN 0–415–25198–2 (v. 4) – ISBN 0–415–25199–0 (v. 5)
1. Languages, Modern–Study and teaching–History.   I. Howatt,
Anthony P. R. (Anthony Philip Reid).   II. Smith, Richard C., 1961– .
PB35.M592 2002
418′.0071–dc21   2001048567

ISBN 0–415–25194–X (Set)
ISBN 0–415–25198–2 (Volume IV)

Publisher's note
The Publisher has gone to great lengths to ensure the quality of this
reprint but points out that some imperfections in the original books may
be apparent.

Printed and bound by CPI Antony Rowe, Eastbourne

CONTENTS

CONTENTS

ACKNOWLEDGEMENTS

The publishers would like to thank the following for permission to reprint works in this volume:

Edinburgh University Main Library for permission to reprint Henry Sweet, *The Practical Study of Languages: A Guide for Teachers and Learners*, London: Dent, 1899.

Anna Marie Lindahl for the Estate of Otto Jespersen for permission to reprint Otto Jespersen, *How to Teach a Foreign Language*, London: Swan Sonnenschein, 1904 translation by Sophia Yhlen-Olsen Bertelsen of Sprogundervisning, Copenhagen: Schuboteske Forlag.

INTRODUCTION TO VOLUME IV

Overview

The Reform Movement derived much both from British philology (in particular, the phonetic work of Ellis, Bell and Sweet) and from Scandinavian scholarship in the fields of phonetics and English studies (Storm's contributions were important early on, as Jespersen's were to be later). Indeed, Storm and Sweet were on particularly good terms, and it had been at the suggestion of the Norwegian scholar that Sweet brought out his *Handbook of Phonetics* in 1877 (see Volume I). However, the Reform Movement was to have a much weaker influence in Britain than in Scandinavia, despite the sustenance it derived overall from the 'English school of phonetics' and the widely-admired contemporary contributions of Widgery (1888) and Sweet (1899) in particular. Jespersen's own (1901) *Sprogundervisning* (translated into English in 1904 as *How to Teach a Foreign Language*) was to constitute a fitting climax to the Reform Movement as a whole, concisely summarising the best of the practical ideas for modern language teaching in schools which had been developed since 1882, particularly in Germany and Scandinavia.

Britain

In Britain, despite the significant early contributions to Reform Movement theory by Sayce and Sweet (see Volumes I and II), awareness of Reform principles remained relatively low in the 1880s and 1890s. Towards the end of the 1880s two teachers in particular, William H. Widgery and W. Stuart MacGowan, did make great efforts to bring Reform principles into Britain from Germany, interpreting them in relation to local conditions and engaging in their own practical experiments (Widgery's (1888) pamphlet was particularly impressive in both respects, and was immediately recognised abroad as a significant contribution to the Reform literature). Together, Widgery and MacGowan organised a conference in Cheltenham in 1890 which was probably the first time for British (as opposed to foreign) teachers of modern languages to gather together, and this led on to the establishment of the Modern Language Association in 1892 (see Viëtor 1891 in this volume). Tragically, Widgery had died from a chronic kidney ailment in the interim, and the nascent movement for Reform in Britain was severely handicapped by the loss of his intellectual leadership.

However, there were many reasons for the slow progress of the Reform Movement in Britain, not just the loss of Widgery. Mainly it was a question of the continuing low status of living languages in schools, there being no equivalent of the Realschulen in Germany with their 'modern', relatively vocational curricula: grammar schools in Britain tended to ape the public schools in paying an excessive degree of attention to classical languages. Indeed, there was still very little training available at university level for potential modern language teachers (very little training in particular, of course, in the spoken forms of French or German) and study trips to the Continent were much more difficult to arrange than they are today. Throughout the period (up until the present day, indeed) modern languages were typically seen as subjects 'for girls' (cf. Bayley 1998). Finally, the continuing dominance of the university-led system of examinations (for some examples of typical questions see Appendix 2 to our General Introduction in Volume I) meant that grammar-translation was likely to remain entrenched in schools so long as the exams stayed the same; and this last factor, combined with the perceived need for enhanced teacher education, partly explains the strong emphasis which was placed on demands for improvements at university level by British reformers (including Sweet). Thus, at the end of his (1888) paper, Widgery calls for reform in the following terms: 'The change must come from the Universities: in particular they must change their method of examining for foreign languages which at present is little short of ludicrous' (p. 58). He goes on:

> Of the four elements of language, hearing, speaking, reading, writing, not a single one is adequately tested. The weight is thrown on translation and the exceptions in the grammar; the former the native speaker never wants, and the latter he absorbs unconsciously. So far can false views on the nature of language mislead us.

Another factor which may have hindered the translation of Reform principles into practice in Britain was the contemporary surge of public interest in the ideas of François Gouin in the 1890s (see Howatt and Smith 2000: Vol. VI), and the way this may have distracted attention away from Reform as this was being undertaken in Germany and Scandinavia. Effective publicity by Howard Swan and Victor Bétis, Gouin's translators, for their interpretation of his 'Series Method' (or, as it came to be called, 'psychological method') and, similarly, by the Berlitz chain of schools for their own favoured method, seem to have contributed to much misunderstanding of the nature of Reform Movement principles, in particular following the establishment of the Direct Method by official decree in France, in 1901–2.

Despite Puren's (1988: 121–67) concern to highlight the different principles or tendencies *within* 'Direct methodology' (or what we might prefer to term the 'Reform-approach') in France, there is no doubt that the well-publicised French official approval of the 'Direct Method' label at the turn of the century, associated with a lack of deep prior understanding of Reform principles in Britain, had some unfortunate consequences. Despite the attempts of Widgery (1888) and, especially, Sweet (1899) to establish a principled, relatively undogmatic basis for language teaching methodology, a certain reductionism tended to set in: ignorance of the true nature of Continental school-based reform was combined with a tendency to associate new methods of teaching with the narrower ideas of Berlitz and Gouin, popular at the time, with the effect that 'Direct Method' came – in most people's, including teachers' minds – to symbolise 'conversation lessons', 'teaching through actions' or 'teaching wholly in the target language', and little more. The association of Direct Method with these relatively narrow and utilitarian procedures simply exacerbated misunderstandings and resistance to new methods among school teachers in Britain, who were not, as a rule, particularly confident of their own abilities in spoken French or German.

Thus, promoters of Reform Movement ideas in the first two decades of the twentieth century (Kirkman and Rip[p]man, for example, and Palmer from 1915 onwards) found it very hard to get the 'true' message of Reform across to other teachers (similar battles against prejudice and misunderstanding were already being won by 1890 in Germany, for example, as has been indicated in Volume III).

By now, the pace of actual reform in Germany had left countries like the UK behind, and the international unity of purpose which had characterised the Movement's early years had accordingly been dissipated. Increasing nationalism and concomitant insularity in the years before the First World War may also have been factors preventing genuine understanding in the UK of the Continental, in particular the German reforms.

Thus, although there is no doubt that the 'Direct Method' was widely discussed and promoted (not least, by publishers) in the UK (and the USA) in the years between the turn of the century and the First World War, even gaining the apparent allegiance of fair numbers of progressively-minded teachers, there was also severe opposition, strengthened by misconceptions that Direct Method was synonymous with utilitarian and monolingual teaching ('courier French' was just one among many terms of disapprobation).

The opposition and reductionism which were involved here are clear targets of Kirkman's (1906: 204) riposte that there is 'not one reform method but several – good, bad and indifferent'. He complains that it is the bad or indifferent that are often being held up to ridicule in the UK and argues therefore for improved teacher training. The most prevalent misunderstanding he notes is that speaking is the goal, but he stresses, like the early Reformers, that it is 'part of a general education' in which reading is also important.

Direct Method teaching, he stresses, does not have a purely practical end, as this would be in the province of the 'technical institute' (that is, the province of the Berlitz or Gouin schools, for example). Similarly, in the USA, Krause (1916) struggled hard to rescue the Reform approach from reductionism on three fronts, stressing that it is not simply 'psychological' (as in Gouin), 'phonetic' (as promoted by some publishers at the time) or 'direct' in the sense of making exclusive use of the target language and conversational teaching (as in Berlitz). Back in the UK, Kirkman was still writing in 1925–6 to correct misconceptions that the Direct Method meant 'exclusive use of the foreigry tongue', but to no avail: Direct Method has now been, probably irretrievably, reduced to this one, single meaning in the English-speaking world.

Gilbert (1954: 15) notes the deleterious long-term effects of this reductionism on the reputation of the late nineteenth-century reformers in Anglo-American discourse on language teaching. Thus, he speaks of 'three illusions widely entertained about the early reformers; namely, that their teaching was superficial and not thorough, that they neglected grammar, and that they never used translation and so created confusion in the minds of their pupils'. As he says, and as Volume III, for example, has shown, 'None of these criticisms is true, at least of the German reformers. Many eyewitness accounts have, moreover, been given of their classroom teaching, all of which testify to its soundness and practical success' (ibid.).

In the UK, then, although the 'Direct Method' enjoyed a certain vogue in theory between 1899 and about 1924 (prompting Krause (1916: 12) in a 1912 report penned in America to say 'England, which is so often called conservative, has taken up the reform most energetically'), misunderstandings by its advocates as much as its enemies conspired to prevent its successful adoption in schools: as Hawkins (1981: 133) writes, 'the ferment of new theories left day-to-day teaching in classrooms little changed'. Nor – unlike on the Continent – was Reform ever officially endorsed; indeed a circular of 1912 cited by Hawkins (1981: 134) supports our assessment above in its sceptical remarks that although 'the impact of the Direct Method is acknowledged in theory, its principles . . . are not always understood'. Seven out of eight schools inspected for this report were seen to be using phonetic transcription (which at last began to enjoy a vogue in British schools in the first two decades of the twentieth century), but the quality of the teachers' work with the texts could hardly be praised. As Hawkins suggests (1981: 137), 'The momentum of change, slight as it was, faltered after 1914', due to factors including the effects of the First World War on staff recruitment, the severance of links with reformers in Germany, and an increase in prejudice against German and Germany generally. Other factors noted by Hawkins include: relatively negative reports by inspectors in 1916, 1918 and 1926, the effect of new national examinations set up in 1918 which further entrenched translation into the target language as the most prestigious component, and the failure of universities to take an interest in the teaching of languages or the problems facing schools (including in-service training). The 1918 Leathes Report summed up the situation by saying 'Direct Method has certain inevitable dangers . . . after all the effort that has been made during the last two decades this verdict is very disappointing . . . the falling off was attributed by our informants to misuse of the Direct Method' (cited by Hawkins 1981: 147). Thus, little was found to have fundamentally changed in schools in practice, despite an apparent dominance of the Direct Method in theory. Schools almost unanimously dropped phonetic transcription in one more swing of the pendulum in the 1920s and 1930s, and grammar-translation retained its dominance.

Although Daniel Jones and Harold E. Palmer (1877–1949) had carried the beacon of reform through the First World War years, and their efforts were to have an enormous influence on the teaching of English as a foreign language, Palmer's disappearance to Japan in 1922 (or 'export' of Reform to that country as it might be interpreted: see Smith 1999) meant, as with the earlier loss of Widgery in 1891, that the reform of modern language teaching in the UK remained leaderless, haphazard and unconvincing. Palmer's (1917) *Scientific Study and Teaching of Languages*, in particular, had been written with French teachers in the United Kingdom mainly in mind, and although this book is probably the most detailed and sustained proposal for reformed methods of teaching French in British schools that had appeared up to that date, he, along with the other, previous British reformers (Sweet, Widgery, Rip[p]man, Kirkman) tended, perhaps, to underestimate the insecurity that teachers feel when faced with having to speak in a foreign language to school children, and in particular to hyper-critical adolescent boys. The reformers also tended to overestimate the potential of phonetics to assist in the necessary process of change although Sweet, for one, believed that phonetic transcription could help in training non-native speaker teachers' own language abilities. What was most needed, probably, were improved courses of study at the universities, improved teacher training and extended periods of stay abroad – and these were relatively slow in coming in the UK. All in all, as Rowlinson (1994: 11) suggests, 'It is probably true to say that the Direct Method did not fail in England: it was never properly tried'.

Scandinavia

In Johan Storm (1836–1920) and J. A. Lundell (1851–1940), Professors at the Universities of Christiania (Oslo) and Uppsala, Sweden, respectively, Scandinavia had its own equivalents to Henry Sweet as intellectual leaders in the early days of Reform, and (as Passy's (1887) report in Volume II makes clear) they were not averse to agitating for Reform themselves. Storm, a Professor of English and Romance Philology, had published his *Engelsk Filologi* ('English Philology') in 1879, and this led, according to Passy (1887:

4) to the formation in Scandinavia of a new school of young phoneticians (called 'Jungfonetiker', after 'Junggrammatiker') who were to be in the vanguard of pressure for reform. Lundell (a Professor of General Phonetics and Slavic Languages) was younger, but also academically well-established enough to serve as a figure-head of reform. Although neither had gone as far as Sweet in offering theoretical statements on language teaching methods, both supported (and in Storm's case inspired) Reform Movement ideals implicitly through their own phonetic work, and explicitly through statements they made at the crucial August 1886 Nordic Philological Congress (see Passy 1887, in Volume II; and Palmgren 1887, in this volume).

The Reform Movement in Scandinavia may be said to have begun, though, with the rapid translation by the (very) young Otto Jespersen of Franke's (1884) pamphlet into Danish. This was published later in the same year, 1884. At the Stockholm Congress, Otto Jespersen rose to even greater prominence, together with a Norwegian teacher, August Western (1856–1940) who had already published a work entitled *Undervisning i nyere sprog* ('Modern Language Teaching') (Copenhagen, 1885, as cited by Passy 1887: 40). Western was a teacher in a school in Frederikstad, and Passy (1887: 31–2) describes a lesson he observed there. In his report Passy (1887: 6) also mentions a slightly later work by Lundell entitled *Om sprokundervisning (sic)* ('On Language Teaching'). Finally, Jespersen had published an influential article in a local journal in the intervening year, which was also cited by Passy (ibid.): 'Den ny sprogundervisningsmetoden' ('The new language teaching methods', in *Vor ungdom*, Copenhagen, 1886).

The Quousque Tandem Society for the reform of modern language teaching which was founded by Jespersen, Lundell and Western following the Stockholm Congress of 1886 (see Passy (1887: 32–3) for the founding statement – in a French translation – and Palmgren 1887 in this volume for a German version) rapidly gained members (as reported by Passy 1887: 33), and it appears to have published a series of newsletters, although Breymann does not list many issues in his (1895) bibliography, in Volume V.

Referring to the activities of this Society, Widgery (1888: 24) even stated that 'at this time, most activity seems to be going on in Scandinavia'. It is unclear, though, whether the initial impetus for reform was translating itself into practice as in Germany at this early stage.

Six years after the Third Congress in Stockholm (1886), the Fourth Nordic Philological Congress was held in Copenhagen, 18–21 June 1892. An anonymous (1892) report – probably by Passy, who attended the Congress – appeared in *Le maître phonétique* later in the same year, and Western and Jespersen are said to have defended Reform principles vigorously against attacks by traditionalists. By the time, six years later still, when Klinghardt (1898) reported on a lecture given by Jespersen to a meeting of teachers' associations in Copenhagen, it appears that the phonetic method was not yet strong in Denmark, although other Reform principles seem to have been making headway. Jespersen was himself, by this stage, firmly established in his professorship at the University of Copenhagen, and involved by virtue of this position in the training of all future secondary school teachers of English in Denmark (Sœrensen 1989: 38).

In the interim, government directives appear to have lent some support to Reform principles. In 1902, however, there was a step in reverse in Sweden, with an official government regulation recommending a return to explicit grammar teaching (Passy 1904). One year previously, Jespersen had published his classic (1901) *Sprogundervisning* (literally, 'Language Teaching', although the title of the (1904) English translation included in this volume was *How to Teach a Foreign Language*). There is no doubting, Jespersen's personal commitment to reform, and the importance of the leadership role he played throughout the period in Scandinavia generally: further detail is provided in our notes relating to his (1901/1904) *How to Teach a Foreign Language* below. This publication itself provided a masterly summary of theoretical and practical ideas developed over the preceding two decades in relation to school teaching, and brought the Reform Movement period to a more than fitting close.

We end this overview of developments in Britain and (to a lesser extent) Scandinavia with the suggestion that, although the contributions of both Sweet (1899) and Jespersen (1901/1904) to the establishment of a principled basis for language teaching in the twentieth century have been acknowledged occasionally in the past (see, for example, Roddis 1968, Titone 1968, Darian 1969 and Howatt 1984), the influence and continuing relevance of these two major works deserve much wider recognition.

Notes on individual works and authors

1. Widgery, W. H. (1888) *The Teaching of Languages in Schools*, London: Nutt.

When he wrote this, his major work, William Widgery (1856–91) was an Assistant Master at University College School, London. The second edition, published in 1903, contains a brief 'Life' by his sister Florence Tozer, on which the following details of his career are based (see also Hill 1894).

Widgery was born and grew up in Exeter, where he attended the local Grammar School. He was successful in his studies, and entered Cambridge University in 1874, primarily to study mathematics, although 'literature, languages, and art were not neglected' (Tozer 1903: ix). He graduated in 1879, despite having had to leave college for a year due to ill-health. After leaving university he began teaching at Dover College, then returned to Exeter, spending some time in the study of languages: 'To Greek and Latin he added French, Spanish, and Italian' (Tozer 1903: ix). At this time he seems to have considered entering the Unitarian Ministry, but he abandoned this idea and set to work on an essay on the First Quarto Edition of Hamlet which was awarded the Harness Prize at Cambridge. From 1880 to 1883 he taught at Brewers' Company's School, Tower Hill, and continued his linguistic studies (this time, Flemish) during a visit to his artist brother in Antwerp. He also found time to study Icelandic, Medieval Latin and Anglo-Saxon at University College, London (later he was also to study Hebrew and Sanskrit). In 1883 he was appointed Assistant Master at University College School, where he welcomed visitors to his classroom. He also began to engage in voluntary public work, becoming a member of the Stepney Committee of the Charity Organisation Society, Secretary of the Education Society, and Librarian and member of Council of the recently established Teachers' Guild.

In 1885 his first book reviews appeared, in the *School Board Chronicle* and the *Journal of Education*, and these were to be followed by many others, on books dealing with pedagogy and philology in particular. As his sister says, 'From this time until his death he was ceaselessly active except, as he said himself, on "days wasted in illness"' (Tozer 1903: x). In 1886 he went to Germany for six months, attending lectures on pedagogy and philology, visiting schools and attending an educational congress. In January 1888, at a Teachers' Guild Conference in London, he gave a paper with the title 'Teaching of Modern Languages' which formed the basis for a series of six articles on 'The teaching of languages in schools' in the *Journal of Education*. Almost immediately, in the same year, this series was reprinted in the form of the pamphlet which is included in this volume.

The breadth of Widgery's interests is apparent from the first pages, which consider the question 'Why do we learn foreign languages?' from a variety of perspectives, beginning with an attempt to show how the status of the teaching of modern foreign languages is linked to the developing status of the mother tongue. The bibliography at the end of the book takes in several recent articles from British educational journals, and Widgery attempts to link his arguments on the reform of modern language teaching to wider educational issues. The breadth of Widgery's reading is apparent also in his long, scholarly account of the origins and development of grammar teaching, going back to the classical period. He then turns to 'a discussion of the principles set up by modern philology, and their application to school teaching' (p. 19), and from this point onwards the influence of the Continental Reformers becomes more marked. Although Franke's influence appears particularly strong, Widgery also shows originality in interpreting Hermann Paul's (1880) *Principien der Sprachgeschichte* to describe what speech is, how it works, and how skill in speaking is acquired through practice and the use of analogy, rather than through grammatical analysis: 'We must learn to think *in* before we think *of* the language' (p. 39). The book is not only theoretical, however, and Widgery presents various very practical suggestions based on his own experience. This is necessary in the case of phonetics, he implies, because (p. 24):

Unfortunately, our [i.e. British] phoneticians are as little school-masters as our schoolmasters phoneticians; the expansive subtilty of Mr. A. J. Ellis, and the curt conciseness of Mr. Sweet, have deterred many from entering on the study.

The influence of the Continental Reformers (particularly, perhaps, Max Walter (see Brebner 1898: 14; Gilbert 1954: 16)) seems clear, also, in Widgery's exposition of practical ideas on the use of the reader and the inductive teaching of grammar (he particularly emphasises here the value of 'the unconscious method of imitation and incessant repetition' (p. 38). These ideas have the additional merit, though, of having obviously been tried and tested in his own teaching. As with grammar, Widgery then takes the reader back to first principles when he asks 'What *is* our object in [teaching] translation?' (p. 44), and the remainder of the essay is given over to considerations on vocabulary lessons (which are recommended) and expositions of etymology based on comparative philology (which are not).

Overall, as Gilbert (1954: 16) has remarked, Widgery is not afraid to state unpopular views (in this, he comes across as a less 'moderate' reformer than MacGowan – see below): he claims that the study of modern languages is superior to that of the classics, that the grammar method has failed completely, and concludes that 'our present method needs a thorough reform' (p. 58), beginning with change in the universities (which must offer more scholarships in modern languages and improve their examinations). Klinghardt wrote the following in a review of Widgery's pamphlet in *Englische Studien* (cited by Hill 1894: 242):

> I anticipate the happiest results from his entry into the continental discussion of reform on the art of teaching and his communication of our views to his English professional colleagues. I have no doubt but that Mr. Widgery will in no distant future be generally acknowledged as standing in the foremost rank of the promoters of a reformed method of language teaching, abreast with the most distinguished leaders of this movement.

Widgery's early death in 1891 put paid to these hopes, although the publication of his 1888 pamphlet made him quite well-known as a writer and speaker on education. A further paper, on 'The history of educational museums', was published by the College for the Training of Teachers, New York, and another, 'Class teaching of phonetics as a preparation for the pronunciation of foreign languages', was reprinted as a pamphlet, after first appearing in the *Educational Times* of January 1890. Widgery's sister remarks that he was acknowledged in Germany, 'not only as an educational reformer, but as a competent Shakespearian critic' (Tozer 1903: xi). He was, in particular, a frequent speaker at meetings of the Teachers' Guild, arguing in favour of, among other things, the improvement of teacher training, and improved methods in the teaching of mathematics. He contributed 'notes' on modern philology, and continued to write reviews until August 1891, when he died at his home in Exeter, having become ill through over-work in preparing for the Cheltenham Conference of 1890. As Gilbert (1954: 16) remarks, 'His untimely death [. . .] was a great loss to the reform movement – he had become absorbed in the German movement, and understood and interpreted it probably better than any other Englishman of the time'.

2. MacGowan, W. Stuart (1891) 'The reading-book as the centre of instruction in teaching a foreign language', ***Phonetische Studien*** **4: 83–90.**

The journal *Phonetische Studien*, founded by Viëtor in 1888 and edited by him since then, frequently carried reports of Reform activities in various countries and general articles on modern language teaching, as well as contributions in the fields of scientific and practical phonetics. The encouragement of reformed methods of language teaching was later made into an even more explicit priority (from 1893 onwards), with *Phonetische Studien* being incorporated within a new journal *Die neueren Sprachen*, which Viëtor also founded and edited.

In the 1891 volume, a full version of the paper read by W. Stuart MacGowan at the Cheltenham Conference of 1890 was followed by a report by Viëtor on the same conference (see below). MacGowan was a French master at Cheltenham College, where the conference was held, and was its chief organiser. In his paper he argues that grammar, as taught at that time, is an abstract and lifeless science: '*we must put it in a concrete form, if we are to give it any vitality*. This is brought about by bringing it into connexion with reading' (p. 84).

MacGowan's views on method as expressed in this paper appear to be similar to those of the more 'moderate' reformers in Germany (Gilbert 1954: 17), whereas Widgery's (in his 1888 pamphlet) appear generally to be closer to those of more 'radical' reformers such as Walter. Thus, MacGowan says, 'I fully recognise the importance of a systematic treatment of grammar in the reading-book, and do not therefore agree with those who would abandon grammar altogether' (p. 85). He is not 'anti-grammar', then, but must be learnt systematically, by a system of modified induction from carefully prepared and connected texts. He also sees a place for translation (p. 88), and even values the 'mental discipline' (p. 86) which modern language study can bring, rejecting a perceived contemporary 'tendency . . . to assign the dominant place to purely utilitarian subjects' (ibid.).

As we explain below, the motion this paper was supporting was carried unanimously at the Cheltenham Conference.

3. Viëtor, W. (1891) 'Dritte Jahresversammlung der Teachers' Guild und erster Englischer Neuphilologentag in Cheltenham', Phonetische Studien 4: 132–8.[1]

In April 1890, 'probably the first real conference of modern language teachers to be held in England took place' (Gilbert 1953: 1). Although the Cheltenham Conference had been preceded in the 1880s by annual meetings of the recently formed Société nationale des professeurs de français en Angleterre (an association for French teachers of French nationality), this was the first time for British teachers to take the lead in coming together, and for this William Widgery and W. Stuart MacGowan were mainly responsible. Like Widgery, MacGowan had made a close study of the Reform literature and visited schools in Germany in the 1880s (Gilbert 1954: 16), and he shared his friend's desire to convey what he had seen and learned to other teachers in England.

Both Widgery and MacGowan were already active in the Teachers' Guild, established a few years earlier, and they took advantage of plans to hold its third annual conference at MacGowan's school, Cheltenham College (10–11 April 1890), to organise a special satellite conference on 'The Teaching of Modern Languages' (11–12 April). From Germany they invited Wilhelm Viëtor and from France Paul Passy, and the programme followed the model of earlier conferences on the Continent, with five propositions being debated and voted upon.

On his return to Germany Viëtor published this quite detailed report on both the main Teachers' Guild meeting (pp. 132–5), attended by more than 500 participants, and the modern language teaching conference (pp. 136–8). Below we focus on the latter, but it is worth first noting the topics of discussions and papers at the main conference:

The conference started on 10 April with discussion of a recently proposed 'Registration of Teachers Bill' (p. 132), and this was followed with a paper read by Reverend T. Field, headmaster of King's School, Canterbury, on the need to establish an 'Educational Museum' (*pädagogische Museum*, p. 133). Widgery had already written a history of the subject (see above), and he contributed to the discussion. In the afternoon, Mr Courthorpe Bowen spoke on the teaching of English (*den Unterricht im englischen*, ibid.), saying that this should be carried on according to correct psychological principles, with less attention being paid to etymology and more to the development of language as a useful tool. Again, Widgery spoke up, supporting the speaker and complaining about the neglect of the mother tongue in comparison with the situation in France (probably he was thinking here of Passy's experiments in teaching children to read using phonetic script). The day ended with a paper by a Mrs Curwen of London on the teaching of music (*den Unterricht in der Musik*, ibid.).

The second day (11 April) opened with a paper on the transition from elementary to secondary school (*den Übergang von der Elementarschule zu einer höheren Schule*, p. 134) by Dr R. Wormell, headmaster of the Middle Class School [*sic*]. His suggestions on the need to expand opportunities for secondary education now that 90 per cent of all children attend elementary school received resounding support, and occasioned many contributions from the floor. Next Miss Beale (Principal of Cheltenham Ladies' College), spoke on the relative status which should be given to written and oral work, especially in girls' schools (*schriftliche und mündliche Leistungen in der Schule*, foot of p. 134), suggesting, in general, that the latter should be more highly valued, and the former kept within reasonable limits. Although her suggestions are not limited to a particular subject, she gives several examples from the teaching of languages. Following a lively discussion of this paper the morning session came to a close, and with it the conference of the Teachers' Guild proper.

This was followed, on the afternoon of 11 April and the morning of 12 April, by the Conference on the Teaching of Modern Languages which Viëtor and Passy had been invited to attend. The conference had been organised primarily by MacGowan under the auspices of the Teachers' Guild and the Grammatical Society (top of p. 136). The conference programme took the form of a series of debates on five motions (*fünf Thesen*, p. 136), each introduced by a short paper, supported by a second speaker (Motion 2 also by a third speaker), opened up to general discussion and finally voted upon. The conference ended up approving all five motions, numbers 1, 3 and 5 unanimously (*einstimmig*, ibid.).

- Motion 1: 'That grammar should be handled similarly in all five school languages' (*Gleichmässigheit in der Behandlung der Grammatik der fünf Schulsprachen ist wünschenswert*, ibid.). Reverend A. V. Vardy spoke for the motion, explaining that different grammatical terms were currently used in the teaching of different languages (the 'five' languages referred to in the motion are Latin, Greek, French, German and English (as mother tongue)), and that this caused confusion. This motion appears to reflect the interests of the Grammatical Society, which co-sponsored the conference with the Teachers' Guild. It was unanimously approved.
- Motion 2: 'That Phonetics should form the basis of all modern language teaching' (. . . *hat die Grundlage des ganzen neusprachlichen Unterrichts zu bilden*, top of p. 137). Viëtor himself spoke for the motion, giving a brief account of the German reform movement and mentioning Sweet. He also listed the resolutions passed at various conferences and expressed the hope that this conference, too, would accept the usefulness of phonetics. Passy spoke next, mainly about his own successful experiences with the 'phonetic method'. The use of phonetic symbols and spelling reform are not the same thing, he said, and he disagreed with those who thought phonetic transcription represented an

additional burden for pupils. Laura Soames (an enthusiastic advocate of phonetics in the British context, who was to publish her own *An Introduction to Phonetics* the following year (Soames 1891)) also spoke for the motion, saying the biggest obstacle to the introduction of the phonetic method in England was likely to be ignorance with regard to the sounds of English itself. The motion was also supported by Widgery, though he took the moderate view that phonetics is a subject for teachers rather than children, and the use of phonetics does not necessarily mean use of phonetic symbols. The motion was approved, though not unanimously.

- Motion 3: 'That the reading-book should be the centre of instruction in teaching a modern language' (*Das Lesebuch muss den Mittelpunkt des fremdsprachlichen Unterrichts bilden*, foot of p. 137). MacGowan's paper in favour of this motion is included in the present volume (see above). Both Widgery and Viëtor himself took part in the ensuing discussion, and the motion was unanimously approved.

- Motion 4: 'That the esteem in which grammar is held and its status in modern language teaching should be urgently reappraised' (*Die Wertschätzung und Stellung der Grammatik im neusprachlichen Unterricht bedarf dringend der Revision*, p. 138). Professor Barbiers of Cardiff began to speak for the motion; there was no time to complete or discuss his paper, but the motion was approved.

- On the following morning (12 April) there was discussion of Motion 5: 'That a proper supply of teachers be obtained by establishing Honours Degrees at the Universities which shall adequately test knowledge of the living language' (*Ein tüchtiges Lehrermaterial wird am besten dadurch gesichert*, etc., ibid.). Professor Meyer of Liverpool spoke for the motion, and it was unanimously approved.

The Cheltenham Conference served to draw attention to the need for reform in England, and it supplied a useful summary of the views of the reformers in Germany, France and England as given by their respective leaders. However, the conference resolutions addressed only some of the main Reform principles, and Widgery's intervention in support of a moderate view of the place of phonetics may have been crucial in ensuring acceptance of this particular motion. (Indeed, British teachers were to be slow to adopt phonetic script (Gilbert 1955: 8), although it did gain more widespread acceptance in the first decades of the twentieth century.) MacGowan's paper, too, presents a relatively moderate view of the role of the reader and inductive teaching of grammar. The final resolution, on the need to ensure an adequate supply of British teachers of modern languages, perhaps conveys the best picture of the state of affairs at the time: modern language teaching was mostly in the hands of 'native speaker' (foreign) teachers, and there was a clear need for reform at *university* level if modern language teaching was to gain anything like the status it was already beginning to enjoy on the Continent.

4. MacGowan, W. Stuart (1893a) 'Modern Language Association', *Die neueren Sprachen* **1: 282–3.**

In 1892, J. J. Findlay, writing in the *Journal of Education*, remarked 'It has been very interesting to notice the stimulus given to the teaching of Modern Languages by the Cheltenham Conference of 1890 and by other efforts of those who were associated with that meeting' (cited by Gilbert 1953: 1). Following Widgery's death in 1891 it was W. Stuart MacGowan who carried the torch of Reform in England, and primarily his efforts which led to the establishment of the Modern Language Association of Great Britain in December 1892. MacGowan himself reports on the steps which led to the formation of the Association in this brief note in the first volume of *Die neueren Sprachen*, under the rubric 'Associations' (*Vereine*). The note ends (p. 283) with an indication of the main focus for current reform efforts: petitioning the Universities of Oxford, Dublin and Durham to institute an honours degree in Modern Languages and Literatures (Cambridge had shown the way in 1884; Oxford was still dominated by the classics, with no honours degree even in *English* language and literature).

The Modern Language Association continued to be the main professional body for modern language teachers in Britain until 1990. Its conferences and journal *Modern Language Quarterly*, founded in 1897, provided much-needed vehicles for debate about all aspects of language teaching (Bayley 1998: 45).

5. MacGowan, W. Stuart (1893b) 'The relative educational value of ancient and modern languages', *Die neueren Sprachen* **1: 309–18 (Part I), 391–9 (Part II) and 437–49 (Part III).**

In 1893 Viëtor incorporated *Phonetische Studien* within a new journal, *Die neueren Sprachen*, expressly designed to focus on modern language teaching, as its subtitle makes clear (*Zeitschrift für den neusprachlichen Unterricht*). The new journal was initially co-edited with two friends from the Marburg region, Franz Dörr and Karl Kühn, both of them well-known 'names' in the German reform movement, and it continued to be the major journal for modern language teaching in Germany right up until the end of the twentieth century.

Following on from his participation in the 1890 Cheltenham Conference, Viëtor was evidently keen to support the nascent movement for reform in Britain, as is shown by his inclusion of contributions from MacGowan both in *Phonetische Studien* (see above) and *Die neueren Sprachen*. Nevertheless, the arguments presented by MacGowan in this particular series of articles were perhaps of most pressing relevance in Britain, where secondary schools (including grammar as well as 'public' schools) continued to be very much in the grip of the classics: there was no equivalent of the successful German attempts to place French and English firmly on the curriculum in the Real-schulen, and modern language teachers continued to feel a strong need to justify their very existence.

This series of three articles started life as an invited lecture given at the Taylorian Institute in Oxford on 17 May 1892. It seems possible that the invitation had come from Max Müller (1823–1900), Professor of Comparative Philology at Oxford, who later in the same year agreed to become the first President of the Modern Language Association (MacGowan 1893a: 282)). It is also more than likely that MacGowan wished to profit from the occasion to rally support in Oxford for the establishment of an honours degree in modern languages (see above).

In his lecture, then, MacGowan reveals himself a pragmatist who realises the necessity of attacking the classicists with their own theories. He studiously avoids utilitarian arguments (see p. 393), although he does refer to the strange belief (or 'anomalous contention', as he puts it) that 'the more Latin and Greek are for all practical purposes, useless; the more are they for all educational purposes, valuable' (p. 394). He goes much further than Widgery (1888) in asserting that the study of modern languages (including English) provides as much mental discipline as the study of Latin and Greek, and goes so far as to claim that 'modern languages are even better adapted than the classics to educate and develop the mind' (p. 445). Whether or not MacGowan was sincerely committed to such arguments, Oxford was to remain resistant to change, delaying until 1903 before finally instituting an honours degree in modern languages (Bayley 1998: 50).

6. Sweet, Henry (1899) *The Practical Study of Languages: A Guide for Teachers and Learners*, London: Dent.

Although the work of Henry Sweet was a major inspiration within the overall Reform Movement (see Volumes I and II), he was not a 'leader' of Reform in Britain in the same way as Viëtor, Passy and Jespersen were in Germany, France and Denmark, respectively. For example, he played no role at the Cheltenham Conference or within the Modern Language Association, with the leadership role being taken on instead by Widgery, then MacGowan, from a younger generation. Above all, Sweet was an academic philologist with a genuine interest in 'practical' language learning, but without a strong commitment to classroom teaching himself. It is interesting, though, to speculate how things might have turned out differently in Britain if he had gained academic influence sooner and been able to engage in classroom teaching at university level earlier in his career.

In 1884 Sweet had given the paper on 'The practical study of language' which is included in Volume II, and at around the same time he was busy producing several learning manuals, including the (1885) *Elementarbuch des gesprochenen Englisch*, also in Volume II. This line of work was to continue in the years up to 1899, for example with the publication of an English version of the *Elementarbuch* in 1890, and a beginner's manual and dictionary for students of Anglo-Saxon in 1897. Although he continued to expound his views on language study in the prefaces to these materials, Sweet was not to make any further significant contributions to language teaching theory until 1899 and the publication, 'out of the blue' as it must have appeared at the time, of his masterpiece, *The Practical Study of Languages*.

Indeed, from around 1885 Sweet's work appears to have undergone a general shift away from previous concerns which may have been linked to his failure to be awarded the newly-established Professorship of English Language and Literature at Merton College, Oxford, in that year (Wrenn 1946: 184). Thus, Wrenn (ibid.) emphasises the way Sweet left behind his pioneering work in the field of Anglo-Saxon studies, and turned his attention instead to the theory and practice of grammar, and comparative philology, publishing major works in these fields which included *A New English Grammar, Logical and Historical* (Part I, 1892; Part II, 1898) and *The History of Language* (1900). This general shift in interests may be one explanation of the apparently delayed publication of *The Practical Study of Languages*, which had existed as a 'complete treatise' in draft form as early as 1876 or 1877 (see the book's Preface, p. viii, and Sweet 1884: 577). In his 1884 paper for the Philological Society on 'The practical study of language' (in Volume II), Sweet had implied that he would soon be getting down to revising and publishing the treatise (Sweet 1884: 577–8). When it finally appeared, however, the book was 'not merely an expansion of these earlier efforts, but [. . .] the result of more matured thought and wider experience' (p. viii).

The Practical Study is unique in the Reform literature for presenting a wide view which extends beyond school teaching and applies general principles 'to different circumstances and different classes of learner' (p. v). Among these learners Sweet includes travellers, missionaries, and dialectologists, and he places special emphasis on self-study (p. vi). He also defines the 'practical study' of languages broadly, taking in not only the learning of modern European languages but also the study of dead and Oriental languages, and the relatively 'philological' pursuits of deciphering writings in unknown languages and dealing with unwritten forms of speech, 'for although such investigations have not always a directly practical aim, their methods are wholly practical' (pp. v–vi).

The book is innovative, also, in constituting an attempt 'first, to determine the general principles on which a rational method of learning languages should be based' (p. v), and only then to suggest particular procedures which might be followed in different circumstances. The same kind of approach was to characterise Harold E. Palmer's (1917) *The Scientific Study and Teaching of Languages* and (1921) *The Principles of Language-Study*, both of which built on Sweet's (1899) work to further establish the study of language learning and teaching on a firm theoretical footing. Sweet's own contribution prefigured post-Second World War 'applied linguistics' by almost fifty years (cf. Véronique 1992).

In 1901, soon after the publication of *The Practical Study* (1899) and *The History of Language* (1900), came 'the most incredible of all [Sweet's] academic defeats' (Wrenn 1946: 193), his failure to be appointed to the Professorship of Comparative Philology at Oxford. His achievements were finally acknowledged in the same year, with his appointment to the newly established Readership in Phonetics, but as MacMahon (1994: 99–100) remarks, 'This was small recompense for . . . the injustices he claimed to have suffered over the years at the hands of less-able academic colleagues'. The key to his lack of conventional academic success, according to many of his contemporaries, even his small circle of friends had been 'quite simply, his personality' (MacMahon 1994: 101): 'In a nutshell, Sweet was exceedingly sharp with his tongue (and pen) to colleagues whose views he did not agree with; diplomacy and tact were rarely in evidence' (ibid.). Sweet's particular love–hate relationship with Oxford was another factor: he had moved back there with his wife in 1894, and refused to consider working for other universities, in Britain and abroad, which had offered him academic positions (MacMahon 1991: 15–16).

Sweet's main publications after 1901 were a revised (1906) version of the *Primer of Phonetics* (originally published in 1890) and his last word on the subject, *The Sounds of English: An Introduction to Phonetics* (1908). He died in Oxford in 1912.

7. Palmgren, F. (1887) 'Verhandlungen zur Reform des Sprachunterrichts auf der dritten Nordischen Philologenversammlung zu Stockholm (10–13 August 1886)', *Englische Studien* 10: 335–52.[2]

In Scandinavia, Reform principles were first debated publicly at the Third Nordic Philological Congress, 10–13 August 1886, in Stockholm. In this report, F. Palmgren, a colleague of J. A. Lundell's at the University of Uppsala, reports on the discussions which took place. As at the two previous meetings, in Copenhagen in 1879 and Christiania (modern Oslo) in 1881, the 1886 Stockholm Conference included a special section on language pedagogy. This was especially well attended and involved a number of foreign specialists (including Paul Passy, whose own report on the conference is included in Volume II). Palmgren's report focuses on the second and final meeting of the section which began on Thursday 12 August and continued the following day. It was in two parts. The first (pp. 335–42) was a normal meeting which heard a paper by A. Drake (Nyköping, Sweden), followed the next day by open discussion. The second half (pp. 342–52) was a second, unprogrammed session involving about fifty participants which began with a discussion of the basic principles of reform (pp. 342–50) and led to an invitation (*Einladung*, p. 350) to set up an independent association dedicated specifically to the improvement of language teaching in Scandinavia. It carried the title 'Quousque Tandem' after the pseudonym used by Viëtor when he first published *Der Sprachunterricht muss umkehren!* (in 1882). The invitation includes a useful summary of the objectives of the Reform Movement at this stage (p. 351).

Part 1 (pp. 335–42) begins by describing how the meeting opened with a paper from Drake which asked the very general question: 'How can we provide a practical and psychologically sound approach to language teaching methodology in our schools?' The paper is more concerned with the organisation (*Anordnung*) of classroom methodology than with its procedures. In particular, it picks up Viëtor's point about the need for homework to consolidate material that has already been taught in class, not to prepare lessons in advance (in a usually inadequate manner). Drake's main points are listed on p. 338:

- The relationship between class work and homework must be rethought;
- The thorough and carefully designed teaching of grammar is central to the school curriculum as a whole;
- All language teaching in individual schools should be co-ordinated;
- Teaching materials should be consistent with the findings of linguistic science;
- The aims of Latin teaching should be re-examined;
- The provision of a comprehensive programme of spoken language activities is still a long way from completion.

Short individual comments from the floor followed and the meeting adjourned until nine o'clock the following morning (foot of p. 339).

The discussion of the Drake paper then involved contributions from at least six participants including Lundell (Sweden), Western (Norway) and Passy (France). Lundell offered four basic points which attracted general support (p. 340):

- Language teaching should be based on everyday spoken language (*die gesprochene Sprache des wirklichen Lebens*), and should therefore make use of phonetic transcription (*Umschrift*);
- Translation (*Übersetzung*) into the foreign language is damaging (*schädlich*) and should be replaced by free expression in the foreign language (*freie Production in der fremden Sprache*). Translation into the mother tongue should be curtailed (*eingeschränkt*);

- The basis of instruction should be connected texts (*zusammenhangende Texte*) and not disconnected sentences (*abgerissene Sätze*);
- Grammar should relate to the class texts (*sich an die Lecture anschliessen*) and be taught inductively (*inductiv*).

August Western (p. 341) repeated Sayce's motto: 'Language consists of sentences not words' (*die Sprache bestehe aus Sätzen, nicht aus Wörtern*), and Paul Passy lent his support to the use of phonetic transcription by describing his own experience with youngsters learning English in Paris. Since he adopted phonetic methods four years previously, the success rate of his pupils in exams had improved dramatically. (Passy 1887: 17–19, presents the above discussion 'verbatim'.)

Part 2 (pp. 342–52) opens with a description of how, after the formal conclusion to the section meeting, most of the participants remained behind to extend the discussion of Lundell's four basic principles of reform (see above), prior to the announcement of a proposal for setting up a new association. Lundell himself was elected chairman of this session. His first two points (referred to as 'theses' in the text) attracted the most comment.

Thesis 1 (pp. 342–5): *Everyday spoken language should be used in teaching and represented in phonetic transcription*. The meeting lent general support to this principle but there was some concern over the problem of homophones (for example, 'night'/'knight'); Western pointed out, however (p. 343), that context should provide a solution. The discussion ended with Passy's enthusiastic endorsement of transcription (pp. 344–5), which in his view should be used in English teaching for at least eighteen months, with another six months devoted to the transition to normal orthography. This became Principle 1 in the constitution of the new Association (see p. 351).

Thesis 2 (pp. 345–7): *Translation should be replaced by free production exercises in the foreign language*. This topic provoked varying views. At least one speaker claimed that the exclusion of translation might work for English but for 'more difficult languages' like French it was necessary, and another objected to the description of translation as 'damaging' (*schädlich*). The word was dropped from the final version: see Principle 4 of the new Association on p. 351.

Thesis 3 (pp. 347–8): *Language teaching should be based on connected texts, not disconnected sentences*. There was a general consensus on this point, with Johan Storm (Norway) saying that the use of disconnected sentences was neither theoretically right nor practically useful (*weder theoretisch richtig noch praktisch nützlich*, p. 348). This became Principle 2 on p. 351.

Thesis 4 (pp. 348–50): *Grammar should be based on the class texts and taught inductively*. The most detailed contribution came from Otto Jespersen (Denmark), who linked this point with the earlier discussion on translation. The basic reason for using connected texts in language teaching was to provide material for the discovery of the language system. Translation emphasised the wrong priorities by focusing the attention of learners on the mother tongue rather than on the specific features of the foreign language.

On pp. 350–1 is the text of the proposal for the new language teachers' association 'Quousque Tandem', with the final version of the four principles. It takes the form of an invitation signed by representatives of three Scandinavian countries: Otto Jespersen for Denmark, J. A. Lundell for Sweden and August Western for Norway. In the association's first year it attracted seventy-five members in roughly equal numbers from the three countries (see the footnote – added, in all probability, by Hermann Klinghardt – on p. 352).

8. Jespersen, Otto (1901/1904) *How to Teach a Foreign Language*, **London: Swan Sonnenschein, and New York: Macmillan, translation by Sophia Yhlen-Olsen Bertelsen of** *Sprogundervisning*, **1901 Copenhagen: Schuboteske Forlag.**

From the beginning Otto Jespersen had been at the forefront of the Reform Movement in Scandinavia, as Palmgren's (1887) report makes clear (see also Jespersen's own early (1887) article on 'Der neue Sprachunterricht' in Volume II), and he was to encapsulate his experience of the previous fifteen years in the book *Sprogundervisning* whose English translation is included in this volume.

After graduating from the University of Copenhagen in 1887, Jespersen spent almost one year abroad, visiting England (where he met Sweet, Ellis, Viëtor and Sayce), Germany (meeting the phoneticians in Leipzig, Sievers in Halle, and Klinghardt in Reichenbach), and France (where he stayed for two months at the Passys' in Neuilly-sur-Seine). During this period Vilhelm Thomsen, who had taught him phonetics at the University of Copenhagen, wrote to advise him to develop a specialism in English language and literature, since an academic post in that field was likely to fall vacant in the future. Jespersen took his mentor's advice and, following a short period in Berlin (where he attended lectures on Old and Middle English), returned to Copenhagen in August 1888. He then started work on a doctoral thesis on the English case system which he was to defend successfully in 1891. To support himself while writing his thesis he taught English and French part-time, and published a *Fransk Læsebog efter Lydskriftsmethode* ('French Primer in Accordance with the Transcription Method') in 1889. This was later (in 1895) to be followed up with the *Engelsk Begynderbog* ('English Primer'), co-authored by Christian Sarauw, which was the most widely-used introductory textbook for English in Denmark until well into the twentieth century.

Having gained his doctorate, Jespersen took up his automatic right to work as an (unpaid) 'Privatdocent' at the University, giving classes in Old English and Chaucer in order to prove his worth beyond 'merely' phonetics. This paid off when a Professorship of English Language and Literature was advertised in 1893. Despite being only thirty-three at the time, Jespersen was judged the most suitable candidate, and he was appointed to the Chair on 1 May 1893.

During the 1890s, Jespersen continued to be best-known as a language teaching reformer and as a phonetician, although he is now remembered among linguists primarily for his (mostly later) pioneering in the fields of syntax and language development. His contributions to phonetics in the 1890s included his (1889b) *The Articulation of Speech Sounds*, in which he presented a new analphabetic system for scientific transcription (in other words, a system, like Bell's 'Visible Speech' – see the introduction to Volume I – which does not employ roman letters). This was in spite of his support for the standardising of Sweet's Broad Romic for more practical purposes which was to characterise developments within the IPA at around the same time (see Volume III). Jespersen's (1897–9) *Fonetik* was also a major contribution, and was translated into German in 1904.

Although Jespersen's pioneering treatments of (English) syntax and the history of language were mostly published in the twentieth century, two fundamental principles on which this work was to be based had already emerged in his early academic work (see Haislund 1943/1966: 151–2), namely (1) his assertion of the close connection between sound and sense (or, as this was later to be expressed, form and function) in language, and (2) his strong belief in the idea that languages tend to 'progress' rather than 'decay', as they adapt to meet new communicative needs.

In both of these areas, Jespersen's emphasis on the importance of 'meaning' or 'function' as fundamental to 'form' continued to represent a refreshingly humane alternative to the predominantly form-focused views which dominated linguistics in the twentieth century (Saussure, Bloomfield, Chomsky, etc.); it is tempting to view this emphasis as a development out of his early work as a language teaching reformer, including his reaction against the sterility of grammar-translation, and the emphasis he placed on the integrity of connected texts as instruments of communication (as Hjelmslev (1942–3/ 1966: 171) has suggested, 'les seules influences qu'il a vraiment subies sont celles de sa première jeunesse. Jespersen est toujours resté ce qu'il était d'abord'). On the surface, though, Jespersen's ideas were developed against a backdrop of linguistic theory: he opposed the German neo-grammarians' 'mechanistic philosophy, according to which sound laws operate blindly [in the history of a language] like the laws of natural science' (Christophersen (1989: 10), asserting instead that many sound-changes are due to semantic, not to internal phonetic factors. In line with this view, Jespersen expressed his opposition to Romantic notions of the 'decay' or 'degeneration' of languages from purer primitive forms: instead, languages make progress, attaining greater clarity, regularity, ease and pliancy as they adapt to convey new meanings.

These developing views were first expounded in early articles, in the introduction to his doctoral thesis, and in his (1894) *Progress in Language with Special Reference to English*. They also found practical expression later on in Jespersen's support for the development of an effective international auxiliary language, with this project engaging his internationalist, progressivist and rationalist leanings. He was a leading member of the committee that worked out 'Ido', a reformed version of Esperanto (see Forster 1982: 126–7). Later, in 1928 and 1930 publications, he presented his own, alternative, system, Novial (NOV = new, I = International, A = Auxiliari, L = Lingue).

The linguistic work for which Jespersen is best remembered, however, was carried out in two or three main areas, mostly in the first three decades of the twentieth century: (1) linguistic evolution, most fully treated in his (1922) masterpiece, *Language: Its Nature, Development and Origin*, and reconsidered in his last book, *Efficiency in Linguistic Change* (1941); (2) syntax, with his points of view being summarised in two main works, *The Philosophy of Grammar* (1924) and *Analytic Syntax* (1937). Earlier, Jespersen had brought together his interests in syntax and the history of language in another original and brilliant work, *The Growth and Structure of the English Language* (1905); finally (3), he had also begun putting his syntactic principles into practice in his monumental *A Modern English Grammar on Historical Principles* (7 vols, 1909–49) (the last volume was published posthumously). His (1933) *Essentials of Grammar* provides a succinct summary of the main body of this work.

As with Sweet's *Practical Study* (and as we hope the above notes have made clear), Jespersen's (1901/1904) *How to Teach a Language* can only be seen as one major achievement among many in the context of a brilliant linguistic career. However, Jespersen, unlike Sweet, had *begun* this career as a language teaching reformer, had been a school teacher himself, and was to remain not only committed to the reform of school teaching but able to promote it in practice throughout his career, by reason of the prestigious academic status he had gained early on in his life (in this sense, his role in the 1890s and beyond was closer to Viëtor's than that of Sweet, who had little contact with (future) school teachers). Thus, during the thirty-two years between his appointment in 1893 and his retirement from the University of Copenhagen in 1925 Jespersen was to make 'an outstanding contribution towards raising the professional level of numerous future teachers of English' (Sœrensen 1989: 38) – indeed, for a generation, *all* future secondary school teachers of English are said to have been taught by him at the University of Copenhagen (ibid.). Jespersen's own prior experience as a (part-time) secondary school teacher made him, like Viëtor in Marburg, particularly well-suited to the responsibility of preparing future teachers, and his familiarity with the practical problems of secondary school teaching is clear throughout *How to Teach a Foreign Language*, which provides a necessary counterweight in this respect to Sweet's *Practical Study*.

In this book, Jespersen advances basically the same principles which he had stated in his 1887 article for *Englische Studien* (in Volume II), though in greater detail: (1) the importance of spoken language and phonetic transcription as a basis, (2) the importance of connected texts with sensible content and limited vocabulary, and (3) the need for grammatical observation in close connection with the study of texts, though this should be limited to a minimum in the initial stages of learning. In this connection, Jespersen reaffirms his support for the analytic(al) method, or, as he terms it, 'inventional grammar' (not approved of by Sweet), which, in his conception, involves students going treasure-hunting in the text for examples on the basis of which they can form grammatical rules for themselves. The text can also be used as a basis for transformational exercises (whereby simple present sentences are transformed to simple past, for example). Jespersen is not against the use of systematic grammatical study, however, especially at later stages. Finally, (4) the role of translation should be severely limited, particularly translation *into* the foreign language. Instead, students should be engaged in more creative exercises, for example retelling the contents of the text, in their own words.

During his career Jespersen received many honours, including honorary doctor's degrees from three universities abroad, was a member of many academies and scientific associations, and was rector of his university for a year (1920–1), but he never ignored the importance of modern language teaching in schools. The effects of this commitment are made clear in the following overall assessment by his close collaborator, Niels Haislund, written in 1943:

> His revolutionary work for the improvement of the teaching of modern languages has had great effects far beyond the boundary of his own country. [. . .] In his opinion scientific work should be done for the sake of mankind, and he has tried to do his share. [. . .]
>
> He has always been a friend of progress and peace and advocated international collaboration. It is to be hoped that he will live to see a world at peace, a world in which collaboration between nations is again possible.
>
> (Haislund 1943/1966: 157)

Although this wish was not to be realised – Jespersen died in the same year, 1943 – his example and teachings live on, not least in his *Sprogundervisning*.

Notes

1 *Phonetische Studien* followed the same practice as *Englische Studien* (see the Introduction to Volume I) in capitalising only proper nouns and the first word in each sentence. However, to avoid over-use of '*sic*', we have capitalised all nouns in the title of this report and in our quotations from it here; the same applies to Palmgren's (1887) report from *Englische Studien*, discussed further below.
2 See note 1.

References

Anon. [Passy, P.?] (1892) 'Congrès philologique scandinave' (report on the 4th Scandinavian Philological Congress, 1892), *Le maître phonétique*, August–September 1892: 118–21.

Bahlsen, L. (1903/1905) *The Teaching of Modern Languages*, translated from German by M. Blakemore Evans, 2nd ed., Boston: Ginn (originally published by Teachers' College, Columbia University).

Bayley, S. N. (1998) 'The Direct Method and modern language teaching in England 1880–1918', *History of Education* 27: 39–57.

Brebner, M. (1898) *The Method of Teaching Modern Languages in Germany*, London: Clay.

Breymann, H. (1895) *Die neusprachliche Reform-Literatur von 1876–1893: Eine bibliographisch-kritische Übersicht*, Leipzig: Deichert.

Christophersen, P. (1989) 'Otto Jespersen', in Juul and Nielsen (1989), pp. 1–11.

Collins, B. and I. M. Mees (1998) *The Real Professor Higgins: The Life and Career of Daniel Jones*, Berlin: Mouton de Gruyter.

Darian, S. G. (1969) 'Backgrounds of modern language teaching: Sweet, Jespersen and Palmer', *Modern Language Journal* 7, 8: 545–50.

Forster, P. G. (1982) *The Esperanto Movement*, The Hague: Mouton.

Franke, F. (1884) *Die praktische Spracherlernung auf Grund der Psychologie und der Physiologie der Sprache dargestellt*, Heilbronn: Henniger.

Gilbert, M. (1953) 'The origins of the reform movement in modern language teaching in England' (Part I), *Research Review* (Institute of Education, University of Durham) 4: 1–9.

Gilbert, M. (1954) 'The origins of the reform movement in modern language teaching in England: Part II', *Research Review* (Institute of Education, University of Durham) 5: 9–18.

Gilbert, M. (1955) 'The origins of the reform movement in modern language teaching in England: Part III', *Research Review* (Institute of Education, University of Durham) 6: 1–10.

Haislund, N. (1943/1966) 'Otto Jespersen', *Englische Studien* 75: 273–83, reprinted in Sebeok, T. A. (ed.) (1966) *Portraits of Linguists: A Biographical Source Book for the History of Western Linguistics, 1746–1963*, Volume 2. Bloomington: Indiana University Press, pp. 148–57.

Hawkins, E. (1981) *Modern Languages in the Curriculum*, Cambridge: Cambridge University Press.

Hill, W. K. (1984) *William Henry Widgery, Schoolmaster: A Descriptive and Critical Account of His Life, Work and Character*, London: Nutt.

Hjelmslev, Louis (1942–3/1966) 'Nécrologie Otto Jespersen', *Acta Linguistica* 3: 119–30, reprinted in Sebeok, T. A. (ed.) (1966) *Portraits of Linguists: A Biographical Source Book for the History of Western Linguistics, 1746–1963*, Volume 2. Bloomington: Indiana University Press, pp. 158–73.

Howatt, A. P. R. (1984) *A History of English Language Teaching*, Oxford: Oxford University Press.

Howatt, A. P. R. and R. C. Smith (eds) (2000) *Foundations of Foreign Language Teaching: Nineteenth-century Innovators*, London: Routledge.

Jespersen, O. (1889a) *Fransk Læsebog efter Lydskriftsmethode*, Copenhagen.

Jespersen, O. (1889b) *The Articulations of Speech Sounds*, Marburg: Elwert.
Jespersen, O. (1894) *Progress in Language with Special Reference to English*, London: Swan Sonnenschein.
Jespersen, O. (1897–9) *Fonetik: en systematisk fremstiling af læren om sproglyd*, Copenhagen.
Jespersen, O. (1901/1904) *How to Teach a Foreign Language*, London: Swan Sonnenschein, and New York: Macmillan, translation by S. Yhlen-Olsen Bertelsen of *Sprogundervisning*, Copenhagen: Schunboteske Forlag.
Jespersen, O. (1905) *The Growth and Structure of the English Language*, Leipzig: Teubner.
Jespersen, O. (1909–49) *A Modern English Grammar on Historical Principles* (7 vols), Heidelberg: Winter.
Jespersen, O. (1922) *Language: Its Nature, Development and Origin*, London: Allen & Unwin.
Jespersen, O. (1924) *The Philosophy of Grammar*, London: Allen & Unwin.
Jespersen, O. (1928) *An International Language*, London: Allen & Unwin.
Jespersen, O. (1930) *Novial Lexike*, London: Allen & Unwin.
Jespersen, O. (1933) *Essentials of English Grammar*, London: Allen & Unwin.
Jespersen, O. (1937) *Analytic Syntax*, Copenhagen: Levin & Munksgaard.
Jespersen, O. (1941) *Efficiency in Linguistic Change*, Copenhagen: Munksgaard.
Jespersen, O. and C. Sarauw (1895) *Engelsk Begynderbog*, Copenhagen.
Juul, A. and H. F. Nielsen (eds) (1989) *Otto Jespersen: Facets of his Life and Work* (Studies in the History of the Language Sciences Vol. 52), Amsterdam: Benjamins.
Kirkman, F. B. (1906) 'Recent proposals in modern language instruction', *Modern Language Teaching* 2, 7: 204–7.
Kirkman, F. B. (1925–6) 'First principles of the Direct Method', *Modern Languages* 7, 1: 11–14; 7, 2: 50–7; 7, 5: 136–41; 7, 6: 163–73.
Klinghardt, H. (1898) 'Der Werth der Phonetik für den Unterricht in der Muttersprache und den Fremdsprachen', *Englische Studien* 24: 239 (Part I); 25: 162–94.
Krause, C. A. (1916) *The Direct Method in Modern Languages*, New York: Scribner's.
MacMahon, M. K. C. (1991) 'Sweet, Europe and phonetics', *Henry Sweet Society Newsletter* 17: 12–18.
MacMahon, M. K. C. (1994) 'Henry Sweet's linguistic scholarship: the German connection', *Anglistik* 5, 2: 91–101.
Palmer, H. E. (1917) *The Scientific Study and Teaching of Languages*, London: Harrap.
Palmer, H. E. (1921) *The Principles of Language-Study*, London: Harrap.
Palmgren, F. (1887) 'Verhandlungen zur Reform des Sprachunterrichts auf der dritten Nordischen Philologenversammlung zu Stockholm (10–13 August 1886)', *Englische Studien* 10: 335–52.
Passy, P. (1887) *Le phonétisme au congrès philologique de Stockholm en 1886. Rapport présenté au Ministre de l'instruction publique*, Paris: Delagrave & Hachette.
Passy, P. (1904) 'Recul', *Le maître phonétique*, September–October 1904: 126–7.
Paul, H. (1880) *Principien* [in later editions, *Prinzipien*] der *Sprachgeschichte*, Halle: Niemeyer.
Puren, C. (1988) *Histoire des méthodologies de l'enseignement des langues*, Paris: Nathan-Clé International.

Roddis, M. F. (1968) 'The contemporary relevance of three early works on language teaching methodology', *International Review of Applied Linguistics* 6, 4: 333–47.

Rowlinson, W. (1994) 'The historical ball and chain', in A. Swarbrick (ed.) *Teaching Modern Languages*, London: Routledge, in association with the Open University, pp. 7–17.

Smith, R. C. (1999) *The Writings of Harold E. Palmer: An Overview*, Tokyo: Hon no Tomosha.

Soames, L. (1891) *An Introduction to Phonetics (English, French and German)*, London: Swan Sonnenschein.

Sœrensen, K. (1989) 'The teaching of English in Denmark and Otto Jespersen', in Juul and Nielsen (eds), pp. 29–41.

Sweet, H. (1884) 'The practical study of language', part of the programme relating to the Thirteenth Address of the President, to the Philological Society, 16 May 1884, printed in modified spelling, in *Transactions of the Philological Society, 1882–4*, pp. 577–99.

Sweet, H. (1892) *A New English Grammar, Logical and Historical, Part I: Introduction, Phonology and Accidence*, Oxford: Clarendon Press.

Sweet, H. (1898) *A New English Grammar, Logical and Historical, Part II: Syntax*, Oxford: Clarendon Press.

Sweet, H. (1899) *The Practical Study of Languages. A Guide for Teachers and Learners*, London: Dent.

Sweet, H. (1900) *The History of Language*, London: Dent.

Sweet, H. (1906) *A Primer of Phonetics* (3rd revised edition), Oxford: Clarendon Press.

Sweet, H. (1908) *The Sounds of English: An Introduction to Phonetics*, Oxford: Clarendon Press.

Titone, R. (1968) *Teaching Foreign Languages: An Historical Sketch*, Washington, DC: Georgetown University Press.

Tozer, F. (1903) 'Life' [of William Henry Widgery], in W. H. Widgery, (1888/1903) *The Teaching of Languages in Schools* (2nd ed.), London: Nutt, pp. ix–xi.

Véronique, D. (1992) 'Sweet et Palmer: des précurseurs de la linguistique appliquée à la didactique des langues?', *Cahiers Ferdinand de Saussure* 46: 173–90.

Viëtor, W. (1891) 'Dritte Jahresversammlung der *Teachers' Guild* und erster englischer Neuphilologentag in Cheltenham', *Phonetische Studien* 4: 132–8.

Widdowson, H. (1984) *Explorations in Applied Linguistics 2*, Oxford: Oxford University Press.

Widgery, W. H. (1888) *The Teaching of Languages in Schools*, London: Nutt.

Widgery, W. H. (1890) 'Class teaching of phonetics as a preparation for the pronunciation of foreign languages', extracted from *The Educational Times*, January 1890. Publisher unknown.

Wrenn, C. L. (1946) 'Henry Sweet', Presidential address delivered to the Philological Society, 10 May 1946, *Transactions of the Philological Society* 1945, pp. 177–201.

1

W. H. WIDGERY

The Teaching of Languages in Schools

Source: London: Nutt, 1888.

THE TEACHING

OF

LANGUAGES IN SCHOOLS

BY

W. H. WIDGERY, M.A.,

ASSISTANT MASTER AT UNIVERSITY COLLEGE SCHOOL.

LONDON:

DAVID NUTT, 270 STRAND.

1888.

TO THE MEMORY

OF

MARY.

TEACHING OF LANGUAGES IN SCHOOLS.

WHY do we learn foreign languages? For two reasons, a lower and a higher—the lower simply utilitarian, the higher to acquire a new soul by penetrating into a new realm of thought. For England and Englishmen both reasons are of prime importance: the growing keenness of modern competition makes the former an imperative necessity if we are to hold our own in the world; we need the latter if we are to free ourselves from insular onesidedness.

Throughout the Middle Ages, and down almost to the French Revolution, the great weight laid on the teaching of Latin in schools was due rather to practical needs than to any claim for it as a superior instrument of culture. The educated man spoke his mother speech for every-day life; with his school speech he could address the whole of Europe. In the time of Shakespeare 70 per cent. of the books published were written in Latin. The need to know only two languages was undoubtedly a great boon, and had Latin been capable of development enough to satisfy the wider spiritual needs of our time the dream of Comenius would have been worthy of all pains to make it a living reality. Now the educated man is saddled with at least five languages, and we try, but try in vain, to carry in our schools the same heavy weight. This is too much of a good thing; something must be cut out.

Our great modern reformers, Rousseau, Pestalozzi, Froebel,

7

have been the sources of mighty inspirations; they have pointed out in the rough the paths along which we must travel. They failed in system. We need now rather some powerful organiser, well trained in philosophy, in logic, in psychology, one who will do actual school work for some years and then clear for us the jungle of educational literature.

Descartes married the algebra of the Arabs to the geometry of the Greeks, and laid the foundations of our modern mathematics. Our new educational reformer must combine the desire of Comenius for widening the realm of positive knowledge with Pestalozzi's enthusiasm for heightening the intellectual powers; he must wed the formal education of the Middle Ages to the spreading science of the moderns. Posterity will not turn to him for fresh inspiration or new life, but his work will be, so to speak, built into the human race.

Greek and Latin stand in the same relation. For new inspiration and hope we must turn ever and again to Greece, the bright home of our literature and art. Latin has had its day. In the intellectual world Rome is but the pale reflex of Athens, and we, more fortunate than the Middle Ages, can go direct to the source. Latin has died twice; once as the language of ancient Rome, a second time as the *lingua franca* of Europe: she is built into the framework of the world; cannot we let her rest there? For the future our school time must be saved by limiting the teaching of the classics strictly to the acquirement of the power to read them, except, of course, for the classical student, a specialist no less than other specialists; his practical control must pass up into conscious and scientific mastery.

But we shall be told we cannot understand modern Europe without a knowledge of antiquity. Well, the study of origins is not everybody's business, and our religion, our politics, our painting do not spring from Greece or Rome. The first small beginnings of our science are indeed found in Greece, but they bear no more comparison to our broadening stream than the aimless movements of a child do to the swift sure steps of a man.

Again, the classics are said to be superior to modern languages as a means of culture. Who has a right to affirm that this is so? The latter have never been seriously tried in schools. Before we can adequately judge any system we must see it from the point of view of its defenders. A greater authority than Boeckh we can scarcely desire. In an oration delivered in 1826 he says:—"Men keenly seeking reasons for the study of the literature and, more especially, the language of Greece and Rome have been able to find none better than that of the so-called 'mental training.' This, however, is not enough for me: as far as my experience goes men who devote themselves to the study of Greek and Latin grammar are not markedly superior to other mortals in the possession of well-balanced minds. Although the classics do indeed afford material fit for mental training, they should, I think, unless some more powerful reason can be brought forward, be banished from our schools." (R. V. Stoy, Encyklopädie, Methodologie, und Literatur der Pädagogik, 1878, p. 66.)

Another great advantage of the modern languages over the ancient as a school subject is the effective criticism to which our work can be subjected. If a Frenchman or a German comes into our class-rooms, he detects instantly the slightest mistakes in our pronunciation, in our language, in our explanations. Can the classical student obtain such efficient supervision? We doubt it.

Again, as we are nearer in time to our modern classics, not only do we understand them, we feel them. Antiquity is a long way off, and we lack the atmosphere in which its thoughts moved. Let us listen to Boeckh again. He finished a lecture on Pindar once with these words:—" Gentlemen, you have just heard the commentaries and the various readings of one of the finest odes of Pindar. I have told you all I know about them. If you ask me to point out the passages that moved Greece to a transport of admiration, I

must answer in all frankness and humility, *I do not know.*"
(Lévy, I., p. 20.)*

We cannot put our finger on the passages where Homer
nodded, nor point out what Vergil wished erased. In school
we must be content to understand the ancients ; the modern
languages we must learn to speak, to feel, to write. If our
scholars like to amuse themselves with the classics, as Littré
did with Old French, that is their business—it does not
belong to the school.

Another important task for the future reformer is the
effective grouping of our school subjects ; at present they run
in unconnected straight lines—they ought to spread in con-
centric circles. What, then, must be the beginning of our
language teaching? It must of necessity be English. Important as it may be for an English boy to learn something of
other tongues, it is still more important for him to know his
own. Around English, and around English alone, can our
teaching be properly concentrated; in English, and in English
alone, can we make any attempt at a proper study of grammar
as such, for in the mother tongue alone have we enough
preliminary knowledge to arrange into a scientific scheme.
And what a language to begin with !

Here let me quote, with especial pleasure, the words of an
English headmaster, one of the very few who have helped
their fellow-teachers by giving them the fruit of a ripened
experience—proud words written when Shakespeare was a
lad of eighteen, when England was gathering up her mighty
strength before she smote back Spain into darkness, to
blossom soon after into the splendour and glory of our
Elizabethan drama :—

"I love Rome, but London better; I favour Italy, but England
more; I honour the Latin, but I worship the English. 'Why,' he
cries, 'must we teach in Latin? Why not all in English, a tongue
of itself both deep in conceit and frank in delivery? I do not think

---

* The full titles of works quoted thus will be found under the
authors' names in the bibliography at the end.

that any language, be it whatsoever, is better able to utter all arguments, either with more pith or greater plainness than our English is, being not any whit behind either the subtile Greek for couching close or the stately Latin for speeding fair; besides. an English profit must not be measured by a Latinist's pleasure, which is not for studies to play with, but for students to practise."—(Mulcaster, p. 259.)

Are these the prejudiced words of an Englishman? We can confirm them three centuries later with the testimony of the father of Teutonic philology :—

" Among modern languages, English has gained more strength and vigour than any other, just because it has abandoned and put to rout its old laws of sound, while losing very nearly all its inflexions. On its wealth of unrestricted intermediate sounds—a wealth that can only be learnt but not taught—depends a genuine power of expression, such as perhaps never before stood at the command of any other human tongue. Its thoroughly intellectual and marvellously felicitous framework and development arose from a striking marriage of the two noblest languages of modern Europe, the Teutonic and the Romance : the one furnished the concrete foundation, the other added the intellectual superstructure. It is not without significance that the greatest and supremest poet of the modern world, as opposed to the classical poetry of the ancients—I mean, of course, Shakespeare— was born and bred in the English tongue ; indeed, it can full well claim to be a universal language, and it seems, like the English themselves, marked out to dominate in the future, in a still higher degree over all the ends of the earth. In wealth, in common sense, in compressed sequence, no other living language can be placed by its side, not even our own German tongue, which is torn and distraught as we are torn and distraught."—(Grimm, 50.)

The mere possession of our language ought to have put us in the very forefront of the world as philologists. " English is of all existing languages perhaps the best for explaining the development of language in general " (Tylor, 133). From the Teutonic words that passed into currency among the Finns and Lapps in the first century, we can follow the course of our language for close on two thousand years. We can see it pass from an inflexional stage, nearly as full as that of Greek or Latin, to the most analytic in the world; and yet, with all this incessant change, with this unceasing incorporation of new elements, we have retained much of the old. Our consonantal system is nearer than any other allied modern language to the Primitive Teutonic.

English may be roughly classed " as an isolating language which is passing into the agglutinative stage with a few traditional inflexions. Hence the value of English as a preparation for the study of language generally, when studied rationally : it enables us to watch many linguistic phenomena in the very process of formation." (Sweet, I., 491.) By a good preliminary training then in our own tongue, we ought to acquire a general framework into which we can place afterwards as many languages as we please. We have not enjoyed a good reputation as linguists, but with a proper change of method there is " no reason to fear that the English will prove in any way inferior to other nations ; in fact, the richness of our sound-system, both consonants and vowels, the delicacy of our intonation and stress distinctions, and the comparatively rational nature of our grammar ought to give us great advantages." (Sweet, III., 598.)

With regard to the study of English I venture to propose the following :—

Increase the reading-lessons in it ; let them be mainly in modern prose. Teach the very first elements of phonetics and grammar purely inductively ; pay special attention to the vocabulary, grouping the words which children meet in their reader under psychologic and grammatical categories. At ten, or earlier, begin to work backwards, say to the age of Anne. With Shakespeare, their attention should be directed to his variations from modern usage, and the beginnings of a sense of the development of language made. At eleven, we might start French, reading at the same time a little Chaucer. Between twelve and thirteen, we might just touch Old English by means of a short Reader with the text on one side and the necessary grammar on the other, some slight knowledge of the laws of language should be introduced, analogy and the regular changes of sound at least being fully illustrated. The child of twelve and a-half is now fit to begin German. After a year's study, bifurcation must come in; the future classical student could begin Latin at fourteen and gradually drop French, begin Greek at sixteen and devote his time to the classics. The student of the modern languages could now begin a scientific study of his three, keeping English always in the centre.

Before proceeding to develop the lines of a new method, we must examine that already in use ; it centres around grammar and translation. The mere phrase "grammar school" shows the great weight universally laid on the study of the formal side of language. Seeing the large amount of time devoted to it, we are justified in assuming that the teachers and the writers of our primers will be eager to appropriate the latest results of science, eager to welcome improvements from each and every source. Alas ! the history of their labours affords a melancholy picture of men's proneness to copy one another, and to repeat obvious errors because they seem honoured by age ; they should rather turn the fresh and free play of thought on their labours. We shall find one author in 1826 elaborately explaining that Latin had no article, and yet keeping *hic, haec, hoc* under that rubric in his grammar because he did not venture to depart from established usage !

GRAMMAR.

As the chief discussion of language teaching, if these lines are lucky enough to cause one, will centre around the grammar, a slight sketch of its history in England will not be out of place here. The materials were not easy to get, and the reader is requested to extend to the attempt the indulgence due to a pioneering effort. In the hope of the subject being taken up by some classical master, a fairly full bibliography will be found at the end.

The beginnings of grammar spring from the discussion whether the relation between a thing and its name is one of necessity or agreement. But the true or the false, said Plato and Aristotle, lies not in the single word, but in its relation to the other words in a sentence: philology thus became the handmaid of logic, and the parts of speech were determined according to its categories.

Through the textual labours of the Alexandrine School, grammar rises into an independent study. The τέχνη γραμματική of Dionysius Thrax, a pupil of Aristarchus, was rounded off by the syntactical labours of Apollonius Dyskolus in the second century A.D. (Brugmann, in Dr. Iwan Müller's "Handbuch der klassischen Alterthumswissenschaft," p. 3.)

At the very outset we find two schools representing the two sides of that duality which we are always meeting in language, "analogy" and "anomaly," the regular and the irregular, the old and new, the conscious and the unconscious; the system recognising the two and allotting to each its proper place has not yet been worked out.

From Chrysippus the belief in "anomaly" as the fundamental principle of language passed to Crates of Pergamus, who visited Rome about 159 B.C. He broke his leg in a sewer, and stayed in Rome to give lectures on Greek grammar. In the time of Pompey Dionysius, Thrax, came to Rome as the representative of the principle of "analogy"; he drew up a Greek grammar, his terminology and system were translated into Latin, and have travelled for two thousand years over the civilised world, serving unfortunately as a Procrustean bed in which other languages have failed to find rest.

Now the terminology of Dionysius was derived from Athens, where "the terminology of formal logic and formal grammar were the same." The categories of language, however, are congruent neither with those of logic, grammar, psychology, nor metaphysics.

Dionysius is the ultimate source of the grammars still in use in our schools: his method was founded on an empirical analysis of one language, and represents only one side of that language; others followed him like the blind led by the one-eyed. The scientific study of grammar thus inaugurated was zealously carried on by Stilo, Lucilius, Caesar, Cicero, Verrius, Flaccus, and Varro. The latter, in his educational treatise, takes grammar as one of the nine disciplines. About 70 A.D. Remmius Palaemon, a successful " coach " who lived the life of a blackguard and made £4,000 a year at Rome, was the first to reduce the labours of his predecessors into a school-book, the "Ars grammatica." He took the "eight parts of speech " from Dionysius. Palaemon, Mr. Nettleship assures us, wrote "without any philosophy at all."*

In Keil's " Grammatici Latini," 1857, we find that Charisius had arranged the Latin nouns into five declensions and the verbs into four conjugations, just as they stand at the present moment in the " Latin Primer." The unscientific intrusion of the consonant into the midst of the vowel stems still stands firm. In the fourth century Donatus, the teacher of St. Jerome, and the author of the famous saying, *Pereant qui ante nos nostra dixerunt*, cast his " Ars grammatica " into the form of a catechism, to which, perhaps, he owed his extraordinary popularity. It is so easy to give a boy so much to learn by heart and to cane him if he doesn't know it !

> Continuo auditae voces, vagitus et ingens
> Infantumque animae flentes in limine primo.

The cane has barred psychology out of our schools too long. The authority of Donatus lasted undiminished through "the age of tears," and his name became a synonym for grammar just as Euclid still stands, at least among us English, for geometry. He was the chief authority for Bede's " Liber de Arte Metrica" and the " Liber de Orthographia," in which he was followed by Alcuin. In 995, Ælfric drew up a Latin Grammar in English, based, as he

---

* " The conclusion to which my argument points is that the main outlines of the traditional Latin grammar, such as we find it in the numerous but often identical expositions which bear the various names of the later grammarians, Charisius, Diomedes, Pompeius, Donatus, Cledonius, and others, were drawn in the first century."—(Nettleship, 212.)

expressly tells us, on Priscian and Donatus. To it he added a Latin-English glossary, topically classified, and a "Colloquium" containing a lively discourse between the teacher and the scholar, types to which we shall have to return (Ten Brink, "Early English Literature," p. 106 ; R. Wülcker, "Grundriss der angelsächsischen Literatur," § 532).

As to the value of Donatus and Priscian, who have reigned so long over Latin Grammar, Mr. Roby tells us that they cannot be recognised as authorities for the grammatical usage of classical Latin, as they would think more of what Caesar or Pliny ought to have said than of what they actually did say (Latin Grammar, Vol. I., xxii.). Indeed, since the discovery of Sanskrit and the rise of comparative philology, our modern scholars *know* a good deal more of the Grammar than the Latins themselves did.

In the hope of finally extinguishing the heathen poets of antiquity, Alexander de Villedieu wrote three didactic poems to serve as a repertory for all knowledge. His " Doctrinale," or Grammar, was written in 1199 or 1209 for the *clericuli novelli*, who were supposed to know their Donatus ; but the latter, as well as Priscian, were gradually displaced by the " Doctrinale," which reigned paramount from the thirteenth to the sixteenth century. We may congratulate ourselves on not having had to learn Latin then.

The syntax for the next four centuries was virtually settled by the " Graecismus " of Evrard de Béthune, written in 1124 : the title of the book is taken from the tenth chapter, which contains some Greek etymologies. The popularity of the book was due to the versification of the rules. Both the " Doctrinale " and the " Graecismus " were pure memory books ; the teacher had to give the explanations.

With the Renascence in Italy matters began to mend. Petrarch awoke a better understanding of the ancients ; and Dante, by writing in Italian, began to make Latin a dead language, incapable of further development. Guarino da Verona and Vittorino da Feltre laid the first foundations of our modern school system, and under them Donatus and Priscian were replaced by the " Orthography" of Gasparino da Barzizza and the " Grammar" of Guarino. Lorenzo Valla was the first to break with Alexander,—" Ego pro lege accipio quidquid magnis auctoribus placuit; abeat iam barbarus Alexander et barbaram cum sua barbarie repetat patriam." Here we have a clear enough statement of the fact that the author rules the grammar and not the grammar the author.

The new impulse to a better study of grammar was brought from Italy by John Colet. In 1513, Linacre wrote " De emendata structura latini sermonis," the first systematic book, according to Eckstein, on the subject; it proved too copious for school use.

In 1525 Robert Barnes, at Cambridge, turned the students from the study of scholasticism to that of the classics; while twenty years later Thomas Smith was bold enough to praise his native tongue. With the rise of Protestantism, Latin, the official language of the Romish Church, began to fall into disrepute, and we now begin to hear of its value as a formal study. Melanchthon praised it for this purpose, as it clearly compels us to think; Johannes Sturm, the *praeceptor Germaniae*, who lamented that infants did not suck in Latin with their mothers' milk, made it his leading principle, and his influence is still felt. In his curriculum more than twenty hours a week were devoted to Latin.

Page after page had to be learnt by heart, and the time was quite taken up in hearing the " lessons." In the explanation of the authors, the connection of the thoughts was quite neglected; it was all grammar. (Eckstein, 557.)

From the preface to Thomas Hayne's "Grammaticae Latinae Compendium," published in 1640, the " judicious reader " will find an interesting sketch of the history of Latin grammar from the time of Henry VII. The source of reform in the beginning of the fifteenth century is at Magdalen College, Oxford. Annaquil, Stanbridge, Whittinton, and Lily carried the movement on; the latter spent some time in Rhodes and afterwards introduced Greek at St. Paul's. Besides the old Donatus and Priscian, the " Opus Grammaticum" of Sulpicius, published in 1494, served them as a model.

The diversity of grammars then was no less a difficulty than now, and Henry VIII. attempted some reform. Before the end of the century Lily's " Brevissima Institutio " held the field, and continued to do so for three centuries, lasting under the guise of the Eton Grammar down to our own time. Editions followed one another with great regularity from 1609 to 1836, in spite of an almost incessant series of attacks, comprising in 1706 a crushing critcism by Richard Johnson in his Grammatical Commentaries.

Even as late as 1861 "The School and University Eton Latin Grammar," by Roscoe Mongan, professed to combine the works of Colet and Lily. During the last century grammar was studied with great ardour in Scotland. The preface to Ruddiman's book on " The Rudiments of the Latin Tongue," Edinburgh, 1714, strikes again the note of dissatisfaction with the books in use. The conflicting opinions of grammarians are complained of, and as those " who are taught the Latin Tongue reap little other Benefit from it, than as it enables them to speak and write English with the greater exactness," he adds scraps of English grammar, while the rules for the Latin are given on the same page in both languages. A German edition by Stallbaum, in 1823, was used by Dr. Kennedy in preparing his " Latinae grammaticae curriculum," 1844. The Rudiments were published as late as 1855.

The change to the system now in vogue seems to date from an address on the study of Latin and Greek delivered by Prof. Long in 1830. He urged the use of the inductive method of modern philology, that in the hands of Bopp and Grimm had achieved such brilliant results. Dr. Allen published his " Etymological Analysis of Latin Verbs " in 1836. He made a " happy experiment " with his exercises, the results of which were published by the Central Society of Education in the

first volume. With 1838 came Dr. William Smith's " Latin
Exercises for Beginners " and the change to the Crude Form
system.

Dr. Kennedy spent five years over his " Curriculum "; in
method it agreed with the Eton Grammar " for it supposes
its rules to be learnt by heart." After again insisting on the
necessity of boys learning " by rote," the author hopes for a
time " when, among other pressing educational improvements,
the best elementary Grammars shall be appointed by authority
to be used in all the Foundation Schools of England," a wish
that unfortunately found a fulfilment. In the recently published " Revised Latin Primer " and " Shorter Latin Primer,"
no real change in method has taken place.

To a student brought up on the latest German philology,
" A sketch of the History of Grammar, being an introduction
to the Public School Latin Primer," published in 1868, reads
like the story of a bygone world. With the discovery of
Verner's law, the investigations on the vowel system of
the Arian languages now made accessible in Brugmann's
" Grundriss," and the beginnings of the study of comparative syntax, the whole aspect of our grammar has been
changed.

The evil of this persistent obstinacy in holding to tradition
we shall only realise adequately when we have completely
broken away from it. Still worse, the same method has been
applied to modern languages, and the grammars persist in
neglecting phonetics, in heaping exceptions upon rules
—or shall we say rules upon exceptions—and in keeping
doggerel, that powerful aid to the production of artificial
stupidity.

What, then, *is* grammar? " Grammatica quid est? Scientia
interpretandi poetas atque historicos et recte scribendi loquen-
dique ratio, ἀπὸ τῶν γραμμάτων " (Keil, VII., 320). This definition we have practically still further narrowed in our Latin
by leaving out the speaking. The source of our troubles is
making the *letter* and not the *sound* the ultimate element of

B

language. Even Grimm did not clear himself from the tyranny of the letter. Until we have a real living faith in the *spoken* language as the source of all our literature, and as the starting-point of all our scientific studies, we shall make no real progress with our language teaching.

Nay, the problems of Greek and Latin grammar, if they are to be solved at all, will be solved by methods and principles derived from the direct study of modern dialects and languages, for in the latter alone are we on ground where our general inductions can be controlled by direct observation.

Can grammar teach us a language? Are the complaints of its inadequacy to give a practical power to speak a foreign tongue confined to our modern reformers? Let us listen to John Webbe, who published in 1622 "An appeal to Truth, for the controversy between Art and Use, about the best and most expedient Course in Languages. To be read Fasting." "Grammar," he tell us, "is become a full-swoln and overflowing Sea, which by a strong hand arrogates to itself (and hath well near gotten) the whole traffic in learning, but especially for languages." In a long passage, bristling with names now happily forgotten, he shows how grammarians from age to age have quoted the defects and errors of each other. "A petition to the High Court of Parliament" a year later, points out with remarkable clearness the weak spot of teaching by grammar :—

"I had rather a scholar should remember the natural and received position of a clause by keeping the words always all together than understand the particular correspondence of the words, and thereby lose their proper places. For discretion and comparison of clause with clause will at length bring the understanding of the words, whether we will or no; but nothing will bring the true position of these words again by reason that our own doth therein still misguide us."

In 1720 we shall find J. Clarke, Schoolmaster at Hull, in a lively "Essay on Education," complaining that "boys of good parts spend five or six years in a Grammar School, without attaining so much of the Latin Tongue as to make sense of half-a-dozen lines in the easiest of the classic Authors."

In the present century, from Grimm downwards, complaints of the powerlessness of Grammar to teach a language effectively have grown in bulk and loudness, and the change they demand must come soon.

We may now pass, with a hope that the above sketch has not been too long or tedious, to a discussion of the principles set up by modern philology, and their application to school teaching. We must first endeavour to get some sort of clear idea of the nature of Language, turning our attention afterwards to Phonetics, the Reader and its connection with the Grammar, Vocabulary, Translation, and Philology.

The enormous advances made in this century, as compared with all that went before, must not dazzle us into the belief that the question of the origin and development of language has been by any means settled : we have made only the first beginnings.

One of the main hindrances to a just view of language has been the use of similes ; words were compared to the leaves of the forest, the old falling, the new putting forth fresh life. Language was looked on as a plant or an animal, as though it had an independent life of its own. Still worse, terms proper to morals were intruded into science ; and we hear of phonetic decay, loss, degradation, corruption, as if languages had in them something inherently wrong. The new recuperative force replacing and improving the old, was conveniently left out of sight. To speak of modern English as a corrupted form of the old is not less inaccurate than to call a modern rifle a corruption of an old flintlock.

The science of language was not so very long ago treated as a natural science ; it has now definitely taken its place as a mental science.

Speech is not a thing that can be handled or seen ; it is mental activity manifesting itself through physiological means. We cannot even strictly speak of speech as living ;

its life is less than the life of summer flies. Excited by the outer world, by the society in which a man lives, the mind sets the organs of speech in activity; the outgoing stream of breath is thrown into vibration. The air pulses to and fro; these strike the ear; the movement travels into the brain, leaving impressions behind that may last for a lifetime. Psychology, physiology, physics, physiology, psychology, these form the circuit along which speech travels (Preyer, 282—290).

When we speak we are quite unconscious of all the complicated movements in our mind and body. The proof of unconscious activity is one of the greatest triumphs of modern psychology; the neglect of this capacity of the mind is the chief defect of our language teaching. All that passes consciously into the mind remains unconscious as a potential working factor. By exercise power consciously acquired can be translated into power manifested unconsciously. In any language the mind forms psychologic groups, such for example as strong and weak verbs, the plurals of nouns, &c.; these groups are allied to others in a perpetual state of change and growth, as Paul has well shown in the first chapter of his *Principien der Sprachgeschichte.**

These groups must not be confused with the categories abstracted by grammatical reflexion, though of course they usually overlap one another. Before doing a piece of German prose, I have sometimes made the class run over the irregular verbs occurring in it; in spite of this precaution many of them come out weak, showing that an English boy forms unconsciously categories for his German. The neglect of this unconscious activity of the mind is the main source of the *stupor pædagogicus* in schools; the fault lies with us, the blame with the boys.

With the acquirement of what we consciously teach runs the unconscious formation of certain beliefs and prejudices.

---

* There is now an English translation by Dr. H. A. Strong.

By beginning Latin too early, we encourage the theory that languages are to be learnt by the eye, that the letter is more important than the sound, that there is no need to express one's own thoughts in a foreign tongue, that languages are built up mosaic-like out of paradigms and syntax rules, and many other views diametrically opposed to the truth. Of course, we do not wish to do all this; but we are guilty none the less, and shall continue guilty as long as we attend to the subjects taught rather than to the psychology of the child.

Language, then, is psychologic activity manifested through physiological means: it must therefore obey all the laws of psychology and physiology.

The whole process of speech consists in the reproduction by memory of forms already heard and in the shaping by analogy of new ones on their model. When a set of these groups has been made in the mind unconsciously, it is found that a considerable number of forms lie outside it: these constitute the " exceptions." Historically, they are the remnants of earlier normal groups which occurred in every-day speech so often that they became fixed in the mind firmly enough to resist change. Now, as these forms can be retained only by a pure act of the memory, the child is more likely to make mistakes in them than elsewhere, and a fair length of time must be allowed before we can expect them to be accurately reproduced. It is hard to imagine anything more unsound psychologically than the method in our grammars of putting a list of " exceptions " immediately after the rule, often without a single example obeying the latter. Apart from their being dug out of various strata of the language by the misguided industry of grammarians, they will probably not be met with in the school life of a boy, and they ought to be felt as "exceptions" when they are first met with—a thing impossible unless the mind has been for some time impregnated with the normal types.

Not only must our rule be invariably derived from the language, but enough examples must be given at a time to make the rule spring up as it were by itself; all that militates against it must be kept in the background. Small points, the writer has practically found, are usually resolved by three examples; harder ones, especially in syntax, by not less than five. This imperatively demands the most careful preparation on the part of the teacher, and a wealth of illustration that only a good practical command of the language can give.

By skilful questioning he must know how to entice out of the child what lies dormant in his mind. Under the right treatment the boy's face grows as still as water, and ripples into a smile when the unconscious knowledge rises into the light of the conscious. The mind comes down with a snap on the example and the rule, and it is no burden to retain them both.

We may now, under the guidance of Preyer (pp. 305—330), pass to a short sketch of the manner in which a child learns its native tongue. Roughly speaking, the conditions are the same at the beginning of a foreign language. At birth the infant lacks the anatomical, physiological, and psychologic means of speech ; all is as yet undeveloped.

In the production of single sounds vowels precede the consonants, those requiring the least exertion of the parts of speech coming as a rule, but not always, first. The law of least effort is not invariably followed in language. This will be more fully treated of under " Phonetics." The child rises slowly from sounds to syllables, from syllables to words, from words to sentences. The tone, the accent, the pitch of the voice arouse the child's attention rather than the separate sounds.

In the majority of children the capacity to understand spoken words precedes the power to reproduce them, as the impressive side is developed earlier than the expressive. In beginning a new language, therefore, the teacher must be content to give for some time before he demands anything in return. The seed must be left for a while in the soil of the unconscious, till the intermediate paths between the sensor centre for sounds and the motor centre for their reproduction have fashioned themselves (Preyer, 289, 320).

The child learns to speak by associating ideas which it already has with sounds imitated at first without any regard to meaning; the meaning is coupled to them later by association.

Again, the child obtains a complete mastery over the language spoken at home without the aid of grammar, dictionary, reading, or translation, of which we see and hear so much in school. The language is learnt entirely by the ear without the intervention of writing; it is concerned only with the needs of every-day life, and is a simple, unconstrained idiom in which all the words employed have a definite fixed meaning.

The thing and the word denoting it call one another up as readily as a ball rebounds from the cushion of a billiard table. The child learns the language as a harmonious whole—accent, intonation, sentence melody, and dialect, as well as the single sounds and words.

A child obtains complete control over the home dialect provided it hears that only and no other : the memory retains what the child can understand and finds interesting; all else is forgotten in two or three days. How many of our works of literature are read in schools because they are interesting to the master rather than adapted to the boy's capacity ?

The question whether a centre for language exists by inheritance in a child that has not yet learnt to speak must be answered in the negative; if it does not hear spoken sounds no such centre is formed. In this case the ganglion cells of Broca's centre are used for other purposes, or they suffer atrophy. In learning to speak, however, first the sound centre, then the syllable and word centre, and lastly the dictorium are gradually built up. By its own activity the brain grows (Preyer, 330). We must reproduce a like activity in our children when they begin a foreign language : and this must imperatively take place through the ear, and not through the eye, as in teaching Latin. This brings us to the discussion of Phonetics.

PHONETICS.

" Ohne Laute, keine Sprache."

To demand a knowledge of phonetics from the language teacher is to ask no more than a knowledge of his notes from a musician. Phonetics as such is not a school subject, but the master must be a phonetician, and happily a little phonetics goes a great way ; the difficult points in the science are very difficult, but there is a good deal of plain sailing. One of the great achievements of modern science is Mr. A. Melville Bell's analysis of the vowel sounds ; the Indians more than two thousand years ago had worked out the consonants with striking accuracy.

Phonetics are the solitary branch of philology in which England has added to the knowledge of the Continent; the young and vigorous school we have set going in Norway has just formed a society, the " Quousque Tandem," for the improvement of the teaching of modern languages. For our national honour, we English teachers ought to be the readiest to apply the results of this science to the art of teaching. Unfortunately, our phoneticians are as little schoolmasters as our schoolmasters phoneticians ; the expansive subtilty of Mr. A. J. Ellis, and the curt conciseness of Mr. Sweet, have deterred many from entering on the study. If the writer may offer any advice to a fellow teacher it would be, Read the portion in Huxley's *Physiology* on the organs of speech, get a human throat from a medical friend, or study a wax model—there is an excellent one at Guy's Hospital—and then work steadily at Mr. Sweet's *Handbook of Phonetics*. Some portions will have to be gone over many times, but when they are once mastered it is convenient to have them so short.

Parallel with the *Handbook*, his excellent little *Elementarbuch des gesprochenen Englisch* may be read. Johann

Storm's *Englische Philologie* is very clear and interesting; in it the reader who desires to extend his phonetic knowledge will find all the best literature mentioned. A more theoretical view of the subject in general can be obtained from E. Siever's *Grundzüge der Phonetik* (3rd edition).

The main objections against phonetics seem to be the learning of a new alphabet, and a vague sort of fear that English literature will die a sudden death if we alter our orthography. But we do not object to spend a little time in learning the Greek alphabet—one, too, that the Greeks themselves never saw ; as for the latter objection, it finds no harbour in the mind of any true philologist, but flourishes among the half-taught, who, if the truth were told, would probably confess that they fondly imagined the spelling of their Shakespeare to be the same now as when he wrote.

Whatever our object in learning a foreign language may be, whether we wish to speak it or only to read it for purely scientific or literary purposes, the actual spoken language of to-day must form the base. For practical purposes, errors of accidence or syntax are of less importance than imperfect pronunciation ; a language mispronounced is a language unrecognisable. On the literary side the beauties of style can only be *felt* by their distinction from the talk of every-day life; the spoken language is the only ultimate source of the literary, it is not by any means a corrupt form of the latter. For educational purposes, the spoken language is obviously superior to the literary as the starting point in our teaching : the vocabulary is limited in range, the words used have fixed definite meanings, the grammar is restricted, and, as the facts lie well within the knowledge of the child, his attention is concerned only with the form, he translates from the very beginning in block, sentence by sentence.

The pronunciation cannot be " picked up." An English boy may hear *Quelle* correctly spoken a hundred times; he will always pronounce it like his own *quell* till his attention has been directed to its formation. Frenchmen cannot understand our confusion of *pécher* and *pêcher*. Each language has its own delicate shades of sound carrying distinct differences of meaning; phonetics alone can enable us to pronounce them properly.

Throughout our language teaching, the study of English must always be several stages ahead, especially in phonetics, as our orthography is the worst in Europe, and consequently, English children have a confused sense of the connection between sounds and their written signs, and hardly any idea at all of their true formation. This blurred feeling is carried into other languages, and it is curious to observe how a scholar who shudders in grammatic pain at a wrong gender or a faulty construction, will make without a qualm gruesome errors in pronunciation, errors which a knowledge of the physiological production of the sound would remove at once.

Just as the infant lacks the physiological and psychologic means of speech, so too does the child lack them in the presence of a new language. Indeed, the child is somewhat worse off, as the tendencies produced by the native language stand in the way. For the physiologic side we need a thorough gymnastic of the organs of speech by means of our phonetics; for the psychologic side we need, by continued exercise *in* the foreign language, by repeating the conscious till it becomes the unconscious, to arrive at length at the *Sprachgefühl* of the foreigner.

The writer hopes to bring out a small book for teaching phonetics in schools. As it is almost impossible to write on the subject without new types, he must content himself now with a few remarks in the hopes of helping other teachers who may be groping towards a method. First write on the board a set of words like *pit, bid ; cab, gap ; cats, cads ; catch, cadge :* the difference between voiced and unvoiced sounds will be soon felt and lead up readily in the endeavour to explain where the vibration comes from, to a short physiological account of the chest, throat, mouth, etc. The teacher will discover that the class has peculiar views of its own—that the heart, for example, is in the backbone or that the alimentary canal is the place for ailments! In case an actual throat cannot be shown to the class, large diagrams should be used. A very good one is F. Techmer's *Wandtafel zur Veranschaulichung der Laut-bildung.*

The next step will be to determine the place in the mouth where the different consonants are produced; in choosing the order of the sounds we must work from the lips inwards. The class must not be helped too much, but left to think for itself. At first the answers will be very wild, but by pitting boys with the most divergent fancies against one another, clearness comes in time. Finally, by arranging the consonants into open (= spirant), shut (= stop), and nasals, we get the scheme shown in the *Elementarbuch* p. xxvii.; this table can be simplified by putting the voiced and unvoiced sounds together, and by describing *h* and *l* below it. Instead of *wh* I employ a "barred w," like a Greek ω with a bar over it, and *y* for *j*.

The boys copy this table on a large scale in black ink, afterwards the French consonants in red ink, and the German in pencil, thus bringing into relief the agreements and differences.

In order to avoid, as far as possible, any confusion between phonetic letters and the alphabet, I always print the latter on the slate with red chalk, made by dipping a piece of ordinary chalk into red ink. Boys will often produce a sound in chorus with the rest of the class that they seem unable to bring out by themselves; a gymnastic drill of the muscles regulating the movements of the parts of speech can be carried out by means of the teacher's hands. Let the left when outstretched mean "unvoiced," the right "voiced;" when the hand is raised the class must pronounce the "shut" sound, when lowered the "open." In going on to the vowels, the mystery "of sometimes *w* and *y*" may be explained by defining the sonant as the "syllable carrier," including not only the vowels but also, at times, *l, m, n,* and *r*; thus

SONANT.	CONSONANT.
i saving	saviour
u nudge	language
l ankle	anklet
m hansom	some
n written	ten
r represent	present

This will thoroughly impress on the class the inadequacy of the Latin alphabet to represent our sounds, and help to develop the feeling that the sound is more important than the letter.

For the vowels I prefer a diagram showing the actual place in the mouth where they are produced to the Bell-Sweet rectangle. The following triangle is very instructive :—

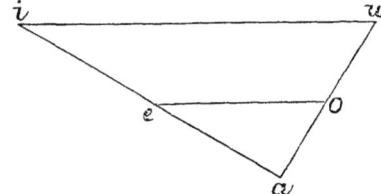

The child feels at once that any number of vowel sounds are possible, and that the signs give, so to speak, only the central positions. The *e* may travel upwards towards *i* and become "close" as in English, pronounced Inglish, or downwards towards *a* and become "open." Similarly for *o*. The reason for the mutation of *a* to *e* is obviously caused by an *i* in the succeeding syllable. When the space between the tongue and the roof of the mouth is still more narrowed *i* and *u* become consonants.

Again, *i* and *e* are "front" vowels, and have a tendency to palatalise *k* and *g*, showing us how *church* and *Sisero*, for example, were developed out of *kirk* and *Kikero*. When the French and German vowels are written in red ink and pencil on the same diagram, the striking differences in the vowel systems of the three languages are clear enough to make the dullest boy feel that he must really train his organs of speech to acquire a passable pronunciation.

The German sounds are thus shown in W. Vietor's *German Pronunciation*, p. 9, and the French by Passy in Vietor's *Phonetische Studien*, p. 24. Beside this, a diagram of the tongue, looked at from the roof of the mouth, should be given ruled in bands, with the corresponding vowels on them; opposite these bands on the right, the lip aperture, and on the left, an angle showing how far apart the jaws ought to be. Particular stress must all through be laid on those points where the English habits will have afterwards to be corrected: thus in "table," the *l* is sonant for English, consonant for French. We have a tendency to make our vowels end in "vanishes": thus pay = pe^i, no = no^u; this hinders us in acquiring the pure vowel sounds of French and German.

In English there is a general tendency to draw the tongue back, with the tip pointing towards the alveolars, while there is a strong disinclination to push the lips out—"It doesn't look nice," as one of my boys once told me. In French the lips are much more active both in rounding and in slit-like formations; in German the tongue is stretched straight out in the middle of the mouth, while the lips are more active than in English, and less so than in French. (Storm, 21; Sievers, 103; Bierbaum, 31; Techmer, 18, 19.)

In what order are we to teach foreign sounds? Here again we must observe the stages through which the child passes in acquiring its native tongue.

Although no general rule can be set up (Preyer, 431), we shall not go far wrong in following a remark of F. Schulze's in his book, *Die Sprache des Kindes*, p. 27. "The order in which the sounds of speech are produced in the mouth of the child begins with those that require the least physiological effort, and passes gradually to those that require the greatest."

At first the sounds are imitated mechanically, without any

sense of their meaning, just as movements of the head or hand are mimicked by an infant. The power to produce the single sounds precedes that of combining them (Preyer, 429—433). In choosing our type words for practice, imperatives should be taken as far as possible, as they satisfy the demand for the sentence as the unit.

Any phonetic system designed for school use should satisfy the following conditions:—

Each single sound must be represented by a single sign, and *vice versâ*; *h* as a diacritic is to be avoided.

It is better to invent new signs than to employ old letters, (as *c*, *j*, *q*) with a new value, nor must letters be taken over from one language to another, e.g., *ç* (= *ch* in *ich*), a phonetic sign in German and a letter in French. The cross associations are too much for boys.

Diacritical marks over the line are to be avoided; it is hard enough to make boys dot their i's.

The new signs should be as far as possible graphic: thus "open *o*" is better represented by an *o* left open at the top than by *ɔ* ("turned *c*"). For "open *e*" the horizontal bar may be left half drawn, and finished for "close *e*."

Names must be given to the new signs, and their place in the alphabet definitely settled.

It would simplify one's way through the maze of various phonetic systems if a list of words were drawn up containing the elementary sounds in English, French, and German; then each author in his own system could equate his signs to the list. This would have the advantage of clearly showing when two languages had the same sound; thus E5 = G8 might mean that the fifth vowel in the English list, say *men*, is the same as the eighth in the German list, *männer*, and so on.

Are we to begin with a phonetic transcription? Yes, decidedly, for French. The modern orthography is a very corrupt representation of the pronunciation in the seventeenth century, and is surpassed in badness only by the English, in which symbols mainly due to Anglo-French scribes of the Planta-

genet period, and imperfectly adapted to an Elizabethan pronunciation, are retained in the reign of Victoria! (Skeat,
Principles of English Etymology, p. 333.)

The first attempt to apply phonetics in teaching the grammar of a foreign language was made by W. Vietor in his
Englische Grammatik. The magic simplicity of our inflexional
system grows clear in its phonetic dress, and we proudly
recognise in our tongue two of the leading attributes of advanced culture, simplicity and wealth ; the swift grace and
easy movement of English are all lost because we make it
wade up to the knee in cacographic mud.

Let us turn to French. Plump go all the plurals of nouns
with the sole exception of the *cheval, chevaux* group, the
singular of the verbs has very nearly given up every sign of
person, the masculine adjective can be derived from the feminine by means of a few simple rules. (Vietor, 15.)

All the elaborate apparatus that we fondly imagined to be
grammar, turns out to be nothing more than the swollen hol-
lowness of a bad orthography. Like the portentous horror of
the genii in the Arabian Tales, the magic sound reduces them
to a small vase where they can be safely kept.

Finally, a few words as to a very real fear on the part of
many teachers. Things being as they are with an imperative
demand on the part of examiners for correct spelling, shall we
not hopelessly confuse our scholars and ourselves by the introduction of a phonetic notation? Experience alone can tell us,
and, as far as we can judge at present, it is not unfavourable.
According to Mr. Sweet (III., 582), it has "certainly shown
that children taught reading phonetically, will master both
phonetic and ordinary reading quicker than a class taught
unphonetically will master the latter only." M. Paul Passy,
a well-known French writer on our subject, says that a four
years' experience has shown the phonetic teaching to be practically superior to the old (*Englische Studien,* X., 335 and 412.)

Vietor's complaint, too, that English orthograghy is "an international misfortune which hits us and our German school-

boys," is worth some attention. The one thing at the present moment in the way of English becoming the universal language is our orthography.

What are the advantages of beginning with phonetics? First and foremost, they compel the child to watch himself, instead of learning parrot-fashion what he is told.

As the ultimate element of language really is the sound and not the letter, we follow the method of nature in placing the sound first. The grammatical forms are abstracted unconsciously from the spoken, and not consciously from the written language; when freed from orthographical confusions, they become few and simple. Compared with Greek and Latin, this simplicity is not poverty but ease.

The work in class grows more lively and interesting; the master influences the boys more immediately and profoundly. It is healthier to use the lungs than the eye and hand.

A theoretic and scientific knowledge of a language cannot be obtained in the future except on the base of a genuine practical mastery over it.

The capacity to express one's thoughts freely and directly in another tongue, demands considerable intellectual activity; the effort to attain it affords far more " training " than an excessive occupation with grammar.

After a little work at phonetics boys learn to "speak out" by themselves; our teaching is heavily discounted by their not hearing one another. A knowledge of phonetics is the foundation of shorthand.

If we still harbour doubt as to the wisdom of beginning with pieces phonetically transcribed, passing afterwards to the traditional spelling, we ought to be very clear on the difficulty of going from the spelling to the sound. Suppose some innocent Spaniard had learnt English by himself in the belief that the spelling and pronunciation agreed as closely as in his own language, while another had confined himself to books written entirely in phonetic characters, which would be the more advanced after six months' residence in England?

In beginning a new language the *form* in which ideas are expressed is new; the ideas, then, must be old and familiar, they must be drawn from every-day life. The mind cannot fix its attention at the same time both on the substance of thought and on the form in which it is expressed. In this first or phonetic stage our chief aim is to give a good pronunciation; if some of the common errors are allowed to pass unchecked at the beginning, they will last through the whole school life.

So far as the matter is concerned, Felix Franke's "Phrases de Tous les Jours" is an admirable model; if it were possible to arrange the material under the same grammatical categories as in Joh. Storm's "Französische Sprechübungen: Mittlere Stufe" (the only part as yet published), we should be fairly near perfection.

At first the weight of the work falls almost entirely upon the teacher; he must be the walking mouthpiece, grammar, dictionary, all in one. "The pupil must hear the sounds frequently, have his ears, as it were, bathed in the sounds, so that he can recall them mentally when he makes the effort to repeat them. . . . Subsequently the teacher should read frequently to the pupils, especially what they know; and do it in his best manner, not in that hurried indistinct fashion, with head depressed over the book, which teachers too often affect" (Ellis, 14). The point to be insisted on is the correct reproduction of *the sounds as sounds;* the meaning can be put into them as soon as they are impressed on the memory and fall trippingly from the tongue. The free English translation on the page opposite the phonetic transcription must be taken in sentences, with a careful avoidance of any attempt at word-for-word translation. We must use it, too, as sparingly as possible; it is generally possible to tell from a child's face and tone of voice whether he understands what he is saying.

As soon as a noun or verb occurs for the third or fourth time we demand the whole sentence in which it made its first and second appearance, thus getting all the help we can from

C

the law of association. In this way the child will unconsciously be getting ripe for the strict scientific view of a word as the molecule of a sentence—the atom being, of course, the sound—and for a sense of the intimate connection between form and meaning.

These sentences will contain most of the future "irregularities" of the grammar, but as they are not yet recognised as such they will cause very little difficulty. Ringing any changes on them should be avoided, as we want to approach the grammar later on with a mass of material under perfect control ; they can be gone over till they are known almost by heart. It is great fun to see two small boys taking the persons of a dialogue, while the rest of the class watches in envious admiration or sweeps down on the smallest mistake with a chorus of correction.

READER.

We now pass to the "reader," the centre of our system, the *corpus vile* from which we learn our orthography, our vocabulary, our grammar. Fables, letters, tales, descriptions of striking historical scenes, all in modern prose, carefully graduated and printed in the usual spelling.

We begin somewhat as follows. Let the teacher learn by heart the first piece, say Lessing's fable of "The Sparrows." A useful little exercise for him will be to transcribe it phonetically beforehand; he will make some interesting discoveries as to the accuracy of his pronunciation. Then with voice, eye, and hand all active, let him declaim the fable to the class, exaggerating just a little the sounds peculiar to the German. After telling the gist of the story in English, he will repeat the first breath-group of the German sounds, and after a slight pause pitch on some boy to repeat purely as a sound sequence. The whole class will be kept on the alert if the rule be observed of never letting the boys know beforehand who is expected to answer. After a whole sentence has been thus repeated, the teacher will give again the breath-groups and with them the English, *taking the words in the German order*, this being the natural one for a German—the object of the bald English is merely to give the meaning. Explanations must at first, of course, be given in English, but as soon as the class knows fairly well what a piece is about, and in all repetition work, the foreign language should be employed—our chief aim being to learn French or German, not English.

When the piece has been finished in this way the books may be opened, and one of the best boys put on to read and to give the English translation with the words in their proper order. Their previous phonetic training and the sound of the teacher's voice will be sufficient to counteract the perturbation caused by the new spelling; mistakes in pronunciation must, of course, be mercilessly rooted out. Again the books are closed, and a lively shower of questions, such as the native teacher would rain down on a reading class of his own, must arouse interest and develop fancy—things as important as the knowledge of genders or the irregular verbs. Halting attempts to reproduce the story can be improved and amplified, the children being encouraged to ask the master questions. Finally, an idiomatic translation from the master is followed by another declamation of the German.

As soon as a few pieces have been done in this way, a systematic exploitation may be commenced of the material acquired. First, the orthography. With the books open the teacher pronounces each word and asks whether the vowel in it is long or short. As the answers are given he writes the words down on the slate as in the annexed table. Curiosity will ask why he puts them in such different places.

VOWELS.

Short	allein, ausgebessert, denn, kommt, verlasst	double consonant.
	als, alt, fand, Glanz, Kirche, Nest, Sperling, ward, welche ...	two consonants.
	das, was	monosyllables ending in single cons.

Vowels.—*Continued.*

Long	gab, dastand, kamen	not denoted.
	wozu	
	nun, suchen, zu	
	grosse	*ss.*
	unzählig, ihr, Wohnung	*h.*
	sie, schreien, wieder	*ie.*
		aa, ee, oo.

The rules in the last column must be discovered inductively by the boys themselves. If the examples are not enough to make the rule show itself, more must be given, or the letters affected may be underlined.

Now for the grammar. Rule the slate in two, putting English on one side and German on the other. Take the nouns first, and elicit from the class the different ways of forming the plural in English; put against them the German, always with the article, saying nothing about gender yet. "We will do the adjectives and verbs a little later on." Below the piece the *primitive words only* should be printed in the same type and arranged in small groups according to the parts of speech; the other words can stand below in smaller type. The "lesson for next time" will be simply to learn by heart the vocabulary of the primitives.

The teacher should know with faultless accuracy the first dozen pieces or so, and, as new points in grammar turn up, refer back continually to examples that have already occurred. Boys are delighted to find that they really know more than they gave themselves credit for.

Preceding the reader should be a grammar containing only the absolute essentials. Here let no "exception" or list, even with the saving clause of being learnt as vocabulary, dare to show its head. "Single words and forms in teaching are a clumsy breach of psychology and pedagogy" (Vietor, 20). Spaces might be left for small important groups, such as the masculines in -*e* without mutation, and entered as they occur in the reader. Later on come occasional lessons devoted entirely to the grammar, the paradigms being taken with the book open and each word embodied in a sentence. Boys are not the only persons who cease to think when they say paradigms by heart: grammarians themselves occasionally do nod; *naissons* is somewhat late, and *ich starb* is forewarned with a vengeance—it will be so useful in the next world!

Another pedagogic error of lists is the juxtaposition of closely allied forms. After *der* Band or *die* See has become firmly fixed in the mind, we can safely confront them with *das* Band or *der* See. To give them all at the same time must produce confusion.

Neither is the power to say the paradigms correctly of very great value, for the good of repetition lies not so much in remembering the same impression of a thing at different times as in the recognition of it as one and the same in different relations (Perthes, iv. 20).

The right-hand side of the grammar should contain the syntax of the accidence on the left; the sentences must invariably be printed above the rule, and they, not the rule, are to be learnt by heart.

Considering the weight laid on grammar in our language examinations, the following more general considerations may perhaps find a place here.

GRAMMAR.

"Magis offendit nimium quam parum."

Grammar is a science presenting the facts of a language arranged under certain categories — descriptive, historical, logical, or philosophical. The science, hard enough in itself, is rendered needlessly harder by the obstinate persistence of grammarians in refusing to recognise that a large portion of language cannot be explained logically; it is retained purely by the memory, and, like a well-worn coin, everybody knows what it stands for, though the time and place of its stamping have been forgotten.

For a modern Englishman, it is no explanation to say that in *the more the merrier*, "the" is an old instrumental: all sense of the instrumental case died out of the English mind long ago. Our language is an abstraction made by taking the average speech of a number of Englishmen who do not differ largely from the normal type, as opposed to other normal types such as French or German. Each member of the English group has, in common with his fellow-countrymen, an individual manner of thought, an individual manner of expressing that thought by spoken sounds.

To learn a foreign language, then, thoroughly is no easy matter; we understand it when the same outward manifestation arouses the same inner movement of the mind, we speak it when the same inner movement is accompanied by the same outward manifestation, as in the case of a native.

All the reformers from Ratke down to Grimm have grown eloquent in combating the mistake that grammar can teach a language. "This," says the latter, "is an unspeakable piece of pedantry that we should find some trouble in making a Greek or Roman, who had risen from the dead, understand" (Bierbaum, 62). Not an exact knowledge of all the rules of the grammar, nor some skill in their application, will give the power of speech. There is no time for conscious reflection, the thought and the word must spring up in the mind simultaneously; and this power, this readiness, will never be acquired by the conscious method of reflection, but only by the unconscious method of imitation and incessant repetition.

The task of the grammar is a purely subsidiary one—it must classify *known* facts by making clear what the child has already half felt, half seen in his reader. Instead of appearing to settle everything, like a despotic governor whose reason or want of reason cannot be seen, the rules must be simply short and concise statements summing up the facts of the language. It might, perhaps, be a wise thing to put in the hands of the children a grammar containing only well-selected sentences *without the rules*, and to leave their induction to the teacher.

How many Englishmen could justify their use of the subjunctive or of the verbs of mood by quoting rules? Then why do we demand from English boys more than the foreigner himself could give? We must learn to think *in* before we think *of* the language. We want to sow with the left hand and reap with the right. Grammar is not elementary in the teaching of languages, and what we now ask from the lowest classes we ought to postpone to the highest. If we demand a legitimation from the rules of the grammar, why not refuse to receive a piece of reasoning unless accompanied by its rules of logic?

As soon as the reader has been finished and the study of works of literature begun, a large grammar, arranged somewhat like a dictionary, may be used. The paradigms given in the reader should be met here in the same type; the arrangement being mainly descriptive, with examples taken entirely from modern prose. In making groups for the nouns and verbs, only those that have at least fifteen or twenty examples should be given, all others being relegated to alphabetical lists. The forms can be marked as they are looked out, and then gone over at stated intervals.

As far as possible the grammar should, by means of different print, distinguish clearly between the logical and idiomatic sides of the language, as well as keep on one side all remarks not immediately useful in learning the language of to-day (Münch, 29, 33).

But to return to our reader. As soon as the first dozen pieces have been read, and the vocabulary of the primitives occurring in them thoroughly mastered, a search can be made for derivatives. Word-formation is as much an integral portion of a language as the accidence or syntax, and ought to receive the same share of attention. As a guide in the selection of the vast number of possible compounds, those forms only are

41

to be given which the child will find later on in the reader. These exercises are peculiarly fruitful, especially in German. A sense of the connection between form and meaning is gradually aroused, and the child is being properly prepared for learning the accidence of a synthetic language. To take an English boy who has no real sense of case, and to suddenly give him five in Latin is to demand from him too great a mental spring.

The teacher will find it advisable to limit himself very strictly as to the main points of grammar to be insisted on during each month ; examples for the accidence may be denoted by dots, and for the syntax by lines drawn under the words. After a while, some sharp boy will probably say, " Please, sir, I think I know why we are marking that word." " Well ? " " It's a comparative that doesn't modify." " Very good; now pick them all out and compare with the grammar." In this way the subjunctive mood can be very well attacked, and rules formulated for the particular cases ; good examples may be committed to memory.

As we work our way gradually through the reader, repetition must be incessant. A thorough and swift command over the back work is really as important in language as in mathematics; inaccuracy or hesitation is a fatal hindrance to the power of speech (Ellis, 11).

Together with many short pieces, fit for *intensive* reading, one or two easy tales of some length should be read *cursorily*, just for the fun of the thing—no more being demanded than a knowledge of the story. These pieces may be printed in one or other of the eight alphabets with which German youth is plagued. Considerable practice in the written characters is needed to decipher many notices posted on museums or University boards. To an Englishman there is some slight solace in this alphabetical luxuriance, as it affords a retort to rude remarks on the stupidity of our weights and measures and spelling.

Parsing at first must be very sparingly indulged in. If a

boy knows the plural of a noun or the parts of a verb, it is immaterial to him at this stage whether they are regular or irregular; that will grow clear when he has gained material enough to classify. A sharp look-out must be kept for idiomatic turns and phrases; they could be entered in an exercise book and learnt by heart. If we use a printed collection, the phrases removed from their context do not make a strong impression, and we run the risk of learning archaic turns.

This incessant occupation with a text in front of him, this continued return to material continually offering new suggestions and displaying unsuspected wealth, cannot fail to work back beneficially on the method of reading books in English. Our main object being to concentrate the child's attention on the language itself, dictation will become important as a substitute for written translation. The almost forgotten art of listening is cultivated, as well as the power of grasping with the ear the foreign sounds—the first and most necessary thing when we put foot on foreign soil. The pieces already studied intensively are the best for dictation, and, since it is hardly possible to write a single sentence in a foreign language correctly unless it is really understood, this exercise gives us a training in exactitude comparable to that of mathematics. Here alone in our language-teaching is there no escape, no loophole for mistakes. The exercises when corrected form good material for repetition work, as the words can be freely underlined. When the boys know that "places" will depend afterwards on a raking fire of questions in the foreign language strictly limited to the words underlined, they mark them with peculiar attention. After the piece has been thoroughly threshed out in this way, the papers are collected and the class left to give the substance in their own French or German, and to invent new sentences on the model of the old.

The main object of the reader being to give a thorough knowledge of the accidence and the first beginnings of the syntax, the number of pieces in it need not be great, and every piece should be read. For the middle classes in the school, French offers us a rich variety of stories in modern prose; good examples are harder to find in German. Some of these may be read chiefly for vocabulary and syntax, in order to prepare us for the poetry and prose masterpieces in the highest classes.

Although a considerable improvement has taken place of late years in the notes to school editions, we are still reminded at times of Goethe's remark that many books seem written not for us to learn out of them, but to show that the author knew something. Lives of the writer, biographical data about unimportant persons, æsthetic disquisitions far above the heads of the children, scraps of etymology, often wrong in themselves, and when right of small value in making the meaning clearer, had better stay away. The fear of the reviewer seems more present than the mind or age of the child. Some editors, wise perhaps in their own generation, credit the teacher with next to no knowledge or industry in preparing his work.

The notes must be worked out on a consistent plan for definite classes; explanations on things such as the foreign boy would need, being kept distinct from points of language. In the latter we need the pronunciation of proper names, the leading examples in the book of any difficult construction, paraphrases in the foreign language of important words with their synonyms, and, above all, the variations in the selected work from the modern prose of every-day life.

While the higher classes are reading the masterpieces of the literature, they might also have very short accounts of the foreign history and literature given them, written in language easy enough to be understood without the need of translation.

For the future commercial man, a short chatty book, somewhat on the lines of Becker's *Charicles* and written in the foreign language, would be extremely useful. To the merest skeleton of the history, geography, and government of the country, should follow accounts of school life, the manners and customs of the inhabitants, the famous sights of the leading towns, the money and metric systems, hints on etiquette, art, music, and the theatre, everything in fact that bears on the life of to-day.

What has become of translation, of exercises? Their limitation and partial extinction we shall endeavour to justify below. After three or four years' study of the vocabulary and grammar, entirely through the reader and easy prose texts, it is hoped the boy will be in a position to read literature as such, leaving all the paraphernalia of the earlier stages well behind him. We must endeavour to give him some foretaste of the sweets for whose enjoyment he has undergone so much drudgery : we approach the æsthetic stage of artistic enjoyment. While we gaze with rapt attention and drink in the beauty of the Venus of Milo, is our delight enhanced by remembering that the marble is made of calcium oxide and carbonic acid gas? It is an indignity to turn a masterpiece of literature into a happy hunting-ground for compound plurals or even for the rules of the subjunctive. Shall we learn anatomy on the bodies of our dead friends?

The crown and summit of the language master's activity is to make some of his sense for the splendour and beauty of foreign literature—some of his sense for the warm breath of humanity glowing in its pages—pass into the souls of his boys; they must catch some of our delight, our joy—joy being, as Goethe finely puts it, the mother of all the virtues. With our over-grown curriculum we lead or drag them up the steps of too many of the fair gardens of knowledge, but, after a brief glimpse through the gates of the sun-lit glades and flower-bordered paths, we turn them back into the turmoil and struggle of life, ill-fed and unsatisfied. " I've forgotten everything I learnt at school; I never found it of much use." Let us fill our children with a genuine love for literature, with a desire to know more than they read with us, and we shall hear fewer and fewer of such unjust remarks. But literature we must read as literature; we must endeavour for the time being to transform ourselves into fellow countrymen of the author. Textual criticism, archæology, philology—these are the veriest handmaids of the school; their work is over when they have left the best possible text at the school gates.

"What happens when you read Homer: do you enjoy the poetry, or are the words all roots?" a distinguished philologist was once asked. "Roots," was the reply given with a melancholy smile. We often see papers set on "Literature," but the questions are almost invariably concerned with the language in which the literature is written—a very different matter. We can imagine Shakespeare in the realm of shades receiving a set of the Clarendon Press edition, and on being told that they were chiefly used in schools, putting them on his shelves under the title "The Revenge of Holofernes"!

TRANSLATION.

What *is* our object in translation? Unless we know where we are going we cannot go there. The native speaker, we may reflect, uses his grammar unconsciously, and never employs translation at all; and yet around these two our method of teaching centres. Our whole system seems planned to give a self-conscious knowledge about the language and not the language itself: we do not place the reasoning of the critic above the spontaneous work of the artist; why then do we rate a knowledge of the visible signs of a foreign tongue so much higher than a practical power over the audible, spoken language, in fact the very language itself?

If our object is to penetrate into the very arcana of another tongue, to think and feel as a Frenchman thinks and feels, then surely this will be accomplished the quicker, the more the English is kept out of sight.

Or is it our aim to turn out future translators of German books? If so we shall be content to leave them "within six weeks of speaking the language."

"We have given your son, Sir, a thorough training in Harmony and Counterpoint; occasionally he has had a little playing on a dumb piano. In six weeks, with continued practice, we hope he will be able to play a tune passably well!" Ought it not rather to be our desire to give a real command over the language, even though that command be limited to things of every-day life? Theoretically we do, indeed, look on the capacity to speak as one of the aims of our teaching, but it "doesn't pay" in examinations—as little as the examinations themselves "pay" in after life—and, worst error of all, the power to speak is put at the end of the school career, or more correctly outside of it, instead of at the very beginning. But, perhaps, we shall be told we translate for the sake of "mental training." Well, training, if it is anything, is the persistent and consistent application of fixed principles, and that the grammar cannot afford simply because grammar and logic are not congruent. But, apart from theoretical justifications made for external consumption, let us try to see a little more closely what happens with the ordinary boy.

He has, say, twenty lines of Latin to do. After reading the first sentence through, he picks out the subject and then the verb*; he turns up the dictionary for his noun, and after sensibly skipping the dubious or antiquated etymology, begins to wonder whether the meaning is under I. A., 1a, or II. B. (b); on the road he has to turn back sometimes to the three pages of abbreviations at the beginning. However, he gets a meaning at last, and the process is repeated with the verb and the other words, with a flying reference, perhaps, to the grammar for some irregular gender. Then comes a hunt through the index to the syntax—that is, if he is lucky enough to have an index—and at last, the meaning is fairly clear; frequently, however, this is by no means the case, and he dives into the dictionary and grammar again. This

---

* For an attack on this method see "The Art of Reading Latin," by W. G. Hall (Ginn & Company).

is a danger to which conscientious boys are liable
patient and misdirected ingenuity, they arrive at a false
construction, but the labour of finding it was so great that the
first impression remains stronger than the later correction.

The good boy works in this fashion; the ordinary boy
leaves his grammar at school, skims through the lines as
quickly as he can, writes down the words that are utterly
foreign to him, turns up the dictionary, puts down the first
meaning he comes across, and is quite happy next day if he
escapes the Task Book. Is this where the training comes in?

In class there is a raking fire of questions directed apparently on the principle of " take care of the grammar, the
æsthetics will take care of themselves." After vivisecting the
author in this manner a translation is made, and the child
does all he can to prevent his weak English from being
twisted quite out of shape by the foreign idiom. Then comes
the turn of the " paper master," with his blue pencil and caba-
listic signs. However, even the ordinary boy gets a fair copy
made at last, and we creep on towards the examination. Then
one morning a strange thing happens. The master touches
the acmé of absurdity by saying, " We haven't time to read
the Latin (or French); get on with the translation." What is
the lesson—Latin, French, English? Not only must the boys
read the French aloud as a connected whole after the details have
been discussed, but the teacher must declaim it to them in the
finest style he can muster; for if we really desire to teach
French, the French must be the first thing to be heard, and
the last thing must be a memory haunted by the clear thoughts
and the clear sounds of the French.

Even if this dictionary and grammar procedure gave what
is claimed for it, we have still to ask whether its intrinsic
value, compared with that of other subjects, is worth the time
devoted to it in the strictly limited number of school hours
in a boy's life.

With regard to the above, it may not be superfluous to
point out that an attack on method is not an attack on a

subject : we may love Vergil without being lost in admiration of the way we were taught to read him. We do not disparage a mountain view by telling a tourist that he could have come up by an easier and better route.

Another branch of the translation method is the veritable " night side " of our system, I mean the exercise-book. Since the vain attempt to teach a language by means of short, disconnected sentences was introduced into Germany about seventy years ago, there has been a steady rise in the number of hours devoted to Latin, but the results are not better, nay, they are worse (Perthes, IV. 11).

After the French Revolution had given the death-blow to the real use of Latin as a means of communication, this new method was gradually evolved in the hope of infusing some show of life into the ghostly dilettanteism of " prose composition," that sickly branch of study kept alive only by the golden sap of prizes and scholarships.

To prophesy the failure of such a system ought not to need any profound knowledge of the nature of language; the merest common sense is surely enough to see the impossibility of making anything homogeneous out of such disparity in difficulty as the two parts of an exercise.

The form in which to clothe a thought is given at once in the mother tongue, and we need know little more than the meanings of the separate foreign words to translate them with fair accuracy ; but with the converse the form is almost entirely lacking. To obtain even a feeling for it we must first and for some time insist on attention being paid to it as embodied in sentences in the foreign language. Models and rules are insufficient at this stage, for the child is quite lost directly a sentence occurs, not slavishly like the old. After little progress with the scales, does the music-master ask his pupil to write down the notes of what he has just played ?

The unconscious absorption of the form through delight in the matter we quite miss, because of the vapid stupidity of the disconnected sentences we inflict on our pupils. Perhaps it might not be unfruitful in results if the reader were to put aside these lines now and to take as literature for half an hour the exercise-book he has been using lately, and then turn to a few pages of the author read in class. Should his conscience grow qualmish, he may solace himself with the reflection that in our generation at least, no power will arraign him before the dread court of Psychology and Pedagogy before casting him into the circle reserved for those who have sinned against youth.

The fundamental error at the base of this system is the belief that language can be reconstructed *a priori* on the model of certain types, or by the exercise of the logical faculty in the correct application of the rules of grammar. This, as we have seen, leaves entirely out of view the portion retained purely by memory, and the mind lost in a mass of details where thought must wait on form, tied in a psychologic knot by the attempt to do two things at once, hobbling through the language on grammar and dictionary as crutches, when suddenly confronted with the lively interchange of thought in conversation, finds itself unable to use the material acquired ; and the British parent complains more in sorrow than in anger, that, after years of patient work at school, his son cannot understand what is said to him, nor stammer out sentences for his most obvious wants.

Teachers can grow eloquent enough about the patience required to teach children. How about the patience of the children with us when we offer them the banausic banality of our exercise-books !

Les premières amours sont les plus vives is certainly highly instructive for a ladies' school, and our comic papers do right in holding such gems up to ridicule. That source of amusement, however, would swiftly dry up if the writer had to replace what he laughs at with two or three good sentences. When some remark not wholly foolish has been found, the noun or verb turns out to be irregular or not yet given, and in changing the forms sense vanishes.

Translations from English into a foreign tongue lie really

outside the school, and, if exercises must be done, they should not come till at least after two years' reading, and then only in aid of the study of the syntax. It is impossible to translate into a foreign language unless the mind feels in it more or less at home.

The ultimate expression of any reform in method is a change in the time-table, and I would seriously urge on all in authority to try at least the experiment of putting the exercise book at the beginning of the second year. Since this sort of work comes early in the school life, a change would not interfere with any public examination; from this lucky fact, the worst fault is most easy of reform.

Instead of spending most of our time in the lower classes in correcting exercises, let us get into the language as soon as possible, and stay in the language as much as possible. Translations, at first, we must of course have, but they should be idiomatic; "the English boy says *this*, the German *that*, when he wants anything."

As soon as possible, however, we must begin to use paraphrases in the foreign language, rather than send the child to a dictionary with English meanings; our object all through being to transplant ourselves into the method and manner of thought of the foreigner. For the French, A. Beaujean's abridgment of Littré, or P. Larousse's *Dictionnaire complet illustré* may be used; Wenig's *Handwörterbuch der deutschen Sprache* is a handy book, in which the new orthography is given.

As long as we think in English and translate into French, we do not know French. However swift the process take place, there must be a great psychologic gap between the conscious arrangement of elements and the unconscious flow of real speech. The knowledge of the medical student will help him little in a race : his chance depends not on theory, but on practice. This practice in a foreign language is the proper work of the school, and can be done better there than afterwards, when the richer spiritual life makes it more and more difficult to clothe thought in a foreign garb.

D

Occasional written translations into English are in their proper place only in the highest classes, and our chief demand on an English translation is that it should be English.

The most interesting way to teach composition is by means of short stories; not only is sufficient material given, opportunity is afforded as well for the individuality of the child to come to the front, a point of capital importance as a corrective to the levelling tendency of class work. Of course, in French and German more discussion and help must be given; this exercise would make an excellent substitute for *Unseens*. In the higher classes a variation can be got by giving a free English translation of some foreign original for retroversion, the work to be done in the class-room without assistance; after a discussion of the papers sent up, two or three of the best may be compared with the original; in this way we can begin to develop a sense of what translation really means.

In close connection with this exercise stands the art of letter writing. That the school should be mainly a preparation for after life seems a reasonable demand, but in the neglect of this pleasant art it shows almost a hostile front. For the mass of people, letter writing is the sole form of original literary work; and although we may not be able to teach grace of style, clearness we can and ought to give. The introduction into schools, even for " commercial boys," of actual business letters, is a grave mistake—they belong to the counting-house. Neither do we want the letters of the great literary men of the last century, but the easy unaffected style of the present day—such as " brother Hermann " writes to his " dear Karl " in *Eine Alpenreise*, by Wagner.

VOCABULARY.

In the Middle Ages it was a daily school task to learn a certain number of words by heart, so fully was the need of a vocabulary recognised. Comenius, indeed, endeavoured with 8,000 words to give a slight idea " of the whole world and the Latin language." The mechanical deadness which such a method induces could not fail to call forth a warm opposition on the part of the reformers of the end of the last century. "Learning by heart" fell into disrepute. Vocabulary lessons, however, we must have again as a regular part of school work. Educated men are said to use about 3,000 words in every-day life; to acquire this store stands in importance next to the pronunciation and the grammar. For practical use after leaving school it is even more important. To say how this is to be done is not an easy matter. On what principle are we to classify the words—by the alphabet, the things around us, the parts of speech, etymology, or psychology?

The first plan hardly needs any discussion; the second somehow grows very dull in practice, nor can it be consistently carried out, as it would be highly inconvenient to get together all the things belonging to any particular class of words.

Now, since the primary office of words is to carry meaning, they must be arranged, as far as possible, in those groups which analogy forms unconsciously in the mind. For this we need very much a small edition of Roget's *Thesaurus of English Words and Phrases*. While avoiding out of the way words, and a pedantic attempt to include everything, the groups should be arranged more in accordance with modern views on psychology, and contain only those words that an educated man uses. The groups of this ideological dictionary should then be sedulously worked over in the English classes, by forming sentences with them. Our orthography is a heavy burden to us with its "spelling lessons." "Meaning lessons" are more needed, as any teacher may convince himself if he will ask his boys to write out the meanings of the technical terms they have been using for years in their Geometry or Algebra. The corresponding French and German vocabularies should be printed in precisely the same way, so that, with the English vocabulary open before him, the child could tell at once from its position in the page the meaning of the French or German word.

Later on, when we wish to drop translation as much as possible, the foreign vocabularies can be taken alone, and cross associations will be avoided. How are we to acquire these groups? First and foremost we must never ask the child to learn a word he has not already seen as an integral part of a sentence. We do not begin to teach anatomy by presenting the student with a confused heap of disjointed bones; a single word by itself has no more meaning than a single bone.

Perthes' plan, as explained in the Reader above, is undoubtedly the best to begin with; but this alone will hardly give a real command over the vocabulary of the primitives. After a fair number of them have been mastered, the words should be ticked off in the vocabulary parallel to the English. As soon as any particular one has a majority of ticked forms, the teacher can make up easy sentences for the others, and the whole group may be learnt by heart. The ingenuity of the class can be exercised by making it use up the material thus acquired in the formation of new sentences.

As soon as the higher classes have acquired a fair store of words, they may be gradually rearranged on etymological principles, so far as these are applied to showing the *inner* construction of the language. This may be done best by a thorough study of the irregular verbs.

It may not be superfluous to point out that some caution is necessary in grouping cognate words : the new theories on the Arian vowel system, adding the European *e, o* to the Sanskrit *a* for the parent speech, have not yet got into the books of reference. We must not couple *shire*, for example, with *shear*, as the *i* does not belong to the same vowel rank.

By this time a number of derivatives will have been unconsciously absorbed, and, as soon as a clear feeling for some of their formative elements has been obtained, we can work over our primitives again by making words (*e.g.*) ending in *-able, -ung, -eur* compound verbs in *be-, er-*, &c., &c. In this way the sense for the connection between meaning and form will be developed, and a good foundation laid for the future study of Latin and Greek.

A useful plan for saving the time of the children is to work through the author set with a note-book cut step-wise into an alphabet, and to enter the leading derivatives as they occur under their respective primitives. Then we can either take one page and explain the family of words on it, or we can work through the note-book and pick out all those that have the same formative element. In this way, by preparing for the coming words, we can read faster, and, even if some are partially forgotten, the right translation will be remembered when it is seen in the dictionary.

Delightful essays have been written on the culture of nations as derived from a study of their vocabulary, but, as far as the writer knows, they are confined entirely to the most ancient periods of the language; for modern times such an investigation would be equally valuable and far more inter-esting. We may, perhaps, get such a piece of work done when the view that the study of the ancients is but one wing in the mighty edifice of the science of language, obtains adequate recognition.

PHILOLOGY.

Like phonetics, philology is not a school subject save in English. The teacher should know a great deal about it, and the children should hear uncommonly little. In mathematics, we constantly feel how our knowledge of the higher branches modifies the particular way in which we present the elementary parts ; in the same way our statements on language should be made as far as possible in that form in which the pupil, if he advance far enough, will meet with them in philology. For example, the vowels of allied words in the Arian parent language are known to belong to certain fixed ranks of which the majority are formed by *e* and *o*, followed by one of the medians *i*, *u*, *l*, *m*, *n*, *r*, as may be clearly seen in the Greek *leipō, leloipa, elipon.* When the word was accented on the ending, the vowels *e* and *o* were assimilated to the following median, which then became sonant. In passing into Teutonic, *e* developed into *i* before another *i* or an *n* followed by a consonant; thus Latin *vertit* = *wird, ventus* = *wind;* *o* became *a* —Lat. *hostis* = *Gast;* the sonants *l, m, n, r* developed a preceding *u,* and under certain conditions *u* became *o.* Hence we have

$$\bar{\imath}, \qquad ai, \qquad \dot{\imath},$$
$$eu, \qquad au, \qquad u,$$
$$e\text{—}i, \qquad a, \qquad u\text{—}o.$$

The first group is preserved in verbs like *ride, reiten;* the second in *seethe, sieden;* the third in *help, helfen—bind, binden.* The last is numerically the most important, so without saying a word to the child about the above we teach the German irregular verbs in this way :

werden—wird;	*ward—wurden*	*geworden*
helfen—hilf;	*half—hülfe*	*geholfen*
	hälfe ;	
binden ;	*band ;*	*gebunden.*

We must learn then to connect these vowels thus :

$$e\text{—}i; \qquad a, u; \qquad u\text{—}o.$$

The first pair we have already noticed in *Hilfe; Berg* and *Gebirge; Wetter* and *Gewitter.*

The imperative of *binden* is *binde;* but those which show the change *e—i* in the present indicative have, almost without exception, an *i* in the imperative without the final *e,* as *helfen* and *hilf, gelten* and *gilt.* In the past tense the vowels in the singular and plural used to be different, as in our *was* and *were;* but, as soon as the reason for this was forgotten, a struggle for existence began between them. In *war* and *waren,* we see that *a* runs right through, but the *r* of the plural has killed the *s;* at the present moment *wurde* for the singular is driving out *ward.* Now, the past subjunctive is made regularly by mutation of the vowel of the *plural,* as *würde;* but, when the vowel in the singular of the past indicative killed the vowel in the plural, the past subjunctive did not correspond, and new forms like *bände, hälfe* were made by analogy.

These double forms are now struggling for life with one another, and grammarians differ as to which of them should be retained; some say *sünge* marks more distinctly the difference between the moods, others ask for uniformity. We must follow the lead of the best authors.

The vowels of the past tense are found in a large number of masculines that modify in the plural—*Band, Spruch, Schlag, Fluss, &c.* Again, factitive verbs are made by mutating the vowel of the past *singular*, so we couple *sat, set; drank, drench; sank, senken.* These strictly should be weak verbs, but in cases like *schmelzen* the primitive and derivative are the same, and confusion between the weak and strong conjugation naturally takes place.

Another large class of nouns ending in *t* may be connected with the verbs by the law that in Primitive Teutonic all gutturals and labials passed into their corresponding spirants before this *t*: thus *drive, treiben—drift, Trift; may, mögen—might, Macht; bow, biegen—bight, Bucht.*

Analogy may be used incidentally to show how *Mittwoch, été* have become masculine through being associated with a group of allied masculine nouns. In the French verb, of course, we show the connection of the future and conditional with the present and imperfect of *avoir*, and form the tenses from their different stems.

Instead of the usual four conjugations it would be better to accept Chabaneau's more scientific division into living and archaic (*Histoire et Théorie de la Conjugaison française*, 1878). In the former the accent is very nearly always on the ending, and from it alone are new verbs made—those in *-er* from nouns, in *-ir* from adjectives; in the latter the accent shifts. This method has been carried out in the *Neufranzösische Formenlehre nach ihrem Lautstande*, by E. Koschwitz.

In the above we have kept to the principle of restricting

philology to showing the *inner* formation of the language; this, however, is not the method most in vogue. Some of our grammars and readers present us with something over which they are pleased to put "Grimm's Law." A mnemonic formula ASH, SHA, HAS is to help us; the sounds apparently are divided, like boiled eggs, into hard and soft. A stands for aspirate and, as we learn by the way, for spirant too: that is *father* and fa*t her* are the same! Unfortunately, this pleasing law breaks down when we compare *father, mother, brother* with *Vater, Mutter, Bruder*. Of course, boys soon get to believe that etymology is a game where the letters of the alphabet are shaken up in a bag and you take out what you like; another firm conviction, which always rouses the wrath of Mr. Skeat, is that English "comes from" German. They cannot believe anything else; after getting, with scant courtesy to the vowels, a hundred words from the German, it is idle to add the saving clause: "You musn't think that English is derived from German."

A curious defence for the retention of Latin in schools, is sometimes put forward on etymological grounds: "to understand the English language thoroughly it is necessary to have a knowledge of Latin." While gratefully acknowledging any expression of the desirability of learning English *thoroughly*, it may be pointed out that the same holds true for half the languages of Europe, including especially Scandinavian, Norman-French, and Old English. When will classical scholars help us to understand our own language thoroughly by giving us a trustworthy etymological dictionary for Greek and Latin? English from Latin? Why not Latin from English, as thus—

sit   *sat*   *ne-st*

"down-sit."

The vowel in *nest* has been lost; the accent was originally on the ending; therefore the Latin *sedeo* must be connected with *nīdus*. The length, then, of the i is due to the loss of a z, springing from an s voiced by the voiced d: nīdus < nizdos

< ni-sd-os; so sēdi < sezdi < se-sd-i, a reduplicated perfect we see. Again, Arian *d* both in English and Latin passes with a following *t* into *ss* : *oida*—*wit, iwiss, wīse* ; so *sed-to-s > sessus*, and the verb *sedeo* is clear. But this we shall scarcely see in our time, as it demands from English masters in English schools a philological knowledge of English.

One point of capital importance is altogether overlooked by these classical philologists—the change of meaning. Even our professed etymologists subordinate it far too much to the changes of sound. The scientific study of the former has only just begun, and the principles are not yet sufficiently settled to apply them to school work. A month's study at vowel gradation in Old English would teach more etymology and philology than years of school Latin ; if we really desire to test the value of this method take any ten pages of the French Reader, write down all the words the boys do not know, and see how many can be explained etymologically. Even then it will often be easier to learn the meaning at once than to follow the various changes from Latin to modern French ; we stand a chance, too, of blurring the scientific sense for language, by putting side by side changes in form that it took centuries to bring about. We set up cross associations, and they are the one thing to be avoided in teaching language; let us take one subject at a time, and get a clear, firm grasp on it before we venture to compare. Let us not confuse the practical mastery of a modern tongue with the scientific study of its origin; we must learn things as they are, before we begin to investigate how they got to be what they are.

In spite of a fondness for the subject, the writer has come, after some considerable experience, to the belief that the intrusion of comparative philology into school work is positively harmful. In a class averaging sixteen years of age and preparing for the London Matriculation a carefully drawn up set of German cognate words was given in the hope of strengthening a weak vocabulary in " Unseens." *Strafe* was soon sent up as " strap "; this gave food for reflection, and the perpetration of the following gave the death blow to Grimm, and killed even the desire to expatiate on Verner :— " The Latin word *hostis* is represented by the runic *gastiz*— no boy can resist a rune—and we see that *o* becomes in Teutonic *a*. Let us take the word *dog* : we have first *dag*, then by metathesis *gad;* now *g* becomes *k*, and *d*, *t*, and so we have *cat*." The class was delighted, and some of the boys in the "Matriculation English" took out their pocket-books to preserve so wonderful a fact. Next morning, when it was demanded why *cat* hadn't become *dog*, they began to see that they had been trifled with. We had no more Grimm that day nor next.

Finally, if the principles laid down in the preceding pages are in the main right, our present method needs a thorough reform. Who is to begin the change? What is the chief hindrance in our way? The change must come from the Universities; our hindrance lies in the exaggerated respect paid by the British public to examinations, while it takes no trouble to see that they will test the capabilities it wants or that the examiners are specially fitted for their work.

We shall not teach either foreign languages or other subjects adequately till scholarships can be freely gained for them at our Universities, and the graduate feels that his future chance for a headmastership is as good as if he had taken up classics, mathematics, or science. Or rather, the particular subject he is to teach ought to be made subordinate to his knowledge of pedagogy. In the past the schoolmaster has been confused with the scholar; now we run the risk of confusing him with the specialist. In appointing a cook, do we select the man with the largest larder or the biggest round of beef?

The scholar lacks intellectual detachment, the specialist a right sense of proportion in estimating the value of his subject. With each the main occupation is with a thing; with the schoolmaster it is a mind. The true doctor is an artist, with his skill based on science; he sees instinctively what the particular individual patient before him wants at that particular moment. We should be artists in the souls of children, but as long as we are allowed to offer great knowledge of a single subject joined to a rough empirical experience, instead of a profound study of the child's mind, we shall rise in matters of teaching, in spite of all our enthusiasm, devotion, and hard labour, no higher than the level of the herb-woman and the bone-setter.

Considering the large number of men and women engaged in education, and the intrinsic value of the subject, is it too much to ask our Universities to give us *Schools* or a *Tripos for Teachers?*

At present our method in examining for foreign languages is little short of ludicrous; in the great majority of cases the highest honours *can* be won by the deaf and dumb! Of the four elements of language, hearing, speaking, reading, writing, not a single one is adequately tested. The weight is thrown on translation and the exceptions in the grammar; the former the native speaker never wants, and the latter he absorbs unconsciously. So far can false views on the nature of language mislead us.

BIBLIOGRAPHY.

The following books were read or consulted in preparing the above. Although making no pretension to be a complete Bibliography, the list is given in the hope of saving the time of other workers on the same subject.

Beda, 672—735 A.D.

Bedae Presbyteri Liber de arte metrica, Liber de orthographia.

1857. **H. Keil** : Grammatici Latini ; VII., 217—294.

de VIII partibus orationis, Cunabula grammaticae artis Donati restituta de schematibus et tropis.

1863. **C. Halm** : Rhetores Latini Minores, pp. 607—618.

De schematis et tròpis sacrae scripturae.

De arte metrica.

1848. **H. Petrie & J. Sharp** : Monumenta Historica Britannica.

The titles of the works in the various authorities vary a great deal; complete ed. J. A. Giles, 1843—44. Migne's Patrologia, 90—95. See W. S. Teuffel, Gesch. d. röm. Lit., § 500, 3.

1880. **J. Zupitza** : Aelfrics Grammatik und Glossar. Erste Abteilung : Texte und Varianten.

The Grammar, based on Priscian and Donatus, is written in English, with skilful translations of the technical terms.

1884. **J. Stürziner** : Orthographia Gallica. Aeltester Traktat über französische Aussprache und Orthographie, nach vier Handschriften zum ersten Mal herausgegeben.

The introduction, pp. i.—xlvi., gives a full account of the MSS., with extracts from other books of a similar nature, written sometime between 1300 and 1377.

See also **P. Meyer** in the "Revue critique," V. 2, p. 373, and **E. Stengel** in the "Zeitschrift für neufranzösische Sprache und Litteratur," I., p. 1.

1495 (?) Here begynneth a treatyse called Peruula.

Picture of master in a large chair with a birch in left hand; at his feet, three boys with caps on : "What shalt thou doo whan thou haste an englyssh to be made in latyne. I shall reherce myn englysshe fyrst ones, twyes or thryes, and loke out my princypal verbe, and aske hym this questyon, who or what. And that worde that answeryth to the questyon shall be the nomynatif case to the verbe." Colophon. Prynted at westmynstre, in Caxtons hous, by wynkyn de worde.

1510 (?) **J. Holt**: Lac puerorum. Mylke for chyldren.

This simple grammar is fully described by Dr. T. F. Dibdin in his edition of the "Typographical Antiquities" of J. Ames, vol. 2, p. 380. In the frontispiece is a picture of three boys seated on a low form in front of the master who, with a birch, seems to be waiting for another pupil to come through the open doorway.

1519. **W. Horman.** Vulgaria uiri doctissimi Guil. Hormani Caesaris-burgensis.

Contains a great number of proverbs, moral sayings, &c., in English, followed by Latin translations in larger print.

1521. **A. Barcley**: Introductorie to write and to pronounce Frenche.

There is an interesting account in the Prologue of the teaching of French in England.

1524. **T. Linacre**: Thomae Linacri Britanni de emendata strvctvra Latini sermonis libri sex.

There were eleven editions published between 1524 and 1559.

1529. **T. Wolsey**: Rvdimenta grammatices et docendi methodus, non tam scholae-Gypsuichianae per reuerendissimum, D. Thomā Cardinalē Eboř. feliciter institutae, q̃ oĩ busaliis totius Anglie scholis prescripta.

The "method" is laid down for each of the eight classes. At the end is a Carmen Guillelmi Lilii, ad discipulos de moribus.

1530. Lesclarcissement de la Langue Francoyse, compose par maistre **Jehan Palsgraue**, Angloys natyf de Londres, et gradue de Paris. Neqve, lvna, per, noctem. M P G anno uerbi incarnati. M.D.XXX.

1532 (?) **G. Duwes**: An introductorie for to lerne to rede, to pronounce, and to speake Frenche trewly, compyled for the ryghte hygh, excellent, and most vertuous lady, the lady Mary of Englande, doughter to our mooste gracious souerayne lorde kynge Henry the eyghte.

In the "Imploration for Grace" and the Introduction, an interlinear translation in French is given. Following the seven rules for correct pronunciation, comes a long vocabulary of the parts of the body, of words for age, dress, white meats, &c., and after a little grammar a long list of verbs.

"Here foloweth the seconde booke of thys lytell worke, in the whych shalbe treated of cōmunications, and other thynges necessary to the lernynge of the sayde Frenche tonge."

This part consists of conversations with interlinear translations, and letters such as

"Another letter sende to the lady Mary by Jhon ap morgan squier, caruer of the same, her grace being somewhat crased."

The octavo edition printed by N. Bourman for J. Reyns is ascribed to 1532. In the quarto edition by J. Waley the second part is "Nwely corrected and amended." It was published probably in 1557.

Palsgrave and Duwes were edited in 1852 by Génin in the "Collection des documents inédits sur l'histoire de France." See also **A. J. Ellis** "On Early English Pronunciation," more especially Vol. III., pp. 794—838.

1540. **Joannis Palsgravi** Londoniensis, ecphrasis anglica in comoediam Acolasti.

"The Comedye of Acolastus translated into oure englysshe tongue, after suche maner as chylderne are taught in the grammer schole, fyrst worde for worde, as the latine lyeth, and afterwarde accordynge to the sence and meanyng of the latin sentences . . ." Anno M.D.XL.

W. Fullonius presented his comedy to the burgesses of Hagen in Holland, in 1529.

1553. **Du Ploiche:** A Treatise in English and Frenche right necessary uud proffitable for al young children . . . . made by Peter du Ploiche teacher of the same . . .

The English is given in Black Letter, with the French in italics on the same page. It contains the Catechism, Litany and Suffrages, evening prayers, "for to speake at the table, for to aske the way, for to buy and sell," &c.

1566. **Claudius Hollyband** [= C. Desainliens]: The Frenche Little-ton : a most easie, perfect, and absolvte way to learn the frenche tongue.

Further editions in 1578, 1581, 1607.

The little book begins with short dialogues in which the author manages to let us know his fees for teaching. A "Traicté des Danses" precedes the rules for the pronun-ciation!

1570. **R. Ascham** : Scholemaster—

"To vnderstand, write, and speak Latin."

1577. A shorte introduction of Grammar, generally to be used : com-pyled and set forth for the bringing vp of all those that intende to attayne the knowledge of the Latine tongue.

After the command from Elizabeth that no other Grammar but this should be used in schools, come three sensible pages to the reader. Great weight is laid on turning some English book into Latin.

1580. Clavdii a Sancto Vinculo [= C. Desainliens] de pronuntiatione lingvae Gallicae libri dvo.

This book was written, the author tells us, as he was "victus quotidianis multorum Anglorum querelis."

Recommends reading of Amadis de Gaule; P. Boaistuau ; Belle-Forestz; Clement Marot ; Sleïdan ; Les vies et morales de Plutharque.

1580. **C. Hollyband** : A treatise for declining of verbes, which may be called the second chiefest worke of the french tongue.

1580. **Cl. Hollyband** : The Treasurie of the French tong : Teaching the waye to varie all sortes of Verbes . . . .

1582. **C. Desainliens** : The Frenche Schoolemaister of Claudius Hollyband, newly corrected. Wherein is most playnely shewed, the true and most perfect way of pronouncing of the Frenche tongue, to the furtherance of all those which doo studye priuatély in their owne study or houses.

1582. **Richard Mulcaster** : The first part of "The Elementarie."

1583. **[C. Hollyband]** : Campo di fior, or else the Flovrie field of fovre Langvages of M. Clavdius Desainliens, aliâs Holiband ; for the furtherance of the learners of the Latine, French, English, but chieflie of the Italian tongue.

Contains a Latin poem by R. Mulcaster. A book of dia-logues and phrases.

1592. **G. Delamothe, N.**: The French Alphabet, teaching in a very short time, by a most easie way, to pronounce French naturally, to read it perfectly, to write it truly, and to speak it accordingly.

   The epistle is dated 1592; the book printed 1647. [Good collection of proverbs at the end.]

1593. **C. Hollyband**: A Dictionarie French and English.

1612. **A. Hume**: Grammatica nova in usum juventutis Scoticae ad methodum revocata ab Alexandro Hvmio. Et auctoritate senatus, omnibus Regni scholis imperata.

   Based mainly on Linacre. The whole book is in Latin.

   "The parliament of Scotland authorized in 1607, as Henry had done in 1545, proper commissioners for settling 'the most approven grammar.'"

   They ordered Hume's Grammar; it was however easier to order it than to get it accepted. See G. Chalmers: "Life of Ruddiman," pp. 23 and 377.

1612. **A. Hume**: Prima elementa grammaticae: in usum juventutis Scoticae ab Alexandro Hvmio digesta.

1622. **John Webbe**: An appeale to Truth, for the Controuersie betweene Art and Use; about the best and most expedient Course in Langvages. To be read Fasting: For the greater benefit of the deluded innocencie of our owne, and other Nations. Drawen and Exhibited by John Webbe, Dr. of Ph., London.

1623. **John Webbe**: A petition to the High Covrt of Parliament, In the behaulfe of auncient and authentique Authors, for the vniversall and perpetuall good of euery man and his posteritie.

   If we had a Pedagogic Society, Webbe's Tracts would be worth reprinting.

1625. **J. Wodroephe**: Marrow of the French Tongue.

1629. The first comedy of **Pvb. Terentivs**, called Andria, or the Woman of Andros, English and Latine: claused for such as would write or speak the pure Language of this Author, after any Method whatsoever, but especially after the Method of Dr. Webbe.

   An elaborate "crib."

1634. **Christopher Syms**: An introduction to, or, the art of teaching the Latine speach . . . Dublin. Black Letter.

"A preface to the Reader, proper only for the Teacher."

At the end of each section there is "An advertisement to the teacher" on the right method to be pursued. "The end and use of learning grammar is to understand the latine speach, to *speak* it, and to write it."

1639. **Hermes Anglo-latinus**; or directions for young Latinists, to speake Latine purely.

1639. **T. Hayne**: Linguarum cognitio: seu de linguis in genere, et de variarum linguarum harmonia dissertatio.

1640. **T. Hayne**: Grammatices Latinae Compendivm, Anno 1637 . . .

"Here also the most necessary Rules are expressed in English opposite to the Latine, that the one may facilitate and give light to the other."

1648. **Sir Balthazar Gerbier**: The Interpreter of the Academie for forrain langvages, and all noble sciences, and exercises. To all fathers of families and lovers of vertue.

This curious example of the puff elaborate is written in French and English, and ranges from the proper pronunciation of the French vowels to fortifications.

1649. A publique Lecture on all the languages, arts, sciences, and noble exercises, which are taught in Sir Balthazar Gerbier's Academy.

1649. **C. Hoole**: An easie Entrance to the Latin tongue.

1651. **C. Hoole**: The Latine Grammar fitted for the use of schools. Wherein the words of Lilie's Grammar are (as much as might bee) retained; many errors thereof amended; many needless things left out; many necessaries that were wanted, supplied; and all things ordered in a Method more agreeable to Children's Capacitie.

1652. **G. Dugres**: Dialogi Gallico - Anglico - Latini. Per G. Dugres, linguam gallicam in illustrissima et famosissima Oxoniensi Academia haud ita pridem privatim edocentem.

1654. **Samuel Hartlib**: The True and Readie Way to learne the Latine Tongue, attested by three excellently learned and approved authors of three nations, viz.: Eilhardus Lubinus, a German; Mr. Richard Carew, of Anthony, in Cornwall; and the French Lord of Montaigne.

1655. **J. Poole**: The English Accidence: or a short and easy way for the more speedy attaining to the Latine Tongue.

E

1668. **A. Huish**: Priscianus Ephebus: or a more full and copious Explanation of the Rules of Syntax.

1669. **A. B. Z. W.** A demonstration how the Latine Tongue may be learn't with far greater ease and speed then commonly it is.

1670. **J. Poole**: The Youth's Guide: or English Accidence. Being a more short and easie way for the speedy attaining to the Latine Tongue.

1672. Ludus ludi literarii: or, school-boys' exercises and Divertisements. In xlvii Speeches: some of them Latine, but most English; Spoken . . . . at several Breakings up, in the Year 1671.

"He that hath something in his mind of Greek or Latine is requested now-a-dayes, to be civil, and translate it into English for the benefit of the Company."

1675. **Elisha Coles**: Nolens volens: or you shall make Latin whether you will or no. Containing the plainest directions that have been given on that subject. Together with the youth's Visible Bible . . . four and twenty copper plates; with the Rude Translation opposite, for the exercise of those that begin to make Latin.

The method consists of a short grammar followed by parallel English and Latin verses out of the Bible. "From a child thou hast knowne the Scriptures."

Some of the wood-cuts are very amusing.

1675. **Elisha Coles**: Syncrisis, or the Most Natural and Easie Method of learning Latin: by comparing it with English together with the Holy History . . . Illustrated in Fourteen Copper Plates: with the Rude Translation opposite for the Exercise of those that begin to make Latin.

1675. The English Guide to the Latin Tongue: or a brief system of all the most necessary rules for the initiating of youth in the Rudiments of Grammar.

1675. A philosophicall Essay for the **Reunion of the Languages,** or the Art of Knowing all by the mastery of one. (Oxford.)

"I had in the end no other course to take, but to throw myself upon the Latin."

This interesting tract gives the philology of the time with the current views as to the families of languages.

1677. **E. Richardson**: English and Netherdutch Academy.

1679. **C. Hoole**: The Common Accidence examined and explained by short questions and answers.

1680. The **High Dutch Minerva** à-la-mode, or, a Perfect Grammar never extant before, whereby The English may both easily and exactly learne the Neatest Dialect of the German Mother-Language, used throughout Europe. London, printed in L. Britain, and to be sold at the Rabbets and Harrow in Jacksons court Blackfrayer.

This Grammar is much livelier reading than most of its successors. Full phonetic transcriptions are given and a set of correspondances of the letters between English and German: "though a certain rule or standing certainty can not be prescribed (as we could wish it were) through the whole language without instances and exceptions."

Later German Grammars will be found in Vietor's Festschrift (1886): Die aussprache des englischen nach den deutschen-englischen grammatiken vor 1750, and in an article in his "Phonetische Studien," Vol. II., p. 65, by W Bohnhardt.

1683. **S. Hoadly**: The Accidence in Questions and Answers... being an Introduction into useful Learning. In a new but Natural Method...

"He had heard and read abundance of sad complaints and confessions of ingenious men both at home and abroad that our way was utterly wrong... Only Mr. Lewis and the Westminster-Grammar, seeing the utter incorrigibleness of Lily, went quite another way, but so unhappily that he thinks he can make it good that there are in each of those three Grammars more gross errours than brakes."

1683. **John Twells**, Schoolmaster: Grammatica Reformata, or a general examination of the Art of Grammar as it hath been successively delivered by F. Sanctius in Spain, G. Scioppius in France, and G. J. Vossius in the Lower Germany; and methodized by the Oxford Grammarian in his observations upon Lily.

A remarkable preface of twenty-six pages gives a mass of valuable information, tracing the history of Latin Grammar from Crates down to 1635. If ever the History of Grammar in England is written these few pages by Twells will be one of the leading authorities. Those who desire "uniformity in grammar" will not derive much pleasure from the history of the attempts made to set it up.

"As for what was afterwards dully and foolishly delivered by the Latins, it ought not to be imputed to one that was a Greek: . . . it is to be ascribed to their Sottishness, who either did not well understand their own Language; or else wholly neglected the use of Grammatical Disputations . . .

"Strange Fate! That a Grammar, which all men, that wear their Senses, acknowledge to be tedious and impracticable. A Grammar, which interferes with all the Principles of true Didacticks, should deceive the World for the space of One Thousand eight Hundred and Fifty Years!"

1683. An English Introduction to the Latine Tongue. For the Use of The Lower Forms in Westminster School.

1693. **William Walker**: Some improvements to the Art of Teaching, especially in the first grounding of a young scholar in Grammar Learning. Shewing a Short, Sure, and easie way to bring a Scholar to Variety and Elegancy in writing Latin.

1698. **A. Lane**: A rational and speedy Method of attaining to the Latin Tongue. In Two Parts. The first containing such Precepts as are common to all languages. The second contains what is more peculiar to the Latin Tongue.

1703. **Ric. Johnson, M.A.**: A treatise of the Genders of Latin Nouns: by way of examination of Lilly's Grammar Rules . . . being a specimen of grammatical commentaries . . . shewing, that system to be in many things false, in most obscure; superfluous in things unnecessary, and defective in things necessary; and consequently an insuperable impediment to the progress of youth . . .

For his Essay Johnson read 47 Latin authors, and he subjects Lilly to a cruel criticism, page by page, by confronting him with the actual usage of the classics.

1706. **R. Johnson**: Grammatical Commentaries: being an apparatus to a new Grammar by way of animadversion upon the falsities, obscurities, redundancies, and defects of Lilly's system.

1707. A defence of the Grammatical Commentaries against the animadversions of Mr. Edward Leeds.

1711. An essay upon education: shewing how Latin, Greek and other languages may be learn'd more easily, quickly, and perfectly, than they commonly are.

> The author insists on conversation for teaching Latin; he says that boys were kept a year and a half at the grammar alone. "Latin may as well be our first Language as English."

1713. H. Felton: A dissertation on reading the Classics, and forming a just style. Written in the Year 1709, and addressed to the Right Honourable, John Lord Roos, the present Marquis of Granby.

1714. T. Ruddiman: The Rudiments of the Latin Tongue.

> Ruddiman complains feelingly of the varying views of grammarians; he attacks the theory that putting the whole grammar into Latin "carries the Learner more directly to the Habit of speaking Latin, a practice much used in our schools."
>
> See "The Life of T. Ruddiman" by. **G. Chalmers**, 1794, and "Great Scholars" by **H. J. Nicoll**.

1718. A. Blackwall: An introduction to the Classics; containing, a short discourse on their excellencies; and directions how to study them to advantage.

1718. R. Johnson: Additions and Emendations to the Grammatica Commentaries with a reply to Mr. W. Symes.

1718. R. Johnson: Noctes Nottinghamicae: or cursory objections against the syntax of the Common-Grammar, in order to obtain a better.

> There is a long "Preface to the School Masters."
>
> "'Tis not to be suppos'd that a Government can have that Passion for, or interest in Lilly's Grammar, as to enjoyn It upon School-Masters against their Will."

1719. A supplement to the English Introduction of Lily's Grammar .. with a preface, in which an account is given of the method used in the two lowest forms of the said school [at Exeter], with the reasons thereof; and a defence of the early and long Use of Terence therein.

1720. John Clarke: An Essay upon the Education of Youth in

Grammar-Schools. In which the Vulgar Method of Teaching is examined, and a New one proposed.

Replaces the Grammar at the beginning by the use of Literal Translations. The whole Essay is full of common sense.

1721. A compendious way of teaching the learned languages, and some of the Liberal Sciences at the same time ; us'd formerly by Tanaquil Faber.

The Introduction contains a good history of Latin Grammar.

1723. A compendious way of teaching Ancient and Modern Languages, formerly practised by the Learned Tanaquil Faber . . . .

1725—31. **T. Ruddiman** : Grammaticae Latinae Institutiones.

The preface to the reader gives an interesting sketch of the history of Latin Grammar. In Scotland there was a 17th edition of the Institutiones in 1815 ; in England, a 24th edition in 1782. A German edition by Stallbaum was published in Leipzig in 1823, and used by Dr. B. H. Kennedy (see 1844).

1731. **J. Clarke** : An Essay upon Study. Wherein Directions are given for the Due conduct thereof, and the Collection of a Library, proper for the Purpose, consisting of the Choicest Books in all the several Parts of Learning.

1733. **J. Clarke** : A New Grammar of the Latin Tongue comprising all in the Art necessary for Grammar-Schools. To which is Annex'd a Dissertation upon Language.

"The sole Occasion the Generality . . . have for the Latin Tongue is to read usefull Books writ in that Language, easily and familiarly "

1733. A Dissertation upon the Way of teaching the Latin Tongue : Wherein the Objections raised against Mr. Ruddiman's . . . Grammar . . . are answered and confuted ; And the vulgar Practice of teaching Latin by a Grammar writ in the same Language, is justified and defended.

A lively defence of Ruddiman's Grammar, and an attack upon the new Latin Grammar by Mr. John Clarke, Schoolmaster at Hull.

1743. **J. Barclay** : A treatise on Education.

1750. **J. T. Philips** : A compendious way of teaching antient and modern languages, formerly instituted by the learned Tanaquil Faber . . . also an Essay on Rational Grammar. To which are now added, Proposals for a new Method of Domestick Education. Fourth edition.

1793. An Introduction to the Latin Tongue for the use of Youth. Eton.

1795. An elementary introduction to the Latin Grammar with practical exercises, after a new and easy method.

" The young scholar may now begin to make some short Latin sentences : this early practice will at once excite his ambition and flatter his pride."

1809. [**Sidney Smith.**] Essays on Professional Education by R. L. Edgeworth. *Edinburgh Review*, Vol. XV., pp. 40—53 : " return our thanks for the courage with which he has combated the excessive abuse of classical learning in England."

The article is written in the slashing style.

1817. Public education, consisting of three tracts, reprinted from the *Edinburgh Review*, the *Classical Journal*, and the *Pamphleteer*, together with the defence of Public Schools, by the late Dean of Westminster.

1818. **N. G. Duflef** : Nature Displayed in her mode of teaching Language to man, being a new and infallible method of acquiring languages with unparalleled rapidity . . .

The method simply consists in learning some thousand phrases before the grammar is touched.

1825. **W. Duverger** : Comparison of French and English Languages.

1826. **T. W. C. Edwards** : The Eton Latin Grammar, a plain and concise Introduction to the Latin Language being Lily's grammar abridged for the use of the young gentlemen of Eton College.

" In this edition the construing is given in a manner far superior to that of any edition published."

1826. Hamilton's Method of Teaching Languages. *Edinburgh Review*, Vol. XLIV., pp. 47—69.

A lively article with a vigorous attack on the loss of time in looking words out in a dictionary.

1827. **Arth. Clifford** : A letter to the Right Honourable the Earl of Shrewsbury on a New Method of Teaching and Learning Languages.

The method really consists in learning a large vocabulary

by heart. The father and mother can teach about 1000 Latin words to the child at the age of 3—5 years !

1828. **George Long** : An introductory lecture delivered in the University of London on Tuesday, November 4th, 1828.

1829. **L. Mühlenfels** : Introductory Lecture on the Study of German.

1829. **A. Clifford** : Instructions to Parents and Teachers respecting the use of the elementary books for the Latin Language.

1830. **L. P. R. Fenwick** de Porquet : The Fenwickian System of Learning French.

1830. **George Long** : Observations on the Study of the Latin and Greek Languages. An Introductory Lecture delivered in the University of London, November 1, 1830.

1836. **Alexander Allen** : An Etymological Analysis of Latin Verbs. For the use of schools and colleges.

The interesting preface of XLIII. pages affords a good view of philological opinions at the time on roots and crude forms. It is based mainly on Pott's *Etymologische Forschungen* and Dr. Struve's book — *Ueber die Lateinische Declination und Conjugation* (1823).

The author apparently imagines the primitive man as one day making up his mind to have a language, and then glueing it together in this fashion—

Prepo-sition.	Redupli-cation.	Connecting Vowel.	Root.	Flection Syllable.	Tense Vowel.	Plural Sign.	Person Sign.
con	*d*	*i*	*d*	*er*	*u*	*n*	*t*

1836. **Rev. M. Russell, LL.D.** : Observations on the Advantages of Classical Learning, viewed as the means of cultivating the youthful mind, and more especially as compared with the studies which it has been proposed to substitute in its stead.

1836. **J. Ward** : A short Introduction of Grammar, generally to be used : compiled and set forth for the bringing up of all those, that intend to attain to the knowledge of the Latin Tongue.

1836. **Thomas Wyse, Esq., M.P.** : Education Reform ; or, the Necessity of a National System of Education. Vol. I.

1838. **Dr. L. Lersch** : Die Sprachphilosophie der Alten, dargestellt an dem Streite über Analogie und Anomalie der Sprache.

1838. **Dr. William Smith**: Latin Exercises for Beginners.

1839. **George Long**: What are the advantages of a Study of Antiquity at the present time?

> Central Society of Education. Third Publication. p. 184.

1839. **William Smith**: On the Study of Comparative Grammar.

> Central Society of Education. Third Publication. p. 315.
> Based on the labours of Bopp, Grimm, and Pott.

1842. **J. S. Blackie**: On the Study of Languages. In Tait's Edinburgh Magazine, Vol. IX., pp. 747—754.

1842. **C. Levert**: A general and practical System of Teaching and Learning Languages, applied to all Languages, especially the French.

1844. **A. J. Beresford Hope**: Essays on the Study of the Latin Tongue. Pp. 71—91.

1844. **Dr. B. H. Kennedy**: Latinae grammaticae curriculum; or, A Progressive Grammar of the Latin Language for the use of all classes in Schools.

> Doggerel verses are given for the gender and some nouns of the third declension; the syntax is in Latin with English interspersed.

1845. **J. S. Blackie**: On the Teaching of Languages. *The Foreign Quarterly Review*, Vol. XXXV., pp. 170-187.

1846. **T. H. Key**: A Latin Grammar on the System of Crude Forms.

> Based on Forcellini, Ramshorn, Zumpt, and Madvig.

1847. **John Robson**: On the Comparative Advantages of some Methods of teaching Latin and Greek. *The Classical Museum*, Vol. IV., pp. 388—427.

1850. **J. Price**: On the Study of Languages. *The Classical Museum* Vol. VII., pp. 196-200.

1852. **J. S. Blackie**: On the Studying and Teaching of Languages.

1852. **Jacob Grimm**: Über den Ursprung der Sprache.

1853. **The School Claims of Languages, Ancient and Modern**. In the *Westminster Review*, pp. 450—498.

> A vigorous attack on the exaggerated claims often made for the Classics.

1854. **C. Richardson**: On the study of Language.

1855. **Steinthal**: Logik, Grammatik und Psychologie.

1856. **Fr. Haase**: De medii aevi studiis philologicis.

> Mediaeval grammarians are full of errors in accidence and

lexicon, but excellent in philosophy ; modern Syntax really follows Ebrard Bethuniensis Graecismus, 1124. (See 1887.)

1856. **Berthold Sigismund** : Kind und Welt.

1857. Grammatici Latini ex recensione **H. Keilii.**

> There are excellent indices in the last volume. According to Mr. Nettleship, all the works given are really based on the labours of not more than twelve grammarians, none of whom lived later than the Antonines.

1858. **J. E. Carlile** : Grammar Schools.

> In " Essays by Ministers of the Free Church of Scotland, edited by W. Hanna."
>
> Gives an interesting sketch of the history of Latin Grammar in Scotch schools.

1859. **Ch. L. Livet** : La Grammaire française et les grammariens au xvie siècle.

1859. **C. E. A. Schmidt** : Beiträge zur Geschichte der Grammatik.

1861. [**W. Lily**]. **Roscoe Mongan** : The School and University Eton Latin Grammar.

1865. **M. B. Lévy, II.** : De l'enseignement des langues vivantes en France.

1867. Essays on a Liberal Education. Edited by Rev. F. W. Farrar.

> I. **C. S. Parker** : On the History of Classical Education.
>
> II. **H. Sidgwick** : The Theory of Classical Education.
>
> III. **J. Seeley** : Liberal Education in Universities.
>
> IV. **E. E. Bowen** : On Teaching by means of Grammar.
>
> V. **F. W. Farrar** : On Greek and Latin Verse Composition as a general branch of Education.
>
> VI. **J. M. Wilson** : On Teaching Natural Science in Schools.
>
> VII. **J. W. Hales** : The Teaching of English.
>
> VIII. **W. Johnson** : On the Education of the Reasoning Faculties.
>
> IX. **Lord Houghton** : On the present Social Results of Classical Education.

1869. **Ch. Thurot** : Extraits des divers manuscrits latins pour servir à l'histoire des doctrines grammaticales au moyen âge.

1870. **D. Nasmith** : The practical linguist ; being a system based entirely upon natural principles of learning to speak, read, and write the German Language.

The distinctive point of the method was to obtain the relative numerical value of words, by reading five books through and ticking off every word as it occurred:—"some words had a numerical value of upwards of one thousand, others fell to and below five." The Vocabulary is divided into permanent and auxiliary. The Accidence has a repellent look: the English in the exercises is first Germanized. "How can I help it?" becoming "What can i [*sic*] therefore?" and so on.

1871. **W. D. Whitney**: Language and Education. In the *North American Review*, Vol. CXIII., pp. 343—374.

Hermann Perthes: Zur Reform des lateinischen Unterrichts auf Gymnasien und Realschulen.

1873 and 1885. Erster Artikel. Über den Plan einer "lateinischen Wortkunde im Anschluss an die Lectüre."

1874 and 1885. Zweiter Artikel.

1886. Dritter Artikel. Zur lateinischen Formenlehre, sprachwissenschaftliche Forschungen und didactische Vorschläge.

1886. Vierter Artikel. Die Principien des Übersetzens und die Möglichkeit einer erheblichen Verminderung der Stundenzahl.

1876. Fünfter Artikel. Erläuterungen zu meiner lateinischen Formenlehre.

The first two articles of this important work appeared originally in the *Zeitschrift für das Gymnasialwesen*. They form the starting point of a movement, since grown very powerful, for a thorough-going change of our method in teaching all languages.

The first, second, and fourth articles are of general interest; every teacher of the Classics ought to read the whole.

Although the German love of system may not suit the English temperament, we cannot but envy the point and precision given to pedagogic discussions in Germany by the fixed limits within which they have to move.

1874. **Julius Jolly**: Schulgrammatik und Sprachwissenschaft.

1875. **A. J. Ellis**: On the Acquisition of Languages. Reprinted from the *Educational Times* for 1st Nov., 1875.

1875. **Dr. F. Pfalz**: Über den Bildungswerth der fremden Sprachen im Schulunterrichte.

1875. **R. H. Quick**: The First Steps in Teaching a Foreign Language, with some accounts of celebrated methods.

1876. **H. Breymann**: Sprachwissenschaft uud neuere Sprachen.

1876. **Henry Sweet, I.**: Words, Logic, and Grammar. Philological Society's *Transactions*, pp. 470—503.

> A remarkably acute paper, especially in the treatment of Grammar.

1876. **M. Taine**: On the Acquisition of Language by Children.

> In *Mind*, Vol. II., pp. 252—259 : A Translation of an Article that appeared in the *Revue Philosophique*, 1876.

1877. **Darwin**: A biographical Sketch of an Infant. In *Mind*, a quarterly review of psychology and philosophy.

1877. **Henry Sweet, II.**: A Handbook of Phonetics, including a popular exposition of the principles of Spelling Reform.

1868. **J. Baumgarten**: Französische Sprache und französischer Unterricht.

> An admirable article in Schmid's *Encyklopädie*, Vol. II., pp. 647—709.

1878. **Fr. A. Eckstein**: Der lateinische Unterricht, in Dr. K. A. Schmid's Encyklopädie des gesammten Erziehungs- und Unterrichtswesens. (First edition.)

> The article in the second edition (1887) has been published separately by **Dr. H. Heyden**.

> Reviewed by **Heller**, in the *Wochenschrift für classische Philologie*, V., 7.

1878. **B. Perez**: Les Trois Premières Années de l'Enfant.

1878. **F. Pollock**: An Infant's Progress in Language. In *Mind*, Vol. III., pp. 392—401.

1879. **A. H. Sayce**: How to Learn a Language. *Nature*, p. 93.

1880. **S. S. Haldemann**: Note on the Invention of Words in *Proceedings* of the American Philological Association.

1880. **M. W. Humphreys**: A contribution to Infantile Linguistic, in *Transactions* of the American Philological Association, XI., 6—17.

1880. **M. B. Lévy, I.**: Les Langues mortes et les Langues vivantes dans l'Enseignement secondaire.

1880. **F. Lichtenberger**: How to teach and learn Modern Languages.

1880. **O. Rade** : Die psychologischen Grundzüge des Unterrichts in der Muttersprache.

1880. **Fritz Schultze** : Die Sprache des Kindes.

1880. **W. Vietor**: Die wissenschaftliche Grammatik und der englische Unterricht. Englische Studien, III., 106.

1881. **Ch. Thurot** : De la Prononciation française.
On early French books from 1521—1800.

1881. **Edward B. Tylor**: Anthropology.
The chapters on Language, pp. 114—181, are sound, and form a good starting-point for the scientific study of language.

1881. **Wyma** : The Mental Development of the Infant of to-day, in the *Journal of Psychological Medicine and Mental Pathology*, VII., pp. 62—69.

1882. **S. Brassai**: Die Reform des Sprachunterrichts in Europa.

1882. **G. Körting**: Gedanken und Bemerkungen über das Studium der neueren Sprachen auf den deutschen Hochschulen.

1882. **Gustav Lindner**: Kosmos.
"Die Beobachtungen von Lindner gehören zu den besten, welche überhaupt vorliegen." (Preyer.)

1882. **J. Müller** : Quellenschriften und Geschichte des deutschsprachlichen Unterrichts bis 1550.
The leading books between mediaeval and humanistic times are given with great fulness and accuracy.

1882. *Quousque tandem*. Der Sprachunterricht muss umkehren! Ein Beitrag zur Ueberbürdungsfrage.

1886. *Quousque tandem* (**Wilhelm Vietor**). Zweite um ein Vorwort vermehrte Auflage.

1883. **C. Bursian** : Geschichte der klassischen Philologie in Deutschland, von den Anfängen bis zur Gegenwart. 2 Bde.

1883. **Richard Hiller**: Die Latein-Methode des J. A. Comenius.
Contains a full bibliography.

1883. **Karl Kühn** : Zur Methode des französischen Unterrichts. Ein Beitrag zur Reform des Sprachunterrichts und zur Ueberbürdungsfrage.
Reviewed by H. Klinghardt, in *Englische Studien*, VII., 491.

1883. **Dr. Wilh. Münch**: Zur Förderung des französischen Unterrichts, insbesondere auf Realgymnasien.

1883. **G. A. Schrumpf**: How to begin French.
An educational essay.

1883. R. P. Scott : English in the Higher Education.

1884. Dionysii *Thracis* ars grammatica, edidit Gvstavs Ohlig.

> This excellent critical edition has full indices at the end. The paradigms taken from a MS. at the Vatican are the earliest I have seen. The edition has been reviewed by Egenolff in the *Wochenschrift für klassische Philologie*, V., 7.

1884. Felix Franke : Die praktische Spracherlernung auf Grund der Psychologie und der Physiologie dargestellt.

> An admirable little tract.

1884. W. Preyer : Die Seele des Kindes. Beobachtungen über die geistige Entwickelung des Menschen in den ersten Lebensjahren.

> There is an American translation by H. W. Brown.

1884. Henry Sweet, III. : On the Practical Study of Language. *Philological Society's Transactions*, pp. 577—600.

1885. — Spelling Reform and the Practical Study of Languages, a paper read before the English Spelling Reform Association, December 16th, 1884.

1885. J. J. Baebler : Beiträge zu einer Geschichte der lateinischen Grammatik im Mittelalter.

1885. H. Breymann : Wünsche und Hoffnungen, betreffend das Studium der neueren Sprachen an Schule und Universität.

1885. J. Neudecker : Das Doctrinale des Alexander de Villa-Dei und der lateinische Unterricht während des spätern Mittelalters in Deutschland.

1885. G. C. Schrumpf : French School Books for English Pupils, published before the 19th century. *Journal of Education*, p. 190, p. 266. See also p. 397.

1885. Henry Sweet, IV. : Elementarbuch des gesprochenen Englisch.

1885. F. Hornemann : Zur Reform des neusprachlichen Unterrichts auf höheren Lehranstalten.

1886. — Zweites Heft.

1885. H. Klinghardt : Die Lautphysiologie in der Schule. Englische Studien, VIII., 287.

1885. F. Techmer : Sprachentwickelung, Spracherlernung, Sprachbildung, in his *Internationale Zeitschrift für allgemeine Sprachwissenschaft*, Vol. II.

1886. H. Nettleship : The Study of Latin Grammar among the

Romans in the first century A.D.   The *Journal of Philology*, Cambridge,   Vol. XV.

1886. **Dr. Julius Bierbaum** : die Reform des fremdsprachlichen Unterrichts.

1886. **Ph. Kuhff** : Le Principe et la Méthode de l'Enseignement scolaire des Langues vivantes.

1886. **H. Paul** : Principien der Sprachgeschichte. (First edition, 1880.) **Prof. Strong** has made an English translation.

> This book is quite indispensable for the student of language ; it is like very stale bread, dry but nourishing.
>
> Reviews on it will be found in :—*Revue critique*, 1887, No. 1 ; *Literarisches Centralblatt*, 1887, p. 215 ; *Berl. philol. Wochenschrift*, VII., p. 531 ; *Modern Language Notes*, II., 8 ; *Internationale Zeitschrift für allgemeine Sprachwissenschaft*, III., 357.

1887. **J. Bierbaum** : Die analytisch directe Methode des neusprachlichen Unterrichts.

1887. **C. Colbeck** : On the Teaching of Modern Languages in Theory and Practice.

1887. *Eberhardi Bethuniensis* Graecismus : Edited by **Dr. Joh. Wrobel** (Breslau) as the first volume of a *Corpus grammaticorum medii aevi*. It is to be hoped that the volumes will rapidly succeed one another.

> Dettweiler gives a full review in the *Berliner philologische Wochenschrift*, VIII., 26.

1887. **K. Foth** : Der französische Unterricht auf dem Gymnasium. Auch eine Reformschrift.

1887. **Hugo Hoffmann** : Über Sprachentwickelung und die darauf sich gründende Einführung in den ersten Sprachunterricht der Elementarschule.

1887. **Otto Jespersen** : Der neue Sprachunterricht. *Englische Studien*, X., 412.

1887. *Journal of Education*. **A. Sidgwick** : The Future of Classical Education, p. 257. **Mr. Colbeck** : On Modern Language Teaching, p. 141. **Dr. R. W. Hiley** : The Study of Modern Languages in England, p. 307.

1887. **Dr. B. Jowett** : On Modern Language Teaching. A speech delivered at the Congress of French Professors. See *Journal of Education*, p. 113, or Dittes' *Paedagogium*, p. 799.

1887. **H. Klinghardt**: Techmer's und Sweet's Vorschläge zur Reform des Unterrichts im Englischen. *Englische Studien*, X., 48.

1887. **H. Klinghardt**: Ziele und wege der modernen sprachwissenschaft. *Englische Studien*, XI., 197—208.

In the same volume will be found several reports of discussions by practical schoolmasters on the Teaching of Languages. By the side of these copious *Verhandlungen* the reports of our Headmasters' Conferences make a very poor show indeed.

1887. **G. Körting**: Neuphilologische Essays.

The chief object of the school is to give the children the power of reading the great works of literature.

1887. **M. Lazarus**: Sprache.

In K. A. Schmid's Encyklopädie des gesammten Erziehungs- und Unterrichtswesens. Second edition, Vol. IX., pp. 41—73.

Students of Paul's *Principien* should read this article.

1887. **H. Neubauer**: Die Reformbewegung auf dem Gebiete des Sprachunterrichts und die höhere Bürgerschule.

1887. **Prof. Dr. Sievers**: Ziele und Wege der modernen Sprachwissenschaft. In the *Paedagogium*, edited by Dr. F. Dittes.

A short and lucid statement of modern views on language.

1888. **A. Thirion**: The Teaching of French in English Schools.

1888. **H. Klinghardt**: Ein Jahr Erfahrungen mit der neuen Methode. Bericht über den Unterricht mit einer englischen Anfängerklasse im Schuljahr 1887, '88.

1888. *Journal of Education.* **H. W. Eve**: Greek or Latin? p. 331. **Dr. E. A. Abbott**: Latin through English, p. 381.

C. F. Hodgson & Son, Printers, Gough Square, Fleet Street.

2

W. STUART MacGOWAN

'The reading-book as the centre of instruction in teaching a foreign language'

Source: *Phonetische Studien*, 4, 1891, pp. 83–90.

THE READING-BOOK AS THE CENTRE OF INSTRUCTION IN TEACHING A FOREIGN LANGUAGE.[1]

The main principle which I shall have to establish in dealing with this question is the following, which I shall now postulate as an axiom, but shall shortly endeavour to prove, viz.: *The reading of connected texts is the basis upon which a sound practical knowledge of a modern language can best be acquired.*

If not, what is our alternative? That great authority on things educational, Dr. Johnson, has furnished us with a doctrine, which, from its apparent logic, has overshadowed all teaching of languages from his day to our own. He says:— "First get a thorough know-ledge of the grammar, and then apply what you have learnt to reading and writing." This seems beautifully simple, but a long and patient trial has proved it to be a fallacy most cunningly con-cealed. Teachers are now awakening to the fact that by giving to the grammar a premier and isolated position, they have for years persistently put the cart before the horse. The result of this has been sorrow and disgust to the teacher, weariness and pain to the pupil. This is hardly surprising. Grammar in the abstract does not appeal to the mind of the pupil; it is uninteresting, unintelligible, and is not remembered for long. It makes the study of language dry even to pupils with strong linguistic tendencies, and leads them to attach an exaggerated importance, to really very unimportant

---

[1] Vortrag, gehalten 11. april 1890 zur begründung der 3. neusprachlichen these: *"That the Reading-book should be the Centre of Instruction in teaching a foreign language"* bei der versammlung der *Teachers' Guild of Great Britain and Ireland* in Cheltenham, 10.—12. 'april 1890.

Die these wurde einstimmig angenommen.

6*

details. Grammar was made for man, and not man for grammar. I am not abusing grammar, in so far as it helps us to understand language; but our stereotyped method of imparting it has brought it into just disrepute. Surely it is possible to write and speak French without knowing all about the plurals of compound nouns. Thus *grand'mères*, but *grands pères; avant-gardes*, but *timbres-poste*, &c.

Is it necessary that an elementary student of German should burden his memory with the differences in meaning of *Länder* and *Lande*, *Tücher* and *Tuche?* Is it absolutely essential that a Latin student should be quite certain of the gender of a *hat,* a *cough,* and a *basin* in that language?

This kind of thing is very nearly useless, even in more advanced prose composition.

A candidate for the "Little Go" or "Smalls" has to show a most unnecessary knowledge of what a French professor quaintly called "les beautés de la langue," which, as neither the "Tripos" nor the "Final Schools" require them at all, he very soon wisely forgets.

Grammar, then, being an abstract and lifeless science, *we must put it in a concrete form, if we are to give it any vitality.* This is brought about by bringing it into connexion with reading. If a boy has seen a form in his reading-book, and has had to translate it, it is no longer an abstract creation of the grammarian, a something shadowy and unreal, which has no part in life, but it has become an objective reality to him, a concrete and tangible object, which will serve him as a basis for an intelligent grammar lesson.

Let us take a form like ὁρῶσα in Greek. The pupil has to find a meaning, fails, and has to be told that it is contracted from ὁρά-ουσα; he will then see the need of some rules for contraction, and will eagerly welcome any assistance which grammar can give. In other words, *we ought never to give a grammatical rule without a preceding concrete instance.* This is really the only logical method, and yet how few Latin or Greek grammars do we see giving numerous examples of a phenomenon, and then deducing their rules from these examples. Don't they nearly all give the rule first, and then illustrate the rule by examples? I remember vividly how, at school, I wasted valuable time by mechanically committing to memory first the rules of the Eton Latin Grammar, and afterwards those of the Public School Latin Primer.

Again, there are some things in a language which no grammar can ever explain, no rule can ever define. Rules and grammar are powerless to cope with what can only be felt; it is useless to explain the vigour of a foreign idiom, we can but feel it or imitate it. It is quite impossible to explain how a thought took a certain form of words; in our rendering we can at best give an approximate translation, or a corresponding idiom. Grammar, then, has very clearly defined boundary lines, which it is powerless to pass.

Therefore, grammar, to be really useful, must be brought into connexion with the reading of carefully selected texts. In this form it will be of real service to the pupil.

The case for the Reader as Centre of Instruction may be very adequately summed up in the words of Bréal: *"Il faut apprendre la grammaire par la langue et non la langue par la grammaire."* — *"Grammar should never be taught before the language and apart from it"* (Kühn, Preface to *French German*).

But I fully recognise the importance of a systematic treatment of grammar in the reading-book, and do not therefore agree with those who would abandon grammar altogether. Grammar is the systematized result of man's labours in the field of language; to throw it away would be a wilful sacrifice of the experience ot our race, and would compel each pupil to begin systematizing for himself afresh.

This would be a terrible state of affairs, and might aptly be termed the method of "plunge and struggle." It has very little to recommend it, and is open to some serious objections.

(*a*) The task of forming a logical series of inductions, in the strict sense of the word, is beyond the power of most pupils. They would be simply bewildered by the maze of forms they would encounter, and without assistance they could never reduce their experiences to anything like order. It has been said by some advocates of this method : One word is as difficult to a beginner as another; but, even if we admit this obvious fallacy for the sake of argument, it by no means follows that the order in which we present words, and facts connected with them, is of no importance. We must help our pupil to introduce order into all his conceptions; all his work must be sytematic; he must see as clearly as we do the goal towards which he is striving; boys resent being taught in the dark. *What we want is modified induction—i. e., induction on the basis of certain carefully prepared texts.*

(*b*) But there is another, and I think a graver objection to the method of "plunge and struggle" than that just mentioned. If we abolished grammar, we should abolish with it that mental discipline which some rate so highly, and which consists in mastering and applying a systematic knowledge of any language. This is a real education to a pupil, and in these days, when the tendency is to assign the dominant place to purely utilitarian subjects, we cannot afford to let him neglect it. It gives him a power of abstract thinking, and may be obtained just as easily from a *modern* as from an *ancient* language.

We may definitely assume, therefore, that grammar is a necessity; it remains to be seen in what form it can best be taught.

Most of our present methods, although they all, from Ollendorff to Prendergast, have some definite underlying principle, are open to the objection that they are unsystematic and inexact, and are thus not calculated to impress the pupil with the idea that languages are really a most scientific study. It would serve no purpose to enumerate the many deficiencies in the more prominent among modern methods of imparting foreign languages; but the main points which have struck me most forcibly in the numerous grammars I have read are the following:—

(i.) Their utter want of organization.

(ii.) The absolute lack of anything like a definite system in dealing with the varied phenomena of language.

The most glaring defect of all, viz., the absolute want of uniformity in grammatical terms, has already been dealt with, so that I need only mention it in passing.

The unfortunate pupils are lost in a wilderness of confused ideas: every grammarian, every author of a "course", uses different terms to still more bewilder the hopelessly befogged pupil. Every one has his own particular fad, his one pet belief, which he trots out regardless of the fact that, while teachers disagree, pupils must suffer.

There are some people, however, who derive great hope for the future from the very multiplicity of our rival systems, on the general ground that "Competition is healthy," or "There is nothing like free trade in education." Nevertheless, our striking lack of uniformity has been, and still is, largely responsible for the low level of knowledge of foreign languages noticeable among us to-day.

Do not let us disperse without formulating the main principles on which the true method of teaching foreign languages can be based.

This brings us to the further question, *What are the conditions which an ideal method ought to fulfil?*

They are numerous, but they may be summed up shortly.

(1) *The Reader must be systematic; i. e.,* it must lend itself to a methodical study of grammar. This may be best achieved by means of carefully prepared texts into which the forms to be learnt are systematically introduced in a prescribed order. This must, of course, be accomplished without doing violence to the literature, and, by diligent search, pieces may be discovered which amply illustrate all the grammatical phenomena of a language. By this method, the pupil will kill two birds with one stone—(*a*) he is developing his sense of language by learning phraseology and vocabulary, and (*b*) he is learning grammar—*inductively*, almost unconsciously. Then, too, his interest must be kept alive no less by the consecutiveness of the passages than of the ideas they embody. There must be no isolated nonsense sentences, so dear to the disciples of Messrs. Otto, Ollendorff, and Ahn, about "My brother's cups of tea," or "The trees of the good baker's wife." Fragments of this sort may possibly be understood, but they cannot form a compact whole in the mind of the pupil, for the very good reason that they have never been conceived as a whole in the mind of the grammarian.

Thus, *a definite and systematic series of graduated grammatical phenomena is an indispensable requisite of any Reader which is to be the centre of instruction.*

(2) Another important feature of this Reader would consist in the *arrangement of the various grammatical phenomena to be acquired.* — These would be so arranged as to present to the pupil the *important* before the *unimportant*, the *less* difficult before the *more* difficult. With two or more Readers, the pupil could be taken through several courses (lasting three or four years); each of these would cover the ground of the whole grammar; but while the first gave merely the barest outline of the language, the successive ones

would cover the same ground with more and ever more detail.
(First *Übersicht*, then *Einsicht*).

The results of this method would be that the pupil, instead
of leaving school with an ill-assorted medley of isolated facts, which
are of very little use for the practical purposes of reading and
writing, would have acquired without difficulty a complete and connected view of the main features of the language. This he would
carry away with him in his memory, and it would be a permanent
possession to him.

(3) The next point of importance in the Reader would be the
position the vocabulary (*Wortschatz*) would occupy. This should be
useful, but not too comprehensive; simple, and yet not vague.   It
should not attempt to replace the teacher entirely, but should yet
be sufficiently extensive to give the pupil a sufficient *copia verborum*.
In this particular, it would fittingly replace the dictionary, the clumsy
use of which causes an immense waste of time among junior pupils.

(4) Another important feature in this Reader *would be graduated
English passages for translation based upon the grammar and vocabulary just acquired in the foreign text.* Writing must always be based
upon reading. The importance of this principle was recognised by
Roger Ascham, and its truth is nowadays reasserted by many prominent modern schoolmasters. In many of the French and German
school books of the present day, one constantly finds after the text
sentences and sometimes connected passages for retranslation. But,
though both Ascham and modern teachers are at one as to the
importance of basing writing upon reading, yet here again there is no
system, though Bacon's dictum, that "writing maketh an exact man,"
is as universally recognised to-day as it was three hundred years ago.
What is wanted now is a Reader which shall combine Ascham's
principles with the research and ingenuity of modern times—*i.e.*,
writing based upon reading combined with systematic grammar. Such
writing as this would be doubly useful, because it would compel a
pupil to arrange and apply his knowledge.

Lastly, it would be an essential feature of the reading-book
that it should be in touch with our examination system, although it
is to be hoped that examiners may shortly see fit to somewhat
modify their present *modus operandi*. Still, any method, to be an

ideal one in a *practical* as well as an *educational* sense, must not be too far removed from the exigencies of our time.

With such a Reader as this, the true order of learning would be somewhat as follows:—

(i.) Read a carefully prepared text under the direction of a teacher.

(ii.) Learn a small piece of grammar arising out of the text just read.

(iii.) Apply the knowledge thus gained to writing.

Efforts have been made of late to embody in practical form the principles for which I contend, and I hope that before long the problem will be successfully solved to which Mr. Henry Sweet refers in an article in the *Academy* of July 17th, 1886, when he speaks of the imperative "necessity of bridging over the formidable gulf between grammar and reading."

But the importance of this subject is not merely technical, or solely educational; it is vital to the best interests of a wider circle than that controlled by the scholastic profession. In view of our vast commerce, no less than our premier position in the van of nations, the public have a right to expect that their sons and daughters shall be practically instructed at school how to read, write, speak, and understand foreign languages. The Press is perpetually drawing attention to the lamentable fact that foreigners are daily supplanting our youth in city appointments, which the latter, owing to their ignorance of foreign languages, are wholly incompetent to fill. It is not for want of ability in the rising generation that our knowledge of foreign languages is of such small practical use: there is no lack of native intelligence in the Anglo-Saxon race,—it is merely the want of a properly organized rational system. It is perfectly useless to expect good "results", if we leave to the unfettered free agency of untutored minds the task of selecting or evolving the method by which these results are to be obtained. The average mind is quite incapable of the initial effort which the evolution of a system demands; hence, in the interests of foreign languages, it is absolutely essential that the majority of teachers should be agreed as to the catholic method of imparting instruction.

It is thus little less than a national calamity that language teachers should regard the chaotic muddle of conflicting methods with complacency, when the country cries aloud for reform. We modern language teachers have a great national duty to fulfil, and one which will brook no delay. It is an urgent educational necessity, that the true method of teaching foreign languages should be laid down in no ambiguous terms. If the Reader were once made the centre of a clearly defined system, most of our difficulties would vanish. In conclusion, I can only express the hope that the Conference, by their vote to-day, will put on record the fact that, in the opinion of a great body of teachers, Order, Uniformity, and Progress can best be attained by the universal adoption of the Reader as the centre of all foreign language teaching in the future.

Cheltenham.   W. STUART MACGOWAN.

3

W. VIËTOR

'Dritte Jahresversammlung der *Teachers' Guild*
und erster Englischer Neuphilologentag
in Cheltenham'

Source: *Phonetische Studien*, 4, 1891, pp. 132–8.

DRITTE JAHRESVERSAMMLUNG DER *TEACHERS' GUILD* UND
ERSTER ENGLISCHER NEUPHILOLOGENTAG IN CHELTENHAM.

Auf einladung des dortigen zweigvereins hielt die *Teachers' Guild of Great
Britain and Ireland* ihre 3. jahresversammlung vom 10.—12. april d. j. in Cheltenham, und zwar in den räumen des *Cheltenham College* ab.   Die zahl der teil-
nehmer belief sich zeitweise auf mehr als 500.

Die verhandlungen wurden eröffnet mit der begrüssung der mitglieder
und gäste durch den bürgermeister von Cheltenham, Col. Thoyts, sowie durch
den vorsitzenden Rev. H. A. James, B. D. *(principal of Cheltenham College).*

Den ersten gegenstand der beratung bildete die vom vorstand des vereins
entworfene bill bezüglich der „*registrirung*" *der lehrer (registration of teachers'
bill)* zum schutz gegen unberufene eindringlinge im lehrfach.   Der entwurf lag
der versammlung gedruckt vor.   Der vorsitzende hob die hauptpunkte hervor,
insbesondere die einsetzung eines unterrichtsrates, welchem die führung der liste
(register) qualifizirter lehrer und lehrerinnen obliegen würde.   Die 30 mitglieder
des rates wären von der königin, den englischen, irischen und schottischen universitäten, dem *College of Preceptors,* der *Teachers' Guild* und mehreren andern
institutionen gemeinsam zu ernennen. — Mr. F. Storr, B. A. *(Merchant Tailors'
School)* beleuchtete das verhältnis der bill zu einer andern ähnlichen inhalts, die
vom *College of Preceptors* ausgegangen sei und dem parlament bereits vorliege.
Der wesentliche unterschied sei der, dass die neue bill auch die elementarlehrer
zur registrirung zulassen wolle. — In der debatte wurde dieser punkt von mehre-

ren rednern beifällig kommentirt. Zum schluss beantwortete Mr. Storr einige von dem Hon. Lyulph Stanley *(London school board)* gegen die bill erhobene einwände.

Es folgte ein vortrag von Rev. T. Field, M. A. *(head master of the King's School,* Canterbury) über das vom verein in aussicht genommene *pädagogische museum.* Ein solches sei besonders nötig für die fächer der naturwissenschaften und der geographie. aber auch z. b. für die der geschichte und der klassischen sprachen. — Ein bild des geplanten museums entwarf Mr. Storr. Es müsse in dem museum zu finden sein: 1. material zur geschichte des unterrichts, insbesondere der lehrbücher; 2. lehrpläne, *examination papers* etc.; 3. schulgeräte, sowie modelle und pläne für ventilation, heizung etc.; 4. ein historischer und geographischer apparat (karten und bilder); 5. ein naturwissenschaftlicher apparat 6. eine anleitung zur anlage von schulmuseen; 7. später auch eine anthropometrische abteilung (nach Galton und Warner); 8. ein pädagogisches auskunftsbureau. — Mme. Armagnac *(Cheltenham Ladies' College)* empfahl in französischer rede das *musée pédagogique* in Paris als muster, während Mr. Lethbridge *(York Place Schools,* Bristol) die dort herrschende unordnung tadelte; Mr. J. S. Thornton, B. A. (London) verwies auf das pädagogische museum in South Kensington, das aber, wie Mr. W. H. Widgery, M. A. (London) bemerkte, ohne aussicht auf wiederherstellung eingegangen ist.

Die mittagspause wurde zur besichtigung der pädagogischen ausstellung (vorwiegend lehrbücher) und zum lunch benutzt.

Am nachmittag redete Mr. Courthorpe Bowen, M. A. (London) über *den unterricht im englischen.* Das englische müsse nach psychologischen grundsätzen gelehrt werden. Die aneignung des wortschatzes habe nicht auf etymologischem wege, sondern durch vergleichung von sätzen zu erfolgen. An sätzen sei auch die kenntnis der sprache als eines werkzeugs zu erwerben; stilübungen seien im anschluss an den anschauungs- und zeichenunterricht vorzunehmen. — Mr. Widgery unterstützte die ausführungen des redners und klagte über die vernachlässigung der muttersprache in den englischen schulen im vergleich mit Frankreich. — In der sehr lebhaften diskussion des vortrags traten verschiedenerlei ansichten zu tage. Mr. T. C. Snow, M. A. (Oxford) glaubte, das englische werde am besten indirekt in den für andre dinge bestimmten lehrstunden gelehrt, was Mr. Widgery nachdrücklich zurückwies.

Auch der sich anschliessende vortrag von Mrs. Curwen (London) über *den unterricht in der musik* war von allgemeinerem interesse. Das ziel des musikunterrichts ist nach ansicht der rednerin nicht die heranbildung ausübender künstler, sondern eines kunstsinnigen und kunstverständigen publikums. Die meisten musiklehrer sündigten gegen die elementarsten grundsätze der pädagogik, wie z. b. die folgenden: 1. Jede lektion muss sich aus der vorigen ergeben und zur nächsten hinführen (der gang der „klavierschulen" nimmt nur auf die schwierigkeit der ausführung rücksicht). 2. Das einfache (zeit, name, intervall etc.) ist vor dem zusammengesetzten (musikstück) zu lehren. 3. Die sache (z. b. rhythmus) vor dem zeichen (zeitlicher notenwert). 4. Das konkrete (töne) vor dem abstrakten (noten). 5. Nur eins auf einmal, und das nötigste zuerst (die vorzeichnungen der tonarten z. b. werden zu früh gelehrt).

Über denselben gegenstand sprach sodann Mrs. Webster, L. R. A. M. (Aberdeen), um für den klassenunterricht im klavierspiel einzutreten. Die methode hätte 4 stufen zu umfassen : *1. stufe:* Noch ausser der gesangsstunde übungen des ohres und der hand; elementare notenkenntniss. *2. stufe:* fünffinger-übungen (ohne noten); zuerst einzel-, dann zusammenspiel; elementare theorie. *3. stufe:* ganz leichte melodien (ebenso). *4. stufe:* einfache stücke zu 4 händen; anfänge der musikalischen analyse. Auf jeder stufe wären prüfungen abzuhalten.

Abends fand im *Ladies' College* eine *conversazione* statt, zu welcher der vorstand des vereins einladungen hatte ergehen lassen.

Am zweiten tag führte der Hon. Lyulph Stanley den vorsitz. Dr. R. Wormell, M. A. *(head master of the Middle Class School,* Cowper street, E. C.) erhielt das wort zu einem vortrag über *den übergang von der elementarschule zu einer höheren schule.* Redner sieht diese frage als äusserst wichtig an, denn nicht nur $^6/_7$, wie man vor 20 jahren erwartete, sondern $^9/_{10}$ aller schulpflichtigen kinder besuchen eine elementarschule. Den hinreichend beanlagten und bemittelten unter ihnen muss der zugang zur höheren bildung eröffnet werden. Diese notwendigkeit müssen die lehrer der höheren schulen, die lehrer der elementarschulen und die vorstände und leiter der letzteren gleichmässig anerkennen. — Principal Barnett, M. A. *(Borough Road Training College)* äusserte ernste bedenken gegen die von dem vorredner empfohlenen stipendien. Wirkliche besserung sei nur von der errichtung höherer und niederer freischulen zu erhoffen. — Rev. Dr. Flecker *(Dean Close School)* warnt vor weiterer überfüllung der höheren schulen — und infolgedessen des mittelstandes — mit nur mittelmässig beanlagtem schülermaterial. Er empfiehlt hebung der volksschulen durch beschaffung von gründlicher gebildeten lehrkräften. — Mr. Thornton tadelt die gründung von gehobenen schulen durch die lokalschulvorstände als einen unberechtigten übergriff. — Mr. C. Hayward *(British School,* Cheltenham) wünscht mittelschulen, die nicht nur für die befähigten schüler der elementarschule geeignet wären, sondern auch solchen, die jetzt eine höhere schule besuchten, eine bessere vorbildung fürs praktische leben bieten würden. Gründliche abhülfe sieht er nur in einem nationalen unterrichtssystem mit einem unterrichtsminister an der spitze. Mr. Richardson (Oxford) verweist auf die bereits bestehenden fortbildungsschulen. Nach prof. Henry Smith gehe nicht ein schüler unter tausend später zur universität über. — Mr. Newbold (Manchester) sieht die der versammlung vorliegende frage darin, ob der höhere (d. h. sekundär-) unterricht durch erweiterung des primärunterrichts ergänzt werden solle. — Mr. Lethbridge (Brighton) erklärt sich gegen stipendien und verteidigt die vom schulvorstand in Birmingham errichtete fortbildungsschule gegen Mr. Thorntons angriffe. — Der vorsitzende, Mr. L. Stanley, will den unterschied zwischen primärunterricht (wohin er auch die deutsche *bürgerschule* und die französische *école primaire supérieure* rechnet) und dem sekundärunterricht gewahrt wissen, jedoch müsse der primärunterricht auch fortbildungsschulen einschliessen. Die frage sei noch nicht reif zur entscheidung, doch greife die überzeugung immmer weiter um sich, dass die nation für die heranbildung aller volksklassen verantwortlich sei.

Hierauf sprach Miss Beale *(principal of the Ladies' College,* Cheltenham über *schriftliche und mündliche leistungen in der schule,* insbesondere der mädchen-schule. Die rednerin beantwortet zuerst die frage, was in bezug auf mündliche leistungen zu verlangen sei, dahin, dass an erster stelle das aufsagen von gedichten zu stehen habe. Dann folgen der reihe nach: 2. das wiedererzählen von geschichten; 3. das übersetzen aus fremden sprachen; 4. das lernen von grammatischen formen (jedoch mit hülfe von tabellen etc.); 5. dialoge und unterredungen im anschluss an bilder; 6. mündliche fragen über alles aufgegebene (in den unteren klassen). Die schriftlichen arbeiten für schülerinnen von etwa 8 bis 12 jahren will die vortragende auf ein geringes beschränkt wissen; die zu hause angefertigten arbeiten dürfen eine halbe bis höchstens eine stunde in anspruch nehmen. Passende aufgaben sind: 1. niederschreiben von auswendig gelernten gedichten; 2. abschreiben englischer wie auch französischer stücke; 3. diktate (nach vorbereitung); 4. grammatische formen (aus dem gedächtnis); 5. übersetzungen und rückübersetzungen und seltener grammatische lesestücke. Für das alter von 12 bis 16 jahren soll die auf schriftliche hausarbeit verwandte zeit 1—1$\frac{1}{2}$ stunden betragen. Was den sprachunterricht betrifft, so gehören folgende schriftliche arbeiten hierher: niederschriften nach dem gedächtnis (englisch, in den höheren klassen in fremden sprachen); desgl. von fremdsprachlichen grammatischen formen; satzanalysen, „*written* vivâ voce", d. h. schriftliche beantwortung mündlich gestellter fragen (in der klasse); wöchentlich mehrere kurze aufsätze (auf grund von fragen über einen behandelten gegenstand etc.). Auch die korrektur der verschiedenen schriftlichen arbeiten wurde eingehend besprochen. — Miss Cooper (*High School*, Edgbaston), Rev. H. A. James und Rev. J. E. C. Welldon *(head master of Harrow School)* legen grösseren wert auf das niederschreiben von notizen seitens der schüler. Miss Burstall *(North London Collegiate School)* glaubt, dass die schülerinnen zuviel zu schreiben, die lehrerinnen zu viel zu korrigieren haben. Auch Miss Ward *(Maria Grey Training College)* klagt über die menge der korrekturen und die starrheit der methode in mädchenschulen. Rev. T. K. Moore *(Church of England Training College,* Dublin) betont die notwendigkeit, vom schüler vollständige und sprachlich korrekte antworten zu verlangen. Mlle. Soult (für höheren unterricht delegirt von dem französischen unterrichtsminister[1]) berichtet hierauf über die an ihrer anstalt, dem *lycée Fénélon* in Paris, befolgten methoden. Anfänglich hätten die schriftlichen arbeiten fast soviel raum eingenommen wie in den englischen höheren mädchenschulen, die erfahrung habe jedoch gelehrt, dass man mit einer schriftlichen arbeit täglich auskomme. Notizen würden nur in den obersten klassen und nur nach diktat gemacht.

Die verhandlungen der *Teachers' Guild* schlossen mit den üblichen dankesvoten.

---

[1] Für den elementarunterricht war delegirt: Mme. Armagnac *(membre correspondant de la Société des instituteurs)*. Ferner hatte der minister entsandt: M. Bonet-Maury *(docteur de la faculté théologique protestante de Paris)*; die stadt Paris: M. Bébin (prof. am *lycée Buffon);* die *Société scientifique et littéraire:* Dr. de Thierry; die *Société des professeurs de français:* M. Huguenet. Auf einladung des ausschusses für die neusprachlichen verhandlungen nahmen M. Paul Passy

Im anschluss an die vorausgegangenen verhandlungen fand am nachmittag des 11. und am morgen des 12. april die von der *Teachers' Guild,* der *Grammatical Society* und Mr. W. Stuart Macgowan, B. A. *(Cheltenham College)* veranstaltete neuphilologische oder neusprachlich-pädagogische versammlung *(Conference on the teaching of modern languages)* statt. Das komitee bildeten laut dem programm: John Peile, Esq., Litt. D. *(master of Christ's College,* Cambridge); Rev. H. A. James, B. D. *(principal of Cheltenham College);* Oscar Browning, Esq., M. A. *(fellow of King's College,* Cambridge); Prof. W. Vietor, Ph. D., (Marburg); M. Paul Passy (Neuilly-sur-Seine); W. M. Baker, Esq., M. A. *(head master of modern department, Cheltenham College);* Prof. Kuno Meyer, Ph. D. *(University College,* Liverpool); Prof. P. Barbier *(South Wales University College,* Cardiff); Prof. E. A. Sonnenschein, M. A. *(Mason College,* Birmingham); W. R. Porcher, Esq., M. A. *(The College,* Cheltenham); L. M. Moriarty, Esq., M. A. *(Harrow School,* Harrow-on-the-Hill); Mons. George Patilleau *(The Charterhouse,* Godalming); Mons. Paul Desages *(The College,* Cheltenham).

Folgende fünf thesen wurden jede durch einen kurzen vortrag eingeleitet, durch einen zweiten redner (these 2 auch durch eine dritte sprecherin) unterstützt, zur diskussion gestellt und endlich zur abstimmung gebracht. Die versammlung nahm sämtliche thesen an, davon these 1, 3 und 5 *einstimmig.* Den vorsitz in der nachmittagssitzung führt Mr. H. W. Eve, M. A. *(head master of University College School,* London).

Zu these 1: *„Gleichmässigkeit in der behandlung der grammatik der fünf schulsprachen ist wünschenswert"* sprach Rev. A. R. Vardy, M. A. (Birmingham). Der redner schildert die namentlich in der bezeichnung der tempora herrschende verwirrung. So führe z. b. *j'ai parlé* in den den englischen schulgrammatiken folgende namen: *„preterite indefinite", „indefinite", „present perfect", „past indefinite", „compound present".* Grössere gleichmässigkeit lasse sich seines erachtens erreichen: 1. in der phonetik (eine gemeinsame lauttafel für alle schulsprachen); 2. in der klassifikation der redeteile; 3. in der einteilung der substantive, adjektive, pronomina und verba; 4. in derjenigen der modi. Auch in der syntax könne manches in gleichem sinne gebessert werden; wie die anordnung der formen des prädikats etc. Redner erhofft von dieser reform ein gesteigertes interesse an linguistischen studien durch die weitergehende anwendung der vergleichenden methode. — Miss Beale (Cheltenham) erwähnt. dass die *Grammatical Society* alle sprachen als dialekte einer und derselben sprache behandle. — Mr. Snow (Oxford) regt die einigung der wichtigsten prüfungsbehörden über ein minimum grammatischer gleichmässigkeit an. Prof. Sonnenschein hebt hervor, dass die *Grammatical Society* der grammatik keine grössere wichtigkeit beilegen, vielmehr einen grossen teil des grammatischen ballasts über bord werfen wolle. Der vorsitzende, Mr. Eve, möchte das *„past indefinite"* im französischen und den „aorist" im griechischen beibehalten wissen. — Die these wurde ohne widerspruch angenommen.

(Neuilly-sur-Seine) und der unterzeichnete an der versammlung teil, so dass auch die internationale *Association phonétique des professeurs de langues vivantes* durch ihren schriftführer und ihren vorsitzenden vertreten war. Die deutschen uuterrichtsbehörden hatten keine delegirten geschickt.

These 2: *„Die these hat die grundlage des ganzen neusprachlichen unter-*
richts zu bilden" führte der unterzeichnete (englisch) ein, indem er, von Sweets vortrag von 1884 *(The practical study of language)* ausgehend, ein bild der seit etwa
zehn jahren in Deutschland wirkenden reformbewegung zu geben suchte.   Die
hierher gehörigen beschlüsse der versammlungen zu Dessau (1884), Giessen (1885),
Hannover (1886) und Dresden (1888) wurden in wörtlicher übersetzung mitgeteilt;
auch wurde darauf hingewiesen, dass die besseren erfolge der phonetischen methode bei den höheren schulbehörden schon mehrfach nachdrückliche anerkennung
gefunden haben.   Hoffentlich werde die versammlung der ansicht sein, dass auch
in England, der „heimat der phonetik", wie Sweet sich ausdrückt, die phonetik
die grundlage des neusprachlichen unterrichtes bilden müsse. — M. Paul Passy
schilderte (englisch) in eindringlicher rede die günstigen erfahrungen, die er mit der
phonetischen methode gemacht habe, und wies die vorurteile zurück, dass phonetische umschrift in der schule und orthographie-reform dasselbe seien, oder dass
die phonetische umschrift eine neue belastung der schüler bedeute. — Miss L.
Soames (Brighton)[1] sah das grösste hindernis für die einführung der phonetischen
methode in England darin, dass man über die laute der eigenen sprache meist
völlig im unklaren sei.   Wenige leute ahnten, dass das *a* in *father, fat, fate, wall,*
want, villa, village sieben verschiedene aussprachen habe.   Phonetische kenntnis
der muttersprache sei daher das dringendste erfordernis. — Mr. Widgery, der schon
am vorigen tage bei anderm anlass nachdrücklich für die phonetik eingetreten
war, ergriff in der diskussion das wort, um nochmals zu betonen, was die phonetik *nicht* sei: 1. Kein neuer gegenstand — in den schulgrammatiken pflegten
die ersten zwei seiten von phonetik zu handeln; leider nur seien sie so voll von
fehlern *„as an egg is of meat"*. 2. Kein gegenstand für das kind, sondern für
den lehrer; der lehrer müsse nicht die prinzipien, sondern die anwendung geben;
einige winke könnten von ungeheurem werte sein. 3. Nicht dasselbe wie phonetische orthographie. 4. Keine rivalin der litteratur; aber die litteratur könne
ohne die phonetik nicht voll gewürdigt werden; mit ihr erst komme leben in
den Horaz und den Virgil.   Ferner sprechen zu der these M. Le François *(Cotham*
Brow Ladies' College, Briston), Miss A. C. Beale (London) und Mr. Storr. — Die
versammlung erklärt sich mit der these einverstanden.

Die 3. these: *„Das lesebuch muss den mittelpunkt des fremdsprachlichen*
unterrichtes bilden" leitete ein vortrag von Mr. W. Stuart Macgowan, B. A.
(Cheltenham) ein, der den lesern der *Phon. studien* an anderer stelle im wortlaut
zugänglich gemacht ist. — Unterstützt wurde die these durch Mr. Moriarty. —
An der debatte beteiligten sich Mr. W. S. Logeman *(Newton House School,* Rock
Ferry), Mr. Widgery, M. Le François, Mrs. Curwen, Miss Cooper, M. Gould

---

[1] Miss Soames *(hon. secretary of the Brighton branch of the T. G.),* unsere
geschätzte mitarbeiterin, hatte nicht nur im ausstellungssaale eine umsichtig aus-
gewählte phonetische bibliothek zur ansicht gebracht, sondern den besuchern der
versammlung auch eine kleine broschüre mit folgendem titel zur verfügung gestellt: *„Notes on Phonetics,* containing a statement of the methods of instruction
recommended to students of phonetics; and an English phonetic alphabet in which
no new letters are used."

(Scarbro'), Mr. Courthorpe Bowen und der vorsitzende. Die abstimmung ergab die einstimmige annahme der these.

Zur gründlichen behandlung der 4. these: „*Die wertschätzung und stellung der grammatik im neusprachlichen unterricht bedarf dringend der revision*" blieb keine zeit. Der (unvollendete) vortrag prof. Barbiers (Cardiff) zur begründung der these wurde beifällig aufgenommen.

Am folgenden morgen (samstag den 12. april) fand unter dem vorsitz von prof. Sonnenschein die schlusssitzung statt.

Prof. Meyer (Liverpool) sprach zu these 5: „*Ein tüchtiges lehrermaterial wird am besten dadurch gesichert, dass an unseren universitäten ein* honours' degree *in neueren sprachen eingerichtet wird, dessen erlangung an die gründliche kenntnis der lebenden sprache geknüpft ist.*" Der vortragende beantwortet die fragen, was unter einem tüchtigen lehrermaterial, und was unter einem *honours' degree* der angegebenen art zu verstehen sei. Der neusprachliche unterricht sei in England fast noch gänzlich ausländischen lehrern, d. h. dem zufall überlassen. Es müsse gelegenheit zum gründlichen studium der neueren sprachen auf den englischen universitäten geboten werden. Das, und nicht allein der akademische grad, sei das ziel des antrags. — Nach einer diskussion, an welcher Mr. Widgery, Miss Soames u. a. teilnahmen, fand die these die einstimmige billigung der versammlung.

Marburg.   W. VIETOR.

4

W. STUART MacGOWAN
'Modern Language Association'

Source: *Die neueren Sprachen*, 1, 1893, pp. 282–3.

III. VEREINE.

MODERN LANGUAGE ASSOCIATION.

The necessity of forming some Association whose main object should be to raise the status of the study of modern languages in England became obvious shortly after the Modern Language Conference held at Cheltenham College in April 1890, when a series of resolutions were passed which, could they have been immediately been carried into effect, would have revolutionised the teaching of modern languages throughout the country.

At that time, despite the efforts of Prof. Sonnenschein and his band of co-workers, the objects and aims of those who wished to reform the empirical teaching of the past 50 years were only partially understood. — No organisation existed which could speak authoritatively on controversial points, or disseminate the latest ideas either for improving the teaching or raising the standard of knowledge in modern languages in our schools und universities. — The Teachers' Guild were doing what they could for education generally, but my suggestion to the Educational Committee of that body, that the resolutions which had been brought forward by Prof. Vietor, M. Passy, Prof. Sonnenschein and many others well known teachers, should be printed and published, was met by the reply that no funds were available for this purpose. Thus the matter dropped for a year. In August 1891 however, Prof. Marshall Elliott of Johns Hopkins University, one of the leading organizers of the Modern Language Association of America, pointed out to me in the course of a long conversation at the British Museum, the benefits which would result to the study of modern languages, not only in England, but also in Germany and America, from the formation of a society, which should serve as a connecting link between the three kindred nations. — Meeting with further sympathy and assistance from Mr. J. J. Beuzemaker—until recently editor of the *Modern Language Monthly* — and others, letters were written to personal friends and other educationists asking for some indication of their opinion if a society of the kind thus briefly outlined would meet with their approval and support. — The body of opinion thus collected being unanimously in favour of the founding of such a society, circulars were issued to leading colleagues at the public schools convening a meeting on Dec. 22nd 1892 at 87, Southampton Row W.C. — After giving the meeting a brief account of what had been accomplished by the American and German societies and reading kindly letters of greeting from Profs. Vietor and Elliott—to both of whom I take this opportunity of offering the Association's warmest thanks—the society was duly constituted. — Since then four meetings of the Committee have been held: the officers elected were: *President*: Prof. Max Müller; *Chairman* of Committees: J. J. Beuzemaker (86, Fleet St. E.C.); *Vice-Chairman*: J. Bentham Dickinson (Rugby); *Hon. Treas.*: J. W. Whyte (Haileybury); *Hon. Sec.*: W. Stuart Macgowan (Cheltenham).

105

The *Memorandum of the Association* has been drawn up and the Association has begun its active work. — The Universities of Oxford, Dublin and Durham are to be petitioned to grant an honours degree in Modern Languages and Literatures, while full inquiries will be made into the position and status of modern languages in our principal schools and colleges. — Owing to the comprehensive nature of its aims, the work before the Association promises to be arduous, but the large measure of support it has hitherto met with augurs well for the success of its future career.

Cheltenham.   W. Stuart Macgowan.

5

W. STUART MacGOWAN

'The relative educational value of ancient and modern languages'

Source: *Die neueren Sprachen* 1, 1893, pp. 309–18 (Part I); pp. 391–9 (Part II); pp. 437–49 (Part III).

DIE NEUEREN SPRACHEN.

ZEITSCHRIFT
FÜR DEN
NEUSPRACHLICHEN UNTERRICHT.

| BAND I. | OCTOBER 1893. | HEFT 6. |

THE RELATIVE EDUCATIONAL VALUE OF ANCIENT AND MODERN LANGUAGES.[1]

CHAPTER I.

For the purposes of this paper, I may at once explain that while by "Ancient Languages" I understand only the dead languages of Athens und Rome, by "Modern Languages" I mean the living languages of France, Germany and England. — "Language," says Milton, "is but the instrument of conveying to us things *useful* to be known," but, except for casual mention, I shall not dwell on the *utilitarian* value of modern languages to-night; that is universally admitted. I will speak rather of modern languages as instruments of intellectual discipline and culture, and as the records of the literature of great nations. — Our chairman (Prof. Nettleship) has spoken of language and literature as "*Human life which has escaped the grave*," and it is upon the broad basis of the general culture and knowledge to be derived from the study of all human life, that I plead for a more serious study of French, German and English in our schools und universities. — As the very body of literature, language is incomparably the finest instrument of education we possess, for it is the record of those choice spirits to whom the gift of utterance has been vouchsafed, and who, amid the weltering chaos of life, have left unto us a memorial of their hopes and fears, their toiling and struggling in the search after truth.

---

[1] Dieser am 17. mai 1892 im Taylorian Institute zu Oxford gehaltene vortrag erscheint hier zum ersten mal im druck.   *D. red.*

The great Universities of Oxford and Cambridge have long recognized this fact, but owing to reasons which need not be detailed here, the study of language has hitherto exclusively meant Latin and Greek. Both Universities hold that a detailed course in Latin and Greek is the best preparation for the man who wishes to acquire an elevated English style, hence up to 1884 Cambridge had no honours degree in modern languages, and Oxford still refuses to set any store on English or foreign languages and literatures. The study is not discouraged, it is true, but it is not thought worthy of an honours degree. In our great schools, the vernacular is not much taught, our literature is not studied; French and German are taught by the help of "Messrs Otto, Ollendorff and Ahn" in a haphazard empirical style, which is practically of no educational value whatever; while foreign literature is never even mentioned. Can it be that our language and literature is poorer than that of say Germany? We have the authority of Jacob Grimm for saying that it is not. Why then should we still hold fast to the mediaeval tradition, which considered modern languages irregular in grammar and structure because forsooth they refused to be restrained by the thraldom of the Latin Primers? Why should we leave to the enthusiasm of German scholars the minute study of our native language and literature? Why allow our cousins to investigate for us this glorious instrument of thought and expression which we have inherited like the sceptre we hold from our fore-fathers?

Let us begin English education with the accurate study of English. It is of the utmost importance in teaching a foreign language, that the language which is to be the medium of instruction should be thoroughly understood. English is not thoroughly understood, and foreign languages are seldom seriously studied at school. This is detrimental even to the study of the classics, for the great thoughts and wisdom of the ancients have survived and are incorporated in modern languages and literatures. It is thus just as important, that classical students of the 19th century should know and understand English, French and German, as that they should be continually nurtured on the ancient literatures, which have already so largely determined our modes of thought and expression. Critical scholarship was formerly a means to an end, now it threatens to become an end in itself. Surely, if the mind merely requires grammatical stimulus, there are difficulties enough and to spare in German accidence and French syntax, even should it find itself confronted by no obstacles when it tackles English grammar. Even if it were not so, a knowledge of French and German is an ever living reality to its possessor. I regret that, with the majority of our fellow countrymen, the classics are not as much appreciated as they deserve to be. Their prestige gains for them a certain *succès d'estime* with minds of a certain culture, but I fear the admiration of the rest does but unconsciously give effect the old adage painfully acquired from the Latin Grammar, "*omne ignotum pro magnifico.*" — "*Wir behalten doch am ende von unseren studien nur das, was wir praktisch anwenden können,*" says Goethe. How many men habitually read the masterpieces — or otherwise — of antiquity in later life? Statistics on this point would, I fancy, put a different complexion upon that fervent admiration for the classics so often expressed by many an antagonist of modern languages. Are the classics really so perfect as to justify the excessive eulogies bestowed upon them? Are we quite without prejudice in forming our judgment? May not our attitude be something similar to that of the Romanist prostrate before the shrine of an ancient and fabled saint? Are we not taking a great deal on trust? Are Latin and Greek as educative for the majority of mankind as we have been led to believe?

Even if we grant that they are absolutely perfect in the abstract, this is not enough; they are only potentially so; for notwithstanding all the labour and ingenuity which has been lavished upon them, they have not been made attractive enough. If boys are to be educated, they must be stimulated, their training should interest them; we must give them something which is relatively attractive, something which they will appreciate and which, in its early stages, will by its inherent interest rivet their attention. This, modern languages and literatures, if taught by educated men upon a rational method, could not fail to do. There is never any visible connexion in the boy's mind between the daily dole of Caesar and Xeno-

20*

phon and the thoughts and experiences of his own life. This study of the classics is often far too abstract. Can it then be wondered at, that after a boy has got up, by the aid of grammar, dictionary and crib, his meagre dole of Virgil or Sophocles, he turns to that lightest of Literature "Tit Bits" or to the sterner delights of the "Penny Dreadful"?

Nor is there anything wonderful in his doing so. The dry formalism of Latin and Greek is intensely repellent to the average boy's active receptive mind. I trust this contention will not be misunderstood. I have no wish to derogate from the claims of the Latin Language — even in its mediaeval stage — to a position of almost unique importance in the history of the culture of the human race; but the intellectual convenience which caused it to be the learned medium of intercourse in Europe no longer exists. It is no longer spoken at Oxford and Cambridge, and it only lingers on in "canine" form as a kind of student's slang at some of the German Universities. None save the more pedantic, pretentious or exclusive of classical or theological scholars ever venture to employ it. It is no longer used for records of proceedings at law.

As in ecclesiastical matters, so in education. Long after forms and ceremonies have lost any significance they may have originally possessed, they have still retained a superstitious hold both on public and on private opinion. From the darkest Ages Latin and Greek have held an honoured place until, as Emerson has it, they have now "become stereotyped as education."

The culture conveyed to the mind by classical study and nothing else cannot fail to be somewhat one-sided. The classics do not stimulate us to action, but rather predispose us to dreams; they are not altogether in sympathy with the spirit of the age. Can we not teach French, German and English quite as scientifically and accurately as we can Latin and Greek? Can we not teach boys to appreciate the masterpieces of English, French and German literature? Surely this is not impossible! Yet it has never been tried.

Can we not free ourselves from our superstitious veneration for empty forms and see if it be not possible to remedy a state of things whereby the exercise of construing Latin and Greek is demanded of all men and of all intelligences? Surely it must be narrowing for the mind and cramping for the intellect of a nation, that each one of its citizens should be passed through the same educational mill. May not the Greek and Roman languages have too long possessed the monopoly in secondary education? Has not our native language been too long ignored? Have not foreign literatures been studiously overlooked? Has the influence of the classical languages always been beneficial? Can we deny that they have blotted out much of our vigorous native vocabulary? Has not our speech been emasculated? Has not our very syntax been warped? Truly we have too long been bound by the classic chain. — Was not the spirit of parochialism upon the Philistines who, at the Renaissance, transplanted into the living body of our native speech, portions from the dead Corpus of the Roman language?

I venture deferentially to suggest that although these pathological operations were successfully accomplished, they were performed by quack practitioners who were ignorant of the principles of "natural selection" and understood not the laws of "evolution." Our native speech has been slandered, vilified and abused. It has been cast out of doors and proscribed. Some good Samaritans, Shakspeare, Marlowe and Ben Jonson, took it up and carefully tended it, till, despite its wounds, it attained a giant-like stature. Since then, notwithstanding many attempts of the learned to sap its strength and cramp its frame, it has grown and multiplied, and this is entirely due to the native inherent vigour of its constitution. Neglect and opposition have merely retarded a growth which they could not crush.

How much longer are we going to neglect Ben Jonson's advice to the English nation "to ripen the wits of our children and advance their knowledge" by the study of our native tongue? One of the main reasons why English education produces such comparatively poor results is that we do not thoroughly understand the language which is the medium of all the instruction we give, viz: English. — With French and German, the case is slightly different. The reason the standard is so low is traceable to the reign of Messrs Otto, Ollendorff,

Ahn, Prendergast and Co. These systems do not edify the mind, they build up no faculty, nor are they even a short cut to the languages they attempt to teach. The *fons et origo malorum* in their case has been the entire absence of any rational method in teaching these languages. As some one has happily put it: "The teaching of French and German has been spoiled by cups of tea."

But henceforward, this complaint cannot honestly be made. Some years ago, a method was formulated, which last January met with the official approval of the highest Educational authority in Europe, — the Prussian Education Department. This new method, while it ensures a complete mastery of a language, also affords as adequate a mental training as that obtainable from classical study.[1] But I must leave the consideration of this most interesting part of my subject, to briefly summarize the history of the study of French and German in England.

CHAPTER II.

If we glance back at the position occupied by French and German in English schools in the 18th century, a melancholy state of affairs is disclosed. We find that though Latin and Greek were taught in the grammar schools, French formed no part of the regular curriculum. Hence it held no very high place in the esteem of young Englishmen. Later on this indifference would not unfrequently develop into contempt, for we were then in a chronic state of war with France, and the patriotic Briton would occasionally boast that he could neither speak nor understand the language of "frog-eating Mounseer." In the case of German, the "insular note" was even more pronounced, for despite the Teutonic extraction of our Royal Family, prejudice was against the language, and it was not studied. Even our great writers appear almost ignorant of the existence of Klopstock, Lessing, Schiller and Goethe.

Thus it is only during the present century, that French and German have gained a permanent place in our school

---

[1] What can be done with the new method has been ably shewn by Messrs Vietor, Passy, Dörr, Klinghardt and others.

time-tables. Only sixty years ago, French was studied as an "extra" which ranked with "dancing and deportment," while German, although at that time (1831) the great Goethe was entering on the last year of his life, was practically an unknown tongue. True, some far-sighted spirits, such as Sir Walter Scott, Thomas Carlyle and Coleridge, had been induced to study the language, but except for such casual attention, German scholarship was non-existent in England.

With the marriage of Queen Victoria to a German Prince, whose encouragement of modern languages at Eton[1] soon gave them a certain vogue in less favoured schools; with the establishment of the French Empire under Napoleon III., and with the institution of Competitive Examinations, French and German received an impetus to which they largely owe the improved position they occupy in our schools to-day. But even under these improved circumstances, as those of us whose experience goes back into the last generation will recollect, French and German, apart from their recognized position as conduit-pipes of the army, were not always viewed in the light of serious studies. The time devoted to them was utterly inadequate,[2] the French or German master was not always in sympathy with his pupils, and in the absence of the stimulus such sympathy produces, the results obtained were frequently very poor.

As an instance of the utter contempt felt until quite recently for all things foreign, one need only quote the oft-told tale, that on the French mastership at Woolwich falling vacant, the Duke of Wellington did not hesitate to appoint the husband of his discharged housemaid or cook. But "a great deal has happened since then." We have seen a United Germany and a United Italy grow up; France has consolidated her power and developed her resources. English scholars have taught their countrymen, that France and Germany have not only languages but literatures. *Faust* and *Les Misérables* have electrified the world.

---

[1] Dr. Arnold of Rugby was, I understand, the first to introduce the study of modern languages at that school.

[2] There is still ground for complaint in this respect.

French art has found numerous admirers; German music is admittedly supreme, while the latest results of research in Chemistry, Geography and Mathematics are published simultaneously in French, German and English. So too, in the domain of History, Philosophy and Educational Science, the latest additions to knowledge are frequently published in French and German.[1] The great science of Comparative Philology owes most of its vigour to the indefatigable diligence of German scholars. Englishmen are gradually becoming less insular and more cosmopolitan in social intercourse, more open-minded in their relations with the outside world.

Although modern languages have now won tardy recognition from a certain section of the public, which has recognized their social, commercial and political value; though they are daily increasing in importance as school subjects, and though their most uncompromising opponents cannot maintain that a knowledge of them does not treble the library whence information can be drawn, yet, in spite of all this, there exists a class of mind which never wearies of bringing forward arguments against French and German as instruments of humanistic culture.

No one, so far as I am aware, has yet deemed it worth while to attempt a serious defence of modern languages as instruments of culture, but they have been strongly attacked on many occasions. Let me quote a few statements out of many.

"Modern Languages," said the late Mr. J. K. Stephen in his defence of Compulsory Greek at Cambridge, "can be learnt partly by guess-work, partly by imitation." "They can be 'picked up' by a few weeks' residence in the foreign country," says another. "They are quite out of place at a University," says a third. "They are out of court at once as a training ground for mind," said the late headmaster of Uppingham (Mr. Thring). "There is not enough in them as subjects," says a fifth, "they contain no history or philosophy." And so on,

---

[1] Indeed, I have been told, that at Oxford, unless a man can read modern German, he finds a difficulty in getting a First class in the Honours School of Literae Humaniores.

but I will not further multiply instances. — The condemnation of modern languages is unanimous in many quarters. But why? Is their educational value really nil?

If we examine the stock arguments, we shall find that most of them are mere stereotyped assertions, and that not one of them is wholly borne out by the facts of the case. In the absence of sound argument, considerable ingenuity has been exercised in getting up a case against modern languages. Latin and Greek, it is urged — being dead — are fixed *languages*, but as French and German are still spoken, they are merely changing *dialects*, and being themselves "undisciplined," it is alleged that they are necessarily incapable of affording mental discipline to the student of them. Now, these statements are either rhetorical, or, they are meant as arguments, in which latter case, the ease with which they can be met augurs well for the speedy recognition of the educational value of modern languages in the immediate future. Yet no less an authority than the late Headmaster of Uppingham devotes some 18 pages of dogmatising to the task of proving that while the modern languages of Europe are valueless as a training subject for the young, "Greek and Latin are the most perfect practice-ground in the world for training mind."

Mr. Thring's whole argument is based on the assumption that modern languages are learnt "as by a baby in the nursery" and that the power of speech does not involve the slightest mental training. These premises being as I shall hope to shew untenable, the whole fabric of argument crumbles to the ground. No one will venture to maintain that a boy at school learns French or German in the same way that he learnt his mother tongue; the maternal method is not in use outside the *Kindergarten*[1]; nor will any one care to dispute the fact that the effort involved in uttering grammatical speech is one involving considerable concentration of thought, judgment and coordinating power. And although I am quite prepared to admit that some teachers of foreign languages — notably Messrs Otto, Ollendorff, Ahn and Co. — may have somewhat

---

[1] M. Gouin's method is a mere organized continuation of the *Kindergarten* process.

overrated the *ear* as an educational medium, yet it is an undeniable fact that classical scholars and teachers have hitherto
woefully underrated it. The ear, like the eye is one of the
entrances to the mind, but the latter has no monopoly as a
medium of education. Ear, eye, tongue and voice; these are
the instruments by means of which we learn a language.

(Fortsetzung folgt.)

Cheltenham.   W. Stuart Macgowan.

THE RELATIVE EDUCATIONAL VALUE OF ANCIENT AND MODERN LANGUAGES.

CHAPTER III.

An ideal education should of course include some knowledge of both ancient and modern languages, the amount being strictly proportioned in accordance with a boy's future career, but our time-tables are already very full. — Quite apart from the ever-present utilitarian aspect of the case, it is rapidly becoming quite obvious that something must be done. — Classical *rersus* Modern is no mere empty cry. It fitly represents the element of discord in the secondary education of to-day. — Education has become so vast that all we can do is to take samples of its various branches. — Both the mind of Humanity and of the Individual have expanded to an appreciable degree, and Latin and Greek are no longer the only representative samples either of knowledge or culture. — Something will shortly have to be curtailed or even sacrificed, or we shall have an *überbürdungsfrage* almost as serious as that which Prussia has had to cope with in her secondary schools, and which had to be faced in our own elementary schools. It would be a sad blow to one class of culture if Latin and Greek were omitted from the curricula of secondary schools. Still, the possibility of such a calamitous eventuality suggests a very pertinent question: Cannot the literary feeling which we rightly regard as part of the normal development of an Englishman be obtained from any other source than Latin and Greek? Has not the field of knowledge already become too wide to be exclusively possessed by these two languages? — When this question arises, unless some provision is soon made for the more adequate study of foreign languages, it may bring another in its train: "Must Modern Languages or Classics

25*

go?" Should this issue ever arise, the decision of the school-masters of the next century can hardly be doubtful. — The Englishman of the future will have to study his own language and his own literature together with that of the nations round about him whatever else goes to the wall.

And if this were done, we should have a nearer approach to classical education — in one sense — than anything we have yet seen. — For what was the education of the Greeks in in the 5th Century, the classic age of Pericles? — They studied their own epic and lyric poetry, and were instructed in the elements of grammar. This was about all. — True, those destined for public life were instructed by the sophists in the art of public speaking, i. e. how to arrange their matter, marshal their arguments und polish their style. This was in outline a Greek classical education, but how far is it a sample of Education in England to-day? Could we learn nothing as regards language from a detailed study of our native poets, nothing in style from our best orators, nothing as to the treatment of matter or the marshalling of arguments from French prose? — Is there no Education in contemporary speech? — These questions will have to be answered soon. —

This brief investigation has shewn us that our so-called classical education is—in one sense of that term—not classical at all. — Let us further enquire: Is it a liberal education? Of what does it consist at school? The average schoolboy "gets up" by aid of his grammar and dictionary certain isolated fragments of Greek and Roman Literature. In so doing, he seldom pays any attention to the subject matter or to the beauty (if existent) of the style, for he regards each fragment merely as a reservoir whence questions on Accidence, Syntax or Etymology may be drawn. — Even when of riper years at the Universities, he may find that, for examination purposes, Philology is of more importance than Literature and the power to give a grammatical account of an involved sentence is deemed more important than the ability to explain the thought which the writer strove to convey.

I should like to quote some weighty words of Prof. John Stuart Blackie on this subject. He says:— "The famous saying of Charles V. that a man is five times a man when he knows five languages, is only true when a certain number of tools are necessary for his work. — That a knowledge of any language outside the vernacular is not necessary in certain cases, the example of the Greeks sufficiently proves:— they taught themselves the highest wisdom and became the recognized teachers of East and West by the use of the mother tongue alone. — Everybody borrowed from them; they borrowed from nobody. But all people are not so highly gifted or so happily situated in this respect as the Greeks. The Romans, when they came to their full imperial stature, found it necessary to study the Greek language for the sake of the Greek wisdom, which neither the sword of the soldier, nor the spade of the agriculturalist, nor the sentence of the lawyer could produce at home. — And in the same way in Modern Times, Great Britain, who in her political function is a compound of ancient Rome and ancient Carthage, while she has inherited a language which is a motley mixture of half a dozen strange tongues, has, by her position imposed on herself the duty of giving languages a prominent place in her educational programme. But, while she has done so largely, she has sadly failed in lack of wisdom, both in respect of the languages she studies and the methods of inculcation which her schoolmasters pursue. — The preference which she gives to Latin and Greek savours rather of scholastic tradition than of practical utility, while the methods used in respect of linguistic training are the outcome of a system in which books have usurped the place of life and the natural functions of the ear and voice have been transferred to the secondary mechanism of the eye. And to this pedagogic abuse must I fear be added a certain 'insular ignorance', which as well as his native insular insolence, makes the Englishman less careful to acquire foreign languages than the German, the Russian or the Modern Greek."

And there are other reasons why we should study modern languages. First and foremost the ever prominent utilitarian argument suggests itself, but I do not wish to enlarge upon that.

I have never seen the fact denied, though I have often heard it sneered at, that some conversational knowledge of French or German was a most useful possession. The complacent Briton who says:— "Dominant races do not require to learn foreign languages," is guilty of a mere empty boast. He does not deny that for the practical purposes of commerce, politics, diplomacy, the army, the navy and in fact for all ranks of society modern languages are rapidly becoming an indispensable qualification. But it is a mere waste of time to enumerate the practical and utilitarian advantages resulting from the study of foreign languages. It is ostentatiously admitted by the opponents of modern languages that both French and German have enormous utilitarian advantages which it is hopeless to attempt to claim for Latin and Greek; nevertheless, like the fox in the fable they hint that it is rather an advantage than otherwise to be thus shorn, and some, like the great headmaster I have already referred to, assert that "the stupendous advantage of their not being spoken languages shall be boldly put forward as the most prominent merit of Latin and Greek."

Hence we have the anomalous contention that the more Latin and Greek are for all practical purposes, useless; the more are they for all educational purposes, valuable. But "there is something rotten in the state of Denmark" here. Why should there be any antagonism between what is practically useful, and what is educationally valuable? What reply do classical students give to this? The orthodox classic will tell you, almost in the same breath with his repudiation of any utilitarian value attaching to classical study, that on purely educational grounds, he gives the palm to Latin and Greek, precisely because their utilitarian value is nil.

Latin and Greek train "faculty," he argues, while French and German do not. This is a somewhat ambiguous phrase; it may mean a great deal or it may mean nothing; I have never seen it satisfactorily explained, — but, in many cases, it means that the chief faculty a boy will develop is a dislike to language learning in general and to Latin and Greek in particular. As an instance of the average layman's appreciation in after life of the facultative training afforded him by a course of classical study in his youth, we have Mr. Labouchere's half-rueful, half-serio-comic utterances from his place in the House of Commons on Feb. 20th 1891.

That gentleman while advocating — it must be admitted

on purely utilitarian grounds — the importance of French and German in the social and commercial world, laments with some indignation, that although he had spent 10 years of his life at school in learning ancient Greek, yet in the course of his wanderings all over the world, he had derived no benefit from his studies at all!

Now though the statesman in question has put his own case in far too unfavourable a light, and has entirely left out of consideration the fact that this long language training probably laid the foundation of his crisp, vigorous and incisive English style, yet his case may be taken as typical — at a moderate estimate — of more than 90 % of those boys in secondary schools, who are now enjoying the benefits of a so-called "classical" education!!

Thus, under what is still our national system of secondary education, thousands of boys are receiving instruction in subjects, which while for *practical* purposes they are admitted to be useless, have not yet been conclusively proved to possess compensating *educational* advantages. Languages after all are not knowledge in themselves, they are only the keys to knowledge. Latin and Greek are not work, they are only tools for work and some think they are rather out of date.

"The ancient languages," as Emerson has observed, "contain wonderful remains of genius, which draw and always will draw, certain like-minded men — Greek men and Roman men in all countries to their study. But by a wonderful drowsiness of usage, they have exacted the study of *all* men. Once, Latin and Greek had a strict relation to all the science and culture there was in Europe." *Mais nous avons changé tout cela.* Latin and Greek are no longer an education in themselves; they have been stranded on the beach for two centuries, yet the schoolmaster still jogs comfortably along, hugging his traditions and happy in his groove, patiently waiting — it may be — till another vision like Ezekiel's shall dawn upon the world, and these dry bones shall live.

And so the weary warfare against common sense goes on. If we look the matter squarely in the face, we must acknowledge that a system of education to be truly liberal, in the widest sense of that term, must satisfy the requirements of the greatest number in the nation with the least possible expenditure of force. We may also fairly expect to have something to shew as the result of our expenditure of time and strength. The present system produces what a friendly foreign critic (Dr. Wiese) has described as "poverty stricken results," it wastes a vast amount of nervous energy, and — on the most generous computation, it only supplies the needs of about 10 % of the pupils. — Now if English, French and German were made the staple of a liberal education, if they were made "class-subjects," if they were studied for the information they contain, the side lights they shed upon our national development, if they were treated, not merely as useful acquisitions but as instruments of mental discipline, — if they were taught — as they can be — so as to train "faculty," we should waste less time, less vital energy, secure a wider training; we should be supplying the needs of the majority and should have what, as a nation, we glory in — something tangible, something practical by way of results.

The time seems really to have come when reasonable beings must ask themselves:— Why is this effete system still tolerated? Why this enormous waste of energy? Why this unquestioning subservience to 16th Century tradition? How long are we to continue in the comfortable belief that a Course of Latin Grammar and a Course of Logic are synonymous terms? How long are we to be asked to accept as a canon of higher education, that the process of aping or caricaturing the style of the ancients is the best method of developing taste and style in the moderns? These and many other questions will have to be answered sooner or later, and stereotyped reiteration of past services rendered will be of no avail. Signs are not wanting that another *zeitgeist* has arisen. There is a phrase which the men of next century will frequently repeat. It is:— *Dic cur hic*; and any ancient institution which relies only on tradition will assuredly be abolished.

CHAPTER IV.

Let us ask ourselves a few questions with regard to the study of the classical languages.

(i) Do they, or do they not, add one iota to the mass of

positive knowledge possessed by mankind? — The answer to this must be: "No, they do not."

(ii) Could the time — 8 to 10 years — now in so many cases wasted at school in acquiring merely a husk-knowledge of two dead languages, not be better utilised by the majority, in acquiring a thorough knowledge of two or even three living languages?

Most laymen would answer this also in the affirmative.

Why then are Latin and Greek studied (together) on an average about 20 hours a week and French and German (together) on an average — I fear it is too high — 6 hours a week? In the earlier part of this paper I have hinted at the reasons. Let me now state them more categorically:

The Classics were *originally* studied:—

(i) Because, at the Revival of Learning, they were the only storehouses of learning reasonably accessible to the Student of Literature.

(ii) Because they were the only subjects which, at that time, had been systematized so as to possess a disciplinary value.

(iii) Because they were the only subjects which the schoolmasters of that time were themselves competent to teach.

(iv) Because, in former times — with the exception of Italian — modern languages and literatures in the sense we understand these terms to-day, were non-existent.

(v) Because Latin was the polite medium of intercourse throughout Europe and the power to communicate with foreign nations was a political necessity for both church and state.

These were the real reasons for studying the classics in the time of Edward VI. It will be seen that they are all practical and utilitarian, and only in a minor degree educational. Do they still hold to-day? I think not. *Tempora mutantur nos et mutamur in illis*, says Horace. But the last part of the line is hardly apt; for the English schoolmaster does not change with the times. Despite our boasted liberalism, we are a conservative people and old traditions die hard. We readily acknowledge as practical men, that the *necessity* which existed in the Middle Ages for acquiring Latin and Greek no longer exists. It is also universally admitted that a general necessity for acquiring modern languages does exist. But then our time-tables are already too full and we often quote another phrase, *non multa sed multum*, which shews that we understand evils of smattering. — Yet we teach French, German, Latin and Greek at school. Overpressure is an evil which has already made itself felt in the elementary schools. All these things we know, and yet the trite old phrase "a scholar and a gentleman" still calls up visions of the classically educated cleric or don, while men of the most varied knowledge or attainments in other subjects, but yet lacking the subtle aroma diffused by classical tomes, scarcely rank as "cultured" at all.

Why then, do the men of *to-day* study the classics?

(i) Because their ancestors did and their instincts are naturally conservative.

(ii) Because a few canonized Head-Masters have extolled them and recommended their study.

(iii) Because they serve to keep up class distinctions. — The Board schools don't teach Greek.

(iv) Because they are heavily endowed studies. [Under this head come several other reasons of a similar nature, which it would serve no purpose to enumerate.]

(v) Because — in the abstract — they *are* educative studies, and a very small minority like them and derive benefit from them. —

Now against those who belong to the last category, I have not a word to say. I have no wish whatever to raise the question as to the desirability or non-desirability of classical studies in themselves. Men of antiquarian proclivities will always exist who will delve in the dust of ages with a certain amount of profit both to themselves and their fellow creatures. Still even here we must draw a very sharp line of distinction between those students who digest and reproduce the thought of past ages with a view either to enlarge the mental horizon of their contemporaries or to warn them from out-lived error, and those whose life is spent in annotating, renovating and furbishing up the mental products of past times. The first are the benefactors of their race; the latter have their reward in the discovery of cryptograms proving (to them) that Shakspere is Bacon, or in counting the number of times that *et* and *mais* occur in a mediaeval poem.

Only very few of us can breathe upon the past and make it live, and most of us, if we attempt to imitate it, will achieve but a feeble caricature. In addition to which, the study of mediaevalism is but a sorry substitute for that of modern life. There are an honoured few for whom the difficulties in the way of acquiring knowledge will but add a fresh zest to research. But it is for the majority of the rising generation that I plead. Speaking of the Latin language, Milton says:— "It is a preposterous exaction to force the empty wits of children to compose themes, verses and orations which are the acts of the ripest judgment."[1] These are abstractions and we must not forget that the abstract *in se* is generally distasteful to a young mind, and that the too early absorption of indigestible matter will stultify rather than develop the faculties. But even if this were not so, it is a truism to repeat that a mind exhausted by linguistic struggles is not in a fit state to receive delicate literary impressions. It is quite impossible to drink in the thoughts of an author or even appreciate his style, if one's mind is crowded with thoughts on gender, etymologies or syntax. What we want is "not slow reform but swift revolution" both in languages and methods, for, as Mr. Welldon shewed at the Head Master's Conference in Dec. 1890, by figures upon which we can all rely, exactly 50 per cent of the boys receiving secondary education in England are still struggling under their mediaeval burden of Latin and Greek.

---

[1] This is a fact which the vigorous intelligence of the present emperor of Germany has not been slow to appreciate.

(Fortsetzung folgt.)

Cheltenham.   W. Stuart Macgowan.

DIE NEUEREN SPRACHEN.

ZEITSCHRIFT
FÜR DEN
NEUSPRACHLICHEN UNTERRICHT.

BAND I. **DEZEMBER 1893.** HEFT 8.

THE RELATIVE EDUCATIONAL VALUE OF ANCIENT AND MODERN LANGUAGES.

CHAPTER V.

But, it may be suggested, surely this is a very one sided statement of the case, and there must be other reasons than these for the persistent retention of Latin and Greek in the forefront of all other educational subjects.

So there are, and it is only fair that I should briefly enumerate them. They are somewhat as follows:— It is urged:—

(*a*) That the classics contain a vast amount of valuable information, which is inaccessible except through the medium of classical speech itself.

(*b*) That they form a capital introduction to Comparative Philology.

(*c*) That structurally these languages are more perfect than any other known speech, and that therefore their prose is unrivalled for exquisite grace, while their poetry is in itself an aesthetic training of the highest value; hence, — they serve to model our taste and style.

(*d*) That for "intellectual discipline," i. e. mental gymnastics, they are superior to modern languages.

(*e*) That also for culture — in the academical sense of the term — they are to be preferred.

Such are the arguments in favour of the classics. I hope I have not left any of them out. They are quite a formidable array. Yet it will require no special pleading to shew that — as regards their bearing on classical study — these arguments, where not mere temporary makeshifts, are generally either illogical or only partially tenable, and that so far from applying exclusively to Latin and Greek, any weight they may possess tells equally in favour of modern languages.

(a) Let us glance briefly at the first argument: *That Latin and Greek contain much valuable information which is inaccessible to a person unacquainted with classical speech.* This sounds like a sensible, businesslike argument, and, if it can be substantiated, Latin and Greek will at any rate have established a *prima facie* utilitarian case. These languages doubtless do contain valuable information, but it has filtered so insensibly into modern languages, that persons who are absolutely ignorant of Latin and Greek may be in full possession of all the positive knowledge possessed by the ancients. Therefore I contend the argument will not hold. Let us take for example what the Germans call by the generic name of the faculties. These roughly represent what we understand by the learned professions. They are *Medicine*, *Philosophy*, *Law* and *Theology*.

If I were to ask any medical or scientific gentleman present:— "What does your science derive from the study of Hippocrates, Galen, Celsus and the ancients generally?" I fancy his answer would be short but to the point:— "Absolutely nothing." Harvey, Jenner and Koch are greater names than any of which the ancients can boast.

In Philosophy there is undoubtedly more. It is difficult to exactly estimate what the world owes to Socrates, Plato, Aristotle and Cicero, but speaking without first-hand knowledge of the subject, I should imagine that we might now make shift with translations, seeing that we possess Bacon, Locke, Hobbes, Pascal, Descartes, Comte, Kant, Schlegel, Schopenhauer and Fichte who have presumably incorporated what is best from ancient systems. Again the fact that all ancient systems are illumined by the light of Christianity must be thrown into the modern Philosophers' scale. Still, ancient philosophy would appear to be a highly educative study, but appeals only to a small minority and can surely be studied apart from its classical garb.

Then there is Law. Latin has undoubtedly a slight utilitarian value in the legal profession, but one can obtain a good knowledge of the Roman Law without much knowledge of the Roman language. Indeed I imagine that the reason why some knowledge of this subject is required from candidates for the Bar, is because it is an expansive study for the mind, for our Common Law is not based upon Roman Law. No knowledge of the classical languages is necessary in the practice of the profession.

If I touch on Theology, it will be to admit that the purely technical value of Latin and Greek for the purposes of reading the New Testament, patristic writings etc. in the original is of undoubted utilitarian value for the clergy, but I would also remark that the power to read Hebrew and German is in these days of doubt and scepticism of perhaps equal importance. Yet the clergy are — as a rule — absolutely ignorant of both these languages, notwithstanding their direct bearing on their profession, and, so far as I am aware, no plea either for Hebrew or German has yet been raised on account of their technical or educational importance for the church.

This argument then, viewed as a whole, will not hold, for all the information the Classics contain is more conveniently expressed in contemporary speech. I will sum up my arguments with the following passage from Macaulay; he is most explicit on this very point:—

"In the time of Henry VIII. and Edward VI., a person who did not read Latin and Greek could read nothing, or next to nothing. Italian was the only modern language which possessed anything like a literature. All the valuable books then extant in the vernacular dialects of Europe would hardly have filled a single shelf........ Latin was, in the sixteenth century, all, and more than all, that French was in the eighteenth. It was the language of the courts as well as of the schools..... It was employed by every writer who desired a wide and durable reputation..... This is no longer the case. The great productions of Athenian and Roman genius are still what they were. But though their positive value is unchanged, their relative value, when compared with the whole mass of mental wealth possessed by mankind, has been constantly falling. They were the intellectual all of our ancestors. They are but a part of our treasures. We believe that the books which

29*

have been written in the languages of western Europe during the last two hundred and fifty years — translations from the ancient languages of course included — are of greater value than all the books which, at the beginning of that period were extant in the world."

These words of a man who could speak as a classic, an historian, a poet and a politician may fittingly clench my first argument.

(*b*) Let us take the next argument: *That Latin and Greek are a capital introduction to Comparative Philology.* This argument is a palpable makeshift and does not readily admit either of proof or of refutation. It is unimportant and does not call for serious attention. It was not urged in the Middle Ages, because, as the extract I have just quoted shews, Latin and Greek were then studied, as French and German should be to-day, mainly for reasons of political expediency and educational utility. Comparative Philology did not then exist. The art of hair-splitting in matters of derivation and phonology had not then been reduced to a science. For mere purposes of philology or glottology however, it is idle to lay such stress on Latin and Greek, for Anglo-Saxon, Old High German and Moeso-Gothic are in their way as valuable, if not more valuable than both Classical Latin and Classical Greek put together. But even if we admit the argument in its entirety, it does not advance the case for the classics much, because the legitimate inference is, that if Latin and Greek are a capital introduction to Classical Philology, English, French and German are just as valuable an introduction to Modern Philology. This argument, therefore does not tell.

(*c*) We now come to our third and most plausible argument of all, that as to *the structural perfection of the ancient languages, etc.* The late Mr. J. K. Stephen of King's College, Cambridge, one of the foremost champions of compulsory Greek suggests "as a commonplace which has never been denied[1] that Greek is a marvellously subtle, flexible and ingenious language which contains mechanical niceties and intellectual devices not

---

[1] *The Living Languages — A Defence of the study of compulsory Greek at Cambridge* by J. K. Stephen, M. A. Macmillan & Bowes, Cambridge.

to be found in any modern language. Of all inflected languages it is admittedly supreme."

This is all very well, and no one would care to deny the supremacy of Greek as among inflected languages, but it has not yet been conclusively shewn either that inflection argues the highest possible state of linguistic development or that the multiplying of auxiliaries and prepositions *is* a coarser, and therefore inferior method of approaching recondite meanings than the almost unlimited variability of the single word. This subject is far too vast to admit of treatment within the limits of a paper, but quite independently of its structure, the English literature alone is a sufficient answer to those who suggest that Modern languages harmonize with the thoughts of a rather common place race and that English is good enough for the "Stock Exchange broker or bagman on his rounds," while the classical languages alone can satisfy the intellectual requirements of the literary and philosophic man. Where is the great superiority of the ancient over the modern languages?

Can it be true that languages which flourished 1800 years ago really express thought more perfectly than the French and English of to-day? If so, what has stayed the laws of natural development in language? How does it come that the classics are superior? These questions will have to be answered sooner or later. The mere reiteration that the classics are the only avenues to culture is no argument. In the days of Pascal when the classical controversy was at its height, that great writer summed up the situation very graphically, when he described the moderns as standing on the shoulders of the ancients. There can be no question as to who has the larger horizon. If this argument applied 200 years ago, it must certainly hold with greater force to-day, for language has still further worked out of the dialect stage; synthetic Latin has become analytic French, and you will pardon me if I consider the daughter is as fair or even fairer than the mother.

This whole argument as to the structural perfection of the ancient languages has always struck me as being so utterly tortuous, so wholly illogical and so absolutely at variance with the laws of nature, that were it not that the point has so long

133

remained uncontroverted by teachers of foreign languages, that our opponents have taken to citing it as a fact which has never been denied, I would not further dwell upon it now. But I cannot for one instant allow that modern languages are inferior either *structurally* as instruments of discipline, or *logically* as vehicles of thought to the ancient tongues. Unless the world has stood still, unless the whole human race has been stationary, unless the men of the present day have become — by overmuch contemplation of the ancients? — mere barnacles on the rock of antiquity, the thing is absolutely impossible. There is such a thing as evolution in the domain of language. Why this unreasoning worship of case and inflection? These are merely mechanical devices. The logical order of words in an English or French sentence, the lucid statement of a complicated thought by means of vigorous carefully chosen words, — these, to a mind untrammelled by superstition, seem to reach a higher level than that attained by any inflected language whatsoever. Inflection in itself is no more a sign of maturity in a language than is an involved sentence of lucidity of thought. A boy who is incapable of understanding the function of *Gallum* in the sentence: *Caesar Gallum occidit*, save by the mechanical addition of the Accusative *m*, will require a somewhat severer course of logic than that afforded by the "Public School Latin Primer" to sharpen his faculties. Again, if he failed to apprehend the function of *Jack* in the two sentences: *Jack sees Gill* and: *Gill sees Jack* because of the absence of inflection, we might add one to help him on his way, but it should be regarded merely as a concession to weakness and a mere temporary expedient. Is not the logical order of the modern sentence which appeals to the *intellect* proof positive of a higher grade of linguistic evolution than the most subtle mechanical devices which appeal solely to the *senses*?

Let me put a case. Suppose that (for the sake of clearness?) we were to resort to mechanical devices in the English language. Suppose it were agreed to print all nominatives red, all accusative blue, all adjectives in various shades of green, according as they qualified masculine, feminine or neuter nouns, and suppose in addition to this, that we decided to print passive verbs in large type, to put finite verbs at the end of the sentence, but that in other respects words might be ticketted or labelled and then jumbled up like lottery tickets in a bag: if we did this, we should practically be doing what the ancients did, but we should be retrogressing, we should be going back one step nearer to the picture-writing and hieroglyphics of the Egyptians and Phoenicians, of which Case and Inflection are after all but a later development. Case and inflection then may be regarded by the student of language much as the modern painter regards the works of the Pre-Raphaelite school, viz. as masterpieces (of their age) and as possessing undeniable historical interest, but, when viewed by the light of our present knowledge, as crudities emanating from an ignorant age which understood not perspective nor the anatomy of the human form. Case and Inflection are like the shell of the chrysalis; they have served their turn; the mind of man has soared to a higher plane; language is now more logical and less material, it is shuffling off its linguistic coil, it would not take it back if it could.

This argument then is both unscientific and contrary to Nature; it will not hold, nor will its logical corollary that the classics should be studied as models of style. In this respect they are of no further use.

As regards vocabulary it is a mere truism to say that the vocabularies of the *kultursprachen* of modern Europe are more copious than those of the classical languages of Greece and Rome. Although, owing to the pathological operations I have already alluded to, we have lost much of our native vocabulary, yet, both through the Norman French and from later direct borrowings, the English language has become largely indebted to the corpus of Latin and Greek. This is not an unmixed blessing, for the process has lost us many of our more forcible native words, yet, on the other hand we have gained a vast wealth of synonym and an infinity of beautifully graded expressions which make the English language the best conceivable medium of expressing thought. Whether the borrowing has been overdone or not is a question for philologists to determine, but the effect of it has been to make modern languages more copious than ancient ones. Another reason for their copiousness may also be owing to the fact, that having more ideas than the ancients we require a larger vocabulary to express ourselves completely. Thus it comes to pass that it is an absolute impossibility to translate a piece of English or French abounding in technical expressions into Latin or Greek, from the very excellent reason that the ancients, not having any ideas on modern Science, have no words or expressions to embody those ideas. Thus modern languages are more copious than and can be used just as concisely as the ancient tongues. In cases where the former display any ponderosity or obscurity, the mischief is generally traceable to a classical source. I imagine that the reason why German prose occasionally exhibits a lack of terseness and lucidity is deducible from the fact that in that country both teachers and professors have, — for more than 300 years — zealously striven to emulate the style of Demosthenes and Cicero. The result of this has been that much of the native vigour of the language has been impaired, though not entirely lost. What can be done with German prose is shewn when Heine, with true poetic and prophetic insight, bases it on French models. But to come back to our own language. Look at the pompous bombast of Dr. Johnson's "large, full well-weighted words" and then turn to the simple majesty of the Psalms! Which is the fitter language for modern Carthage? Which of these two more truly breathes the spirit of our race? Surely the language of Shakspeare and Chaucer has drawn deep enough from the wells of antiquity! Surely it can now shake itself loose from the shackles of the past!

The question as to the aesthetic training to be derived from the study of classical verse would involve a long discussion, into which this is not the place to enter; but it may well be that it is of high value to the very few who are capable of appreciating it.[1]

(d) We now come to our fourth argument, that as regards the *mental training* or *intellectual discipline* to be derived from

---

[1] The question as to whether Latin and Greek verse composition is or is not a waste of time has now been pretty generally answered in the affirmative.

a course of classical study. The arguments I rely on to demonstrate the value of modern languages are almost identical with those usually urged by others in favour of Latin and Greek. I shall hope to prove that, as regards the training of faculty, modern languages are in no way inferior to the classics. And here I join issue with nearly all the authorities on the subject. I rely, however, on a very simple argument. It is the indisputable arithmetical fact that *two* is greater than *one*. If we assume that language is the finest instrument of culture we possess, I will venture to contend that modern languages are even better adapted than the classics to educate and develop the mind.

And this for the following reasons: Modern languages can be acquired at an early age by what classical scholars have scornfully termed "soaking" or "imitation."[1] But these processes are perfectly natural. Being living tongues, French and German exercise the faculty of hearing. Latin and Greek, being dead languages, neglect the ear altogether, whereas memory, the lowest of all our faculties, is often put to a totally depraved use. Both ancient and modern speech exercise equally the sense of sight. Both too, when properly taught, will train a child's judgment and imagination. In the early stages of learning, the classical languages suppress the imitative faculties so strongly present in children; modern languages — if taught rationally — develop them. Modern languages are living and concrete, classical languages are too often dead and abstract. Now children hate the abstract, which is quite normal, for this faculty does not develop until later, — and they glory in the concrete.[2] And yet Modern languages have been decried on the ground that they afford "no intellectual discipline whatever."

I must own that my mind is too coarse to apprehend the logic by which it is maintained that because modern languages develop *two senses* (sight and hearing) they are therefore in-

---

[1] I attribute the noticeable lack of this faculty in the boys of the present day to the abstract way in which languages are presented to them. The imagination is thus starved, and in after life they cannot appreciate poetry for this reason.

[2] It is this fact which has made M. Gouin's method so successful in the teaching of young children.

ferior to the classical languages which admittedly develop but one (sight); that languages which develop two elementary faculties (memory and mimicry) are therefore inferior to those which develop but one (memory);[1] that, in short, languages which develop the mind fully and naturally are therefore inferior to those which develop it only partially and abnormally; and yet this is what too often takes place. I am not maintaining that modern languages are at present taught so as to produce these results, or that the ancient languages never do produce beneficial results, but modern languages have potentialities, which the classics no longer possess. The latter are far too exclusive in their action: some faculties — as I have shewn — they cramp and confine; others they scarcely touch at all, and their champions rather plume themselves on this lack of comprehensiveness: in fact Mr. Thring calls it "a stupendous advantage." But all classical Headmasters do not take this extreme view. Mr. Welldon[2] of Harrow in some powerful articles written in the autumn of 1890 sums up my argument very adequately when he says: "Whatever intellectual discipline is derivable from the languages of Athens and Rome is derivable also from the languages of Paris and Berlin."

CHAPTER VI. CONCLUSION AND SUMMARY.

(e) I now come to my fifth and last argument that *for Culture, modern languages are in no way inferior to the classics.* I understand this word in the late Matthew Arnold's connotation of the term, *viz*: as an appreciation of "what is best in literature." The time has long gone by when the seeker after culture could range over the whole field of literature. Cannot the student of modern languages gain culture from *his* study? Cannot the modern man gain culture from the study of Shakspeare, Milton, Voltaire, Goethe or Dante? I only mention a few names.

No one can now say like Bacon did to Lord Burleigh: "I have taken *all* knowledge to be my province;" the passage

---

[1] The faculty of Judgment is perhaps more exercised by the classical languages while the Imagination is more affected by modern languages.

[2] Headmaster of Harrow.

I have quoted from Macaulay sufficiently illustrates that this merely meant the classical literatures of Greece and Rome with such knowledge and culture as could be obtained from them.

The men of to-day then will have to be more discriminating than their ancestors if they would attain "culture." They will have to study modern languages above all things, for while these have incorporated nearly everything worth preserving from the classics, they possess in addition a vast literature of their own.

Even among schoolmasters there are signs that the belief in the orthodox smattering of two dead languages as the only means of culture is now on the wane; the classical languages are no longer a kind of Fetish to conjure with, they almost threaten to become a kind of Frankenstein-monster on our educational horizon.

There is no sound educational or practical reason why such a large amount of time — 8, 9 and even 10 years of a boy's life — should be devoted to them. *Was man nicht nützt, ist eine schwere last,* says Goethe.

The conditions of modern life are such that no one can afford to be unduly weighted in running the race which is set before him. Truly in this matter as Locke says: *Custom serves for Reason.*

Is it not a startling anachronism that at the end of the 19th century we should still cling so slavishly to the traditions of the 16th? Surely there is a middle course. Can we not divest ourselves of mediaeval superstitions in the teaching of languages without in any way derogating from the services which Latin and Greek have rendered us in the past and which they may still render in the future? Can we not cease to draw arbitrary distinctions between modern languages and the classics, — always to the disadvantage of the former? Surely it could be done. The position which the study of our own and of contemporary speech occupies in our national education is detrimental alike to the study of ancient and modern languages. The purely classical education is somewhat out of date, but the so called "modern" education is often mere empty cram, and neither classical nor modern schools have been fair to French, German and English. No system of education can be complete which does not provide for the adequate study both of the vernacular and of Modern Languages and Modern Literatures. But we can break down artificial barriers and overcome existing prejudices without abolishing classical study. There is no real antagonism between classical and modern languages. No true student of modern languages would wish to see the study of the classics abolished. Still less should there be any differences between the students of ancient and modern literature. Both have one great aim in common; they study, — in its native dress — the various manifestations of the minds of man though in different stages of this world's history. As sources of information the student of modern languages possesses advantages over the student of ancient tongues. Both ancient and modern speech are of vast importance to the student of Comparative Philology. Both ancient and modern languages have a certain aesthetic value; both can and do train literary taste. In the matter of "intellectual discipline" and "culture," although individuals may differ as to the precise value of these attributes, when obtained from ancient or modern languages, yet here again, there is no fundamental difference between them; both are students of "human life which has escaped the grave." [1]

But we must allow to our own language and to those of the great nations around us, a position of at least equal honour and importance in our educational curricula, as that which we have for centuries assigned to Latin and Greek. We must be fair to modern languages. It is in the power of this great University to infuse new life into the study of the classics by instituting an honours school in English, French and German. These great monuments of the past would soon be viewed in a new light; they would be studied by a new race of men who would ponder over and read them as carefully and lovingly as the son cons the letters of his father, when that revered

---

[1] As I correct these lines for the press I see announced in the "Times" the death of Prof. H. Nettleship, who was my chairman when this lecture was delivered at Oxford in May 1892. It may interest some of my readers to know that in the opinion of this liberal minded professor of Latin at our oldest University, modern languages were considered just as worthy of serious study as Latin and Greek.

parent has passed away. No one has a greater veneration for the classics than the student of modern languages. The classics will always remain the "intellectual ancestors" of our race, but we must not forget that we ourselves possess a language whose "sound has gone out into all lands" and which is destined to wield a mighty influence over the nations of the earth. If we study other languages, it should be because we wish better to understand our own. With a thorough knowledge of his own language and literature and those of France and Germany, an Englishman becomes a citizen of the civilized world; whereas without such knowledge, he cannot he said to possess a "liberal" education at all.

What we want now-a-days is — *pace* the classics, not exclusively a classical or *class*-education nor — *pace* the scientists, is it a mere technical or *mass*-education, it is in the widest sense of the term a "liberal education."

Our education — in the past — has been far too narrow; it is the duty of the educator to so co-ordinate his efforts, that he can develop the child equally on every side of his nature. This is the most fitting preparation for manhood and for life. But the mediaeval gospel: "Study first Latin and Greek and their peculiarities, and every thing else shall be added unto you," has not produced this result. Men are both *viri et homines*; they may be specialists in the community, but they should be complete units, rounded off entities in themselves. An incomplete system of education cannot produce a complete man.

Yet so long as the students of ancient and modern languages are at variance as to the educational value of their studies, — so long will the unification of educational effort, so sadly needed in this country, be put off.

Unification is sure to come, sooner or later. When it does, the Classics will be so fused with Modern Languages that no sharp line of demarcation will separate the old from the new, and the present distrust and estrangement will be healed. Perhaps by that time, even the schoolmaster of the day may recognize, that for intellectual discipline, knowledge and culture, the modern languages of England, France and Germany are in no way inferior to the ancient languages of Greece and of Rome.

Cheltenham. W. Stuart Macgowan.

6

HENRY SWEET

The Practical Study of Languages: A Guide for Teachers and Learners

Source: London: Dent, 1899.

THE PRACTICAL STUDY

OF

LANGUAGES

A GUIDE FOR TEACHERS AND LEARNERS

BY

HENRY SWEET, M.A., Ph.D., LL.D.

CORRESPONDING MEMBER OF THE MUNICH ACADEMY OF SCIENCES
FORMERLY PRESIDENT OF THE PHILOLOGICAL SOCIETY

With Tables and Illustrative Quotations

LONDON

J. M. DENT & CO.

BEDFORD STREET, COVENT GARDEN

1899

PREFACE

THIS book is intended as a guide to the practical study of languages. Its object is, first, to determine the general principles on which a rational method of learning foreign languages should be based, and then to consider the various modifications these general principles undergo in their application to different circumstances and different classes of learners.

The want of such a guide has long been felt. All the works on the subject that have hitherto appeared have either been short sketches, or else have only dealt with portions of the subject, such as the teaching of classical or modern languages in schools.

I have given careful attention to these questions, but have by no means confined myself to this branch of the subject. I have rather endeavoured to give a comprehensive general view of the whole field of the practical study of languages, as far as lay in my power. I have not only given special sections on the learning of dead languages and of Oriental languages, but have also added a chapter on the methods of deciphering writings in unknown languages and of dealing with unwritten forms of speech; for although such investigations have not always a directly practical aim, their methods are wholly practical. This part of the book ought to be welcome to travellers and missionaries, who often feel great perplexity when confronted with the difficult problem of reducing an illiterate language to writing and analysing it grammatically. The same remarks apply with equal force to dialectologists, the results of whose labours are often worse than useless through their want of proper method. Another class of students whom I have had specially in view are self-taught learners of foreign languages, who often not only waste time, but fail to attain their aim through following bad methods and using unsuitable text-books.

My examples are taken from a variety of languages, partly to avoid one-sidedness of treatment, partly to interest as many different classes of readers as possible.

In discussing methods, I have drawn my illustrations from those books which I know best. The time has not yet come for an historical survey and critical estimate of the vast and increasing literature of linguistic pedagogy, either of that portion of it which deals with generalities and criticisms of methods, or that still larger portion which carries out—or professes to carry out—these general principles in practical text-books—reading-books, grammrs, text-editions, 'methods,' etc.

In giving warning examples of mistakes into which learners may fall, I have confined myself to those made by foreigners in speaking and writing English, for the simple reason that the mistakes made by English-speakers in the use of other languages, though in themselves equally instructive and amusing, would have no point for the majority of my readers.

From the point of view of the purely practical learner, my treatment may perhaps appear not only too comprehensive, but also too ideal. He will ask, What is the use of recommending a method of study which cannot be followed because of the want of the requisite helps in the way of text-books? But this is precisely one of the objects of my book. My object is both to show how to make the best of existing conditions, and to indicate the lines of abstract research and practical work along which the path of progress lies.

In the present multiplicity of methods and text-books, it is absolutely necessary for real and permanent progress that we should come to some sort of agreement on general principles. Until this is attained—until every one recognizes that there is no royal road to languages, and that no method can be a sound one which does not fulfil certain definite conditions —the public will continue to run after one new method after the other, only to return disappointed to the old routine.

My attitude towards the traditional methods is, as will be seen, a mean between unyielding conservatism on the one hand and reckless radicalism on the other. There are some fundamental principles on which I insist, whether they are popular or not, such as basing all study of language on phonetics, and starting from the spoken rather than the literary language. But, on the other hand, the reader will find that while I agree with the Continental reformers in condemning the practice of exercise-writing and the use of *à priori* methods such as Ahn's, I refuse to join with them in their condemnation of translation and the use of grammars.

As regards my qualifications for the task, I have, in the

first place, acquired a considerable knowledge of a variety of languages of different structure; and in studying them I have always paid as much attention to the practical as to the purely philological questions that have suggested themselves. I may also claim the merit of having made the scientific historical study of English possible in this country by the publication of my numerous practical helps to the learning of the older stages of our language, especially Old English. At the same time, my *Elementarbuch des gesprochenen Englisch* has done something towards making genuine spoken English accessible to foreigners. I have, lastly, had considerable experience in lecturing and teaching in connection with various branches of the study of languages, so that this work is as much the outcome of varied practical experience as of scientific theorizing.

The first draft of this work was written out as far back as 1877, but for various reasons was never published, although an abstract of it appeared in the Transactions of the Philological Society for 1882–4, under the title of *The Practical Study of Language*. I need hardly say that the present work is not merely an expansion of these earlier efforts, but is the result of more matured thought and wider experience, so that it is an entirely new book, except that the chapter on 'mind-training' is taken without alteration from the first draft.

OXFORD,
  February, 1899.

CONTENTS

CHAPTER IV

FOREIGN ALPHABETS

CHAPTER V

VARIETIES OF PRONUNCIATION

CHAPTER VI

GENERAL STUDY OF PHONETICS

CHAPTER VII

BEGIN WITH THE SPOKEN LANGUAGE

CONTENTS

CHAPTER XI

GRAMMAR

CHAPTER XII

THE DICTIONARY; STUDY OF THE VOCABULARY

CHAPTER XIII

TEXTS ; THE READING-BOOK

CONTENTS xiii

CHAPTER XIV

RELATIONS BETWEEN DIFFERENT LANGUAGES ; TRANSLATION

CHAPTER XV

CONVERSATION

CHAPTER XVI

LITERATURE ; LITERARY COMPOSITION

CHAPTER XVII

DEAD LANGUAGES

PHONETIC SYMBOLS

Phonetic writing enclosed in ( ).   Length marked by doubling, strong stress by ('), medium by (:), and weak by (-) before the syllable.

a   *as in* 'cut;' also short of (aa).
aa   ,,   'father.'
a   ,,   French 'pâte.'
ã   ,,   French 'sans.'
ä   ,,   'bird.'
æ   ,,   'man.'
c = front stop.
ç *as in* German 'ich.'
d = emphatic Arabic *d*.
ᶑ ⎫
δ ⎭ *as in* 'then.'
e   *as in* French 'été;' also = (e).
e   ,,   'men.'
ẽ   ,,   French 'vin.'
ə   ,,   'sofa.'
ε   ,,   'men, air.'
ʒ   ,,   German 'sagen.'
h = Arabic throat-sound *hā*
i *as in* French 'fini;' also = (i).
i   ,,   'fin.'
ï   ,,   Welsh 'dyn.'
j   ,,   'you.'

ɟ = front stop voice.
ḳ = deep Arabic *k*.
l*h* = Welsh *ll*.
ñ *as in* Italian 'ogni.'
o   ,,   French 'eau;' also = (*o*).
o   ,,   German 'stock;' also 'not.'
õ   ,,   French 'son.'
œ   ,,   French 'peur.'
œ̃   ,,   French 'un.'
ɔ   ,,   'not'; 'saw.'
ø   ,,   French 'peu.'
ṣ = Arabic emphatic *s*.
ʃ *as in* 'she.'
ꝑ ⎫
θ ⎭   ,,   'thin.'
u   ,,   French 'sou;' also = (*u*).
u   ,,   'good.'
w*h*   ,,   'what.'
x   ,,   German 'loch.'
y   ,,   French 'une.'
ʒ   ,,   'rouge.'

157

THE PRACTICAL STUDY
OF LANGUAGES

CHAPTER I

THE STUDY OF LANGUAGES

Practical and Theoretical Study

IT is hardly necessary to enlarge on the distinction between the **practical** and the **theoretical** study of languages—between learning to understand, read, speak, write a language on the one hand, and studying its history and etymology on the other hand.

But it is important to realize at the same time that the practical study of languages is not in any way less scientific than the theoretical.

The scientific basis of the practical study of languages is what may be called 'living philology,' which starts from the accurate observation of spoken languages by means of phonetics and psychology, and makes this the basis of all study of language, whether practical or theoretical. The opposite of living is 'antiquarian' philology, which regards the present merely as a key to the past, subordinating living to dead languages and sounds to their written symbols.

Necessity of General Principles

The first thing, therefore, is to determine the general principles on which the practical study of languages should be based. It is evident that if these principles are to be really general, they must be based on a survey of the whole field of languages : that is, while giving due prominence to French and German, as being the two modern languages most generally studied in this country, we must not neglect the remoter languages, confining ourselves, of course, to an examination of a sufficient number of typical ones.[1]

Having settled our general principles, the next thing is to consider what modifications, what special combinations of them may be required under special circumstances. It is evident that a method which suits an inflectional language may require modification when applied to a language of a different character; that learning to read a dead language is a different process from learning to speak a living one; that self-instruction and teaching children in school require different text-books, and so on.

As the tendency at present is to exaggerate rather than under-rate these differences, I shall confine myself as much as possible to general principles, leaving special modifications and applications to be made by others. It would, indeed, be presumptuous in me to say much about such subjects as the school-teaching of languages, in which I have no practical experience—at least as teacher.

I am not much concerned with such questions as, Why do we learn languages? Is learning languages a good or a bad training for the mind? Is Greek a better training for the mind than German or mathematics? I start from the axiom that as languages have to be learnt, even if it turns out that the process injures the mind, our first business is to find out the most efficient and economical way of learning them.

Good and Bad Methods

The plan of this book involves, to some extent at least, a criticism of existing methods.

In this connection it is significant to observe that though there is great conservatism in scholastic circles—as shown in the retention of antiquated text-books, in the prejudice against phonetics, and so on—there are, on the other hand, many signs of dissatisfaction with these methods.

[1] Besides English, French, and German, I have drawn my illustrations chiefly from those remoter languages of which I have some practical knowledge, that is, Sanskrit, Welsh, Old Irish, Finnish, Arabic, and Chinese.

This dissatisfaction is strikingly shown by the way in which new 'methods' are run after—especially the more sensational ones, and such as have the good fortune to be taken up by the editor of some popular periodical.

But none of these methods retain their popularity long—the interest in them soon dies out.   There is a constant succession of them ; Ollendorff, Ahn, Prendergast, Gouin—to mention only a few—have all had their day.   They have all failed to keep a permanent hold on the public mind because they have all failed to perform what they promised : after promising impossibilities they have all turned out to be on the whole no better than the older methods.

But the return to the older methods is only a half-hearted one : even Ollendorff still has his adherents.   In fact, things are altogether unsettled, both as regards methods and text-books. This is a good sign : it gives a promise of the survival of the fittest.   Anything is better than artificial uniformity enforced from without.

The methods I have just mentioned are failures because they are based on an insufficient knowledge of the science of language, and because they are one-sided.   A method such as Gouin's, which ignores phonetics, is not a method : at the most, it gives hints for a real method.   Gouin's 'series-method' may in itself be a sound principle, but it is too limited in its applications to form even the basis of a fully developed method.

A good method must, before all, be comprehensive and eclectic.   It must be based on a thorough knowledge of the science of language—phonetics, sound-notation, the grammatical structure of a variety of representative languages, and linguistic problems generally.   In utilizing this knowledge it must be constantly guided by the psychological laws on which memory and the association of ideas depend.

CHAPTER II

PHONETICS

THE main axiom of living philology is that all study of language must be based on phonetics.

Phonetics is the science of speech-sounds, or, from a practical point of view, the art of pronunciation. Phonetics is to the science of language generally what mathematics is to astronomy and the physical sciences. Without it, we can neither observe nor record the simplest phenomena of language. It is equally necessary in the theoretical and in the practical study of languages.

Phonetics not an Innovation

The necessity of phonetics has, indeed, always been tacitly recognized—even by its opponents. Even such a simple statement as that 'English nouns take -*es* instead of -*s* in the plural after a hiss-consonant' involves elementary facts of phonetics; the terms 'vowel' and 'consonant,' 'hard' and 'soft,' all imply phonetic analysis. What the reformers claim is not that phonetics should be introduced—for it is there already—but that its study should be made efficient by being put on a scientific basis.

In fact, phonetics is almost as old as civilization itself. The Alexandrian grammarians were not only phoneticians—they were spelling-reformers! Few of those who mechanically learn the rules of Greek accentuation by way of gilding the refined gold of their scholarship have any idea that these to them unmeaning marks were invented by the Alexandrian grammarians solely for the purpose of making the pronunciation of Greek easier to foreigners. The Romans, too, were phoneticians: they learnt Greek on a phonetic basis, as far as their lights allowed them. The Sanskrit grammarians were still better phoneticians. It is the unphonetic, not the phonetic methods that are an innovation.

The efficient teaching of phonetics is impeded by two popular fallacies.

4

Fallacy of Imitation

The first of these is that pronunciation can be learnt by mere imitation. This is as if fencing could be learnt by looking on at other people fencing. The movements of the tongue in speaking are even quicker and more complicated than those of the foil in fencing, and are, besides, mostly concealed from sight. The complicated articulations which make up the sound of such a French word as *ennui* cannot be reproduced correctly by mere imitation except in the case of an exceptionally gifted learner.

Even in the case of children learning the sounds of their own language, the process is a slow and tedious one, and the nearer the approach to maturity, the greater the difficulty of acquiring new sounds. Indeed, the untrained adult seems to be often absolutely incapable of imitating an unfamiliar sound or even an unfamiliar combination of familiar sounds. To the uneducated even unfamiliar syllables are a difficulty, as we see in 'familiarizations' such as *sparrow-grass* for *asparagus*.[1] Even those who devote their lives to the study of languages generally fail to acquire a good pronunciation by imitation—perhaps after living ten or twenty years in the country and learning to write the language with perfect ease and accuracy.

Fallacy of Minute Distinctions

The second fallacy is that minute distinctions of sound can be disregarded—or, in other words, that a bad pronunciation does not matter. The answer to this is that significant distinctions cannot be disregarded with impunity. By significant sound-distinctions we mean those on which distinctions of meaning depend, such as between close and open *e* in French *pécher*, *pêcher*. We see from this example that significant sound-distinctions may be very minute—or at least may appear so to an unaccustomed ear. To a native ear they always seem considerable. Thus to English people the distinction between the vowels of *men* and *man*, *head* and *had*, seems a very marked one, while to most foreigners it seems but a slight one: many Germans are apt to confound *head*, *had*, *hat* under the one pronunciation *het*.

---

[1] I knew a child who used to make *giraffe, facsimile, chiffonier* into *edgiruff, face smile*, and *shove anear* respectively.

Nor can we tell *à priori* what sound-distinctions are significant in a language : a distinction that is significant in one language may exist as a distinction in another, but without being significant, or one of the sounds may be wanting altogether.   Thus in ordinary Southern English we have no close *e* at all ; while in the North of England they have the close sound in such words as *name* without its being distinctive, for it is simply a concomitant of the long or diphthongic sound of *e*.

Experience shows that even the slightest distinctions of sound cannot be disregarded without the danger of unintelligibility.   The friends of the late Guðbrand Vígfússon, the well-known Icelander, still remember how he used to complain that the country people round Oxford could hardly be made to understand him when he asked for eggs : ' I said *ex*—I ought to have said *airx*.'   Here the remedy was almost worse than the disease ; and yet what suggested *eks* to an English ear differed only from the correct pronunciation in having whisper instead of voice in the first as well as the second consonant !

Methods of Study : Organic and Acoustic

The first business of phonetics is to describe the actions of the organs of speech by which sounds are produced, as when we describe the relative positions of tongue and palate by which (s) is produced.   This is the **organic** side of phonetics. The **acoustic** investigation of speech-sounds, on the other hand, describes and classifies them according to their likeness to the ear, and explains how the acoustic effect of each sound is the necessary result of its organic formation, as when we call (s) a hiss-sound or sibilant, and explain why it has a higher pitch—a shriller hiss—than the allied hiss-consonant (ʃ) in *she*.

It is evident that both the organic and the acoustic sense must be cultivated : we must learn both to recognize each sound by ear and to recognize the organic positions by which it is produced, this recognition being effected by means of the accompanying muscular sensations.

We all carry out these processes every day of our lives in speaking our own language.   All, therefore, that we have to do in the case of familiar sounds is to develop this unconscious organic and acoustic sense into a conscious and analytic sense.

Isolation of Sounds

The first step is to learn to **isolate** the sounds and to keep them unchanged in all combinations and under all the varying conditions of quantity and stress (accent). Thus the learner may lengthen and isolate the vowels in *pity*, and observe the distinction between them and between the vowels of *pit* and *peat*.

This method of isolation is a great help in learning foreign sounds. A teacher of French who has learnt to cut up such a word as *ennui* into (ãã, nyy, ii) will, without any knowledge of phonetics, be able to give his pupils a much better idea of the pronunciation of the word than by repeating it any number of times undivided.

Analysis of the Formation of Sounds

The next step is to learn to analyze the formation of the familiar sounds. This analysis must be practical as well as theoretical. It is no use being able to explain theoretically and to hear the distinction between a breath consonant such as (f) and the corresponding voice consonant (v), unless we are able to *feel* the difference. Let the beginner learn to isolate and lengthen the (f) in *life* and the corresponding (v) in *liver* till he can feel that while (f) is articulated in one place only, (v) is articulated in two places—not only between lip and teeth, but also in the throat. If he presses his first two fingers on the ' Adam's apple,' he will feel the vibration which produces the effect of voice in (v), which vibration is absent from (f). If he closes both ears, he will hear the voice-vibration very distinctly.

Deducing Unfamiliar from Familiar Sounds

The great test of the practical command of such a distinction as breath and voice is the power it gives of deducing unfamiliar from familiar sounds. Repeat (vvff) several times in succession, and try to carry out a similar change with the voice-consonant (l), and the result will be the Welsh (l*h*) in *llan*. Again, to get the German or Scotch (x) in *loch* it is only necessary to exaggerate and isolate the ' off-glide ' of the (k) of the English *lock*. Often, indeed, mere isolation is enough to deduce an apparently unfamiliar sound. Thus the peculiar obscure *a* and peculiar (s)-sound in Portuguese, as in *amamos*, are simply the first element of the diphthong in English *how* and the second element of the English (tʃ) in *chin*, which is distinct from the (ʃ) in *fish*, being really a sound intermediate between (ʃ) and (s).

It is interesting to observe that hearing such an unfamiliar sound as (lʰ) is a hindrance rather than a help to the beginner, who, hearing a sound which is partly a hiss and partly an (l), tries to do justice to the acoustic effect by sounding separately the familiar English hiss (þ) in *think* and an ordinary voice (l), so that he makes (lʰan) into (þlæn). This is an additional argument against the imitation fallacy.

But, as already remarked, the acoustic sense must be thoroughly trained, for in many cases the acoustic does help the organic analysis. 'Listen before you imitate' is one of the axioms of practical phonetics.

Relation of Native Sounds to Sounds in General

Before beginning the study of foreign sounds, it is important to get a clear idea of the relations of our own sound-system to that of sounds in general, and especially to learn to realize what is anomalous and peculiar in our own sound-system. Thus, when the English learner has once learnt to regard his (ei) and (ou) in such words as *name* and *so* as abnormal varieties of monophthongic close (ee, oo), he will find that much of the difficulty of pronouncing such languages as French and German will disappear; he will no longer have the mortification of betraying his nationality the moment he utters the German word *so*. Indeed, speakers of the broad London dialect in which (ei) and (ou) are exaggerated in the direction of (əi) and (au) often become unintelligible in speaking foreign languages. Two young Englishmen abroad once entered into conversation with a French curé, and one of them had occasion to use the word *beaucoup*; the Frenchman was heard repeating to himself (bauky) and asking himself what it meant. Each language has its own 'organic basis,' and the organic bases of French and English are as distinct as they can well be. Hence the importance of a clear conception of the character of each basis, and their relations to one another.

CHAPTER III

PHONETIC NOTATION

NEXT to analysis, the most important problem of practical phonetics is that of sound-notation, or spelling by sound.

The first and most obvious advantage of a phonetic notation is that the learner who has once mastered the elementary sounds of the language, together with the elementary symbols of the notation he employs, is able to read off any phonetically written text with certainty, without having to burden his memory with rules of pronunciation. To such a student the distinction, for instance, between close and open *e* and *o* in Italian offers no difficulties : he learns from the beginning to pronounce each word with the correct vowel.

Another advantage of a phonetic notation is that as the learner sees the words written in a representation of their actual spoken form, he is able to recognize them when he hears them with comparative ease—or, at any rate, he is better prepared to recognize them. Most English people, when they first go to France, are unable to understand a word of the language when spoken, however well they may be able to read it. This is simply because the unphonetic French spelling they are used to represents not the spoken French of to-day, but the French that was spoken in the sixteenth century—being a very bad representation even of that. But if a foreigner has learnt to decipher such written forms as (aksebo) or (a k s e bo !), (kɛksɛksa, kjɛski), he would certainly be better prepared to understand them when spoken than if he had first to translate them in his mind into (aa kə sə ei bou) or something of that kind.

Phonetic notation helps the ear in many ways. The spoken word is fleeting, the written word is permanent. However often the learner has the elements of such a word as *ennui* repeated to him, it is still a help to have the impressions of his ear confirmed by association with the written symbols of such a

9

transliteration as (ăănųi). If the phonetic notation, instead of confirming, *corrects* an impression of the ear, its utility becomes still more manifest.

Teaching by ear alone throws away these advantages. It is certain that even the quickest linguist is helped by phonetic notation. Even if it were not absolutely required for the purpose of saving him from mishearings and mispronunciations, it would still serve to strengthen his hold of the spoken word.

The consideration that the written word is permanent is enough to refute the objection sometimes made to phonetic spelling, namely, that it makes the language more difficult to understand. It is clear that if the learner cannot solve such a riddle as (aksebo) at his leisure, he will certainly not be able to solve it when he has only the fleeting impression on his ear to rely on.

Unphonetic Spelling; Nomic Spelling

The question of phonetic notation is complicated by the fact that the traditional or 'nomic' orthography of most languages is only partially phonetic. But even French and English are not wholly unphonetic. Even in English we find hundreds of such spellings as *send*, *if*, *not*, which even the most radical spelling-reformer need not alter, together with many others which would require only a slight change to make them wholly phonetic. Indeed, it is easy to see that a wholly unphonetic system of spelling—one in which every word was written with an absolutely arbitrary combination of letters—would be too much even for the most retentive memory.

But even a little unphoneticness may cause a good deal of confusion and perplexity, as we see in the case of the two pronunciations of Italian *e*, *o*, *z* and of Welsh *y*—a language whose spelling is often said to be entirely phonetic. The want of stress-marks in English, and still more in Russian, is one of the greatest obstacles to learning to speak these languages, and sometimes gives rise to ludicrous misunderstandings. Thus a German staying in an English house, when summoned to dinner, told the servant that he was 'occupied' and could not come yet; but he put the accent in the wrong place, the result of which was that the assembled company was startled by the information, 'Please, sir, Dr. A. says he's a Cupid!' As Dr. A. was short and stout, amazement soon yielded to amusement.

So difficult is the Russian stress, that an Englishman in Russia, when asked by another Englishman who was learning Russian to give him some simple rules for the accent, told him to try and find out what syllable the accent ought to fall on, and then to put it on some other syllable. Although German stress is on the whole regular, yet such a distinction as that between 'übersetzen, 'leap over,' and über'setzen, 'translate,' is puzzling enough to the beginner.

Fullness of Transcription

Besides unphonetic writing which is positively misleading, there is another way of being negatively unphonetic by simply suppressing—not perverting—the phonetic information required. Thus, when a foreigner has to read aloud about 'the reform-bill of 1830,' it is no help to him to have it phonetically transcribed into (ðə rifɔmbil əv 1830), if the numerals are not transcribed in full at the same time. It is still worse when an Englishman has to read straight off in French such a number as 1789. Vietor and Dörr are quite right in giving such texts as the following in their *Englisches Lesebuch*—except, of course, that it ought to be in phonetic spelling :—

'In the course of last month Jack saved elevenpence. Out of this he bought a few steel pens, for which he paid threepence, and a pot [1] of ink, which cost him twopence. The rest of his money was then just one small silver coin; what is its name?'

But they spoil it all by going on to give such 'texts' as the following :—

ADDITION TABLE.

1 and		2 and		3 and		4 and	
1 are	2	1 are	3	1 are	4	1 are	5
2 ,,	3	2 ,,	4	2 ,,	5	2 ,,	6
3 ,,	4	3 ,,	5	3 ,,	6	3 ,,	7
4 ,,	5	4 ,,	6	4 ,,	7	4 ,,	8
5 ,,	6	5 ,,	7	5 ,,	8	5 ,,	9
6 ,,	7	6 ,,	8	6 ,,	9	6 ,,	10
7 ,,	8	7 ,,	9	7 ,,	10	7 ,,	11
8 ,,	9	8 ,,	10	8 ,,	11	8 ,,	12
9 ,,	10	9 ,,	11	9 ,,	12	9 ,,	13
10 ,,	11	10 ,,	12	10 ,,	13	10 ,,	14
11 ,,	12	11 ,,	13	11 ,,	14	11 ,,	15
12 ,,	13	12 ,,	14	12 ,,	15	12 ,,	16

[1] Ought to be 'bottle.'

169

So also such a formula as $a^2 + 2ab + b^2$ ought to be also written in full (ei -skweə :plas tuw :ei bij :plas bij -skweə), although, of course, it would be out of place in an elementary book.

On the same principle such contractions as *lb.*, *cwt.*, *oz.*, *Ry.*, ought to be written in full.

But here a caution is necessary. It would be quite wrong to expand *P.M.* into (poust miˈridjem), for we always pronounce this contraction literally—(pij em). *M.A.* may be read either as (:maastər əv aats) or (em ei), as also *M.P.* and many others, the literal pronunciations being the most common.

Relation of Nomic to Phonetic Spelling

The first and most obvious objection brought against the use of a phonetic notation in teaching a foreign language is the danger of confusion between the phonetic and the nomic spelling of the language. A-priori theorists have argued that the result of beginning with a phonetic spelling will inevitably be 'to spoil the learner's spelling for life.' But all who have ever given the phonetic method a fair trial maintain that this objection has no practical weight. They assure us that their experience shows that when a language has once been thoroughly mastered in a phonetic notation, the learning of the ordinary traditional spelling offers no difficulty: those who have begun phonetically end by spelling orthographically just as well as those who began at the same time with the ordinary spelling, and learn no other spelling, and thus were able to give much more time to it. The explanation of the quicker progress of the phonetic learners is, of course, that they are able to grasp the general idea of sound-representation easier and quicker by beginning with an easier—that is, a phonetic —spelling.

It cannot, of course, be denied that the study of such a language as French would be easier if the divergence between its nomic and its phonetic spelling did not exist. But the difficulty of which this divergence is the expression is not the fault of phonetics: ignoring phonetics does not get rid of the divergence between the spoken and the written sounds of the language. All we can do is to minimize the difficulty; and the first step towards this is the adoption of a phonetic transcription.

The next question is, Which should be learnt first? This amounts practically to the question, Which associations ought to be strongest? Clearly those with the sounds: in speaking the associations between sounds and ideas must be instantaneous, while in reading or writing we have time to stop and think. This is the order we follow in learning our own language: we speak before we spell.

If children learnt by eye first, they would never speak properly—they would speak like foreigners who have begun with the literary language.

The same kind of reasoning which forbids us to begin with the nomic spelling, forbids us also to learn the two simultaneously. The only way of avoiding cross-associations is to begin with one of them and use it exclusively, and then—either for a time or permanently—use the other as exclusively. As we have seen, there is every reason why we should begin with the phonetic spelling, which, when it has served its purpose, may be put aside entirely.

The relation between phonetic and nomic spelling is analogous to that between the tonic sol-fa notation and the ordinary staff-notation in music. The advocates of the former notation argue that the first thing is to learn the thing itself in the easiest way possible. They then go on to state as a fact, the result of experience, that when the thing music is once learnt, it does not matter so much what notation is used. The result of beginning with the tonic sol-fa notation is that thousands who would be quite unable to learn music from the ordinary notation, master it perfectly on the new system, and are then able with a little practice to read music at sight from the staff notation, so that even if their sole object is to learn the latter, they save themselves much toil and trouble by beginning with the tonic sol-fa notation.

Remedies: Additional Marks and Letters

The difficulties caused by unphonetic writing may be met in a variety of ways.

Such a difficulty as that of the place of stress is only a negative one, and can easily be remedied by the addition of accents or other marks without any alteration of the nomic spelling. Nor does this kind of difficulty involve the same amount of cross-association as the confusion between close and open *e* in Italian. Still worse are cross-associations involved in such a group of spellings as the English *plough, enough, trough* = (plau, inaf, trɔf), or those two which made the witty French philosopher express a wish that the *plague* (pleig) might take half of the English people, the *ague* (eigju) the other half.

The defects of such comparatively phonetic orthographies as the Italian can be easily remedied by the application of diacritics as in *ora* (close), *ôro* (open), or by the use of italics, which may also be used to indicate ' silent letters.'

But any system which involves retention of the nomic spelling practically breaks down in the case of such languages as English and French. Here we must sooner or later come to the conclusion that instead of trying to teach pronunciation not *through* but *in spite of* the nomic spelling, it is better to start with an entirely new phonetic spelling.

The defects of the ordinary Roman alphabet may be supplemented in a variety of ways :—

1. By adding new letters—either entirely new, or taken from other alphabets : ʃ, ȝ, η; þ, ð, θ, δ.
2. By adding diacritics : ā, é, ñ.
3. By utilizing superfluous letters : c, q, x.
4. By turned letters : ə, ɔ, ɾ.
5. By italics and capitals : *a, ʔ*, ʀ.
6. By digraphs : th, dh, n*j*, l*h*.

Of these expedients the first is the most popular. As a general rule, the more ignorant and inexperienced the reformer, the more reckless he is in adding new types, although nothing is more difficult than to invent a new letter. The main objection to new types is, of course, the trouble and expense of procuring them.

The same objections apply also, though in a less degree, to diacritics, which, as Ellis says, ' act as new letters.' The best known of the diacritic alphabets is Lepsius's *Standard Alphabet*, in which seventeen diacritics are used above and fourteen below the letters, the number of lower-case letters employed being more than 280, of which 200 have to be cut specially for each fount.

The four other expedients have the advantage of not requiring new types to be cut.

Principles of Phonetic Notation

The first requisite of a good alphabet is that it should be capable of being written and read with ease and written with moderate quickness.

Simplicity.—For ease of reading, it is desirable that the letters should be as simple as is consistent with distinctness. From this point of view, the Roman letters are superior to the black-letter or Gothic forms still used in Germany, as we see especially in the capitals. Dots and other diacritics, which must be made small, tend to indistinctness.

Compactness.—Ease of reading depends also greatly on compactness. Hence syllabic systems of writing like Sanskrit, in which such a syllable as *skra* is expressed by a single character, are in many respects easier and pleasanter to read than the corresponding Roman transcription. It is often a matter of surprise that the Chinese characters try the eyes so little, in spite of the great complexity and minute distinctions they often involve. The reason is that every word is represented by a compact square character, all the characters being of uniform size, the strain on the eyesight being further reduced by the arrangement of the characters in perpendicular columns. The superiority of the syllabic principle is strikingly shown by the fact that both the Protestant and the Catholic missionaries in Canada use syllabic alphabets in teaching the Crees and other native tribes to read, on account of the length to which the words run when written in Roman letters. These alphabets consist of simple characters expressing consonants, such as **V**, turned different ways—**< >**—to indicate what vowel follows.

Joining.—Ease and quickness of writing require that the letters should be easily joined together, as may be seen by comparing a passage written in Greek letters with one in Roman letters.

The most accurate way of estimating the comparative merits of letters as regards ease and quickness of writing is to count the number of strokes of which they are composed on some uniform plan. Thus *i* without a dot consists of one stroke, scrpit *s* of two, *š* of four.

But this method of calculation leaves out of account the 'aërial movements' of the pen from the line of writing to the diacritic and back again. We see now that writing the single letter *š* takes as much time as writing the five letters *seeee*!

Printed Forms.—In printing, the complexity of the letters does not influence speed or ease : the main thing is to have as few types as possible. This is an additional reason for abolishing the use of capitals in phonetic writing—except for special distinctions. In printing it is easiest to have the letters detached. This is highly objectionable in writing, but is generally an advantage in reading.

As regards the relations between the written and printed forms of the letters, it is evidently desirable to avoid unnecessary deviation without, on the other hand, attempting to make print into a—necessarily imperfect—imitation of handwriting. The disadvantages of such an attempt are well shown in Arabic, with its superfluous distinction of initial, medial, and final forms of one and the same letter, the maximum of discomfort being reached when the short vowels are indicated by diacritic strokes printed on separate lines, so that the reader is sometimes in doubt whether the diacritic is to be read above the consonant of the line he is reading or below the consonant of the line above.

Some phonetic transcriptions—such as that of the Swedish Dialect Society and of Trautmann in his *Sprachlaute*—consist entirely of italics, so as to diminish the difference between the written and printed characters as much as possible, and also to make the phonetic writing stand out distinctly in a page of Roman type. But as italics are required for a variety of other purposes, and as it is a waste of existing material not to utilize the distinction of Roman and italic, it seems better to make the more legible Roman the basis, and use italics for various supplementary purposes; it is always easy to mark off phonetic writing by enclosing it in ( ). The transcription of the Danish Dialect Society *Dania* is so far an advance on the other italic systems that it utilizes Roman letters for special distinctions of sound.

Having thus determined the general principles on which the choice of symbols is founded, we come to the still more difficult question, how to use these symbols—what sounds or what phonetic functions to assign to them.

National and International Basis

The most obvious way of making an unphonetic orthography phonetic is to select some one out of the various traditional representations of each sound, and use that one symbol exclusively, omitting at the same time all silent letters, and adding marks of stress (accent) if necessary, as in the following specimen of Ellis's ' English Glossic : '—

' Ingglish Glosik iz veri eezi too reed. A cheild foar yeerz oald kan bee taut too reed Glosik buoks.'

A system which, like Glossic, writes short and long vowels with totally different symbols (i, ee) is only half-phonetic : it is phonetic on an unphonetic basis. Again, this unphonetic English basis breaks down altogether in some cases. It fails, for instance, to supply unambiguous symbols for the vowels in *child* and *book*, *full* and the consonant in *the*, which Ellis writes (dh).

The following specimens of French and German spellings formed in a similar way on the basis of the respective nomic orthographies of these languages are taken from Soames's *Introduction to the Study of Phonetics :*—

' Deû pti gars*on* d la vil, Richa:r é Gusta:v, s égarè:r *eun* jou:r da*nz* un épè:s foré.

'Äs 'ist doch gevis, das 'in der Vält den Mänshen niçts nohtvändiç macht 'als dih Lihbe.'

A fully phonetic system, in which long vowels and diphthongs are expressed by consistent modifications or combinations of the simple vowel symbols, and in which simple sounds are, as far as is reasonable and convenient, expressed by single letters instead of diagraphs, must necessarily discard any one national traditional basis. The best basis on the whole is obtained by making the later Latin pronunciation the foundation, with such modifications and additions as may be necessary. We thus get the ' Romic' or international as opposed to the Glossic or national basis. Thus the passage quoted above appears as follows in my ' Broad Romic' notation :—

' iŋgliʃ glosik iz veri iizi tə riid. ə tʃaild fɔə jiəz ould kən bi tɔt tə riid glosik buks.'

Observe that on this basis the vowel in the English *book*, French *jour*, and German *gut* would be expressed uniformly by (u) in writing all three languages (buk, ʒuur, guut) instead of in three different ways, as on the Glossic basis.

c

175

It is evident that as soon as we have to deal with more than one language there can be no doubt of the superiority of the Romic basis.

A Universal Alphabet Unpractical

If a universal alphabet were constructed which provided symbols for every possible sound, then each language would simply have to select from it the symbols required for its own sound-system. On the other hand, it is desirable for ordinary practical purposes that each language should utilize the simplest and most convenient letters. Thus, if in the universal alphabet (e) were restricted to the close sound of French *é*, the corresponding open sound being represented by (ε), this arrangement would suit French very well. But if it were applied to English, which has not any close (e) at all, the result would be that the simplest and easiest to write of all letters would not be used at all.

Significant Sound-distinctions

Again, for practical purposes we have to distinguish between differences of sound on which differences of meaning depend— significant sound-distinctions—from those which are not significant. Thus the distinction between (e) and (ε) is significant in French, as in *pécher*, *pêcher ;* but in those languages in which the short *e* is always open and the long *e* always close there is no necessity to employ (ε) at all : the distinction of quantity in (e, ee) is enough. Even if the distinction of close and open is made in the long *e*, there can be no ambiguity in writing *e* for the short sound if it is always open, as in German and English, in both of which languages such a spelling as (men) is perfectly unambiguous.

So also the distinction between the first elements of the English diphthongs in *high, how* is un-significant, and although neither of them is identical with the vowel of *ask*, we do not hesitate to write all three uniformly with *a*—(hai, hau, aask). And as the pronunciation of these diphthongs varies considerably, and as it would be impossible to do justice to all these minute distinctions without a much more elaborate system of notation than is required for ordinary practical purposes, we regard (ai, au) simply as general symbols for a variety of diphthongs, all of which may be classed under one of two distinct types, both beginning with back or mixed non-rounded vowels and ending with approximations to (i) and (u) respectively.

Superfluous Sound-distinctions

This is connected with another common-sense principle, namely, that of omitting superfluous distinctions. Thus, if a language always has the stress on the first syllable, the stress does not require to be marked at all. If the majority of words have the stress on the first syllable, then it is necessary to mark it only when it falls on some other syllable. It is evident that on this principle the 'smooth breathing' in Greek ought to be omitted, as there are only two breathings, and the absence of the rough breathing is enough to show that the other one is meant. In English it is necessary to distinguish the long open *o* in *naught* from the short open *o* in *not*, which we ought strictly to do by writing (nɔɔt, nɔt). But as there is no short close *o* in English, there is no reason why we should not write *not* with the easier *o*. Hence it becomes superfluous to mark the length in *naught*, which finally brings us to (not, nɔt) as the shortest and most convenient phonetic spellings.

Modifiable General Basis

We see, then, that the ideal of a general alphabet for practical purposes is one which gives a basis which is, on the whole, generally acceptable, but can be freely modified to suit the requirements of each language. The better the basis, the less inducement there will be to diverge from it.

If we accept certain mechanical principles, such as utilizing *c, x,* and the other superfluous letters, avoiding diacritics, testing new letters with regard to their distinctness and ease of writing, and return where practicable to the original Roman values, we shall have little difficulty in arriving at a basis of agreement. No one, for instance, who has given any thought to general principles could hesitate long between *ü* and *y*, *š* and *ʃ*.

In comparing the sounds of a variety of languages—still more in dealing with sounds generally—we require a much more elaborate system of notation than in dealing with a single language; we can no longer content ourselves with marking

177

significant distinctions in the simplest and shortest way: it becomes necessary to mark such distinctions as that between the first elements of English (ai, au), for the unsignificant distinction between the first element of English (au) and the (aa) of *ask* may be a significant one in some other language—as it actually is in Portuguese, one of whose *a*-sounds is like English (aa), while the other is the first element of English (au).

My Narrow Romic (see my *Primer of Phonetics*) is a general, minutely accurate scientific notation on the same basis as Broad Romic. Narrow Romic is to some extent based on Ellis's ' Palæotype,' a Romic system in which no new letters are used, the ordinary letters being supplemented by turned, italic, and small-capital letters, and by many digraphs. Ellis afterwards had the unhappy idea of constructing a ' Universal Glossic' on the English-values basis, which is a complete failure. It has had disastrous effects on the phonetic investigation of the English dialects, for which it was specially intended.

My Romic systems were made the basis of the alphabet of *Le Maître Phonétique* (MF), which is the organ of *L'Association phonétique internationale* directed by Mr. P. Passy. This alphabet is now widely used on the Continent, and Mr. Passy hopes that it will be universally adopted by linguists in all countries. But, slight as the differences are on the whole between my Romic and the MF alphabet, I cannot bring myself to adopt the latter, which I feel to be still in the experimental stage. It is surely best to be contented with the amount of agreement already reached, and leave the rest to the survival of the fittest, which will certainly eliminate some of the details of the MF alphabet in its present form.

Non-Roman Basis: Organic Alphabet

It is, indeed, questionable whether it is possible to construct a really efficient universal alphabet on the basis of the Roman alphabet. All such alphabets tend to degenerate into an endless string of arbitrary and disconnected symbols. It is impossible to build up a really consistent and systematic notation on such an arbitrary and inadequate foundation.

The only way out of the difficulty is to discard the Roman alphabet altogether, and start afresh.

What is wanted is a notation built up on definite principles, in which there is a definite relation between symbol and sound. This relation may be either organic or acoustic—that is, the symbol may indicate either the organic positions which produce the sound, or indicate the pitch and other acoustic characteristics of the sound. No one has ever attempted, as far as I know, to construct a phonetic notation on a purely acoustic basis. The tendency of the earlier attempts at a universal alphabet was to symbolize the consonants organically, the vowels acoustically, as in Brücke's *Phonetische Transscription* (Vienna, 1863). It is now generally acknowledged that the vowels as well as the consonants must be represented on a strictly organic (physiological) basis. This is the great merit of Bell's *Visible Speech*, which appeared in 1868, and, in a shorter form and with some modifications, in 1882, under the title of *Sounds and their Relations*.

I studied Bell's system under the author himself, and afterwards gave an elaborate criticism of Visible Speech in a paper on *Sound-notation* (Phil. Soc. Transs., 1880 1), in which I described a modification of it—the Organic Alphabet. This system is merely a revised form of Visible Speech, in which I attempted to get rid of what seemed objectionable features in the older system without attempting any radical changes. A full description of the Organic alphabet will be found in my *Primer of Phonetics*.

The Narrow Romic notation already mentioned (p. 21) is practically a transcription of the Organic alphabet into Roman letters, so as to make the principles of Bell's analysis more accessible to the world at large. In the Primer of Phonetics I use this notation, together with Broad Romic, concurrently with the organic symbols.

All these notations are alphabetic : that is, they go on the general principle of providing separate symbols for each simple sound.

In the Roman alphabet such symbols as *v, f,* are arbitrary. In a physiological alphabet such as the Organic, each letter is made up of elements presenting the components of the sound ; thus in the organic symbol of (v) we can clearly see the graphic representation of its components ' lip, teeth, voice.' It is not, of course, necessary that all the components should be explicitly represented in the symbol. Thus, if there is a special mark or modifier to express voice, the absence of that modifier necessarily implies breath. A further simplification is attained by the consistent use of differences of projection above and below the line of writing, and of size—as in the distinction between Roman 1 and i (without the dot), o and °, and of direction, as in the Cree alphabet (p. 15). All these devices are fully utilized in the Organic alphabet, the result often being that the letters are simpler than the corresponding Roman ones. The simplicity of the system is shown by the fact that in its most elaborate form it requires only 109 types compared with the 280 of Lepsius's alphabet (p. 14).

Analphabetic Basis

An 'analphabetic,' as opposed to an alphabetic basis was first definitely advocated by Jespersen in his *Articulations of speech-sounds represented by means of Analphabetic symbols* (Marburg, 1889), the system being further developed in his *Phonetik*.

In this system the elementary symbols do not denote sounds, but the components of sounds, each simple sound being represented by a group of symbols resembling a chemical formula, as if we were to denote the lip-teeth-voice consonant by *ltv* or *lt'* instead of *v*. In this way Jespersen avoids what he considers the great defect of Bell's notation, that is, its want of elasticity. He claims for his own system that it allows perfect freedom in combining the elementary symbols, while Bell's vowel-symbols, for instance, can be used only by those who accept all the details of his analysis as enshrined in his famous 'chess-board' arrangement of the 36 elementary vowels. Another great advantage which he claims for his system is that the symbols consist mainly of the first six letters of the Greek and the first twelve letters of the Roman alphabet together with the numerals, so that it can be printed anywhere, and thus made generally accessible.

The two main defects in Jespersen's working-out of these ideas appear to be that his choice of symbols is not good, and that his symbolization is too abstract.

As regards the first criticism, when we consider how unwieldy and sprawly such a notation must necessarily be, we have a right to expect that these drawbacks will be compensated by the symbols being as accessible and easy to handle as possible, especially when we consider how few of them are required. One does not understand, therefore, why the inventor should have gone out of his way to mix up Greek with Roman letters;

for the former are not to be met with in every printing-office, so that many missionaries in out-of-the way regions would not be able to use the Analphabetic notation at all. He also occasionally uses Greek capitals, and a small capital R together with a turned 2—z, all of which are symbols which would be avoided by any one constructing an ordinary alphabetic phonetic notation, although their use would be much more excusable there.

The second defect is shown in the use made of these symbols. The Greek letters denote the moveable organs, such as the lips and the different parts of the tongue; the Roman letters denote such organs as the teeth and the different parts of the palate. The alphabetic order of both sets of letters is made to correspond to the order of the articulatory organs, beginning with the lips: β = tip of the tongue, d = teeth, k = uvula. The result of this is that there is no direct association between symbol and organ. And, indeed, to those accustomed to the opposite order, which makes the stream of breath follow the direction of ordinary writing, thus—throat, back of tongue and palate, front, lips (Primer of Phonetics, § 35)—so that the lips come last instead of first, it is almost impossible to learn and remember the meaning of these symbols.

This notation would surely be greatly improved (1) by getting rid of the out-of-the-way symbols and by substituting italics for the Greek letters; (2) by making the latter correspond as far as possible to the Roman letters, so that, for instance, the upper and the lower lip, the middle of the palate and the middle of the tongue, should be respectively denoted by the same letter, one Roman, the other italic; and (3) by giving each place of articulation a symbol which could be directly associated with it. Thus, the upper teeth might be denoted by *f*, the lower by f, because this consonant necessarily involves teeth articulation. It would certainly be less confusing to find j used to denote the middle of the palate than the back, as in Jespersen's scheme.

But however much this notation were capable of improvement, certain radical defects would always remain. In the first place, no possible choice of Roman letters could entirely obviate cross-associations with their existing values. And the formulæ are too lengthy for the eye to be able to take them in at a glance or remember them: they can never make a definite picture to the eye as the organic symbols do.

In short, the gain is so questionable that it would perhaps be best in the end to fall back on descriptions of the sounds in contractions of ordinary words, denoting, for instance (v) by *lp tth vce* if *ltv* is too brief.

Nevertheless, it cannot be denied that the system is an ingenious one, and worthy of trial, especially at the present time, when there seems little prospect of agreement as to a general scientific alphabet on a non-Roman basis.

Jespersen's notation has one great advantage over Bell's in being based on a more advanced phonetic analysis. But this, of course, has nothing to do with the fundamental question whether the universal alphabet of the future is to be on an alphabetic or an analphabetic basis.

The Alphabetic Basis the Best

Many of the objections which Jespersen makes to Bell's alphabet could be easily got rid of without giving up the alphabetic basis.

In the first place, the Organic alphabet is made much more elastic than Visible Speech by the 'modifiers' introduced by me, some of which have been found so useful that they have made their way into the Romic transcriptions of Passy and others. Again, it would be easy by a slight modification of the vowel letters to construct symbols denoting narrow or wide vowels indifferently, and so on. In fact, this can easily be done as it is by adding the 'wide-modifier' to the narrow vowel. In fact, many years ago I constructed a general algebraic phonetic notation on this basis, in which there were symbols for whole classes of sounds—one to denote all stopped consonants, another to denote all mixed vowels, and so on. With a little management, and the temporary use of Roman letters, such as v = 'vowel,' x = 'consonant,' combined with the modifiers, this can be effected with the Organic alphabet in its present shape.

We must not forget, moreover, that all alphabets—even the most scientific—are intended to serve practical purposes.

Practice implies compromise. Hence every alphabet must in some respects be a compromise between opposite principles. Thus the Organic alphabet is so far analphabetic that its elementary symbols mark only those distinctions of sound which, as far as can be judged *à priori*, are likely to be significant (p. 18). Thus they involve the division of the palate into three parts only, the minuter intermediate positions involved in Jespersen's symbols being indicated by the modifiers, which are graphically subordinated to the elementary symbols. So in this respect the Organic alphabet partially adopts the digraph or analphabetic principle.

Again, in a practical alphabet, the distinctions of nature must often be exaggerated so that there may be no hesitation in distinguishing the symbols of similar sounds. From this point of view Jespersen's objection to Bell's symbolizing consonants and vowels on different principles, so that, for instance, there is no resemblance between the symbols of lowered (j) and non-syllabic (i), appears of little weight. The real objection here seems to be that Bell confuses analysis with synthesis. But, again, if it is more practical and convenient to embody such distinctions as vowel and consonant, syllabic and non-syllabic, in the elementary analytic symbols, then he is justified in doing so till some one else hits on an arrangement which is more scientific and as practical.

Universal Alphabet not suited for Connected Writing

A universal notation is, in the nature of things, generally used only to write a few words at a time, sometimes only a single sound. In writing connected texts in one particular language, an alphabet of the Broad Romic type is infinitely more convenient : all the learner has to do is to associate each Broad Romic symbol with the pronunciation of the corresponding Narrow Romic, Organic, or Analphabetic symbol of the sound in question, so that, for instance, when he meets (i) in his texts, he knows that it stands for the high front wide—or whatever shade of sound it is—in the language he is studying.

But it is evidently a great help to the learner—especially if he has not a teacher—to have his texts accompanied by a minutely accurate notation for at least the first page or two. Here an analphabetic notation is perfectly useless.

The advantages of the Roman alphabet for connected transcription are evident : it is an alphabet which has been developed partly by a slow process of spontaneous evolution, partly by conscious reforms and endless experiments.

But it has many defects. From a mechanical point of view, its worst defect is want of compactness (p. 15). In a universal scientific alphabet like the Organic, a certain amount of sprawliness is inevitable; but in a practical alphabet, which has to supply only a limited number of characters, it is an inexcusable defect.

Again, although our script or running-hand alphabet is fairly quick to write, it ought certainly to be quicker than it is. In most of the languages which use the Roman alphabet speed is further impeded by diacritics, such as the accents in French. Even in English the dot over the *i* and *j* wastes much time.

Superiority of Phonetic Shorthand

These and other considerations point clearly to the adoption of a system of phonetic shorthand on a general basis capable of being adapted to the special requirements of each language. As the basis of such a shorthand would be necessarily quite independent of the Roman alphabet, the danger of confusion between phonetic and nomic spellings would be reduced to a minimum. The introduction of a phonetic shorthand would, at the same time, be the real solution of the problem of spelling-reform. Lastly, all modern systems of shorthand are based more or less on organic or acoustic associations: they all show some connection between the form of the symbols and the sounds they represent, although, of course, in a practical system of writing theoretical consistency must always yield to considerations of speed and convenience.

Speed.—The term 'shorthand' is, in itself, only a relative one. Our ordinary script is a shorthand, if compared with the Roman capitals out of which it developed. The highest development of shorthand as regards speed of writing is, of course, reporting shorthand, whose definite aim is to enable the writer to keep up with a moderately fluent speaker: that is, it must be capable of being written at the rate of about 150 words a minute, which is five times as much as the rate of quick longhand writing.

As speech would outrun the quickest fingers, if every syllable —not to speak of every sound—had to be indicated, if only by a single stroke, high speed necessarily involves contraction —the wholesale omission of vowels, syllables, or even words —

the result being generally unintelligible to the writer himself unless copied out into longhand immediately after being written.

Distinctiveness.—A system of shorthand which is to take the place of longhand and retain the latter's advantages must, on the other hand, subordinate speed to legibility. For linguistic purposes it must be more than legible : it must be phonetically distinctive, that is, it must be capable of being transcribed accurately into such a notation as Broad Romic. In its contractions, too, it must be rigorously distinctive : each word, however much contracted, must have its own outline, by which it can be recognized immediately and with certainty without any guessing by the context.

All we can expect, then, from this point of view, is a system of writing as much shorter and more compact than ordinary longhand as the requirements of distinctness and legibility will allow. None of the three systems most in use at the present time—Pitman's in England and America, and the German systems of Gabelsberger and Stolze on the Continent—can be said fully to meet these requirements : they all sacrifice efficiency to brevity, the brevity being often only apparent.

My Current Shorthand is an attempt to supply this want (A Manual of Current Shorthand, Oxford, 1892). In the preface to the Manual I sum up the characteristic features of the system as follows :—

1. It is the first workable pure script [as opposed to geometric] shorthand that has been brought out in England.

2. It affords the first satisfactory solution of the vowel problem, by providing separate symbols for them, which, though joined to the consonants, are subordinated to them, so that the vowels can be omitted without altering the general appearance of the word.

3. It is the first system which makes a systematic use of projection above and below the line of writing to indicate the different classes of consonants.

4. It provides a purely orthographic and a purely phonetic style of writing for concurrent use.

5. It discards not only thick and thin, but all other sham distinctions.

6. It is rigorously linear, so that it can be used for all the purposes of ordinary longhand.

7. It could be printed from moveable types with comparative ease.

8. It is on a strictly syllabic and alphabetic basis.

Modified Nomic Spelling

As already remarked (p. 14), the defects of a comparatively phonetic orthography such as that of Italian or German can be easily remedied without substituting a new orthography.

A nomic orthography can be supplemented in the six ways enumerated on p. 14.

Of these methods, the use of diacritics is peculiarly applicable to the orthographies of dead languages, especially those in which it is desirable to reproduce the varying spellings of the original manuscripts, as in printing Old English or Old Irish texts. It is often a great advantage to have such texts printed in such a form as to enable the reader to see at a glance what is the original manuscript spelling, while at the same time he is supplied with the additional information required for the discrimination of the distinctive sounds of the language as far as they have been determined with any degree of probability. Thus in Old English there are two sounds of c, namely (k) and (c), the former being sometimes written k in the manuscripts. If our manuscript has k, we print it so; if the manuscript has c, we print it c when it stands for (k), $\dot{c}$ when it stands for (c). If we were constructing a new phonetic transcription of Old English, we should transliterate the two sounds by k and c respectively, as being more distinct and convenient than c and $\dot{c}$. But this is inadmissible if we wish faithfully to preserve the evidence of the manuscripts. So also it is better to mark long vowels in Old English with (ˉ) than by doubling—which we might prefer in a free phonetic transcription—or the addition of (′), for quantity is occasionally marked in these last ways in the manuscripts, but never by the macron or circumflex, either of which may therefore be employed. Hence such spellings as *kēne, cyning, cīese, ċīese*, in my Anglo-Saxon Reader serve both to indicate the exact pronunciation of these words, and to allow the reader to infer that the original manuscript spellings are *kene, cyning, ciese, ciese.*

Although diacritics have peculiar advantages as regards restitution of the original manuscript spellings, there is no objection to substituting other letters which do not occur in the ordinary orthography of the language in question. Thus if *k* never occurred in Old English manuscripts, there would be no harm in using it instead of *c*, so that the other sound could be represented by simple *c*. In the same way we could substitute *ɔ* for *č*, or use it to distinguish the open *o* in *lond* as opposed to the close *o* in *on*, *boren*, for none of these substitutions would hinder the recovery of the manuscript spelling. Italics are often very convenient for such discriminations of pairs of sounds.

Italics are specially useful in indicating silent letters, such as the final *e* in many words in Chaucer's English. As silent letters do not occur in Old English, italics can be used there to mark the omission by the manuscript of a letter required by strict phonetic spelling, as in *man*n for the manuscript spelling *man*.

Even modern English might be written phonetically in this way. Thus *through*, *though*, *thy* might be written (throūgh, thōugh, ᴛhȳ). But any such method breaks down practically with such an orthography as the English; and it is much simpler in the end to start with an entirely new phonetic spelling, as distinct from the nomic spelling as possible.

CHAPTER IV

FOREIGN ALPHABETS

THE difficulty of learning national alphabets does not much trouble the linguist as long as he confines himself to European languages.

But even the German black letter causes some difficulty to the beginner, although it is nothing but a late modification of the Roman alphabet. The printed capitals are especially difficult: of those who have learnt to recognize them perfectly by eye, not one in a thousand is capable of drawing them from memory. I remember, when I began to learn German by myself as a boy, that I at first confused the capital *s* with *g*, so that I read the word for 'care' as *gorgfalt*. By a similar confusion I read *neunauge*, 'lamprey,' as *reunauge*. This I found a hindrance to remembering these words; as soon as I read them correctly, I recognized their etymology and remembered them without difficulty.

So also the Greek and Russian alphabets are easily mastered by those who have an eye for form, while to others they may cause considerable waste of time. Thus I was told by the late Prince L. L. Bonaparte that he never could learn Russian or any Oriental language solely because of their alphabets: he did not care how difficult a language was as long as it was in the Latin alphabet.

It would be superfluous to enlarge on the difficulties of such systems of writing as the Arabic, Sanskrit, Chinese, and Japanese. The Chinese running-hand is said to take eight years to learn, even when the learner has thoroughly mastered the printed characters—itself a task of great difficulty.

The multiplicity of alphabets is a source of inconvenience in many ways, and also of expense.

Transliteration of Foreign Alphabets

Fortunately there is a growing tendency to substitute the Roman for the national alphabet in many languages. Holland, Sweden, England, and many other countries have given up the black letter, and others are following in their steps. The practice of transliterating into the Roman alphabet has extended to many of the Slavonic languages.

Transliteration is now the rule in quoting words from a variety of dead languages, as in comparative grammars. In such a book as Horn Tooke's *Diversions of Purley* (published towards the end of the last century) we still find the Gothic and Old English words printed in Gothic and Anglo-Saxon types. Now no one thinks of using these characters even in connected texts. So also Bopp, in his Comparative Grammar, gave Zend words in Zend types, and so on; all his successors transliterate the Old Arian languages except Greek. It is a curious illustration of the force of habit and prejudice that we still persist in printing Greek in late Byzantine characters which no ancient Greek would be able to read.

From a psychological point of view, the relations between national alphabets and transliterations are exactly parallel to those between nomic and phonetic spelling. The first thing is to learn the language itself in the easiest possible way, which involves beginning with transliterated texts. When the language itself has once been learnt, it can be easily read in any alphabet: Greek is still Greek in a Roman as well as in a Byzantine dress, Arabic is still Arabic even when written with Hebrew letters, just as English remains English in all the hundreds of systems of shorthand in which it has from time to time been written.

The argument most generally brought against transliteration is that it unsettles the learner's associations with the national alphabet.

The mere fact of any one's bringing forward this objection shows that his method of learning languages is a radically wrong one: it shows that he learns them exclusively by eye. There have been German Orientalists who made no distinction whatever between the Arabic hiss-sounds ذ, ث, ظ, ز, ص, س, pronouncing them all (s), and recognizing them only by the form of their symbols. But even in an extreme case like this there ought not to be any great difficulty in establishing visual associations between the Arabic letters and their transliterations s, s̤, z, z̤, θ, δ (or þ, ð).

This, however, only elicits fresh objections. The opponents of transliteration say, ' This would be plausible enough if we had only one fixed transliteration to learn; but unfortunately almost every text-book has a special transliteration of its own : one cannot even get a grammar and a dictionary with the same transliteration. It is therefore impossible to carry out your advice of keeping to one transliteration till one has mastered the Arabic alphabet.'

The multiplicity of transliterations is certainly to be deplored, but it is no more an argument against the principle of transliteration than the multiplicity of phonetic notations is against the phonetic method. The same influences which are steadily bringing us nearer to our ideal of a general basis of phonetic notation will doubtless bring about uniformity in the transcription of remoter languages as soon as the results of our experience with European languages become known to Orientalists and others, who are still hampered by bad traditions and the unscientific methods of their native authorities to a degree which is incredible to those familiar with the phonetic method as applied to European languages.

The great safeguard against confusions that arise from conflicting transcriptions is the principle already insisted upon— that of beginning with the language itself, which of course means beginning with a mastery of its sounds. The beginner in Arabic who has once learnt to distinguish *ṣaif*, ' summer,' from *saif*, ' sword,' by the combined associations of the peculiar sound and the special muscular sensations which accompany the utterance of the ' emphatic ' *ṣ*, will be independent of transliterations, for the ideas of ' summer ' and ' sword ' will at once suggest to his mind combinations of sounds as well as combinations of letters, the former associations being the stronger and more direct : he will be in quite a different position from the student whose only definite associations are with the written

صيف and سيف

Orthographic Transcription.

If the national alphabet itself is phonetic, the transcription will be phonetic also : it will be a key to the pronunciation, and at the same time it will be a key to the original spelling of each word, so that any one who is acquainted both with the method of transcription and the national alphabet will be able to transliterate the transcription back into the original writing.

If the national alphabet is unphonetic, but only moderately

so, the most obvious course is to follow the same method as in reproducing the manuscript spellings of dead languages; that is, to add the necessary diacritics, or make whatever modifications may be found convenient for the purpose of indicating pronunciation, so that all that is necessary to transliterate back into the national writing is to ignore these supplementary distinctions. If the national writing makes unphonetic distinctions by having two or more letters or combinations of letters to express the same sound or sound-group, then the diacritics will have an orthographic, not a phonetic value, and will therefore be ignored except as giving the key to the original writing.

We thus have a distinction between a purely phonetic and an orthographic transcription, the characteristic of the latter being that it can always be transliterated back into the national writing whether the latter is phonetic or not. It need scarcely be said that every orthographic transcription ought to be phonetic at the same time, or at any rate not markedly unphonetic, although in many cases it is most practical to sacrifice rigorous phonetic consistency whenever an unphonetic detail of transcription does not cause real difficulty. Thus in transcribing German it is better to keep the distinction between *sz* and *ss* in *füsz, musz, müssen,* than to run the risk of subsequent confusion by writing *füss, muss;* for such a spelling as *füss* is only a compromise between *fusz* and the fully phonetic (fuus), and not even a beginner would think of trying to pronounce *sz* exactly as it is spelt.

The method of orthographic transcription has been successfully applied to Persian by H. Barbs, a full account of whose transcription by K. Feyerabend will be found in *Phonetische Studien,* iii. 162. Persian in itself is generally considered one of the easiest and simplest of languages, but in its written form it is distinctly a difficult language because of the irregularity, complexity, and ambiguity of its alphabet and orthography. Without the help of a skilled and patient teacher it is hardly possible to learn it in its nomic form, because, as Feyerabend remarks, 'one can only read out of it what one has already learnt and knows.' Persian has the disadvantage of being written with an alphabet in every way alien to its genius—the Arabic. Hence such a defect as the omission of the short vowels—which in Arabic occasions much less difficulty than might be supposed because of the regularity and symmetry of the Arabic vowel-system—becomes very serious in a language

D

like Persian, where there are no rules for determining *à priori* the vowel-structure of a word, as is to a considerable extent the case in Arabic. Persian is, besides, full of Arabic words, which are written in the Arabic orthography, while the pronunciation is only imperfectly preserved. The slavish application of Arabic rules of orthography to Persian words is a further source of unphonetic spellings. Barbs' transcription seems fully to solve the double problem of giving a phonetic transcription which can at the same time be transliterated back letter for letter into the national writing. The student begins with a Reader in which all the texts are transcribed on these principles. When he has gone through it, he begins again, and at the same time he is gradually introduced to the Persian alphabet and the rules of Persian orthography. Then a parallel Reader in the Persian writing is put into his hands, and the work of deciphering begins. Feyerabend assures us, as the result of personal experience, that this causes no difficulty in the second third of the first year's course; for, as he says, 'we soon learnt to recognize our old acquaintances in their new dress.'

Nomic Pronunciation

The principle that in learning a language through written texts we should strengthen our associations with the characters by associating each character with its proper sound, and should avoid giving the same sound to letters which are pronounced differently (p. 30), cannot always be carried out literally.

Sometimes the learner has not access to a native teacher or to reliable information about the pronunciation. These difficulties are of course greatly increased if he is learning a dead language.

Under such circumstances the learner need not hesitate to make up a pronunciation of his own on the principle of accompanying every written distinction with a corresponding difference of sound, so as to strengthen as much as possible his visual associations.

Many foreigners have begun English in this way, pronouncing, for instance, *knowledge* in three syllables (knovledge), not because they thought this was the real pronunciation, but simply as a means of fixing the spelling in their minds.

G. von der Gabelentz—who united many of the qualifications of the theoretical and the practical linguist—goes a step further, and advises the beginner in Arabic who cannot pronounce ع ‘ēn to substitute (η)—a sound which does not occur in Arabic, and therefore cannot be mistaken for anything but a substitute for ‘ēn (Gab. 75). Before I saw Gabelentz' book I had hit on the same device, and had extended it to all the difficult sounds in Arabic: pronouncing ‘ēn as (v), ḥ as (wh) in what, the hamza or glottal stop as (p), the emphatic consonants as front or front-modified consonants. None of the substituted sounds occur in Arabic, except that (v) is sometimes developed by assimilation in colloquial pronunciation. The subsequent transition to the real pronunciation caused no difficulty whatever: after changing (v)s into ‘ēns for a day or two, the substitution is made mechanically. So also in learning Old Slavonic the important and rather confusing distinction between i and ĭ, u and ŭ may be easily made by giving i and u the narrow, ĭ and ŭ the corresponding wide sounds. This may, indeed, very well have been the actual distinction made.

Perhaps the most hopeless distinctions to learn without a teacher are those of intonation. And yet the tones in Chinese and other East-Asiatic languages cannot be ignored, for they are essential to intelligibility. A very simple memoria technica pronunciation for the Chinese tones consists in adding sounds to the monosyllabic Chinese root-words. Thus, if we adopt the deep sound of (u) as the symbolic exponent of the low level tone, (i) of the rising and (a) of the falling tone, we are able to differentiate (wenu) 'hear' from (wena) 'ask,' (waηu) 'king' from (waηi) 'depart.' If the word ends in a vowel, corresponding consonants may be added, of which there is a considerable choice, as only a limited number of consonants occur finally in the pronunciations of Chinese ordinarily adopted by European beginners. Here, again, the student who afterwards gets access to native teachers will have the great advantage of knowing beforehand the intonation of each word, and will have no difficulty in dropping his phonetic props and substituting the real tones; while if he had attempted to pronounce them theoretically, he would certainly have got into wrong habits of pronunciation which it would perhaps be difficult for him to get rid of.

Learning a Foreign Alphabet

The process of learning new alphabets and new systems of writing implies the establishing of various visual associations. But these associations may be of different kinds, and some may be much easier to establish than others.

In the first place, it makes a good deal of difference whether the language is already familiar—as when English people learn an English shorthand system, or Chinese boys learn to write the Chinese characters—or unfamiliar, as in the traditional method of learning Oriental languages. An extreme form of this method is well described in the following extract from Derembourg and Spiro's *Chrestomathie élémentaire de l'Arabe littéral* (Paris, 1892): 'the only practical method of beginning the study of a language is to take a piece written in the language one wishes to learn, and force oneself to translate even before one knows how to decipher the characters.' With such a method as this one can hardly be surprised to learn from the same preface that 'the first burst of enthusiasm in those who begin Oriental studies is often followed, even in the case of the most talented, by a profound discouragement, when they recognize the difficulty of an exploration undertaken without guide or compass.' But there *is* a guide and compass, and it is—a transcription such as that used by Barbs in teaching Persian (p. 33). If approached in the way advocated by Messrs. Derembourg and Spiro, Arabic is certainly what they call it— 'the most inaccessible of the Semitic languages.' With a transcription it is no longer inaccessible.

The method of beginning with transcriptions put the foreign on a level with the native learner. In fact, as regards most Oriental languages, the foreigner will have the advantage over the native, to whom his own written language is often a foreign language, near enough, however, to the colloquial language to cause constant cross-associations, as we see in comparing the vowel-structure of the present tenses in classical and modern Arabic. The foreigner can, if he chooses, begin his study on a transliteration of the old classical form of the language, although at present there do not seem to be any text-books on this principle for classical Arabic.

Next to a good transliteration, the greatest help in learning an alphabet is to establish definite associations between the symbol and its sound. If the required associations are not already provided, it is advisable to make artificial ones by means of 'nomic pronunciation.' If the system of writing is a mixture of disguised pictures and phonetic elements, as in Chinese, such associations are generally difficult and often impossible to establish. Such writings must be learnt mainly by eye.

But there are some general principles which apply to all systems of writing.

One of the most important of these is that we should learn to recognize the characters by eye before attempting to write them. The general fault of those who learn a new system of writing is that they are in too great a hurry to begin writing it. Nothing is more common than to hear people who have learnt a little shorthand say, 'I gave up Pitman's shorthand because even after I had learnt to write it at the rate of sixty words a minute I could not read what I had written.' The beginner should, therefore, resolutely abstain from writing until he can read with a certain fluency.

When he can do this, he may begin to write. It is, indeed, advisable to give some time to writing, even if the learner only wants to read the language, for the muscular sensations that accompany the act of writing undeniably strengthen the associations of the eye. If the characters are complicated, the learner will do well to get into the habit of writing with his forefinger—that is, imitating the movements of the pen or brush—simultaneously with his reading. He must take care to write each stroke in its proper order—writing, for instance, the top stroke last in Sanskrit. In Chinese the order of the strokes is of the greatest importance, and is an essential help in learning the running-hand.

An equally important principle is that of learning the characters, as far and as soon as possible, in connected texts, or at least in sentences and complete words. It is, of course, best to begin with texts with which one is already familiar in transcriptions. Under such circumstances there is really no harm in following Messrs. Derembourg and Spiro's advice by beginning to read before mastering the details of the alphabet. The usual method is to give the learner the complete alphabet with all its complexities, then suddenly to cease all transliteration, and give him a string of disconnected words to decipher without even translations, or anything to identify the words.

CHAPTER V

VARIETIES OF PRONUNCIATION

PHONETIC notation does not necessarily imply phonetic spelling. If we found *picture* written in Broad Romic (piktjuə), we should not admit this as a spelling of English as it actually exists: we should shrewdly suspect the speller of a burning desire to reform English spelling and English pronunciation at one blow. If our reformer were to go into the other extreme, and write (piktə), we should admit the correctness of this spelling, but only for the vulgar dialect: we should refuse to admit any spelling but (piktʃə) as a representation of the educated spoken English of the present day.

Artificial Pronunciation

This use of a phonetic notation to represent imaginary and non-existing pronunciations is especially frequent in the case of 'gradations,' such as (ðæt) demonstrative and (ðət) relative pronoun and conjunction, the tendency being to confound these two distinct words under the fuller form (ðæt). So also those who wish to make phonetic spelling a protest against the natural development of the spoken language ignore such 'weak' or unemphatic forms as (im) pronoun and (kaant), and insist on writing the 'strong' forms (him, kæn not) everywhere, regardless of distinctions of emphasis and position in the sentence. Even those who admit that the obscurer and shorter forms are under certain definite conditions of want of stress and emphasis universal in natural educated speech, maintain that the fuller forms are more 'correct' and elegant, and, at any rate, that foreigners ought to discard the weak forms, and thereby make their pronunciation more distinct, while at the same time setting a good example to the natives.

38

The answer to this is, that the first aim of foreigners who come to England is to understand the natives and make themselves understood by them. If the foreigner has never seen such a form as (kaant) written, he will not be able to understand it when he hears it spoken; while, on the other hand, even if he does not make himself unintelligible by saying (kæn not) under circumstances where every one else says (kaant), it is in the end the simplest and best course to content himself with speaking as well as the average educated Englishman. In some German schools great care is taken to teach the pupils the correct English sounds by phonetic methods—and with remarkable success; but when, as is too often the case, the weak forms, such as (ðət, ðə = ðɛə, ʃəl), are ignored, and such words as *holiday*, *Oxford* are made to rhyme with *day* and *ford* instead of being pronounced (holidi, oksfəd), the result is that the pupils speak a language which, though made up of English sounds, is as a whole quite un-English, so that when they come to England, they have to unlearn their pronunciation, and make the—generally unsuccessful—attempt to construct a new one on the basis of the laws of gradation. It is a pity their teachers do not realize that even so slight a change as that of (hau d ju duw) into (hau du ju duw) makes the sentence un-English, however perfect the individual sounds may be.

There is more excuse for teaching an artificial pronunciation of such languages as German and Italian, where the multiplicity of educated dialects resulting from want of centralization has made it difficult to settle which is the standard, or how a standard is to be formed. Nevertheless, the foreigners who adopt the so-called 'theatre-German' (*bühnendeutsch*) pronunciation would certainly make themselves ridiculous, as this well-meant attempt to set up a standard of pronunciation is not founded on any rational linguistic principles. Nothing, for instance, can be more monstrous than the recommendation to pronounce final *g* as a voice stop.

In all languages the pronunciation of the stage is merely a special development of the ordinary educated colloquial pronunciation. In such languages as French and English, where all educated people speak practically the same dialect, there need be but little separation between the colloquial and the oratorical pronunciation; and with us, at least, the stage has no authority in questions of pronunciation.

But in French and most other languages there is still a

tendency—which may be observed in English also—to make the pronunciation not only of oratory but of mere reading aloud distinct from that of everyday life, as is shown very clearly in the *liaisons*. Thus, in reading aloud, a Frenchman would sound the (t) of the ending *-ment* before a vowel, but never in speaking.

Here the principle of association comes in. To a Frenchman the ending *-ment* suggests primarily the pronunciation (-mã) before a vowel as well as a consonant; but when he speaks or reads to an audience, he makes an effort to sound the (t) before a vowel; just as an Englishman in speaking slowly and solemnly may make (kaant) into (kæn not), although in English there is no necessity felt for departing from the colloquial pronunciation. It is evident that the first and most immediate associations of the foreign learner ought to be with the colloquial forms. When he has learnt these, he will be on a level with the educated native, and, like him, can afterwards learn the more artificial pronunciation, and thus establish a series of secondary oratorical associations. If his associations are primarily with the oratorical forms, his ordinary conversation will be unnatural and offensive to the native ear.

Degrees of Colloquialism

But there are degrees of colloquialism. In all languages the pronunciation may vary according to the degree of familiarity between the speakers. Even in England a young man will sometimes unconsciously modify his pronunciation in speaking to a strange lady or an older man.

The mood of the speaker, too, may have an effect. Tension of mind—as in giving definite directions, explaining a difficulty, impatient command — is naturally accompanied by greater vigour of enunciation; while indifference and languor show themselves in half-finished consonants and curtailed sound-groups. We can hear in English the sharp snap of *what!* degenerate in the mouth of the same speaker into the languid (woh) or almost (waa), which may further degenerate into a mere grunt.

Again, the pronunciation of the same person may vary according to the speed of utterance. This is very marked in French, where the elimination of the weak (ə) depends greatly on speed. In Passy's *Elementarbuch* the texts are given in the pronunciation of medium speed, a quicker and a slower pronunciation being occasionally given in the notes. Thus to the normal (õ vjẽ d sɔne msjɸ) and (i j ãn a də tut le kulœœr) correspond the slow (õ vjẽ də sɔne məsjɸ) and the quick (j ãn a d tut le kulœœr), and to the medium (ɛstrɔrdinɛɛr) (si vu plɛ), the slow (ɛkstraɔrdinɛɛr) and the quick (sj u plɛ).

It is evident that the foreigner should aim at what may be called a medium colloquial style of pronunciation. It is painful and incongruous to hear the rapid pronunciation of clipped speech reproduced in a slow, solemn, oratorical tempo. On the other hand, it is much more irrational to teach a foreigner pronunciations which never occur in the colloquial speech of natives. The best general advice is therefore : never be oratorical ; be colloquial, but not too colloquial.

The revolt against artificial standards of pronunciation sometimes tempts phonetic enthusiasts into constructing colloquial monstrosities when dealing with a foreign language—they become more colloquial than the most slovenly native. Thus a foreigner who has learnt to obscure weak-stressed vowels in English—who has learnt to say (kæriktə, maagit, izri-əl) in spite of the associations of the written forms *character, Margate, Israel*—is apt to get reckless, and go too far in this direction, making perhaps (nɔ'wijdʒən næpsæk) into (nəwijdʒən næpsək), pronunciations which I remember having seen actually given.

Vulgarisms should be avoided ; not because they are in themselves ugly or less logical, or in any way more objectionable than the corresponding polite forms, but simply because they belong to a different dialect. But we must distinguish between real and theoretical vulgarisms : that is, between forms which, as a matter of fact, do not occur in educated speech, and those which are commonly called ' vulgar,' and yet do occur in educated speech. Of theoretical vulgarisms, some are simply universal in educated speech, such as the loss of the consonant (r) in *lord* by which this word becomes identical in pronunciation with *laud*, others widely spread, such as the (r) in *idea(r) of, India(r) Office*. But as this latter colloquialism is not universal, the insertion of the (r) generally occurring only in rapid speech and in closely connected groups of words, so that its omission does not produce any effect of unreality or artificiality, it would be mere perversity in the foreigner to imitate it in his slow pronunciation. But while it is a real vulgarism to omit (h) in full-stressed words, it is a disagreeable affectation not to drop it in such collocations as *tell him*. This affectation is widely spread; but it is always artificial; so that the speakers who try to keep it up consistently are always liable to fail. For these reasons a foreigner should avoid it: that is, he should say (tel -im), keeping the (h) for the emphatic (tel him not həə).

The statements of unphonetic natives about vulgarisms and other varieties of pronunciation are never reliable, and should be listened to with great caution. A foreigner once asked a learned Englishman which was right, (aast) or (aaskt), as the preterite of *ask;* and was told that there was no such pronunciation as (aast). A minute after the learned man was heard to say (sou ij aast im ən aast im ən aast im əgen). On another occasion a well-known authority on the English language began in a mixed company to denounce the vulgarisms in my *Elementarbuch des gesprochenen Englisch*. A German pupil of mine who was present sent a whisper round the circle, telling them to listen carefully for these very vulgarisms in the authority's own pronunciation. The latter then began a lengthy harangue; and, to his surprise, was continually interrupted by bursts of laughter from his audience.

Standards of Pronunciation

As the educated pronunciation of a language is never absolutely uniform, the question arises, which is the standard? To the foreigner this is not a sentimental or æsthetic question, but a purely practical one.

As the literary languages of most countries are simply the fossilized dialects of their respective capitals—literary French being nothing but the written form of the older Parisian dialect, literary English of the older London dialect—there seems every reason why the dialect of the capital should be taken as the standard of the spoken language as well. Practical considerations point to the same view. First, there is the numerical preponderance of the speakers of the dialect of the capital. Secondly, foreigners naturally gravitate to the capital, or, at any rate, make it their starting-point. Even in Germany, where there is much less centralization than in France and England, it is surely more practical for the foreigner to learn the educated speech of Berlin than that of some provincial town where on abstract grounds 'the best German' is said to be spoken.

Even within the narrowest limits there may be differences of pronunciation. Even in educated Southern English we sometimes find a word pronounced in several ways. When Dr. Johnson was asked by a lady whether he pronounced the word *neither* as (naiðər) or (niiðər), he replied (neeðər, mædæm). The last pronunciation is now extinct, but the other two still seem to be about equally frequent. The fluctuations of French pronunciation are even greater. In such cases the learner must select one pronunciation and keep to it. It follows, of course, that his text-books should, as far as possible, give a uniform pronunciation, no matter how arbitrary the selection may be.

Pronunciation of Rare Words

For rare words which the learner meets for the first time in nomic texts, he will require a pronouncing dictionary. Such a dictionary may be shortened and made more convenient by the omission of all the commoner words which the learner who has read a few phonetic texts cannot help knowing thoroughly.

The learner should not be too scrupulous about the pronunciation of rare foreign words in the language he is studying, such as barbarous geographical names, which may fill the newspapers for a few weeks, and then be quite forgotten. When a foreigner wants to know exactly how such a name as *Ujiji* ought to be pronounced, he should be told to guess at it by analogy, taking care not to anglicize it—in fact, to do what an English reader would do with an unfamiliar word he had never heard spoken, but only seen in print. When a foreigner reflects that such a word as *Zulu* is not pronounced (zjuwljuw) but (zuwluw), he must see that it would be contrary to analogy to give the first *i* in *Ujiji* the English value (ai); it must be either (ij) or (i)—it does not matter which. Such a word cannot have a fixed traditional pronunciation.

In introducing words from our own language into the foreign language we are speaking, we must be careful about trying to adapt its pronunciation to that of the foreign language; where there is doubt, it is safest to keep the native pronunciation unchanged. I remember having constantly to correct a Norwegian who pronounced the name of the Norwegian town *Bergen* as (bəədʒən). I told him that if he must anglicize it, let him call it (bɛəgən), which would be the average educated

Englishman's imitation of the native pronunciation. So also, when an Englishman uses such a German name as *Beethoven* in speaking French, it is much safer to keep the German pronunciation than to try and make up a French pronunciation with a final nasal vowel.

If, on the other hand, a native name has two pronunciations, one of which agrees with the spelling, the latter is generally sure to be the most modern one, and should therefore be adopted by a foreigner, who, for instance, will find himself on the side of the increasing majority if he pronounces such names as *Cirencester* and *Abergavenny* as they are written. If he does the same with *Coke*, *Home*, *Cowper*, instead of calling them (kuk, hjuwm, kuwpə), he will at least have many mispronouncers on his side.

CHAPTER VI

PHONETICS, like all other branches of knowledge, has its own special difficulties. But much of it is perfectly easy, if approached with an unprejudiced mind. It is a subject in which a little knowledge goes a long way.

In dealing with a single language there is no absolute necessity for the pupils' going through a complete course of phonetics: the teacher can give them what they want from time to time.

Nevertheless, there can be no doubt that the best results are obtained on the basis of a previous course of general phonetics, which, again, must be based on a practical analysis of the learner's own sounds. Divergencies of pronunciation and many other considerations make it impossible to tell beforehand whether or not a knowledge of a given sound will be a help in acquiring the pronunciation of a given language.

There is every reason why the study of phonetics should begin at an early age. It requires no precocity of mental development, and there is nothing abstract about it: on the contrary, it appeals mainly to the love of the concrete and the experimental, and the tendency to imitation which are characteristic of the undeveloped intellect. It trains the young mind to habits of observation. It gives a command of the organs of speech which has a most beneficial effect on the learner's pronunciation of his own language.

Apparatus : Diagrams, Models, Phonograph

The methods of teaching phonetics already indicated may be supplemented in various ways.

One is the use of diagrams of the organs of speech and their

45

positions in forming the sounds. Vietor's *Elemente der Phonetik* will be found useful in this respect. The best diagrams of the vowel-positions will be found in Grandgent's *German and English Sounds.*

Models of the organs of speech would be useful, if it were possible to obtain satisfactory ones. Those recommended by Vietor are not very good; the best of them seems to be the enlarged model of the larynx and glottis.

We hear a good deal nowadays about the phonograph and the help it is in studying languages. But it must be borne in mind that whenever we have access to native speakers, the phonograph is superfluous, for, at the best, it cannot speak better than a native. And where we have to rely entirely on the phonographic record, its testimony is sometimes defective on points where information is most needed: it fails to reproduce shades of breath-sounds and the less sonorous elements of speech. It succeeds best with sounds of full vocality, and in giving the general effect produced by the organic basis, and by stress and intonation. Its chief use will probably be in reviving recollections of pieces heard direct from native speakers.

The idea that the phonograph can be used in schools as a substitute for a trained phonetician shows a misconception of the problem of teaching phonetics.

Experimental Phonetics

Of late years we have heard still more about experimental phonetics, that is, the exact determination and measurement of the organic positions and actions by means of special apparatus. But as yet the performance of experimental phonetics has fallen far short of its promise. What ought to be its most important problem—the exact determination of the vowel-positions—is still beyond its reach, except by the laborious and sometimes uncertain method introduced by Grandgent, the results of which are described in his above-mentioned book. But his apparatus has the merit of extreme simplicity. All attempts, too, to determine by purely objective experimental methods the pitch of spoken vowels and to record the intonations of natural speech have hitherto been failures.

In fact, wherever we really want information it leaves us more or less in the lurch. Most of its results are simply confirmations of what we know already. The really great results have been obtained without any apparatus. We do not require apparatus to round and unround vowels systematically and exhaustively, and it is by such simple methods that Bell's vowel-scheme was constructed.

One awkward fact about experimental phonetics is that most of those who work at it have no adequate practical knowledge of phonetics: they are unable to lengthen a vowel without modifying it; some of them persist in regarding their own imperfect pronunciation of foreign languages as perfect, and cannot write the simplest phonetic notation.

The apparatus of the experimental phonetician is often expensive and inaccessible, delicate and complicated, so that it requires an expert to manipulate it with any chance of success.

It also requires some practice to speak into the funnel of a phonograph or one of the above-mentioned apparatus, without either becoming inaudible on the one hand or unnatural on the other.

That experimental methods may lead to very unsatisfactory results is shown by Czermak's analysis of the Arabic gutturals, which is an analysis not of actual sounds, but of his own, apparently very defective imitations of them.[1]

We cannot wonder, then, that there is a certain antagonism between the unphonetic physiologists and physicists who work at experimental phonetics and the practical phoneticians.

At the same time, it cannot be denied that simple apparatus with which we could measure exactly instead of going by subjective impressions would be a great boon to all phoneticians. Experimental phoneticians may rest assured that as soon as they succeed in providing such apparatus, it will be warmly welcomed by all classes of phoneticians. At present it would be a great mistake in the beginner to neglect acquiring a thorough practical command of his organs of speech and of sounds in general for the sake of working at experimental phonetics.

Phonetic Dictation

Phonetic dictation[2] is very stimulating to the pupils, and serves as a useful test of their acoustic powers, while at the same time it obliges them to free themselves from any trammeling associations with the nomic spelling, and thus developes

[1] See my paper (ði ærəbik þroutsaundz) in MF 1895. 4.
[2] See J. Passy's paper (la dikte fɔnetik) in MF 1894, pp. 34, 50.

the dormant faculty of phonetic observation. At first the dictation should be in the pupil's native language, and he should be expected only to write down the significant distinctions of sounds in some easy Romic notation without any attempt to mark stress or intonation. It is surprising to see what mistakes are made, partly through confusion with the nomic spelling, partly through complete absence of the faculty of observing even the broadest distinctions when unaided by visual associations. When the pupils can write with fluency and correctness on this basis, they should be trained to add stress-marks, and then simple tone-marks. Then the same stages should be repeated in the foreign language. Advanced pupils in general phonetics may be cautiously exercised in writing down nonsense-words consisting at first of a certain limited number of sounds. Thus the teacher may tell them that all the vowels will be narrow, that there will be no mixed vowels, no front consonants, and so on. For this advanced dictation the organic alphabet should be used.

Advantages of Phonetics

The first and most evident advantage of phonetics is the independence it gives us. In the first place, it makes us independent of residence abroad. Even if the learner intends to go to the country where the language is spoken, it is a great advantage to him to start with a thorough practical knowledge of the sounds in which he is to practise himself.

Secondly, phonetics makes us independent of native teachers. It is certain that a phonetically trained Englishman who has a clear knowledge of the relations between French and English sounds can teach French sounds to English people better than an unphonetic Frenchman who is unable to communicate his pronunciation to his pupils, and perhaps speaks a dialectal or vulgar form of French.

Again, phonetics enables an intelligent adult to get a sound elementary knowledge of the sounds of a foreign language without any help from outside—that is, if he has an adequate phonetic analysis and transcription to work with.

But the gain of a phonetic grasp of a language extends far beyond such special considerations. A secure grasp of the sounds of a language is a great strengthening of the mastery of its forms and meanings.   A minute discrimination of similar sounds in closely allied languages is the surest safeguard against otherwise inevitable confusions, as when we keep up the slight distinction between the Norwegian and the Swedish (ü) in *hus*, 'house,' the Swedish sound being more advanced and nearer (y).

Hence also the literary and æsthetic use of phonetics. Phonetics alone can breathe life into the dead mass of letters which constitutes a written language; it alone can bring the rustic dialogues of our novels before every intelligent reader as living realities, and make us realize the living power and beauty of the ancient classical languages in prose and verse.

Phonetics is not merely an indirect strengthener of grammatical associations, it is an essential part of grammar itself.   It enables us to state grammatical and philological laws with a brevity and definiteness which would be otherwise unattainable, as when we condense the information that under certain circumstances in a given language *d* becomes *t*, *g* becomes *k*, and *b* becomes *p*, into the simple statement that 'voice stops become breath.'   In Eliot's *Finnish Grammar* (p. 11) we find the following statement : 'The final *e* of a dissyllabic stem disappears in nouns before terminations commencing with *t*, and in verbs before terminations beginning with *k* or *n*, provided that *e* is preceded by any simple consonant but *k*, *p*, *v*, *m*, or by a double consonant of which the last letter is *t* or *s* (except *ht*). Thus from the stem *une*, 'sleep,' *vuore*, 'mountain,' *vete*, 'water' (nominative *vesi*), come the forms *unta*, *vuorta*, *vettä* . . .'   If in this statement we substitute for the negative and purely abstract conception of 'any simple consonant but *k*, *p*, *v*, *m*,' the positive enumeration of the consonants left after this subtraction, namely *r*, *l*, *s*, *t*, *n*, we are able to simplify it still further by saying that in nouns *e* is dropped before *t* when the *e* is preceded by a forward consonant, the evident reason being that these consonants are formed in the same place as *t*.

A knowledge of sentence stress and intonation is not only an essential part of elocution and correct pronunciation, but is also an integral part of the syntax of many languages.[1]

In short, there is no branch of the study of language which can afford to dispense with phonetics.

[1] See my *New English Grammar*, Part II.

E

CHAPTER VII

BEGIN WITH THE SPOKEN LANGUAGE

THE second main axiom of living philology is that all study of language, whether theoretical or practical, ought to be based on the spoken language.

The distinction between the literary and the colloquial form of the same language has considerably complicated the problem of learning languages. This distinction is not solely the result of the use of writing and printing, for even such unlettered savages as the Andaman islanders have an archaic poetical dialect which differs considerably from their ordinary spoken language; but writing—and, still more, printing—have naturally increased the divergence. In many Oriental languages the divergence is so great that the colloquial is no longer a mere variation of the literary form, but the two practically constitute distinct, mutually unintelligible languages.

The Spoken the Source of the Written Language

In European languages, where the difference is much less, most grammarians tacitly assume that the spoken is a mere corruption of the literary language. But the exact contrary is the case: it is the spoken which is the real source of the literary language. We may pick out the most far-fetched literary words and forms we can think of, but we shall always find that they are derived from the colloquial speech of an earlier period. Even such forms as *thou hast, he hath*, were ordinary colloquialisms a few centuries ago, though they now survive only as fossil, dead colloquialisms side by side with the living colloquialisms *you have, he has*. Every literary language is, in fact, a mixture of colloquialisms of different periods.

Every literary language must indeed in its first beginnings be purely colloquial. It is certainly difficult to realize that such a language as the classical Italian of Dante and Petrarch was originally nothing but a rough attempt to write down what were then considered the slovenly colloquialisms of Late

50

Latin; but nevertheless such is the origin not only of Italian, but of all the other Romance languages as well. The tradition of the origin of Italian is still kept up in the word for 'translate,' namely *volgarizzare*, literally 'make popular.'

Accordingly, it is now an axiom not only of Romance philology, but of philology generally, that the real life of language is better seen in dialects and colloquial forms of speech than in highly developed literary languages, such as Greek, Latin, and Sanskrit.

Practical Considerations

Important as this principle is from a scientific point of view, it is still more so from a practical one, and for the following reasons :—

If we compare the written and spoken language of a given period, we shall find that the literary language is full of superfluous words and phrases, which the spoken language nearly always gets rid of. Thus in the English spoken language the idea 'sky' is expressed by this word only, while in the literary language it may also be expressed by *heaven, heavens, firmament, welkin*. So also the form *hath* was still used in literary prose in the last century in such phrases as *the author hath ...* , and it is still used in poetry and in the liturgical language of the Bible and Prayer-book, while in the spoken language the only form used is *has*. Again, nothing is more difficult than to give definite grammatical rules for the use of the subjunctive mood in literary English; in the spoken language the subjunctive is not used at all except in a few perfectly definite constructions, such as *if it were*. So also in spoken French the two most difficult tenses of the verb, the preterite indicative and subjunctive, have been supplanted by the perfect. So completely is the preterite obsolete that Passy, in his translation of the Gospel of Luke into modern French, discards it entirely, as in the beginning of the parable of the vineyard : ŏen ɔm a plããte yn viñ, i l a lwe a de viñrŏ, e il e parti pur lŏŏtã (20. 9). According to Passy (Elementarbuch, 156), it occurs only in comic imitations of the South French dialect. Even in German the complicated rules for the inflection of proper names—*Luise*, gen. *Luise'ns, Cato, Cato's,* plur. *Cato'ne, Leibnitz,* plur. *Leibnitz'e*—are swept away bodily in the spoken language, which, as a general rule, does not inflect such words at all.

Again, in literature the context is often vague, as in the Homeric *méropes ánthrōpoi*, where *méropes* may mean any quality that can be predicated of men generally. So also in the Sanskrit Vēdas we have whole hymns, which, when epitomized, leave not much more than 'the bright shiner (that is, the sun) shines brightly.' In simple colloquial prose, on the other hand, the meaning of a word is generally quite clear from the context. The spoken language, too, is far stricter in its use of epithets: it hardly ever introduces an adjective or other qualifier except to convey some definite information. Thus in ordinary speech we do not talk of 'the bright sun' or 'the silver moon,' simply because the epithets convey no information —tell us nothing that is not already implied in the words *sun* and *moon* themselves. Even such a phrase as 'the sun shines brightly' has an uncolloquial ring about it, although it is not exactly anti-colloquial. We could say 'the moon is bright to-night,' because this really conveys information. The spoken language also prefers a simple paratactic arrangement of sentences. The complicated periods of literary prose would, indeed, often be unintelligible in speech.

We see, then, that the advantage as regards clearness and definiteness is on the side of the spoken language: by starting from the spoken language we have less to learn, and we learn it accurately. Everything therefore points to the conclusion that in learned foreign languages we should follow the natural order in which we learn our own language: that is, that we should begin with learning the spoken language thoroughly, and then go on to the literary language.

The psychological arguments for beginning with the spoken language are precisely analogous to those for beginning with a phonetic transcription (p. 12): if we learn the literary and the spoken language simultaneously, cross-associations are inevitable; and the only possible way of avoiding or minimizing these cross-associations is to learn the two forms of the language separately.

The question, which of the two we ought to begin with, is easily answered.

It is evident that our strongest and most direct associations ought to be with the spoken language, for in speaking we must have all our associations between ideas and words in perfect working order: we have no time to pick and choose our words and construction, as when we are writing. So also when others are speaking to us, we must understand each sentence at once, or the whole statement becomes unintelligible, while in reading, as in writing, we can pause and consider as often as we like.

If, then, we first get a thorough knowledge of the spoken form of the foreign language, and then proceed to learn its literary form, we shall be in exactly the same position as regards relative strength of associations as the natives themselves : we shall think in the spoken language, because our associations are directly with it, while at the same time we are able to understand the literary language, and, with a little effort at first, to write it; but we are no more able to *speak* the pure literary language than a native is.

As it is, we too often reverse the process, and so do foreigners who learn English. They first of all imprint firmly on their memories the obsolete phraseology of the Vicar of Wakefield, or, at the best, of Washington Irving's Sketch-book, then add a few choice Shakespearisms, and finally season this heterogeneous mixture with such modern colloquialisms as they can gather from the pages of Punch and Dickens. The result is always unsatisfactory, and often leads to unintelligibility. Thus I remember a case in which a German, on being asked how a certain lady was, replied that she was (ræpt). As he tapped his forehead at the same time, the Englishman thought he meant to say that she had had a rap or knock on the head ; but after a long discussion and many vain attempts to get at his meaning, it turned out that he was thinking of Shakespeare's phrase in Macbeth, ' how our partner's rapt ' (= transported, in an ecstasy), and meant to convey the idea that she was out of her mind. Another foreigner, a Spaniard, was observed to speak English with perfect grammatical correctness, but with a curious old-fashioned stateliness of diction, which was at first assumed to be the natural accompaniment of the blue blood of Spain; it turned out, however, that the sole source of his colloquial English had been the dialogues in Dr. Samuel Johnson's Rasselas. I remember myself that when I first began to talk German, I was complimented on the poetical diction I used. It is said that when Sir Walter Scott talked French to the ambassadors of Charles IX., they were amused and often puzzled to hear a Scotch adaptation of the language of Froissart and Joinville.

CHAPTER VIII

DIFFICULTIES OF LANGUAGE

LEARNING a language means overcoming difficulties, and each language has its own peculiar difficulties.

External Difficulties

Some of the difficulties may be purely external—due not to anything in the language itself, but to the circumstances under which it is learnt. Perhaps there is a want of text-books and other helps; the beginner is perhaps met with the cheerful warning, 'You will have to make your own dictionary, you know.' Or there may be text-books, grammars, dictionaries in plenty, but not in the learner's native language; thus no one can learn Finnish without knowing Swedish, and to many languages Russian is the only key.

The difficulties caused by the written form of the language, such as the complexity of its alphabet—which, again, may be the result of the writing being partly hieroglyphic—the ambiguity or unphonetic character of its orthography, are all purely external: Arabic is still Arabic when transcribed into Roman letters, nor is Japanese any the more Japanese for being written in a mixture of disguised hieroglyphs and syllabic alphabetic writing, both borrowed from China. No existing system of writing is anything but an external disguise borrowed from some other language: Arabic is disguised Syriac writing, and the Russian alphabet is Byzantine Greek.

Relations to the Native Language

There is another class of difficulties which may be regarded as partly external, partly internal—those which depend on the

54

212

relations of the foreign language to the learner's native language, especially as regards similarity in vocabulary and structure.

We are naturally inclined to assume that the nearer the foreign language is to our own, the easier it is. A Spaniard soon learns to understand Portuguese, and a Portuguese soon learns Spanish enough to understand it, a Dane soon learns to understand Swedish, and an Englishman soon learns to understand broad Scotch, because in all these pairs the two languages are practically only dialects of one another—in other words, because knowing Spanish or Danish or English implies knowing two-thirds of Portuguese, Danish, or Scotch respectively. Hence also we are often told that ' Italian is very easy if you know Latin and French.' Hence also Old English (Anglo-Saxon) is easier to a German than to an Englishman, so that, as I have remarked in the preface to my Anglo-Saxon Reader, ' he (the German) is able to acquire a practical knowledge of it from a crabbedly theoretical exposition of it that would baffle an English learner.'

But this very likeness is often a source of confusion. It is a help to the beginner who merely wants to understand the allied language, and is contented with a rough knowledge ; but it is a hindrance to any thorough knowledge, because of the constant cross-associations that are sure to present themselves. Thus in German *werden* is present and infinitive, *worden* is past participle ; but in Dutch *worden* is equivalent to the German *werden*, while the Dutch *werd* is the preterite, being equivalent to German *ward*. And yet the general resemblance between German and Dutch is much less than that between such a group of languages as Danish, Norwegian, and Swedish. The resemblance between these three is, indeed, so strong that it is practically impossible to keep them apart : a foreigner who has learnt to speak Danish fluently, and then goes on to learn Swedish, will soon lose the power of speaking the former language, and will not regain it till he has forgotten his Swedish. A further study of Norwegian, which is intermediate between Danish and Swedish, will cause still greater confusion.

Differences in the vocabulary are an even greater snare than differences of grammatical structure, because they cannot be brought under definite rules. Thus it is very difficult for an English speaker to realize that when a Frenchman ' demands permission,' he does not mean to imply the slightest imperativeness. It is dangerous to guess at the meanings of words in closely allied languages, or in languages between which there is any borrowing of words; thus in German *gottesdienst* means 'divine service,' but in Dutch *godsdienst* has the wider meaning 'religion.' So also in Swedish *rolig* means 'pleasant, amusing,' while in Danish and Norwegian it has only the older meaning 'quiet, tranquil,' in accordance with its derivation from *ro*, 'rest,' cognate with the German *ruhe*. Hence a Dane would be puzzled if a Swede told him that he had found the Carnival or the Lord Mayor's Show 'rolig.'

In learning a remote, unconnected language the difficulties are reversed. The beginning is much more difficult, and, of course, it takes a much longer time to understand the language. But when the initial difficulties have been once overcome, it is easier to get a minutely accurate knowledge of the language, because the learner is less disturbed by cross-associations.

Internal Difficulties

We will now consider those difficulties which are, in the strict sense of the word, internal—inherent in each language apart from external circumstances and from its varying relations to other languages.

The difficulties of language in general may be classed under the four heads of (1) logic or reasonableness, (2) definiteness, (3) fullness of expression, and (4) simplicity.

(1) As regards **logic**, most untrained minds regard everything in a foreign language that differs from their own as essentially irrational. But apart from such prejudices, there are some grammatical constructions, some methods of expression in special languages, which all foreigners—as well as unprejudiced natives of a philosophic mind—would agree in considering irrational. Such a construction is that by which in classical Arabic the numerals from three to ten are put in the feminine before masculine nouns, and in the masculine before feminine nouns, as in þalāþatu banīna, 'three sons,' arba‘u banātin, 'four daughters.' The contradiction here is purely formal.

We have an example of an equally striking logical contradiction in the French *plus de soupe!* 'no more soup!' an expression which every Englishman would naturally and instinctively use instead of the correct *encore de la soupe!* Such constructions are absolute paradoxes. As an example of an ordinary irrational construction we may quote the English use of *up* in *pack up*, *lock up*, *wrap up*, which is opposed both to common sense and to the usage of most other languages, in which the literal translation of 'pack up' would mean the exact opposite—'unpack.'

Of antigrammatical constructions—those constructions which cannot be parsed in accordance with the general grammatical rules of the language in question—some are logical and rational in themselves, such as the construction of a singular collective noun with a plural verb or a word implying plurality (*the committee are of opinion that* . . . *many cattle*), while others are irrational, such as that almost incredible German construction in *ich habe kommen müssen*, 'I have had to come,' where the infinitive *müssen* is used as if it were a preterite participle.

Over-abstraction sometimes leads to difficulties which defy direct logical analysis, such as the curious use of the verb 'to be' in the passive, which is common in the Celtic languages, as in the Old Irish *cëin both oc aurgnom dōib*, 'while they were being served (waited upon),' literally ' while it-was-being-been with-serving to-them,' as if we were to say in Latin *dum eratur ministrando eis*.

The use of the preterite in English and other Arian languages to imply rejected condition in such sentences as *if I knew*, implying ' I do not know,' is not wholly irrational, but certainly shows a certain intellectual clumsiness, as compared with the sensible Arabic use of two words for 'if,' one of which (*lau*) always implies rejection of the condition, so that there is no occasion to throw the distinction on the verb.

Some difficulties are what may be called 'negatively illogical.' Thus to a foreigner the distinctions of gender in German and Old English by which hands are feminine and fingers masculine, while feet are masculine and toes feminine, appears to 'have no sense in it.' I remember a young Welshman correcting me, when I called the pair of bellows *y megin* instead of *y fegin*, by saying, 'We call a pair of bellows a she, sir;' he was then evidently struck by the absurdity of it, for he added after a pause of reflection, 'I don't know why we do so.' The difficulties connected with grammatical gender are purely mechanical difficulties, which cannot be overcome or evaded by any exertion of the reasoning faculties.

Another—and perhaps the greatest—source of difficulty is

that the same fact may be regarded from a variety of different points of view, all of which are perhaps equally logical and reasonable. Thus in such a sentence as ' she held her hands before her face,' we should expect those languages which use the accusative case to express motion and the dative to imply rest to put *face* in the dative, as the hands are supposed to be at rest; but in German the accusative would be used in such a construction, showing that the speakers who first framed this construction were thinking of the movement which brought the hands before the face rather than of the resulting position of rest. This difference of point of view is one of the chief sources of difficulty in idioms. Thus in French the idea of ' back numbers' of a periodical is expressed by (kɔlɛksjõ dy ʒurnal), where the element of ' backness' is entirely ignored, the whole idea being approached from a totally different point of view. Sometimes the difference of point of view is the result of different circumstances or way of life, as when a German translates ' he followed me all over the house' by ' he ran after me through all the rooms,' because Germans generally live in flats, and seldom occupy a whole house.

(2) As regards **definiteness,** one language may make more minute distinctions than another. Hence to an ordinary Englishman who contents himself with roughly designating objects in space as ' this' or ' that,' or as being ' here' or ' there,' the threefold distinction involved in the Scotch *this, that, yon,* or *here, there, yonder,* the Latin *hic, iste, ille,* or the Welsh *yma, yna, acw,* occasions great difficulties—especially some of the special idiomatic uses of the Welsh *acw*—although he cannot help admitting that the threefold division is in some respects logically superior to his one twofold one.

Want of definiteness, on the other hand, may cause just as much difficulty. How often in speaking a foreign language do we hesitate, vainly trying to find a word or phrase which corresponds definitely and exactly to the idea in our mind, till at last we have to fall back on a periphrase ! Those who have lived long abroad sometimes hesitate even in speaking their own language, because they feel tempted to use some foreign word, such as the German *gemüthlich* or the French *flâner.* Nouns, such as the German *philister* and the French *flâneur,* are, indeed, so easily incorporated into the native speech that they soon become actual denizens, unless some translation or adaptation takes their place, as when *philister* is adopted in the form of *Philistine*.

This want of definiteness may sometimes amount to positive ambiguity, as in the English use of *will* and *shall* to express wish and compulsion on the one hand and futurity on the other, an ambiguity which is completely avoided in German by the use of *werden* to express pure futurity only. This makes an Englishman hesitate sometimes to use *wollen* or *sollen* in German where he ought to do so ; he does not feel the slight shade of wish or compulsion implied by the substitution of these auxiliaries for *werden*, and is therefore afraid of introducing an anglicism.

A frequent source of indefiniteness and ambiguity is reliance on the context. In all languages a word may have a great variety of meanings distinguishable solely by the context, as when in English we apply the adjective *sharp* to knives, distinctions, answers, and tempers. But the function of grammatical forms is also largely dependent on the context, as we see in the English inflectional *-s* in *sheep's, trees, he knows*. In Chinese this reliance on the context is carried to extreme lengths : thus *sam yuet*, literally 'three month,' may mean either 'three months' or 'the third month,' and *laú laú*, literally 'old old,' means 'to treat old people as they ought to be treated (that is, with respect),' the first *laú* being converted into a transitive verb 'to old.'

(3) **Fullness** of expression may go to the extremes of redundance on the one hand, as in *the reason why, my future address will be . . .* , and ellipse on the other, as in *at his brother's (house)*.

It is not these clearly marked cases, but the less defined ones, which cause real difficulty. Thus many of the Greek particles seem redundant and superfluous when compared with those of most other languages. So also do many of those used in classical Chinese, especially the finals, which practically in many cases seem to a foreigner to be little more than marks of punctuation, serving to show that the sentence is completed.

But Old Chinese in most cases is almost incredibly concise and elliptical. Thus it has no word for the pronoun of the third person in the nominative—that is, it has no word for *he, she, it, they*, the absence of a pronoun being supposed to imply the third person; but not content with this, they omit the pronoun freely in the other persons as well, whenever the context seems to allow it, so that, for instance, *yuet* may mean not only 'he says, she said, they will say, one may say,' and so on, but also 'I say, we have said,' etc.

(4) **Simplicity** of expression implies in the first place regularity. As every one knows, irregular inflections are one of the most formidable difficulties in the study of inflectional languages.

Simplicity also leads to generalization and abstraction, which, when unfamiliar, may require an effort to grasp, as in the many idiomatic uses of the Chinese indefinite pronoun *cĕ*, which has the function of making the preceding word or word-group into a noun of general meaning, so that, for instance, *govern cĕ* means 'the abstract conception of government,' *able mend fault cĕ* means 'one who is able to reform his faults,' *grass firewood cĕ* means 'cutters of grass and gatherers of firewood.'

The opposite extreme of want of abstraction which leads to over specialization is a more frequent source of difficulty. It is most clearly seen in those savage languages, which often have no word even for so concrete an idea as that of 'washing,' but only separate words for 'wash the hands,' 'wash the feet,' 'wash dishes,' and so on. In the language of Tierra del Fuego no verb implying place can stand alone—the point of the compass must be indicated: they cannot say 'he stood' by itself, but only 'he stood in the north, in the south . . . ,' these local determinations being used also in a variety of metaphorical uses, 'in the north,' for instance, implying 'away from the fire.'

But want of abstraction is by no means confined to savage languages. Even in English we have no word to express the 'running' of a horse: we must define the pace as trotting, galloping, etc. German has no general word for 'handle.' In Swedish there is no general word for 'aunt' or 'uncle,' these ideas being expressed by contractions such as *father-sister, mother-sister* (*faster, moster*), so that it is always necessary to state expressly whether the maternal or paternal aunt or uncle is meant, just as in the older languages.

One of the greatest sources of difficulty is that caused by superfluous distinctions—that is to say, distinctions which are invariably and unmistakably shown by the context, such as the Swedish and Norwegian distinction between *ja* and *jo* in the sense of 'yes,' the former being used after a positive, the latter after a negative question. Equally superfluous is the German distinction between *herauf* and *hinauf*, 'up towards the speaker,' 'up away from the speaker.' In such cases the fact that the distinction is always implied unambiguously by the context makes the foreigner inclined to ignore it; unless, indeed, he carries it too far, saying, for instance, *gerade hinaus* instead of *gerade aus* in the sense of 'straight on.' The use of the subjunctive mood in indirect narration is almost equally superfluous; it is instructive to observe that modern French, which is otherwise strict enough in its use of the subjunctive, has in this case substituted the indicative, a change which also took place very early in the transition from Old to Middle English.

Some minute distinctions may be justified logically on the ground that they do sometimes express shades of meaning which are more or less independent of the context, and may yet be, on the whole, practically superfluous. This is the case with the difficult Welsh distinction of four verbs 'to be'—*sydd, mae, yw, oes*—whose use depends on subtle distinctions of definiteness and indefiniteness, emphasizing the predicate and so on. As these verbs are incessantly employed in the numerous substitutes for 'yes' and 'no,' it is impossible in Welsh to express simple affirmation or negation without a thorough knowledge of the syntax.

Another equally fruitful source of difficulty is unnecessary complexity. This is frequent in numerical expressions, such as *threescore and ten* for *seventy*, French *quatre-vingt-onze*, 'four-twenty-eleven' = 'ninety-one,' Danish *halvtredsindstyve*, 'half three times twenty,' that is 'threescore minus half a score' = 50, with which compare German *halb zwei*, 'half two' = 'one and a half.' Very curious also are Finnish numerals, such as *kaksikymmentä*, 'two tens' = 20, *yksikolmatta*, 'one of (the) third (set of tens)' = 21. Even the English numerals are complex as compared with the Chinese ones, such as *ʃip riˆ*, 'ten two' = 12, *ŋuˊ ʃip yit*, 'five ten one' = 51. The difficulty of the English vocabulary is the result of the complexity of its root-system, as shown in such groups as *sun, sol-ar, helio-centrical*, and *sour, acid, oxy-gen*. In German or Greek two roots would suffice for these six words.

Phonetic Difficulties

As regards phonetic difficulties—difficulties of pronunciation—there are three main considerations. The first is, that the difficulty of a sound depends more than anything on whether it is familiar or unfamiliar, which is not an intrinsic, but a relative or, we may almost say, an external difficulty. To the unphonetic learner all unfamiliar sounds are difficult, or even impossible—at least, he thinks so. This applies also to unfamiliar combinations of familiar sounds. Thus even initial (ts) may be difficult to English speakers, as well as such combinations as (ʃtʃ) in Russian, because, although (ts) is a familiar combination, it is unfamiliar when initial.

Hence a language may have a very simple and normal sound-system, and yet be difficult to pronounce, as we see in the case of Finnish, where it is necessary to make a strict distinction between long and short vowels, double (or long) and single consonants in unstressed as well as stressed syllables, the stressed syllable—which is always the first in the word—having a very strong stress, the others a very weak one, besides being uttered with great rapidity, so that the only way to keep up the necessary distinctions of quantity is by making the short sounds excessively short; hence such a word as *opettamattomuudessansa*, 'in his want of instruction (in his ignorance),' requires much practice.

As the number of distinctive sounds of natural occurrence is rather limited, there is always an *à priori* probability of meeting at least some familiar sound in every new language. Hence there is, on the whole, a tendency to a balance of difficulties in foreign languages. Thus the English speaker meets his soft and hard *th* and his *w* hardly anywhere till he comes to Arabic, where, however, the first two are lost in most of the modern dialects. The Dane, again, finds his 'stödtone' again in the Arabic hamza, and something, at least, of the sound of his *r* in the Arabic *'ēn*, for I certainly hear the same kind of throat-contraction in both sounds (I mean the Copenhagen *r*), although the Danish phoneticians do not agree with me in this.

The second consideration is, that no sound that actually exists in a language for any length of time can be intrinsically difficult; for sounds are so easily and so imperceptibly modified in their transmission from generation to generation that their retention, unchanged for only a few generations, is enough to prove that they cannot be difficult in themselves. Thus, if the two Arabic throat-sounds, the *ḥā* and the *'ēn*, were as difficult in themselves as most foreigners imagine them to be, they would not have been preserved, as they have been, unchanged in Arabic for at least ten thousand years. Nor do Arab-speaking children find them so difficult to learn as some of the other consonants, such as the deep *k̯*.

Lastly, practical training in general phonetics gets rid of many difficulties at once, and tends to make a complete mastery of the pronunciation of a foreign language simply a matter of practice and perseverance, ample time for which is afforded by the difficulties of mastering the grammar and vocabulary of the language. As our knowledge of phonetics and our methods of teaching it are gradually perfected, the easier it will be to clear away the remaining difficulties, especially if the practical study of phonetics is begun young enough—that is to say, in the nursery.

General Difficulty of each Language

In estimating the general difficulty of one language as compared with others, it is necessary once more to insist on the elimination of all external and irrelevant considerations, such as those caused by a defective or complicated system of writing, by want of grammars and dictionaries, by want of suitable texts. Latin is difficult partly because most of its literature is rhetorical and artificial—hardly ever naïve and simple. Browning and Hegel are difficult and obscure writers, but that has nothing to do with the question whether English and German are in themselves difficult. Old Slavonic, on the contrary, is comparatively easy partly because most of its literature consists of translations of ecclesiastical writings. Gothic is easy because the whole language—texts, grammar, glossary, and all—can be comprised in one volume, and this in addition to the texts being mostly Biblical translations.

Most people, if asked what constitutes the real difficulty of such a language as Greek or Sanskrit, would answer without hesitation, 'the complexity of its inflections.' Most schoolboys have wondered how the Greeks ever could have learned to conjugate the verbs in -*mi*. These people assume that all inflectional languages are necessarily difficult, and that the only real progress in language as regards ease of learning is getting rid of inflections. They are inclined to assume that a language such as Sanskrit or Russian, with its eight cases, must be more difficult than one which has only four, such as German, and that Finnish, with its fifteen cases, must be nearly twice as difficult as Sanskrit—at least, from the point of view of noun-inflection.

But when we look a little closer into the question, we see that there are generally compensations for an increased number of inflections. We find that, as a general rule, the greater the number of cases, the more regular they are, and, what is equally important, the more distinctive in form, and therefore the easier to remember. Thus in Finnish all ablatives end in -*lta*—which under certain definite and simple phonetic conditions is regularly modified to -*ltä*—all 'translatives' end in -*ksi* without any distinctions of gender, the endings being the same in the plural as in the singular; the only difficulty in Finnish are the changes undergone by the stem, which, though often considerable, are not so difficult as in more advanced inflectional languages. In Sanskrit there is much more irregularity than in Finnish, but many of the endings—such as -*bhyas*—are so full-sounding and heavy that they are as easy to remember as if they were independent words. German, on the other hand, has only four cases, which are expressed by a very limited number of endings : -*e*, -*en*, -*em*, -*es*, -*er*. But this formal simplicity is in itself a source of difficulty, for most of these endings have such a multiplicity of grammatical functions that they lose all individuality and become mere abstractions, which are absolutely meaningless apart from their context. It is a question whether the modern German inflections are not as difficult as the Finnish. The German dialects seem to think the noun-inflections difficult, for most of them get rid of them more or less completely.

Again, the Finnish inflections enable the language to dispense with prepositions to a great extent. Thus 'without money' is expressed by putting money in the 'caritative' case, or, in other words, making *without money* into *money-without*, so that having fifteen cases, which sounds so formidable at first, means, from this point of view, having only fifteen prepositions in common use. The result often is that a grammatical category which in English can be expressed only by a variety of prepositions of complicated meanings and functions is in Finnish expressed by a single case which is often as distinct and tangible as an independent word.

We thus arrive at the conclusion not only that a larger number of inflections does not necessarily increase the difficulty of a language, but also that inflections may in some respects be easier to learn than the prepositions, particles, and auxiliaries which take their place in 'analytical' languages such as English and French. No inflections can possibly be more difficult than the English distinction between *will* and *shall* in the future, or the French uses of the prepositions *à* and *de*.

Then, again, inflections are not the only formal irregularities in language. The student of spoken English has not only to learn the syntactical use of *will* and *shall*, but has also to learn to recognize these words in their various formal disguises in such combinations as (ail, ai wount, ai ʃaant), and so on. So also French, after substituting *de* for the various inflections of the Latin genitive, goes on to develope fresh irregularities, such as *du*, *des*.

The epithet 'analytic,' too, is often applied too sweepingly. If we compare Italian with Latin, we see that the loss of the cases is to a great extent compensated, as regards irregularity and complexity of form, by the difficulty of the verbs, and by the various forms of the pronouns and the other new developments. It is clear, therefore, either that the intrinsic ease of Italian as compared with Latin has been exaggerated, or that it is the result of other changes than mere loss of inflection.

If, indeed, we put ourselves in imagination in the place of an intelligent Asiatic who knows nothing of any European language, we shall have reason to doubt whether Italian is, after all, easier than Latin. The comparative ease of Italian to Europeans is mainly the result of purely external conditions, the most important of which is that most of those who learn it, really know it partially beforehand through knowing French and Latin—languages which no European can help learning to some extent through the French and Latin words imported into his own vocabulary.

If inflections, and grammatical irregularities were the main cause of difficulty, then Chinese ought to be the easiest language in the world, for it has no inflections, no grammatical genders, no irregularities of form, and its particles and auxiliaries are few in number : Chinese grammar is all phonology and syntax —there is no accidence whatever. And yet the construction of classical Chinese is as difficult as that of Latin, quite apart from any external difficulties.

F

The Real Difficulty is in the Vocabulary

The fact that the languages commonly learnt by Europeans belong mostly to the same Aryan stock, and have besides a large vocabulary in common of borrowed Latin, French, and Greek words, is apt to blind them to a recognition of the fact that the real intrinsic difficulty of learning a foreign language lies in that of having to master its vocabulary.

Mastering the vocabulary of most European languages means simply learning to recognize a number of old friends under slight disguises, and making a certain effort to learn a residue of irrecognizable words, which, however, offer less difficulty than they otherwise would through being imbedded in a context of familiar words. The higher vocabulary of science, art, and abstract thought hardly requires to be learnt at all; for it consists either of Latin and Greek terms common to most European languages, or of translations of them.

It is very different with a remote disconnected language such as Arabic or Chinese. The abstract vocabulary of Arabic shows Greek influence, although this affords very little practical help; but the terminology of Chinese philosophy and science is independent of Western influence, so that every extension of the vocabulary requires a special effort of memory and reasoning. The task of mastering such languages is literally an endless one. Enough Arabic grammar for reading purposes is soon acquired, the construction being always perfectly simple—at least in ordinary prose, but the student may read one class of texts for years, and then, when he proceeds to another branch of the literature, he may find that he can hardly understand a word, this being almost entirely the result of the unfamiliarity of the new vocabulary required.

In short, we can master enough of the grammar of any language for reading purposes within a definite period—generally less than six months—but we cannot do the same with the vocabulary unless it is already partially familiar to us in the way that the vocabulary of Italian is to all English speakers.

All Languages Equally Difficult

All these considerations, if summed up impartially, lead us finally to the conclusion that, as regards ease of learning, all languages are intrinsically on a level—they are all equally easy or equally difficult; that is, of course, if we rigorously eliminate all external considerations, and disregard the special relations between individual languages.

But as it is practically impossible for any one who has not an equally perfect knowledge of all languages to test this by experience, it must remain an abstraction, like the dogma of the absolute regularity of sound-changes. We may also say of the dogma of the intrinsically equal difficulty of languages, as of that of the absolute regularity of sound-changes, that even if it is not true, it has a certain value as a corrective to one-sidedness and inaccurate reasoning.

The external considerations have been already discussed. One reservation only remains to be stated. When we talk of the difficulty of a language, we must strictly define the limits of the language; we must be careful in speaking of a language to make sure that we are not really speaking of a group of languages, or—what is the same thing from our present point of view—a group of dialects. Thus an ordinary Greek grammar would give us a very exaggerated estimate of the difficulty of the verbs in -mi if we reckoned up all the divergent forms without regard to difference of dialect. It must also be remembered that the Homeric dialect is a confused mixture of forms of different periods and dialects with artificial monstrosities invented by grammarians: it never could have been an actual language. So also Italian is not so difficult as its conventional grammars are.

The conclusion to which we have just arrived is strengthened by some *à priori* considerations. The history of grammatical irregularities is very instructive from this point of view.

The tendency of unrestrained phonetic change is to cause increasing complexity and irregularity in language. The origin of inflections is to be sought mainly in phonetic changes which caused originally independent post-positions to become incorporated into the preceding word, as we see in the Icelandic reflexive inflection -*sk*, which is simply a shortening of the reflexive pronoun *sik*, as in *būask*, 'prepare oneself,' whence our verb *busk*. The phonetic changes which brought inflections into being tend to complicate more and more both the inflections themselves and the inflected words. We see the result in such English forms as (wumən), plural (wimin), where there are only traces left of the original Old English forms *wīfmann*, plural *wīfmenn*, the second element of (wimin) being also completely isolated from modern English (mæn) or its plural (men).   So also in Old Irish *ben*, 'woman,' plural *mnā*, where the change of *b* into *m* is purely phonetic.   So, again, in Welsh the word *potatoes* was borrowed in the form of *tatws*, which was regarded as a collective plural, from which on the analogy of native words a new singular was formed by vowel-change and the addition of *-en*, the whole word being afterwards shortened to *tysen*, the singular being thus completely isolated from the plural, as if they were unconnected words.

In languages as they exist, such difficulties are allowed to accumulate up to a certain point.   When they threaten to undermine the whole structure of the language—as they certainly would do in any language if left to themselves—they are got rid of by means of the process of levelling by analogy.   Thus, in some dialects of Welsh the divergence in the words just mentioned is got rid of by forming a new singular *taten* from the plural, so that the comparatively regular inflection *taten*, *tatws* is developed.   So also in English we might make the inflection of *woman* regular by giving it a regular plural *womans* on the analogy of the vast majority of English nouns.   We might make the plural of *man* itself regular in the same way. But as these two words are of extremely frequent occurrence, it is easy for us to remember them, especially as the whole number of irregular plurals is but small.

Different languages tolerate different irregularities.   Thus Welsh is very irregular in the formation of its plurals, but it makes up for this by getting rid of all its case-inflections. Finnish, as we have seen, has many cases, but they are, on the whole, very regular.   If a language is very regular and simple in one department, we may expect it to be irregular and complex in another.   In this way there is a balance of difficulties, although this is often ignored through taking a one-sided view. Thus in English the formal part of the grammar is fairly simple and regular ; but the vocabulary shows the greatest complexity and irregularity, which in the spoken language extends to the form as well as the meanings of the words, as we see in such a group of words as (foutəgræf, foutə·græfik, fə·togrəfə), where there is not only divergence in stress but also in sound, so that the first and last have very little resemblance to the ear.

It is evident that every language in its colloquial form must be adapted to the average capacity of its speakers. Although each language is constructed to a great extent by the philosophers and poets of the race, it cannot in the form of it which serves for ordinary intercourse go beyond the capacity of the average mind. Learning a language, therefore, is not in any way analogous to learning mathematics or metaphysics : it does not imply any attempt to enter into higher regions of thought —to commune with a higher mind. On the contrary, as the greater part of all existing languages was evolved by people in a rudimentary state of civilization, it implies the very reverse. Hence, as we shall see hereafter, it is often a positive obstacle to learning a language to be rigorously logical and minutely analytical.

From the admission that all languages are in themselves equally difficult, it does not necessarily follow that we are never to apply the word 'difficult' to languages. But it must be understood that when we say that one Oriental language is more difficult than another, we only imply that the external obstacles are greater, or that the structure of the language differs more from that of the average European language.

CHAPTER IX

GENERAL PRINCIPLES OF METHOD

WE now come to our main problem—how to overcome these various difficulties.

Language Only Partly Rational

Before going any further it is important to realize clearly the fact that language is partly rational, partly irrational and arbitrary. Thus, when a language enlarges its vocabulary by systematically utilizing material words to express abstract ideas, as when it uses such words as *spring* or *source* to express the idea of 'origin,' it is rational ; so also when it indicates different grammatical relations between words by the order in which they follow each other. When, on the other hand, language developes such a system of grammatical gender as we find in French and German, or when it allows inflections to become irregular and ambiguous, it is irrational. It is true that we can prove by historical philology that there was once a reason for grammatical gender, and that the inflections that are now irregular and anomalous were once the regular ones, or that at any rate they are the result of regular sound-changes ; but this does not in any way alter the fact that they are now, from a practical point of view, irrational. We might as well argue that the buttons that are still put at the back of men's dress coats are useful because our dress coats were originally coats with long tails which were buttoned up in riding.

The arbitrariness of language is most strikingly evident in its vocabulary. The type of a rational word is such a one as *cuckoo*, which, to those who already know the object it represents, is as self-interpreting and as easily remembered as any gesture or picture. But in all languages the vast majority of primitive words have no connection with the meanings they

70

express, and, what is worse still, one sound-group often stands for a variety of ideas, which are sometimes quite disconnected, as in the various meanings of such English words as *bear* and *box*. Again, in a rational vocabulary words similar in form would have allied meanings, and similar meanings would be expressed by similar words, but in English such formally almost identical pairs as *bit* and *beat*, *bed* and *bad*, have nothing in common as regards their meanings, and even such ideas as 'good' are expressed by a variety of distinct words, such as *good, well, virtue.* The only rational part of the vocabulary is that which forms new words by composition and derivation, and gives words new meanings by means of metaphor, simile, and other processes of the same kind; but all these processes are often irregular and arbitrary both in their operation and their results.

Irrational Combinations in Language : We Cannot Speak by Rule

Language is often irrational even in the way it combines words into sentences—in its synthesis. If language were perfectly rational in this respect, we should be able to handle words like the nine digits in arithmetic, and combine them into sentences at pleasure by applying a few simple grammatical rules. In practice, however, we find that a great part of all languages consists of a limited number of natural sentences, only some of which admit of being formed *à priori* and freely modified by the substitution of other words, as when from *have, ink, pen* we make up such sentences as *I have the ink; who has the pen? who has the ink? he has the ink,* and so on.

But just as we cannot go on speaking long without using irregular inflections, so also we cannot go on speaking naturally for any length of time without using irregular combinations of words—combinations which cannot be constructed *à priori.* The sentences which make up natural speech are of two kinds—**general** sentences, such as those which have just been given, and **special** sentences or idioms, such as *how do you do? never mind,* which are really on a level with simple words, such as *salutation, indifference,* and, like them, have to be learnt one by one, in the same way as the iregularities of the grammar. Many of them, indeed, have meanings inconsistent with those of the words of which they are made up. Thus *do* by itself never has the meaning it has in *how do you do?* and *help* in the idiomatic expression *I could not help being late* has the meaning 'prevent,' 'avoid,' which is the exact contrary of its ordinary meaning.

Again, even in those cases in which the grammar and dictionary allow us to express an idea by various combinations of words, there is often only one of these combinations in actual use. Those who have had to do Latin prose composition know that the main difficulty of the art consists in having an instinctive knowledge what combinations to avoid. French has a similar character. English and Greek are much freer in this respect, a fact which many foreigners find it difficult to realize. When they ask me such questions as 'can one speak of an "elegant supper"?' 'can you say, "he was bad last night"?' I always answer that English is a free language, and that there is nothing to prevent any one calling a supper 'elegant,' although I do not remember ever doing so myself. Nevertheless, English has its limitations as well as other languages. Foreigners' English often presents the curious spectacle of a language constructed on strict grammatical principles, but with hardly a single genuinely English sentence in it. The following extract from the published works of a distinguished French Orientalist who lived many years in England, and wrote most of his books in English, will illustrate this. The writer is Prof. Terrien de la Couperie (The Pre-Chinese Languages, § 235), and he is protesting against the systematic study of phonetics :—

'Another point which requires due consideration is that of pronunciation. The scientific achievements lately obtained in perfection of transcription by several English and German scholars go beyond human looseness. They have reached the high level of the respective idiosyncrasies of the speaker and of the transcriber, above the common average of speech. The activity of man's speaking-organs and also that of his ear-sense, have nowhere the mechanical and permanent precision which their principles and those of the new school of grammarians imply. Uncultured populations and uneducated men are not naturally bent in the material of their speech to the yoke of steady precision which is only the result of a training in educated social surroundings through several generations. Audition and articulation of language, except in the higher races, seldom arrive together at some sort of perfection in their effectiveness. For instance, we may quote the well-known fact that the acuity of the ear among the races paying peculiar attention to the colour and pitch of the vowels exists only at the expense of precision in the articulation.

'Tribes in a rude state of culture have a looseness and uncouthness of pronunciation and hearing, which escapes, in its group's fancies or individual distortions, from any unflinching law of regularity. The cases and causes of variance from analogy, relative easing, symbolical strengthening or weakening, scorn anything like a formulated law. The segmentation, dispersion, and migration of tribes grown from a homogeneous linguistic stock in that state of unculture, combined with the complication from the frequent though often unknown super-imposition of races and languages in a similar condition or otherwise, imply large divergences of pronunciation apparently inconsistent with their genuine derivation from common parents. And the efforts at reducing the whole of the divergences to regular and somewhat mechanical equivalence cannot lead otherwise than to numerous confusions and misapprehensions.

'After the disturbance of ideologies, the most important result for all the languages engaged in the struggle, a result produced at the same time by the intermingling of blood, concerns the phonesis.'

The Arithmetical Fallacy

The 'arithmetical fallacy,' as we may call it, is well illus-trated in the practice of exercise-writing and translation into the foreign language, a subject to which we will return later on.

In the well-known methods of Ahn, Ollendorff, and Arnold it is developed into a regular system, intended as a substitute for the ordinary grammar and dictionary method—at least for the beginner. The result is to exclude the really natural and idiomatic combinations, which cannot be formed à priori, and to produce insipid, colourless combinations, which do not stamp themselves on the memory, many of which, indeed, could hardly occur in real life, such as *the cat of my aunt is more treacherous than the dog of your uncle | we speak about your cousin, and your cousin Amelia is loved by her uncle and her aunt | my sons have bought the mirrors of the duke | horses are taller than tigers.* At one school where I learnt—or rather made a pretence of learning—Greek on this system, the master used to reconstruct the materials of the exercises given in our book into new and strange combinations, till at last, with a faint smile on his ascetic countenance, he evolved the following sentence, which I remembered long after I had forgotten all the rest of my Greek—*the philosopher pulled the lower jaw of the hen* (tou tijz ɔˈnaiþos ænou gnæþos). The results of this method have been well parodied by Burnand in his *New Sandford and Merton*, thus: *the merchant is swimming with (avec) the gardener's son, but the Dutchman has the fine gun.*

Isolated Phenomena of Language: Grammar and Dictionary

One result of language being partly rational, partly irrational, is that some of its phenomena can be brought under general rules, some cannot. Thus in English the fact that *tree* is made into *trees* when we speak of more than one tree is a general one; for we can add *s* in the same way and with the same change of meaning to nearly all other names of things. But the fact that *t, r, e, e* expresses the idea 'tree,' and not any other idea, is an isolated one; for, given these sounds, we cannot tell beforehand what the meaning will be, and given the idea 'tree,' we cannot tell beforehand what combination of sounds will express it.

This constitutes the whole distinction between grammar and dictionary. Grammar, like all other sciences, deals with what can be brought under general laws, and relegates all the other phenomena of language to that collection of isolated facts which we call the dictionary: It need hardly be said that there is no absolute line of demarcation between the two; thus the prepositions and many other particles belong both to the grammar and the dictionary. It also follows from our definition that what belongs only to the dictionary in one language may fall— partially, at least—under grammar in another, and *vice versa.* Thus in that remarkably symmetrical family of languages, the Semitic—of which classical Arabic is the best type—many of the details of the formation of roots and the structure of the primitive vocabulary are rightly included in the grammar. Again, such languages as German and Russian—though in many respects they fall short of the Semitic languages in word-forming power—still have great resources in the way of composition and derivation. In English, on the other hand—which, from the point of view of the vocabulary, must be regarded as a degenerate language—even such a simple matter as the formation of an adjective from a noun is often the business, not of the grammar, but of the dictionary, as in *sun, solar, man, human, virile.*

We see, then, that the existence of grammars and dictionaries is founded on the nature of language itself.

The Natural Method

But many undeniable abuses in the use of these helps have led some reformers to a revolt not only against the use of grammars and dictionaries, but also against all system and method whatever in learning languages. This revolt against method has further led to an advocacy of the 'natural method' by which children learn their own language.

These enthusiasts forget that the process of learning one's native language is carried on under peculiarly favourable circumstances, which cannot be even approximately reproduced in the later study of foreign languages.

In learning our own language, we begin young, and we give our whole time to it. Our minds are perfect blanks, and we come to it with all our faculties fresh and unworn. The fact, too, that we generally learn new words and new ideas simultaneously, and that the word is often the key to the idea, gives a peculiar vividness and interest to the process of word-learning.

But the process has also its disadvantages. It is a very slow process; and the results are always imperfect. Indeed, so imperfect is this natural method, that even with the help of school-training and the incessant practice of everyday life, very few ever attain a really thorough mastery of their own language. When we say that any one is 'eloquent,' or that he 'has a good style,' or 'is a good speaker,' or 'can tell a story well,' we hardly mean more than that his command of his own language is rather less imperfect than that of his fellows. If languages were learnt perfectly by the children of each generation, then languages would not change : English children would still speak a language as old at least as 'Anglo-Saxon,' and there would be no such languages as French and Italian. The changes in languages are simply slight mistakes, which in the course of generations completely alter the character of the language.

The disadvantages we have to labour under when we learn a

foreign language are evident enough, and the later in life we begin, the more evident these disadvantages become. The power of imitation has greatly decreased, which is especially noticeable in the pronunciation. Not only has the power of imitation decreased, but also the desire to use it: the mind has lost its freshness and susceptibility to new impressions.

On the other hand, the mind is formed: it is capable of generalization and abstraction; it has an immensely wider and more accurate knowledge of the things and ideas represented by words and their combinations; it has greater powers of concentration and methodical perseverance. And these advantages more than compensate the disadvantages we have just mentioned.

Nevertheless, there is one disadvantage which turns the scale; that is, the fact that the student has already learnt another language—his own. Hence in learning the new language he has, as it were, to try to unlearn the other language, to struggle continually against the formidable difficulties caused by cross-associations. When he tries to pronounce a new sound, his tongue tends to slip back into the position for forming the nearest native sound. So also with word-order, grammatical construction generally, and the whole fabric of the language.

The fundamental objection, then, to the natural method is that it puts the adult into the position of an infant, which he is no longer capable of utilizing, and, at the same time, does not allow him to make use of his own special advantages. These advantages are, as we have seen, the power of analysis and generalization—in short, the power of using a grammar and dictionary.

Residence Abroad

The natural method almost necessarily implies a residence in the country where the language is spoken. But residence abroad has also its own linguistic drawbacks.

It sounds well to talk of ' picking up a language by ear in the country itself,' but most good linguists will confess that they learnt nearly everything from books, especially in the beginning of their study of the foreign language, and but little from conversation. There are, indeed, many obstacles to learning from conversation. In the hurry of talk we are apt to mishear and forget, so that what we pick up in that way is never reliable. Conversation is really not a means of learning new words and expressions, but only of practice in hearing and reproducing what we have already learnt. In conversation we also have the disadvantage of hearing only the answers to our questions, while we have no means of knowing whether our questions are expressed correctly, for it is very difficult to overhear the natives asking questions which will serve as patterns for our own. Rash reproduction of what we hear casually may land us in vulgar, ludicrously slangy, or otherwise objectionable expressions. The results of picking up a language entirely by ear from the beginning may be seen in uneducated adults who come among a population speaking a strange language : after years of residence in the country they are often unable to utter anything but a few words and phrases.

In fact, a residence in the country itself before the elements have been mastered at home is positively injurious, for it forces the learner to improvise incorrect expressions on the spur of the moment; and these incorrect expressions then tend to become stereotyped by incessant repetition, so that they can scarcely be got rid of. This is specially the case with the equivalents of such particles and phrases as *Oh ! to be sure, don't you know.*

Nor must the learner expect too much from a residence abroad. There are many external obstacles, especially in the case of English-speakers. Thus it is often almost impossible for an Englishman to learn educated colloquial German in the country, because all the Germans want to practise their English upon him; and, besides, he is often thrown by circumstances almost exclusively among English-speakers in foreign schools and boarding-houses. I heard of one case in which an English boy was at Bonn for a year ; when he came home, he said he had not spoken a single word of German the whole time, not even in the shops.

Then there is the difficulty of avoiding confusion of dialects, even if the learner is able to choose his place of residence exclusively from that point of view; in a University town the professors and students come from all parts of the country, and therefore often speak different dialects.

Many people, however, who admit the utility of grammars and dictionaries, are inclined to discard systematic study as soon as they have mastered the elements of the language, especially if they have an opportunity of pursuing their studies in the country itself. A little reflection ought to convince them that systematic study is almost as necessary at the end of the course as at the beginning. After what has been said about the difficulty, or rather impossibility, of picking up reliable knowledge by hearing—which applies also, though perhaps in a less degree, to cursory reading—it is evident that giving up systematic study means simply giving up learning. After we have once given up systematic study, we cannot be said to learn the language, we only 'keep it up.'

Those who wish to derive the fullest benefit from residence in the country itself should, therefore, be guided by the following principles: (1) prepare yourself thoroughly beforehand; (2) choose a place where you will have an opportunity of hearing a good standard of pronunciation and language generally, as unmixed as possible; (3) keep up systematic study till the last.

Speaking Foreign Languages at Home

There are several substitutes for residence abroad. One is, to converse with foreigners in one's own country. In this way many foreigners get a good knowledge of colloquial French and English. It is evident that the success of this method depends to a great extent on the number of foreigners who come to the learner's country, and on the extent to which they learn the language of the country, the most favourable conditions being for the learner to speak the language of a small country much frequented by foreign tourists, as when a Norwegian learns English from tourists of that nationality.

But this course has its drawbacks and dangers, which become more and more evident the more the conditions diverge from those sketched above. A tourist, who stays only a short time in the country, preserves his national habits of thought and speech, which are generally those of an educated man; but foreigners who settle permanently in another country may partially lose their nationality in speech as well as in other respects, and may be bad models from the beginning.

The greatest of these drawbacks is, of course, that the surroundings are not foreign, so that we miss a good deal of what we should learn spontaneously in the country itself, and what we do learn is learnt under wrong surroundings and associations. Thus instead of learning the words and phrases associated with the national games and amusements of the foreigner, we hear perhaps the description of a game of cricket or lawn tennis, interlarded, of course, with many English words and phrases.   German clerks in our large towns may be heard using such expressions as *die bill of lading ist noch nicht da*, and, of course, *da hab' ich einen kep* (= cab) *genommen*.   Foreigners who have lived long in the country often import even its idioms into their own language.   Thus Germans in America in conversation with each other have been heard to say *backen Sie nicht aus*, ' don't back out (of your promise) ! '

Similar objections apply to the practice of letting children learn languages from foreign nurses and governesses.

Of course, the younger the child, the more perfect its imitation of the foreign language.   But if this is carried too far, it implies that the child does not learn its own language.   Then, again, if young children learn easily, they forget still more easily : in extreme cases a child may learn a little of its own language, then learn a foreign language tolerably well, forgetting its own language in the process ; it then begins to learn its own language again, and forgets the foreign language, the final result being simply to delay its learning of its own language.

The results, too, are generally unsatisfactory in many ways : the child learns to speak the little it learns with great fluency, but the pronunciation is not good, nor the construction perfect ; and if there is a large family of children, they soon invent a French or German of their own with a pronunciation made up exclusively of English sounds.   Good results are due either to exceptional ability on the part of the child, or to exceptionally favourable circumstances which make the child bilingual from the beginning.   Thus when the children of foreign parents settled in England speak the two languages perfectly, this is not a case of learning a foreign language in the ordinary sense of the word, any more than when children are taken abroad by their parents.

Natural Aptitude

Every one knows that the natural aptitude for learning foreign languages varies greatly in different individuals.   It varies in children as well as adults, though perhaps not to the same degree.

Children show different degrees of quickness and accuracy in learning to speak their own language. Gabelentz says, in speaking of children learning their own language (Gab. 65): 'Some take years to overcome the difficulties of pronunciation and grammar, while for others these difficulties seem scarcely to exist. I could mention German children who, from the very beginning of their attempts to speak, pronounced the gutturals and the consonant-groups of their own language and even foreign words with ease and correctness, and seldom violated the rules of German gender, or the irregularities in the formation of the plural and the conjugation of the verbs. Other children built up independently a language of their own with special laws.' He goes on to mention a child who, of its own accord, developed a system of modifying the vowels of the German words it learnt for symbolic purposes, somewhat as in the Semitic languages, and thus constructed a language of its own, in which, for instance, the vowel u was associated with bigness, the vowel i with littleness.

This is interesting, as illustrating what we shall have occasion to notice hereafter, that originality of mind does not make a good linguist. In fact, a talent for languages does not imply any higher intellectual development of any kind. The truly original mind seizes instinctively on the most efficient means of expression at its command—that is to say, it prefers to express itself in the language it knows best, which is its own. Such minds avoid learning foreign languages as much as possible. Swedenborg would no doubt sooner have written in Swedish than in Latin, were it not for his wish to have his books read as widely as possible. As for those who are drawn to the original investigation of the science of language, they do not, as a rule, speak them any better than other people—often worse. We need only mention the bad Latin in which the great founder of comparative philology made his first discoveries known.

The considerations to which we were led before, namely, that languages are only partly rational, show that their acquisition must be, to a great extent at least, a mechanical process. Mechanical learning does not require originality of mind or a critical spirit. These are, indeed, hindrances rather than helps. What is required is the faculty of observation, quick imitation, adaptiveness to grasp the phenomena of the new language, and memory to retain them.

All these qualifications are required in the highest degree in speaking, ease in which—especially, of course, with the more remote languages—is the greatest test of the born linguist as opposed to the scientific philologist. One of the most perfect types of what the latter would call 'the parrot linguist' was Palmer the Orientalist; and it used to be said of him at Cambridge that when he talked to Orientals in their own language, he seemed to speak faster than they did. This excessive fluency often blinds the superficial observer to the defectiveness of the imitation, especially in the pronunciation, which in the born linguist of the highest type is always good, but apparently never perfect, unless with the help of phonetic training. It is said that when Palmer talked to the Arabs of the desert, they thought he was an Arab of a different tribe.

There is also a lower type of general linguist who cannot speak, but reads a large number of languages, and, perhaps, writes them. This type is the natural result of the combination of a less quick mind with a retentive memory and a natural taste and enthusiasm for polyglot linguistics.

Although originality and independence of mind are to some extent anti-linguistic, they are not positive bars to the acquisition of languages. Strength of purpose, based on a conviction of the utility or perhaps the absolute necessity of learning a given language, will work wonders, especially if there is a real love of the study, which does not necessarily imply any special talent.

It is difficult to define the opposite extreme of the purely anti-linguistic mind except as the negation of the other extreme, that is, as the result of slowness of mind, want of adaptability and power of imitation, together with shortness of memory. Such an absolutely anti-linguistic mind is the slave of the associations of its own language : when it expresses itself in a foreign language, it tries to do so by translating the native expression of each idea word for word into the foreign language, perhaps grammatically, but regardless of idiom and the genius of the foreign language, as when an Englishman of the old-fashioned John Bull type said to a German *ich habe einen groszen geist Sie niederzuklopfen.* This anti-linguistic mind is not uncommon among grammarians and philologists.

It must, of course, be understood that the intellectual qualities which constitute linguistic talent are of a special kind : the quickness must be linguistic quickness, the memory must be a linguistic memory, however much it may extend to other subjects as well. In the same way the adaptability and

G

sympathy must be linguistic sympathy : the feeling which makes us feel an interest in the individuality of each language—in the way in which it expresses ideas.

The linguistic interest, though allied to the literary, is not identical with it—least of all, in the higher developments of the latter. Thus the great linguist Palmer wrote verses with great facility, but these verses had nothing of poetry beyond the mere form, which was itself generally trivial. No phenomenal linguist has ever produced real literature, nor, what is more remarkable, ever made any great contribution to the science of language.

National Aptitude

There does not seem to be any valid reason for supposing that one nation has more talent for languages than another. The great linguists have not been confined to one country any more than the phenomenally strong men.

But nevertheless the observations we have made concerning individuals apply, to some extent, to nations also.

In the first place, original and intellectually independent nations which have a long civilization behind them, do not generally take kindly to learning foreign languages. A Frenchman in a mixed company abroad expects every one to talk French, even if he is the only Frenchman present. Englishmen are less egotistical, but they generally prefer to talk English with foreigners, even if they can speak the foreigner's language better than the foreigner speaks English. The Germans, on the other hand, whose sense of nationality has been of later growth, never speak their own language if they have a chance of speaking a foreign one ; but, as might be expected from the most intellectual nation in Europe, they seldom speak foreign languages really well.

The imitative Russian and the supple Oriental seem to be often better linguists than the slower and more independent European. But the Russian aptitude for learning languages has been doubtless much exaggerated. Foreigners who have lived long in the interior of Russia have often assured me that the Russians, as a rule, do not speak foreign languages better than other nations. Tolstoi, too, in one of his novels, remarks of one of his Russian characters that 'he spoke that excellent French which is so seldom heard now.' The fact is, that those

Russians who used to speak perfect French had to pay the price in expatriation and partial oblivion of their own language. We may safely prophesy that as the national life of the Russians developes, they will become worse and worse linguists.

Some of the conditions of national linguistic skill are purely external. Belgians, Swiss, Dutchmen, and Danes are better linguists than Englishmen partly because the smallness of their respective countries obliges them to learn other languages. The Russians were obliged to be good linguists, partly because their retarded civilization obliged them to be imitative and adaptive with regard to the older civilizations of Western Europe, partly because the newness and inaccessibility of their own language prevented foreigners from acquiring it.

One Method for All

However great the differences may be between individuals and between nations as regards ease of learning foreign languages, these differences are differences of degree only. All minds work by the same fundamental psychological laws. No one can learn a language without exerting the faculties of association and memory. However bad his linguistic memory, however weak his linguistic associations may be, he must have *some* linguistic memory and be capable of forming *some* linguistic associations, or he will not be able to learn any language at all—not even his own. The mere fact of his having learnt his own language shows that he is capable of learning other languages as well.

That the difference between the dull learner of languages and the born linguist is one of degree only, seems to be confirmed by the fact that even such a prodigy as Mezzofanti used to learn paradigms by heart like any schoolboy. The only difference was that Mezzofanti learnt them quicker and remembered them better, and was more ready in applying them to the grammatical analysis of the texts he read. His memory was so retentive that he could repeat a whole folio page of a Greek Father by heart after reading it through once.

These considerations will help us to settle the important question, how far the method of learning languages ought to be the same—that is, of course, the same for all normally and fully developed minds.

241

If one linguist gives another linguist an account of the method by which he has learnt—or professes to have learnt—a language, the other may agree with him, or may think some other method better.   But he may also take an agnostic attitude : he may say that every one has his own method of learning languages, and that it is impossible to set up any general principles.

But the facts we have been considering certainly tend to show that even if there is not one absolutely invariable method, there are at least general principles.   If in learning languages by whatever conceivable method we must all make use of the same fundamental psychological processes, and if these faculties are present in all minds, differing only in degree, it seems reasonable to assume that all learners will have to travel by the same road, although some will take a longer time for the journey.

The comparison of the process of learning languages with a journey is halting in this respect, that most of the learners can hardly be said to reach their destination at all; that is, they fail to learn the foreign language perfectly.   But this, again, is only a question of degree ; for it is doubtful whether even the best linguists learn foreign languages perfectly—unless, of course, they learn it under circumstances in which any one might reasonably be expected to become perfectly bilingual. Thus, as already remarked, Palmer was taken for an Arab, but never for an Arab of the tribe he was among, showing that he did not really speak any one dialect perfectly, but took the Arabs in partly by his amazing volubility and powers of mimicry generally.   It must be remembered that he was not only a linguist, but also a powerful mesmerist and a most expert conjurer.   All this helped the illusion.

It is very difficult to get at the exact truth about these born linguists, most of whom are surrounded with a mist of exagge-ration and fable.   Indeed, one does not quite see how such a statement as that such-a-one 'speaks forty languages like a native' is to be tested.   One would first have to collect forty indubitable natives ; then to confront them with the linguist ; and then to make sure that their complimentary criticisms of his speaking were to be taken literally.   As it is, such statements are generally made by people who know nothing of the lan-guages in question, and who draw their conclusions solely from the fluency of the speaker, or take his statements on trust.   The achievements of Mezzofanti have certainly been exaggerated in this way. I was told by Prof. Johan Storm, who got his information from a Norwegian who had had an interview with the great linguist, that the current statements about his being able to distinguish the different Norwegian dialects were pure fable, and that he kept his visitor waiting a long time in the antechamber, while he primed himself with a selection of Norwegian phrases, which he uttered slowly and with considerable hesitation. It is really not difficult to get, or make, the reputation of speaking a foreign language perfectly. An Englishman travelling in out-of-the way parts of South Germany has only to speak anglicized book German to be taken for a Prussian, and then to go home and tell people he was taken for a German everywhere.

But even if we grant that some adults are practically incapable of learning to speak a remote language with fluency, or even of reading its classics with ease, this does not invalidate our conclusion that all must travel by what is essentially the same road : the fact that the traveller does not reach his destination by one road does not prove that he would have got any further by another road.

It is lastly to be observed that the doubts and objections we have had to meet are founded on the results obtained by the antiquated methods of study still generally employed in this country. One of the most important results of the perfection of rational methods will be that differences in natural aptitude will be more and more levelled by systematic training. The same adult who would otherwise be incapable of imitating a single unfamiliar foreign sound, would certainly, if he had been trained in phonetics from his infancy, be able to reproduce every foreign sound with ease and perfect accuracy, and would therefore in this important respect be completely on a level with—or rather, superior to—the most highly gifted linguist trained on the old system.

No training will ever make a slow mind or a bad memory equal to the mind and memory of a great linguist : we can never expect that all learners will reach the goal with the same ease and quickness. But perfected methods will reduce these inequalities to a minimum ; and we may reasonably hope that they will bring the goal within the reach of all who are ready to make the necessary sacrifices of time and trouble.

Another consideration is, that nothing will ever make the learning of languages easy : it will always be a difficult and unnatural process—unnatural because it involves constant conflicts with the associations of the learner's native language. It is not true that 'to learn to speak no matter what language is a thing as natural and easy to a child as learning to fly is to a bird.' This was said by Gouin in praise of his own system, the great merit of which, according to Gouin's disciple Swan, is that ' the stupidest scholar can learn it as easily as the smartest ' because 'all intelligences are sensibly equal' (Br. G. 29). This last statement is only an extravagant exaggeration of the one-method-for-all principle. The preceding statement may be true, but, unfortunately, learning Gouin's method does not imply knowing the language.

The Historical Method

With the rise of comparative philology and its great development during the present century came the historical view of language. It was shown that the irregularities and anomalies of language could be explained by comparison with their older forms as preserved both in the earlier stages of the language itself and in the cognate languages belonging to the same family, and that the further a language is traced back, the more clear and regular does its structure seem to become.

Hence it was inferred that the historical treatment of language would also lighten the drudgery of acquiring a practical mastery of its grammar.

Although the scientific study of language is impossible without historical method, it is possible to carry the historical view of language too far. The historical study of language degenerates into one-sided antiquarianism when, as is often the case, it concentrates all its energies on the determination of the oldest formations in a language or group of languages, valuing the inflections and other forms of modern languages only in as far as they throw light on those of the older stages.

The great defect of antiquarianism is that it ignores the fact that every language and every stage of a language has an individuality of its own. It is not enough to trace the forms of a language back to what we conventionally regard as their original forms ; we must also gain a clear idea of the structure of the language of a given period as an organic whole without regard to the antiquity of its morphological characteristics or their older forms. From this point of view it is, for instance, of primary importance to know that the modern Scandinavian languages have a passive voice, while the fact that this inflection is of late origin is comparatively unimportant. Again, a knowledge of the fact that such a plural as *feet* is exceptional and anomalous, and that the great majority of English plurals are formed by adding -*s*, is essential to the comprehension of the structure of English, while the historical explanation of the origin of the form *feet* through *fōti*, *fǣti*, *fǣt*, *fet*, *fīt* does not materially assist that comprehension.

It is no doubt interesting to know that such plurals as *men*, *feet*, *mice* were once perfectly regular, and interesting to trace the steps by which they gradually assumed their present forms; but this does not in the slightest degree modify the fact that these plurals are now isolated forms or irregularities. The difficulty the foreign learner feels in mastering such forms lies in the effort of forming associations supported only by a few words, and directly opposed to those involved in acquiring the regular plurals; nor is the tendency to expect *mans*, *foots*, *mouses* instead of *men*, *feet*, *mice* and the effort of overcoming this tendency at all affected by the learner's conviction that the forms that are now isolated irregularities were once regular.

Mischievous as one-sided antiquarianism is in the scientific study of language, it is still more so in the practical study of language. As we see, the anomalies and irregularities of language retain all their practical difficulty, however much they may be illuminated by the light of history; and the main result of the application of the historical method is to add to the effort of overcoming the cross-associations involved in the anomalies and irregularities themselves, the further one of mastering a number of theoretical statements and of learning a number of hypothetical forms which afterwards have to be unlearnt.

The Crude Form System

An extreme development of the historical method is the so-called 'crude form' system.

It is strange that the advocates of this system do not see that the student who has learnt, for instance, the Greek paradigm *ánax*, *ánaktos*, etc., by heart has learnt exactly as much as another who has been first taught that the crude form is *anakt*, that the nominative is formed by adding *-s*, and that *anakts* is then contracted into *anaks*, *ánax*, the only difference being that the crude-former not only has to learn the actual forms *ánax*, *ánaktos*, but also a variety of hypothetical forms, besides having to make the additional effort of remembering that the forms *anakt*, *anakts*, etc., do not exist. So also in Finnish the mere juxtaposition of such forms as nominative singular *käsi*, 'hand,' illative *käteen*, plural nominative *kädet*, together with the possessive nominative singular *käteni*, 'my hand,' is enough to give a practical knowledge of the fact that the stem or crude form is *käte*, from which the nominative singular *käsi* and the nominative plural *kädet* are formed by perfectly regular sound-changes. Putting *käte* at the head of the paradigm simply unsettles the learner's associations with the nominative *käsi*; and the confusion is made worse, when, as is sometimes the case in Finnish grammars, nouns are given sometimes in their nominative singular, sometimes in the form of the bare stem. If the learner only has two such forms as *käsi*, *käteni*, or *käsi*, *kädet*, he has material enough to enable him to construct the stem together with all the inflectional forms.

The Etymological Fallacy

Similar criticisms apply also to the 'etymological fallacy.' The meaning of a word in a given period of a given language is a matter of usage, and the fact of its having had a certain meaning at some earlier period or in some cognate language does not necessarily afford any help in determining, and still less in remembering, its present meaning. Etymological translation should, above all, be avoided in dictionaries. Thus in Old English dictionaries we find *geþofta* defined as 'one who sits on the same rowing-bench, companion;' but the only meaning the word has is the second one, the former being an inference from the etymology of the word. The inference is no doubt correct in as far as it assumes that the word had the other meaning once; but this does not alter the fact that in the language as known to us this meaning does not occur. Besides, any one can draw the inference for himself; so it is a waste of space first to give the etymology, and then to interpolate the inference drawn from it among the meanings. Etymological translation often takes the silly form of translating an Old English word by some obsolete or dialectal word which is assumed—sometimes erroneously—to be etymologically connected with the other word, as when the Old English *bearn* is translated by the Scotch *bairn*—as if modern English were such a poverty-stricken language that it could not find a word for ' child ' !   Then the German *lied* and the Old English *lēoþ* is translated *lay*—a French word which has nothing to do with *lied*.   This practice is carried to an extravagant extent in many translations from the Icelandic.   On this principle we might translate the German *jener kleine knabe ist nicht faul* by *yon clean knave is naught foul*.   It has also been suggested to me that the lines in Faust—

> *Bist du es, Faust, dess stimme mir erklang,*
> *Ein furchtsam, weggekrümmter wurm ?*

ought to be translated—

> *Be'st thou it, Fist, whose voice to me did clink,*
> *A frightsome 'way-ycrumpled worm ?*

Comparison with Cognate Languages

Even when the historical method does not require the help of hypothetical, non-existent forms, it involves the importation of words from other languages into the text-books of the language which is being studied.

Now it is true that, for instance, a knowledge of Latin considerably facilitates the acquisition of Italian and the other Romance languages.   But where the connection between the two languages is self-evident, the help of scientific historical philology is not needed : every one sees for himself that *padre* is connected with *patrem*, *aimer* with *amare*.   If the connection is not self-evident, the question arises, Is a knowledge of the etymology of any practical use ?   How, for instance, can the Latin *sitim* help us to remember the French *soif !*   Why, they have only a single sound in common !   ' That is true,' says the philologist; ' but when the learner has once mastered the intermediate stages, the connection becomes perfectly clear.'   Very likely it does; but when it turns out that these intermediate stages involve no less than nine distinct sound-changes, some of them very difficult to understand, we are forced to ask, Is it practical and rational to seek our object in so roundabout a way ?   So also a knowledge of Sanskrit is a great help in learning Zend; for the languages are so closely allied that whole passages of Zend can be translated into Sanskrit word for word simply by applying the laws of etymological sound-change. But, as we have seen (p. 55), this very closeness is a source of difficulty; so that, instead of wishing to have his associations with Sanskrit strengthened, the learner ought rather to try to forget his Sanskrit as soon as it has helped him over the first difficulties; and consequently he is only exasperated when he finds he cannot look at a paradigm in his Zend grammar without having his mind confused by the constant intrusion of parallel Sanskrit forms. Nor does the beginner in Arabic want to be reminded of Hebrew. It is besides conceivable that the study of Zend or Arabic may be begun without any previous knowledge of the two other languages, in which case the confusions resulting from cross-associations become still more serious.

Comparative Philology Sometimes Useful

But our scepticism with regard to the help afforded by comparative philology and etymology must not be exaggerated into an unreasoning rejection of it.

Cognate forms may be just far enough from one another to make it a matter of doubt whether or not the learner will recognize their affinity; under such circumstances it seems reasonable to give the learner a hint which may perhaps enable him to establish many other similar associations which would otherwise have escaped his notice. Thus, if the learner fails to see that German *zehn* is cognate with English *ten*, a statement of the correspondence between the initial consonants in the two words will not only help him to remember *zehn*, but will also enable him to establish an association between German *zeit* and English (*noon*)*tide*, and so with hundreds of other words. But there is always a danger of going too far; the teacher must be careful not to allow himself to be drawn into an elaborate exposition of Grimm's Law or any other philological generalization until he is quite sure that the practical gain will outweigh the expenditure of time and trouble.

In most cases it certainly will not. Fifty years ago, the main laws of Aryan and Romance etymology could be tabulated in a brief space and with delusive simplicity; but nowadays the phonetic changes from Latin to French alone can hardly be mastered even by specialists, and Grimm's Law has been developed and subdivided into a whole series of laws with endless complications.   Under these circumstances, the dream of making comparative philology and etymology a part of ordinary education has to be abandoned.   But there is no great harm in occasionally introducing scraps of comparative philology into elementary books, if only the information is correct—which it often is not.

Chance Resemblances between Languages

Not that this matters much from a practical point of view; for it often happens that a false etymology is a greater help to the learner than the correct one.   Thus every beginner in Greek remembers the meaning of *hólos* by its similarity in form to the English *whole*, while its real affinity with the Latin *salvus* is mastered only by an effort.   Such accidental resemblances are instinctively seized on by the beginner as the natural foundation of his new vocabulary, and none the less if they appeal only to his sense of the ludicrous or paradoxical, as when Hood says of the French 'they call their mothers mares, and all their daughters fillies.'   A Latin primer was once published in which, among other similar suggestions, the learner was told to remember that *hasta* meant 'spear' by thinking of the warning not to be *hasty* with it.   This is really more sensible than giving the Sanskrit cognate form.

These chance resemblances are especially valuable in learning remote and unconnected languages, where, therefore, there is no scope for comparative philology, and where the new vocabulary is the main difficulty.   Thus in Arabic it is some help to note that the first numeral, *wāhid*, begins with the same consonant as the English *one*, and that the seventh numeral *sab'* resembles German *sieben*.   So also in learning Finnish we cannot help associating *poika*, 'son, boy,' with English *boy*, whether or not we are inclined to believe in any closer connection between the two words.

Borrowed Words

There are few languages of any degree of culture from which our Western languages have not borrowed to some extent.   At any rate, we are generally familiar with some of the proper names in the language. In the case of Latin, the number of borrowed words is so great that we really know the vocabulary beforehand. English gives us, too, a fairly full vocabulary for Greek also, where affinity with known Latin words is often a further help. Of the remoter languages, Arabic is particularly well represented by borrowed words. When we consider the great difficulty of the Arabic vocabulary, it is a pity that our elementary text-books do not make a systematic use of this link of association. Thus, starting from *salaam* = Arabic *salām*, originally meaning ' peace,' we get to the verb *salim*, ' be safe and sound,' whence the fourth form *aslam* by the regular process of dropping the second vowel and prefixing *a*, the meaning being ' give oneself up, resign oneself (to the will of God), become a Mahommedan,' whence by equally regular changes the infinitive *islām*, ' true faith,' and the present active participle *muslim*, ' true believer,' while in the name *Muḥammad*, ' praised ' or ' praiseworthy,' we have the corresponding passive participle of the second class of verbs, formed by doubling the middle consonant. In this way a few Arabic loan-words can teach us not only a good deal of the vocabulary, but of the grammar as well.

So also in Chinese, if we bear in mind that the native forms of *Pekin* and *Nankin*, namely *pek king* and *nam king*, mean ' north capital ' and ' south capital ' respectively, and that *kuań tung*, the native name of Canton and the province in which it is situated, means ' extensive east,' and that the name of the neighbouring province *kuań si* means ' extensive west,' we have a memoria technica which helps us to recall the Chinese names of the points of the compass.

The associations with borrowed words have this great advantage over those with cognate words that the connection between the borrowed word and its original form is generally simple and direct, both in form and meaning. Borrowed words do not generally require any Grimm's Law to explain them. If they are disguised, the disguise is generally a simple one. Thus the fact that Welsh *rhwyf*, ' an oar,' is the borrowed Latin *rēmus*, though not self-evident, is soon made clear by a few of the numerous parallel cases.

CHAPTER X

Rules; Mechanical Isolation

ONE result of language being only partly rational is that only part of it can be brought under general rules, so that while some linguistic phenomena can be learnt by bringing a number of them under a general statement, others have to be learnt disconnectedly, one by one.

With those that can be brought under general statements or rules, the question still remains to be answered for each particular fact of language, Is it worth while referring it to a rule, or is it better to learn it simply as an isolated fact?

The usefulness of a rule depends: (1) on its extent—that is, the number of examples included under it; (2) on its efficiency —that is, the number of exceptions it has to admit, the rule that has the fewest exceptions being the most efficient; (3) its definiteness, clearness, and simplicity—that is, the ease with which it is learnt and applied, independently of its extent and efficiency. Such a rule as that for the formation of the plural of nouns in English stands high in all three respects: its meaning and scope are definite and clear, and its extent and efficiency make it applicable to every noun in the language, with few exceptions. A still more perfect rule is that of Latin grammar, by which in indirect narration finite verbs are in the subjunctive mood.

This example illustrates the fact that syntactical rules are, in the nature of things, more perfect than those which deal only with the forms of words. Many syntactical rules, indeed, hardly admit of exceptions; when there are exceptions, they are the result of crossing by other syntactical rules, or, at any rate, the exception is one for which a clear reason can be

93

given. Thus in Old English, where the verb is in the subjunctive in indirect narration, as in Latin, it is nevertheless put in the indicative in such a sentence as *I wish to say that I am ready to start*, because the whole sentence practically means the same as the direct statement *I am ready to start*, the clause *I wish to say* being almost an 'empty clause.' The subjunctive is here also avoided because it would imply that the speaker wished to make a false statement.

It is evident that our first two criteria balance one another to some extent. If a rule has no exceptions—or none but self-evident and necessary exceptions—it is worth learning, even if it applies to only a few words. If a rule covers a great many words, it may be worth while learning it even if there are a good many exceptions. The exceptions must be in the minority to make a rule worth learning; if the regular forms are at least twice as numerous as the exceptions, then the rule is generally decidedly worth learning—that is, if a rule is really useful or necessary. Thus, as we shall see hereafter, the genders of nouns in such languages as French and German are better learnt one by one than by rule; hence it is not worth while to give any rules for gender in these languages except those which practically admit of no exception.

All rules of any extent have this great utility, that they tell us how far the analogy of the form we are dealing with extends. Thus suppose a foreigner began the study of English with the word-group *hands and feet*, or *men, women, and children*. In either case he would be puzzled by the variety of plural-forms, and would instinctively feel a wish to know whether any one of these methods of forming the plural predominated in the language, and if so, which. The answer, 'the regular way of forming the plural of nouns is shown in the first word; nearly all English nouns form their plural in this way; the others are irregular forms which you need not trouble yourself with at present,' gives him the information he wants, enabling him to concentrate his attention on those forms which he can associate together by bringing them under a simple rule.

Where there is greater complexity and irregularity, we may either make our rules correspondingly elaborate, adding long lists of exceptions, or we may content ourselves with giving only those rules fully which are most efficient, and then content ourselves with general statements. Thus in dealing with the complicated noun-plurals in Welsh, we may content ourselves with stating that Welsh nouns form their plurals by about a dozen vowel-changes (*dafad*, 'sheep,' plural *defaid*), and by adding various endings (*pen*, 'head,' plural *penau*), which are sometimes accompanied by vowel-changes (*mab*, 'son,' plural *meibion*). This very general and vague rule may then be supplemented by such statements as that the most frequent endings are *-au*, *-iau*, *-on*, *-ion ;* that the ending *-od* is used chiefly with names of animals (*llwynog*, 'fox,' plural *llwynogod*). In Arabic the difficulty of bringing the plurals under simple and definite rules is still greater.

Under such circumstances it is safest to err on the side of ignoring rules rather than that of elaborating them. The beginner will find the simple mechanical method of associating each singular form with its plural the most effectual : that is to say, he must repeat such pairs as *dafad*, *defaid*, till one form instantaneously recalls the other. When he has accumulated a stock of examples in this way, he will then be able to derive all the more benefit from learning rules of increasing elaborateness. So also with grammatical gender : the simplest way of learning them is to associate each noun with the definite article or any other word which marks the gender. Thus the learner of German who has learnt to repeat *das haus*, 'house,' *häuser*, has a practically exhaustive knowledge of the word.

There are other considerations by which the choice between the method of rule and that of mechanical isolation is guided. Such plural formations as those of Welsh and Arabic are very distinctive : they are full and sonorous, and make a strong impression on the ear, so that they have greater individuality, and consequently are easier to discriminate and retain in the memory. But in a language such as German, where the endings are more worn away, the inflections have a more abstract character, so that such an ending as *-e*, though frequently used to form plurals, does not in itself suggest any such idea, because it is used for a great variety of other grammatical purposes, besides being in itself of little phonetic weight. Hence German plurals, though simpler than those of Welsh and Arabic, are much more in need of rules to prevent otherwise inevitable confusions.

Again, the isolating method does very well with purely formal distinctions such as those of grammatical gender, because these require no thought—nothing but a mechanical asssociation between the noun and certain accompanying words, such as the definite article. But with syntactical rules such as those for the use of the subjunctive, purely mechanical methods are rarely effective, or, indeed, available : the different constructions can only be discriminated by the help of reason and logic. Hence syntactical rules not only tell us how far the analogy of any particular construction extends (cf. p. 94), but they also save us the labour of finding out for ourselves why such a construction as the subjunctive mood is used in any particular sentence. So also it would be hopeless to try to master the initial mutations in modern Welsh without knowing the rules which govern their highly abstract and varied syntactical functions.

We see, then, that the syntax is the most important part of the grammar, and that it requries a much fuller and more detailed treatment than the accidence. Fortunately, too, syntax lends itself to such a treatment more easily and naturally than accidence does (p. 93).

We are now able to answer the general question, Should languages be learnt with or without the help of grammatical rules ?

The tendency among reformers now is to revolt against rules, and lay stress on such facts as that ' we learn to speak by pattern rather than by rule' (Paul, 89), and that ' we learn living languages more by imitation than by rules' (Storm, Forbedret Undervisning, 20). As Storm remarks, ' those who learn such a language as French mainly from grammars are often greeted by Frenchmen with the remark, " What you say is certainly very correct, but it is not French !" '

But it must be remarked that such results are generally due not to using grammars, but to using the wrong grammars—those which ignore the living language in favour of the oldfashioned literary form of it. No grammar that really restricts itself to modern French can possibly teach anything that is not modern French.

It is true that we can often dispense with rules in modern European languages, because they have so much in common grammatically that to a great extent we know their grammar beforehand, just as we do their vocabulary. Thus any one who has learnt the rules for the subjunctive in Latin or German will soon pick up those which govern its use, say, in Italian. Most European languages show a certain similarity in the construction of sentences through the great influence Latin has had on their prose.

Nevertheless, while admitting the importance of the imitative principle, we must, even from the limited point of view of the modern European languages, add that 'rules are often a great help'—we may say 'an indispensable help.' Those foreigners who try to learn the English verb without definite rules for its modern use, generally fail to master its delicate syntactical distinctions.

This is partly because English lies to some extent off the beaten track of modern European linguistic development. Hence also English learners are at a disadvantage when they learn one of the ordinary European languages : grammatical gender, the subjunctive mood, the accusative case, are all novelties to them, unless they are already familiarized with them from Latin grammar.

In remoter languages the necessity of definite rules is felt from the beginning. We can pick up a knowledge of Italian by desultory reading of the Italian New Testament, but this method would break down with such a language as Welsh, although it, too, is an Aryan language : no ordinary learner could be expected to find out for himself the mutations and the different uses of the verb 'to be,' or the principles on which the various equivalents of 'yes' are formed—without a detailed grammatical analysis all this would be a chaos of apparently arbitrary distinctions.

The more unfamiliar the language, the greater the amount of grammatical analysis required, and the more elaborate and detailed it must be. Old English differs considerably from modern English grammatically, and yet I have in my *First Steps in Anglo-Saxon* been able to give all the grammatical information absolutely required by the beginner in 25 pages, comprising not only accidence and pronunciation, but also syntax and full examples. Even the much fuller grammar in my *Anglo-Saxon Primer* takes up only 54 pages. Classical Chinese, on the other hand—a language which has no accidence whatever, in which nouns have not even a plural, and in which verbs have neither person, tense, nor mood distinguished by form—takes up 84 pages in Gabelentz's *Anfangsgründe der chinesischen grammatik*. And yet the most thorough knowledge of this book will not enable the learner to read a single line of the Chinese classics by himself—so great are the difficulties of

H

the grammatical construction in Chinese, which can only be overcome by long-continued and elaborate syntactical training carried on side by side with a careful study of the texts.

Analysis and Synthesis

Although language is made up of words, we do not speak in words, but in sentences. From a practical, as well as a scientific, point of view, the sentence is the unit of language, not the word. From a purely phonetic point of view words do not exist. As I have said in my *Primer of Phonetics* (p. 42), ' No amount of study of the sounds only of a sentence will enable us to recognize the individual words of which it consists. We may write down every sound, every shade of [phonetic] synthesis, but we shall never be able to analyse the sentence into separate words till we know its meaning, and even then we shall find that word-division postulates much thought and comparison of sentences one with another.' Thus the sound-group (telə) may stand for the single word *teller* or the two words *tell her*, there being no more pause between the words of a sentence than between the syllables of a word. In French, where word-division is much less clearly marked by stress and other formal criteria than in English, it is still more difficult to mark off the divisions of words by ear only. Thus the title of Darmesteter's well-known popular book on etymology, *La vie des mots*, is pronounced (lavidemo) with practically equal stress on all the vowels, and nothing to show, as in English, whether the internal consonants form groups with the preceding or the following vowel, so that if we did not know what it meant, we might transcribe it into nomic spelling in half a dozen ways, especially if some unknown proper name entered into it : *la vie . . . , l'avis . . . , l'avide et . . . , . . . des mots, . . . dé maux, Lavy . . . , . . . Maux, . . . Desmaux.*

We see, then, that there are two ways of dealing with languages : (1) the synthetic, which starts from the sentence; (2) the analytic, which starts from the word.

From the point of view of the practical study of language the synthetic method implies that the analysis of the language is not carried further than, at the most, cutting it up into sentences, which are grasped and learnt as wholes, instead of being separated into words, and put together like pieces of mosaic, as on the analytic method.

As the division of sentences into words is an essential preliminary to grammatical study, the synthetic principle is as opposed to grammatical analysis as it is to the analysis of a sentence into words.

The great development of analytic methods in modern times is partly the result of our fixed word-division in writing and printing, partly of the increasing elaboration of grammars and dictionaries, and partly of the growth of minute scholarship, philology, and etymology.

These analytic methods are often carried to a monstrous and almost incredible extreme in the historical and 'scientific' study of dead languages, as elaborated in Germany, and now being imported into this country. On this system, the words of an Old English or any other text are taken word by word and discussed etymologically, each word being transliterated into the form it assumes, or ought to assume, in the other cognate languages. The result of such a method is that the students learn a good deal about words, but nothing about the language itself, the sense of whose individuality is completely lost amid the chaos of conflicting associations.

Paradigms

A knowledge of the grammar by no means necessarily implies a knowledge of the language itself : the grammar with its rules and paradigms merely gives the materials for acquiring that knowledge. The schoolboy who has learnt his *túptō*, *túpteis*, *túptei*, *túptomen*, *túptete*, *túptousi* by heart has simply established a series of external associations between these six words, an association which is at first so strong that he is unable to get to his *túptei* or *túptousi* without repeating all its predecessors in order—an association of which the actual language knows nothing. It is not till such a context as 'the master beats the boy when he does not know his lesson' has been learnt in Greek, so as to establish an instantaneous association between thought and sound, that any real knowledge can be said to be gained. Nor does being able to state that *lune* in French is feminine necessarily imply a practical knowledge of its gender. When the student has learnt to associate *lune* with the article *la* or with the adjectives *belle*, *blanche*, he really knows its gender; till then he has simply transferred the '*lune*, subst. fem.' of his dictionary to his own memory, and has, after all, only facilitated his reference to a statement, not mastered the fact it involves. In the case of paradigms such as *túptō, túpteis, túptei*, there is a certain amount of natural association between the words— although so weak that we can scarcely imagine them ever coming together in one sentence—and this is one of the justifications of the practice of learning paradigms. But there is no natural association between *lune* and the word 'feminine,' or the letters *s.f.*, or with printing in small capitals—LUNE—as has been actually proposed as a means of learning the genders, and consequently these associations are useless; while the simple rule of never repeating *lune* without a preceding *la* establishes a natural association, and at the same time gives all the information contained in the statement that the word is feminine.

Learning Lists of Words

The worst kind of isolation is to begin the study of a language by learning lists of words by heart: 'if I learn two hundred words a day, I shall have a perfect knowledge of German in a fortnight.' It is conceivable that there may be a period when the learner finds it worth while to sum up his knowledge of the vocabulary of the language he is studying by running over ' *kopf* head, *auge* eye, *ohr* ear,' and so on; but the beginner is not concerned with isolated words, but with their combinations into natural sentences: it is no use telling him that *kopf* means 'head' when he wants to say 'the head' or to speak of 'heads;' nor would even the information contained in *der kopf*, 'head,' plural *köpfe*, be of any use to him till he had learnt some grammar, which again implies previous text-reading.

Detached Sentences; Context

As already remarked, we speak in sentences. But we do not generally speak in detached sentences; we speak in concatenations of sentences. In ordinary speech sentences are connected together in the form of a dialogue, which, again, often consists of an alternation of questions and answers. In books sentences are joined together into larger groups called paragraphs, which again form chapters, which again constitute a complete connected text.

The relations between sentences and texts are analogous to

those between words and sentences: both are relations of context.

Just as a word apart from its context may be ambiguous both in grammatical form and in meaning—for even in Latin we cannot tell, apart from the context, whether *boni* is genitive singular or nominative plural—so also, though in a less degree, the grammatical construction or the meaning of a sentence may be ambiguous when it is detached from its context. Hence, also, the meanings of words are brought out more clearly in connected texts than in detached sentences.

These considerations point clearly to the conclusion that the main foundation of the practical study of language should be connected texts, whose study must, of course, be accompanied by grammatical analysis.

But in a grammar, the rules must be illustrated and justified by examples, which also serve to strengthen the learner's hold of the rule, and to make it easier for him to recognize the working of the rule in the texts he reads. These examples must in the nature of things be detached words or detached sentences.

For this and other reasons we cannot dispense with detached sentences. But we must be careful to employ as far as possible only those sentences which will really bear detaching. Such a sentence, for instance, as *the sun rises in the east and sets in the west* conveys a perfectly definite and distinct meaning, and requires no further context. In grammars in which the examples are taken from the higher literature we often meet sentences which are almost unintelligible.

One of the great weaknesses of the *à priori* methods of the Ollendorff type is that they involve the substitution of detached sentences for connected texts. But detached sentences are not peculiar to these methods. They are the natural and inevitable result of all methods which make the grammar the centre of instruction instead of the texts. Widgery remarks (p. 47), quoting partly from Perthes :—

'Since the vain attempt to teach a language by means of short, disconnected sentences was introduced into Germany about seventy years ago, there has been a steady rise in the number of hours devoted to Latin, but the results are not better, nay, they are worse. After the French Revolution had given the death-blow to the real use of Latin as a means of communication, this new method was gradually evolved in the hope of infusing some show of life into the ghostly dilettanteism of "prose composition," that sickly branch of study kept alive only by the golden sap of prizes and scholarships.'

Storm remarks (Forbedret Undervisning, 17) with special reference to modern languages : ' It is but little relief in the study of a difficult grammar to have to ruminate hour after hour dry, detached sentences without a trace of connection, indeed often without intelligible meaning.' He then gives an extract from a manual of French, which he says is in pretty general use in Norway : *The more merit one has, the more modest one is. Thy sisters ate apples, and mine ate nuts. Receive, sir, the assurance of my high respect. These (!) threw bombs into the fortress in order to compel the besieged to surrender. Yield to his importunity, if you do not possess enough strength to make a resistance.* As he remarks, ' an intelligent pupil will ask, Who are *these ?* But such unintelligible language has simply a stupefying effect on most learners ; the meaning is entirely lost to them ; and how much they retain of the French form it is not difficult to imagine.'

In that form of the Ollendorff system developed by Prendergast in his ' Mastery Series,' each detached sentence is regarded as a bag into which is crammed as much grammatical and lexical information as it will hold. The following are examples of this ' sentence-cramming ' method as applied to French and German :—

' Pourquoi ne voulez-vous pas me faire le plaisir de passer avec moi demain chez le frère de notre ami dans la rue neuve ?

N'avez-vous pas besoin d'aller à Londres aujourd'hui, avant votre promenade du matin, chez le cordonnier français, pour faire élargir vos bottines ?

Dites au garçon, je vous prie, de m'apporter tous les jours sans faute, à sept heures ou plus tôt s'il peut, un pot d'eau chaude, une tasse de café au lait, et mes habits bien brossés.

Savez-vous comment se nomme cette vieille dame anglaise qui demeure près du pont neuf, dans la même maison ou il y a une famille française, et un jeune ministre allemand ?

J'ai eu pour moins de deux francs dans un grand magazin de Paris où tout se vend bon marché, du papier à lettre très-beau, des plumes métalliques excellentes, et un joli petit buvard.

Da er, der junge Freund des reichen Mannes, dem Diener den Brief nicht hat geben wollen, so werden Sie mir ihn gleich holen lassen müssen.

Wenn der alte und kluge Lehrer uns den guten Rath selbst gegeben hätte, würden wir diesen grossen Fehler kaum gemacht haben können.

Die kleine Freundin der schönen Dame liess sich die neue Kutsche nach der nächsten Station der Eisenbahn schicken, um in derselben zu der Stadt zu fahren.

Aber endlich schickte die Alte aus, und bestellte ihre Kiste, weil sie die Absicht hatte, die schon oft vorgehabte lange Reise sobald als nur möglich zu unternehmen.

Ich höre, dass das schon gestern Morgen früh erwartete Schiff selbst heute Abend, wie ich glaube, wegen des schlechten Wetters, schwerlich mehr hier ankommen wird.

Ein dringender Brief eines kranken Geschäftsfreundes, welcher mir so eben gebracht worden ist, nöthigt mich zu einem kurzen Ausflug, um einen keinen Badeplatz an der Nordküste von Deutschland zu besuchen.'

This attempt to give each word a context without overstepping the boundaries of a single sentence must be pronounced a failure. The sentences are quite as insipid as those of Ahn, and even more unnatural and impossible; the last sentence is practically nonsense as it stands. The construction of the German sentences is stiff to the last degree; observe the repetition of the 'split article' construction in two consecutive sentences (the fourth and the fifth). The incessant heaping of epithets—'the young friend of the rich man, the old and sagacious teacher'—is alone enough to give an uncolloquial, or rather exaggeratedly literary, character to these sentences (p. 52).

Association

The psychological foundation of the practical study of languages is the great law of association, to which we have frequently had occasion to allude already.

The whole process of learning a language is one of forming associations. When we learn our own language, we associate words and sentences with thoughts, ideas, actions, events.

The words themselves are associated into groups of various kinds. Thus such words as *tree, wood, forest* form an association-group by virtue of their meaning; the words *trees, woods, forests* also constitute a group in another way, namely, by all having the same plural inflection; all six words, lastly, are associated together by forming part of the grammatical group ' nouns.' These groups are independent of any linguistic context : even if we never met *tree* and *wood* associated together in one sentence, the mind would still pick them out and associate them together by virtue of the meaning and grammatical function they have in common. These groups often cross one another in different ways; thus *wooden* by its meaning belongs to the preceding group, but from a grammatical point of view it is outside it, and belongs to the same group as such words as *good, green.* These associations are unconscious, but none the less real : every speaker of English, even the most uneducated, knows instinctively what a noun is. The sole problem of grammar is to make these unconscious associations into conscious and analytic ones by defining and analyzing them, and stating them as briefly and clearly as possible by means of a suitable terminology.

The function of grammar is, therefore, to sum up the associations by which we all understand and speak our own language as well as any foreign languages we may learn. When we say that certain nouns are feminine in French, we mean that they are associated with certain forms of the definite article and other adjectives, which we call ' feminine,' because these forms are to some extent also associated with the idea of the feminine or female sex. We have seen that the practical way of learning genders is to start, not with the abstract grammatical statement, but with the actual associations themselves.

But when we have accumulated in our memory a certain number of direct associations such as that between *la* and *lune, maison, femme,* and between *le* and *soleil, garçon,* it is a help to have all these associations summed up in a brief statement, the more so as some of the associations connected with gender are complicated and contradictory. Thus the learner of French finds that (la) and (bɔn) are regularly associated together (la bɔn mɛzõ), while (lə) is generally associated with (bõ); he is then puzzled to find the collocation (lə bɔn ɔm). Here the grammar comes in, and saves him the trouble of collecting a large number of examples and comparing them, by informing him that such masculine forms as (bõ) assume the feminine form before a word beginning with a vowel.

Unconscious association is not, as we have seen, necessarily dependent on the actual juxtapositions which occur in language itself : there is a real unconscious association between the forms *túptō, túpteis, túptei*, between *see, saw, seen*, and between *am, is, are, be*, in spite of these four words not having a sound in common ; although, as these forms could hardly occur together in a sentence, the association is not so strong and direct as, for instance, between *la* and *maison* in French.   But they may easily be associated together in two connected sentences ; and such a dialogue as *are you ready? yes, I am ready, but he is not ; he will soon be ready though*, implies a definite association between the four verb-forms that occur in it; the dialogue would, indeed, be impossible if the second speaker had not a clear feeling that *I am* stands in the same relation to *he is* as *I see, I hear*, do to *he sees, he hears*.   There are two association-groups connected with every inflected word : one which connects it with all other words having the same inflection, as in the group *he sees, he hears, he comes, he is ;* another which groups together all the inflections of the same word, as in the group *I see, he sees, saw, seen—am, is, was, been, be—tree, trees—man, man's, men, men's*.   So also there are groups formed by derivation and other formal changes, such as *big, bigger, biggest— happy, happily, happiness, unhappy*, which again involve such groups as *bigger, stronger, less—biggest, least—happiness, goodness, unselfishness*.

This is an additional proof of the utility of grammatical paradigms.   A paradigm of the Latin declensions is simply a brief summary of these unconscious associations which we have just been describing.   A paradigm is useful both as a guide through the mazes of these often conflicting associations, and also as a test of the learner's practical mastery of them.   In this way, the being able to repeat a paradigm by heart, useless as it would be to the beginner, is a gain to the more advanced student, for it strengthens and reduces to order associations already partially formed—or, at any rate, prepared—by a natural process.

The following are the main axioms of the principles of association :—

(1) **Present the most frequent and necessary elements first:**

The first associations are the strongest, because they are the least disturbed by conflicting associations, because they have the longest time to establish themselves, and because the greater effort required in mastering the first elements fixes them more strongly in the mind. It is evident that in learning a language we should establish the strongest associations with —that is, we should begin with—the commonest and most necessary words, phrases, idioms, and constructions of the ordinary spoken language before proceeding to the vocabulary and style of the higher literature.

This principle has been well illustrated in our discussion of the relations of the spoken to the written language (p. 52), where we have also seen its importance in cases where cross-associations arise. When a foreigner learns archaic literary and modern colloquial English simultaneously, he constantly hesitates between such forms as *he hath* and *he has*, *quotha* and *he said*. But if he first forms strong associations with *he has* and *he said* exclusively, he can then form weaker secondary associations with *he hath* and *quotha* without much fear of their interfering with the primary associations.

(2) **Present like and like together,** and then
(3) **Contrast like with unlike till all sense of effort in the transition ceases:**
Thus in learning the English noun-plurals, the beginner may have the regular inflections exhibited in a variety of nouns. Then, when these are firmly fixed in the mind, he will have the mutation-plurals, such as *men, geese,* brought before him in a group, till they also are firmly fixed in the mind. Lastly, the regular and irregular forms may be contrasted in carefully selected natural collocations such as *hands and feet, ducks and geese, men and animals,* till not only the sense of discontinuity of association is overcome, but a new special association is formed between the contrasted words, so that the one suggests the other, and both in common suggest, and are suggested by, the idea of plurality. It is to be understood that this is not intended as a model way of learning English, but simply as an illustration of how the principle of association works under certain given conditions. So also in teaching German, it is a violation of the principles of association to put before the beginner such a contrast as that between *der band,* 'volume,' and *das band,* 'ribbon;' these words ought at first to be kept entirely apart and mastered separately, each in its natural

context. But when they have been learnt in this way, it is not only allowable but advisable to confront them, and call the learner's attention to the difference of gender. Otherwise he might be tempted to transfer the gender of the word he was more familiar with to the less familiar one.

(4) Let the associations be as definite as possible:

Thus in giving examples of the use of the ablative case in Latin, the grammarian should be careful to choose, as far as possible, sentences containing words whose ablative case is distinct from their dative. So also no text should be published for beginners without full phonetic information in the way of quantity-marks, stress-marks, and so on, in addition to all the helps that can be given by the use of the ordinary marks of punctuation, the use of italics, etc.: if the learner of Latin were taught from the beginning to recognize the distinction between such pairs as *labor*, 'labour,' and *lābor*, ' I slip,' *populus*, 'people,' and *pōpulus*, ' poplar tree,' by eye and ear, instead of having to rely entirely on the context, he would certainly learn to understand Latin quicker.

The common practice of withholding information of this kind with a view to exercising the learner's intellect and testing his knowledge is an example of the violation of this principle of association. Thus in text-books of Oriental languages it is usual to give transliterations only on the first few pages, not to mark the short vowels (in Arabic) after a certain page, adding them only when the learner is supposed to want them. But as no one can possibly tell beforehand the weak places in another person's memory, each learner complains that the information he wants is withheld, and that which he does not want is repeated over and over again. Gabelentz, in his Chinese grammars, shows his practical good sense by invariably giving transliterations however frequently the word may occur. It is a pure fallacy to imagine that withholding information and forcing the learner either to guess or waste time in seeking elsewhere for the information withheld adds to his knowledge: on the contrary, it not only puts superfluous mental labour on him, but also weakens his associations, and leads him into inevitable errors, which can be corrected only by still greater and more painful efforts. All examination and testing of knowledge should be reserved till there is reasonable ground for supposing that the learner has a firm grasp of the subject.

(5) Let the associations be direct and concrete not indirect and abstract :

The crude form system (p. 87) is an example of the fallacious substitution of indirect for direct associations : the learner has first of all a non-existent crude form or stem presented to him, and then is taught how to deduce from it the actually existing form which ought to have been presented to him at the outset.

All associations which involve remembering a certain order —first class, second declension, third conjugation—are indirect, just as calling a certain class of people 'the third estate' is less direct than calling them 'the commons,' which does not involve any knowledge of what the other two estates are, and what the order of the three estates is. All associations of order should be made direct, as when we call that group of strong verbs to which Old English *cēosan* belongs the 'choose-class' instead of expecting the learner to identify it by remembering its order in a series. The objection to going entirely by numbers is not only that it is difficult to remember the order, but also that all numbering is essentially more or less arbitrary, so that there is always a possibility of a variety of orders. Thus in my arrangement, the choose-class is the seventh, in Germany it is the second, while the name 'choose-class' has the double advantage of conveying information instead of being purely negative, and of being entirely independent of any changes of order.

Of course, if the order is part of the meaning of the words, the mere repeating of them in their order—which, on this supposition, is always a fixed and definite one—does establish a direct association with the meaning of each separate word, as when we repeat *one, two, three . . . , first, second, third . . . , Monday, Tuesday, Wednesday . . . , October, November, December, January . . . ,* and in a less degree in such groups as *north and south, east and west,* and *men, women, and children,* or *ladies and gentlemen,* because these orders may differ in different languages. Thus in Chinese the order of the four quarters is *nam, pek, si, tuη,* 'south, north, west, east.' The order in such groups is very strict in Chinese, and has great grammatical importance, for any deviation from the fixed order implies change of construction. Thus *tsï′ niü′,* 'son daughter,' means 'sons and daughters' on the principle of the male preceding the female; if this normal order is inverted, *niü′ tsï′,* the combination becomes attribute + noun instead of being co-ordinate : = 'female child.'

266

As a further illustration of the distinction between direct and indirect associations, if we wanted to distinguish between the two Mills, we might either state it abstractly by saying 'the elder Mill's christian name was *James;* he wrote the *History of British India* and . . . the younger Mill's christian name was *John Stuart;* he wrote a *System of Logic* and . . .,' or we might simply repeat to ourselves 'James Mill history of British India, John Stuart Mill system of logic . . .' It is evident that the latter method would establish more direct associations, because the association of ideas would be helped by the sounds and organic formation of the words themselves. Such mechanical and external associations are of the greatest help in learning languages.

(6) **Avoid conflicting associations** (cross-associations):

Attempting to teach a language through its nomic form and its phonetic transcription simultaneously would be an example of the violation of this principle. It also involves basing the study of a language at first exclusively on one definite dialect and period. Thus it involves not beginning to read Herodotus till one has a firm grasp of Attic Greek.

A striking example of the ill effects of cross-associations is afforded by the gender-lists which figure so prominently in some French and German grammars, especially the older ones. In these grammars we are told that a certain ending is feminine except in four words, which are given together with, perhaps, two words to serve as examples of the regular feminine gender. The result is that a stronger association is established with the irregular than with the regular forms. This is really worse than cross-association, it is 'inverted association.' A further objection to this procedure is that the lists of exceptions must either comprise a large number of rare and useless words, or else be incomplete and comparatively useless, for it is impossible to draw any definite line between rare and frequent, useful and useless words.

It is to be remembered that this axiom is only meant as a protest against unnecessary cross-associations caused by defective methods of teaching or defective statements of the phenomena of language. Those cross-associations which are inevitable— that is to say, which exist already in language itself, are dealt with under (3).

Memory ; Repetition

The next problem is, how best to retain these associations in the memory.

As even the strongest associations are liable to be weakened by disuse and lapse of time, the principle of **economy** is all-important : that is, of giving the learner only such material as he wants at the time or is likely to want within a short period. Thus, if he is to give a certain time to reading nothing but Cæsar's Commentaries, in which the verb occurs only in the third person, it is evident that if he is to be provided with a special Latin grammar for that purpose, it ought to exclude the first and second persons of the verb. In the German grammar I began with the word *hornung*, ' February,' was given as an exception to the rule that nouns in *-ung* are feminine, and for many years no German word was more familiar to me, except perhaps *petschaft*, ' seal,' whose acquaintance I made at the same time and in the same way. But to the present day I cannot remember having met with either of them in any Modern German book, still less of ever having heard them in conversation, *hornung* being now entirely obsolete except in some German dialects. At last, when I began Middle High German, I met with it for the first time in my life in a poem of Walther von der Vogelweide, but by this time I had forgotten all about it, and so failed to recognize it, especially as it appeared in the slightly disguised form of *hornunc*, which, I know not why, made me guess it to mean ' hornet.' I am glad to see that this and other words of a similar character are now often omited from German grammars.

Economy teaches us to begin with as small a vocabulary as possible, and to master that vocabulary thoroughly before proceeding to learn new words. In this, and in many other ways, it confirms the general principles of directness and simplicity.

Repetition is essential both for forming associations and retaining them in the memory.

It is an additional argument for working as long as possible with a limited vocabulary, for the smaller the vocabulary, the greater chance the different words, forms, and constructions have of being repeated.

But there is a point beyond which repetition becomes wasteful —and in two ways. In the first place, the excessive repetition of one detail hinders the due repetition of other details. Secondly, such excessive repetition is wearying to the learner, who is already familiar with the detail in question, and so any further repetition of it causes his attention to flag. This is the great danger of using grammatical illustrations made on the impulse of the moment by the writer instead of being collected from a variety of texts by different authors. In such illustrations certain words and constructions tend to recur with a frequency of which the writer is unconscious until he revises what he has written from this special point of view. He will then find that in a chapter on the syntax of the numerals he has, perhaps, given one particular numeral five times as often as any other, and has omitted to give any examples at all of some of them, when he might just as well have utilized his sentences to give each of the more important numerals a fair proportion of examples.

The various devices of artificial memory or memoria technica are of even less use in language than in other branches of study. The whole business of learning languages consists in establishing associations, which can often be effected only by long-continued effort. It is therefore a waste of energy to take on oneself the additional burden of the extraneous associations by which an artificial memory is built up.

Such devices as printing feminine nouns in a dictionary in capitals are liable to similar objections, and are quite superfluous (p. 100).

Of course, if extraneous associations come unsought, they should—and, indeed, inevitably will—be utilized, as in the cases already discussed under the head of 'accidental resemblances' (p. 91). But most of these are not strictly parallel to memoria technica—at least, not those in which the association between the two words is direct, as in *hólos* = whole, and does not require the introduction of a third element.

Some of the methods recommended under the head of 'nomic pronunciation' (p. 34) have also a resemblance to memoria technica, but they are simply cases of the modification of the materials of existing associations.

Learning by heart should not be attempted till the piece has been thoroughly studied from all sides. To learn a piece by heart before it has been properly studied and grammatically analyzed is often rather injurious than otherwise, as it tends to take away the sense of interest and freshness, and to deaden and blunt the observing faculties.

Besides, by the time the piece has been thoroughly studied, the knowledge implied in learning by heart will have come of itself if the learner has a fairly good memory. If he has not, learning by heart is simply a waste of time. If he cannot retain in his memory even a short, simple poem in his own language, he cannot be expected to learn by heart in a foreign language; and if he can learn his own language by imitation and reproduction after a pattern without learning by heart, he can do the same with a foreign language.

Interest

Memory depends also on attention, and this partly on the interest taken in the subject. If we take no interest either in the language itself or the text we are reading, our attention inevitably flags. The genuine linguist, on the other hand, is only stimulated all the more by difficulties. Oriental languages are more difficult than European languages, but they have the charm of remoteness and complete novelty, and stimulate curiosity and interest to the highest degree, so that in learning them we endure drudgery which would seem intolerable if spent on a comparatively insipid Romance language, which we half know beforehand.

But we must be careful not to confuse interest in the literature with interest in the language. An absorbing interest in what we are reading, speaking, or hearing, so far from helping us to remember and observe the phenomena of the language, has the opposite effect. If the reader is 'panting to arrive at the thrilling *dénouement*' of a sensational novel, he is certainly not in the mood for observing niceties of syntax.

Another difficulty is that the unfamiliar is what is interesting, while all sound principles of linguistic study tell us that we ought to begin with the expression of those ideas and the descriptions of those things and circumstances which are most familiar to us, or will be so when we have acquired the language. In learning French we ought to begin with what is common to both France and England, French and English life, and when we pass beyond English associations, to be initiated gradually into French ones: we do not wish to

270

accompany Jules Verne into the heart of Africa. Nor will reading about exciting adventures of Englishmen in New Guinea give a foreigner a good vocabulary for a visit to London.

Then, again, all reading that is profitable from a linguistic point of view must at first be very slow, and interrupted by incessant repetitions; and no text can be very interesting under these conditions.

If the learner is interested in the language itself, that is enough. If he has a strong motive for learning the language as quickly as possible as a means to an end, or simply because he wants to get through the drudgery as quickly as possible, he will regard those texts as most satisfactory which bring him to the goal with the greatest ease and quickness; that is, he will prefer texts in which the meanings of words and their constructions unfold themselves easily from a simple context of progressive difficulty, in which there is repetition enough to help the memory, and yet variety enough to keep the attention on the alert. He will prefer such texts as long as they are not ostentatiously trivial and vulgar, to more interesting ones with which he feels he is not making the same linguistic progress. If he has to choose between an anecdote of a Lacedemonian and an Athenian, a fable about a fox and a goat, a funny story about a red rose, 'Twinkle, twinkle, little star,' and a description of the furniture of a drawing-room, he may possibly choose the latter for a variety of reasons : because he knows the anecdotes already, because he does not care for poetry, but mainly because he thinks the description of a drawing-room may teach him some words which he cannot find explained in his dictionary, and which may be useful to him when he visits the country itself.

The Gouin-method is a good instance of the 'interest-fallacy.' According to Gouin himself, his series-method was first suggested to him by observing a nephew of his, who, after seeing a mill for the first time, began to play at being a miller, talking all the time to himself, 'First I fill the sack with corn—then I put it on my back and carry it to the mill . . . the water falls on the mill-wheel, and the wheel goes round—the wheel turns the millstone—the millstone grinds the corn,' and so on. Gouin fails to see that there is a wide difference between taking a lively interest in a novelty and being interested in the

I

vocabulary connected with the object after it has ceased to be a novelty. Even while the child was playing at being a miller, its interest was not in the words, but in what the words expressed: the attitude of its mind was that of the absorbed novel-reader. We know how soon the child's mind tires of any one object of interest; and we may be sure that if a year afterwards M. Gouin's nephew had had to go through the same mill-series in a foreign language, the old interest would not have been forthcoming, and the youth would perhaps have declined to take part in any series in which tin soldiers and a popgun did not figure. If the old interest had been forthcoming, it would have been as much a hindrance to mastering the details of the foreign language as in the case of the novel-reader. Besides, all children are not equally interested in the construction of a mill, even when it is a novelty; and certainly some of the series, such as that which gives a detailed description of opening and shutting a door—'I walk towards the door, I approach the door, I approach nearer, I approach nearer still, I put out my arm, I take hold of the handle'—are as uninteresting as they are useless.

As I have indicated already, the only safe concessions that can be made to interest are negative: be dull and commonplace, but not too much so.

Thus, although repetition is essential, there are some kinds of repetition which are so wearisome to the learner that they can hardly be used in teaching, in spite of certain special advantages they possess. I mean such methods as that of repeating a long Latin speech in *oratio obliqua* in order to show the accompanying changes of construction, or of conjugating a whole sentence through a variety of moods and tenses. It is strange that Gouin, who attaches so much importance to stimulating the pupil's interest in the subject-matter, should advocate teaching the verb by means of such repetitions as these: 'To-day the postman will come before we have breakfast—while we are at breakfast—after we have had breakfast. Yesterday the postman came before we had breakfast . . . to-morrow the postman will come before we have breakfast . . .' Such methods should only be used occasionally in the grammar, not made a standing feature of the method.

Relations between Texts, Grammar, and Vocabulary

We have seen that the traditional division of the materials and apparatus for the practical study of languages into

(1) Connected texts—the reader,
(2) Grammar,
(3) Dictionary, vocabulary,

is founded on the nature of things.   We now have to consider the relations between these three.

We have already come—either expressly or tacitly—to the following conclusions on this subject : that the beginner's grammar ought to deal only with the inflections and constructions which actually occur in the texts he is reading, and that the dictionary—if a dictionary is used at all—ought to take the form of a special glossary to those texts.   My *Anglo-Saxon Primer* is a simple typical example of this threefold division in a single book.

Deducing Grammar from Texts.—But some reformers go further than this.   Some of them go so far as to abolish grammar altogether, at least in the elementary stages, and train the pupils to deduce the laws of the language—the rules of grammar—from the texts they are reading.

An obvious objection to this plan is the time it would take. The most practical way of collecting materials for grammatical investigations is to write each quotation on a separate slip of paper, adding the necessary headings, and then to sort the slips under these headings.   I am told that the great English lexicographers of the present day look down with contempt on anything less than a ton of such materials ; but I am sure that by the time the boys had sorted a hundredweight or so of slips, they would have had enough of it ; and by the time the master had gone over the work of a biggish class of boys, he would have had enough of it too, and would perhaps welcome the suggestion of one of the German reformers, namely, that of using copybooks with printed headings and blank spaces to enter the quotations in.   But even when all the boys' mistakes had been corrected, the material would still be defective, and would require to be supplemented from other texts.   To make a long story short—the master would find it best in the end to do the work himself; and at last, perhaps, a happy thought would dawn on him : Why not print the whole thing? The book would be useful to other teachers, and it might pay. When the book was published, the author would discover to his astonishment that the result was nothing more or less than an ordinary grammar.

These considerations show that this method would be a failure, if carried out on any large scale. It would involve great waste of time and effort as compared with the ordinary grammatical methods. And there would be a sense of unreality about it : teachers and pupils alike would feel that they were only playing at grammar—pretending that they had to make their own grammar, while they knew perfectly well that the work had been done for them long ago, and that the results were accessible in hundreds of grammars of every degree of elaborateness. This method of 'inventional grammar' would be highly useful as an occasional stimulus and exercise for the pupils, but there its legitimate sphere of usefulness would end.

Such inventional methods—of which Spencer's *Inventional Geometry* is a good type—have often been tried in various branches of education. There is certainly something plausible in the idea of making the learner's progress consist in finding out by himself the solution of a series of problems of progressive difficulty and perplexity, till at last he stands on the highest pinnacle of knowledge with the proud consciousness of having arrived there entirely by his own efforts. But although these inventional methods excite great interest at first in the minds of the more gifted pupils, those who are less original and slower in mind instinctively rebel against them, and all, sooner or later, get tired of their sham originality.

As regards the difficulty of the problems or other work involved in inventional methods, if we look at the question from the point of view of the average learner, we have to face this dilemma : if the work really requires much thought or originality of mind, it will be too difficult for them, or, at any rate, will cause them to make so many mistakes that the labour of establishing correct associations will be far greater than it is worth; if, on the other hand, the work is so easy as not to tax the intellectual powers of the pupils, it will cease to excite their interest.

But there is a method allied to the inventional which may

form an integral part of a systematic course of linguistic study—that is, the method of **inductive grammar.**

It is only the fully developed mind of the adult that can plunge straight into the study of the grammar of a foreign language. A less developed mind, one which is less used to dealing with general and abstract statements, requires to start with something more individual and concrete. There is, besides, as we shall see hereafter, a pre-grammatical stage in every progressive course of linguistic study—whether for children or adults—in which no grammar is taught, but only the materials on which grammar is based, that is, sentences and short texts. In the case of very young children, the pre-grammatical stage is, indeed, the only one suitable for their intelligences.

Now, although the grammar is rightly banished from this stage, it is possible to familiarize the pupils with some of its principles almost from the beginning, that is, as soon as they have read or heard enough to furnish a few examples of some grammatical category. Thus, as soon as they have met with three or four examples of a certain case or other inflection, the teacher calls their attention to this category by writing the words containing that inflection on the blackboard, and making them see what these words have in common, as far as is possible without using any technical or abstract terminology. In the same way he can collect together on the blackboard from the texts already read the scattered words which make up such a paradigm as *I am, you are, he is.* When this has gone on for some time, the teacher may expect the pupils to find out for themselves what grammatical category a word belongs to. This, then, is the deductive method of teaching grammar, or rather of preparing for the systematic study of grammar. It is capable of various stages of development, according to the mental development of the pupils, according as the grammatical categories are left undefined, or are stated explicitly in more or less technical and abstract language. As already remarked, there will be no harm in varying the course of inductive grammar by an occasional application of the inventive method—letting the pupils find out some of the categories by themselves—although, for the reasons already given, this ought not to be made an integral part of the course.

After all, the main thing is that the texts and the grammar should be intimately associated, and studied as much as possible simultaneously—the exact order is generally of less importance.

Stages of Progressive Method: Irregularities

I will now give a general sketch of a rationally progressive method of linguistic study on the principles already discussed.

The complete course may be divided into five stages: (1) the mechanical; (2) the grammatical; (3) the idiomatic and lexical (dealing with the vocabulary of the colloquial language); (4) the literary; (5) the archaic.

(1) The first stage, the **mechanical,** begins with a thorough mastery of the pronunciation of the language which is being learnt, which presupposes a general practical knowledge of phonetics based on the sounds of the learner's own language. Every sentence must be practised till it runs glibly off the tongue without effort or hesitation. Even with a thorough preliminary training in phonetics, this will take long practice at first, until the learner is familiar with the organic basis of the language. The result will be that at first everything will practically be learnt by heart. Hence the importance of carefully choosing the most instructive words and sentences for these phonetic exercises, and of associating every word and sentence with its exact meaning—in the case of sentences by means of idiomatic translations, together with a translation of each word separately.

As the energies of the pupil will be mainly taken up by phonetic difficulties—especially if his previous phonetic training is either defective or altogether wanting—there will be no time for grammatical analysis. Even the analysis into separate words need not be carried farther than the translation of the ' full words,' the meaning of the form-words—the prepositions and other particles—being left to be gathered from the context. Such idioms as *how do you do?* in which words are used in special meanings which they do not otherwise have, might also be left unanalyzed—partially at least. But it would be advisable, perhaps, to exclude such idioms from the first stage. To omit word for word translation altogether would be carrying the mechanical principle to an irrational extreme : we do not wish our pupils to fall into the error of the student who was being examined in the Greek Testament, and after translating *néos oînos* correctly as ' new wine,' was asked ' which is *new* and which is *wine*,' whereupon, suspecting a trap, and distrusting the similarity between the Greek and the English forms of the words, he answered '*néos* wine, *oînos* new.'

Irregularities.—The phonetic exercises should, as already implied, include some of the most necessary and frequent elements of the grammar and vocabulary, and, perhaps, some of the most indispensable idioms.   In this way many of the irregularities could be learnt in this stage, and they would be learnt without effort, for the learner would not know that they were irregularities.   Thus to a foreign beginner who has not learnt any English grammar, the regular singular *feat* and the irregular plural *feet* are on exactly the same level—they are purely phonetic difficulties, the difficulties being identical in both—and it is not till he learns the grammar that such a collocation as *hands and feet* causes any hesitation through associations which tend to make him change it into *hands and foots*.   It is indeed possible that *foots* is more difficult to him than *feet*—of course on phonetic grounds.

This would be the solution of what from a strictly grammatical point of view is an insoluble dilemma.   The dilemma is this: the irregular forms are the most frequent, and should therefore be learnt first; but in the grammar the irregular forms must necessarily be subordinated to the regular ones.   The answer is, as we see, that irregularities are psychological, not mechanical difficulties, and should therefore be mastered in the mechanical stage.

When some progress has been made in the first stage, the learner may be allowed to read short texts of the simplest character—still without any grammatical analysis.

The time spent on the first stage will depend on the conformation of the learner's mind.   If his mind is mature and quick to grasp general principles, he will remain in this stage only as long as is necessary to give him a thorough command of the pronunciation, which, again, will depend partly on his natural aptitude for phonetics, partly on the degree of training he has had in practical phonetics.

In the case of immature or slow minds the first stage may be indefinitely prolonged.   The more it is prolonged, the more will phonetic considerations be subordinated to those of grammatical structure and the acquisition of a useful vocabulary, so that the texts will become longer and more varied, and

277

the method of grammatical induction will be more and more applied.

(2) The **grammatical** stage. It is evident from what has been said that the transition from the first to the second stage may be either quick and abrupt or slow and gradual, and that the two stages may overlap in various ways.

This second stage presupposes a thorough mastery of the pronunciation and the acquisition of a certain amount of materials for grammatical study in the shape of words, sentences, and texts whose meanings are known. What further preparation for grammatical analysis has been made will depend on the length and character of the first stage.

In this stage the texts will be so chosen as to embody the different grammatical categories in progressive order of difficulty as far as is compatible with employing genuine texts which reproduce the actual language. The texts will naturally become longer and less simple in style and subject, and will embody a more and more extensive vocabulary. But as the vocabulary is in this stage entirely subordinated to the grammar, there will be no attempt to develope the vocabulary systematically. It will be taken into account only from the negative point of view of keeping out rare and superfluous elements, and using as small a vocabulary as is consistent with general efficiency.

In most cases the grammatical training will consist in a gradual expansion of the deductive method, till the learner is able to read with profit a grammar founded on the texts he is studying together with those he has learnt in the first stage. When he has gone through his first grammar, he will begin again at the beginning and revise all the texts in the first stage from a grammatical point of view.

The study of grammar is not confined to the second stage, but is necessarily continued through all the following stages. At the end of the second stage the learner will be able to read a general grammar—one that takes its material from the whole of the language, not merely from the texts already read—but this grammar will necessarily deal only with the modern colloquial language. The student will not be able to read a grammar that includes the literary language till he is in the fourth stage, and for historical grammar he will have to wait till he has finished the fifth stage.

The historical study of grammar lies outside the domain of the practical study of languages. Even if we admit, with Storm and the majority of German linguists, that the study of historical grammar and comparative philology 'is practical in a higher sense, because it facilitates the comprehension and acquisition of the facts,' we cannot admit that it is an essential part of the practical study. We only have to ask ourselves the question whether three years spent in the exclusively practical study of a language, or the same time spent partly in practical, partly in theoretical studies such as historical grammar, would yield the better results. We cannot hesitate in answering that the latter method would be a failure as compared with the former, if only because it would not allow time for acquiring the necessary practical knowledge of the older periods of the language. If we extended the period to five years, the disparity as regards practical results would not be so glaring, but the advantage would still be on the side of the purely practical course.

(3) In the **idiomatic** and lexical stage the idioms will be learnt systematically, partly from reading idiomatic texts, partly from a phraseology in which the idioms will be classed under psychological categories, as will be explained hereafter.

At the end of this stage the learner will have acquired a thorough command of a limited number of words and phrases and idioms expressing the most necessary ideas. His vocabulary will not be large—perhaps not more than three thousand words—but he will command it with ease and certainty.

Those who learn a language through its literature often have as wide a vocabulary as the natives, but have no command of the elementary phraseology: they know words, but do not know how to combine them, except from a purely grammatical point of view. They are, indeed, often unable to describe the simplest mechanical operations, such as 'tie in a knot,' 'turn up the gas,' or express such ideas as 'make haste' or 'what is the matter?' As Storm remarks (Forbedret Undervisning, 22), there are hundreds of expressions in French, which, although they occur incessantly in conversation, are seldom or never taught in the ordinary school-books because they cannot be brought under the conventional rules of grammar. Hence even those who have learnt French for years do not know that, for instance, the French for 'it is kind of you' is *c'est aimable à vous*, not *de vous*, and that 'it smokes here' cannot be translated by *il fume ici,* which means 'he smokes,' but only by *ça fume ici.* 'Very few have the gift of being able to learn such expressions from books. The material afforded by literature, even in that form of it which approximates most closely to the colloquial language, namely, novels and comedies, is such a medley, so varied, and so mixed, and often so difficult, that one expression drives out the other; the reader has enough to do to understand the contents, and has not time to concentrate himself on the separate expressions. The great art is, not to learn everything, but to take note of the special expressions that one really requires; but this is an art which only very few are capable of.'

All this points to the necessity of a systematic study of the vocabulary and phraseology of the language, which should begin in this stage, and be carried on in the next stage as well, where it will have the further use of helping to prevent confusion between the colloquial and the literary language.

It must be understood that the study of the phraseology is only a part of the study of the vocabulary, as given in an ideological dictionary, as explained hereafter. The learner should begin with phrases and idioms, and then study the whole of his vocabulary from the ideological point of view.

(4) The **literary** stage. As our ideal student advances, he will be able to choose his texts with greater freedom and with less subordination of matter to form, till at last he is able to enter on the fourth stage, and begin to read the actual literature unmodified and uncurtailed, beginning, of course, with ordinary prose, and proceeding gradually to the higher prose literature and to poetry.

There is no reason why some literary texts of exceptional simplicity should not be read in the previous stage. In fact, simple poetry might be read almost from the beginning, for the metrical form is generally an effectual bar to any cross-associations with the divergent forms of colloquial prose. The greatest danger of confusion is with the antiquated or artificial colloquial style of the drama.

In the course of this stage the learner will begin to acquire the nomic spelling of such unphonetically written languages as French and English. In dealing with less unphonetic languages, the nomic spelling may be begun earlier. With others the nomic spelling will be used almost from the beginning.

The learner will henceforth be able to dispense with the phonetic transcription altogether, except when he wishes to refresh his memory for purposes of conversation.

(5) The **archaic** stage presupposes a thorough mastery of the modern literary language in its most important branches, as far, at least, as understanding it goes.

In proceeding to the older literature of such a language as English, he may either work his way back through Milton to Shakespeare and Spenser, or he may begin at once with Old English (Anglo-Saxon), and work his way down through Chaucer to the modern period.

The choice between these two main lines of study and the details of the study will, of course, depend on what his objects are—especially on whether his interests are purely linguistic, or whether he means to use his knowledge of the language as a key to literary, historical, or other non-linguistic studies and investigations.

CHAPTER XI

GRAMMAR

GRAMMAR, like all the other divisions of the study of language, has to deal with the antithesis between form and meaning.

Accidence and Syntax

The fact that in language there is generally a divergence between form and meaning—as when the idea of plurality is expressed by a variety of forms, and sometimes by none at all (*trees, men, sheep*), or when the same form is used to express distinct grammatical functions (*he sees the trees*)—makes it not only possible, but in many cases desirable, to treat grammatical form and grammatical meaning apart.

That part of grammar which concerns itself simply with forms, and ignores the meanings of the grammatical forms as far as possible, is called **accidence** or 'forms' (German *formenlehre*); that which concentrates its attention on the meanings of grammatical forms is called **syntax.** Thus under accidence an English grammar describes, among other details, those of the formation of the plural of nouns—how some add -*s*, some -*es*, while others mark the plural by vowel-change, and so on. In the syntax, on the other hand, the grammar ignores such formal distinctions as are not accompanied by corresponding distinctions of meaning, or rather takes them for granted, and considers only the different meanings and grammatical functions of noun-plurals in general. The business of syntax is, therefore, to explain the meaning and function of grammatical forms, especially the various ways in which words are joined together to make sentences. As the form of a sentence depends partly on the order of its words, word-order is an important part of syntax, especially when it serves to make such distinctions as

124

in the English, *the man saw the fox first*, and *the fox saw the man first*. In fact, word-order is the most abstract part of syntax, just as word-order is the most abstract grammatical form.

In accordance with its etymology, syntax is by some grammarians regarded entirely from this latter point of view, so that it is by them identified with the analysis of sentences, the meaning of grammatical forms being included under accidence. Thus the peculiar meaning of the plural inflection in such words as *sands, leads, waters of the Nile*, would by such grammarians be discussed under accidence, on the ground that accidence deals with isolated words, syntax only with combinations of words into sentences.

Although the application of grammatical terms cannot be allowed to depend on their etymology, yet, as we cannot avoid saying something about the meaning of grammatical forms under accidence—if only to discriminate between such inflections as *trees, John's, comes*—it is often convenient to clear off this part of the grammar under accidence, especially if the variations of meaning are only slight, or else so great that they cannot be brought under general rules.

The whole question is, after all, one of convenience. The separation of meaning from form is a pure matter of convenience, and is not founded on any logical necessity, but only on a defect of language as it is, for in an ideally perfect language form and meaning would be one—there would be no irregularities, no isolated phenomena, no dictionary, and what is now dictionary and grammar would be all syntax. Even in languages as they exist form and meaning are inseparable, so that the separation of accidence and syntax must always be a more or less arbitrary one, which may vary in different languages, quite apart from any questions of convenience.

Formal and Logical Syntax

The duality of form and meaning allows us to study syntax from two points of view. **Formal** syntax starts from the grammatical forms, and explains their uses ; **logical** syntax starts from the grammatical categories expressed in language generally, and describes the different forms by which they are expressed, as when we describe the different ways in which predication is expressed—by a single verb, by the verb *to be* with an adjective or noun, and so on. So also in logical syntax the two constructions *man's disobedience* and *the disobedience of man* would be treated of under the same head, while in formal syntax the one would go under 'inflections of nouns,' the other under 'prepositions.'

It is evidently the first business of syntax to deal with the phenomena of language from the formal point of view, reserving logical groupings till all the grammatical forms have had their functions explained.

G. v. der Gabelentz seems to have been the first to insist on the distinction between formal and logical—or, as he calls them, 'analytic' and 'synthetic' grammar (Gab. 86, 90). In his larger Chinese grammar he has tried to carry out the distinction in detail.

Grammar and Dictionary

We have seen that grammar deals with those phenomena of language which can be brought under general rules, while the dictionary deals with isolated phenomena—especially with the meanings of separate words.

But not of all words. It is clear that while the meaning of such a word as *man* or *house* belongs to the dictionary, that of such a word as *of* in *the disobedience of man* belongs to the grammar, for it has exactly the same function as the *-s* of the genitive case : it cannot, indeed, be said to have any meaning of its own at all.

From the point of view of the practical study of languages, such a question as whether or not the prepositions are to be treated of in the grammar as well as the dictionary, and the further question whether all of them, or only some of them, are to be included in the grammar, must be answered by showing whether or not the acquisition of the language will be facilitated thereby ; and this will depend on the structure of each language.

Accidence and Syntax Taught Together

We have seen that there is no real necessity for the separation of accidence and syntax. Although practical convenience often seems to call for a separation, there may be circumstances under which it is desirable to treat forms and their grammatical functions and meanings together.

In Beyer and Passy's *Elementarbuch des gesprochenen Französisch* this principle has been carried out consistently. Thus, under 'definite article' first the forms are given (la mɛɛr, le pɛɛr, dy pɛɛr), and then under the heading 'gebrauch' (use) the syntax of the definite article is given. In dealing with the verb, the forms are first given in a lump, the periphrastic forms as well as the inflected being given, and then the 'gebrauch.' But this arrangement is only a compromise : it simply amounts to giving a chapter of accidence and a chapter of syntax alternately, instead of printing all the chapters on accidence together, and then giving the chapters on syntax together. In going through such a book as this, one feels doubtful whether it is not after all more convenient to have the accidence all together, so as to facilitate reference to the paradigms and other sources of information, instead of having to search through the whole grammar for them.

In my *First Steps in Anglo-Saxon* I have also tried the experiment of teaching accidence and syntax together. So far from subordinating syntax to accidence, I have in some cases advocated teaching syntax first, and for the following reasons, as stated in the preface to the book : ' Inflections may be recognized in two ways : by their form—as when we know that a noun is in the dative plural by its ending in *-um ;* and by their function—as when we infer from a word expressing more than one person and standing in the indirect-object relation that it is a noun in the dative plural. Of these two methods of parsing —the formal and the ⸗syntactical—sometimes one is easier, sometimes the other. There is therefore every reason why elementary syntax should be learnt simultaneously with accidence. It seems irrational to oblige a beginner to recognize such a grammatical category as the subjunctive mood solely by irregular and perplexing inflections, when such a simple rule as "it is always used in indirect narration" may enable him to recognize a large number of subjunctives with mathematical certainty.'

In accordance with these principles, I have in the grammar to *First Steps in Anglo-Saxon* blended accidence and syntax together more closely than in Passy's book. Thus under 'cases' I first describe the formal peculiarities of each case, and then describe its functions. One of the advantages of this arrangement is that the syntactical examples serve to imprint the formal details more firmly on the learner's memory, being, in fact, chosen partly for that purpose. In beginning the verbs, I confine myself at first to the indicative mood together with the infinitive and participles. Then, when I have given a general sketch of the different classes of verbs from this limited point of view, I go on to describe the forms of the subjunctive mood, and how they differ from those of the indicative, which takes up only half a page; I then devote two pages to stating the chief rules for the use of the subjunctive, with examples. In this way the danger of confusing the forms of the subjunctive with those of the indicative—and in Old English these two moods are especially liable to be confused—is reduced to a minimum.

Stages of Grammatical Analysis

In this book I have also tried to do justice to another important principle of practical grammar, namely, that grammatical analysis has two stages, one of **recognition** or identification, and another of **reproduction** or construction. As I say in the preface, ' The first requisite is to understand written texts, which involves only the power of recognizing grammatical forms, not of constructing them, as in the further stage of writing or speaking the language. Thus in beginning the second text in the present book, a learner in the first stage is expected to find out for himself that *manna* is in the genitive plural, and that *cræftum* is in the dative plural, and to infer from the ending -*ne* in *hwelcne* that *cræft* is masculine. He will then be able to infer with tolerable certainty from what he has learnt in the grammar that the plural of *cræft* is *cræftas*, but this inference belongs really to the second stage : a learner in the first stage is only expected to recognize the inflection of *cræftas* when he meets it. The first object, therefore, of a simplified grammar is to give what is necessary to enable a beginner to recognize the grammatical forms in the texts he is about to read. . . . The first thing is to explain the general structure of the language— that in Old English, for instance, nouns have three genders, that the gender is partly grammatical, that nouns have four cases— and to state those general rules which admit of no exception, such as that all nouns in -*a* are masculine, and that compound nouns follow the gender of their last element. Those irregular forms which are of very frequent occurrence—such as the inflections of the definite article—must of course be learnt by heart at once, the learner relying on their incessant repetition

286

to fix them in his memory. Less frequent irregularities need not be included in the grammar at all, their explanation being relegated to a note [to the texts]. . . . In dealing with the strong verbs, it will be seen that after giving a general account of their formation and a few general rules —such as that in the preterite the second person singular always has the same vowel as the plural—I content myself with giving the typical forms of each verb in a note to the passage where it first occurs. . . . In some cases where there is more than one form, but without there being any great complexity or irregularity, I steer a middle course : I mention the various forms, but without giving any rules for their use. Thus I merely say that most strong neuters take -*u* in the plural or else remain unchanged. . . . In the grammar I have been careful to group parallel forms together as much as possible. Thus under " cases " I give the inflections of nouns, the definite article, and the personal pronouns all together, so that, for instance, the learner may make *them, her* stepping-stones to *pǣm, hire, pǣre*, and afterwards to the corresponding strong adjective inflections. The occasional paradigms are in most cases not intended to be learnt by heart, but serve only to sum up the scattered information already given.'

I then go on to say, ' All these principles are those which are carried out—consciously or unconsciously—by most linguists. An experienced linguist in attacking a new language begins with the shortest grammar he can find. He first takes a general bird's-eye view of the language, finds out what are its special difficulties, what has to be brought under general rules, what to learn detail by detail, what to put off till a later stage. The rash beginner who starts with a big grammar forgets two-thirds of it soon after he begins independent reading. Such a grammar as the one in the present work simply attempts to give him the really useful residue which, when once learnt, is not and cannot be forgotten.'

Grammar Learnt Unconsciously

We have already seen how the first or mechanical stage of learning a language, being the pre-grammatical stage, may be utilized to convey a good deal of grammatical information not directly through rules, but indirectly through examples, so that when the learner comes to the rule, he finds that he knows it

K

already, or, at any rate, has advanced half way towards knowing it—a result which is a special help in mastering irregularities (p. 119). Thus in the grammar to *First Steps* I give under the phonology, among other examples of the vowels, *twā handa*, 'two hands,' *twēgen fēt*, 'two feet,' *twēgen menn*, 'two men,' so that when the learner comes to the numerals, he finds that the paradigm

$$\underbrace{tw\bar{e}gen \quad tw\bar{a} \quad tw\bar{a}}_{\substack{tw\!\!\!\!^{\bar{æ}}m \\ tw\bar{e}gra}}$$

offers hardly any new difficulties; for he finds the above examples repeated with a reference to the place where they occur, but without any translation, together with *mid twǣm handum* as an example of the dative, whose ending -*m* is already familiar to him, from the nouns and adjectives. The only remaining form *twēgra* is sufficiently illustrated by the parallel genitives *prēora* and *prītigra*, of which I proceed at once to give examples in sentences. The form *twēgra* is only added to complete the paradigm, as it does not occur in the texts in *First Steps*, for which reason no special example is given of it.

It will be seen that after the learner has gone through such a book as *First Steps*, in which the grammar is kept strictly within the limits of the recognition-stage, a great part of his grammatical knowledge will be unconscious instead of analytic and systematic. Thus he will know a good many individual forms of strong verbs, but will know nothing of the distinctions of class. Thus he may know that *brecan* has preterite *bræc* and preterite participle *brocen*, but he has not learnt to refer it to the bear-class, although he may have noticed the parallelism between *bræc*, *brocen* and *bær*, *boren*, and may have strengthened this association by remembering the further parallel *stelan*, *stæl*, *stolen*. In this way he will be well prepared for the classification of the strong verbs. A few weeks' work at the *Anglo-Saxon Primer*, which is constructed on the rigorous grammar-and-glossary historical method—though otherwise made as simple and easy as possible—will then, as I have said in the preface to *First Steps*, enable him to 'systematize his knowledge and round it off, and he will proceed to the elements of historical and comparative grammar with all the more zest through not having had them crammed into him prematurely.'

Evils of the Separation of Syntax from Accidence

The evils of the separation of syntax from accidence are well shown in the way in which the dead languages are taught in schools. Boys are made to learn paradigms by heart, and are then set to read the classical authors with the help of a dictionary before they have acquired any real knowledge of the meanings of the inflections they are expected to recognize in their texts—much as if they were taught the names of tools without being taught their uses. Thus in learning Greek they are taught to recognize the optative mood entirely by its form without having any idea of its meanings and functions as distinguished from those of the subjunctive, of which, indeed, they come to regard it as an arbitrary and unmeaning variation; to which may be added that their ideas about the meaning and function of the subjunctive mood itself are vague enough. When they are afterwards made to learn the rules of syntax, they are unable to apply these rules to what they are reading, and in most cases the possibility of doing so never enters their minds: they prefer to go on as before, and to guess at the meaning from the context without paying any regard to the moods. It is not very long ago that the rules of Greek syntax were learnt in Latin—an effectual bar to any intelligent application of them.

Examples

It is now generally admitted that a grammatical rule without an example is of no practical use: it is an abstraction which is incapable of entering into any direct associations with anything in the language itself. The example, on the other hand, is concrete: it can be imprinted firmly on the memory by the mere force of the mechanical associations involved in carefully reading it and carefully pronouncing it aloud; while, on the other hand, it is logically associated with the rule, which it explains, illustrates, and justifies. The example serves also as a standard or pattern by which the learner can recognize other examples of the rule as they occur in his reading. The example is thus a link between these other examples and the rule itself.

Many of the older grammarians, while expending much

thought and care on elaborating their statement of the rules, considered the choice of examples as of subordinate importance. They forgot that the first object of grammatical study is not the acquisition of rules, but of a practical command of the language itself; so that instead of the examples being intended solely to illustrate the rules, the true relation is almost the reverse: the rules are mere stepping-stones to the understanding of the examples; so when the latter are once thoroughly understood, the rules become superfluous and may be forgotten.

These considerations have led some reformers to advocate putting the example before the rule, the idea being that the learner is thereby led to study the example carefully and then deduce the rule for himself, and finally compare his deduction with the rule as formulated in the grammar. This is the old inventional fallacy (p. 116) over again. Experience shows that when the learner knows that the work of deducing the rule from the examples has been already done for him, he naturally declines to do it again, so that, if the rule is put after the example, he simply reads the rule first, and then returns to the example. If, however, he prefers to read the example first, there is nothing to prevent him from doing so, whether it precedes the rule or not. Most learners prefer to read the rule first in order to know what the example is about, and what to look for in it—for a sentence may be, in itself, an example of a dozen rules of grammar—and if they do not understand the rule, they then read the example and return to the rule again, and when they finally understand the rule, they concentrate their attention on the example. We may say, in short, that the order of rule and example is of no importance compared with their mutual relations.

The number of examples depends partly on the nature of the rule, partly on the scope and size of the grammar.

Some rules hardly require any example at all through being practically of universal application, or self-evident, or because they are of no intrinsic importance, and are added only for the sake of completeness. But it is a safe principle never to take for granted that a rule does not require an example: if adding a few words in parentheses will make the statement or rule any easier to grasp, or prevent some misunderstanding that the writer never thought of, they certainly ought to be added. If they are superfluous, no harm is done. Besides, what is superfluous to one reader may be helpful or even necessary to another. German writers often exasperate the reader by giving half a page of examples of some pet truism that requires only two words to illustrate and prove it, and then make a series of abstract generalizations expressed in unfamiliar and arbitrarily defined terminology without any help in the way of example, so that they often become unintelligible even to their own countrymen.

If every rule is to have an example, it follows that a compound rule ought to have an example of each division of the rule. Thus, such a rule as that 'verbs expressing joy, desire, memory govern the genitive' requires at least three examples. But in such a case as this many short grammars would give only one, on the mechanical principle that each paragraph is to have only one example. Even in the shortest grammar space may generally be found for a full number of examples by omitting some of the irrelevant matter of which such ill-planned books are generally full.

If there is not room for more than one example to those rules which really seem to require it, additional examples to those rules that most require it may be given in a separate book.

A good example must fulfil two conditions: (1) It must illustrate and confirm the rule unambiguously. Thus, as already remarked (p. 107), examples of the use of the ablative in Latin should, if possible, be forms which cannot be taken for datives. (2) The example must be intelligible as it stands, without any further context. If the example is a sentence or is contained in a sentence, the sentence should be one which will bear isolation from the context. In dealing with separate words, it is often a great help to the learner to give them in natural groups such as *hands and feet, buy and sell, past, present, and future, dead or alive, neither here nor there*. The more concrete a word is, the better it will bear isolation. It is mere waste of space to give bare lists of prepositions, conjunctions, and other form-words in an elementary practical grammar.

It need scarcely be said that the examples must be in the language with which the grammar deals. Thus no one would think of illustrating a rule of Spanish syntax by a Portuguese example. But it is almost as great an absurdity to illustrate rules of modern English syntax by examples taken from Shakespeare, except in special cases where the earlier constructions have been imitated by modern writers. All of this would, however, be quite out of place in a practical grammar for beginners.

Carrying this principle a little further, we must be careful that our examples in an elementary grammar do not contain any specially difficult or rare words or irregularities of construction which do not directly illustrate the rule.

Examples made up extempore for the purpose of illustrating a rule are not so good as those which have been collected from a variety of writings. There is, first of all, the danger of monotonous repetition of words, ideas, and constructions. In the effort to frame collocations of words to illustrate some rule, the grammarian is apt to produce unnatural, trivial, or otherwise objectionable sentences, such as *the golden sun shines brightly | the happy children of our teacher sing sweetly enough from their book of hymns*, both taken from an English grammar of some repute in its time.

Every example ought to be explained—even in the phonology. The translation of a new word not only gives a useful piece of information, but serves also to identify the word.

But the explanation need not necessarily take the form of translation. There is one objection to translating the examples in a grammar: the learner is tempted to read them carelessly, and so not get all the benefit that would result from a conscientious analysis of them. In my *First Steps in Anglo-Saxon* I have therefore tried the experiment of putting the explanation of the examples in the grammar on the same footing as the words in the texts, as far as possible, so as to oblige the learner to read the examples with the same care as the texts themselves. At the beginning of the grammar each example is translated in full. When a word or word-group or sentence is repeated in the grammar, it is not translated, but the learner is referred back to the place where it is translated; and after the first few pages each new word in the examples is explained in the notes at the end of the book. Hence the reader is obliged to study each example carefully, and with constant comparison of what he has already learnt, while at the same time he has every inducement to learn thoroughly every page before proceeding to another.

Paradigms

The paradigms and tabulations in an elementary grammar ought to be regarded mainly as summings up of what has already been learnt indirectly or in the form of scattered details (p. 129).

The principle of combining words into groups rather than presenting them singly (p. 133) should be carried out in paradigms for beginners as far as possible. Thus, in dealing with an inflectional language, nouns should be accompanied by the definite article or some similar word, adjectives by a noun whose gender is known. In Old English and German the weak inflection of adjectives should be exhibited in its natural surroundings, that is, with the definite article as well as a noun. This, I believe, is generally done in the German grammars used in England. To take an example from Old English, it is evident that such a collocation as *þone gōdan witan* must strengthen the associations by which the learner has already learnt to recognize *þone* and *witan* as accusative masculine singulars, so that the weak inflection *gōdan* offers no new difficulty, while the preceding definite article always reminds him of the syntactical conditions on which weak adjective-inflection depends.

From this point of view the Middle-Age grammarians with their incessant *hic, haec, hoc* were really more practical than their successors. It was not the old grammarians' fault that Latin had no article; and they certainly took the best substitute they could find. So also were the old-fashioned French grammars when they indicated the subjunctive mood by the addition of *que: que je sois, que tu sois . . .* I need hardly say that I follow this precedent in my *First Steps:* indicative *ic wearþ*, subjunctive *þæt ic wurde*.

In a paradigm, the first requisite is clearness and simplicity: such words must be chosen as will best bring out the grammatical phenomena in question without perplexing the learner by complications arising from special sound-changes and other disturbing factors. Hence it may happen that the number of words suitable for the purpose is but small. Thus in Old English, if we look for a simple adjective to show the feminine ending -*u* without any accompanying vowel-change in the body of the word, we shall hardly find any but *sum*, while there is a wide choice among those which drop the -*u*.

The question now arises, whether we ought to keep the same word throughout a paradigm or series of paradigms, or whether the examples ought to be varied as much as possible. In such Old-English paradigms as

Sing. Nom.	*gōd crǣft*	*gōd cild*	*gōd cwēn*
Acc.	*gōdne crǣft*	*gōd cild*	*gōde cwēne*

·   ·   ·   ·   ·   ·

and

Sing. Nom.	*sum crǣft*	*sum cild*	*sumu cwēn*
Acc.	*sumne craft*	*sum cild*	*sume cwēne*

·   ·   ·   ·   ·   ·

which are intended to bring out the distinction just mentioned, there is the minimum of variety: we must have two different adjectives, and we must have three different nouns to bring out the three different genders. It might now be urged that the associations of gender would be strengthened by giving each noun a different adjective—thus *gōd crǣft, geong cild, wīs cwēn*. But the scarcity of adjectives with feminines in -*u* would make it difficult to carry out this variation in the second paradigm. It must also be remembered that by keeping one adjective throughout in each of the two paradigms the contrast between the two is made more definite, and at the same time the unity of each paradigm is asserted more strongly. The principle of variety is carried to an extreme in the following paradigms taken from Bernay's German Grammar and German Exercises :—

ich wurde gelassen	I became very calm
du wurdest böse	thou becamest angry
er wurde gehorsam	he became obedient
wir wurden ungehorsam	we became disobedient
ihr wurdet blasz	you became pale
sie wurden ausgemergelt	they became emaciated
ich sey hell-blau oder himmel-blau	I may be light-blue or sky-blue
du seyst purpur-farbig oder scharlach-roth	thou mayest be purple or scarlet

294

ich habe den muth des kriegers gelobt	I may have praised the courage of the warrior
du habest die farben des gemäldes gelobt	thou mayest have praised the colours of the picture
er habe den inhalt des werkes gelobt	he may have praised the contents of the work

It must be understood that these are not given as substitutes for the ordinary paradigms, but as an appendix to the grammar. They are in fact strings of detached sentences, or 'exercises' which are not written, but learnt by heart. All the objections that can be made against the system of detached sentences apply with double force to such paradigms. They are intended to serve the double purpose of fixing the inflections in the learner's mind and at the same time systematically enlarging his vocabulary; but as there is no association between the sentences except the indirect one of their belonging to the same logical category, and as the association between the head-word of the paradigm and the added words is very slight, learning these paradigms does not help us to remember the vocabulary they embody much more than if we fell back on the old plan of learning bare lists of words (p. 100).

But the unity of paradigms may be carried too far. In Arabic the connection between the different conjugations or classes of verbs is so close that the same verb-root can occur in a variety of classes—sometimes in nearly all. It is therefore usual in Arabic grammars to make up the paradigms as far as possible with one verb-root, such as *fa'al*, 'do,' or *qatal*, 'kill,' thus—

    I. *qatala*, II. *qattala*, III. *qātala*, IV. *aqtala*, V. *taqattala*, VI. *taqātala*, VII. *inqatala*, VIII. *iqtatala*, IX. *iqtalla*, X. *istaqtala*.

This is as if in Latin we were to make *am-* the sole basis of our paradigms of all the conjugations: I. *amare, amat;* II. *amēre, amet;* III. *amere, amit*; IV. *amīre, amit.* The parallel is not a fair one, because many of the forms of *qatala* given above actually exist. But, on the other hand, such a form as the ninth is a complete monstrosity, this class being practically confined to expressions of change of colour. It is clear, therefore, that the only appropriate verb-root for this class is such a one as *safar*, 'be yellow;' in fact, it is doubtful whether any one would be able to give the ninth form of *qatal* or *katab* except with much hesitation and comparison with a genuine ninth-class form such as *isfarra*, 'become yellow.' It is a question, therefore, whether it would not be better for Arabic grammar to follow the example of Latin, and exemplify each class with a distinct verb-root, thus:

I. *kataba*, 'write;' II. *sallama*, 'give up;' III. *qātala*, 'fight;' IV. *arsala*, 'send;' V. *takallama*, 'speak;' VI. *tarāhana*, 'bet;' VII. *inkasara*, 'be broken;' VIII. *iktasaba*, 'gain;' IX. *isfarra*, 'turn yellow;' X. *istahsana*, 'approve.'

It will be observed that the formation of the eighth class by insertion of a *t* after the first consonant of the root is clearer in *iktasaba* (from root *kasab*) than in *iqtatala* with its two *t*'s.

On the whole, this method has the double advantage of keeping the different classes more distinct, and giving each a greater individuality, while at the same time it enlarges the learner's vocabulary—a point of great importance in the study of Arabic, whose vocabulary is so exceptionally difficult.

Fullness of Treatment

As regards fullness of treatment, there is an obvious distinction to be made between a grammar—whether for beginners or advanced students—which is to be assimilated completely so that the learner at last practically knows it by heart, and one which is only for reference.

The latter will aim at being exhaustive wherever reasonable and practicable, and will perhaps give information on a variety of subjects which would be omitted altogether in the learner's grammar. Thus it may give rules for the gender of nouns with almost exhaustive lists of exceptions—all of which would be superfluous to the ordinary student, who learns his genders simply by associating each word with the definite article, or some such equivalent as the Latin *hic, haec, hoc*. So also the reference-grammar ought to give information on a variety of subjects which belong to the debateable land between grammar and dictionary. The alphabetic index to such a grammar and the lists scattered through it will, indeed, be almost dictionaries —or at least the foundations of dictionaries.

Brevity is, of course, in itself a desirable quality in any grammar, especially in one intended for reference: the more matter is brought together on a page, the easier and quicker the reference is, in a grammar as well as in a dictionary. In an elementary grammar, where fullness of explanation and illustration is indispensable, brevity can only be obtained by strict limitation of plan and exclusion of everything irrelevant or in any way superfluous. Brevity in an elementary grammar must never be obtained by omitting what is essential—by omitting examples, translations, transliterations, or any other necessary helps. Most of the grammars of the *Porta linguarum orientalium* series err in this respect.

Such grammars often waste space by giving information which has nothing to do with the practical elementary study of the language, such as histories of its literature, sketches of its dialects, long bibliographies, weights and measures, not to speak of etymologies and comparisons with cognate languages. I do not mean to say that much of this information is not useful in itself, nor would I deny that in some cases an appendix to a grammar may be its proper place, but it must not be allowed to encroach on what is essential from the purely grammatical point of view.

As examples of legitimate condensation I would mention Gabelentz' *Anfangsgründe der chinesischen grammatik* and Ásbóth's *Kurze russische grammatik.*

CHAPTER XII

THE DICTIONARY; STUDY OF THE VOCABULARY

IT will, perhaps, be most convenient to begin with that aspect of the dictionary which makes it the reverse of the grammar. From this point of view we have already defined a dictionary as a collection of the isolated phenomena of a language—those which cannot easily and conveniently be brought under general rules. It follows from this that the main function of a dictionary is to give the meanings of separate words. Some dictionaries confine themselves strictly to this function. But a dictionary which does not sacrifice everything to giving as large a vocabulary as possible in the shortest space ought to give a good deal more than this.

Idioms fall entirely within the province of the dictionary, because the meaning of each idiom is an isolated fact which cannot be inferred from the meaning of the words of which the idiom is made up : a dictionary which explains the meaning of *do* without explaining that of *how do you do?* is useless as a guide to the meanings of words.

A thoroughly useful dictionary ought, besides, to give information on various grammatical details, which, though they fall under general rules of grammar, are too numerous or too arbitrary and complicated to be treated of in detail in any but a full reference-grammar : such a dictionary ought to give full information about those grammatical constructions which characterize individual words, and cannot be deduced with certainty and ease from a simple grammatical rule. Thus it ought to give full information about the prepositions by which verbs are connected with the words they govern (*think of, think about, think over, part from, part with*). Such a dictionary ought further to give the anomalous and irregular forms, especially those which are of only occasional occurrence, so

140

that the learner cannot reasonably be expected to be perfectly familiar with them.

A full dictionary of this kind is obviously suited for reference only. All grammars—even the most detailed reference-grammars—can be read through with profit; but few would think of reading through an ordinary dictionary. It need scarcely be said that M. Gouin, who tried every conceivable method of learning German—that is, all except a rationally progressive one on a phonetic basis—tried this also. He took a dictionary of three hundred pages, and not only read, but learnt by heart ten pages a day, so that in a month he knew the whole dictionary by heart. Such, at least, is his statement. The result was what might have been expected: he could not understand a word of German, and in a month he forgot all he had learnt.

Ease of reference involves alphabetic order, as in the index to a grammar. In fact, an ordinary alphabetic dictionary is, in some respects, simply an expanded index to a reference-grammar.

We will now consider the principles on which such dictionaries ought to be constructed.

Scope

As convenience of reference requires that a dictionary should be as little bulky as is consistent with efficiency, it is advisable that its scope should be distinctly defined and strictly limited. A dictionary of English for practical use by foreigners, or a French or German dictionary for practical use by English speakers, is, in the nature of things, mainly a dictionary of the present stage of these languages: its foundation is the modern colloquial and literary language, which involves, of course, the inclusion of a certain number of archaic words used in the higher literature, together with a certain amount of slang and vulgarisms and those dialectal words which have found their way into general literature and conversation.

Such a dictionary as the *New English Dictionary*, which attempts to include the whole English vocabulary from 1200 to the present day, is not, even from a purely scientific and theoretical point of view, a dictionary, but a series of dictionaries digested under one alphabet. Such dictionaries have no practical interest. This applies with still greater force to comparative dictionaries, such as Fick's *Indogermanisches wör-terbuch.*

Most of our larger English dictionaries are also compromises between an expanded dictionary and an abridged cyclopedia. The fundamental distinction between a dictionary and a cyclopedia is, that the dictionary has to explain *words*, the cyclopedia has to explain *things*. The main function of the dictionary is to identify each word with its meaning or meanings, and give the details of its linguistic use as far as they do not fall entirely and exclusively under the province of grammar. This is clearly shown in the use we make of dictionaries of foreign languages. If we are ignorant of the meaning of the French word *fleur*, we look it up in our French-English dictionary, where we find the English translation 'flower,' without any further comment, it being assumed that we know what a flower is. We feel that the translation is a surer guide to the meaning than the most elaborate definition. In an English dictionary for English people the same method of translation is followed as far as possible : *commence* and *purchase* are defined by being translated into the simpler 'begin' and 'buy,' and we fall back on definition only when absolutely obliged to do so. Some of the more naïve among the older dictionaries openly give up the attempt to define by such evasions as telling us that *dog* is 'the name of a well-known animal.' Even Walker's celebrated definition of a *flea* as 'a small insect of remarkable agility' would be of little use to any one who did not know already what a flea was.

But it may happen that in reading French we come across the name of some flower that is not found out of France, or, at any rate, not in England, so that when we look up the word in the French dictionary, the only explanation we find is 'name of a flower' with, perhaps, the botanical name, which probably conveys no meaning to our minds; we have not, therefore, learnt anything from the dictionary beyond what we could probably have gathered from the context without any further help. Nevertheless, the dictionary has done everything in its power to identify the word with the thing expressed by it; it is our want of knowledge of the thing itself which prevents us from profiting by the dictionary's identification. If we look up the botanical name in a cyclopedia, we can acquire a more or less definite idea of the thing itself—the flower.

There can be no question of the usefulness and convenience of the brief explanations of the ideas and objects expressed by rare words which our larger dictionaries give: these explanations afford the reader enough information to enable him to form an idea of the real nature of the thing represented by the unfamiliar word without obliging him to wade through a sea of detail.

But it is a question whether it would not be better to publish such information in a separate book than to mix it up with the legitimate material of a dictionary—namely, the identification of familiar ideas with the words which express them. An educated Frenchman just beginning English is ignorant of the meaning of the commonest verbs and adjectives in English, but he will not require to be told what *oxygen* is, or how *lithography* is carried on. It is not meant that these words should be excluded from a practical dictionary; on the contrary, they are examples—especially the latter—of a numerous class of words which form a debateable ground between necessary, everyday words and purely special and technical words.

A further reason for separating the special or encyclopediac from the general or lexical words lies in the different treatment they require. While the former demand, or, at least, allow, a more or less elaborate and lengthy description of the thing they denote, accompanied, perhaps, with pictures or diagrams, they are generally barren from the linguistic point of view, for they offer neither varied shades of meaning nor irregularities of form, nor do they enter into idiomatic combinations or special grammatical constructions. With the lexical words the relations are reversed: the greater the number of irregularities of form a word offers, and the more complex and varied its meanings and idiomatic combinations and special constructions are, the more indispensable for expressing ideas, and the more independent of encyclopediac treatment it is sure to be.

We arrive, then, at the result that for purposes of practical study of modern languages we require dictionaries which are strictly limited to the modern language, and exclude all encyclopediac elements—that is, all words of which it is conceivable that an educated native might say that he had never seen them in literature or that he did not know what they meant. Such a dictionary would, of course, include debateable words, unless it were intended for very elementary purposes, in which case it might exclude even such words as *abacus, habeas corpus, iambic, nabob, oxygen.*

But it would be very difficult to lay down any general principles by which we could exclude all encyclopediac words without hesitation, and the ordinary compromise has its practical advantages.

Pronouncing Dictionaries

Most dictionaries of modern languages are at the same time pronouncing dictionaries, the pronunciation being indicated either by the addition of stress-marks and other diacritics, or by a complete phonetic transliteration of each word, the last method being the only practical one with such languages as English and French. Separate pronouncing dictionaries are the most convenient for reference. It might be worth while to shorten them by the omission of all words in frequent use, which no one could help knowing who had learnt the language in a phonetic transcription, but it would be difficult to draw the line. A complete pronouncing dictionary ought to include proper names.

The usual arrangement in a pronouncing dictionary is to give the words in their nomic spelling and add the phonetic transcription. Michaelis and Passy's *Dictionnaire phonétique de la langue Française* is an interesting example of the reverse order, which is more scientific, but less convenient for reference.

We have hitherto assumed that the dictionary covers the whole field of the language it deals with. A dictionary which deals only with the words occurring in certain definite texts is called a glossary. Of such nature are the glossaries to primers and readers. Glossaries admit of the same variety of arrangement and scale of size and fullness as complete dictionaries. Such glossaries as those to Grein's edition of the Old English poetry and to Windisch's *Altirische texte* are on the scale of a large scientific dictionary.

The field of a dictionary may also be diminished negatively —by excluding certain classes of books. This can only be done in dead languages like Latin, where we have excellent school dictionaries such as Smith's, restricted to the vocabulary of the books read by schoolboys, which are numerous enough to give the complete elementary vocabulary of the language.

Such an abridgement has the great advantage of making the dictionary smaller without diminishing its efficiency for its special purpose. The practice of cutting down a big dictionary by simply omitting all quotations and shortening the definitions and other details results in an inferior book of the type of Liddell and Scott's *Abridged Greek-English Lexicon*.

Fullness

Most dictionaries contain much that is superfluous. Many of them, while excluding idioms and other really indispensable details, retain hundreds of compound and derivative words which any one acquainted with the meanings of their elements can understand and form himself without any difficulty and with perfect certainty. Such a word as *hatless*, for instance, has no more claim to be included in a practical English dictionary than the phrase *without a hat* has. The same applies also to most of the compounds found in German and Dutch dictionaries. Thus in a Dutch dictionary I find nearly half a column of words such as *tijgerbek*, 'mouth of a tiger,' *tijgerkop*, 'head of a tiger,' *tijgerpoot*, 'foot of a tiger,' *tijgeren*, 'belonging to a tiger.' So also the explanation of such German compounds as *knopfmacher*, 'button-maker,' *salzsteuer*, 'tax on salt,' is for most practical purposes superfluous. Not till a compound or derived word has developed a meaning which cannot be inferred from the meanings of its elements is it necessary to give it an independent place in the dictionary. Even in an exhaustive thesaurus it is not necessary to do more than simply enumerate self-interpreting derivative and compound words under the first element without definition or translation.

Besides these 'half-superfluous' words, all dictionaries contain a large number of words which might safely be omitted from a dictionary intended for foreigners on the simple ground that many educated speakers of the language in question might be found who have never met with them, or, at any rate, have forgotten their meaning. Some of these are encyclopediac words (p. 142), some are completely obsolete, some are coinages of some more or less obscure writer which no one else has ever used or quoted, and some, lastly, are simply mistakes—spurious, non-existent words. As a specimen of the way in which our

L

dictionary-compilers heap up useless material—mainly, it would seem, to be able to boast of ' having ten thousand words more than any other dictionary '—I may quote the following series of words taken in their order without omission or addition from an English dictionary for foreigners published not so very long ago : *bezan, bezant, bezel, bezoar, bezola, bezonian, bezzle, bhowanee, bhung, bia, biangulate, biangulated, biangulous, biangular.* A student might read English literature for ten or twenty years without meeting with any of these words, although some of them are quite genuine.

Such words might be collected into a special dictionary for occasional reference, the space gained in the ordinary dictionary being then utilized for the fuller presentation of idioms and other necessary details.

Most dictionaries are not at all liberal in giving space to idioms and phrases. When they are, they ought to exercise the same criticism as with single words. A practical elementary dictionary for foreigners ought to exclude all completely obsolete phrases and idioms ; and all dictionaries, whether for foreigners or natives, ought to let the reader know whether each idiom is still in use or not. As a specimen of idioms which foreigners are taught to regard as genuine modern colloquialisms, I will quote the following choice expressions which I find under the word *back* in an English dictionary for foreigners published in the latter half of the nineteenth century : *the back side of a knife* | *a strong back* = ' a rich man' | *I can make neither back nor edge of him* | *to show one's back* = ' act in a cowardly manner' | *to beat a person back and belly.* I doubt also whether many English people know what *dancing the Paddington frisk* is, which the same dictionary gives as an idiomatic expression for being hanged. In none of these cases does this dictionary give any indication of the idiom being at all antiquated or obsolete.

Conciseness

The greatest drawback to the use of a dictionary is bulkiness. The mere physical labour of pulling volume after volume of a big dictionary off the shelf and then replacing them is alone enough to deter the student from the attempt to utilize the material stored up in them. And few can spare the time to search through the mass of material accumulated under the common words ; so that such dictionaries are used mainly as sources of information about rare and encyclopediac words.

However much the scope of a dictionary may be reduced by rigid adherence to one period of the language, and by exclusion of everything extraneous or superfluous, it is always worth while to reduce its bulk still further by carrying brevity and conciseness as far as is consistent with clearness and convenience.

The first requisite is a sense of proportion, by which the amount of space taken up by a word is proportionate to its importance from a linguistic, not from a historical or scientific or any other extraneous point of view. The test of this in an ordinary dictionary is the fullness of treatment of the commonest words and the relatively small space given to rare words. A short dictionary or glossary which gives whole columns to historical or biographical details, and dismisses prepositions in a few lines, shows the want of proportion in its extreme. The glossary to Derembourg and Spiro's *Chrestomathie élémentaire de l'Arabe littéral* is an example of this want of proportion.

The next condition of conciseness is the systematic use of contractions. Thus in my *Student's Dictionary of Anglo-Saxon* instead of the lengthy *w. dat. of pers. and gen. of thing* I write simply *wdg.*, which is unambiguous and easy to remember, especially as I shorten *dative* itself into *d.* Again, in the same dictionary, by adding to each strong verb the number of its class, I dispense with the addition of *str. vb.*, while, at the same time, the omission of any number shows that the verb is weak.

Much, too, may be done in the way of shortening and saving space by the use of marks, such as the familiar * to indicate hypothetical or non-existent forms, † to indicate archaic or poetical words or forms. Muret's *Encyclopedic English-German Dictionary* and the other similar dictionaries published by the firm of Langenscheidt in Berlin make a systematic and extensive use of these and other devices for securing the greatest possible conciseness and convenience.

Surveyability

Surveyability—what in German is called *übersichtlichkeit*—is the greatest help in finding a word in a dictionary. It implies, in the first place, getting as much as possible on to each page.

The pages ought, therefore, to be square and three-columned, except in 'pocket-dictionaries,' most of which, however, will hardly go into an ordinary pocket. The other condition of surveyability is the judicious use of varieties of type and special marks to catch the eye. Lastly, everything that tends to promote conciseness necessarily works in the same direction.

The larger the dictionary, the more urgent does this consideration become. When a word extends over several pages of quotations, only occasionally interrupted by the definitions of the meanings, it is often a matter of great difficulty to find any one meaning in this sea of quotations, as every one knows who has had occasion to consult Littré's large French dictionary or the *New English Dictionary*. This difficulty is met in an ingenious manner in the Langenscheidt dictionaries. In them the meanings and definitions are given in a lump without any quotations, being merely numbered; then the quotations are given in a lump immediately after the body of meanings and definitions, the number of the definition being repeated before each group of quotations by which it is illustrated, the body of quotations being marked by a vertical waving line on one side of it.

Meanings

The first business of a dictionary is to give the meanings of the words in plain, simple, unambiguous language. There must be no 'etymological translation' (p. 88), no translation into obsolete or dialectal words. When we look up *lǣce* in an Old-English dictionary and find it translated 'leech' as well as 'physician,' we ought to be quite sure that *leech* here has its genuine modern meaning, and is not a mere repetition of the meaning of the other word.

Again, some dictionary-makers think it necessary to translate every slang or colloquial word or expression in one language into a slang word or expression in the other language. The result is that they sometimes use some provincial or obsolete word or expression which may be quite unintelligible to the majority of their readers, and, indeed, may soon become unintelligible to all of them, for nothing becomes obsolete sooner than a certain class of slang colloquialisms. Most languages are so ambiguous in themselves that it is folly to go out of one's way to make them more so; and in a dictionary everything is detached and isolated, so that there is but little context to help. In fact, without the help of quotations it is almost impossible to define meanings with certainty. As I remark in the preface to my *Student's Dictionary of Anglo-Saxon*, the best method is to add part of the context in ( ): thus I explain *ādragan* by 'draw (sword),' *seomian* by 'hang heavy (*of* clouds),' where the italic *of* stands for 'said of' or 'applied to.'

Quotations

Quotations are next in importance to definitions. Indeed, in a large dictionary or thesaurus, the quotations are *the* dictionary, and their arrangement is a matter of almost subordinate importance. They cannot, of course, be given with any great fullness in most short dictionaries. But in some cases a quotation is both shorter and clearer than a definition. All sentences that have anything of the character of proverbs or formulæ deserve a place in every dictionary. Such sentences, indeed, can hardly be regarded as quotations, any more than idioms, which are as much a part of the common stock of the language as the words themselves: like them, they cannot be constructed *à priori*.

References

References in a full dictionary of a dead language for scientific purposes should be to the line and page of the text where the form occurs or whence the quotation is taken. But as the number of the page may vary in different editions, it is better to number the paragraphs, the reference to which is enough, if they are short; if the paragraphs are long, or if accuracy of reference is required, the lines of each paragraph may be numbered, and a reference made to the line as well as the paragraph. In referring to such a work as the Saxon Chronicle, the lines of each year should be numbered separately in this way, except, of course, where a year takes only a few lines. In my *Anglo-Saxon Reader* each piece is numbered from beginning to end, and in the glossary the references are to the number of the piece and its line. The advantage of such methods of reference over that of referring to the page is not only that the references are independent of the size and number of the pages of different editions, but also that the reader soon learns to remember each piece by its number, while in the case of such a work as the Saxon Chronicle it is of the greatest importance to know what year each reference belongs to.

Where exact reference is impracticable or superfluous, it is still a great advantage to know at least what book or author or what larger dictionary a word is taken from—thus, in an English dictionary it may make a good deal of difference whether a word is taken from Bailey's dictionary or from some such writer as Rudyard Kipling. Marks such as † often serve the purpose of such general references.

Grammatical and Other Information

Grammatical information is especially necessary in the case of constructions, such as what case or preposition a verb or adjective takes after it, and of irregularities.

Information about pronunciation and varieties of spelling is indispensable in many languages. In a Chinese dictionary every character—that is, every word—must be transliterated. In Giles's great Chinese-English dictionary every character— of which this dictionary contains about eleven thousand—is transliterated into the pronunciation of eleven dialects with their tones, the standard rhyming word being also given.

This last example might be followed with advantage in many other dictionaries—at any rate, so far as to mark words that occur in rhyme, or at the end of the line; thus in such a text as the Middle-English Ormulum the fact of a dissyllabic word occurring at the end of the line shows that the last syllable but one is long; so if a word like *fader* were quoted from the Ormulum in such a dictionary without any indication of its occurring at the end of the line, this would be an argument in favour of the *a* being short. It need hardly be said that in a full scientific English dictionary information should be given as to the history of the pronunciation of each word whenever it shows any special features or irregularity of development. It is, for instance, much more the business of such a dictionary to tell us how Hart, Bullokar, and the rest pronounced than to give us the cognate forms of the words in the other Germanic languages.

Arrangement, Word-order

The ordinary alphabetic arrangement followed in European dictionaries has the merit of being fixed and uniform, with a few exceptions, such as the Scandinavian practice of putting *ä* and *ö* together at the end of the alphabet. The German practice of ignoring the distinction between *ä* and *a*, *ö* and *o*, is more practical.

But this alphabetic arrangement has no other merits, for the order of the letters is entirely arbitrary. It is a question whether it would not be worth while to alter it in one respect in which it would be easy to agree, that is, in putting all the vowels together: *a, æ, e, i, o, ö, u, y, b, c, d* . . . It is most inconvenient in an Old English dictionary to follow such a word as *ierfe* through its various spellings *ærfe, erfe, ierfe, irfe, yrfe* from one end of the alphabet to the other. And similar fluctuations may occur in any language which has not a fixed orthography. It is also unfortunate that *c, k, q, x* do not follow in immediate succession. Any further attempts to remodel the order of the alphabet on phonetic principles would be a failure; for, much as we may envy the Sanskrit alphabet its rational order, it would be hardly possible to choose between the great variety of more or less reasonable arrangements—as, for instance, between *tdnpbm* and *tdpbnm*. But we are always at liberty to make certain obvious concessions to the peculiarities of each language, such as putting all words beginning with *k* under *c*, or *vice-versa*.

All deviations from the traditional alphabetic order which are not recommended by considerations of direct utility and convenience should be regarded with suspicion, unless, of course, they amount to a complete abandonment of the alphabetic order, and the substitution of a logical for a formal arrangement. To this we shall return hereafter. Otherwise, as the whole justification of the existing alphabetic order is its convenience, there can be no rational motive in departing from it except convenience. All such innovations as separating long from short vowels—*ab, ac, ad* . . . *āb, āc* . . . instead of *ab, āb, ac, āc*—on the ground that this will oblige the learner to pay attention to distinctions of quantity, are inconsistent with the first principles of the alphabetic arrangement.

But different languages require different arrangements. In

English we expect to find every word in the dictionary simply by looking it up under its initial letter. In Welsh, with its initial consonant-mutations, this will not do : we may have to look up such forms as *dad* and *nhad* under *tad*, and *fam* under *mam*. Even in German we cannot expect to find *genommen* under *g-*, while, on the other hand, we do find *gebirge* under *g-*, not under *b-*. As *ge-* is a still more moveable prefix in Old English, it seems legitimate to disregard it entirely in the alphabetic arrangement of an Old English dictionary, and make it an invariable rule that all words beginning with *ge-* are to be sought under the letter following the *e*. The practical justification of this arrangement is that it saves much space, and also saves waste of time in referring to two entries of what is practically one and the same word.

Again, in the Semitic languages—where one root branches off into a great variety of remarkably regular and transparently symmetrical derivatives formed partly by vowel-changes, partly by prefixes—it becomes practically necessary to group all these formations under their root. Thus, in an Arabic dictionary there is no difficulty in finding such apparently disconnected words as *salām, islām, muslim* under their common root *slm*. With a few cross-references for disguised and irregular forms this method works very well, and effects a great saving of space.

In the first half of this century, during the intoxication which followed the rapid development of comparative philology, many attempts were made to arrange the vocabularies of different Germanic languages under roots, as in Ettmüller's *Lexicon Anglosaxonicum*, where, for instance, the words *beran, forberan, gebyrd, bearn,* together with many others, are all included under *beran*. A milder form of this arrangement consists in uniting words into families comprising all the words which are clearly connected according to the laws of the language itself. Thus *bearn* and *gebyrd* are evidently connected with *beran*, but we cannot say that they are, from an exclusively Old English point of view, so clearly connected, as *gebyrd*, for instance, is with *gebyrdlic*.

In its still more cautious form, this arrangement would confine itself to grouping together regular derivatives and compounds, such as *synn, synfull, syngian, forsyngod* in Old English. There is a tendency now to carry this out wherever it does not involve any great disturbance of alphabetic order ; that is, in Old English to keep *beran* and *forberan*, *syngian* and *forsyngod*, apart, but to put *synfull* under *synn*.

It must be confessed that there is a certain antagonism in this respect between the compiler and the user of a dictionary. There is in the compiler a tendency to try experiments, to subordinate mechanical regularity of arrangement to higher considerations of a logical character, to sacrifice convenience to brevity, and to expect what he calls ' a certain amount of intelligence' in the user of a dictionary, and also, perhaps, an elementary knowledge of the language. The latter, on the other hand, is apt to expect an impossible combination of brevity, small size and cheapness with such a fullness of information and cross-references as will enable him to read the language without any previous grammatical study.

Every complete bilingual dictionary is twofold : a German-English implies as its complement an English-German dictionary. For many purposes it is convenient to have both dictionaries on the same page—thus German-English on the upper, English-German on the lower half. In this way there is only one alphabet throughout the whole book. In fact, this arrangement ought always to be adopted whenever the two dictionaries are not made into separate volumes, which, of course, depends partly on their size.

Logical Dictionary

Just as there is a distinction between formal and logical grammar, so also we can have a logical as opposed to the ordinary conventional formal or alphabetical dictionary; that is, instead of seeking the meanings of words, we may seek the words which express meanings—given the meaning, we may inquire what are the words and phrases by which it is expressed. Thus, instead of taking the word *good*, and enumerating its various meanings of ' pleasant to the taste, morally good, property, possessions,' and so on, we may take such an idea as that of ' morally good,' and enumerate the various words and phrases by which it can be expressed, such as *good, goodness, well, virtue, morality, moralist, bad, vice.*

This, then, is the logical or synthetic as opposed to the formal or analytic side of the study of word-meanings, and a logical or ideological dictionary is one in which words, idioms, and phrases are grouped under the different categories of space, time, matter, sensation, emotion, etc., with as much logical continuity as is possible.

The best example we have of such a dictionary is Roget's well-known *Thesaurus of English Words and Phrases*, which first appeared in 1852, after nearly fifty years' preparation. In giving a short account of the plan of this work, I quote from the third edition of 1855, as giving the author's own matured views, although there are later editions revised by other hands. The words are grouped under the following heads :—

I. Abstract relations: existence, relation, quantity, order, number, time, change, causation.

II. Space: generally, dimensions, form.

III. Matter: generally, inorganic, organic.

IV. Intellect: formation of ideas, communication of ideas.

V. Volition: individual, intersocial.

VI. Affections: generally, personal, sympathetic, moral, religious.

In the body of the work words expressing opposite and correlative ideas are arranged in two parallel columns on the same page, so that each group of expressions can be contrasted with that which forms its antithesis. Such ideas as 'increase and decrease,' 'easy and difficult,' 'truth and falsehood,' 'teacher and learner,' are contrasted in this way.

It is to be observed that the vocabulary is so far defective that under 'matter' the author gives only the words of general meaning: he does not go into details by enumerating the different minerals, etc. Nor does he give lists of plants, animals, etc.

The following extract will give an idea of the material given in this dictionary and the method of its arrangement :—

3. *Time with reference to an Effect or Purpose.*

132. Earlyness, timeliness, punctuality, readiness, promptness, promptitude, expedition, quickness, haste, acceleration, hastening (684),[1] anticipation.

133. Lateness, tardiness, slowness, delay, cunctation, procrastination, deferring, postponement, dilation, adjournment, prorogation.

---

[1] These numbers refer to places where the same or allied ideas are grouped under other categories.

Suddenness, abruptness (111).

V. To be early, to be in time, etc., to keep time.

To anticipate, forestall.

To expedite, hasten, haste, quicken, press, dispatch, accelerate, precipitate, hurry, bustle.

Phr. To take time by the forelock ; to be beforehand with ; to steal a march upon ; to be pressed for time.

Adj. Early, prime, timely, punctual, matutinal, forward, ready, quick, expeditious, summary, prompt, premature, precipitate, precocious, prevenient, anticipatory.

Sudden, abrupt (111), unexpected (508), subitaneous, extempore.

Adv. Early, soon, anon, betimes, rath, apace, eft, eftsoons, in time, ere long, before long, punctually, to the minute.

Phr. In good time ; in military time ; in pudding time ; at sunrise ; with the lark.

Beforehand, prematurely, before one's time, in anticipation.

Suddenly, abruptly, at once, on the point of, at short notice, extempore ; on the spur of the moment, *instanter*.

Phr. The Fabian policy, *La Médecine expectante*.

Protraction, prolongation, leeway.

Phr. An afternoon man.

V. To be late, etc., tarry, stay, wait, bide, take time, dally, dawdle, linger, loiter, bide one's time (275, 683).

To stand over, lie over.

To put off, delay, defer, lay over, suspend, shift off, stave off, waive, remand, postpone, adjourn, procrastinate, prolong, protract, draw out, prorogue.

Phr. To tide it over ; to push, or drive to the last ; to let the matter stand over.

Adj. Late, tardy, slow, behindhand, postliminious, posthumous, backward, unpunctual, belated.

Delayed, etc., suspended, in abeyance.

Adv. Late, backward, after time, too late, *sine die*.

At length, at last, at sunset.

Slowly, leisurely, deliberately.

Phr. Nonum prematur in annum ; a day after the fair ; at the eleventh hour ; after meat, mustard ; after death, the doctor.

Roget's book was adapted to German by Dr. D. Sanders, the well-known German lexicographer, under the title of *Deutscher Sprachschatz*, from which I quote an extract corresponding to the beginning of the above one :—

Nr. 91.   Das Frühsein.

Substantiva.

a. das Frühsein ; Frühzeitigkeit, etc. ; Frühe ; Morgenfrühe, etc. ; Eile u.s.w. ; Schnelligkeit ; Geschwindigkeit ; Flinkheit ; Hurtigkeit ; Gewandtheit ;

Nr. 92.   Das Spätsein.

Substantiva.

a. das Spätsein, Zuspätsein, Zuspätkommen, etc. ; Verspätung ; Langsamkeit ; Saumseligkeit ; Saumsal ; Zögerung ; Verzögerung ; Verzug, etc. ;

Raschheit ; rasches, expedites Wesen, etc. ; Bereitheit ; Pünktlichkeit ; Exactheit ; Promptheit ; *promptitude*, etc. ; übereiltes Wesen ; Überhastung ; Hast ; Unüberlegtheit ; Beschleunigung, etc. ; Vorwegnahme ; Anticipation, etc.

Abtrift ; Aufschiebung ; Aufschub ; Hinausschiebung u.s.w. ; Hinhaltung ; Verschleppung ; Protraktion ; Vertagung ; Prokrastination ; Perendination ; Prorogation ; Prolongation ; Verlängerung ; das Lavieren ; das Abwarten ; ab-, zuwartende Politik ; . . .

Zeitwörter.

b. früh statthaben, stattfinden, etc. ; . . . Nichts versäumen, verpassen ; die Gelegenheit bei der Stirnlocke fassen, etc. ; . . . dieıKelle nicht an der Pfanne kleben lassen ; sich beeilen ; eilen, etc. ; sich übereilen ; sich hasten ; sich überhasten ; sich überstürzen ; . . .

Zeitwörter.

b. spät, zu spät kommen ; . . . nicht aus der Stelle (vom Fleck) kommen ; schlendern ; zögern ; . . . auf die lange Bank (Bahn) schieben ; auf die lange Bank ziehen, spielen, weisen, bringen ;† in die lange Truhe legen ; in die Länge hinausziehen ; . . .

These extracts will give an idea of the nature of the problem, and its extent and difficulties. It will also be observed that the work is a genuine thesaurus : it gives all the words and phrases the author could collect, whether old or new, literary or colloquial. It is, therefore, quite unfitted for the use of a foreigner learning English, just as Sanders' adaptation would be useless as a guide to the practical study of German idioms. It was intended by the author 'to facilitate the expression of ideas, and assist in literary composition '—for which purpose it has been found very useful.

As regards the general question of the classification of words according to the ideas they express, I may quote the following remarks from a paper of mine on *Words, Logic, and Grammar* (Philological Society's Transs., 1875-6) :—

' In the first place, it must be borne in mind that the ultimate ideas of language are by no means identical with those of psychology, still less with those of metaphysics. Language is not in any way concerned with such psychological problems as the origin of our ideas of space and matter ; for at the time when language was evolved, these conceptions were already stereotyped in the form of simple ideas, incapable of any but deliberate scientific analysis. Even such universally known facts as the primary data of astronomy have had little or no influence on language, and even the scientific astronomer no more hesitates to talk of "the rising of the sun" than did the astrologers of ancient Chaldæa. Language, in short, is based not on things as we know or think them to be, but as they *seem* to us.

'But though the categories of language do not require so deep an analysis as those of psychology, they are, on the other hand, far more complicated. Each word we use suggests a large number of ideas at once, varying always according to the context, and it is a matter of extreme difficulty to select the really characteristic and essential idea or ideas, which alone can be made the basis of classification. It is the great defect of Roget's system that he often classes his words by some extraneous idea that they suggest. Thus *food* is considered as something purely mechanical, as a mode of 'insertion,' and hence is included under "directive motion," whereas it clearly comes under "volitional functions of living beings," with, of course, a cross-reference to "insertion" and its other mechanical associations. . . . For many words special compound categories are required. It is, for instance, misleading to class *sharp, edge, knife* together under "superficial form," as Roget does; the essential difference between *knife* and the other two is, that while they denote—or can denote—natural objects, *knife* always implies human agency: we require, therefore, a special category "inanimate things + volition," or something of the sort. Similarly *meadow* as opposed to *heath* requires a special complex category.'

The double difficulty of classifying the words and of finding them naturally suggests a compromise, such as that adopted by Boissière in his *Dictionnaire analogique de la langue Française*. In this work each page is divided into an upper and a lower portion by a cross-line. The upper portion contains all the words in alphabetic order; the lower portion gives the head-words for the logical categories, also in alphabetical order. If the word sought in the upper portion is at the same time the head-word of a category, it will be found in that capacity immediately below; otherwise, a direction is given, 'see such and such a category.' To keep the two portions of the page abreast of one another, the author has been obliged to sub-divide his categories to an extent which would not otherwise be tolerated; thus *arbre* and *forêt* are separated from one another. The words under each category are again arranged in alphabetical order; thus under *arbre* the words are given in two groups, one a list of trees—*ablanier, abricot* . . .—the other comprising the more general words relating to trees: *abreuvoir, abrouti, agrément, allée* . . . To make reference easier, the words are arranged in vertical columns. The inevitable separation of words that ought, from a logical point of view, to come together in these lists is to some extent remedied by a system of numbering, by which all the words forming a group of their own within the alphabetically arranged group have the same number prefixed to them, so that they can be quickly found by running the eye along the margin.

But all attempts to combine such opposed systems of classification as the alphabetic and the logical must be unsatisfactory. It seems better to carry out the logical arrangement unhampered by any concessions to the alphabetical order, and then give an alphabetic index, as is done in Roget's Thesaurus. The more perfect the logical arrangement, the less need will there be for such an index.

The scope, fullness, size, and other features of a logical dictionary may be varied in the same way as with a formal dictionary.

Its size will, of course, depend on whether it includes quotations or excludes them, as Roget does, who only admits phrases and idioms in addition to single words.

Study of the Vocabulary of a Language

At first, the meanings of words will be learnt mechanically one by one by associations with their context. In every language there are a certain number of words which the learner remembers at once, either because they are borrowed from or are cognate with words already familiar to him in his own or some other language, or through some chance resemblance to known words (p. 91). These words are, as it were, centres round which other words crystallize, each new association leading to further associations, till at last the chief part of the elementary vocabulary of the language forms a solid mass of associations each connected in various ways with others.

To any one practised in the use of a dictionary the trouble and time expended in looking up words in such a glossary as that to my *Anglo-Saxon Primer*—which takes up only twenty-four pages—is but slight, but to a beginner it may be an irksome and slow process. Indeed, even to the most practised dictionary-user the peculiar discontinuity and abruptness of the associations formed and broken in a minute between the words in the text and the words in the dictionary becomes after a time wearying to the brain and irritating to the nerves.

If the beginner starts with a dictionary or glossary of wider scope, so that the chief meanings of the commoner words are given, he must inevitably waste still more time in looking his words up. And if he conscientiously reads over each article in his dictionary, he takes away still more time from his study of the texts themselves. It must also be remembered that the only parallel or supplementary uses and meanings of a word which it is profitable for him to study are those which he has already met with: it only confuses his mind to have to take note of those with which he has no practical acquaintance. Now it is evident that if the only use of looking up a word in the dictionary is the chance of being referred either directly or indirectly to some other passage in the text he is reading, it would be simpler to give him that reference at once without sending him to the dictionary. Widgery, in his *Teaching of Languages in Schools* (p. 45), thus describes the process, as carried out by the ordinary boy :—

'He has, say, twenty lines of Latin to do. After reading the first sentence through, he picks out the subject and then the verb; he turns up the dictionary for his noun, and after sensibly skipping the dubious or antiquated etymology, begins to wonder whether the meaning is under I.A., 1*a*, or II. B. (*b*); on the road he has to turn back sometimes to the three pages of abbreviations at the beginning. However, he gets a meaning at last, and the process is repeated with the verb and the other words, with a flying reference, perhaps, to the grammar for some irregular gender. Then comes a hunt through the index to the syntax—that is, if he is lucky enough to have an index—and, at last, the meaning is fairly clear; frequently, however, this is by no means the case, and he dives into the dictionary and grammar again. This is a danger to which conscientious boys are liable: by patient and misdirected ingenuity, they arrive at a false construction, but the labour of finding it was so great that the first impression remains stronger than the later correction.

'The good boy works in this fashion; the ordinary boy leaves his grammar at school, skims through the lines as quickly as he can, writes down the words that are utterly foreign to him, turns up the dictionary, puts down the first meaning he comes across, and is quite happy next day if he escapes the Task Book.'

Notes instead of Dictionary.—In accordance with the principles of comparison and progressive gradation, I have, therefore, in my *First Steps in Anglo-Saxon*, substituted for the glossary an explanation of each new word in the notes, or else a reference to an earlier explanation. The reference is sometimes not to the explanation itself, but to the last passage in which the word occurs, where a reference to the explanation itself is found. When a word has occurred often enough to imprint itself firmly on a careful reader's memory, the references cease.

One good result of this method is that the learner, instead of being able to rely on finding a word in the glossary if he forgets it, has every inducement to master each page of the book thoroughly before proceeding to the next. As remarked before (p. 134), the same principle may be carried out with the examples in a grammar: in the grammar to *First Steps* the examples are not translated after the first few pages, but explained in the notes exactly in the same way as the texts themselves.

In *First Steps* the notes are put together at the end of the book, not at the foot of each page. The former is, of course, the less convenient arrangement, but it has the advantage of affording the learner a better opportunity of testing his progress, while at the same time it gives him an inducement to read the notes carefully.

Interlinear Translation.—Great use was made in the Middle Ages of interlinear glosses or translations, of which the eleventh-century colloquy of Ælfric in Latin with an Old-English translation is a well-known and favourable example. This method was revived in modern times under the name of 'the Hamiltonian system.' It is now little used, as being too mechanical, and as tending to deaden the learner's linguistic sense by forcing his native language into unnatural constructions and order of words. Idiomatic translation accompanied by parsing has all the advantages without the defects of the interlinear method.

Use of the Dictionary.—We now come to the dictionary stage. It may be asked, Why use a dictionary at all during the systematic course of study? Why not leave it to the finished student, who has begun to read the literature on his own account, and to whom a dictionary is, therefore, really a necessity?

But when the learner has acquired a fairly extensive knowledge of the ordinary vocabulary of the language, he feels an instinctive desire to unite and systematize his scattered impressions. Just as collecting the scattered inflections of a word into a grammatical paradigm helps him to remember the separate inflections, so also gathering the different meanings of words together helps him to remember and discriminate these meanings.

Formal Study of Meanings.—Just as formal precedes logical syntax, so also the study of meanings ought to begin from the formal side; for it is difficult to distinguish the mass of often formally unconnected words and phrases by which a given group of ideas is expressed—*good*, *virtue*, etc.—without some knowledge of the various meanings of each word, and the way in which these meanings are connected.

This preliminary study of word-meanings may be regarded as a sort of lexical syntax. It is only concerned with those words whose variety of meanings causes real difficulty, such as particles, the more primitive verbs and adjectives, and some nouns of more general or abstract meaning, such as *man, thing, manner, way*. In this way it might include many words which have an equal right to a place in the dictionary and in the grammar, such as the prepositions.

This formal study of word-meanings by no means involves reading through an ordinary dictionary, or even reading part of it. As the total vocabulary of the learner even up to the end of the third stage need not exceed three thousand words, and as the meanings of many of these would not require any special study, his 'Primer of formal word-meanings' would have to deal only with a small fraction of the words in an ordinary dictionary.

Under these circumstances, there would be hardly any inducement to keep the alphabetic order of the words, for the book would not be for reference, but for study, and would, besides, have an index. There would, therefore, be no obstacle to

M

arranging the words in any logical order which was found most to facilitate the study of each word's meaning. The result would be something like an improved dictionary of synonyms —expanded in some respects, curtailed in others.

Logical Study of Meanings.—The logical or synthetic study of meanings includes the whole vocabulary—by which we mean, for the present, the limited vocabulary of which we have just spoken. It is not, however, absolutely necessary that every concrete word should be included in it—such words, for instance, as the different names of trees. A typical selection of such words would be enough. We have seen that even Roget's Thesaurus does not include such words (p. 154).

The learner's ' Logical primer of word-meanings ' would be an abridgement of a full logical thesaurus. It would consist of a selection of the most frequent and indispensable words and idioms arranged under their logical categories with illustrative sentences wherever necessary. These sentences would, as far as possible, be connected logically one with another so as— occasionally, at least—to form a continuous narrative or description. The *Colloquial sentences* in my *Elementarbuch des gesprochenen Englisch* will give an idea of how this can be done, although it has been carried out only imperfectly. Franke's *Phrases de tous les jours* gives a similar—but fuller—collection for the study of French, but the sentences are more disconnected than in my Colloquial sentences, from which Franke apparently got the idea.

The utility of such a course of study will depend mainly on how far the learner is prepared beforehand ; for it presupposes some practical knowledge of the meaning of most of the words and word-combinations. It would be a mistake to try to master the vocabulary of a language straight off by learning such a book by heart. The associations must be formed more gradually, and from a more varied context. But when the necessary foundation has once been laid, a systematic study of the meanings already learnt cannot fail to strengthen the associations between sound and sense, and revive associations which may have become weak, or even have been lost entirely ; for even in the best-planned course of reading it is not possible to ensure each individual word and idiom its due amount of repetition at regular intervals, by which alone it can be retained in the memory. Such a study will also teach the learner to realize delicate shades of meaning of which he would otherwise be conscious either vaguely or not at all.

The logical primer of word-meanings would naturally be used for reference also, and for this purpose would be provided with an alphabetical index. But when we have arrived at a satisfactory classification of word-meanings, it is to be hoped learners will be trained to find their way through a logical dictionary or vocabulary without such help.

Such a selection would have the great advantage over the material given in artificial ' methods ' such as Ollendorff's and Gouin's, that it would give the actual language in all its aspects, not a one-sided selection embodying ideas which no one either hears expressed by others or has occasion himself to express.

The full logical dictionary—the ideological thesaurus—would also have its practical uses for the foreign learner, but, of course, only for those who are well advanced. Such a complete dictionary would enable a foreigner to master the vocabulary of any new branch of knowledge, any new pursuit at a short notice, for it would give all the technical terms and phrases required in their natural connection.

Such a dictionary would be useful to natives as well. As it is, Roget's Thesaurus is much used by literary workers and others who wish to find the most suitable expressions for their ideas.

As Roget himself observes, a comparative dictionary on this plan would be of the greatest utility and interest, both from a practical and a scientific point of view. Apart from any systematic study of etymology and the development of word-meanings, it is often interesting to run through the various meanings of a word in some remote language, and observe how the characteristics and life of the speakers of it are faithfully reflected in their vocabulary. Thus I remember the first word I saw in a Sanskrit dictionary was *tapovana* or *tāpasavana*, ' forest inhabited by ascetics,' and the next word had something to do with an elephant. If we open an Arabic dictionary at random, we may expect to find something about a camel : ' a young camel,' ' an old camel,' ' a strong camel,' ' to feed a camel on the fifth day,' ' to feel a camel's hump to ascertain its fatness,' all these being not only simple words, but root-words.

CHAPTER XIII

TEXTS; THE READING-BOOK

WHEN the sounds of a language have once been mastered, the main foundation of its study will be connected texts: the reader will henceforth be the centre of study, to which the grammar, dictionary, and other helps must be strictly subordinated. It is only in connected texts that the language itself can be given with each word in a natural and adequate context.

Classification of Texts

We have now to consider the different kinds of texts from the point of view of their fitness to serve as means of linguistic training. We have also to consider the question of sequence —to determine the order in which the different kinds of texts should be read.

There are certain broad distinctions of mood and style which we may consider first. In the following pairs of extremes—

> concrete, objective—abstract, subjective
> matter of fact, dry—imaginative, poetical, ideal
> commonplace, trivial—strange, sensational
> juvenile—adult

the first members are more suited for purposes of elementary linguistic teaching than the second, as being more likely to comply with the primary requisites of directness, clearness, simplicity, and familiarity. Of the other extremes, the imaginative tends to develope literary peculiarities, and so as to diverge from the colloquial, while the strange and sensational tends to take us away from the familiar. Lastly, all literature suited for young children necessarily suits most of our linguistic

164

requirements; even when it becomes imaginative and abstract, it still retains the qualities of simplicity and directness.

Of wit and humour we need only remark that they are generally colloquial in their expression, and generally deal with familiar and homely themes, and are therefore well suited for our purposes—that is, if they are modern. Unfortunately nothing becomes sooner obsolete than wit and humour.

As regards their subject-matter, we may distinguish three main classes—

(1) Descriptions (of things and phenomena), statements of abstract laws or principles such as those of arithmetic;

(2) Narratives, tales, stories;

(3) Dialogues, conversations—

together with combinations of these, as when a story or novel is made up partly of narrative, partly of dialogue, partly of description, or when descriptions and narratives are introduced into a dramatic work.

The most important distinction between dialogue on the one hand and purely descriptive and narrative pieces on the other hand is a purely grammatical one, namely, that while in the latter two the verb appears only in the third person, it appears in all three persons in the former.

There is also a grammatical distinction between descriptive and narrative pieces, namely, that the former favours the present, the latter the past tenses. As regards the tenses, the dialogue form shows the same variety as in the persons, especially as regards its free use of the future.

From a grammatical point of view it is evident that dialogues ought to come last, as being most complex. On the whole, it seems that descriptions ought to come first, because it is convenient to begin the study of the verb with its present tenses, and also because dialogue can be excluded from them, which is often difficult in narratives. It need hardly be said that no historical presents ought to be allowed in the narrative pieces; otherwise the greatest confusions may arise between present and past tenses.

Examples of almost purely descriptive texts will be found in my Elementarbuch. The following are some of the subjects treated of :—

nature : the earth, the sea, the river Thames, the sun, the seasons, the months, the days of the week, light, colours.

man : different races of men, tools and weapons, food, houses, clothes, language.

Other descriptions may be found in my *Primer of Spoken English* : sun, moon, rain. These are adapted from Mrs. Barbauld, and will therefore serve to show how the treatment of the same subjects may vary according to the individuality of the writer. The descriptive texts in the Elementarbuch are mainly adapted, as far as the matter is concerned, from Huxley's *Physiography*, Tylor's *Anthropology*, and Wright's *Domestic Manners and Sentiments in the Middle Ages*, but the language is entirely my own.

Of the following descriptions, the first is from the *Primer of Spoken English*, the other from the *Elementarbuch*. It will be observed that I sometimes give my specimens in nomic, some-times in phonetic spelling, for the benefit of both classes of readers—phonetic and unphonetic. In the phonetically written pieces I omit stress-marks, etc.

rein ·

' rein kamz frəm ðə klaudz. luk ət ðouz blæk klaudz ! hau faast ðei muwv əloŋ ! nau ðei v hidn ðə san . . . ðə z ə litl bit əv bluw skai stil. nau ðə z nou bluw skai ətɔl : it s ɔl blæk wið ðə klaudz. it s veri daak, laik nait. it l rein suwn. nau it s biginiŋ tə rein. whot big drops ! ðə daks ə veri glæd, bət ðə litl bəədz ə not glæd : ðei gou ən ʃeltə ðəmselvz andə ðə trijz. nau ðə rein z ouvə. it wəz ounli ə ʃauə. nau ðə flauəz smel swijt, ən ðə san ʃainz, ən ðə litl bəədz siŋ əgen, ənd it s not sou hot əz it woz bifɔr it reind.'

' The air is always full of water, though we cannot see it, because it is in the state of vapour, like the gas we burn in the streets and in our houses. The heat of the sun draws up this vapour from all the water it can get at—especially the sea. When the air is cooled, the moisture it contains becomes visible in the form of clouds or mist. A cloud consists of very small drops of water, light enough to hang in the air without falling, like dust. Mist is nothing but clouds close to the earth ; and a cloud is nothing but a mist or a fog high up in the air. A fog is only a thick mist. London fog, as it is called, is mixed with smoke, which gives it a yellow colour. When the drops run together, and get so heavy that they fall to the ground, we have rain.'

A short description may be disguised in the form of a riddle.

A special class of descriptive texts are those which deal with abstract ideas, especially numbers, elementary notions of arithmetic and geometry, space, boundaries, shape.   These may be treated somewhat as in Clifford's *Common-sense of the Exact Sciences*.

Another class of descriptions are those involving action. This kind of text may assume the character of a narrative, as in the section on 'Food' in my Elementarbuch (§ 10), which begins, 'At first men had to live on what they found wild. They used to gather fruits . . .'   Generally they have more of the dramatic character, as in the description of a fair in Passy's Elementarbuch (Nr. 7), of which I quote the beginning :

la fwaar

' a ty ʒamɛ vy yn fwaar? i j ãn a yn tu lez ã dã nɔt vilaaʒ. o mwa d ʒyjɛ õ vwa vniir də tu le koote booku d grããd vwatyyr ki rsããbl a de vagõ d ʃəmẽ d fɛɛr. dədã j a de famiij də bɔemjẽ : ɛz i viiv kɔm dã de meezõ. i võ tuus syr la grããd plas, e la i kõstrɥiiz de barak u i mõõtrə tut sɔrt də ʃooz kyrjøøz : de bɛɛt ferɔs, de ʃjẽ savã, dez ɔm ki fõ de turdəfɔrs ɛtsɛtera. s ɛ trɛ drool də vwaar tu sa.'

In narrative pieces the first thing to be considered is their length.   Three-volume novels are evidently not suited for beginners.   The other extreme is represented by anecdotes, which play a great part in most reading-books.   Anecdotes may be historical, moral, humorous.   They may be in a purely narrative form, or they may be partly or entirely in the dialogue form.   The following are time-honoured specimens of different kinds of anecdotes :—

Lakonische Verordnung.

Alexander schrieb an die Griechen, dasz sie ihn für einen Gott erkennen sollten.   Die Lacedemonier faszten demnach einen Beschlusz in folgenden Worten : 'Weil Alexander ein Gott sein will, so sei er einer.'

Der gute Mensch und die bösen Menschen.

Jemand bedauerte Rousseau wegen der Menge seiner Verfolger, und setzte hinzu : ' Die Menschen sind böse.'   ' Die

Menschen,' antwortete der Bedauerte, 'ja,—aber der Mensch ist gut.'

Die rothe Nase.

Ein Greis, der vom Weintrinken eine rothe kupferige Nase hatte, sagte einst zu seinem Enkel, einem Knaben von sechs Jahren, der alle Speisen ohne Brod asz : 'Liebes Kind, du musst hübsch Brod essen; Brod macht die Wangen roth.' 'Dann hast du wohl viel Brod geschnupft, Grossväterchen,' sagte der Knabe.

Was ist der Mensch.

Plato definirte den Menschen, ein zweibeiniges Thier, ohne Federn. Hierauf rupfte jemand einem Huhn die Federn aus und sagte zu Plato : 'Dieses is auch ein Mensch.'

The anecdote in its shortest form is apt to degenerate almost into a definition—as in the last example—or proverb, so that at last it shrinks almost to a single sentence, and loses all claim to the title of ' connected text.' Such anecdotes ought not to be given by themselves, but only as insertions into longer connected texts, as in § 56 of my *Elementarbuch*, where I give an anecdote of two Englishmen and a Frenchman to illustrate the meaning of ' reserve.'

The simplest kinds of narrative pieces of moderate length which at the same time deal with familiar incidents are short tales of everyday life, short modern biographies, fairy tales. As examples of the simplest and most trivial type of short story, almost devoid of incident, I may mention (egare dǎ la fɔrɛ) in Passy's *Elementarbuch* (Nr. 9) and (ðə kauədli litl boi) in my *Primer of Spoken English*.

Historical narratives are not generally suited for our purposes, as they generally deal with unfamiliar subjects, and are often necessarily technical, as when battles are described. Narratives of adventure are good when the subjects and scenes are not too remote. A good specimen of a narrative of boyish adventure is (ði ould tʃæpl) in my *Primer of Spoken English*, which is, however, rather old-fashioned, as it is an adaptation of a story by William Howitt.

Special dialogues are not required by the beginner, as there is sure to be some element of dialogue in the narrative texts.

326

Specimens of dialogues in purely colloquial language will be found in my *Primer of Spoken English* under the following titles : Wild Life, A Railway Excursion, At the Seaside, Education, Socialism, Skating. These are not suited for any but very advanced foreigners. Less difficult dialogues will be found in my *Elementarbuch*. Dialogues such as these, which are intended to help the learner to gain a general mastery of the language, must be distinguished from those which are intended specially for travellers abroad.

We now have to consider the requirements which these different kinds of texts have to satisfy.

Connectedness

The first requisite is that each text should form a connected whole, so as to establish as many associations as possible in the mind of the learner between each word and its context, and in order that each repetition of a word in the same text shall strengthen the learner's hold of it. Collections of proverbs and riddles are objectionable from this point of view ; and as they are generally also objectionable on the score of form, as containing archaic words and constructions, besides being often elliptical and otherwise anomalous in form, they had better be omitted entirely. Such a proverb as *waste not, want not*, for instance, is not modern English at all ; the modern colloquial form would be *do not waste, and you will not be in want.*

It is easy to see that in some texts the individual sentences are more closely connected together than in others. In dialogues there is generally less logical continuity than in descriptions and abstract statements, especially arguments and proofs. The conversations of everyday life are often disconnected and elliptical in the highest degree, so that a faithful reproduction of them would be unsuited for ordinary learners.

These considerations are a warning against carrying too far the reaction against the use of detached sentences in teaching languages. A collection of detached sentences, each of which is good in itself—that is, capable of being isolated without becoming obscure—may be better than a connected text which is obscure in language or whose subject is unsuitable, or a dialogue of disjointed and practically disconnected remarks.

Length

The question of the relative length of the pieces in a reading-book depends partly on the stage of progress of the learners. At first they can advance only slowly, and hence even a moderate amount of variety can only be secured by keeping the texts short. If the book is intended for young children, there is all the more reason for making them short.

On the other hand, it is possible to make too great concessions to variety : an unbroken succession of very short texts is more wearisome than restriction to a single long one. A great part of Vietor and Dörr's *Englisches Lesebuch* is, through the excessive use of nursery rhymes and riddles, little more than a collection of detached sentences in archaic English. Thus, the first two pieces they give are—

1.

' He that would thrive
Must rise at five ;
He that has thriven
May lie till seven.

2.

Early to bed and early to rise
Makes a man healthy, and wealthy, and wise.'

Then come some short poems, including, of course—

' Twinkle, twinkle, little star,
How I wonder what you are !
Up above the world so high,
Like a diamond in the sky.'

.   .   .   .   .

Then Section II. begins with a prose piece, ' The fatal quarrel of saucer, mug, and spoon ; ' then comes—

2.

' Molly, my sister, and I fell out,
And what do you think it was about?
She loved [1] coffee, and I loved tea,
And that was the reason we could not agree.'

Then a poem, ' Too clever ; ' then another piece of prose, ' The wonderful pudding ; ' then—

[1] Archaic for *like*.

6.

' Everything has an end and a pudding has two.
The proof of the pudding is in the eating.
Which is the left side of a round plum-pudding ?

First come, first served.
Hunger is the best sauce.
Enough is as good as a feast.
Half a loaf is better than no bread.
They that have no other meat [1]
Bread and butter are glad to eat.

After dinner sit a while,
After supper walk a mile.'

Then a prose piece, ' Food.'   Then no less than nine pages headed ' Nursery Rhymes, Riddles,' etc., among which we find ' This is the house that Jack built,' ' If all the seas were one sea, what a great [2] sea that would be ! . . .' ' Solomon Grundy, Born on a Monday,' together with verses such as—

' Swan [3] swam over the sea ;
Swim, swan, swim.
Swan swam back again ;
Well swum, swan.'

And riddles such as—

' Which is the strongest day in the week ?

SUNDAY, BECAUSE ALL THE REST ARE WEEK-DAYS.

What is that which you and every living person have seen, but can never see again ?

YESTERDAY.

What is that which no man ever yet did see,[4]
Which never was, but always is to be ?'

TO-MORROW.

And sayings such as—

' No rose without a thorn,'

which does not even constitute a sentence.

[1] Archaic for *food.*   [2] Archaic for *big, large.*
[3] Archaic for *the swan.*   [4] *Did see* archaic for *saw.*

All this is surely carrying the principle of variety too far. One does not see how the pupils are to carry away any definite associations from such jerky transitions, in spite of the care taken by the compilers to preserve unity by giving each section a special subject, such as 'getting up and going to bed,' 'meals,' etc. But the section 'nursery rhymes and riddles' is made up of absolutely detached pieces, many of which, as we see, are extravagantly short.

It is evidently impossible to come to a definite agreement on the subject of length, for what seems short to a slow, retentive mind may seem intolerably long to a quicker or more superficial one. It is evident, therefore, from this point of view, that the compiler of a reading-book ought to vary the length of his pieces on both sides of the average length. This average length ought, from a purely linguistic point of view, not to be less than a page or two, and anything shorter ought to be given only exceptionally, riddles and proverbs being entirely excluded unless quoted in a clear context.

Clear Context

It is of the greatest importance that each word—especially each new word—should, as far as possible, have such a context as to leave room for the minimum of hesitation as to its meaning. Thus the context of the word *east* in such a statement as *the house faces east* may suggest to the learner that *east* denotes one of the four quarters, but it will not tell him which it is, while such a statement as *the sun rises in the east and sets in the west* enables him to identify the quarter in an unmistakeable manner : indeed, if he only knows the meaning of *sun* and *rise*, he will be able to infer the meaning of the other three full words with almost complete certainty. In such a statement as *the first day of the week is called Sunday, the second Monday, the third Tuesday* . . . the associations between the numbers and the days are so definite that any one who has learnt the complete statement by heart in the language he is learning will have no difficulty in recalling any one of the words by repeating the series till he comes to it. In this case we have two independent associations of order—*first, second* . . . , *Sunday, Monday* . . . —each of which strengthens the other.

We see that where, as in the last example, there is a known fixed order. the mere enumeration of the words in this order would be enough to fix the meaning of each word in the memory—the mere repetition of *Sunday, Monday, Tuesday* . . . by itself is enough to teach us the meaning of each word. But if there is no definite order of associations, mere enumeration gives only the information that a certain number of words have some meaning in common, without affording the learner any further means of discriminating them. Thus I once saw an elementary French reading-book in which the different things in a house were simply enumerated, thus 'in the kitchen are plates, dishes, saucepans, kettles . . . ,' so there was nothing to correct the English learner's natural assumption that *plat* means 'plate' instead of 'dish.' So also with such a statement as 'all kinds of flowers grow in the fields : daisies, buttercups, primroses, cowslips . . .'

It need scarcely be added that the context, to be clear, must be familiar. Thus a European beginner should not be allowed to read in a description of scenes in the southern hemisphere that the sun was hot because it was the middle of December.

Limited Vocabulary

As we have frequently had occasion to say, the learner's vocabulary should not be large. Even up to the end of the third stage he will not require more than three thousand words. But these he will command with perfect ease and certainty, and will find them enough to make himself understood in speaking of any topic of ordinary life without going into technical details.

Those who learn a language through its literature often have almost as wide a vocabulary as the natives, but have no real command of the elementary combinations, the phrases and idioms, so that, as already observed, they are often unable to describe the simplest mechanical operations, such as 'tie in a knot,' 'turn up the gas.' Nor, when they come to study English, for instance, do they know that the antithesis of *finding* in the spoken language is not *seeking* but *looking for*. So also, instead of *getting wet*, they *become wet*. Those who learn a language on a colloquial basis generally have no difficulty in expressing what they want by idiomatic paraphrases. Thus I remember a foreign child who, not knowing, or having forgotten, the name for a 'pen-wiper,' described it without hesitation as *the thing you make dirty pens clean with*. Such a learner, so far from substituting *seek* for *look for*, would probably not even know what the former meant.

The Most Necessary Elements given First

The more limited the vocabulary, the greater the care that must be exercised in its selection. It is evident that the first and strongest associations of the learner, ought to be with those elements of the language which are the common foundation of the colloquial, the literary, the familiar, and the scientific and technical strata of the language. As already remarked, he ought not to be confronted with words which would still be unintelligible to him when translated into his own language. His reading-book ought not to give him a description of a candle-manufactory. Even a description of a game of cricket is out of place, for few foreigners are likely to join in it, and such a description would involve technicalities that even Englishmen might be ignorant of, or, at any rate, unable to define accurately.

The distinction between necessary and unnecessary idioms and phrases is especially important. All proverbial idioms, and most of those containing similes, are mere ornaments—often only vulgar ornaments—of speech, and therefore superfluous for the foreigner who can only just manage to express himself in a straightforward way : he requires only to understand, not to be able to use them himself. Equally superfluous are the idioms and expressions constituting slang or argot; except when what is called slang really serves to supply a want —to give expression to some idea which could not otherwise be expressed—in which cases it ceases to be slang, and becomes simply colloquial. Another reason why foreigners should not attempt to imitate such expressions is that they are constantly changing, and nothing is more out of place than antiquated slang.

But besides these, there are thousands of idioms which, although quite unobjectionable in themselves, are superfluous to a beginner because they express ideas which could be expressed just as well by a normal and unidiomatic combination of words. Thus in English, *I must be off now* can be expressed just as well by *I must be going now* or *I must go now*, which, though less forcible, is less familiar, and therefore safer for a foreigner to use. So also *it caught my eye* may be para-phrased into *I happened to see it* without becoming un-English. Such idioms should not be allowed to stand in the way of really indispensable idioms which cannot be paraphrased.

There are, of course, gradations in the indispensability of idioms. For conversational purposes questions are at first more necessary than answers: the idioms used in questions must be mastered perfectly, while those used in answers require only to be understood. But many questions are not so indis-pensable as they might at first sight appear. One of the first idioms we learn in beginning to speak a foreign language is *what o'clock is it?* But as every foreigner who is educated enough to be able to use a phrase-book is sure to bring a watch with him, he simply sets his watch by the station clock when he arrives in the foreign country. The only case in which he is likely to ask the time is that of his watch stopping unexpectedly, and then he would prefer to put his question in a less abrupt form, such as *can you tell me what the right time is?* which is hardly an idiom, but an ordinary normal sentence, *what is the time?* being on a level with *what is the hour? which is the way?*

Familiarity of Subject

The subject of the texts ought to be in harmony with the language they are intended to teach, both as regards place and time: an English reading-book for French learners ought to deal with scenes of modern English life rather than with Lacedemonians. Nor would the English learner of French care to have French adaptations of insipid and antiquated English children's stories put before him.

But when the learner has got a firm hold of the foreign language, it is instructive for him to read descriptions of his own country written in the foreign language, for although such descriptions are not a preparation for either a stay in the foreign country or a study of its literature, they have the advantage of dealing with objects and ideas with which he is familiar, so that the resulting associations, though less directly useful, are more definite and distinct. Descriptions and defini-tions of familiar objects and ideas are peculiarly instructive.

In dealing with languages embodied in old-established literatures such as English and French, and still more with dead languages such as Latin, there is often a great difficulty in finding texts which are at once genuinely national in character and at the same time simple in matter and style.

The difficulty is that highly developed literatures are apt to be too rhetorical or too ornate, too epigrammatic or too cynical, and, generally speaking, wanting in naïvety. Hence the foreigner in search of simple texts is apt unconsciously to select old-fashioned pieces, which, while fulfilling the requirements of simplicity of language and familiarity of subject, do not fulfil them with reference to the present day, the life and language being those of past generations. Such a book as Vietor and Dörr's *Englisches Lesebuch* is pleasant reading to an English adult, precisely because it brings back half-faded associations of childhood and traditions of the eighteenth century, but for that very reason is in many respects a misleading guide for Germans who wish to learn to understand English life and language as they now are. There is no fault to be found with such texts as 'London (in 1880),' but it is difficult to see how the choice of such a nonsense rhyme as

'A diller, a dollar, a ten o'clock scholar,
 What makes you come so soon?
You used to come at ten o'clock,
 But now you come at noon,'

can be justified, for a dollar is not an English coin, and the word *dollar* in the above rhyme is not connected with the context, and when the learner looks up *diller* in the glossary, he gets full information about its pronunciation, but is disgusted to find that he has taken all this trouble about a word which is only a 'scherzwort.'

Even when perfectly suitable modern texts exist, the difficulties of copyright come in. Hence in my *Elementarbuch*, being in want of a short story, I took *The Gypsy Party* by Thomas Hood (in his *Hood's Own*), and modernized the language and, to some extent, the incidents, changing the title to *The Picnic*, the original title being quite an antiquated expression, which many English people would not understand. In this way I have combined the advantages of good matter and modern language. The story of *The Old Chapel* in my *Primer of Spoken English* was obtained in the same way. Although the language of both these pieces as given by me is purely modern, the spirit of them is not so. But, on the other hand, if every reading-book had to be perfectly up to date, we should have to write new ones every five years or so, and they would then embody many very transitory elements, confined perhaps to a limited sphere. But, fortunately, there is a certain foundation of English style and phraseology which is even older than the nineteenth century; there are whole pages even of such writers as Swift and Arbuthnot which, with a very little alteration, are good colloquial English of the present day—in fact, it is only by its being so good that we know that it is not Present English.

Simplicity of Language

Simplicity of language demands, in the first place, that the texts should be colloquial rather than literary: that they should be written in short sentences, not in long and complicated periods, that they should be as free as possible from metaphors and other figures of speech. But colloquial tendencies must not be pushed to an extreme. It must be remembered that in the beginning we do not advocate colloquialism so much for its own sake as because, as a general rule, a colloquial style fulfils certain requirements better than a literary one. But when colloquialism developes into abrupt, elliptical, disconnected dialogues full of unnecessary idioms and slang, it becomes almost as unsuited for elementary practical purposes as the opposite extreme. Again, many considerations point to descriptions of nature as the best texts to begin with; but such descriptions cannot be colloquial in the strict sense of the word, for continuous descriptions constitute not a dialogue but a monologue, which would be hardly possible in real life. Such texts are, in fact, almost as much literary as colloquial, but they give the literary style simplified to the utmost degree in the direction of the spoken language.

Hence, too, as already observed, there is no harm in giving at an early period pieces of simple poetry. For there are many poems whose language is so simple and free from archaisms that it diverges but slightly from colloquial speech as regards vocabulary and grammatical structure, while the marked character given by the metre and diction serve to diminish the danger of cross-associations with the colloquial language. The little poem, *Past and Present*, given at the end of my *Elementarbuch*, is an example of this. In its thirty-

N

two lines the only uncolloquial features I notice are *morn* for *morning*, *bear away* for *carry away*, *'tis* for *it's*, *he* instead of *it* (said of the sun), and the compound *lily-cup*, together with some trifling divergences in word-order. Note, on the other hand, the pure colloquialism, *I'm* for *I am*. We might also substitute *it's* for *'tis* without injury to the metre.

Variety

The great advantage of natural, idiomatic texts over artificial ' methods ' or ' series ' is that they do justice to every feature of the language, if only representative pieces of the three great classes of texts are chosen. The artificial systems, on the other hand, tend to cause incessant repetition of certain grammatical constructions, certain elements of the vocabulary, certain combinations of words to the almost total exclusion of others which are equally, or perhaps even more, essential. Thus the Ollendorff and Ahn methods result in the total exclusion of idioms, even the most necessary; and Gouin's ' series ' deal only with concrete and objective words, and almost entirely exclude the abstract and subjective elements of the language, so that he is obliged to supplement his objective series with a subjective course—or, rather, to promise such a supplement, for, as might be imagined, he soon found the task far beyond his strength. In its present form the Gouin method is incapable of teaching the pupil to say, ' I think so,' or ' I would rather not do it,' or, indeed, to express anything that falls under the categories of emotion or intellect. As Brekke remarks (Brekke, Gouin, 44), the series method results in the most astounding grammatical limitations : only principal sentences, verb only in the first or third person, only assertive sentences (no interrogative or negative sentences), everything in the present tense, and so on.

Gradation of Difficulties

After what has been said, there can be little doubt as to the true principles of the gradation of texts. The simplest in grammatical structure are descriptive pieces, in which the verb can be restricted to the present tense and the third person. The practical value of this restriction will, of course, depend on whether the language is highly inflected or not. Even in

English it would save the learner some difficulties, such as those of the preterites of strong verbs. With such a language as Chinese it would have no grammatical meaning at all. But descriptive texts have the further advantage of affording the clearest, most definite, and most connected and continuous context. With these, therefore, the beginning should be made. They agree with Gouin's series in giving mainly the concrete and objective elements of the vocabulary. Our texts would differ, however, materially from them in giving only the really useful combinations.

The grammatical forms which are wanting in the descriptive texts are supplied by colloquial dialogues, which, in their highest and freest development, are the most difficult of all.

The maximum of variety is attained by that mixture of description, narrative and dialogue, which is exemplified in a novel or short story. This kind of text has the advantage of being infinitely elastic, so that it admits of almost as great simplification as a purely descriptive text, from which it then differs only in giving greater variety of grammatical construction, vocabulary, and idioms. This, then, should be the central type of text: it is at the same time a preparation both for reading and speaking the language.

Interest

The remarks already made on the question of interest (p. 112) will, I think, be confirmed by a consideration of the different ways of studying texts. To be interested in a thing, we must be in the mood for it, and the thing itself must be a novelty. The learner who is struggling with the combined difficulties of pronunciation and grammatical analysis, together with all the difficulties caused by an unfamiliar vocabulary, is not in the mood to appreciate jokes or national humour, which, even if not already stale to him, or uncongenial through national prejudices of his own, will certainly lose their novelty by the time he has learnt to pronounce them and to parse their linguistic embodiment. There are many passages in my *Elementarbuch* and *Primer of Spoken English* which hardly ever fail to elicit signs of amusement from English readers, but I have seldom known any of my foreign pupils show the slightest signs of appreciation of them from this point of view.

And even if it were advisable to make use of sensational

narratives of shipwreck, piracy, murders, and apparitions, our fundamental principles of slow reading and incessant repetition would soon take the interest out of them. The teacher would not fail to hear the remark frequently made by those who begin the study of a foreign language with this kind of literature, ' I should like to read this book in a translation—I cannot remember the plot of the story when I only read twenty lines a day.'

But if learners are often callous to the literary or humorous merits of their texts, they are, on the other hand, very ready to criticize their defects. Young children, in particular, have a great dislike to being condescended to, and being offered what is aggressively babyish, or too obviously intended to serve moral and pedagogic interests. Often, indeed, they prefer the other extreme : they like to have glimpses of something just a little beyond them. We all dislike unnecessary triviality.

This is why I based my descriptions in the *Elementarbuch* mainly on popular scientific and sociological works (p. 166), although this involves some slight deviations from the principle of familiarity. But even when I introduce details out of the life of the Middle Ages or any other unfamiliar scene, I take care to describe them in language which recalls ideas familiar to the modern reader.

Another insuperable obstacle to making texts positively interesting and not merely non-trivial or non-objectionable, is the variety of tastes. Descriptions of nature are soothing and pleasing to some minds even if a little commonplace. To others even the most eloquent and imaginative descriptions of nature are as tedious and depressing as nature itself is to them : those who do not care to hear about

> ' The new soft-fallen mask
> Of snow upon the mountains and the moors '

cannot be expected to be interested in a matter-of-fact description of atmospheric or marine phenomena. Storm objects to my descriptions of nature that 'the children have enough of them at school,' and Passy says that 'no French boys would have the patience to go through them.'

These divergences of taste depend partly on nationality and changes in public taste. A certain style of literature goes out of fashion in one country, and is then introduced into another, where it is welcomed as a novelty, just as extinct German philosophies find a sleepy home elsewhere. Hence it is possible that the 'goody' stories in Passy's *Elementarbuch* may be acceptable to German children, although they certainly were not so to English children even thirty years ago, at which period they had already become old-fashioned in this country. I am certain that such a piece as (l ekɔl bɥisɔnjɛɛr) in Passy's book (nr. 42) would provoke lively antagonism in most English readers, not on account of the sentiments conveyed in it, but of the manner in which the moral lesson is put forward. Nor can I believe that school-children care to read descriptions of schoolrooms and of pedagogues swaggering before a big black board chalk and duster in hand, such as Passy gives in his first piece (la kl*aa*s). I do not make these remarks with any intention of depreciating this valuable book, but simply as an illustration of the impossibility of making linguistic texts permanently interesting to the majority of learners. It is with texts and selections as with pronunciation : every one likes his own best. I find, too, as regards my own books, the *Elementarbuch* and the *Primer of Spoken English*, that every reader has different tastes.

Besides avoiding triviality and over-childishness and naïvety, it is evident that the texts should be of moderate medium length—neither as long as three-volume novels on the one hand, nor as short as proverbs on the other (p. 172).

As to monotony, the principles of variety and gradation already discussed will fully obviate that.

Literary Texts

The language of purely literary texts is generally inconsistent with our principles of selection. It is tolerably sure to be more or less archaic from a strictly colloquial point of view, or to contain unnecessary words and phrases, or to be accompanied by complications of grammatical structure, or vagueness of context. But if a literary piece is exceptionally suitable for any linguistic purpose, or seems to fit in well with the context, or to illustrate it and make things clearer, there can be no very strong objection to admitting it, if the divergences from the colloquial standard are not too marked or such as to cause linguistic confusion.

Many of these divergences can, indeed, often be removed

without injury to the general character of the piece, and this should always be done when practicable.

Useful texts may be constructed by retelling the story of some literary composition in simple language. Epic and narrative poems may be dealt with in this way in languages otherwise wanting in prose texts, such as many dead languages. Thus one of the texts in my *First Steps* is a simple prose paraphrase of the epic poem of Beowulf, which in its metrical form bristles with obscurities and difficulties. I here give a specimen, first of the poem itself, and then of the corresponding portion of my own paraphrase into simple Old English prose :—

'Sþwā ā dryhtguman   drēamum lifdon
ēadiglīce,   oþþæt ān ongann
firene fremman,   fēond on helle.
Wæs se grimma giest   Grendel hāten,
mǣre mearcstapa,   sē þe mōras hēold,
fenn and fæsten.   Fīfelcynnes eard
wansǣlig wer   weardode hwīle,
siþþan him Scieppend   forscrifen hæfde
in Cāines cynne,   þone cwealm gewræc
ēce Dryhten,   þæs þe hē Ābēl slōg.
Ne gefeah hē þǣre fǣhþe,   ac hē hine feorr forwræc
metod for þȳ māne   manncynne fram ;
þanon untȳdras   ealle onwōcon :
eotenas and ielfe   and orcnēas,
swelce gīgantas   þā wiþ Gode wunnon
lange þrāge ;   hē him þæs lēan forgeald !
Gewāt þā nēosian,   siþþan niht becōm,
hēan hūses,   hū hit Hringdene
æfter bēorþege   gebūn hæfdon.
Fand þā þǣrinne   æþelinga gedryht
swefan æfter symble ;   sorge ne cūþon
wansceaft wera.   Wiht unfǣlo
grimm and grǣdig   gearo sōna wæs,
rēoc and rēþe,   and on reste genam
þrītig þegna ;   þanon eft gewāt
hūþe hrēmig   tō hām faran,
mid þǣre wælfylle   wīca nēosan.'

' On þisse blisse þurhwunode Hrōþgār cyning and his menn lange tīd, oþþæt him fēond onsǣge wearþ. Þæt wæs unfǣlu wiht, Grendel hātte. Sē būde on þǣm mearclande, and hæfde him fæsten geworht on fennum, onmiddan þæm sweartum mōrum.

Sume menn cwædon þæt Grende wære of Cāines cynne. Forþæm, þā Cāin ofslōg Ābēl his brōþor, þā wear þ him se ælmihtiga gram, and hine on wræcsīþ āsende, and hēt hine on wēstenne wunian, feorr mancynne. Þanon onwōcon ealle unfæle wihta, dweorgas, and ielfe, and eotenas, þe wiþ God wunnon.

Þā ne mihte Grendel þolian þæt hē ælce dæge blisse gehīerde on Heorote, and hē self ūte wunode on þīestrum.

Þā on niht æfter þæm gebēorscipe, þā þā menn slēpon on þære healle, þā wearþ se rēþa Grendel sōna gearo : hē him on ungearwe on bestæl, þā hīe him nānes yfeles ne wēndon, and hira þrītig genam, and mid him ferede hām tō his fæstenne, þære herehȳþe fægniende ; forþæm hit wæs his þēaw þæt hē hlāf ne æt, ne wæter ne dranc, ac æt manna līchaman and hira blōd dranc.'

But such paraphrases must be into a simple, colloquial style of language, as far as possible. Such books as Lamb's *Tales from Shakespeare* are useless for our purposes because written in an artificial archaic style.

In dealing with dead languages we cannot be so fastidious, especially with one that has only a limited prose literature, such as Old English. Thus in the above paraphrase of Beowulf I have made no attempt to keep to the language of one period, but wherever I have found a suitable model or pattern for any portion of it, I have followed it, whether it comes from Alfred or Ælfric, or from the early or later parts of the Chronicle.

Condensed Treatises

Advanced students of a language often feel the want of a knowledge of the vocabulary of some special technical or scientific subject which they cannot expect to pick up by ordinary general reading — such subjects as commerce, gardening, management of a sailing-boat, cycling, trigonometry, chemistry, electricity.

A full logical dictionary would, of course, give some information as to the vocabulary of such subjects, but necessarily in a very concise form, especially in the wider branches of knowledge. For mastering the vocabulary of these, it would be desirable to have condensed special treatises resembling the science primers and practical guides with which we are familiar, but differing essentially from them in strictly subordinating actual information to explanation and illustration of the special vocabulary and terminology of the subject in question.

This might be extended to more general subjects. Thus we might have a series of ideal condensed histories of different periods with typical battles, sieges, sea-fights, insurrections, trials for treason, embassies and so on, the information—which may be imaginary—being only just as much as will suffice to give a certain number of examples of the terminology required.

Subordination to Form ; Grammatical Texts

We have seen that the general character of a text determines to some extent the character of its vocabulary and grammatical forms—that, for instance, in descriptions and narratives the verbs may be exclusively in the third person. In Cæsar's Commentaries even the dialogues have their verbs in the third person through being put in indirect narration. If, then, for any pedagogic purpose we wanted a text of this description, it would be perfectly easy to make one without doing any violence to the genius of the language.

It is a different matter when we try to write a text under formal limitations which do not naturally follow from the general character of the text. Even so apparently natural and reasonable a restriction as using only the present tense in descriptions of nature might cause embarrassment, although it is partially founded on the character of the text. Thus the very first verb in my descriptive texts in the *Elementarbuch* is a preterite (*used*). Nor must it be forgotten that even if all the verbs are made present in meaning, we cannot avoid the preterite in clauses of rejected condition, as in *if it were* implying ' it is not.'

English has so many monosyllabic words that it is quite possible to write long texts in words of one syllable ; and this has often been done from a mistaken idea that such texts facilitate learning to read. But when we consider that such a restriction allows us to mention only a single season of the year, only three out of the twelve months, and not a single day of the week, it is evident that such texts must be hampered by many unnatural omissions and awkward circumlocutions.

In China, where all the words of the language are monosyllabic, a book written under much more embarrassing restrictions is still used as a primer for teaching boys to read and write. This is the famous *Book of a Thousand Characters* (*ts'ien tsi` wen*). The origin of this book is a curious story. It is said that one of the emperors summoned the best scholar of the time, and gave him a thousand slips of paper, each with a different character—that is, a different word—written on it, and told him to arrange them so as to make sense. The scholar solved the problem in a single night; but in the morning his hair had turned white. The peculiar difficulty of the task lay, of course, in the restriction that no word was to be used twice over—not even the commonest particle. The result was a text that was never really intelligible throughout, not even with the help of the many commentaries that have been written on it. Such a task could not have been even attempted in any other language but Chinese, which, at a pinch, can dispense entirely with auxiliaries or particles of any kind, and express every grammatical relation by mere position.

Other Oriental languages can show long poems written entirely to illustrate grammatical and lexical forms. Thus in Sanskrit there is an epic written for the express purpose of giving examples of verb-forms found in the grammars but non-existent in the literature. The artificiality lies here not in restriction, but simply in finding a connected context for a certain number of words. But comparatively easy as the task is, we cannot believe that the result can be anything but insufferably tedious.

In Europe such texts are constructed in a less ambitious spirit. Our Ahns and Ollendorffs do not write poems; they do not even try to write consecutive prose. Franke's *Phrases de tous les jours* contains excellent materials, but has the same defect of want of continuity. As Storm remarks (*Forbedret Undervisning*, p. 26), 'we have here a good selection of idiomatic material, but not a single actual conversation, nor any arrangement according to the grammar. The material is as disconnected as in the ordinary manuals. We meet, for instance, every minute pronouns without being able to see who is referred to, and questions without answers. It is of little use having good material, if it cannot be assimilated. When the sense is interrupted every moment and the context becomes unintelligible, it is impossible to adapt oneself to the situation, and feel at home in the surroundings.' I may add that Franke probably thought that the arrangement of his idioms under logical categories would be enough to associate them together in the learner's mind. But this seems not to be the case; as they stand, Franke's idioms are of no use except as a summary of what has already been learnt from connected texts. And this was the main object of my colloquial sentences in the *Elementarbuch*, although at the same time I was fully alive to the advisability of making the sentences as connected as possible. But I soon saw that to carry this out fully would require much more space than I could afford. In a full thesaurus or in a primer which dealt only with the commonest words there would, I think, be little difficulty in making the ex-amples form continuous dialogues or narratives or descriptions of some length. The continuity would, of course, be logical, not formal—that is, not according to grammatical categories.

Storm himself has, in his *Dialogues Français*,[1] attempted to construct connected texts for systematic practice in the chief rules of grammar, so arranged that the rules are learnt more by unconscious imitation than by deliberate grammatical analysis. The author has taken the principle of beginning with the spoken language literally by giving his texts in the form of dialogues. But it must be remarked that the book is not intended for beginners, but for grown-up students who have already worked at French for two or three years. From this point of view the choice of dialogues instead of more elementary forms of texts is fully justified, and, perhaps, to some extent, the complete absence of any phonetic transcription.

Considered from the purely grammatical point of view, it must be admitted that these dialogues have been adapted to their purpose with great skill. But it must also be admitted that this subordination of matter to form has made many of them rather trivial and uninteresting in themselves. But the dialogues are frequently interspersed with little anecdotes and occasional literary pieces (cf. p. 181), among which we find the well-known passage from Molière about M. Jourdain speaking prose without knowing it.

One danger of writing texts for a certain purpose is the tendency to spin them out indefinitely by heaping up illustra-tions and dwelling too long on one rule. Even with the most

---

[1] There is an authorized English edition by G. Macdonald under the title of *French Dialogues by Joh. Storm*.

rigid limitations the attempt adequately to embody all the rules of grammar in such texts would probably result in a book of impracticable length.   Storm himself seems to feel this difficulty, for he often interrupts his dialogues to give groups of detached proverbs, phrases, and idioms, which have not even the logical connection of Franke's sentences, being associated solely by grammatical considerations.

I will now give a few examples of Storm's texts :—

'II. L'article partitif.
Avez-vous du vin ?[1]
Je n'ai pas de vin, mais le marchand de vin en a.[2]
A-t-il du vin rouge, du vin blanc, de bon vin,[3] de mauvais vin?
Il n'a pas de mauvais vin, il n'en a que de bon.
Quel vin désirez-vous, du rouge ou du blanc?
Donnez-moi du rouge.   Ce n'est pas du vin, c'est du vinaigre.
J'en ai d'autre ; j'en ai de meilleur ; en voici.
Voilà du vrais bordeaux, et du meilleur.   Vous avez de si bon vin, que je vous en demanderai encore.   Cela fait du bien.
Un peu plus de vin ne vous fera pas de mal.
Il me faut peu de vin et beaucoup d'eau.
Vous mettez trop d'eau dans votre vin ; mettez moins d'eau et plus de vin.
Il n'y a pas de vin ; moi du moins je n'en ai pas.   Il n'y a plus de vin.   Je n'ai plus de vin.
Il n'y en a plus?
Il n'en reste plus.
Si, il en reste encore.
En avez-vous ?
Oui, j'en ai.   En voulez-vous?   Désirez-vous encore du vin ?
En voulez-vous encore ?
Oui, donnez-m'en encore un peu.
Garçon, encore du vin, s'il vous plaît.
Encore un peu de vin, s'il vous plaît.   Encore un verre de vin, s'il vous plaît.
Mais vous avez un verre de vin devant vous.
Pardon, il y a bien un verre [à vin], mais pas de vin.
Un peu plus de vin, monsieur ?

[1] All the texts have translations in parallel columns.
[2] This is Ollendorffian.
[3] In a note the author tells us that the colloquial form is *du bon vin.*

Merci. [Je ne veux]¹ plus de vin.
Monsieur n'en veut pas davantage ?
Pas davantage, je vous remercie.
Du vin, mon ami ?
Merci. Pas de vin. Je ne bois pas de vin. Je ne veux pas de vin. Il y a un verre de trop, ôtez-le.

_____

' Avez-vous du pain ?
Non, je n'ai pas de pain, mais le boulanger en a (il y en a chez le boulanger).

•　•　•　•　•　•　•

_____

' Allons dîner. Garçon, la carte, s'il vous plaît.
Quel potage désirent ces messieurs ?

•　•　•　•　•　•

_____

' Messieurs, en dînant, je vais vous raconter une petite histoire. L'autre jour un Anglais, assis dans un restaurant, criait à tue-tête, à plusieurs reprises : " Garçon ! plus de soupe ! Garçon ! plus de soupe ! Garçon ; n'entendez-vous pas ? plus de soupe !" Le garçon répond d'abord : " Bien, monsieur." A la fin il dit : " Monsieur, j'entends très-bien ; vous ne désirez plus de soupe ; aussi ne vous en servirai-je plus." L'Anglais, très-étonné, s'écrie : " Mais c'est justement plus de soupe que je veux." " Ah," dit le garçon, " c'est différent ; alors il fallait vous expliquer plus clairement. Si vous m'aviez dit que vous désiriez encore du potage, je vous en aurais servi tout de suite." Notre Anglais, honteux et confus, s'est remis à prendre des leçons de français.

•　•　•　•　•　•

' Il n'y a pas de règle sans exception.
Il n'est point de roses sans épines.
Il n'y a pas de fumée sans feu.
Nécessité n'a point de loi.
Faire de nécessité vertu.
A bon entendeur peu de paroles.
A sotte question point de réponse.
Ventre affamé n'a point d'oreilles.
On prend plus de mouches avec du miel qu'avec du vinaigre.

_____

¹ These additions in [ ] might be relegated to notes, as they confuse the learner, who ought to have only one form presented to him at a time—that is, in this case, *Merci. Plus de vin.*

Il n'a ni feu ni lieu.
Il n'a ni foi ni loi.
Cela n'a ni rime ni raison.'

. . . .

The difficulty of constructing grammatical texts may depend on the nature of the language. The more highly inflectional a language is, the more easily it seems to lend itself to such *à priori* construction; while, on the other hand, the complexity of its forms is an additional inducement to make such texts. It will therefore be worth while to notice a Finnish analogue to Storm's book, intended to teach Finnish to Swedish-speaking natives of Finland—Kallio's *Finsk Elementarbok*.[1]

The plan of this book differs, however, widely from that of Storm's Dialogues. It is divided into four parts: (1) texts, (2) vocabularies, (3) general index to vocabularies (4) grammar. Each text has its own vocabulary, in which the meanings of the words are explained in the order in which they occur in the text. The index to these vocabularies is an alphabetic list of all the words in the texts, each word having a reference to the number of the text where it occurs first, which is, of course, also the number of the corresponding vocabulary, no further information being given. The object of this is to induce the learner to master as thoroughly as he can the vocabulary of each piece before going on to the next, so as to save himself the trouble of looking up the word in the index and then referring to the vocabulary there indicated. This is one of the weak points of the book: the learner ought to be referred not to a dry list of isolated words, but directly to the text itself, so that he can take in the context. As it is, if he wishes to compare the context of the first appearance of a word, he has to make three different references—two to lists of words, and another to the text itself. Notes like those in my *First Steps in Anglo-Saxon* are simpler and more effective than these short glossaries, which neither give full information nor are convenient to refer to through not being alphabetic. It would really be simpler to do away with the special vocabularies, and have an alphabetical glossary, and nothing else. The learner cannot be expected to remember every word at once —least of all in a strange language like Finnish—so that

---

[1] I know it only in its fourth edition, in which it has undergone some modifications by another hand.

practically he is obliged to look up many words at least three times, besides occasional references to the grammar. There is, in short, too much to and fro work—there is more turning over of pages than with the ordinary grammar and dictionary method.

The grammar begins with two pages of introduction dealing with the phonology. After that it is divided into numbered sections, each number referring to that of the piece in which the grammatical rules given in that section are exemplified. Thus the first section (p. 139) gives part of a verb-paradigm with analysis and rules :—

'(*minä*) *mene-n*   I go
(*sinä*) *mene-t*   thou goest
(*me*) *mene-mme*   we go
(*te* or *Te*) *mene-tte*   ye go *or* you go
Stem : *mene*. Personal endings : *-n, -t, -mme, -tte*.

Rule 1. In an inflected Finnish word we distinguish *stem* and *ending*.

Rule 2. By adding different endings to the stem we get different inflections of the word.

Rule 3. The subjects *minä, sinä, me, te* (or *Te*) can be omitted if there is no emphasis on them.'

All this seems rather dry and unnecessarily pedantic; but it must be remembered that the book is intended for teaching children in classes, not for self-instruction.

The corresponding text (p. 1) and its glossary (p. 73) are as follows :—

1. *Puheharjoitus.*

'Hyvää päivää ! Kuinka te voitte ?—Kyllä me hyvin voimme. Kuinka sinä voit ?—Kiitoksia, hyvin minä voin.—Mihin menet ? —Minä tulen teille ja toivon, että te huomenna [1] tulette meille.— Kiitoksia ! Kyllä me tulemme, jos minä voin hyvin huomenna.—Toivon, että Te voitte hyvin.

Hyvästi nyt ! Hyvästi, hyvästi !—Siis tulette huomenna ?— Kyllä me tulemme.

1.

puheharjoitus, speaking-practice. *kuinka*, how ?
hyvää päivää, good day !   *te, Te*, ye, you ; *teille*, to you.

[1] Pronounced *huomena*.

voin, be (ill or well).
kyllä, certainly.
me, we ; *meille*, to us.
hyvin, well.
sinä, thou.
kiitoksia, thanks.
minä, I.
mihin, whither ?
menen, go.

tulen, come.
ja, and.
toivon, hope.
että, that.
huomenna, to-morrow.
jois, if.
hyvästi, good-bye !
nyt, now,
siis, so, therefore.'

We cannot expect much of a text produced under such conditions, but it is certainly a great advance on Ahn and the rest of them. At any rate, it is connected. The average length of the later pieces is about a page. The following are translations of some of the headings, to which I have occasionally added the first sentence or two of the piece: Father (Father often goes away early in the morning. Sometimes he comes home late in the evening . . .) ; the Neighbours ; the Poor Woman (Yonder is a cottage. The cottage is old and bad. There dwells a poor woman . . .) ; the Gardiner ; What do we buy and sell? ; Journey abroad ; On the Ice (Near us there is a skating-rink) ; the Eagle's Nest ; the Months ; the Lighthouse ; Norway ; Wolves ; a Fairy-story ; Kalevala (the Kalevala tells of the life of our ancestors. There are fifty cantos in it. The chief personages are . . .). It will be seen that the texts are of a very varied character, only a few of them being in the dialogue form. Some of them are necessarily rather trivial, especially the earlier ones, and sometimes the constructions are a little unnatural, through the necessity of avoiding certain difficult forms, such as most of the infinitive and participle constructions, which are the great difficulty of the language. There is a second part, on the same plan as the first, in which the rest of the grammar is worked out in the same way, accidence and syntax being kept abreast throughout.

On the whole Kallio's *Finsk Elementarbok* gives as good a compromise between free texts and grammatical texts as could reasonably be expected. But the general question still remains, Which method will yield best results within a given time—that of progressive grammatical texts, or of free texts accompanied by a complete grammar founded on the texts ?

These considerations bring us face to face with the problem, How are we to bridge over the gulf between grammar and reader? The dilemma is this: If the texts are perfectly free and natural, they cannot be brought into any definite relation to the grammar. If the learner reads a sufficient number of systematically varied texts, he may depend on finding examples of all, or nearly all, the rules of grammar; but the examples will occur practically at haphazard without any natural grouping and without any regularity of reoccurrence. Thus in a descriptive text all that we can promise *à priori*, from a grammatical point of view, is that the verbs shall be in the third person present, while from a logical point of view we can determine with definiteness and certainty what concrete or other categories shall be represented.

The other horn of the dilemma is that if we try to make our texts embody certain definite grammatical categories, the texts cease to be natural: they become either trivial, tedious, and long-winded, or else they become more or less monstrosities, or, finally, they are broken up into detached sentences. Storm, as we see, openly adopts the detached sentence method; and this is better than giving texts which are outwardly connected, while in reality their sentences are detached.

We may, then, repeat our question in a different form: Is it really worth while trying to construct grammatical texts? Is it not simpler to rely on natural texts on the one hand, and detached sentences on the other?

If we resign ourselves to this compromise, we shall find that detached sentences are the real bridge across the gulf between texts and grammar. The bridge is constructed by taking the detached sentences used as examples in the grammar from the texts the learner is either reading at the moment or is about to read. This is the method I adopt in my *Anglo-Saxon Primer*: all the examples in the syntax are taken from the texts which follow. In this book I have, like Storm, supplemented the texts and the grammar by adding a selection of detached sentences, arranged so as to illustrate the different grammatical categories. In *First Steps in Anglo-Saxon* I generally follow the same principle, though here, not being bound to adhere strictly to the texts, I frequently modify the sentences in the grammar which are taken from the texts, so as to make them more instructive for the immediate purpose I have in view.

This method acts well either way, whether the learner begins with the texts or with the grammar. In the first case, he remembers the context of his sentence when he meets it in the grammar, so that it is no longer isolated to him. In the second case, when he meets his sentence in the texts, he sees more easily what grammatical rule it illustrates. By going through grammar and text alternately several times, both these advantages may be secured.

It is evident that the question of the relation between texts and grammar cannot arise till the systematic study of grammar has been begun. Kallio's book introduces grammatical analysis, with its stems and cases, at the very beginning. In my *First Steps in Anglo-Saxon* I utilize the section on pronunciation as a preparation for the grammar, but, as Old English in the nature of things is not learnt by very young or linguistically untrained beginners, it was not worth while giving much space to lengthening and systematically developing the pre-grammatical stage. If this were done, the gulf between texts and grammar would be partially bridged over beforehand : when the learner came to the grammatical stage, he would not only be better able to understand the detached sentences in his grammar, but would also be familiar with many of them individually.

Another important result of the development of the pre-grammatical stage would be that very elementary and consequently trivial and unnatural grammatical texts would no longer be needed at all, and grammatical texts generally would perhaps become superfluous.

O

CHAPTER XIV

RELATIONS BETWEEN DIFFERENT LANGUAGES; TRANSLATION

IT is evident that any general plan of study cannot be applied to any one language without certain modifications of detail. There are, moreover, further modifications of detail dependent on the special relations between the language to be learnt and the student's own language. Thus German offers certain special difficulties to an Englishman, other special difficulties to a Frenchman, not only in pronunciation, but also in grammar, vocabulary, and phraseology. But all these special relations are governed by the same general laws of association as the ideal general plan of study itself.

Begin with a knowledge of one's own language.— The first preparation for the study of a foreign language is the acquisition of a thorough knowledge of the peculiarities of one's own language. We have already seen that the first requisite for acquiring foreign pronunciations is a practical knowledge of the sounds of one's own language. So also the first requisite for understanding the grammatical structure of another language is a thorough knowledge of the grammatical structure of one's own language. This is one of the reasons why we should from the first be taught to regard the grammar of our own language from the point of view of general grammar. Just as in the study of the phonetics of a foreign language we are often surprised to find that the germ of an unfamiliar sound exists already in our own pronunciation, so also a systematic study of English grammar enables an English learner to point out analogies to unfamiliar foreign constructions which might otherwise escape his notice. Thus in Welsh and many other languages, adjunct-words or modifiers follow the word they

194

352

modify instead of preceding it as in English. Thus the Welsh *gwr gwellt*, 'straw man, effigy,' means literally 'man straw.' But in English an adjunct-group consisting of a preposition and a noun follows the same order as in Welsh, and we only have to think of *man (of) straw* with the *of* dropped to get the Welsh order, so that by degrees we can feel at home even in such complicated series as *llonaid llwy de llaeth*, 'tea-spoonful of milk,' literally 'fullness spoon tea milk.'

It is as important in grammar as in phonetics to have a clear idea of the defects and anomalies of one's own language; which, again, points to the importance of regarding the grammatical structure of our own language from a general linguistic point of view, as is done in my *New English Grammar*. Thus in English we have a group of defective verbs, such as *may*, *can*, which have no infinitives or participles; so that when we have occasion to use them in the functions of infinitives or participles, we have to substitute other words for them : *I can come, I shall be able to come, I have not been able to come.* Other English verbs are defective in other ways ; thus we cannot transfer *he used to go there every year* to the present without a complete change of construction : *he goes there every year*, or *he is in the habit of going there every year.* A distinct consciousness of these defects in English helps the English learner to get over the hesitation he feels when in speaking foreign languages he has to use such a construction as *I shall can . . .* , especially in a language such as German, which expresses these ideas with etymologically allied word *(ich kann,* infinitive *können).* So also, as already observed, the use of English *up* in *pack up* is contrary to that of most other languages, in which 'pack up' suggests the idea of unpacking, these languages generally expressing the idea of our *pack up* by 'pack in,' or some such construction, unless they use separate words. So if the English learner has once learnt to recognize that his native use of *up* in such constructions as *tie up, pack up, shut up,* is illogical, or, at any rate, contrary to the genius of other languages, he will be more ready to accept their divergent constructions.

Difficulties also arise from the opposite reason, namely, that the native language is more normal and rational or simpler than the foreign language. Thus the English speaker is apt to feel impatient of the distinctions of grammatical gender in most other European languages. He learns easily enough to associate feminine definite articles with feminine nouns, and so

353

on, but is continually liable to relapse into calling a tree or a house 'it' instead of 'he' or 'she,' even when he knows the gender. That *son frère* in French should mean 'her brother' as well as 'his brother' seems confusing and irrational to him : he feels it ought to be *sa frère*. It sounds even more absurd to him to talk of women as *le beau sexe*: he feels the adjective ought to be feminine. The only remedy for these and similar wrong associations is to regard the matter from a rigidly formal and mechanical point of view—to suspend the reasoning power, or, in some cases, to divert it into purely grammatical as opposed to logical channels.

The utilization of resemblances between the two languages—whether the result of affinity or accident—has already been discussed (p. 89).

Cross-associations.—We have already seen (p. 55) that the closer the connection between two languages, the greater chances there are of confusions arising from cross-associations. But cross-associations extend far beyond the limits of comparative philology, and may occur between any two languages however remote they may be from one another genealogically. But in such cases they are confined mainly to the syntax and phraseology and general structure of the two languages. But it is evident that if two languages have any general principles of structure in common, there must be a tendency to level differences of detail. Thus the main principles of word-order are the same in English and Chinese, so that the English learner is tempted in cases where the order differs to make the Chinese words follow the English order. If the word-orders of two languages follow fundamentally distinct principles, there is less effort required to keep up differences in detail. So also the general similarity in structure and word-order in English and French, and also in phraseology—all of which is the result partly of independent development, partly of borrowing—makes an English speaker more apt to introduce English constructions, word-order, and phraseology into French than into German, which, although more directly cognate to English, is nevertheless further removed in general structure.

Distrust of Similarity.—A linguist who has learnt a certain number of foreign languages of different families and different morphological structure, and has found certain constructions, idioms, or developments of word-meanings of his own language uniformly rejected by these foreign languages, gets at last quite instinctively into the habit of mistrusting the associations of his own language on these points, so that instead of feeling inclined to translate such a sentence as *ask him to come* literally, saying, for instance, in German, *fragen Sie ihn zu kommen*, he gets into the habit of always expecting something quite different. Hence when he comes to a language such as Arabic, in which, as in English, the meaning 'interrogate' develops into that of 'request,' he resists the tendency to reproduce this usage as strongly as he was once carried away by it. So also it is a surprise to an English linguist to find the Chinese *kien*, 'see,' used in the sense of 'visit.' The French *apprendre par cœur* we do not distrust because we at once conjecture that the English *learn by heart* is simply a translation of it; but we should not venture to transfer it to any other language.

Cross-associations between two foreign languages.— It is evident that the more foreign languages we learn, the greater our liability to form cross-associations. We not only form associations between our own language and a foreign language, but between the foreign languages themselves, especially between the one we are learning and the one last learnt. If an Englishman, after learning to speak Welsh fluently, were to go to Egypt and begin Arabic there, he would find that, in spite of the total want of affinity between the two languages, he would be constantly substituting Welsh for Arabic words in his attempts at conversation. This influence of the language last learnt implies not only that the language last learnt has been recently acquired, but also that it has been acquired with an effort, so that the resulting associations are strongly impressed on the mind in such a way as to be easily called forth by the slightest external stimulus; if our Englishman had been familiar with Welsh from his childhood so as to be perfectly bilingual, the influence of cross-associations derived from Welsh would be no stronger than cross-associations derived from English.

But although want of affinity is no safeguard against cross-associations, there is, of course, much greater danger of confusion when the foreign languages are cognate. Every comparative philologist knows this by experience.

Safeguards against confusion.—The great safeguard against confusions between different languages is, of course, to learn each language separately, and bring one's study of it to some definite conclusion before beginning another language.

But a good deal of help might be afforded by systematic summaries of the conflicting associations—the confusions and divergences—in each pair of languages.

Thinking in the Foreign Language; Not Translating

The remedy usually prescribed is to 'learn to think in the foreign language.' But we cannot think in a foreign language till we have a thorough and ready knowledge of it; so that this advice—sound as it is in itself—does not alter the fact that when we begin to learn a new language we cannot help thinking in our own language.

Thinking in the language implies that each idea is associated directly with its expression in the foreign language instead of being associated first with the native expression, which is then translated into the foreign language. This has led many into the fallacy that if we were only to get rid of translation in teaching a foreign language, substituting pictures or gestures, we should get rid of the cross-associations of our own language. But these cross-associations are independent of translation. They arise simply from the fact that each idea that comes into our minds instantly suggests the native expression of it, whether the words are uttered or not: and however strongly we may stamp the foreign expression on our memories, the native one will always be stronger. This is proved by the well-known fact that in moments of great excitement, we invariably fall back on our native language or dialect. Even if we admit that translation strengthens such cross-associations, we cannot admit that it is the cause of them. If it were, how can we explain those confusions between two foreign languages which we have been considering? It is not even necessary that we should be very familiar with the language last learnt to cause confusion with the one we are learning: all that is necessary to establish cross-associations is that we should have made an effort to learn the former one.

Translation from the Foreign Language

Translation is of two kinds : from the foreign language into our own language, and into the foreign language from our own language. The great practical difference between them is that the latter presupposes a thorough knowledge of the foreign language.

Translation from the foreign language stands on quite a different footing. It does not imply any previous knowledge of the word or sentence translated, and is at the same time the most obvious and convenient way of explaining its meaning. But some reformers wish to exclude even this kind of translation from the beginning.

The Picture-method.—This revolt may be seen carried to its extreme in the plan of teaching the vocabulary of a language by means of pictures. This old idea met with a warm champion in Franke (Fr. S. 34). He argues that the ' translation-method' involves a complicated psychological process : by this method a German learns the meaning of the French word *chapeau* by first associating it with its German equivalent *hut*, and then associating *hut* with the idea 'hat;' but show him the word *chapeau* in connection with a picture of a hat, and he will be able to establish a direct association between the word and the idea.

Such reasoning involves the fallacy that a psychological process must necessarily be difficult because it is complicated. The fact is that to a German the word *hut* and the idea 'hat' are so intimately connected that the one suggests the other instantaneously and without effort. Again, the picture gives us only part of the ideas associated with the word *chapeau ;* the shape and size of a hat varies, and is, besides, a secondary matter compared with the fact that a hat is meant to protect the head from the weather. Now the great advantage of a word as opposed to a picture is that it is practically an epitome of this whole group of ideas, and the equation *chapeau = hut* enables a German to transfer bodily such a group of ideas from his own to the foreign word. This the picture cannot do; for even if we ignore everything but the shape of the hat, we must either give pictures of every conceivable shape of hat—tall, hard felt, soft felt, clerical, sailor, cocked, etc.—or else risk implying that *chapeau* means ' tall hat,' not ' hat in general.'

The picture-method is, besides, very limited in its application. Pictures and diagrams are often useful, and sometimes almost indispensable, but in other cases they are either inadequate or useless, or absolutely impracticable, as in dealing with abstract ideas.

Explanation in the Foreign Language.—A less extreme view is that translation should be used only as a crutch for the beginner, to enable him to grasp the meaning of the foreign words and sentences, and should then be thrown away, the new foreign words being henceforth explained in the foreign language itself. Several advantages are claimed for this method by its adherents. The only incontestable one is that it affords additional practice in the foreign language. The other advantage claimed for it as well as the picture-method, that it diminishes the risk of cross-associations between the two languages, is, as we have seen, of more theoretical than practical importance. We find as a matter of fact that cross-associations cannot be got rid of by ignoring them : on the contrary, they have an awkward habit of cropping up when we least expect them. We cannot get rid of them for the simple reason that every idea is indissolubly associated with some word or phrase in our own language.

The main argument against explaining in the foreign language is that as long as we are learning the foreign language it is our first business to have it explained to us as clearly and unambiguously as possible. Therefore all explanations ought to be in the language we know—that is our own—not in the one we do not know. Again, definitions, like pictures, may be ambiguous : if I define a hat as ' a covering for the head,' the learner may think I mean a cap, or a bonnet, or a hood, or a helmet. Or the definition, like the picture, may be too precise. Thus, if I define a hat as ' a cylindrical head-covering with a brim,' or show the learner a picture of such a hat, he may think I mean to restrict the meaning of the foreign word to ' tall hat.' It is further evident that a misleading or obscure definition will not be made clearer by being expressed in a partially unknown language.

But translation or paraphrase in the foreign language may occasionally have its advantages for the more advanced student. Nor can there be any objection to it in cases where we can rely with certainty on the learner understanding it perfectly :

even if it does no other good, it will at least, as remarked before, serve to give him practice in the foreign language.

There is one application of such translation which is directly useful and instructive. When the advanced student comes to read the literature itself, he will derive much benefit from having the more out-of-the-way words and phrases translated into the corresponding simpler forms in the same language. This will teach him to discriminate clearly between what is general, modern, and colloquial on the one hand, and what is exceptional, archaic, or purely literary on the other hand. And this advantage would be lost if the translations were into his native language only.

It would, indeed, be useful, not only for practical, but also for critical and philological purposes, to have complete idiomatic translations of older standard works of literature into the modern language—to have, for instance, a translation of Shakespeare into Modern English prose, a translation as literal as the divergences of the two periods would allow. Such a translation would be more useful in many ways than a commentary, which, however lengthy, can never be made exhaustive.

Translation makes knowledge more exact.—Translation from the foreign into the native language has other and higher uses than that of being a temporary link between the foreign word and its meaning. When the learner has once clearly grasped the meaning of all the words in a phrase by means of translation, and has also grasped the meaning of the whole phrase, it is well that he should put aside his explanation-crutches for a time, and learn to associate the phrase directly with its meaning, without thinking of the corresponding phrase in his native language more than he can help. He can then begin to think in the foreign language—'to live himself into it,' as the Germans say.

But, as Storm remarks (Forbedret Undervisning, 29), ' the living oneself into the foreign language has also its dangers. One easily accustoms oneself to a partial understanding; one does not form a definite idea of the special shade of meaning, because one has not thought of corresponding expressions in the native language. It is not till one can translate the word, that one has complete mastery over it, so that one not only understands it, but can use it.' In fact, translation has much the same function in the vocabulary as grammatical rules and parsing have in construction: it tells us how far we can go in our unconscious or half-conscious associations. Thus, when an Englishman hears a Frenchman say in French, 'I ask myself (*je me demande*) what this means,' he feels that this makes perfectly good sense as it stands, being, indeed, a possible English expression of incredulity or astonishment. But when he has it translated into its exact English equivalent, 'I wonder what it means,' he sees that what he assumed to be an exceptionally strong expression is a mere expletive, and that he was quite wrong in translating it mentally word for word. Again, without this translation he would be at a loss to find the French equivalent of the English 'I wonder . . .' In this way translation is a most valuable means of testing the accuracy and correcting the mistakes in our unconsciously and mechanically formed associations between our ideas and their expressions in the foreign language.

Three Stages in translation.—We may distinguish three stages in the use of translation. In the first stage translation is used only as a means of conveying information to the learner: we translate the foreign words and phrases into our language simply because this is the most convenient and at the same time the most efficient guide to their meaning. In the second stage translation is reduced to a minimum, the meaning being gathered mainly from the context—with, perhaps, occasional explanations in the foreign language itself. In the third stage the divergences between the two languages will be brought face to face by means of free idiomatic translation. To these we may perhaps add a fourth stage, in which the student has so complete and methodical a knowledge of the relations between his own and the foreign language that he can translate from the one to the other with ease and accuracy.

Translation into the Foreign Language; Exercises

As already remarked, translation into the foreign language presupposes—or ought to presuppose—a thorough knowledge of the foreign language.

If the arithmetical fallacy were true—if sentences could be constructed *à priori* by combining words according to certain definite rules—then all that would be required for translating into a foreign language would be a knowledge of the grammar and the possession of a good dictionary. This is the fallacy on which the old practice of writing exercises was based.

In its crudest form the exercise-method consists in giving the beginner half a dozen words and a few rules, and then giving him detached sentences embodying these rules for translation from and into the foreign language either *viva-voce* or in writing or in both—and this from the very beginning. Thus Ahn's *New Practical and Easy Method of learning the German Language*, after a page or two on pronunciation, begins thus :—

1.

'Masc. *der Vater*, the father ;
Fem. *die Mutter*, the mother ;
Neut. *das Buch*, the book.
gut, good ; *grosz*, tall, big ; *klein*, small, little ; *ist*, is.

Der Vater ist gut. Die Mutter ist gut. Das Buch ist gut. Ist der Vater grosz ? Ist die Mutter klein ? Ist das Buch gut ?

2.

The father is tall. The mother is little. The book is good. Is the father good ? Is the mother tall ? Is the book small ?'

After sixty or seventy pages the learner has only got as far as the following sentences :—

129.

'*bitten*, to beg, to pray, to entreat ; *der Krieg*, the war.

Do you know of what I am speaking, of what I am thinking ? It is not the same street through which we passed this morning, the same house where we have been yesterday. Are you speaking of the war ? Yes, we are speaking of it. Are you thinking of the concert ? We are not thinking of it. Are you satisfied with that ring ? I am. Why do you not come up ? Tell your brother that I shall come down immediately. Come in, my friends. I beg of you to come in. Shall you go to-night to the play ? We shall not. Do you know where that gentleman lives, who he is, and where he is going ? We do not.'

Of the more advanced use of exercises as a supplement to

the detailed study of the grammar, the following are examples from Bernays' *German Exercises* :—

'R. 23. *a.* Of the spoon *Löffel;* of the broom *Besen;* to the father *Vater.* We have a governor *Gouverneur.* Of the tea and to the coffee.

b. Of the chain-of-mountains *Gebirge;* of the evil *Uebel;* to the seal *Siegel;* of the knife *Messer;* of the young-lady *Fräulein;* to the little-man *Männchen* (R. 15).

c. Of the assessor *Assessor;* to the author *Autor.*'

   .   .   .   .   .   .

'R. 161. His cattle is run away, and his pigeons are flown
        Vieh   laufen   *Taube fliegen (ir.)*
away; nevertheless he has worked on, as if (R. 304) nothing
      dennoch   *arbeiten fort*
had (R. 164) happened.—The labourers have run after the
      vor-fallen   *knecht*
horses.—They have run in-imitation-of the rope-dancers.—
               nach   *Seil-tänzer*
Their pond is fished out; now they have done fishing.—He
     fischen   *aus*
has jumped after me.'
  springen (ir.)

It is instructive to compare these examples of Ahn's and Bernays' methods. It is evident that the impossible task of translating into an unknown or only partially known language can be accomplished only under restrictions which make it either an evasion or a failure.

In the first place, translation from one language into another ought to imply as a matter of course that what is translated has a meaning—that it is, if not a complete text, at least a sentence with an independent meaning of its own worth stating—and, of course, that it as well as the translation is grammatically and idiomatically correct. But such groups of words as *of the tea and to the coffee* and *they have run in imitation of the rope-dancers* are neither of them fit objects of translation from English, the first because it cannot have any meaning, the second because it is not English. Nor is it enough that the texts or sentences should fulfil the negative conditions of making sense and being expressed correctly in both languages; it is also necessary that they should express something useful, something worth saying, even if it were only a trivial dialogue between a traveller and a waiter at a restaurant.   But although it is conceivable that any one of the sentences quoted from Ahn might occur in real life, yet taken as a whole they are impossible : instead of the first exercises introducing the learner to sentences and constructions which will help him to understand and express what he is most likely to meet with first, they give him a string of disconnected ideas which he might never have occasion to hear expressed or to express himself, even if he lived for years in the country where the language is spoken.

Again, although the sentence about the ' rope-dancers ' is not English, yet the result of the translation will certainly be a fairly good German sentence, if a perfectly useless one.   But this result is only obtained by giving so many helps in the way of glosses and direct references to the rules of the grammar that the work of translation becomes almost as great a farce as if the learner were set to copy from a book first the English original and then the complete German translation.   In fact, such a process would in most respects be a more instructive and improving one ; for the learner would have the advantage of being able to compare the two languages in their correct idiomatic forms.

We have also to realize what is meant by making mistakes in our exercises and correcting them afterwards.   It means the laborious formation of a number of false associations which must be unlearnt before the labour of forming the correct ones can be begun.   Even when no positive errors are made, the writing of exercises which require any thought must produce vague and hesitating, instead of the clear and instantaneous associations which constitute a real practical command of a language.

And yet this process of going out of one's way to make mistakes, and then laboriously correcting them, is almost the only way of learning languages—at least, of learning grammar —that some people can conceive.   I remember, when I first went up to Oxford as an undergraduate, I told my tutor that I was rusty about some point of Greek grammar ; so he said, ' You had better do a paper on it.'   I could not help thinking even then that strengthening one's false associations by ' doing a paper' was a curious preliminary to getting rid of them.

It must also be remembered that the knowledge and conviction that a certain linguistic combination is erroneous does not necessarily get rid of the false association itself, for that is a matter of habit, not only of conviction. Thus, if in speaking German I once get into the habit of making 'bread' masculine instead of neuter, even when I am told that *brod* is neuter, I am still liable to fall back into saying—as I once heard an Englishman say—(haabən zij kainən vaisbroud) through pure force of habit. Getting rid of this habit may imply that I must repeat *das brod* at least as often as I formerly repeated *der brod*. There was once a professor who taught some Oriental language by correspondence. One of his pupils—a middle-aged military man—after going through a course, asked to be allowed to go through it again, so as to perfect the knowledge already gained before going any further. When he did so, he made exactly the same mistakes over again. He then asked to be allowed to go over the same course for the third time. The professor, who seems to have been a good-natured fellow, was inclined to grant this request, but was dissuaded by his wife.

As we see, the only way to avoid the necessity of making mistakes is either practically to do the work for the learner by giving him a more or less complete word-for-word translation; or to make the exercises so easy that they cost no effort, and afford no real practice at all, so that they slip through the mind without making any impression, these very easy exercises being at the same time necessarily unidiomatic and consequently of little or no use when learnt.

These facts are now generally recognized among reformers. This is, indeed, the one point on which there is the greatest unanimity among them, namely, that everything of the nature of exercise-writing ought to be abolished, not only in the beginning but throughout the whole course.

Free Composition; Question and Answer

There is also a general agreement among reformers that the place of exercises and translations into the foreign language should be taken by free composition in the foreign language on subjects taken from the texts already studied, so that the compositions are reproductions of what is already known.

Continental reformers also make great use of a system of question and answer carried on in the foreign language by the teacher and pupils, the former asking the questions, the latter answering them, or the teacher telling one pupil to ask a certain question of another pupil. The subjects of the questions are, of course, taken from the texts which the pupils have just been reading. Thus even a short sentence such as *we can easily see that the earth is round by watching a ship sailing out to sea* can be made the subject of a number of questions, such as *what is the earth?* or *what is the earth like?* or *what shape is the earth?* | *how can we see that it is this shape?* or *how can we see that the earth is round?* | *what can we see by watching a ship sailing out to sea?* Of course, if any unfamiliar word, such as *shape*, is used in the questions, it must be explained, unless its meaning is quite clear from the context.

This method of question and answer is older than is commonly supposed. As I have several times drawn on Bernays for examples of bad methods, it is a pleasure to me to be able to quote the following remarks from the introduction to his *German Reader:—*

' I have always found it very advantageous to my pupils, both in *private lessons* and *classes*, to let them translate back again into German. For this purpose I make use of the third section, generally beginning with this kind of exercise about the time the student has reached nearly the end of the first section, proceeding at the same time with the construing of German into English. When the learner is thoroughly master of a piece, however short, I question him on it in German, and receive his answers in the same language. By this means, his ear becomes familiarized with the pronunciation of another person without the aid of the eye, while he insensibly acquires the habit of speaking German himself. Take, for instance, the first short anecdote, page 119 [I have given this very anecdote on p. 167]; I ask :—

> Question. *Wer schrieb an die Griechen?*
> Answer. *Alexander.*
> Q. *Was that Alexander?*
> A. *Er schrieb.*
> Q. *An wen schrieb er?*
> A. *An die Griechen.*
> Q. *Was schrieb er an die Griechen?*
> A. *Dasz sie ihn für einen Gott erkennen sollten.*
> Q. *Für was sollten sie ihn erkennen?*
> A. *Für einen Gott.*

Q. *Wen sollten sie für einen Gott erkennen ?*
A. *Alexander.*
Q. *Wer sollten ihn für einen Gott erkennen ?*
A. *Die Griechen.*

'This exercise may be continued and varied to any extent, if directed by any person capable of conversing in German, provided he is sufficiently familiar with the grammar to correct the mistakes of the student.'

I do not know when this preface was first published—certainly before 1856, the date of the seventh edition of the *Reader*. Dr. A. Bernays, who was professor of German language and literature in King's College, London, and was, I believe, more successful in the combination of language and literature than is always the case, began to publish his helps for the study of German about 1830. Although he was under the full influence of the methods of detached sentences and exercise-writing which attained their most extravagant development about his time, his books contain many good ideas. It is strange he did not see the absurdity of teaching his pupils to converse in German about Alexander and the Lacedemonians.

The purely oral exercises of question and answer in the foreign language should precede any attempts at written reproduction of what has been learnt, partly on the general ground that the fixed associations of the ear should precede the secondary and perhaps variable associations of the written form of the language, partly because of the facility and quickness with which they can be worked. They have the further advantage of training the pupils both to understand what is said, and reproduce it with accuracy and ease. They are, in fact, the best possible substitute for a phonetic method, although they will be ten times more efficient if preceded by systematic training in phonetics. They are also in the highest degree stimulating to the pupils, and develope quickness, presence of mind, and the power of observation.

This reproductive or 'imitative' method has the great advantage of being progressive. The questions and answers may be exact literal reproductions of what has been learnt, or they may be free paraphrases of it. The questions may also embody new words, which, again, may be expressly pointed out, and explained, either beforehand or afterwards, or left to be inferred from the context.

So also with the written compositions. At first the pupils will simply be expected to write down from memory the subject of what they have been studying. Then they may be set to write an essay on a subject analogous to that of the text they have been studying. In this way the written compositions become gradually more and more independent of the texts, and more and more general in their subjects, as the learner's command of the language is widened, till at last he is able to express himself both in speaking and writing on any ordinary topic.

Visualizing

By visualizing we understand the establishment of a direct association of the words and sentences of the foreign language with the ideas they express by means of a direct appeal to the sense of sight. This can be effected in three principal ways, namely, by—

(1) Object-lessons—the presentive or object-method: 'here is a piece of chalk,' 'this is called a black board,' 'this is my nose.'

(2) Models, pictures, diagrams—the representive or pictorial method.

(3) Gestures, mimicry—the dramatic method.

It is also possible to establish direct associations independent of the help of a second language by appealing to the other senses. Thus the teacher may illustrate 'cock' or 'fowl' not only by exhibiting a picture of the bird, and by the dramatic method of flapping his arms and raising himself on tiptoe, but also by an imitation of its crow. So also the pupils may be invited to taste sugar, salt, tartaric acid, and alum in connection with a study of the foreign words expressing the accompanying sensations of taste. But the visual impressions are evidently the only ones of which any extended use can be made.

Of the purely visualizing methods, it is evident that the first two are best suited for words expressing concrete ideas, the last for words expressing phenomena and actions.

But they are all limited in their application. And of those associations which can be established by visual means, many are, as we have seen, vague and ambiguous as compared with those established by means of translation. It is so even with the object-method. Thus a cube of boxwood may just as well

P

suggest the idea of ' wood ' as that of ' cube ; ' a piece of sugar may suggest the idea of 'sugar in general,' or it may suggest the narrower ideas of 'loaf sugar' or 'white sugar'—which, again, may be subdivided into 'cane sugar' and 'beet-root sugar'—or 'lump of sugar.' It ought also to suggest the idea of 'lump' or 'piece' in the abstract; but even if a piece of chalk, a piece of coal, and a piece of bread were exhibited together with the lump of sugar, it is by no means certain that the class would grasp what was meant.

Pictures are even more liable to be misunderstood. Let us suppose two pictures, one of a human head, the other of a railway station, with numbers and dotted lines leading to various parts of the pictures, these numbers referring to an accompanying vocabulary of the foreign words expressing the ideas supposed to be excited in the learner's mind by the contemplation of these pictures—a contemplation which, if he is not much interested in the subject of either picture, he will perhaps enter on only with a certain effort and without much attention to details. His first difficulty will be a mechanical one ; as the pictures are shaded in some parts, he sometimes cannot see clearly where the dotted lines lead to : a certain line may point to the pupil of the eye, or the iris, or the cornea, or it may indicate the bridge of the nose. Then comes the old difficulty of determining the degree of generality of the ideas called forth by the pictures : is the eye, or only the pupil of the eye, meant ? is the number to be taken literally as indicating the dial of the clock, or does it imply ' clock ' generally ? does the other number refer to the railway carriage as a whole, or only to its roof ? In fact, did I not possess enough knowledge of the foreign language to know that whatever *wagon* may mean, it does not mean ' roof,' I should find these pictures most misleading guides.

Gestures are equally liable to be misunderstood.

The argument that the substitution of visualizing methods for translation prevents cross-associations is, as we have seen, a fallacy.

If we did not use a phonetic notation, there would indeed be something in the argument that visualizing methods enable us to save the learner the confusions that result from letting him see words written in an unphonetic spelling. But no teacher who has once used the phonetic method will ever think of wasting time over such an inefficient method of teaching pronunciation.

CHAPTER XV

CONVERSATION

CONVERSATION in a foreign language may be regarded from two very different points of view : (1) as an end in itself, and (2) as a means of learning the language and testing the pupil's knowledge of it. But there is, of course, no reason why the second process should not be regarded as being at the same time a preparation for the first.

The difficulty and, at the same time, the utility of conversation, is due to the quickness and presence of mind that it requires. What we speak we have to know perfectly ; and we must have it ready at a moment's notice. Even the elementary question-and-answer method described above requires that the pupil should have thoroughly mastered the little he knows.

Hence every speaker's knowledge must be definitely limited within comparatively narrow boundaries. Even in our own language we can only speak one special form of it. It is true that our knowledge is not confined to the spoken language, but extends to the literary language, and even to the archaic literary language. But although we know the literary language well enough to be able to read it with perfect ease, and perhaps to write it in its modern form, we cannot speak it for any length of time without the risk of continual relapses into the colloquial. The language of a few generations back we can neither speak nor write.

We speak our own colloquial language without hesitation in spite of the confusing associations of the written language, because our associations with the former are by far the stronger ; and the only way to acquire a colloquial style of speech in a foreign language is to make our associations with the spoken language stronger than those with the written language—by beginning with the spoken language and confining ourselves

211

exclusively to it till we can handle it with ease and certainty. We have seen also that this is the rational method, whether we wish to learn the language for conversational purposes or not.

This does not by any means imply that the beginner should learn dialogues about railway travelling and life in hotels, but merely that his elementary training should not be such as to unfit him for doing so hereafter, if he has occasion to travel abroad or converse with foreigners.

Phrase-books

We will now consider what ought to be the character of the dialogue- or phrase-books intended for this special purpose.

As regards the ordinary phrase-books, the want of phonetic notation is alone enough to make them useless.

But they are often quite as defective in their idioms. Not only is there a want of system in selecting the really useful and necessary idioms, and rejecting or subordinating the others, but the idioms and phrases given are often incorrect from the point of view of ordinary speech, being archaic, or literary, or vulgar, or, what is worse still, the result of mistranslation or over-literal translation of some foreign idiom.

Most phrase-book writers fail to reproduce the natural spoken language, partly from want of preparatory training in the practical study of languages, partly from fear of being thought vulgar, but also from pretentiousness and conceit, which leads them into a spurious literary style, so that their dialogues read like extracts from badly written novels. Thus Franke remarks that German grammars and phrase-books for foreigners generally give *eilen Sie!* | *dieses ist mein Bruder* instead of the colloquially idiomatic *beeilen Sie sich* or *machen Sie schnell* | *das (hier) ist mein Bruder*. I find in English phrase-books such fossils as *may I have the pleasure of drinking wine with you, Miss?* | *your health, Sir!* together with dinner-table comments such as *this beef is delicious : it melts in the mouth* | *I love fat.* In some of these books a wife is still *a good lady.* On these principles learned foreigners might address impudent cabmen with *zounds, sirrah!* or even *'sdeath!* Some compilers of phrase-books seem to forget that we no longer cut our pens or snuff our candles. Storm quotes from Otto's French conversation-grammar *la servante nettoie la chambre*, which, he says, would make the same impression on a Frenchman as *the handmaiden cleanses the chamber* would on an Englishman; the correct modern form is *la bonne fait la chambre.*

It is interesting to compare the modern phrase-books or 'parleurs' with a much older specimen of this kind of litera-ture—the *Hermeneumata* or *Interpretamenta* of the Greek Julius Pollux, who was born 150 A.D. and died in 208, and was pro-fessor of literature at Athens under the reign of Commodus. His book was intended primarily for the use of Greeks who wished to learn to speak Latin. The following extracts are from A. Boucherie's edition in *Notices et extraits des manuscrits de la Bibliothèque Nationale, Tome xxiii., seconde partie* (1872), with most of the peculiarities of the orthography unaltered (the manuscript is a ninth-century copy of an older text), but with the text written continuously instead of in two columns of mostly single words, one column Greek, the other Latin, as in the original :

'Epidē orō pollous epithu-mountas ellēnisti dialegesthai kai rōmaeisti, mēte eukerōs dinasthai, dia tēn diskerian kai poluplēthian tōn rēmatōn, ouk ephisamēn touto poiēsai, eina en trisin bibliois ermēneumatikois panta ta rēmata sungrapsōmai.

Arkomai graphin apo alpha eōs ō.

Quoniam video multos cupi-entes graece disputare et latinae, neque facile posse propter diffi-cultatem et multitudinem ver-borum, non peperci hoc facere ut in tribus libris interpretoriis omnia verba conscribam.

Incipio scribere ab alpha usque o.'

I will now give the Latin text only :—
'Bona fortuna, dii propitii.

Preceptor, have. Quoniam volo et valde cupio loqui graece et latinae, rogo te, magister, doce me.

Ego faciam, si me adtendas.

Adtendo diligentur.

Quoniam ergo video te hujus rei, hoc est, ejus interpreta-tionis quae dicitur latinae, cupientem, demonstrabo tibi, fili, quoniam non est cujuslibet hominis deprehendere, sed docti et ingeniosi esse doctrinam. Propter hoc etiam tibi magis, qui nescis nihil disputare, exponam. Opus ergo tibi est quae praecipio : auditus, memoria, sensus ; usus cotidianos artificem facit.

Hoc tibi, si praesteteris mercedes, potes discere. Duo ergo sunt personae quae disputant, ego et tu : tu es qui interrogas, ego respondeo. Ante omnia ergo lege clare, diserte.

Libenter te vidi | Et ego te.

Quis pulsat ostium ? | A Caio ad Lucium. Si hic est, nuntia. Venit a Caio. | Roga illum.

Quid est, puer ? | Omnia recte, etiam domine. Misit tibi epistolam signatam. | Da legam. Scripsit mihi de negotio. Vade, puer, et nuntia quoniam venio.

Date mihi calciamenta; adfer aquam ad faciem; da subar-male, cinge me; da togam, operi me; da penulam et annulos.

Quid stas, sodalis ? Tolle quae opus sunt, et veni mecum; festino ad amicum antiquum, senatorem populi Romani, qui a Romulo deducit genus, a Trojanis Aeneadarum.'

It will be seen from these specimens that Pollux' dialogues are, on the whole, neither better nor worse than most modern ones. Although generally simple and to the point, the pedant has certainly triumphed over the practical linguist in the last sentence, of which Ollendorff himself need not be ashamed. The succeeding dialogues deal in the same way with such subjects as going to the shops, taking a bath, dining. The writer often falls into the mistake of bare enumeration of words belonging to the same category without adding anything to differentiate them (p. 173), as in *praecide cervum et gallinam et leporem et colliculos*. Indeed, he soon tires altogether of such trivial compositions, which afford him no opportunity of displaying his learning and rhetorical skill, and his book degenerates into a mere vocabulary of words arranged roughly under categories. He begins with the names of divinities, then goes on to the signs of the zodiac, enumerates the constellations and stars, then gives words relating to the atmosphere and its phenomena, the winds, seasons, divisions of time, terms relating to medicine, navigation, civil government, military organization, agriculture, names of trees, edifices, relationship, serpents (!), parts of a city, the different trades and professions, and so on.

If we compare the *Hermeneumata* of Pollux with the *Colloquy* of Archbishop Ælfric and his disciple Ælfric Bata, composed about 1000, we cannot hesitate to give the palm to our own countrymen. The full title of the work is *Colloquium ad pueros linguae Latinae locutione exercendos, ab Ælfrico primum compilatum, et deinde ab Ælfrico Bata, ejus discipulo, auctum, Latine et Saxonice*. These dialogues are not only good from a pedagogic point of view, but have intrinsic merits of their own. They are inspired by a liberal and humane spirit, and are full of graphic descriptions and incidents. Accordingly, in my *First Steps in Old English* I have taken the Old English interlinear version of them, and made it into an idiomatic Old English text. The following are specimens of the original Latin :—

' Nos pueri rogamus te, magister, ut doceas nos loqui Lati-aliter recte, quia idiote sumus, et corrupte loquimur.

Quid vultis loqui ?

Quid curamus quid loquamur, nisi recta locutio sit et utilis, non anilis aut turpis ?

Vultis flagellari in discendo ?

Carius est nobis flagellari pro doctrina quam nescire ; sed scimus te mansuetum esse, et nolle inferre plagas nobis, nisi cogaris a nobis.

Interrogo te quid mihi loqueris ? quid habes operis ?

Professus sum monachum, et psallam omni die septem sinaxes cum fratribus, et occupatus sum lectionibus et cantu; sed tamen vellem interim discere sermocinari Latina lingua.

Quid sciunt isti tui socii ?

Alii sunt aratores, alii opiliones, quidam bubulci, quidam venatores, alii piscatores, alii aucupes, quidam mercatores, quidam sutores, quidam salinatores, quidam pistores loci.

Quid dicis tu, arator ; quomodo exerces opus tuum ?

O mi domine, nimium laboro. Exeo diluculo, minando boves ad campum, et jungo eos ad aratrum. Non est tam aspera hiemps ut audeam latere domi, pre timore domini mei; sed junctis bobus et confirmato vomere et cultro aratro, omni die debeo arare integrum agrum aut plus.

Habes aliquem socium ?

Habeo quendam puerum minantem boves cum stimulo, qui etiam modo raucus est pre frigore et clamatione.'

Neither Pollux nor the Archbishop need fear a comparison with the following extract from Waddy's *English Echo* (10th edition, 1877), in which I have enclosed superfluous words and word-groups in ( ), so as to enable the reader better to realize the Gladstonian verbosity of the language :—

' A little bread, (if you) please.—Will you be good enough to pass (me) the salt? I do not think this soup is sufficiently seasoned.—My husband is so very fond of salt and (of) sugar. I tell him sometimes that if he eats so much sugar he will get shockingly stout.—Do not terrify me in that way; I should be horrified if I thought I was likely to be a fat man.—I remember when you were in Germany you were very slim and agile.[1] Our friends gave you the nickname of the active Englishman.—I do not think I could run or leap as I used to (do) then. I have not tried anything in that way since I became sedate so many years ago.—Why, then, we must now call you the lazy Englishman.—(Oh dear!) that is worse than ever; I hate to be thought slow and torpid.—May I have the pleasure (, Madam,) of assisting you to some wine?—Thank you (, Sir,) that is Sherry; if you will allow me I will trouble you for some of the Bucellas. It is in the other decanter.—Adolph, you and I must drink a bumper (with each other) in memory of bygone times.—Your very good health, my old friend!—And yours, and that of your wife and family!—Will you let me send you some of this grouse, or would you prefer some venison?—Thank you, I will wait for a piece of your old English roast beef, of which I have heard so much.—I am sorry (that) we have none to-day. But there is a very nice shoulder of mutton.—I will ask you for some of that macaroni pudding.—Charlotte, you are drinking with your mouth full, that is very unlady-like indeed. John, remove these things and bring us the dessert and wine.—Try some port, Adolph; I think you will approve of it; or would you prefer claret? You always had the reputation of being a good judge of wines,[2] so I will accept your recommendation.—Emily, here are your walnuts; I will break them open[3] for you.—Charles! Charles! you are cracking those nuts with your teeth; you should use the nut-crackers.—I have not got any, mama.—There is a pair just under the edge of your plate; what a careless little fellow you are.—Now, my children, go with your mama. May this little gentleman, Charley, stay with us once? Yes, if he will behave himself very well.—We will rejoin you, my dear, directly. Now, Adolph, draw your chair nearer the fire and fill your glass again.—These pears are very large and fine. Do you grow them yourself?—No, I have no garden here of any size. My wife got them in Covent Garden Market.—Really, I must felicitate[4] you upon having so beautiful and amiable a wife. I am delighted with her.—You will like her better the more you know of her. Her beauty is her least recommendation. She is my greatest treasure.'

This could never have been genuine English conversation,

[1] = active; the word *agile* is put to avoid the repetition of *active*; but this is literary, not colloquial.
[2] = wine.   [3] break open = crack.   [4] = congratulate.

not even in 1860, about which time Storm supposes this book was first published, although it must be admitted that the matter of these dialogues is generally good. Strange to say, Jeaffreson and Boensel's *English Dialogues* (1891) are even more stilted, though in a different way. Take such a sentence as this:

'The practical results of science during that period are doubtless unsatisfactory, but still I think they have been underrated. If Nature was not interrogated as she has been since, there was notwithstanding a considerable improvement in the mechanical arts, so far as they affect the daily comforts of life. Besides, we cannot deny that the foundations of chemistry and optics were laid in that period. The art of navigation, even before the invention of the compass, was greatly improved, and you must not forget that the printing-press belongs to what are called the middle-ages, though coming within a few years of their expiration. There are many other points I might urge in favour of a more respectful attitude towards the science of the middle-ages, but I must leave you now, as I have an appointment.'

This is preaching, not talking. But even in the lighter dialogues there is a constant substitution of unnecessary artificialities for plain colloquialisms, such as *your very humble servant* for *I*, together with archaisms such as *how is that, pray?* and, what is strange in a book for foreigners, unnecessary insertion of foreign expressions such as *nuit blanche, auf wiedersehen!*

As a further illustration of the difficulty of getting really idiomatic conversational language, I may refer to *Spoken English: Everyday Talk*, by E. A. True, which was originally a translation of Franke's *Phrases de tous les jours*. How misleading a guide it is, may be seen from the following examples:

'Since the month of August we have constantly had fine weather (= we have had constant fine weather since August). Please, put a fire in my room. He resembles his eldest brother. Put the lamp on the piano; it is too much exposed here and might be upset. Mary, pick up your hat, it is lying on the floor, and then don't let your toys lie about everywhere. Remove these things from the table; they are in my way. On his way to Paris he must needs pass through this place.'

Prof. Jespersen, who re-edited this work, has got rid of most of the worst faults of the original, but it is hopeless to try to make idiomatic dialogues by translation; one of the languages must sacrifice its individuality.

In short, it should be clearly understood that to write plain colloquial dialogues is a task of great difficulty, and should not be undertaken without preparation—quite apart from a knowledge of phonetics. No one but a native should ever attempt it.

In the present dearth of really useful and reliable phrase-books, the safest way of learning conversational idioms is to read novels and comedies, selecting those idioms which seem most useful and passing over the rest. But this is a slow and difficult process, and requires a peculiar linguistic tact and a special kind of memory to produce good results (p. 122). It is also difficult for the foreigner to know whether the idioms are really modern colloquialisms such as he can safely assimilate without fear of falling into archaisms on the one hand, and vulgarity or slanginess on the other. Plays are, on the whole, not so good as novels for this purpose, as the stage in most countries seems to develope a traditional and conventional colloquial style of its own.

The difficulty of learning the spoken language from literature lies deeper than this: it is the result of the literary being necessarily anti-commonplace. We do not go to literature to find a photograph of our everyday life and talk: we seek the flavour of originality and divergence from the associations of ordinary life. Even when humorous literature is founded on descriptions of the commonplace, the result is seldom anything that the foreign learner can assimilate with advantage.

We must, therefore, have books specially written for this purpose, and for no other. The best book of the kind that has hitherto appeared is Storm's edition of Bennett's *Norwegian Phrase-book*.[1] But as it is mainly intended for tourists who know little or nothing of the language, it does not claim to be anything but a rough guide, the idioms being arranged alphabetically for ready reference.

[1] This book has since been re-edited by another hand, and the phonetic transcription has been discarded.

CHAPTER XVI

LITERATURE ; LITERARY COMPOSITION

In a rationally progressive method of learning languages the approach to the literature of the foreign language will be made gradually. The learner, as he advances, will be able to choose his texts with greater freedom and with less subordination of matter to form, till at last he is able to read with profit the actual literature itself, unmodified and uncurtailed.

As there are gradations in the approach to the literature, so also there will be gradations in the study of the literature itself. The student will, of course, begin with modern prose in its simplest form and that which approximates most closely to the spoken language. In fact, some of this simpler literature will perhaps be already familiar to him in the pre-literature stage (p. 181). He will then proceed gradually to the higher rhetorical and imaginative prose, and then to archaic prose and poetry.

This procedure is quite opposed to the older method of not only introducing the learner to the literature of the language before he has mastered its vocabulary and grammar, but of making its classics the vehicle of elementary instruction. This is much as if a music-teacher were to give his pupils classical sonatas to learn the notes on instead of beginning with scales and exercises. Even in Latin there is no necessity for beginning with such an author as Virgil, whose literary merits no beginner can be expected to appreciate ; in a modern language there is no excuse whatever for such a course.

Besides, when the classics of a language are ground into pupils who have neither knowledge enough of the language to appreciate their stylistic merits, nor maturity of mind and taste to appreciate their ideas, the result is often to create a disgust for literature generally.

Composition

The ambitious student who aspires to original composition in the higher literary style of the foreign language must work his way up cautiously and slowly, beginning with more or less free reproduction (of what he has read, at first in an almost colloquial style, then in a higher literary diction.

The simplest and most spontaneous form of literary composition is letter-writing, which is at the same time the most useful. Letter-writing is, indeed, the only form of literary composition that most people ever attain to, even in their own language.

Even in letter-writing we must firmly resist the temptation to imitate ornate literary models in the foreign language. I have already remarked that a too early introduction to the masterpieces of literature often inspires the learner with a dislike for literature generally. But it may have the opposite effect of rousing too much enthusiasm—a too burning desire to emulate the example of the great masters of literary style. There was once a firm of German merchants at Hamburg who had a native clerk to do the foreign correspondence, which he did very well on the whole, his only failing being a weakness for fine writing, the result of assiduous devotion to the works of Byron and Bulwer Lytton. It happened in course of time that the firm received a consignment of leeches from England. The passage was rough, and as the leech is a delicate insect, the result was that the German clerk wrote a letter to the English firm in which he said, 'Dear Sirs, we beg leave to acknowledge receipt of the consignment of leeches as per invoice, but regret to be obliged to add that the greater part of them have gone to glory.'

In many Oriental languages there would be no incongruity in such a mixture of styles; for in them the inflation and artificiality of the literary language often goes to such a length that all sense of congruity and proportion is lost, and the style is valued according to the degree of its departure from the plain colloquial style. This is why many Hindoos who have a perfect knowledge of English for speaking purposes, become entirely un-English when they write even an ordinary letter, not by making mistakes in grammar, but by using words and idioms in unappropriate surroundings. A Hindoo clerk in whose charge a pony had been left by his employer, wrote thus to him : ' I have the honour to report that the little horse, since your honour's departure, has assumed a devil-may-care attitude, and has become violently obstreperous. This morning, at 6 a.m., the said little horse eloped from my custody, but, with the favour of heaven, he may return.' In a well-known biography written by a Hindu, a description of the confusion caused in the house by some calamity calls forth the ejaculation, ' Here was a pretty kettle of fish ! ' In the same book it is said of the hero of the biography that 'in his youth he was filamentous, but he afterwards became plump as a partridge.'

Next to the imitation of unsuitable models, the greatest snare in composition in a foreign language is originality of style. We can be original in our own language only, although even there we cannot deviate far from the beaten track : in a foreign language we must adhere rigidly to our models. This is why original writers are seldom good linguists : they know instinctively that their own language is the only instrument of thought they can hope to handle freely, and so they have no inducement to try to master any other. However wilful the deviations of a native may be from rule and tradition in his attempts to frame new expressions for new ideas, or to express more forcibly the old ones, the result will always have a native flavour—it may be uncouth or obscure English or French, but it will always be unmistakeably English or French as the case may be. But if we try to be original in a foreign language, there is always a danger of our originality assuming a native form. The result will be a language which is incorrect in grammatical construction or in phraseology, not merely incongrous, as in the examples last given—that is to say, it will use forms which are not only non-existent, but which no native writer could possibly have evolved.

A foreigner's style may of course have a quaint and apparently original character simply through being tinged with reminiscences of his own language, not through any originality of mind in himself. Dialectal influences may have the same effect. Thus much of the supposed originality of Carlyle's style is the result of the influence of the Scotch dialect. When he speaks of newly built suburban houses as ' the human dog-hutches of the period,' an English reader is struck by the picturesqueness of the word ' dog-hutch,' which he thinks is an original creation of Carlyle's, perhaps the result of his supposed imitation of German; but this picturesqueness was quite unintentional on Carlyle's part, being simply the result of his ignorance of the correct expression 'dog-kennel.' It is, of course, often difficult or even impossible to distinguish these two factors. The passage already quoted from Terrien de la Couperie (p. 72) is a specimen of the style into which a foreigner may insensibly lapse who lets himself go under the impression that he has a perfect mastery of the language.

CHAPTER XVII

DEAD LANGUAGES

It need hardly be said that the study of dead languages should be based on the same general principles as that of living languages, with, of course, such special modifications as experience and common-sense show to be advisable.

It must, in the first place, be realized that there is no essential difference in structure between a dead and a living language. The dead Latin and the living Italian differ widely in structure; but this is not because all dead languages are inflectional, all living languages analytical. On the contrary, we need not look far to find in Russian a language whose inflections are quite as complicated as those of Latin. In Hebrew, on the other hand, we have a dead language of comparatively simple structure, the simplicity being, like that of Italian, mainly the result of phonetic change.

External Difficulties

As the study of dead languages is subject to various external difficulties of its own, resulting from their being no longer spoken and being preserved in a limited number of texts which are sometimes fragmentary and often obscure, it is even more necessary than in the case of living languages to remove as many of the other external difficulties as possible.

Hence texts in dead languages should be printed with all the helps that transliteration, quantity- and stress-marks and other phonetic diacritics, can afford, not to speak of punctuation, quotation-marks, capital letters or other marks to indicate proper names. If these are found helpful with modern languages—if we do not like to dispense with them even in our own language—they must be still more useful in such

223

languages as Sanskrit, which, as it is, is printed not only without most of these helps, but without even the help of word-division !

Normalizing

Some dead languages have been handed down to us in a more or less fixed conventional orthography like those of the modern European languages. Other languages died out without ever having developed a fixed orthography, so that in these languages the spelling may vary not only from generation to generation, but also from manuscript to manuscript. Old English, Middle English, Old French, Old Irish afford examples of this extreme, while Sanskrit is an example of the other. In Sanskrit the orthography is so absolutely fixed that even the archaic language of the sacred hymns of the Rig-Veda is written with the spelling of the much later classical Sanskrit, in spite of the fact that this later spelling often does violence to the metre, as when the Vedic *sūria, āria* are written *sūrya, ārya.*

The worst of these fixed traditional orthographies is that they are generally much more modern than the language they profess to represent, so that they may be really quite unauthoritative. Thus the present Sanskrit devanagari alphabet and its whole system of orthography was not evolved till long after Sanskrit had ceased to be a living language. This is also the case with the orthographies of Greek and Latin, which are full of misleading spellings, the result of mistakes and confusions of comparatively modern times, as is soon seen by comparing the traditional spelling with that of the few texts—mostly inscriptions—preserved in contemporary documents. Such spellings as *Virgilius* and some of the details of Greek accentuation are simply modern monstrosities.

It is evident that an unfixed orthography such as that of Middle English and the Greek dialectal inscriptions, which attempts—however imperfectly—to do justice to the peculiarities of its period and locality without regard to tradition, is far more valuable for purposes of scientific research than any fixed orthography.

It must not be imagined, however, that the chaotic orthographies of such languages as Middle English and Old French give a really faithful picture of the languages themselves any more than the fixed orthographies do ; for language is as little lawless on the one hand as it is unchangeable on the other. The varying spellings of one and the same word in the unfixed orthographies are distortions of the truth just as much as the other extreme of writing all the words in a certain period of the language just as they were written several centuries before. The value of these variations—these hesitating attempts to do justice to imperfectly understood distinctions of sound—lies in the varied evidence they afford us by which we are often able to determine with certainty the one sound or grammatical form which lies behind them. Thus when we find an uneducated Englishman sometimes writing *father* for *farther* and *farther* for *father*, and sometimes writing the correct spellings, we cannot resist the conclusion that in his pronunciation the two words have the same sound (faaðə). The various early Modern English spellings *lif*, *lyf*, *life*, *lyfe*, *lyffe*, etc., point to one single form just as much as the Modern English *life* does.

Hence a normalized orthography gives, as a whole, a truer representation of a language than an unfixed orthography does, although the latter is a great help in correcting the former. For the practical study of languages normalized orthographies are indispensable, for the practical learner cannot afford to waste his time and labour on forming conflicting associations with divergent spellings the value of whose evidence he is not yet able to appreciate. It matters little to him whether or not the spelling of a particular word that is adopted in his normalized texts is the best one or not; even if there are downright mistakes in the normalized spelling, it is still worth his while to use it, if it materially assists his mastery of the language. When he has once learnt the language, he can easily correct any errors of this kind, and the divergent spellings will cause but little confusion. If he is studying the language for scientific philological purposes, or if he intends to read manuscripts and original documents, it will be necessary for him to make a thorough study of them. Even those who do not intend to make investigations of this kind will still derive benefit from such a study because of the training it affords in habits of linguistic observation.

Pronunciation

The practical exigencies of teaching make the adoption of some system or other of pronunciation a necessity in dead as

Q

well as living languages; and where the facts of pronunciation are fairly well established, it is often just as easy to pronounce correctly as incorrectly. Thus in Latin it is just as easy to pronounce *nōn, Caesar* correctly (noon, kaisar) as in the English way (non, sijzə). Even if we make the vowel of *nōn* into the diphthong (ou), that is at least better than making the word rhyme with *on*. So also if we distinguish Greek *nómos* from *nomós* by treating the accent as a mark of strong stress, we do not do full justice to what was probably the actual distinction, but we certainly get as near to it as is practicable from our point of view, while at the same time—and this is the really important consideration—we greatly strengthen our hold of the distinction between the two words.

Even when the correct pronunciation offers difficulties, it is generally worth while to make some efforts to overcome them, without, of course, allowing this to take too much time from the general study of the language. For they may be difficulties which will confront the learner in some modern language. In this way, pronouncing a dead language with theoretical correctness may be a valuable help to the learning of living languages. Thus when the learner has once mastered the difficulty of pronouncing double consonants in Latin in such words as *collō* compared with *colō, appellare*—where he must be careful to double the unstressed *p* as well as the stressed *l*—they will cause him no difficulty in Italian, Swedish, or any other modern language. So also the English learner will find that pronouncing such a word as Latin *nōn* with a pure long monophthongal close (o) will greatly improve his pronunciation of almost every foreign language, living or dead.

If the correct pronunciation cannot be ascertained, or if its acquisition takes up too much time, the learner may, for the sake of distinctiveness, adopt a schematic, nomic pronunciation (p. 34), which he can, of course, afterwards modify or discard by the light of further knowledge without any practical difficulty.

For practical purposes it is specially important to make distinctions of pronunciation in two cases: (1) when the distinctions of pronunciation are significant (p. 5); and (2) when they affect the metre of the verse. Thus in Latin it is absolutely necessary from both points of view to pronounce a real double (l) in *collō*, for *colō* not only has a different meaning, but also a different function in verse. It makes no difference, on the other hand, from either point of view whether we pronounce Latin *v* as (v) or (w). In pronouncing Chaucer we must pronounce the weak *e* in *shoures swōte*, or else destroy the metre, so that, while we are about it, we may as well restore his genuine pronunciation throughout. With Shakespeare there is no general metrical necessity for a change, so there is no practical inconvenience in reading him with the modern pronunciation.

Teaching through the Literature

The evil effects of teaching through the literature are even greater in dead than in living languages, for in dead languages every natural obscurity is increased tenfold by our unfamiliarity with ancient circumstances and trains of thought. Such a language as Latin ought to be taught by means of the simplest possible texts, from which every literary complexity or exceptional form has been carefully weeded. Even after the learner has begun the study of the literature itself, he should not be allowed to look at such authors as Virgil, Tacitus, or Juvenal till he is able to read simple prose and poetry with perfect ease.

In modern languages this principle amounts practically to beginning with the spoken language. But as we do not learn Latin to speak it, there is no necessity that the texts should be strictly colloquial in character: all we require of them is that they should imitate the simplicity, definiteness, and directness of the colloquial language—or, at least, that they should not be unnecessarily literary, rhetorical, and artificial.

As these requirements are rarely to be found in the actual literatures, it is often advisable to make special texts for our purpose by simplifying and abridging or paraphrasing literary texts suitable in matter but not in style (p. 182).

Cross-associations with Modern Languages

It is in one sense incorrect to call such languages as Greek and Latin dead languages, for Modern Italian and Romaic or Modern Greek are simply classical Latin and classical Greek which by gradual and perfectly continuous changes have developed into their present form without any change of place. We do not call Italian 'Modern Latin' on the analogy of

Modern Greek, simply because we find it more convenient to give distinct names to Italian, French, Spanish, and the other dialects of modern Latin. The fact that the speakers of Italian and Modern Greek are probably not the descendants of those who spoke the ancient forms of these languages does not alter the fact that Latin and Italian, for instance, differs only in degree, not in kind, just as the Latin of Tacitus differs from that of Ennius. The only languages which can be called really dead are such as Accadian and Hebrew, which have left no direct living descendants.

From a practical point of view, however, we are fully justified in calling such a language as Latin a dead language, differing essentially from a living language (1) in being no longer accessible to direct observation, and (2) in being no longer capable of producing literary works—in having a limited and definitely completed literary development.

But from this point of view the earlier stages of a modern language are also dead. The deadness of such a language as that of Shakespeare differs only in degree from that of Latin. The language of Shakespeare is no more accessible to direct observation than that of Virgil. In fact, as regards its phonology, it is perhaps even less so. We cannot speak, and it is doubtful whether any of us can write Shakespearian English. And from a literary point of view the Tudor period is as finished and shut off from the present period as any ancient literature. If we go a little further back, no one will deny that the Middle English of Chaucer and the Old English of Alfred are dead languages. Old English, indeed, is so remote from Modern English that the learner is often inclined to regard it as a dialect of German.

The divergence between these periods is very gradual. Shakespeare's language was perceptibly easier to the middle of the eighteenth century than it is to our period, and although he was taken less seriously, he was more generally read in the first half of the eighteenth century than at any subsequent period. Chaucer, again, was nearer to the Tudor period than the Tudor period is to us, and was connected by insensible gradations with Old English.

Hence there is a danger of confusion and cross-association to the foreigner who attempts a historical study of a language. Even a native is not exempt from this danger. The difference is that while the foreigner is apt to import Shakespearisms into his Modern English conversation, the Englishman is more apt to misunderstand Shakespeare through giving Present English meanings to his words and phrases.

This suggests two cautions.

The first is: Do not work back from Modern to Old English through Middle English! There is much less risk of confusion if the student, after mastering Modern English thoroughly, goes straight to the other extreme, and masters Old English before making himself acquainted with the intermediate Middle and Early Modern (Tudor) periods. So also the student of German should begin his historical study of the language not with Middle, but with Old High German. In the historical study of French it is still more important to begin with the real Old French, not with fifteenth-century Parisian texts or Anglo-Norman ones.

The second caution is: Do not compare the different periods more than you can help! All the comparisons that are of any use will suggest themselves spontaneously, together with a large number of misleading ones, which unfortunately will be confirmed by the etymological translations in the learner's text-books. When the learner first meets with Old English *sōna*, the important thing is not to tell him that it is cognate with Modern English *soon*, but that it does not mean 'soon,' but 'forthwith, immediately,' just as *presently* in Edinburgh English does not mean 'after an interval,' but 'at once.' So also Old English *smæl* does not mean 'small' (which is expressed by *lȳtel*), but 'narrow:' Norway is a *smæl*, not a *small* country.

Some well-meaning people, misled by one-sided antiquarianism and Freeman's monomania about the continuity of the English language—the only philological generalization he ever seems to have grasped—are incapable of seeing these self-evident facts. They protest that 'we must not isolate Old English from Modern English'—that is to say, that it is wrong to protect ourselves from confusions and mistakes by refraining from comparisons which encourage the formation of cross-associations. The isolation is only a temporary one: when the older periods have once been learnt separately, then is the time to do full justice to the fact of historical continuity.

Dead Methods in Modern Languages

There is another fallacy which requires a brief notice. There is a certain school of educationalists who have a strong conviction of the great value of the study of Greek and Latin as a means of training the mind : many of them, indeed, when reminded of the fact that the majority of those who learn these languages at school never acquire even an elementary practical knowledge of them, reply that this really does not matter much, as they still get the benefit of the mental training. Those who hold these views also urge the convenience of the study of dead languages which is the result of not having to attend to pronunciation, and having to deal only with a limited literature which has been thoroughly worked up for educational purposes.

Many of them further believe that the present methods of teaching modern languages have the contrary effect of weakening the mind and making it more superficial. Some of them think this is inherent in the nature of modern languages. Others, more liberal-minded, think that the fault lies in the methods of instruction. They argue that if modern languages were taught like dead languages, they would have the same beneficial effect on the mind.

Hence instead of assimilating the study of dead to that of modern languages, we are advised to reverse the process. These views are often further combined with antiquarian and etymological fallacies. Thus I was once told by an American pupil of the late Professor Zupitza, of Berlin, that it was a mistake to suppose that Zupitza was not interested in Modern English literature; that, in fact, he had been lecturing on Shelley's *Prometheus Unbound*, but in a more scientific spirit than a purely literary specialist. It turned out that this superiority consisted in his making his pupils translate the beginning of the drama into Anglo-Saxon so as duly to impress on them the continuity of the language !

There is something very unreal about this ' dead-alive ' philology. Some—often insignificant—modern text is taken, and elaborately commented upon with a long historical and critical introduction, and elaborate notes are added on points of grammar, etymology, style, and perhaps metre, the editor not being conscious of the absurdity of teaching metre without a previous knowledge of phonetics on the part of the students.

The text is hardly ever genuinely colloquial, and is often anti-quated, so that the method practically means teaching one language by means of another language. It is not that this kind of study is necessarily objectionable in itself; but it is not the thing to begin with—it should come at the very end, not at the beginning of the course.

The reader may be reminded once more that the question whether the study of dead or of modern languages affords the best training for the mind is one which has nothing to do with the question, which is the best way of learning languages. The only question we have to deal with is whether the extension of the old methods of studying dead languages to the study of living languages would make the acquisition of the latter easier. Our answer to this question must be an unhesitating negative.

CHAPTER XVIII

ORIENTAL LANGUAGES

THE study of the Oriental and of the other remoter languages has many analogies with that of dead languages.

In the first place, the inaccessibility of these languages, and the difficulty of obtaining native teachers, generally obliges the beginner to approach them from the point of view of the study of dead languages.

Secondly, in these languages the true colloquial element is generally even more inaccessible than in European languages, and the divergence between it and the written language is nearly always much greater : classical and vulgar Arabic, written and spoken Japanese, are distinct, mutually unintelligible languages, which have to be treated in separate handbooks and grammars. Even the books which profess to deal with the colloquial form of these languages often give only an approximation to the true colloquial. Thus Green's *Practical Arabic Grammar*, which 'was originally undertaken to meet the requirements of English officers in Egypt,' gives a language which is a mixture of classical with modern Egyptian and Syrian Arabic, containing forms which would be quite unintelligible to an uneducated Egyptian, such as *hāza*, 'this' (classical *hāðā*), the learner's confusion being further increased by the occasional insertion of texts in the classical form. Yet this book—which is mainly on the Ahn plan—has lived through at least three editions (third edition 1893).

Under these circumstances the learner is often obliged to master a dead form of the language as the only stepping-stone to its colloquial form. When the colloquial language is split up into a number of local dialects which are often practically independent languages, the unity of the literary language is certainly an inducement to beginning with it ; thus classical or

232

literary Arabic is the only link by which the different 'vulgar' Arabic dialects of Syria, Egypt, Marocco, etc., can be realized as variations of one language.

But when we have really practical guides to the genuinely colloquial forms of each living dialect or language, the only rational course will be to begin with one definite modern dialect, and then work back to the literary language. To learn classical Arabic as a preparation for modern Egyptian Arabic, or written as a preparation for spoken Japanese, would then be as absurd as to learn Latin as a preparation for the practical study of modern Italian.

Adherence to Native Methods

One of the greatest external hindrances to the study of Oriental languages is the adherence to the native methods of exposition and the native terminology in each language.

It is evident that a method which suits an Oriental may not suit a European. Indeed, we may go a step further, and say that a method which suits the one is tolerably certain *not* to suit the other. To the Oriental 'time is no object,' for he can give his life to his one object of study—the literary form of his own language — which, besides, he already knows to some extent. To him, writing and learning grammar merely means writing and analyzing something that he is already partially familiar with. He learns to read his own crabbed and defective alphabet with comparative ease, not only because he has plenty of time to give to the study, but also because the solution of each orthographic riddle is more or less known to him beforehand. For the same reason in his grammars and dictionaries he can find his way through an abstract and complicated arrangement which baffles the foreign learner, to whom the matter is as unfamiliar as the form.

The difficulties of terminology are alone a serious obstacle. Thus, in Arabic the unhappy beginner is expected from the first to remember the three short vowels by their Arabic names *fatḥa, kasra, damma,* and has, besides, to remember a number of other technical terms relating to orthography and pronunciation which are not clearly explained to him, and even then are difficult to understand and remember—and all this in addition to having to learn a new alphabet. When the learner has at last mastered sixteen or more pages of orthographic absurdities, he has not learnt a single fact about the language itself. The details of Hebrew orthography—which take up nearly twenty-two pages in the very brief grammar of Strack— are even more repulsive and irritating to any one used to a rational method of learning languages.

One cannot blame the scribes who evolved these preposterous orthographic complexities for they knew no better; although it is a pity that when the Arabs borrowed their system of writing from a Christian people, they did not adopt the Coptic instead of the Syriac alphabet. But there is no reason why European learners should be hampered with them just at the time when they require to be able to give their undivided attention to the very real difficulties that encounter them in the language itself. So also it is excusable in the Chinese that they regard the addition of a stopped consonant to a vowel as a kind of tone, because the peculiar character of their writing made it possible for them to dispense with any minute analysis of sounds; but it is nevertheless annoying to look up a Chinese word or 'character' in a dictionary, and then to be told merely that it has the 'entering' tone (ʒip ʃiŋ), or, in plain English, that it ends in some one of the stopped consonants *t, k, p;* the result being that unless we know how the word is pronounced in those modern Chinese dialects which still keep the final stops, and are able to check their often conflicting evidence by knowing the pronunciation of some word given as a rhyme to our word, we are left in an unpleasant state of uncertainty as to its pronunciation.

In many Oriental languages the same difficulties of unnecessary technicality and confused statements follow us through the grammar and dictionary. Everywhere a new terminology and new arrangements, which have to be learnt over again in each language.

Hence even Sanskrit, which in itself is not more difficult than Latin, and whose alphabet is remarkably rational and phonetic in spite of its complexity, was at first considered unattainable by Europeans.

Texts

The want of texts suitable for beginners is as keenly felt in Oriental as in dead languages. There are few of them that can show such a collection of comparatively simple and colloquial texts as those contained in *The Thousand and One Nights*, which, however, have the disadvantage of being neither classical Arabic on the one hand nor fully modern on the other. So great is the dearth of simple texts in Chinese that Summers, in the chrestomathy to his *Handbook of the Chinese Language*, actually includes a translation into Chinese of some of Æsop's fables by an Englishman ! In fact, almost the only texts that are even approximately colloquial in Oriental languages are those which have been taken down from dictation by European scholars. Spitta's *Contes arabes modernes* are an excellent specimen of such work, although unfortunately they are written down so badly from a phonetic point of view as to be misleading to those who have not an independent knowledge of Egyptian Arabic.

CHAPTER XIX

Time and Effort

In learning a language we must advance steadily at a certain speed—neither too fast nor too slow.

Hurried reading either of text or grammar results in the learner forgetting half of what he reads, or in his forming vague instead of definite associations with what he does remember. The nearer the language is to those which he already knows, the greater the temptation to hurry. Thus, the beginner in Italian, finding that when he has once learnt to recognize a certain number of disguised particles such as *anche*, 'also,' *pero*, 'therefore,' he can often guess at the general meaning of whole paragraphs, gets into the habit of superficial reading, until by a succession of gross blunders he is obliged to confess to himself that he has been confusing *di*, ' of,' with *da*, ' by,' that he does not know one pronoun from another, and so on. He then sees that he has simply thrown away so many months, and that he must either give up Italian, or else begin again at the beginning, and go through the tedious drudgery of unlearning false associations and going through the elements of the language again after the study has lost the charms of novelty.

In fact, in dealing with such a language as Italian, it requires a determined effort on the part of the learner to read as slowly and carefully as he ought. Here we see one of the indirect uses of phonetics: if the learner tries conscientiously to do justice to the pronunciation—if only to the extent of distinguishing the close and open vowels, and sounding the double consonants distinctly—he will have to read each sentence so often that there will be no fear of anything in it escaping his attention.

236

If, on the other hand, the language is remote and unfamiliar, there is no temptation to quick reading, which is, indeed, impossible at first. Even if the language is not presented to the learner in an unfamiliar alphabet, the unfamiliarity of the vocabulary will enforce a slow progress. The progress, indeed, may be so slow that the learner is unable to keep up the sense of continuity: by the time he comes to another example of some word or construction, he has forgotten the former one.

Hence most Oriental languages cannot be learnt by merely reading at the rate of an hour a day: a slow learner might go on at this rate for ten years without making any real progress. Such languages must be studied intensively, with a concentration of effort. Thus it is more economical in the end to give four hours a day for a year to such a language than to spread the same number of hours over three years. Sir Thomas Wade used to tell his pupils that they ought to give eight hours a day to their Chinese; but this was addressed to those who were qualifying themselves to serve as interpreters, and therefore had to learn a variety of subjects which would be superfluous to the purely literary or philological student. His method, too, was an imperfect one. Under any circumstances most learners would do well to reduce these eight hours to six; for when tired brain and irritated nerves make the attention flag, the associations necessarily become weaker, and the discrimination of minute points becomes almost impossible.

If the student is perfectly free, and his sole object is to learn the foreign language with the maximum of thoroughness in as short a time as possible, he must work at it continuously every day as long as he feels that he is getting his full value out of his time and labour. How many hours this means will depend on the idiosyncrasies of the learner—on the degree of his interest and enthusiasm, the strength of his motive in learning, his surroundings, his health, and lastly on his intellectual capabilities. At first, too, his progress will depend much on his method of study, and on the character of his helps. Most learners of remote languages waste many years through using bad methods and bad books, although enthusiasm and perseverance will always triumph in the end.

If the time given to the study of a language is to be utilized to the utmost, a certain portion of it will be set aside for repetition.

The thorough student whose memory is not exceptionally quick should always read over again every day what he read the day before. After a month or so, when he has come to a convenient halting-place, he should then go over everything again, so as to pick up those threads of association which have been dropped through the slowness of his progress. He should then read for another month, and then revise his month's reading in the same way. At the end of, say, six months, he should then revise the whole.

The more difficult and remote the language, the oftener this process should be repeated. In fact, each text should be gone through over and over again till the learner feels that he is getting no more good out of it—that he must strengthen and freshen his associations with the words in it by meeting them in new texts and in different contexts.

Results ; Stages and Degrees of Knowledge

Perfect Knowledge.—A perfect knowledge of a living foreign language would imply the power of conversing on ordinary topics with such fluency and correctness as not to be taken for a foreigner, together with that of writing a letter correctly on any familiar subject, and of course being able to read what is written in any branch of general literature. To expect more than this would almost be to expect the foreigner to know the language better than an educated native : by perfect knowledge from a practical point of view we mean a knowledge which puts the foreigner on a level with the average native in all ordinary affairs of life.

It need hardly be said that this ideal is seldom attained purely by systematic study. Such a mastery of a foreign language is generally the result of quite exceptional linguistic talent—aided, however, in most cases by some kind of systematic grammatical study—or of favourable circumstances. If the circumstances are so favourable as to result in the learner partially or wholly forgetting his own language, the victory cannot be said to be a fair one.

This leads us to the question, Is it possible to be truly and perfectly bilingual ? The answer is, Yes, it is just barely possible. But generally what at first sight seems perfect bilingualism is not really perfect : one of the languages has to suffer. Even when a practically perfect command of two such languages as French and English is kept up by alternate residence in the two countries, the respective speakers of the two languages will generally find that there is something queer, something foreign in the pronunciation of one of the two languages—perhaps in both of them. Where the pronunciation is not perfect, the construction may be theoretically perfect, but is seldom practically so.

When bilingualism is the result of living on a linguistic border—as that between England and Wales—the children often learn to speak the two languages with apparently equal ease. But then the languages they learn are themselves already mixed. The children on the Welsh border speak neither pure English nor pure Welsh—they speak anglicized Welsh or celticized English.

When our methods of studying languages are perfected, it is probable that perfect bi-, and even poly-lingualism will become more common, though it will be attainable only by those who have special gifts.

Thorough Knowledge.—The ordinary learner can aim only at what is called a thorough knowledge of the foreign language. A thorough, all-round knowledge implies speaking with moderate fluency and sufficient accuracy of pronunciation to insure intelligibility, and, of course, the power of understanding the natives, and sufficient command of the grammatical structure of the language to avoid grammatical errors, a knowledge of the necessary idioms, and being able to write a letter and read the literature. All this without implying the being taken for a native. Even this degree of knowledge is not common in this country, and where it exists, is generally the result of infinite expenditure of time and perseverance.

Generally this thorough knowledge is one-sided. It often applies only to the written language, a sound critical knowledge of which is often accompanied by complete inability to speak.

Polyglot or 'parrot' linguists may be divided into two main classes : (1) those who can speak their languages—or the majority of them—fluently, and (2) those who can only read them. The former alone fully deserve the appellation of 'born linguists ;' with the latter, the acquisition of many languages is rather the result of concentrated patience and enthusiasm aided by a good memory than of any special talent.

Elementary Knowledge.—A sound elementary knowledge implies only the power of reading at sight any simple prose text. Thus, if the learner could translate a page of Grimm's *Mährchen* which he had not seen before with moderate accuracy and without any great omissions, we might say that he had an elementary knowledge of German.

This knowledge might be attained in about six months of moderate work—an hour a day—by an English adult of average linguistic intelligence, working with good books and with a good method. With a remoter language, offering, however, no special external difficulties, such as Modern Arabic in a Roman transliteration, or Finnish, more time would be required—perhaps a year. With external difficulties, such as those caused by the Sanskrit or Arabic alphabet, the time would have to be largely increased : three years would be a short time in which to learn to read simple texts in Arabic or Sanskrit in their national alphabets. Chinese or cuneiform writing would require still longer time, both as regards number of years and number of hours of daily work. Many learners would require a teacher to reach this standard of progress, especially in the remoter languages ; some, however, advance more rapidly by themselves. Some may take twice as much time, and fail after all.

Elementary Theoretical Knowledge.—Such an elementary knowledge—modest as it seems—is more than sufficient for the purposes of theoretical linguistics and comparative philology. Every one who begins comparative philology is struck first by the limited range of the vocabulary it deals with, and secondly by the fact that a large number of the words quoted do not occur at all in the ordinary literature of the language : half the Greek words seem to come out of Hesychius and Suidas, half the Latin words out of Festus and Varro. In short, lecturing on comparative Greek grammar does not necessarily imply any practical knowledge of Greek : it is enough to have a general knowledge of the structure of Greek so as to be able to avoid mistakes in quoting the few hundred words that reappear over and over again in the comparisons on which Aryan comparative philology is founded.

Thus we arrive at a still lower stage of knowledge, which we may call the elementary theoretical knowledge of a language. This kind of knowledge implies only the power of translating certain strictly limited texts which have been already learnt, it being understood that the texts altogether are long enough to give examples of the main features of the structure of the language in its simpler form. This is the kind of knowledge that would be acquired by going through my *Anglo-Saxon Primer*; that is, the result of learning about fifty pages of grammar, and thirty-five pages of texts. A remoter language would, of course, require more grammar and, perhaps, more texts.

As this kind of study necessarily presupposes a rather high standard of intellect and a certain enthusiasm for the subject, it need not require more than a month, or even less, according to the nearness of the language. With a remoter language more time would be required, and, as already remarked, longer primers. In Gabelentz' *Anfangsgründe der chinesischen Grammatik* the grammar of the classical language takes up eighty-four pages, thirteen of which, however, are given to the explanation of the system of writing, the bulk of the grammar being also increased by everything being given twice over, in the Chinese character and in transcription. The classical Chinese texts at the end, which are accompanied by transcriptions and translations, take up only thirteen pages.

General Stages of Knowledge.—In all practical study of languages there are two main stages, one in which everything is strange to us—in which we feel uncomfortable and not at home—the second, in which the main features of the language are familiar, and we begin to know what to expect, and feel instinctively whatever is contrary to the genius of the language.

These two stages occur in every branch of the study. Thus in learning the peculiar word-intonation of such a language as Swedish, our own imitation of it sounds at first strange and affected, and we feel as if we were making ourselves objects of ridicule, however correct our imitation may be; but after a time we have the exactly opposite feeling: we feel that our own intonation is more or less in harmony with that of the natives, and when we hear our own countrymen speaking the language with English intonation, it sounds as strange to us as to the natives. This is a proof that we have learnt to appreciate the native intonation with our ears at any rate.

So also when the particles of Old Greek or classical Chinese seem useless encumbrances to the learner, he ought to acknowledge that this is a proof of his not having a real knowledge of

R

these languages; when the absence or misuse of one of the particles jars on his linguistic sense, then he may boast that he has really begun to 'live himself into the language.'

Epitomes and Note-books

In the case of languages and dialects which have hitherto been little studied, there may be a want of the necessary helps, so that the student may have to make part, at least, of the grammar for himself, and may have to make his own dictionary as he goes along. But this is an extreme case. And such independent work is neither an essential element of any practical method of learning languages nor even a supplement to it: it is simply filling up a gap in the materials on which the method is founded.

Even when there is a complete grammar, it may be advisable for the learner to make a special abstract of it for his own use. But this, again, is merely filling up a gap in the materials; for such an abstract ought to have been already provided for the use of other learners as well; and if we accept the principle of one method for all, there can be no particular object in each learner making a special epitome of grammar for his own use. Indeed, we may ask, How can a beginner know with certainty before-hand what parts of the grammar he will require? Of course, if his grammar is manifestly unpractical and impossible to work with, then he must do his best; but it is much better for him to have it done for him by some one who knows the language.

So also the use of note-books, in which the learner writes out the words as they occur in his texts with particulars of meaning, inflection, gender, or construction, may be regarded as supplying a defect in the text-book—as supplying the want of notes such as those in my *First Steps in Anglo-Saxon*.

But it may also be regarded simply as a means of strengthening the learner's associations. Thus the learner looks up the German word *haus* in his glossary, and finds that it is a neuter noun with plural *häuser*, so in order to fix this knowledge more firmly in his memory, he enters in his note-book *das haus neut.* ' *house*,' *plur. häuser*, or something of the kind.

The great danger of this method is that it tends to distract the learner's attention from the texts to the isolated word. Instead of thinking of the word in connection with its natural context, the learner gets into the habit of thinking of it as an isolated abstraction—he sees it as a mental picture of the entry in his note-book. This does not matter so much with concrete words of definite and simple meaning, but when it comes to entering abstract words which have hardly any palpable or definable meaning apart from their context, it becomes a pure waste of time. Even in the case of a word which can be easily isolated in thought, it is much better for the learner to read on till he finds such a word as *haus* associated with the neuter article, and then to repeat the whole context till it is fixed in his mind, and then to read on till he comes to the plural *häuser*, and make himself realize in like manner the meaning of the form by association with its context. If he meets the plural before the singular, it does not matter much : he will not have to wait long for the singular.

It is much worse when the learner enters in his note-book further particulars about the etymology and history of the word, giving, perhaps, the cognate forms of a German or Old-English word in Gothic and Icelandic, with an occasional Sanskrit root. This is mere madness from a practical point of view. It is the very antipodes of the principle of making the texts the centre of study.

The Subject-matter of the Texts

We often hear and read complaints about text-editions that the treatment is too exclusively grammatical, linguistic, philological; that the subject-matter—the *realien*—is not commented upon, that the social life of the speakers of the language is not described, that no attempts are made to rouse the learner's interest in the literary merits of the texts or their historical value, and so on.

It is certainly desirable that the learner should understand the subject-matter of what he is reading. But, on the other hand, it is equally desirable that the texts put before the beginner should deal as far as possible only with topics with which he is already familiar. If they must deal with subjects that are unfamiliar to the learner, they ought themselves to give the required definition or explanation, not of course directly, but indirectly, through the context. Any further information about the subject-matter in the earlier stages is therefore superfluous.

In fact, the question can hardly be said to arise at all till we come to the study of the literature itself. Even here, the explanations of and comments on the subject-matter should be limited to what is absolutely necessary for making the meanings of the words clear—that is, to what is really useful from the point of view of the practical study of languages. Any further elaboration of comment and illustration is irrelevant from our point of view. If the learner in the course of his linguistic reading comes on an allusion to Manichæism, or feels a great curiosity as to whether Shakespeare was really a Freemason, or what Milton's diet was, there is no harm in his looking these subjects up in a cyclopedia or biographical dictionary, but this has nothing to do with the question what is the best way of learning languages.

Even a sketch of the history and literature of the language has nothing to do with this question, although, of course, not even the most narrow-minded linguist would quarrel with his teacher for giving him this information.

Teaching Children

The most important difference in the classes of learners of languages is that which depends on age. Within childhood itself, again, there are different stages.

The different subjects which make up a child's education must be begun at different ages, partly because there is not time to carry them on all abreast, and partly because of the natural gradation and dependence of the different branches one on another. It is of the greatest importance that the succession of studies should correspond with—or, at least, not go directly against—the progressive development of the child's mind. These considerations, combined with the conclusions we have already arrived at as to the right method of learning languages, point to the following order in a child's study of languages :—

The foundation of all study of language must be laid by that of the native language. Correct and clear pronunciation of it should be insisted upon from the beginning. The reading-lessons should be made the centre of instruction as soon as possible. The first elements of phonetics and of grammatical analysis should be deduced from them. Great attention should be paid to word-meanings. There is no reason why children should not be taught almost from the beginning of their reading to group the words they meet with into logical as well as grammatical categories—of course, with as little terminology and abstract definition as possible.

The same principles apply also—with some necessary modifications—even to the pre-reading stages of education. Phonetics, of course, should be begun in the nursery. The time will come when ignorance of practical phonetics will be held to disqualify a nurse as much as any other form of incapacity. If the infant's attempts to speak were guided into the channel of systematic all-round phonetic drill, it would on entering into school-life be already a thorough practical phonetician: all it would have to learn would be the use of a phonetic notation. The pronunciation of foreign languages would then offer no initial difficulties whatever: it would simply be a question of remembering what particular sounds occurred in the foreign language, and associating them with the symbols of the phonetic alphabet for that language.

The reading-books in the native language should at first be mainly in simple prose, with only occasional pieces of simple poetry. They would, of course, be entirely in phonetic spelling on a Broad Romic basis, and with accurate marking of stress and intonation.

The further development of the study of the native language would consist in widening the vocabulary, and providing reading of a higher character, and at the same time making the linguistic analysis—both grammatical and psychological—more conscious and more abstract, and framing it more and more into definite rules.

The next great step will be that of emerging from the mono-lingual into the bilingual condition. The first foreign language must, of course, be one which admits of being grasped concretely in all the details required; that is, it must be a living, not a dead language. French seems to satisfy our requirements best on the whole. It might be begun at ten. After two years, German may be begun—at twelve.

The only dead languages that children ought to have any-thing to do with are the earlier stages of their own language. For reasons already stated (p. 229), I think English children ought to begin with Old English. German and Old English will afford mutual help. On the whole, it would be best to postpone beginning Old English till the elements of German are fixed in the memory—that is, till the age of fourteen. It is not necessary that much should be read of Old English literature. After a year of Old English, the learner may go on to Chaucer, and then work his way rapidly down to Tudor English.

If Latin is to be studied at all at school, it ought not under any circumstances to be begun before the age of sixteen. Greek should be put on a level with Hebrew, Arabic, Russian, Chinese, and other languages, which, in spite of their great intrinsic interest and the importance of the literature they embody, have no necessary direct connection with modern European culture; in other words, Greek should be regarded as a linguistic specialism to be entered upon, if at all, at the University. As regards literary culture, the schoolboy who has learnt something of the classics of English, French, and German literature will have as much of that kind of culture as is good for him—perhaps too much.

These are the main features of a linguistic course for children. To show a different scheme—though founded on similar principles—I quote the following passage from Widgery's *Teaching of Languages in Schools* (p. 10), as embodying the opinions of a liberal-minded and progressive practical school-teacher who was at the same time well versed in the literature of his subject:—

'With regard to the study of English, I venture to propose the following:

'Increase the reading-lessons in it; let them be mainly in modern prose. Teach the very first elements of phonetics and grammar purely inductively; pay special attention to the vocabulary, grouping the words which children meet in their reader under psychologic and grammatical categories. At ten, or earlier, begin to work backwards, say to the age of Anne. With Shakespeare, their attention should be directed to his variations from modern usage, and the beginnings of a sense of the development of language made. At eleven, we might start French, reading at the same time a little Chaucer. Between twelve and thirteen, we might just touch Old English by means of a short Reader with the text on one side, and the necessary grammar on the other; some slight knowledge of the laws of language should be introduced, analogy and the regular changes of sound at least being fully illustrated. The child of twelve and a half is now fit to begin German. After a year's study, bifurcation must come in; the future classical student could begin Latin at fourteen and gradually drop French, begin Greek at sixteen and devote his time to the classics. The student of the modern languages could now begin a scientific study of his three, keeping English always in the centre.'

It will be seen that the main point on which I differ from Widgery is that I would rather begin the study of the older stages of English at once with Old English itself, while he prefers to work gradually backwards. I should advocate great caution in introducing children to classics such as Milton, for which their minds are hardly matured enough. As already remarked, I think Greek—and perhaps Latin too—ought to be excluded altogether from schools. This would obviate the ridiculous bifurcation into a classical and a commercial side. The phrase 'classical education' has no longer any meaning; learning Greek and Latin is neither education nor a preparation for it. The future man of science or scholarship wants modern languages as much as the future merchant. What remote or dead languages he or the practical man may require will depend entirely on the details of their pursuits. I would also keep all scientific, theoretical, historical study of languages in schools within very narrow limits, and draw the materials for it exclusively from the native language and from French and German.

Methods for Adults ; Self-instruction

The methods of linguistic study by adults are more varied than with children, for the aims and conditions of study are more varied. The adult can specialize, and he can devote the whole of his time to one language, thus making up by intensiveness of study for what he has lost in quickness and adaptability of mind.

With a Native Teacher.—Another important factor is that the adult can be self-taught. Even if he has a foreign teacher, he may still be self-taught. In fact, he must be so, unless his teacher is a skilled phonetician with a good method. This, it need hardly be said, is rarely the case. So that the teacher is simply a more or less passive object of observation and experiment to the learner, provided, of course, that the latter has had the necessary phonetic and linguistic training.

If the teacher is naturally intelligent, the learner will find it worth his while to try to interest him in the improved phonetic methods. If he succeeds, the gain on both sides will fully repay the time and trouble spent on it.

If the teacher is prejudiced against phonetics, and persistently withholds information about the natural colloquial pronunciation and idioms, the only method is, not to let him see the printed page, but to get the information required entirely by putting such questions as ' what do you say when you meet people— when you go away—when you do not understand what is said to you—when you want some one to pass the salt ? ' and so on, and writing down the answers phonetically. But as this is difficult and slow work, especially at the beginning, it is often better to get a dialogue- or phrase-book, and look through it beforehand, so as to get what information one can from the nomic spelling, and then read over the English translation to the native, without letting him see the book, and ask him how he would say that in his own language ; in this way the danger of his simply reading aloud the perhaps incorrect colloquialisms of the book in an artificially distinct pronunciation will be averted, and if he gives the same idioms as the book, the nomic spelling of the latter will be sure to give some help in distinguishing the sounds.

If the learner finds he cannot get clear ideas of the sounds by hearing them in connected sentences, he should draw up tentative lists of words containing the elementary sounds—as far as he can ascertain them from his grammar and pronouncing dictionary and other helps—in combinations which present the least difficulty to him. These words must be practised diligently by first listening to the teacher's pronunciation while he repeats each word at least three times, and then trying to imitate. When each word has been gone over in this way, the teacher should read the whole list over several times. At first the learner should confine himself mainly to careful listening, till the sounds are definitely fixed in his ear, so that even if he is unable to pronounce a certain sound during the lesson, he is often able to reproduce it successfully when he practises it by himself.

As regards phonetic notation, it is often most convenient at first to improvise a system of diacritic marks—dots, circles, etc., over and below the letters—not attempting to form a complete system of transliteration till the sounds are better known.

At first, while the student is still unfamiliar with the grammar, he will be able to read only a very short piece—less than ten lines—every day, the pronunciation of which can therefore be studied with some care. Each day's portion should be read over by the teacher and then by the learner, first in very short groups of words; as soon as enough of these groups have been read to make up a complete sentence, the whole sentence should be repeated, and similarly with the paragraph. The preceding day's reading should be repeated every day before going further.

The learner who has not had a phonetic training should often exercise himself in repeating short sentences after the teacher without looking at the book. This will train his ear, and make him less liable to be misled by unphonetic spelling.

Start with Definite Knowledge; with a Translation. —In self-study, without any help from a teacher, the first requisite is to start with a definite and exact knowledge of every sentence in the texts. This should always be aimed at under all circumstances; but it is doubly important when the learner has to depend on his own vigilance in detecting any mistakes he may have fallen into. It is a fallacy to regard the texts as puzzles to be solved by the help of grammars and dictionaries, thereby forming vague and often false associations which have to be modified or unlearnt. The beginner should from the first provide himself with a fairly literal translation, unless, of course, he is working with such a book as my *First Steps in Anglo-Saxon*, where everything is explained without a continuous translation. At the beginning he should make a point of reading each sentence in the translation before he begins to read and analyze the corresponding passage in the original.

The dictionary should be referred to only when the information so gained is indispensable, or at least instructive, as in determining the nominative case of a noun, the infinitive of an irregular verb, or the original meaning of a word used figuratively in some special construction. Of course, as soon as the translation has made the sense of the passage clear, it should be put aside, and every word and construction should be carefully analyzed, as far as the student's knowledge will allow. When some progress has been made, the student should occasionally practise himself in making out the sense of a passage with the help of grammar and dictionary only; but this must be regarded as a test of knowledge and a stimulus, not as a method of study.

The current prejudice against the use of translations is founded on the erroneous assumption that the learner requires to be trained in guessing and unravelling the meaning of sentences, just as any one who is learning to shoot has to make many unsuccessful attempts before he learns to hit the mark with any certainty. It is assumed that a learner who has not been set to guess at the meaning of sentences will never acquire the power of reading without a translation. But there is an essential difference between reading and shooting. While the art of shooting can be acquired only by a series of unsuccessful efforts, a knowledge of the meaning of sentences can be obtained without guessing, that is, by the use of a translation. Not till this knowledge is obtained, is it possible to analyze intelligently. The objection to schoolboys using ' cribs ' is a purely practical one, namely, that they are apt to learn the crib by heart instead of comparing it with the original, while the exclusive use of a dictionary forces them both to study the texts themselves, and to do a certain amount of grammatical analysis. It need hardly be said that an intelligent teacher will have no difficulty in testing the soundness of their analysis, whether they have used a translation or not. It is, of course, most satisfactory if the boys can be taught without either a dictionary or a translation, the latter being the special resort of the self-taught adult.

Pronunciation.—The learner should start with a definite pronunciation, which may, however, be only a nomic pronunciation (p. 34). He should, if possible, read everything aloud, and get into the habit of listening to and criticizing his own utterance as if it were that of a stranger.

The Grammar.—Of those principles which are of general application, many are especially important to the self-taught learner, such as that of beginning with a general survey of the language, so as to know beforehand where the difficulties lie, and the degree of attention to be given to each group of linguistic phenomena. Another important general principle is that of beginning with a short grammar.

But every short grammar is not suited for self-taught

beginners. As I have remarked in the preface to my *Anglo-Saxon Reader*, many of the elementary grammars and other text-books published abroad ' are intended as companions to the author's lectures, so that he naturally does not care to put his book into such a form as will make his lectures superfluous ; hence such books are generally not suited for self-instruction.' To this I may add that even when they profess to be fitted for purposes of self-instruction, they are often not so, through the author being unconsciously under the influence of the traditional methods.

In going through his grammar for the first time, the student should without hesitation cut out all superfluities : he should draw his pen through all comparisons with cognate languages, all archaisms in the paradigms or lists. Even when he is entirely unacquainted with the language, common sense will often enable him to distinguish between the really indispensable and the superfluous. Thus, suppose he is in the third declension in Latin, and has come to the words with accusatives in *-im* instead of *-em ;* a little consideration of the meanings of the words *amussis, buris, ravis, sitis, tussis,* and *vis* will show that the chances are much against his meeting the first three during the first year of his study of the language, and, in short, that the only words in the list that can possibly occur with any frequency are *sitis* and *vis.* These therefore he will learn, and ignore the rest, at least for the present. In going over rules for gender, lists of derivative syllables, and so on, those rules should be singled out which are easily grasped and remembered, which include the largest number of important words and have the fewest exceptions, while those which apply only to a few words or are weakened by numerous exceptions should be passed over. The student should content himself at first with obtaining general ideas of the structure of the language, and should never forget that even the most accurate and exhaustive knowledge of the grammar is in itself only a step towards a real knowledge of the language.

The same principles should be followed in studying the syntax as well as the forms. All syntactical rules which are common to language generally, or apply to the native as well as the foreign language, should be passed over. At first the student should confine his attention to those rules which are absolutely necessary for the comprehension of the structure of the language, leaving the others to a later stage.

The first time the piece for the day is read over, after its meaning has been learnt from the translation, it should be studied analytically, till the learner understands the meaning and construction of every word, as far as his then state of knowledge will allow him. In revising the same piece the day after, its sentences should be read over and studied more as wholes, analysis being now subordinated to synthesis. Each sentence should be read over and over again till it can be repeated without hesitation and without looking at the book. This method gives all the advantages of learning long passages by heart without taking so much time. Of course, if the learner has so good a memory that with a little more trouble he can learn by heart whole paragraphs and pages, by all means let him do so.

Attention should at first be concentrated mainly on the particles and commonest words together with the general principles of the syntax. Unless these subjects are thoroughly mastered at the outset, the learner will get into the habit of disregarding them, and will then never acquire them properly, however much practice he may have in reading and speaking.

This knowledge and that of the vocabulary require distinct methods of study : the former can be acquired only by careful and repeated study of a very limited portion of the literature, while the latter demands an extensive, and therefore necessarily rapid and less careful reading of all the representative branches of it. It is evident, therefore, that no attempt at acquiring the general vocabulary of the language should be made till the particles and commonest words are fully mastered.

Of course, as the learner advances, he will be able to read with greater ease and rapidity. Nevertheless he should always set apart a portion of his time every day for slow and careful reading with frequent repetition, and continue this practice up to the very end of his course. The beginning of a new work on a new subject should also be read with special care till the more important elements of its special vocabulary have been well learnt, after which it can be read more cursorily.

Careful study of the grammar should be carried on concurrently with text-reading, and this should go on during the whole course of study : there should be no idea of getting up the grammar at one stroke, and then throwing it aside. In reading, special attention should be paid to those words and constructions which bear on that section of the grammar which is being studied at the time.

This is an additional reason for frequent repetition of what has been read during the last few months. Thus, if a certain text has been read while the learner is studying the syntax of noun-inflections, he will necessarily neglect the syntax of the verb, especially if he has not yet studied that part of the grammar in detail. Hence, when he has come to the syntax of the verb and has mastered it fairly well, he ought to go over the text he read before, partly to get fresh examples of the syntactical rules he has just been learning, partly to perfect his knowledge of the text by means of his newly acquired syntactical knowledge.

For those words and constructions which offer special difficulties the learner may collect further illustrations from the texts either on slips or in his note-book. The use of note-books and collections generally should, however, not be carried so far as to interfere with the study of the texts themselves ; nor is anything gained in itself by removing words from their natural context to the isolation of the note-book. The learner should always bear in mind that there is no short cut to the knowledge of a language, and that this knowledge can only be obtained by persevering study of the language itself as embodied in the actual literature, and that the whole machinery of grammar, dictionary, and note-book is merely a preparation and an aid for this text-study, not a substitute for it. No plan of study can be a sound one, in which reading the texts themselves does not take up, on an average, two-thirds of the whole time.

It need, therefore, hardly be said that the less time given to composition and elegant translation—not to speak of exercise-writing—the better. Idiomatic translation from the foreign language is beneficial in many ways, but should not be attempted too early. When a firm grasp of the language has been attained, it will be time to contrast its characteristic features with those of the native language by means of such translation. In the intermediate stage between this and the very beginning, the student should learn new words and phrases as far as possible by associating them directly with the ideas they express rather than through the medium of his own language.

411

Translation into the foreign language, and, in a less degree, original composition in it without direct imitation of any known text, is a task of great difficulty, even when a tolerably full command of the foreign language has been attained. Indeed, most students of modern languages should not attempt anything more than a mastery of the ordinary forms of letter-writing. In dead languages of limited literature, all attempts at translation into them or original composition in them must deal with subjects and styles for which patterns can be found in the literature of the language. Thus the only kind of translation into Gothic that could be attempted would be from such books as the Pilgrim's Progress.

No study requires more judgment and common-sense than the practical study of languages. The various capacities of different learners also make it difficult to lay down general rules. The three requisites—sympathetic insight into the structure of language, ear for sounds and power of reproducing them, together with a good memory—are generally combined in different proportions. Almost total want of the two first may also be combined with high intelligence and power of dealing with abstractions. Such learners often show a deceptive quickness in learning the grammar, to which their progress in the practical command of the language by no means corresponds.

So varied are the capacities and circumstances of different learners and their aims and ideals of thoroughness, that it is important to cultivate a sound and independent judgment on questions of method, so as to avoid being led astray by preconceived theories, and to acquire the power of profiting by experience, and modifying the plan of study accordingly.

Especial judgment is necessary in settling the amount of time to be given to each day's work. Each extreme is equally hurtful. If the learner hurries over his piece of reading, he will himself feel that he has carried away only a blurred mass of associations which are soon forgotten. If, on the other hand, he studies too elaborately, sits too long over his work, and revises too often or at too frequent intervals, his powers of observation become blunted, and at last he feels that his reading makes hardly any impression on his mind, and that he gets nothing more out of it. He should, therefore, abstain from all attempts at exhaustive analysis, and content himself with acquiring as many new associations and new ideas as can be firmly fixed in his mind by one or two repetitions, while at the same time he seizes every opportunity of confirming earlier associations.   He must also remember that by the mere process of careful reading he is acquiring a number of unconscious associations, many of which he will be able to analyze consciously hereafter, while many he will not find analyzed in any grammar, some of them, indeed, practically defying all analysis.

CHAPTER XX

ORIGINAL INVESTIGATION

WE have hitherto confined ourselves to that study of languages which deals with a language that has been already reduced to writing and analyzed grammatically. We have also generally assumed the existence of dictionaries and reading-books and of texts for further practice in the language. This kind of study does not, therefore, require any originality or independence of judgment on the part of the learner beyond that of selecting his helps and forming a plan of study suitable to his special needs and idiosyncrasies, and this only when he is self-taught.

Decipherment

The task of the investigator who aims at reducing an unwritten language to writing, and then analyzing it grammatically and lexically, is a very different one. It calls not only for original research, but also for enterprise, tact, and perseverance of a higher kind than is required in the more plodding work of learning a language by means of helps already provided by others.

The unfamiliarity of the language may be of any degree. It makes a good deal of difference whether the language is isolated in its affinities or is cognate with some other accessible language or group of languages. In the latter case the study of the new language may mean little more than the investigation of a new dialect of a known language. But even the investigation of the spoken form of one's own language is really to some extent the investigation of a new language, especially if the real features of the spoken language are concealed by an unphonetic traditional orthography. Thus the investigation of the complicated phenomena of gradation

256

414

in spoken English—such distinctions as those between (kæn, ðæt, wil) and their weak forms (kən, ðət, l)—is practically the study of an unknown language, for the written language generally ignores not only the details, but the very principle itself of gradation. So also with the colloquial elision of the ' mute *e* ' (ə) in French. Wherever we have to construct a new system of phonetic notation, there we may be said practically to have to deal with a more or less new language.

It may happen that the language has been written down by its speakers, so that we have written texts to start with, but that nothing further has been done in the way of linguistic analysis, or that more remains to be done.

The most important cases of this kind are those of dead languages made known to us by inscriptions and other documents whose traditional reading has been lost. Such are the inscriptions in the cuneiform writing which from the valley of the Euphrates spread over the adjacent countries, and was used to write a variety of languages ; first, the Sumerian or Accadian language spoken by the Finno-Tartaric founders of the old Babylonian or Chaldean civilization and the neighbouring nations of the same stock, and then of the Semitic Babylonians and Assyrians, and lastly of the Aryan Persians and Cypriote Greeks, together with some other languages. The hieroglyphs of Egypt seem also to be of Babylonian origin ; in their oldest forms they preserve the pictorial foundation of the cuneiform writing. Fresh riddles are afforded by the Hittite inscriptions and those of Southern Arabia, together with the much later hieroglyphs of Central America.

With all unknown texts the method of decipherment is the same in its general principles, however much it may vary under different conditions.

In the first place, no decipherment is possible without some known quantity. Shelley tells us of the youth in his poem of *Alastor* that

> ' His wandering step,
> Obedient to high thoughts, has visited
> The awful ruins of the days of old :
> Athens, and Tyre, and Balbec, and the waste
> Where stood Jerusalem, the fallen towers
> Of Babylon, the eternal pyramids,

S

Memphis and Thebes, and whatsoe'er of strange
Sculptured on alabaster obelisk,
Or jasper tomb, or mutilated sphynx,
Dark Ethiopia in her desert hills
Conceals.   Among the ruined temples there,
Stupendous columns, and wild images
Of more than man, where marble dæmons watch
The Zodiac's brazen mystery, and dead men
Hang their mute thoughts on the mute walls around,
He lingered, poring on memorials
Of the world's youth, through the long burning day
Gazed on those speechless shapes, nor, when the moon
Filled the mysterious halls with floating shades,
Suspended he that task, but ever gazed
And gazed, till meaning on his vacant mind
Flashed like strong inspiration, and he saw
The thrilling secrets of the birth of time.'

But this is a description of what may be, not of what is : with
our present faculties we must go to work in a slower and more
methodical way—we must have something to start from.   It is
the want of this starting-point, this known quantity, which still
baffles us in the Etruscan inscriptions.   The Etruscan alphabet
offers none of the formidable difficulties of the cuneiform and
the Egyptian writing, being, indeed, almost as easy to read as
the Greek alphabet from which it is derived ; but the key to
unlock the meaning of the words has not yet been found.
We know that certain words are numerals, but we do not know
in what order to take them, nor have we yet found any solid
basis of comparison with other languages.   Until a bilingual
inscription is found into which some known language enters,
it does not seem likely that we shall advance further than
guesses at a few isolated words.

In the case of the cuneiform inscriptions, the known quantities
were certain proper names in the Persian inscriptions, which led
to the discovery of a genitive plural ending, the language itself
being practically known beforehand through being an Aryan
language closely allied to Sanskrit and practically almost
identical with Zend.   In the Persian inscriptions the complicated syllabic writing of the Babylonians had been simplified
into a comparatively easy system which had nearly emerged
into the simplicity of the Phenician alphabet with its single
letter for each consonant.   If we had had only the original
Sumerian inscriptions to go upon, the problem would have been

hopeless. As it was, the numerous bilingual and trilingual inscriptions into which cuneiform Old Persian entered soon enabled the decipherers to read the Semitic inscriptions first in the Assyrian and then in the more difficult and archaic Babylonian writing. But the great difficulties of the task could hardly have been surmounted if Assyrian and Babylonian Semitic had not been practically little more than dialects of classical Arabic and Hebrew. When the Semitic inscriptions had once been read, the bilingual inscriptions in Semitic and Sumerian made the discovery of the latter language and its cognates a matter of certainty.

So also with modern texts. Even if the strange language is presented to us in Roman transcription and in a connected text of some length, we can do nothing in the way of deciphering it till we either know what known languages to compare it with, or have a translation, or, at any rate, know what the text is about. If we know, for instance, that it is a translation of the Gospels or of the Prayer-book, the decipherment is only a question of time.

Help afforded by Comparative Philology

Of all helps, that of comparative philology is the most uncertain and the most liable to mislead unless severely controlled by a critical and scientific habit of mind. One page of translation is worth any number of comparisons with other languages and conjectural etymologies. All that a comparison of a certain word with some other word in a known language can do is to give hints which may lead to the discovery of its true meaning.

First there is the difficulty of proving that the similarity is anything but accidental. If the two languages are only distantly connected, the trained philologist distrusts any great similarity. It takes very little theoretical divergence to make languages mutually unintelligible. A speaker of High German who does not know Platt-Deutsch can hardly understand a word of Dutch, nor can a Dutchman understand Frisian, nor a Frisian an Englishman, although Frisian is more closely related to English than to any other Germanic language. Even two dialects of the same language may be mutually unintelligible. Philological dilettantes who have learnt to pick out similarities between cognate languages and to ignore the differences, often rush into the most extravagant statements about the similarities between languages. Thus they look into a Dutch book, and boast that with nothing but a knowledge of German and English to help them, they can read the language at sight, not considering that a great many of the words they recognize by their forms have quite different meanings from what they have in German and English, and that some of the resemblances may be accidental and misleading—that, for instance, *of* has nothing to do with English *of*, but has the meaning ' or ; ' *os*, plural *ossen*, does not mean ' horse,' but ' ox,' and so on.

When Leibnitz first noticed the agreements in vocabulary between Persian and German which are the result of both being Aryan languages, he was so carried away by his discovery that he ventured on the astounding assertion that the similarity between the two languages was so great that an educated German could understand whole strophes of Persian poetry. The simple answer to this is, that if a North German cannot understand more than a word here and there of a South German dialect, it is not likely that he should understand more of a language which is not only non-Germanic, but belongs to the most remote subdivision of the Aryan family. There are certainly some very remarkable resemblances between English or German on the one hand, and modern Persian on the other, some of which are due to real affinity, but these few similarities are not enough to counterbalance the divergences in the rest of the Aryan portion of the vocabulary, together with the fact that about half the vocabulary is Arabic. The comparative philologist, of course, ignores the latter element, but to the practical linguist a modern Persian word of Arabic origin is just as much a Persian word as one of Aryan origin ; and the decipherer has to approach his problems from the practical point of view.

The decipherer will then always distrust great similarity. The degree of average similarity that he expects will depend on the closeness of affinity between the two languages. Thus, if he is comparing a Germanic with a Slavonic language, he will expect on the whole greater divergence between them than between the Germanic language and any other Germanic language. So also if he is comparing the Germanic languages as a whole with the Finnic languages, he will expect the general divergence between the two families—the Germanic and the Finnic—to be greater than that between the most distant members of the Aryan family or the most distant members of the Finnic family.   If he meets in Finnish such words as *kuningas*, 'king,' which are almost identical in form and meaning with words in the Germanic languages, while the corresponding cognate words in such closely allied Aryan languages as the Slavonic are mostly so different that their affinity with the Germanic words requires elaborate proof, he at once assumes that most of such agreements are the result of borrowing on one side or the other—in this case on the Finnish side.

It need hardly be said that borrowed words are among the most valuable aids to the decipherer, just as they are to the practical linguist.   Although their identity may be occasionally disguised by changes of form and meaning, their evidence is generally of a much more direct character than that of cognate words, and if the borrowing is of recent date, there is no reason why there should be any divergence at all in meaning or any but a slight divergence in form.

Etymological affinity, on the other hand, proves nothing—it only raises expectations which may be fulfilled or not.   Thus, if in learning German I come on the word *fusz*, I guess, on the analogy of the identity of the form and meaning of German *hand* with that of the English *hand*, that it is cognate with the English *foot* and has the same meaning.   But if I were to go on to assume on similar grounds that German *kopf* is not only cognate with English *cup*, but has the same meaning, I should find myself as much hampered in my attempts at decipherment by this correct etymological identification as by any incorrect one.   Of course, when I once find out that *kopf* means 'head,' my knowledge of the changes of meanings in other languages would enable me to prove that this change of meaning is quite a natural one.   I might, indeed, have been prepared at the outset for this change of meaning; but experience shows that such flights of *à priori* imagination may lead to results which are as baseless as they are plausible.

Hence we find that while the older school of cuneiform investigators made great use of comparisons with Hebrew and the other Semitic languages, and thereby obtained many valuable hints towards decipherment, the later scholars have got their best and most reliable results by the comparison of parallel uses of words in the texts themselves, so that the testimony of comparative philology has now only a secondary weight: the evidence of the texts settles the etymology, the etymology does not settle the meaning of the text.

Decipherment a Practical Problem

We see, then, that decipherment is more a practical than a theoretically scientific problem, and that even when it calls in the help of comparative philology, its methods still are more allied to those of the practical linguist than of the comparative philologist. Gabelentz has some interesting remarks on this subject (Gab. 76); in speaking of the method of dealing with languages in which we have only texts in a known alphabet to start with, without any help beyond a translation or general knowledge of the contents, he says—

'It might seem that in dealing with texts in a foreign language we should have to rely from the beginning entirely on learned investigations. But this is not the case : here, as elsewhere, a purely naïve attitude (naives verhalten) is best at first. Let the student read a few pages, aloud if possible, in order to help the memory by the ear as well. In doing so, he need not trouble himself particularly about the correctness of the pronunciation, taking care only to distinguish whatever is written differently [p. 34]. He will soon notice that words, perhaps also word-stems and word-forms, repeat themselves, and perhaps occasionally discovers their meaning. In this way the instinct of analysis gradually asserts itself, the text talks to us, and we learn to understand it better page by page. Any one who learns by heart easily, and only wants to get a practical command of the language, will probably attain his object quicker in this way than if he conscientiously set to work to make collections (collectanien) like a philological investigator.'

Gabelentz then goes on to recommend this method of learning languages as a useful training for every linguist and philologist; he says—

'If he chooses some remote, but not too difficult language, such as one of the Bantu family, a Malay, Polynesian, Melanesian, or a Ural-altaic language, he can be certain of success, even if he has no previous acquaintance with any of the languages belonging to the family. He will at the same time receive a quantity of entirely new scientific ideas, his sagacity will be exercised, and after a short spell of certainly rather dry labour, he will have the enjoyment of self-gained knowledge which increases hour by hour. And skill in this method of investigation is immensely increased by practice. We all know that a talent for languages does not always imply scientific capacity. But he who is trained in this school may expect that his scientific judgment will increase in the same proportion as his linguistic knowledge, for in such work theoretical speculation comes of itself.'

Work of this kind might well form part of the training in an ideal seminary of comparative philology in its wider sense in which it is equivalent to the German 'allgemeine sprachwissenschaft.'

All Text-reading Implies Originality

The methods of studying languages we have just been considering all imply a considerable amount of originality. But there is no absolute line of demarcation in this respect between the most difficult decipherment of an unknown inscription and the reading of the easiest text in the most familiar language. All free text-reading implies a certain amount of independent thought. Even in reading our own language we may at any moment come upon unknown words and obscure or ambiguous constructions without being able to get help from any dictionary or grammar.

Text-editing : Original Research

In deciphering a new text in a known language, as when a philologist copies and edits a hitherto unpublished manuscript text, the originality reduces itself to explaining such meanings of words and phrases and grammatical constructions as cannot be found in the existing dictionaries and grammars and other helps. If the text is a literal translation whose original is accessible, the originality may be reduced almost to a vanishing-point. A good deal of what is grandiloquently called 'original research' is purely mechanical work, requiring almost less originality than the routine of a bank clerk. The 'researcher' looks through a catalogue of manuscripts, and finds, say, a *Treatise on the Seven Deadly Sins* in the Kentish dialect of the fifteenth century, or a fragment of a translation of the French romance of *The Adventures of Sir Arthur and the Green Lady*, which his professor assures him has never been published. Our student copies it by the help of a facsimile of the handwriting of the manuscript, translates it with the help of the Latin or French original, and then publishes the text with a glossary and introduction, two-thirds of which perhaps is written by his professor. On the strength of this original research he is then himself made a professor—a professor who never in the whole course of a long and laborious career shows the slightest glimmering of originality.

The evils of the German system which requires, if not the reality, at least the semblance of originality from every candidate for a doctor's degree are manifold and self-evident. Any measure that would stop this over-production would be welcome. Some kind of tax on useless and superfluous literature is much needed.

Investigations of Unwritten Speech

The investigation of unwritten forms of speech requires much higher qualities than publishing a manuscript text. Phonetic training, quickness of observation, presence of mind, are here essential.

Equally important is the power of recording one's observations in phonetic writing. I remember a young foreign philologist showing me his notes of the pronunciation of some Turkish dialect, written in a phonetic notation he had hastily improvised on a French basis, the result being that he had to confess that he was quite unable to remember what sounds his symbols stood for. He was no phonetician, and made no pretence of a knowledge of phonetics. But there are many who profess to be phoneticians, and are almost equally helpless when they have to face the difficulties of having to write down a dialect for the first time.

Such work requires not only accuracy, but quickness. For really good dialectal work, a phonetic shorthand will in future be regarded as indispensable.

But however well-equipped with theoretical and practical knowledge the investigator may be, and however much practice he may have had, the phonetic analysis of a new dialect and the writing down of its sounds must always be a slow and difficult process at first. Let the beginner be under no delusions on this point: no one can write a language down straight off under such circumstances. All who profess to be able to do so deceive themselves. Even familiar and easy distinctions such as that of close and open vowels are often confusing in a new language: what is, relatively speaking, the close sound may be a little opener than in other languages, so that the observer perhaps writes it down roughly and tentatively as (ε); but when he finds a still opener sound which is, however, not so open as the (æ) in English *man*, he sees that he has made a phonetic shifting or 'verschiebung,' so that what he at first wrote (ε) must be written (e), and what he at first wrote (æ) must be written (ε).

Again, many beginners, in listening to the speech of a native, will often confidently assert that the pronunciation of a certain sound varies from word to word; and when the natives assure them that they are mistaken, they only regard it as a proof of their own superior acuteness of hearing; they do not know that it is one of the surest signs of unfamiliarity with the sound in question: the impressions of the ear sway, as it were, from side to side in the vain attempt to identify the unfamiliar sound with some familiar one; and when the sound is thoroughly mastered, this fluctuation ceases.

This leads to another consideration. We cannot write down a strange language or dialect till we know it practically. We can only write down what is familiar to us. Till the elements of the language are familiar to us we can only take rough provisional notes. The only way to describe the formation of the strange sounds is to describe the organic actions by which we imitate them. Experimental phonetics may some day alter this, but at present it is practically the way in which we have to analyze strange sounds. It is the same with the idioms and constructions of the language: at first we can only write down what we have assimilated ourselves.

Help from Natives.—An evident objection to this method is that unless our knowledge is perfect, our description of the new form of speech cannot be perfect. As the only people who have this perfect knowledge are the speakers themselves, a second method suggests itself, that of training an intelligent native to do the work under the supervision of the foreign investigator.

The investigator should first try to find some speaker of the dialect who is intelligent enough to be able to learn to use a phonetic notation, and sufficiently interested in the subject to take the trouble of writing down the tales, songs, riddles, or other traditional pieces he remembers, or making dialogues and other texts on topics suggested by the investigator. A young village schoolmaster will often prove the best help in this way.

At first the native will write his texts in a mixture of dialectal and literary forms. The investigator, by comparing parallel passages and noting apparent inconsistencies, will soon find these out, and by degrees will be able to train the native to write phonetically. The first prejudices once overcome, the latter will soon take a pleasure and pride in being as purely colloquial as possible, and will perhaps feel something of the charm of exploring a country which is at once strange and familiar.

This last method always implies practically a combination of it with the preceding one. Compared with this combined method of learning the language oneself, and training a native to write it down, all other methods are mere makeshifts.

Questioning.—The one that is most frequently employed is, perhaps, that of questioning. If the investigator has to deal with the language of illiterate savages, of whose language he is ignorant, he has, of course, to begin with gesture. Here he will meet with the difficulties already discussed under 'visualizing' (p. 209). If he points to his mouth, he may get the word for 'mouth,' but he is just as likely to get 'bite, eat, teeth, lip.' If he is certain that it is 'teeth' and not lips, he is still in doubt whether the plural or the singular is meant.

Prolonged questioning is apt to tire the intelligent European schoolmaster, still more the flighty barbarian. Many a traveller who has attracted crowds of dusky natives into his tent by displaying his stores, has soon found himself alone when he begins to ask them questions about their language and religious views.

If the natives have a keener sense of humour than of the obligations of veracity, they may revenge themselves by giving misleading answers. A missionary who had been in the South Seas was once observed to burst into repeated fits of laughter while reading what professed to be a list of numerals in a Polynesian language with which he was familiar. He explained that, knowing that the speakers of this language could not count beyond twenty, he was at first surprised and interested to find the numerals given as high as ten thousand, but found that all the higher numbers were simply strings of words of the most ludicrous and improper associations.

The European peasant of the north is apt to turn sulky, if questioned beyond a certain point. A story is told of a Swedish dialectologist who, wishing to know what was the preterite of the verb *die* in a certain Swedish dialect, asked one of the natives whether he said *I died* or *I dew*. The only answer he could get was, 'When we are dead, we don't speak.'

Still more hopeless is the method of investigating a dialect by means of correspondence, although it must be confessed that Ellis by this means accumulated a vast mass of information about the English dialects which would otherwise have been lost. But such information cannot under ordinary circumstances be reliable. It must be remembered also that the information given in the fifth part of Ellis's *Early English Pronunciation*, although originally obtained by correspondence, was in many cases checked by personal interviews with his authorities.

The only possible way of dealing satisfactorily with a whole body of dialects such as the English, is to have a school of phonetics at some real University which will attract speakers of the different dialects, each of whom will pursue his investigations under his teacher on a uniform plan.

Collecting Materials

Every one has his own methods of literary work, and every investigator of unwritten dialects has his own way of collecting his material. But this does not prove that there are not certain broad principles of general application. A method which makes elaborate and carefully digested collections useless to others cannot be a sound one.

Handwriting.—The first requisite is to write clearly. Business men and those who keep secretaries can afford the luxury and distinction of writing an illegible hand. Scientific investigators, who seldom do good work after starting a secretary, and who often have to read nothing but their own handwriting for months together, must learn to write.

425

Their writing should be as small as is convenient for their sight, and as compact as possible, the letters being nearly upright and close together, without more separation between the words than is necessary. They should get into the habit of always leaving a margin—which may be marked by folding the paper—of writing in paragraphs and on one side of the paper only, so as to be able to make additions on the back—unless they are writing in a book, and then only when saving of space is essential. If they can write evenly without ruled lines, their handwriting will be all the better.

Such a system of writing as my Current Shorthand will be found to add greatly to the speed and ease of literary work, as it can both be written quicker and packed into a smaller space than ordinary longhand, even if written without any special contractions.

Notes that are to be kept for any length of time should never be written in lead pencil, but in ink, or, if that is inconvenient, with a solid ink pencil. If it is desired to make the writing with the latter specially distinct, the paper should be slightly moistened, and the pencil carefully sharpened. For rapid and continuous work several of these pencils should be kept in readiness.

Form.—As regards the form of the paper on which the collections are written, they may take the form of slips, of loose sheets, or of bound books.

For the first preliminary rough work of collecting isolated words or quotations for a dictionary or grammar, **slips** are the most convenient. The proper average size of a small slip is about four and a half inches by two, or less for a fine writer; a short-sighted writer will find three and a quarter inches by one and a quarter large enough; he will be able to write the Lord's Prayer many times over in Current Shorthand on one side of such a slip.

If the slips are required only for temporary use, and a great number is required, they may be of thin paper. If the collection of slips is intended to be more permanent and for reference, they should be of stiffer paper, the best for continuous use being evenly cut thin cards.

They can be kept in boxes like cigar-boxes, or, better, in shallow trays with divisions.

For purposes of further division and classification, stiff cards with 'tabs' or square pieces in the middle projecting above the general level may be inserted at intervals among the slips, so that the eye can see the letters or other index-marks on the tabs at a glance.

If accuracy of reference is essential, the slips should be kept in their boxes in the exact order in which they were first written, which of course will be the order in which the words or quotations they contain occurred in the text which was excerpted ; and then each reference should be verified before the slips are sorted into an alphabetic or any other order which interferes with their original order.

The heading—the word, the grammatical category, etc.—should be written at the top left-hand corner of the slip, the reference—name of text, number of page or paragraph and line—at the right-hand lower corner, the quotation itself between.

The more mechanically the work of slip-writing is done, the better. It is a good rule never to put two entries on one slip. There is no occasion to economize in paper.

The great advantage of slips is that they require no previous calculation of space ; a collection of slips is perfectly elastic. Their other advantage is the speed with which they can be written, as they involve no reference, no turning over of pages. But the sorting of them is a most wearisome and irritating, to some minds intolerable, drudgery ; nor can the sorting be left to others unless it is purely mechanical. When sorted, they are easily misplaced or lost. Altogether, they are difficult to handle and refer to, each of the hundred slips which make up perhaps only a page of print being practically on a page by itself.

For less mechanical or more comprehensive collections **loose sheets**, nearly square, so as to allow room for a margin, are very convenient, five inches by four being the medium size for a fine shorthand-writer. The deductions from the materials collected on slips may be summarized on such sheets. If there is any doubt about the sequence of ideas, or any probability of additional matter coming in, each sheet may be restricted to what would be a paragraph in a book. Indeed, this will be found the most convenient way of preparing a book for press, as the paragraphs can be rearranged at pleasure till the book is complete, and can then be transcribed into longhand.

The sheets can be kept in boxes or drawers, or can be kept together with indiarubber bands passing over sheets of stiff cardboard at both ends of the pile of sheets. Larger sheets can be kept in portfolios, subdivisions being made by keeping each lesser group inside a folded sheet of thicker paper.

Bound books, according to Gabelentz, are suited only for travellers, who cannot afford to risk the loss of slips or sheets. The advantages of books are not only that the leaves do not get lost or mislaid, but also the perfect facility of reference, which, again, is increased by the greater amount of matter that can be included in one page. But they postulate that we know beforehand how much space will be required, or else involve a great waste of space, which, of course, diminishes the ease of reference. Then, too, the order of the quotations or the categories under which they are put cannot be altered without causing confusion and waste of space. The bigger the book, the greater the waste of time in making entries. Some, however, still prefer, even in doing a glossary, to enter the head-words in a book—or paste the headings from a printed dictionary along the margin—with ample blank spaces, to going through the drudgery of sorting slips which can never be made easy to refer to.

Some make their slips more easy of reference by pasting them into a book. For this purpose any strongly bound printed book will do. It is only necessary to cut out every sixth leaf or so in order to allow for the thickness of the slips. The work of pasting down the slips is irksome, but it may be shortened by simply running two lines of paste down the page, and then putting down the slips without having to apply the paste to each separately. But the result is always untidy and wanting in compactness. A practical shorthand-writer would hardly hesitate between this method and the slower but far more satisfactory one of simply copying his slips into a book in shorthand.

It is never worth while to **interleave** printed books such as dictionaries unless we are certain of having to make numerous entries into them. Otherwise it is better to write on the margin, and, if necessary, insert a sheet occasionally, either loose or pasted. Many have noticed that interleaved books in libraries often have a few entries on the first few sheets, which are then left completely blank.

For many special purposes it is convenient to make one's own manuscript books by fastening together sheets of folded paper either by stitching, or by simply making holes and putting a piece of thin string through, by which the paper is less liable to be torn; the back may be strengthened by pasting on a narrow strip of cloth.

Principles of Collecting

Collect everything at first.—In working at a text, for the first few pages one should, as a general rule, collect everything. If the collections are for a dictionary, every word should be noted, with, of course, such exceptions as common sense dictates, such as the conjunction *and*. After a time, the text should be read over again cursorily, and the method of collection for the future carefully considered and methodically planned out.

Collect mechanically at first.—The work should also be done mechanically at first. No *à priori* generalizations should be allowed to interfere with the first aim of the investigator, that is, gathering together enough material to form the basis of sound deductions.

When a certain definite amount of material has been collected, or when the most important texts have been gone through, the investigator may well pause and review his gains from a higher and freer point of view, lest prolonged drudgery and impracticable ideas of fullness or exhaustivity of collection lead him into working on a scale which will make it impossible for him to complete his enterprise within reasonable time, until at last he sinks into a monomaniac machine incapable of any higher work. It should never be forgotten that it is much easier to heap up material than to utilize it. It is easy for the dictionary-compiler to brag of the tons of material, the millions of slips that have been collected for him, but when it comes to sorting these slips according to the meanings of the words, and weighing the evidence of each, he often wishes he had started with a ton or two less. Let us, then, take warning by Browning's grammarian—

> ' That low man seeks a little thing to do,
>   Sees it and does it :
> This high man, with a great thing to pursue,
>   Dies ere he knows it.'

Let us be low men—at least at first.

Classification.—We have arrived, then, at the stage of a logical classification of a moderate and reasonable amount of material which, without pretending to be exhaustive, may be relied on for giving a sufficient number of examples to illustrate the general principles we are investigating. The ideal for a dictionary would be to have enough examples of the rarer words and rather more than enough of the very common words.

If our classification is partly arbitrary—as in an alphabetic dictionary—then the classification of the materials will be partly mechanical. The logical classification will then consist mainly in arranging the quotations under the meanings expressed by the head-words. If the quotations are intended to form the foundation of a syntax, then the classification will probably be purely logical from the beginning.

In all logical classifications the investigator should proceed cautiously at first, so as not to start with prejudices or hastily formed generalizations. The material should at first be sorted only into definitely marked off main groups which interfere with one another as little as possible.

At first, the language should be explained as far as possible out of itself. There should be no comparison with cognate languages till this has been done. Otherwise the investigator runs the risk of importing into the language tendencies which do not really belong to it, and so missing, perhaps, some explanation which would otherwise be obvious to him.

CHAPTER XXI

MIND-TRAINING; CLASSICAL AND MODERN LANGUAGES

WE will now examine the grounds of the widely spread assumption that ancient languages—that is, Greek and Latin—are more perfect and more highly developed in structure than modern ones, and that consequently their study is a better training for the mind.

Now that the question of subordinating ancient to modern languages—even to the exclusion of Greek from the general scheme of education—is being earnestly discussed, and is winning more and more adherents, the statement of the innate superiority of ancient languages is incessantly repeated by the advocates of Greek and Latin.

Some of them, indeed, go so far as to hint that the study of modern languages is not only useless as an instrument of intellectual training, but is even positively injurious, as tending to create a superficial turn of mind.

A thorough examination of the reasons of these assumptions, and of the real distinctions between ancient and modern languages, will lead us to the very opposite conclusions in every respect. We shall see that the arguments of the supporters of ancient languages are based on an erroneous idea of the nature of language, which has been further supported by the one-sidedly historical method which has hitherto prevailed in philological investigation.

The assertion of the higher development of ancient languages may be reduced to the more precise one that ancient languages have a more copious grammar than modern ones. The comparison of the two extremes, Greek and English, has often prompted the remark that English has 'no grammar.' And, indeed, if we compare the numerous cases and declensions in

273   T

Greek and Latin with the English genitive and plural -*s*, and the interminable complexities of the Greek verb in all its voices, moods, tenses, numbers, and persons with the few endings which make up the inflections of the English verb, we are apt to accept the statement as a matter of course.

But even the most superficial observer cannot but be struck by the evident contradiction implied in the generally admitted fact that English is one of the most expressive and concise languages that have ever existed, and that ideas can be expressed in it with as much facility and accuracy as in Greek and Latin. Thus the idea, or rather ideas, expressed by the Latin *amat* can be expressed with the same brevity by the English *he loves*, which, like *amat*, consists of only two syllables, and with greater precision, for the English form denotes not only the person, but also the gender. Again, the Latin *amabit* has not only a corresponding *he will love* in English, but also a shorter dissyllable form *he'll love*.

The supposed superiority of the Latin over the English forms consists in the former being able to express their meaning with one, while the latter require two or more words. But the distinction is really a purely graphic one. The actual spoken language admits no division into words, its lowest unit being the sentence, within whose limits there is no division or pause of any kind. Historically considered, moreover, the Latin *amat* is really two words, as much as its English representative, the final *t* being originally a pronoun signifying 'he,' 'she,' or 'it,' and it is only reasons of practical convenience that prevent us from writing *am at* or *ama t* as two, and *heloves* as one word.

It may, of course, be urged that the *s* of *loves* is historically the same ending as the Latin -*t*, and consequently that *he loves* is really three words, but this does not apply to *I love*. Besides, these historical views lie outside of the practical question, and the *s* of *loves* is in English practically nothing but a fossilized archaism.

The really essential difference between *amat* and *he loves* is that in the former the pronominal element is expressed by a suffix, in the latter by a prefix. The end of a word being more hurried over and slurred than the beginning, it naturally follows that in those languages which express general relations, such as the persons of verbs or the cases of nouns, by means of suffixed words or syllables, these elements will be much more liable to various phonetic changes and shortenings, which will vary greatly according to the sounds which precede them, as when the *s* of the nominative in Greek is preserved in *ánax* but dropped in *daímōn*, lengthening the preceding vowel.   Hence have arisen the varied and complex inflections of the ancient languages.

English, on the other hand, prefers to denote general relations by prefixes, which are not liable to be modified, or incorporated into the root-word.   The practical result in writing is that most English modifiers can be written as separate words, and regarded as such, even when their meanings are quite as abstract as those of the inflections of the old languages.   The preposition *of*, for instance, in *of a man* is quite as abstract as the *is* in Latin *hominis*, and, like it, is absolutely unmeaning when separated from its noun, although the accident of its being written as an independent word blinds us to the fact.   The real functional distinction between the two is that while *of* is always perfectly distinct and recognizable in all its combinations, the Latin *-is* is both ambiguous in itself, being used to express a number of other cases as well, and is only one of a large number of means of denoting the same case, as may be seen by comparing the endings of *hominis, mensae, dominī, domūs*, which have not a single sound in common.   What must strike an impartial observer is the waste of power involved in employing so many forms, most of which have at the same time a number of other vague and contradictory meanings, to express an idea which in a modern language like English can be expressed by a single unambiguous word.

By the side of their useless complexity of inflection, ancient languages show a remarkable vagueness of thought, both in grammar and vocabulary.   Compare the extreme vagueness of the meanings of the half-a-dozen cases in Greek and Latin with the precision of the numerous English prepositions which correspond to them.   The same want of differentiation is shown in the vocabulary as well.   Even in those cases in which an ancient language has a considerable number of words to express a given group of abstract ideas, it often happens that each single word runs through and exhausts the whole series of ideas, so that nothing at all is gained by the fullness of the vocabulary.   In such a case a modern language utilizes each word to express a definite idea.

The traditional character of ancient languages often leads them into downright absurdities, such as the use of grammatical genders, which, strange to say, are still retained more or less in all the Aryan languages of Europe with the exception of English. In fact, there can be no question that the highly inflected Aryan languages are in many respects far more irrational than those which stand on a lower scale of development, and that such a language as English owes its superiority as a means of expression in a great degree to developments which have many analogies to those of non-Aryan and even savage languages.

The statement that English has little or no grammar simply means that the grammatical structure of English is so regular and transparent that a very moderate amount of analysis is enough to enable the learner to find his way through it. But regularity and symmetry are by no means inconsistent with complexity, and, as a matter of fact, English is one of the most complex languages that has ever existed. If grammar be defined as the expression of general relations, whether that expression be effected by suffixes or prefixes, by inflections or prepositions and auxiliaries, then English has the most copious grammar of any in the world. The difference between the complexity of an ancient and of a modern language is that that of the former is to a great extent unmeaning and useless, while that of the latter implies a correspondingly full and minute analysis of the ideas expressed by it.

Of course, it must not be forgotten that all languages are extremely defective, if compared with an ideal standard, and that consequently the difference between them can only be one of degree; but if those languages are the most rational which express ideas most clearly, simply, and regularly, there can be no question of the superiority of the modern languages in rationality, and consequently as a means of intellectual training also. If, on the other hand, the mechanical acquisition of irrational distinctions of form, and familiarizing oneself with vague and loose expressions of thought, is the best training for the mind, then there can be no question of the superiority of ancient languages.

It cannot be denied that the defects of ancient languages are compensated by many real advantages, although these advantages have nothing to do with intellectual training. One superiority of most ancient languages is the simplicity, clearness, and sonorousness of their phonetic structure. The very vagueness of their meanings, again, although in itself a serious defect, brings with it great freshness, freedom, and picturesqueness of metaphor, which, together with their fullness of sound, eminently fit them for poetry and oratory, and for æsthetic purposes generally.

The assimilations, contractions, and other phonetic changes of modern languages not only diminish their harmony and fullness of sound, but also make them indistinct by diminishing the individuality of the older distinctions, or even, as is so often the case in English, by confounding originally distinct words under one common form. But even these defects do not affect the value of modern languages as instruments of intellectual training.

The defects of the inflectional languages are most clearly shown in those cases in which an inflectional system has been retained after it has been made superfluous by the development of prefixes, auxiliaries, etc., and a fixed word-order. Modern German is a marked example of such a transition language. Although it has adopted the fixed word-order of a modern language, and makes an extensive use of auxiliaries, prepositions, etc., it still retains many of the old inflections, together with the three grammatical genders. The result is that while in some cases the old inflections still express an independent meaning, as when the distinction between the English *in* and *into* is expressed by *in* with the dative and accusative respectively, in others they are superfluous, the idea being already fully expressed by means analogous to those employed by such a language as English. Such distinctions, for instance, as those between *guter* and *gute* in *ein guter mann* and *der gute mann* are really quite useless, being fully expressed by the *ein* and the *der*. Again, in the old languages the distinctions of grammatical gender, together with the laws of concord, allowed the separation of adjectives from the nouns to which they belong, which, although of little use for purposes of expression, yet added greatly to the harmony and picturesqueness of the language by causing variety, and especially by preventing the repetition of the same heavy endings close together; but in German, with its fixed word-order, they are almost useless, and, indeed, the agreement between adjective and noun is abandoned when the adjective stands predicatively —curiously enough, in the only position in which it would be of any use—although it is superfluously retained in the attributive position of the adjective.

Such a language as Swedish, on the other hand, with its simplicity, its clearness and harmony of phonetic structure, and its few, but clear, simple, symmetrical inflections, really combines, to a great extent, the advantages of ancient and modern languages. German has also the antique clearness and sonorousness of sound, in which it is infinitely superior to English and French, which certainly carry off the palm for simplicity and precision, English, again, being unquestionably foremost in many-sidedness and power.

In comparing the ancient languages among themselves, it must be borne in mind that Greek, owing to the greater intellectual activity of those who spoke it, and the consequent necessity of precision and many-sidedness of expression, is in many respects more modern in structure than Latin. The excessive use of the article and the heaping of particles in Greek are characteristic contrasts with the Latin usages.

It must further be remembered that archaism of structure by no means implies that the language is a dead one. We have in Russian an example of a living language of great literary, social, and political importance, which vies in inflectional complexity with Latin and Greek ; and it is a question whether a study of it would not prove as good a practical training in the use of an inflectional language as that of the classical languages.

Of course, if modern languages are to be studied at all, they must be studied properly. The superficial study of modern languages certainly tends to deteriorate the mind, just as every other superficial study does, but it is equally possible to study dead languages superficially, as also in a narrow and unscientific spirit.

APPENDIX

BIBLIOGRAPHY

THE following notices do not aim at any fullness, but are merely intended as a first guide to those who wish to pursue the subject further. Many of the books here given themselves contain more or less full bibliographies.

General Works

Paul, H.: Principien der Sprachgeschichte. Halle, ²1886. [Purely theoretical and abstract.]

Von der Gabelentz, G.: die Sprachwissenschaft. Leipzig, 1891. [Deals with the practical as well as the theoretical study of languages.]

Storm, J.: Englische Philologie. Leipzig, ²1892. [Purely practical; gives incidentally much information about general phonetics, together with many details about other languages besides English.]

Periodicals

Maître phonétique, la; organe de l'Association phonétique des professeurs de langues vivantes, edited by P. Passy. Address: Fonetik, Bourg-la-Reine, France.

Phonetische Studien, Zeitschrift für wissenschaftliche und praktische Phonetik, edited by W. Vietor, I–VI. Marburg, 1888–93. Continued in the form of an Appendix to *die Neueren Sprachen*, Marburg, 1894, foll. [This publication, like the previous one, is not confined to phonetics, but contains articles of a wider linguistic interest, both theoretical and practical.]

Modern Language Quarterly of Language and Literature, edited by H. Frank Heath, London.

Phonetics

Sweet, H.: Primer of Phonetics. Oxford, 1890.

———— Sketch of Phonetics in *Primer of Historical English Grammar*. Oxford, 1893.

Grandgent, C. H.: German and English Sounds. Boston, U.S.A., 1893. [Very good diagrams of the tongue-positions.]

Sievers, E.: Grundzüge der Phonetik. Leipzig, ⁴1893. [Deals with phonetics mainly from the point of view of comparative philology.]

Vietor, W. : Elemente der Phonetik. Leipzig, ³1893.
Jespersen, O. : Fonetik. Copenhagen, 1897. [Not yet completed.]

Passy, P. : Les sons du Français. Paris, ⁴1897.
Michaelis et Passy : Dictionnaire Phonétique de la langue Française, 1897.
Hempl, G. : German orthography and phonology. Boston, U.S.A., 1897.

General Method

Widgery, W. H. : The Teaching of Languages in Schools. London, 1888.
Vietor, W. : Der Sprachunterricht muss umkehren ! Heilbronn, ²1886.
Franke, F. : Die praktische Spracherlernung. Heilbronn, 1884.
Klinghardt, H. : Ein Jahr Erfahrungen mit der Neuen Methode. Marburg, 1888.
——————— Drei Weitere Jahre Erfahrungen mit der Neuen Methode. Marburg, 1892.
Storm, J. : Om en forbedret Undervisning i Levende Sprog (Universitets- og Skoleannaler II.). Christiania.
Brekke, K. : Gouins Methode (Univ.- og Skoleannaler, 1894). Christiania.
Western, A. : Om Undervisningen i Nyere Sprog. Christiania, 1885.

Text-books

Sweet, H. : Elementarbuch des gesprochenen Englisch. Oxford, ³1891.
——————— Primer of Spoken English. Oxford, ²1895.
Passy, P. : Élémans d'Anglais parlé. Paris, ²1887.
Brekke, K. : Lærebog i Engelsk for folkskolen. Christiania, 1892.

Beyer und Passy : Elementarbuch des gesprochenen Französisch. Cöthen, 1893.
Passy, J. : Chrestomathie Française. Paris, 1897.
Franke, F. : Phrases de tous des jours. Leipzig, ⁵1893.
Storm, F. : Dialogues Français. Copenhagen, 1887.

Sweet, H. : Anglo-Saxon Primer. Oxford, ⁷1893.
——————— First Steps in Anglo-Saxon. Oxford, 1897.

7

F. PALMGREN

'Verhandlungen zur Reform des
Sprachunterrichts auf der dritten Nordischen
Philologenversammlung zu Stockholm
(10–13 August 1886)'

Source: *Englische Studien*, 10, 1887, pp. 335–52.

VERHANDLUNGEN ZUR REFORM DES SPRACHUNTERRICHTS AUF DER DRITTEN NORDISCHEN PHILOLOGENVERSAMMLUNG ZU STOCKHOLM (10.—13. AUGUST 1886[1]).

Wie auf den vorhergehenden nordischen philologenversammlungen zu *Kopenhagen* (1879) und *Christiania* (1881), so trat auch auf der Stockholmer versammlung eine pädagogische section zusammen. Die im schosse derselben abgehaltenen, ungewöhnlich zahlreichen vorträge bezogen sich, gemäss dem charakter der ganzen versammlung, vorwiegend auf den sprachunterricht. Mehr jedoch als die übrigen sollte éiner der vorträge die allgemeine aufmerksamkeit auf sich lenken, und zwar sowohl wegen der eigenen vorzüge in seinen erörterungen über ziel und methode des unterrichts, als auch — und vielleicht nicht. zum mindesten — wegen der discussion, die sich demselben anschloss. Glückliche umstände hatten es nämlich gefügt, dass aus verschiedenen ländern hervorragende vertreter der neuen reformideen dieses gebiets sich jetzt zum ersten male bei uns zusammenfanden und die gelegenheit erhielten, ihre ansichten in der öffentlichkeit vorzutragen bzw. dieselben gegen die mehr oder weniger herkömmlichen anschauungen, welche gleichfalls ihre vertreter zu der versammlung entsandt hatten, in den kampf zu führen.

Und hiermit treten wir in unseren bericht über die verhandlungen ein.

Donnerstag, den 12. aug., hielt die section ihre zweite und letzte officielle versammlung ab, wobei oberinspector [schulrath] *Synnerberg* aus Finnland den vorsitz führte. Zunächst nahm nun lector [oberlehrer] *Axel Drake* (aus *Nyköping)* das wort zu einem vortrage über die frage:

»Wie lässt sich für den sprachunterricht unserer schulen eine praktische und zugleich psychologisch richtige anordnung und methodik gewinnen?«

Die vorwürfe, welche man dem bestehenden sprachunterricht machen kann, waren nach ansicht des redners folgende: »derselbe ist zu abstract, trennt in ungebührlichem masse inhalt und form, ist überaus ermüdend und leidet an fehlerhafter vorbereitung im einzelnen, Alles dies hat nun zur folge, dass weder in theoretischer noch in praktischer hinsicht das endlich erreichte resultat zu der aufgewandten arbeit in einem irgendwie angemessenen verhältnisse steht.«

»Dass der sprachunterricht einen allzu abstracten charakter trägt, ist eine natürliche folge der herrschenden einrichtung unserer elementarbücher, in denen schon von anfang an neben den, zur einübung der betr. regeln dienenden fremdsprachlichen sätzen auch übungssätze zur übertragung aus der muttersprache in die fremde auftreten. Da nun letztere sehr viel sorgfältigere grammatische studien erheischen als jene, und da ihre durchnahme an sich schon weit mehr als die doppelte zeit fordert im vergleich zu den fremdsprachlichen übungssätzen, so ist es zweifellos klar, dass auf diesem wege der beginn zusammenhängender texte ganz bedeutend ver-

---

[1]) Der nachfolgende, höchst willkommene bericht ging der redaction im manuscript zu, ist aber schon vor veröffentlichung dieses heftes fast gleichlautend auch in *Verdandi* 1886 h. 4/5 erschienen.   Red.

zögert wird. Ziel und zweck des elementarbuchs kann aber doch gar kein anderer sein, als das lesen zusammenhängender texte vorzubereiten. Nur wenn es zu diesem behufe nöthig ist, kann es überhaupt für berechtigt gelten! Und da die fremdsprachlichen übungen zumeist aus einzelsätzen bestehen, die ausschliesslich nach grammatischen gesichtspunkten, aber ohne alle rücksicht auf ihren inhalt zusammengestellt sind, so wird man möglichst eilen müssen, dass man damit zu ende kommt, und sich nicht länger mit ihnen aufhalten dürfen, als für den angegebenen zweck eben schlechterdings geboten ist.«

»Was sodann ferner dem unterricht ein abstractes gepräge aufdrückt, das sind die allzu grossen anforderungen an das lateinische und französische[1]) extemporale der abiturienten. Infolge derselben nimmt das grammatische allzuviel zeit und aufmerksamkeit in anspruch und gereicht der lebendigen einsicht in diese sprachen eher zum schaden als zum nutzen.«

»Der zweite fehler, dass man mehr, als gut ist, inhalt und form von einander trennt, fällt grossentheils mit dem vorhergehenden zusammen. Seinen grund hat derselbe zunächst in dem oben berührten elementarbuch-unwesen. Er beruht aber ferner auch auf der noch immer herrschenden verkehrten ansicht über die hauptaufgabe der schulgrammatik, als ob nämlich dieselbe darin bestünde, dem jungen menschen ein abstractes schema, so zu sagen eine karte zu gewähren, worin er gut orientirt sein soll und angeben könne, an welchem punkte eine jede einzelnheit ihre stelle hat. Auf die erklärung der sprachlichen erscheinungen kommt es dabei nicht so sehr an als darauf, dass der schüler nur sicher weiss, es heisst so oder so. Endlich zeigt sich der genannte fehler auch darin, dass man bei der interpretation der zusammenhängenden texte die aufmerksamkeit so ausschliesslich auf das formelle und grammatikalische richtet, dass man den inhalt daneben oft ganz und gar aus dem auge verliert.«

»Dass der sprachunterricht unter solchen umständen höchst ermüdend und langweilig werden muss, ergiebt sich eigentlich von selbst. Oder ist es etwa denkbar, dass dieses ewige herumexerciren mit grammatischen formen (flexionen und constructionen) dem schüler irgend welche befriedigung gewähren sollte? Muss nicht vielmehr dieser sprachunterricht mit seiner geist- und gedankenlosen arbeitslast und seiner zustutzung auf sogenannte regeln, über deren grund man gewöhnlich nicht die geringste vorstellung hat, mehr wie niederdrückend wirken?«

»In früheren zeiten war die »vorbereitung« der häuslichen arbeit ein nahezu unbekannter begriff im schulunterricht, und die gewöhnliche formel beim aufgeben von pensen lautete: »von hier an bis da und dahin!« Aber auch noch heutigentags hört man vertreter und gesinnungsgenossen der alten unterrichtsweise behaupten, dass mit der vorbereitung der häuslichen arbeit in der schule »die geistige selbständigkeit in den studien« einfach vernichtet werde. Wie es sich indess hiermit verhält, werden wir ausführlicher weiter unten sehen.«

»Im zusammenhang mit einer besseren methode ist aber auch eine bessere anordnung des sprachunterrichts geboten. Seitdem man, wie es für uns Schweden in der that allein das richtige ist, das studium der fremden sprachen mit dem

---

[1]) Ein griechisches extemporale kennt die schwedische maturitätsprüfung nicht mehr, wie denn überhaupt seit dem 10. märz 1869 das Griechische aus der reihe der obligatorischen gymnasialfächer gestrichen ist. Dagegen ist für den realistischen (nichtlateinischen) abiturienten ausser dem französischen auch noch ein deutsches oder ein englisches extemporale vorgeschrieben.   H. Kl.

Deutschen begonnen hat, muss man auch — im gegensatz zu dem gegenwärtigen lehrplan — zunächst das französische folgen lassen, um vermittelst dessen ausreichend das studium des Lateinischen vorbereiten zu können, welches uns nach anschauungsweise und satzbau ungleich ferner liegt. [1])«

Damit nun abhülfe geschehe gegen die hier hervorgehobenen missstände, will redner an drei anerkannte axiome der pädagogik erinnern, um dieselben als ausgangspunkt und zugleich als leitfaden zu benutzen für seine vorschläge über die im sprachunterricht nothwendigen veränderungen. Diese axiome sind: a) man muss beim unterricht vom concreten ausgehn und darf das abstracte erst an zweiter stelle folgen lassen; b) in bezug auf die gegenstände des unterrichts ist mit dem näher liegenden zu beginnen und erst danach zum weiteren und ferneren überzugehen, wie denn auch rücksichtlich der verschiedenen übungen der fortschritt vom leichteren zum schwereren stattzufinden hat; c) das rein theoretische moment muss möglichst mit einem praktischen in verbindung treten, sodass man auf keiner stufe mehr theorie giebt, als für gewisse praktische bedürfnisse nothwendig ist.

Rücksichtlich des letztgenannten satzes verkannte redner freilich nicht, dass andere wohl abweichender meinung seien, aber er seinerseits sah denselben jedenfalls als axiom an. Der sprachunterricht der schule müsse nämlich nicht nur einen guten grund legen für solche schüler, welche später sich tiefer gehenden sprachstudien widmen wollen, sondern auch der grossen menge derer, welche vor dem reifeexamen ihre schulstudien abbrechen, um sich der industrie oder dem gewerbe zuzuwenden, eine in diesen berufszweigen praktisch verwerthbare mitgabe sichern [2]). Und wiederum für diejenigen, welche sich auf der universität den medicinischen studien widmen wollen, ist aus ganz anderen gründen eine gute sprachliche ausbildung (in den modernen sprachen) nothwendig als diejenigen sind, welche in dieser hinsicht für den künftigen juristen vorliegen; denn für diesen haben die sprachstudien der schule kaum mehr bedeutung als die einer philosophischen propädeutik.

---

[1]) Vgl. Vietor's vorwort zu seiner Hannoverschen festschrift: »mir erscheint die reihenfolge »Englisch, Französisch, Lateinisch, Griechisch« die vernunftgemässe.« In der that kann selbst die schlechteste methode nicht so unheilvoll wirken, wie die verkehrte aufeinanderfolge der sprachen auch in unserem lehrplan. H. Kl.

[2]) Während der deutsche lehrplan für höhere schulen lediglich die ausbildung der abiturienten ins auge fasst, berücksichtigt der schwedische in hervorragender weise auch die bedürfnisse der grossen, ja überwiegenden zahl jener, welche die schule bereits am schluss von obertertia (ein einschnitt wie bei uns thatsächlich derjenige am schluss von II B, um den indess unser lehrplan sich schlechterdings nicht kümmert), z. th. auch schon von quarta verlassen: letzteren wird in 3jährigem deutschen unterricht mit wöchentlich 7 st. eine praktisch verwerthbare grundlage für diese sprache gewährt, jenen überdies eine solche auch im Englischen, welchem in den beiden tertien gleichfalls wöchentlich 7 st. gewidmet sind. Die vorbildung für akademische studien beginnt eigentlich erst mit II B: in dieser classe setzt wenigstens u. a. (für theologen und philologen) das Griechische ein, und bereits verlangt man energisch, es solle auch der anfang des, für den besuch der universität z. z. noch obligatorischen Latein aus III B nach den oberclassen verschoben werden. Auf diesen verhältnissen beruht obige forderung des redners. H. Kl.

»Unter diesen verschiedenen bestimmungen des sprachunterrichts der höheren
schulen muss man nun diejenige, welche allen lehrgegenständen gemeinsam sind,
nämlich die formale bildung, in erste linie stellen. Hierzu darf man weiterhin
für die sprachen die praktische fertigkeit, das ästhetische moment fügen, sowie die
mannigfaltigen sachkenntnisse, unter denen vor allem jene wichtig sind, welche
einige vertrautheit mit den nationalen eigenthümlichkeiten des betreffenden volkes
gewähren können.«

»Was schliesslich die a n o r d n u n g der sprachen betrifft, so ist dieselbe so
einzurichten, dass jedenfalls alle bisher an der höheren schule gelehrten sprachen
dem lehrplane derselben erhalten werden können.« —

Alle diese vorerwägungen bilden die grundlage, auf welcher redner zu einer
beantwortung der vorliegenden frage gelangt ist, eine beantwortung, die inhaltlich
bereits angedeutet ist durch die anklagen, welche er gegen die bestehende methode
gerichtet hat.   Sie zerfällt in folgende sätze :

1) »schularbeit und häusliche arbeit müssen in ein ganz anderes verhältniss
zu einander treten, als bisher zumeist der fall gewesen ist ;«

2) »grammatisch genaue und sorgfältig den inhalt berücksichtigende lectüre
muss den mittelpunkt bilden für den sprachunterricht der schule ;«

3) »der unterricht in den verschiedenen sprachen muss sich systematisch mehr
zusammenschliessen, so dass man besser als bisher die ergebnisse eines voraufgehenden unterrichts für den nachfolgenden nutzbar machen kann ;«

4) »bei der abfassung von lehrbüchern ist es nothwendig, dass die verf. sich
mit grösstmöglicher sorgfalt die resultate der fortschreitenden wissenschaft
aneignen ;«

5) »das ziel für den lateinischen unterricht der schule ist anderweitig festzu-
setzen ;«

6) »die forderung umfassender sprechübungen, welche sowohl innerhalb des
grösseren publicums wie von einzelnen vertretern der wissenschaft geltend gemacht
wird, scheint nicht vollberechtigt zu sein.«

»Wenn die häusliche arbeit immer genügend vorbereitet würde, so müsste
dieselbe nicht nur viel leichter, sondern auch viel fruchtbringender als gegenwärtig
ausfallen.   Man würde damit sowohl dem geistlosen dumm-fleisse vorbeugen, wie
den häufigen missverständnissen, welche hinterdrein oft schwer zu beseitigen sind ;
man würde aber dadurch ferner auch der verschwendung, die noch allgemein mit
zeit und arbeit des schülers getrieben wird, vorbeugen, sowie jener abnutzung
ihres interesses und ihrer wissbegier, die vordem förmlich zum system erhoben
war.   So ist es z. b. nach allen seiten hin empfehlenswerth, wenn der schüler während der ersten jahre eines jeden sprachunterrichts die fremdsprachlichen beispiel-
sätze vollständig vom lehrer erklärt bekommt, auf die art nämlich, dass letzterer
ihm die erforderlichen andeutungen giebt, oder vorkommenden falls ihn nöthigt,
seinerseits ein wenig nachzudenken, um in möglichstem umfange an der gemein-
schaftlichen übersetzung theilzunehmen.   Denn man muss wohl beachten, dass
die peinvolle seelenarbeit, welche mit ungenügend vorbereiteten übungssätzen (in
der fremden spr.) oder häuslichen exercitien verknüpft ist, keineswegs als identisch
mit wirklicher gedankenarbeit angesehen werden darf; dass aufsuchen in der
grammatik und nachschlagen im wörterbuch oft die hauptsache sind bei der ganzen
zeittötenden plackerei; und endlich dass, in keineswegs seltenen fällen, die ein-
prägung von fehlerhaften auffassungen den einzigen lohn der ganzen anstrengenden

mühen bilden. Gewiss ist das gedächtniss bei der jugend das am besten ent-
wickelte seelenvermögen, aber es muss doch auf eine naturgemässe weise angewendet
werden! Als missbrauch des gedächtnisses ist es dagegen anzusehen, wenn man
— was früher als allgemeine sitte herrschte — den anfangsunterricht auf gedanken-
loses einpauken von katechismussätzen sowie paradigmen und regeln der lateinischen
sprache gründet, oder wenn man, was noch heute gelegentlich empfohlen wird,
den schüler vocabeln auswendig lernen lässt, die er noch nicht im zusammenhange
kennen gelernt hat. Nein, die aufgabe der häuslichen arbeit kann nur darin bestehen, solche dinge in das gedächtniss einzuprägen, die in der schule bereits
erörtert und vom schüler unter leitung des lehrers entwickelt worden sind. Auf
diese weise werden sich die schüler gewöhnen, das, was sie lesen, auch zu verstehen und darüber nachzudenken, und man braucht wahrlich nicht zu fürchten,
dass bei diesem verfahren die »wissenschaftliche selbstständigkeit« leiden könnte!«

In bezug auf die übrigen punkte fasste sich redner etwas kürzer und betonte
hauptsächlich folgendes:

»Da die aufgabe der elementarbücher keine andere sein kann, als die lectüre
zusammenhängender texte vorzubereiten, so reicht es für diesen zweck aus, wenn
der gebrauch des elementarbuchs auf den dritten theil der gegenwärtig von ihm
eingenommenen zeit beschränkt wird. — Schriftliche übersetzung aus der muttersprache in die betreffende fremde sollte niemals aufgenommen werden, bevor das
lesen zusammenhängender texte 1—1$^1/_2$ jahr geübt worden ist, und während des
ersten jahres nur unter der unmittelbaren leitung des lehrers erfolgen, sodass exercitien (extemporalien) nicht eher geschrieben würden, als im vierten jahr des betr.
sprachunterrichts.«

Rücksichtlich des dritten punktes forderte redner, dass, da schriftliche arbeiten im Deutschen und Englischen dem Französischen, und solche im Latein
dem Griechischen zu gute kommen, in den je an letzter stelle genannten sprachen
schriftliche arbeiten wegzufallen hätten, infolgedessen sich das einüben der griechischen grammatik stark beschränken und das der englischen fast beseitigen liesse.
— Redner warnte hierbei vor den versuchen künstlicher gleichmachung bei aus-
arbeitung von parallelgrammatiken.

»Das lateinische extemporale muss bedeutend eingeschränkt werden, wenn
das Latein in seiner stellung als ein wichtiger unterrichtsgegenstand noch soll ge-
rettet werden; dabei ist dasselbe als mittel anzusehen und nicht als ziel.«

Was schliesslich die übungen im sprechen betrifft, so führte redner aus, dass
diese den abschluss des sprachunterrichts auf der schule bilden sollten und dass
übersetzung wie grammatik und schriftliche arbeiten eigentlich nur die vorbereitung
dazu wären. Gleichzeitig wies indess redner auch hin auf das hinderniss, welches
das auswendiglernen künstlicher grammatischer regeln für das sprechenlernen
bildet. Ausserdem sei es zur zeit völlig unmöglich, eine genügende zahl lehrer
zu beschaffen, die sowohl die sprache des schülers wie die zu lehrende fremde
sprache mündlich voll beherrschten — und beides sei doch unumgänglich
nöthig. —

Soweit der redner. Mit dem schluss von herrn *Drake's* vortrag war auch die
zeit für die letzte reguläre sitzung der section abgelaufen, und man einigte sich
demzufolge dahin, dass behufs meinungsaustausches über den vorliegenden gegenstand am nächsten tage vorm. 9—10 uhr noch eine extrasitzung stattfinden solle.

22 *

Zu beginn dieser letzteren wurde nun die discussion eröffnet von lector *Törnebladh-Stockholm*, welcher bestritt, dass die von *Drake* gegen die bestehende unterrichtsweise erhobenen anklagen wirklich allgemeine berechtigung hätten. Was aber die vorgeschlagenen mittel zur abhülfe der übelstände betreffe, so sei ja wohl gesagt worden, man müsse vom leichteren zum schwereren fortschreiten: allein da erhebe sich nun die frage, was denn das leichtere sei, und unter diesem gesichtspunkte dürften sich die elementarbücher wohl vertheidigen lassen. — Eine verständige vorbereitung habe natürlich ihren werth, aber darum brauche keineswegs alles zum voraus im classenzimmer vom lehrer durchgegangen zu werden. — In der frage der praktischen übungen dürfe man leicht noch etwas weiter gehen als *Drake*, und redner sei der meinung, dass man gerade jetzt auf dem besten wege sei, das praktische mit dem gründlichen zu vereinigen.

Docent *Lundell-Upsala* konnte sich im ganzen genommen mit dem vortragenden durchaus einig erklären — doch würde er die geissel über dem derzeitigen sprachunterricht noch wesentlich empfindlicher geschwungen haben. Was den erfolg desselben angehe, so halte er sich zu der behauptung berechtigt, dass im durchschnitt die studenten nach ihrem maturitätsexamen die fremden sprachen noch nicht ohne schwierigkeit zu lesen wüssten. Mit rücksicht auf so bedauerliche ergebnisse erachtete redner eine radicale reform für geboten, besonders bezüglich der modernen sprachen, doch nicht minder auch für den lateinunterricht. Der gegenwärtige unterricht sei sowohl aus psychologischen wie aus rein praktischen gründen im höchsten grade mangelhaft. Redner stellte hiernach folgende 4 sätze auf:

1) »Nicht die buch- oder schriftsprache mit ihrer veralteten orthographie ist dem unterricht zu grunde zu legen, sondern die gesprochene sprache des wirklichen lebens. Man muss demgemäss mit texten in lautgetreuer umschrift beginnen.«

2) »Uebersetzung in die fremde sprache hat als unnütz und schädlich fortzufallen und ist durch mündliche und schriftliche reproduction zu ersetzen, sowie durch freie production in der fremden sprache unter anschluss an die lectüre. Uebersetzung aus der fremden in die muttersprache wird eingeschränkt und durch ausgedehnte cursorische lectüre ersetzt.«

3) »Der unterricht hat schon von anfang an auszugehen von zusammenhängenden texten, nicht von abgerissenen sätzen.«

4) »Die grammatik muss sich in der weise an die lectüre anschliessen, dass der schüler angeleitet wird, mit hülfe des lehrers aus dem gelesenen nachträglich und inductiv die sprachgesetze herauszulösen. Erst später mag ein systematisches lehrbuch behufs repetition in gebrauch genommen werden.«

Diese forderungen seien eine ungefähre zusammenfassung dessen, was von *Sweet* und *Vietor* verlangt werde, und bereits sei eine höchst lebhafte bewegung nach dieser richtung hin im auslande vorhanden.

Prof. *Cavallin-Lund* schloss sich in der hauptsache ganz herrn *Törnebladh* an. Im übrigen verdiene *Drake* gewiss vollen dank, dass er die wichtigkeit der realienkenntnisse beim studium der alten sprachen nicht unterschätzt habe, doch könne man auch in dieser hinsicht zu weit gehen. Es sei unberechtigt, über schüler den stab zu brechen, weil sie nicht die ganze classische zeit von innen und aussen kennen, wie man ebensowenig von einem schüler, der französische schriftsteller aus der zeit Ludwig's XIV. lese, verlangen dürfe, er solle in allen möglichen dingen aus der culturgeschichte jener zeit beschlagen sein. Doch sei darum keineswegs der schluss zu ziehen, dass der unterricht nur formal sein müsse. Wenn der schüler Latein und Griechisch zu lernen habe, so sei es undenkbar, dass er dies erreiche, ohne dass dabei auch starkes gewicht auf den inhalt gelegt werde. Das elementarbuch sei sehr wichtig, um zu verhindern, dass der schüler die gewohnheit annehme, sich vom inhalt aus durchzurathen und um ihm sicherheit in den formen beizubringen. Solche, die sich auf privatem wege zur reifeprüfung vorbereitet haben[1]), lesen ihre schriftsteller vielfach so, dass sie das elementarbuch lieber ein wenig mehr hätten studiren sollen: sicherheit in den formen mangelt! In den modernen sprachen hält man sich zu lange mit dem elementarbuch auf, in den classischen sprachen nicht lange genug.

Western-Fredriksstad (Norwegen) war der meinung, dass die debatte etwas in eine falsche bahn gekommen sei. Zur discussion des altsprachlichen unterrichts liege eine veranlassung gar nicht vor; denn hätte man all die jahrhunderte lang nicht gelernt, diesen recht zu betreiben, so würde man das wohl kaum je lernen. Jedenfalls sei sicher, dass man die bestehende altsprachliche unterrichtsmethode nicht auf die neueren sprachen anwenden könne. Es sei darum am besten, zu diesen zurückzukehren, und redner schlug darum vor, die von *Lundell* aufgestellten punkte zum gegenstande der erörterung zu machen. Und zwar hob er in dieser hinsicht hervor, dass das elementare in der sprache vor allem und in erster linie der laut sei, und danach der einfache natürliche satz. Die sprache bestehe aus sätzen, nicht aus worten. Aber die sätze müssten so gewählt werden, dass sie für die sprache typisch wären; und schon von anfang an sollten sie zusammenhängen und vernünftigen inhalt haben.

P. Passy-Paris (im auftrage der franz. regierung anwesend) äusserte sich hiernach auf schwedisch, wie folgt: »Ich möchte nur ein wort über herrn *Lundell's* ersten punkt sagen, nämlich dass der sprachunterricht mit texten in phonetischer umschrift zu beginnen hat. Ich habe jetzt 9 jahre lang an der Pariser normalschule unterrichtet, und seit 4 jahren wende ich die methode phonetischer umschrift an: da kann ich denn nun mit aller bestimmtheit erklären, dass diese methode nicht bloss theoretisch, sondern auch praktisch besser ist als die alte. Dies geht schon aus folgendem hervor. Als ich anfing, an der normalschule zu unterrichten, hatte noch kein einziger schüler im — wahlfreien — Englischen ein reifezeugniss erhalten, denn die aussprache desselben galt für zu schwer. Auch so lange, als ich nach der alten methode unterrichtete, erhielt durchschnittlich nur je 1 schüler jährlich ein diplom im Englischen. Aber als die schüler, welche ihren anfangsunterricht nach phonetischer methode erhalten hatten, zur abgangsprüfung gelangten, bekamen das erste mal 7, das zweite mal 8 das diplom. Dies scheint mir in der that den werth der phonetischen methode zu beweisen.«

Bischof *von Schéele-Visby*[2]) schloss sich jener richtung an, die es als eine

---

[1]) Deren zahl ist in Schweden verhältnissmässig sehr gross.   H. Kl.
[2]) In Schweden steht jeder bischof, unterstützt von einem aus den 6 oberlehrern der stiftsschule gebildeten consistorium, an der spitze des gesammten schulwesens (auch des höheren) seines bisthums und bildet auf diese weise eine zwischeninstanz zwischen den einzelnen lehranstalten und dem ministerium. So erklärt sich die anwesenheit und das auftreten des bischofs *von Sch.* in einer sitzung von pädagogischen fachmännern.   H. Kl.

erniedrigung des sprachstudiums ansieht, wenn dasselbe sein ziel anderswo als in
sich selbst haben soll. Und dieser standpunkt sei gleichzeitig praktisch wie psychologisch wohl begründet. Unter die praktischen ergebnisse zähle unter anderm
auch die aus solchem sprachstudium hervorgehende fähigkeit, die eigenen gedanken
angemessen ausdrücken zu können. Dazu gelange man indessen nicht, wenn man
das elementarbuch zu frühzeitig aufgebe. Schliesslich habe die schule doch auch
die aufgabe, den charakter zu bilden: wie könne diese aber erfüllt werden, wenn
man die schüler nicht sicher und bestimmt anweise, richtiges und unrichtiges d. i.
recht und unrecht zu unterscheiden, und sie von der unmöglichkeit überzeuge,
noch ein drittes anzunehmen, welches weder das eine noch das andere sei? —

Da nunmehr die knapp bemessene zeit dieser sectionssitzung zu ende
gegangen war, erklärte der vorsitzende die thätigkeit derselben für geschlossen
und sprach insbesondere den herren, welche durch theilnahme an der discussion
zur klärung der vorliegenden frage beigetragen hatten, den dank der section aus.

Unmittelbar hierauf versammelten sich indessen gegen 50 mitglieder derselben, um die begonnenen erörterungen privatim fortzusetzen. Zum vorsitzenden wählte man herrn docent *Lundell*, zum schriftführer herrn dr. *Örtenblad-
Upsala*; auch wurde beschlossen, man möge aufnahme der verhandlungen auch
dieser versammlung in den allgemeinen bericht zu bewirken suchen. Als gegenstand aber der folgenden debatte wurden die in der section von *Lundell*
formulirten punkte angenommen.

These I.

»Nicht die buch- oder schriftsprache mit ihrer veralteten
orthographie ist dem unterricht zu grunde zu legen, sondern die
gesprochene sprache des wirklichen lebens. Man muss demgemäss
mit texten in lautgetreuer umschrift beginnen.«

Zu diesem punkte ergriff an erster stelle herr *Palmgren-Upsala* das wort.
Dieser wollte zunächst nur einige worte äussern über bedeutung und nutzen der
phonetik für den praktischen schulmann, der sich zum eigenen besten wie zu dem
der schüler mit derselben vertraut zu machen habe. Es sei ja ganz schön, wenn
sich jemand selbst »praktisch« durch unmittelbare nachahmung die betr. aussprache angeeignet habe, und dieselbe danach andern auf die gleiche weise bei-
bringe; auch dürfe gern zugegeben werden, dass man ohne dieses verfahren
überhaupt nicht sonderlich weit kommen könne. Aber es fänden sich verschiedene
laute, die man erst mit hülfe der phonetik sicher und weit rascher als durch
blosse nachahmung hervorzubringen lerne. Dies gelte z. b. schon von der frage
über den unterschied der »weichen« und »harten« consonanten, die man freilich
besser als »tönende« und »tonlose« oder als »sangbare« und »nicht-sangbare« bezeichnen sollte, da der unterschied der beiden lautgruppen schon aus diesen namen
allein hervorgehe. Im Französischen z. b. werde die hauptschwierigkeit in der
einübung des $\check{z}$-lautes, — die sonst so viel und meistens fruchtlose arbeit mache —
binnen wenigen minuten erledigt, wenn man dabei auf die »wissenschaftliche«
weise zu wege gehe, und diese dürfte dann wohl in diesem falle zugleich auch
die »praktische« sein. Sobald der schüler nur erst wisse, dass der *j*-laut sangbar
sei, könne er an dem zittern im kehlkopf controliren, ob er $\check{z}$ oder $\check{s}$ spreche.

Was aber die phonetische umschrift betreffe, so sei es ja klar, dass man

die erlernung der aussprache einer fremden sprache erleichtere, wenn man jedem
laute sein eigenes zeichen gebe, und zwar, soweit möglich, ein solches, welches
an ein entsprechendes zeichen und dessen lautwerth in der muttersprache erinnere.
Solche umschriften würden angewandt für das Englische von *Jespersen* in seiner
»Kortfattet Engelsk Grammatik for Tale- og Skriftsproget« und von *Sweet* in
seinem epochemachenden »Elementarbuch des gesprochenen Englisch«,
für das Französische von *F. Franke* in dessen *»Phrases de tous les jours«* und
von *Passy* in *»Le français parlé«.* — Redner war demnach bereit, dem ersten
punkte beizustimmen.

Western meinte, dass darüber, ob es methodisch richtig sei, mit phonetischen
texten zu beginnen, ein zweifel gar nicht existiren könne. Es sei ein immer mehr
anerkannter pädagogischer satz, dass man vom bekannten zum unbekannten, vom
leichteren zum schwereren zu gehen habe, von den neueren sprachen, die uns zunächst liegen, zu den classischen, als den weiter abgelegenen, und so müsse man
auch innerhalb der neueren sprachen ausgehen von der sprache der gegenwart zu
derjenigen der früheren epochen. »Aber z. b. die englische sprache, die man in
unseren schulen lehrt, ist keineswegs Neuenglisch, sondern vielmehr eine art
Mittelenglisch. Wenn der schüler seine erste bekanntschaft z. b. mit dem worte
nait (»ritter«) macht, muss sich ihm dasselbe in *dieser* form darstellen und
nicht in seiner mittelalterlichen gestalt *knight,* welche jetzt nur noch ein abbild der
aussprache vergangener zeiten ist. Man fürchtet freilich, dass der schüler dadurch
verwirrt werden könne, wenn er das wort in seiner neuen tracht, phonetisch geschrieben sehe; diese befürchtung hat aber nur einen sinn für denjenigen, der
die sprache mit der gewöhnlichen orthographie erlernt hat, nicht für einen schüler,
der erst im begriff steht, Englisch zu lernen; für ihn kann es ja völlig gleichgiltig
sein, in welcher form er das wort zu sehen bekommt. Ein einwand anderer art
besteht darin, dass man sagt, worte, die orthographisch weit von einander ver-
schieden sind, würden in der phonetischen form zusammenfallen. Solche verwech-
selung kann doch aber nur stattfinden, wenn das wort vereinzelt auftritt — was
für den schüler nie vorkommen sollte — nicht wenn es im zusammenhange steht.
— Bischof *von Schéele* hatte, soweit redner ihn recht verstanden, geäussert, man
müsse den charakter durch herstellung bzw. beibehaltung von schwierigkeiten
entwickeln. Das wäre, als ob man, um zu einer schönen aussicht zu gelangen,
nothwendig einen mühsamen und steilen bergpfad hinauf klettern müsse, anstatt
sich der gebahnten, bequemen strasse zu bedienen. Die absicht eines unterrichts-
gegenstandes der schule ist doch aber nur dieser gegenstand selbst und sonst
weiter nichts; will man die schüler die aussprache lehren, so muss man sich
des nächsten weges zu diesem ziele bedienen, und das ist die phonetische methode. Freilich wird es wohl noch eine zeit lang nicht gestattet werden, phonetische texte in die schule einzuführen, und darum muss man suchen, mit dem
mündlichen unterricht auszukommen, indem man nicht mit der orthographie, sondern mit dem laut beginnt, nämlich so, dass man zuerst die einfachen laute
ganz praktisch einübt — mit hülfe der finger, soweit es sich um unterscheidung
der tönenden und der tonlosen handelt [1]) — danach die lautcomplexe und zuletzt

---

[1]) Neuerdings ist bei uns mit recht darauf hingewiesen worden, dass der
unterschied noch stärker hervortritt, wenn man die schüler beim einüben der

ganze sätze. — In derselben weise hat man übrigens auch beim unterricht in der muttersprache vorzugehen.«

Docent *Noreen-Upsala:* Phonetik wird im allgemeinen mit unfreundlichen augen angesehen, und dies nicht völlig ohne grund; es empfiehlt sich deshalb, den ausdruck »phonetische umschrift« in these I lieber noch näher zu bestimmen, sonst könnte leicht ein missverständniss hervorgerufen werden; es handelt sich hier nämlich nicht um wissenschaftlich strenge genauigkeit der lautdarstellung, wie z. b. im dialektalphabet [1]), sondern nur um eine »annähernd lautgetreue umschrift, die eben für den vorliegenden zweck ausreicht,« und darum wünscht redner, dass die fassung von these I in diesem sinne abgeändert werde.

Vorsitzender *Lundell* erklärte, der von ihm gebrauchte ausdruck sei »lautgetreu«, nicht »phonetisch«, könne aber recht wohl im angegebenen sinne näher bestimmt werden.

Lector *Sturzen-Becker-Stockholm* wünschte zu wissen, wie lange phonetische transscription wohl in der schule angewendet werden solle. An lehrbüchern der angegebenen richtung fehle es in Schweden nicht: so finde sich solche umschrift schon seit langem bei *Öman* [2]), und auch redner selbst habe eine arbeit mit phonetischer umschrift herausgegeben. [3]) Wenn er also der sache nach mit den übrigen rednern einig sei, fürchte er doch, dass es, wenn ausschliessliche umschrift zu lange angewandt werde, dann schwierigkeit bieten werde, zu der gewöhnlichen »veralteten« orthographie überzugehn und der schüler hierdurch mit zweierlei schreibweisen belastet werde.

Lundell erklärte, s. e. sei phonetische transscription so lange zu benutzen, als bedarf dazu vorliege, d. h. bis die schüler in der aussprache so ziemlich sicher seien — wahrscheinlich das ganze erste jahr hindurch. [4])

Western gab zu, dass phonetische transscription sich allerdings nicht ganz ohne ungelegenheit anwenden lasse, aber es seien ja wenige dinge in der welt, die man gratis bekomme, und auch die englische aussprache sei nicht ganz umsonst zu haben; bei dem gegenwärtigen unterricht gelange man überhaupt nicht zu einer solchen. Man müsse ein lehrbuch haben, welches systematisch über aussprache und schreibung aufschluss ertheile.

Schliesslich nahm auch noch *Passy* das wort, nachdem er um erlaubniss gebeten, sich der deutschen sprache zu bedienen, indem er folgende, auf persön-

---

tönenden laute veranlasst, mit ihren fingern die ohren zu schliessen: das summen in diesen tritt sehr viel stärker und unzweideutiger hervor, als das zittern des kehlkopfes. H. Kl.

[1]) Das »dialektalphabet« ist von *Lundell* im auftrage der schwedischen dialektvereine für deren bedarf sowie überhaupt für die zwecke der schwedischen dialektologie ausgearbeitet worden und umfasst 100 lautzeichen, von denen ein jedes irgend einen besonderen, in einem oder mehreren schwedischen dialekten vorkommenden laut bezeichnet. P.

Vgl. *Lundell's* aufsatz in *Techmer's* Internat. ztschr. I, s. 308—329. H. Kl.

[2]) *V. E. Öman: Teoretisk-praktisk lärobok i engelska språket, efter Toussaint-Langenscheidska metoden, 1867.*

[3]) *Dr. Vilh. Sturzen-Becker: Engelsk språklära for menige man, 1872.* P.

[4]) Also durch ganz untertertia, wobei aber zu bemerken ist, dass in dieser wie in der folgenden classe der schwedische lehrplan wöchentlich 7 st. für das Englische ansetzt. S. o. H. Kl.

lichen erfahrungen beruhende mittheilung machte: »Was das Englische betrifft, so hat sich mir aus meiner erfahrung die thatsache ergeben, dass schüler ganz ausserordentlich leicht von der phonetischen zur gewöhnlichen orthographie übergehn können, wenn dieselben nämlich zunächst in der ersteren einen gründlichen unterricht genossen haben und infolge dessen sich die worte so fest eingeprägt haben, dass sie dieselben auch unter jeder beliebigen verkleidung leicht wiedererkennen können. Hierfür ist aber 1 jahr nicht genug, wenigstens 1 1/2 jahr ist erforderlich. [1]) »Die übergangszeit, während deren man den text erst phonetisch und danach in gewöhnlicher orthographie liest, mag etwa 1/2 jahr dauern; dann aber sind die schüler völlig fest in der üblichen orthographie, ohne dieselbe also eigentlich je förmlich gelernt zu haben. So unglaublich dies auch erscheinen wird, ist es doch einfach eine mir vorliegende thatsache.« [2])

Hiermit schloss die discussion über These I, welche von der versammlung mit der von *Lundell* vorgeschlagenen abänderung angenommen wurde.

These II.

Uebersetzung in die fremde sprache hat als unnütz und schädlich fortzufallen und ist durch mündliche und schriftliche reproduction zu ersetzen, sowie durch freie production in der fremden sprache unter anschluss an die lectüre. Uebersetzung aus der fremden in die muttersprache wird eingeschränkt und durch ausgedehnte cursorische lectüre ersetzt.

Sturzen-Becker erklärte, dass er einer in gemässheit dieser these ausgeführten einrichtung des sprachunterrichts durchaus sympathisch gegenüberstehe, aber fürchte, dieselbe möchte sich praktisch unausführbar erweisen. Wie sollten denn z. b. die schüler lernen, einen englischen brief schreiben, wenn jede übersetzung aus der muttersprache dabei ausgeschlossen wäre? Und wie sollten die lehrer überhaupt ihre schüler controlliren können, wenn diese nicht übersetzen dürften? Jedenfalls sei die methode noch zu wenig erprobt, und darum schlug redner vor, über diese these eine ausdrückliche beschlussfassung auszusetzen.

Western wies darauf hin, dass es vielmehr gerade ein hauptzweck der these sei, zu schriftlichen abfassungen in der fremden sprache anzuleiten. Gegenwärtig werde verlangt, man solle mit hülfe eines nordischen textes, eines wörterbuchs und einer grammatik in der fremden sprache schreiben können, aber natürlich sei das ergebniss ein schlechtes. Dem wolle man nun gerade vorbeugen, indem man dem schüler nicht irgend einen bestimmten text zur übertragung vorlege, sondern statt dessen ihn anleite, durch nachahmung in der fremden sprache schreiben zu lernen. Redner beginnt bei seinem unterricht im Englischen so, dass er, sobald die schüler erst zwischen haupt- und nebensatz zu unterscheiden gelernt haben, dieselben veranlasst — natürlich nicht unter vermittelung durch die muttersprache —, sätze aus der directen rede in die indirecte umzu-

---

[1]) Die fragliche zeitbestimmung hängt jedenfalls immer zugleich von der wöchentlichen stundenzahl ab.   H. Kl.

[2]) Seit mai 1886 erscheint, mit 1 nummer monatlich: »*Dhi Fonètik Ticcer, èdited bai Paul Passy. 8rue Labordère. Neuilly-sur- Seine*, 1 franc pro jahr.
                                                                                                   P.

setzen u. ä. Er habe selbst als lehrer die besten erfolge mit dieser methode gehabt. Wenn die schüler dann etwas weiter vorgerückt seien, könne man ein leichteres stück vorlesen, zuerst 3—4 mal nach einander, dann seltener, und die schüler dann das gehörte mündlich wiederholen lassen.

Sturzen-Becker erwiderte hierauf, dass er schon vorher des redners und seiner gesinnungsgenossen ansicht und methode gekannt habe, hob aber den umstand als hinderlich hervor, dass man, wenigstens in den schwedischen schulen, über zu wenig zeit für dieses verfahren gebiete. Im übrigen liegen im Englischen auch nicht so grosse schwierigkeiten vor, wie im Deutschen und Französischen, zwei sprachen, bei deren erlernung man an der übersetzung in und aus der muttersprache sicherlich eine gute hülfe habe. Das wort »schädlich« in these II müsse deswegen gestrichen werden.

Noreen war in der hauptsache mit *Lundell* einig, schloss sich aber gleichwohl *Sturzen-Beeker's* meinung an, dass es sich empfehle, von einer beschlussfassung über diese these abzusehen, da dieselbe ohne zweifel ziemlich scharf abgefasst und die praktische erfahrung in diesem falle doch noch ziemlich beschränkt sei.

Palmgren betonte, dass der streit zwischen den verschiedenen richtungen sich vorzugsweise eben um diesen punkt drehe: übersetzung oder nichtübersetzung! Er für seine person stehe auf dem alten standpunkte und schliesse sich *Sturzen-Becker's* auffassung an, sowohl in hinsicht auf das principiell empfehlenswerthe der neuen methode, wie rücksichtlich der schwierigkeit, dieselbe praktisch zuzurichten. Uebrigens besitze wohl die s. g. neue methode recht alte ahnen, wennschon die vorzüge derselben erst in unseren tagen theoretisch nachgewiesen und ihre einführung in die schule beantragt worden seien. Von England und Deutschland ausgegangen, habe dieselbe nun auch im norden ihren einzug gehalten und hervorragend befähigte vertreter gefunden, wie *Jespersen* in Dänemark, *Western* in Norwegen und *Lundell* in Schweden. Der letztere habe sich nämlich durch ein ausgezeichnetes referat über eine ausgezeichnete schrift *(Western's* vortrag »U e b e r d e n u n t e r r i c h t i n d e n n e u e r e n s p r a c h e n«) als einen getreuen anhänger der neuen methode gezeigt. Redner stimmte vollständig allen dort vorgetragenen ansichten zu, mit ausnahme derjenigen punkte, welche die übersetzungsfrage beträfen. »Um seine ansicht, dass übersetzungen ebenso unangemessen wie unnöthig sind, zu stützen, beruft sich *Lundell* in der genannten anzeige auf seine persönlichen erfahrungen beim erlernen des Russischen. Das beispiel ist ganz vortrefflich als beitrag zur beantwortung unserer frage, und ich mache selbst davon gebrauch. Wir haben demselben zufolge auf der einen seite: herrn *Lundell*, ein jahr lang ununterbrochen in Russland ansässig, also unaufhörlich veranlasst, fern von jedem störenden einflusse, an ort und stelle, sowie von competentester seite die sprache zu hören und die verschiedenen situationen zu beobachten, welche oft besser als irgend eine übersetzung die ausdrücke verdeutlichen, von denen sie begleitet sind; sodann genöthigt und gezwungen, gerade die in frage stehende sprache zu gebrauchen, dabei weiterhin unterstützt von dem moralischen muth, der sich dem zuvorkommenden fremden gegenüber regelmässig einstellt, während er ebenso regelmässig vor dem kritisirenden landsmann verschwindet — und auf der anderen seite in unseren schulen die schüler X, Y und Z, jahrelang glücklicherweise noch mit anderen dingen als mit sprachen beschäftigt, in Schweden, ihrem vaterlande, ansässig etc. etc. Es ist überflüssig, die parallele weiter auszuführen. Nun sagt man aber, »das alles ist ja in der that

hinderlich genug, aber man schaffe nur das schlimmste hinderniss, die muttersprache, hinweg, lasse die sprache sich selbst erklären: derselbe ausdruck kommt
einmal ums andere bald in der nämlichen, bald in seiner etwas abweichenden
bedeutung vor, und so gewinnt man allmälich klarheit und einheitliche gesammt-
anschauung über seinen ganzen umfang.« Ja, das kann wohl so kommen; aber
das gegentheil ist auch möglich, und auf der stufe des schulmässigen lernens
dürfte die möglichkeit zur regel werden. Der sicherste weg zur erklärung der
fremden sprache dürfte darum gerade der durch die muttersprache sein; und giebt
man einmal dies zu, bekennt man sich zum übersetzungsprincip, dann möchte wohl
kaum irgend jemand sich mit einer »ungefähren« oder einer wortgetreuen (»inter-
linearen«) übersetzung begnügen; beide arten führen nothwendig zu einer nebel-
haften und verschwommenen erfassung der fremden sprache und verderben überdies die muttersprache.«

Örtenblad schloss sich dem vorredner an und wollte keinesfalls so weit gehn
wie die männer der neuen richtung. Der gerade weg könne bisweilen recht
halsbrechend sein. Mit dem Englischen möge die methode sich noch durchführen
lassen, mit dem schwereren Französisch, fürchtete er, dürfte dies nicht möglich sein.

Lundell giebt, nachdem einmal auf ihn und seine persönlichen erfahrungen
bezug genommen worden sei, die erklärung ab, es sei seine bestimmte überzeugung, dass er in der schule die sprachen unendlich viel rascher und besser
gelernt haben würde, wenn man mit ihm das verfahren eingeschlagen hätte, welches er für das Russische beobachtet habe.

Noreen möchte nur ein paar worte zur ergänzung hinzufügen. Bei der
vergleichung sei nämlich der wichtigste punkt ausser acht gelassen worden: herr
Lundell habe die fragliche sprache lernen wollen, unsere schuljungen aber wollten
alles andere eher, nur nicht dies. Auch fänden sich unter ihnen sowohl besser wie
minder gut begabte, und da der unterricht doch auch den letzteren zu statten
kommen solle, so sei eine minder gute methode schliesslich gerade die beste.

Schulvorsteher *Olsen-Tönsberg* (Norwegen) befürchtete störung der so wich-
tigen einheit des unterrichts am gymnasium, wenn verschiedene methoden angewandt würden für den unterricht in den classischen und in den modernen
sprachen.

Western erwidert hierauf, dies sei eine sache, an der sich nun einmal nichts
ändern lasse: die lehrer der neueren sprachen könnten sich doch nicht nach denjenigen der classischen sprachen richten! —

In übereinstimmung mit dem oben gestellten antrage wird hierauf beschlossen,
sich mit der stattgehabten erörterung zu begnügen und von einer eigentlichen
beschlussfassung über these II abzusehen.

These III.

Der unterricht hat schon von anfang an auszugehen von zusammenhängenden texten, nicht von abgerissenen sätzen.

Es verging einige zeit, bis eine debatte über diese these zustande kommen
wollte, und der vorsitzende nahm dies als ein anzeichen, dass ein meinungsaus-
tausch überflüssig sei und die versammlung den satz als selbstredend ansehe. Dies
war auch *Noreen's* meinung: für ihn habe diese forderung immer den werth eines

axioms gehabt. *Sturzen-Becker* dagegen bat um eine begründung desselben, da er seinerseits nicht gänzlich davon überzeugt sei.

Lundell meint, man müsse sich doch eben mit der s p r a c h e beschäftigen, nicht mit abgerissenen sätzen, aus denen jene erst zusammengesetzt sei.

Prof. *Joh. Storm-Christiania* fand die methode der abgerissenen sätze weder theoretisch richtig noch praktisch nützlich. Die gegenwärtigen elementarbücher ermüdeten die schüler durch ihre jähen übergänge von einem vorstellungskreise zum andern. Doch seien darum nicht unbedingt längere erzählungen nöthig; auch stücke, die nur in einem natürlichen zusammenhang unter einander stünden, sowie leichtere gespräche seien vortrefflich geeignet — besonders solche, welche einen bestimmten gegenstand zum mittelpunkt hätten. E s l ä g e e t w a s t r o s t l o s e s d a r i n, d a s s d i e s c h ü l e r n a c h l a n g j ä h r i g e m u n t e r r i c h t n i c h t s o w e i t k ä m e n, u m a u c h n u r l e i d l i c h s i c h i n d e r f r e m d e n s p r a c h e a u s - d r ü c k e n z u k ö n n e n o d e r d i e s e l b e z u v e r s t e h e n.[1]) Im übrigen wolle indess redner erklären, dass er nicht ebenso weit gehn möchte wie die neue phonetische schule.

Western schloss sich rückhaltslos *Storm's* ansicht über die zweckdienlichkeit von g e s p r ä c h e n an und meinte, das seien doch eben an sich schon »zusammenhängende texte.«

Herr *Hagelin-Stockholm* sprach sich gleichfalls gegen den gebrauch abgerissener sätze aus: »die elementarbücher, welche an der mehrzahl der schwedischen lehranstalten für den deutschen unterricht im gebrauch sind, nehmen der regel nach die beiden ersten jahre, sowie vom dritten das erste semester in anspruch[2]), und während dieser ganzen langen zeit bekommt der schüler mit nichts zu thun als mit abgerissenen sätzen und grammatik. Unter solchen umständen wird der unterricht zu einer mühseligen arbeit, die auf schüler und lehrer unendlich schwerer lastet, als es sein könnte und sollte; es muss nothwendig das interesse, welches eine neue sprache wecken sollte, bei der ewigen »gedankengymnastik« abgestumpft werden. Erwünscht wäre demnach für die elementarstufe des deutschen unterrichts ein elementarbuch, welches gleichzeitig die nöthige unterlage für einübung der deutschen grammatik darböte und daneben verschiedene dem lebendigen leben, dem m o d e r n e n Deutsch entnommene proben der deutschen sprache, in form etwa von anecdoten oder kleinen gesprächen enthielte.

Hiernach gelangte these III zur annahme, und man ging weiter zur behandlung von

These IV.

»D i e g r a m m a t i k m u s s s i c h i n d e r w e i s e a n d i e l e c t ü r e s c h l i e s s e n, d a s s d e r s c h ü l e r a n g e l e i t e t w i r d, m i t h ü l f e d e s l e h r e r s a u s d e m g e l e s e n e n n a c h t r ä g l i c h u n d i n d u c t i v d i e s p r a c h g e s e t z e h e r a u s - z u l ö s e n. E r s t s p ä t e r m a g e i n s y s t e m a t i s c h e s l e h r b u c h b e h u f s r e p e t i t i o n i n g e b r a u c h g e n o m m e n w e r d e n.«

Prof. *Storm* glaubte, dass wohl im allgemeinen einstimmigkeit bestehe bezüglich des bisherigen missbrauchs der grammatik. Für die, welche jetzt ihre

---

[1]) Vollkommen einverstanden!   H. Kl.
[2]) Reichen also von sexta bis mitte quarta.   H. Kl.

schulzeit abgeschlossen hätten, erscheine die grammatik wie ein grosser raum mit gewissen lichtpunkten und dazwischen vielen dunklen zwischengebieten. Praktischer wäre es jedenfalls, erst dem schüler die sprachlichen erscheinungen vorzuführen und danach ihn die sprachlichen gesetze daraus finden zu lassen. Es fänden sich aber andererseits auch in den modernen sprachen viele fälle, die sich überhaupt nicht unter irgend welche regel bringen liessen, sondern welche nur praktisch gelernt werden könnten. Warum heisse es denn z. b. *»ça me fait de la peine«* dagegen *»ça me fait plaisir?«* Jedenfalls sei redner bereit, sich in diesem punkte dem antragsteller anzuschliessen; doch werde immerhin ein kurzes grammatisches lehrbuch noch nöthig sein, welches der lehrer dann nach belieben erweitern könne.

Örtenblad wünschte eine erklärung, wonach in vorliegender these auch eine empfehlung des auswendiglernens fremdsprachlicher texte inbegriffen sein solle. Selbst vom rein grammatischen standpunkte aus gäbe solches auswendiglernen z. b. bezüglich des genus bessere resultate als die regeln.

Jespersen-Kopenhagen. »Dieser punkt steht im engsten zusammenhange mit der auf die übersetzungen bezüglichen these II. Wie jetzt der unterricht betrieben wird, befinden sich die meisten lehrer und demgemäss auch so gut wie alle schüler unter dem einflusse der vorstellung, dass das vorlesen eines fremden textes nur die vorbereitung zur übersetzung bildet. Infolgedessen sind die gedanken des schülers, während er vorliest, vorzugsweise mit dem gedanken beschäftigt: »was bedeutet dies oder jenes auf Dänisch? wie soll ich das übersetzen?« Den fremden ausdrucks-formen widmet er dabei kaum irgendwelche beachtung. Ein ganz tüchtiger schü-ler, der mehrere jahre Französich getrieben hatte und dasselbe nun wieder auf-nehmen wollte, übersetzte mir *ex tempore* ein stück aus einem französischen roman; den schluss desselben gab er wieder mit »und er weinte wie Pietri's sohn weinte.« Ich machte ihm darauf das buch zu und forderte ihn auf, den letzten satz noch einmal auf französisch zu wiederholen. Es war ihm unmöglich! nur auf das Dänische konnte er sich besinnen, und dieses übersetzte er nun langsam und stockend mit: *»et il pleurait comme le fils de Pietri pleurait«.* Im franz. text aber stand: *»et il pleura comme pleurait le fils de Pietri«!* Es ist klar, dass, wo eine so geringe aufmerksamkeit auf die fremde sprache verwendet wird, alle grammatikregeln der welt nicht im stande sind, eine lebendige und werthvolle erfassung, z. b. des unterschieds zwischen den beiden französischen verbalformen für die vergangenheit zu erzielen. Wird dagegen der schüler angehalten, seine aufmerksamkeit nicht sowohl auf die übersetzung in die muttersprache zu richten, sondern auf die fremde ausdrucksweise, und lässt man ihn recht häufig und aus-giebig die fremden sätze und satzverbindungen reproduciren, so werden sich bei ihm eine menge grammatische erscheinungen rein instinctmässig im bewusstsein festsetzen, so dass er beim gebrauch der sprache sich nicht gegen deren gesetze versündigen wird. Und übt man ihn ferner anhaltend darin, s e l b s t aus einem oder mehreren gelesenen stücken auf inductivem wege die regeln für den gebrauch z. b. von *je* und *moi* zu bestimmen, so erhält er dadurch ein grammatisches wissen, welches mehr werth ist als das gewöhnliche, weil es — wie alles selbst-erworbene — fester im gedächtniss sitzt, und weil es später durch eine systema-tische grammatik leicht ergänzt und geordnet werden kann. — Vielleicht auch liesse sich die grammatik auf die art mit der lectüre in nächste verbindung bringen, wie einer der deutschen vertreter der reform des sprachunterrichts *(Klinghardt)* mir brieflich vorgeschlagen hat, nämlich durch ein lehrbuch auf schreibpapier, wo nur die regeln sich gedruckt fänden, die zugehörigen beispiele aber nachträglich vom schüler aus der lectüre eingetragen würden. Doch scheint dieses verfahren aus rein praktischen gründen nicht recht empfehlenswerth. [1]

Palmgren konnte nicht leugnen, dass der vorredner recht habe mit seinem hinweis auf die gefahr, welche das übersetzen darbiete für die erlernung der fremden sprache. Aber das habe man auch erkannt und dem übelstande zu begegnen, ja wohl sogar nutzen aus dem verfahren zu ziehen gesucht. Erst wenn der fremde text übersetzt, und, wo die übersetzung für das verständniss nicht hinreiche, auch erklärt worden sei, lasse man den fremden text vorlesen und concentrire nun alle aufmerksamkeit auf diesen. Der inhalt bereite dann keine schwierigkeit mehr: man wisse, was man lese, und könne sich ausschliesslich der betrachtung der form widmen. Bei geschlossenen büchern müssten die schüler grössere oder kleinere stücke des gelesenen unmittelbar mündlich wiedergeben und gelegentlich dieselben wohl später auch noch auswendig [lernen. — Im übrigen stimmte redner der forderung einer k u r z e n grammatik durchaus bei und bezeichnete in dieser hinsicht als vortrefflich die von *Mathesius* und *Jespersen;* unter den »vollständigen« schien ihm *Plattner's* französische schulgrammatik mustergiltig. —

Nachdem nunmehr auch these IV annahme gefunden hatte, wurde die sitzung geschlossen.

Als nächste praktische folge der vorstehend im auszuge mitgetheilten verhandlungen ist ein verein zu bezeichnen, der sich die umgestaltung des sprachunterrichts zum ziel gesetzt und dieser tage sein programm nebst aufforderung zur theilnahme versandt hat. Dasselbe lautet wie folgt:

Einladung:

Im anschluss an die debatte über die methodik des sprachunterrichts, welche auf der dritten nordischen philologenversammlung zu Stockholm stattfand, erlauben sich die unterzeichneten ihre berufs- bzw. fachgenossen und -genossinnen[2]) zum eintritt in den verein

---

[1]) Ich halte noch immer mit aller entschiedenheit an meinem vorschlage fest. Herr *Jespersen* wandte s. z. ein, dass solche lehrbücher unter den händen der schüler beim eintragen und gebrauch leicht das aussehen von schmierheften bekommen könnten, was aus allgemeinen pädagogischen gründen durchaus zu vermeiden sei. Allein ich würde ein solches lehrbuch den schülern nicht vor secunda in die hand geben, und auf dieser altersstufe wäre wohl eine saubere ausführung beim eintragen der mustersätze aus der lectüre zu erwarten bezw. leicht zu erzielen. Was man aber bei seiner durchführung der neuen methode mit abgerissenen beispielen anfangen soll, die der verfasser der betreffenden grammatik entweder selbst construirt oder aus allen ecken und enden zusammengelesen hat und die jedenfalls dem schüler völlig fremd sind, sehe ich nicht ein. Möglich wäre nur noch eine systematische grammatik ohne alle beispiele, welche vielmehr vom schüler unter anweisung des lehrers in ein besonderes heft einzutragen wären. Das käme aber sachlich völlig auf meinen vorschlag hinaus, nur wäre das verfahren in dieser form wesentlich unbequemer. H. Kl.

[2]) Das töchterschulwesen nimmt im norden, zumal in dem mir vorzugsweise bekannten Schweden neben dem unterrichtswesen für die männliche jugend eine erheblich angesehenere stellung ein als bei uns. Eine reihe von töchterschulen sind den gymnasien parallel eingerichtet und mit dem recht der abiturientenentlassung ausgestattet (im december 1886 hatte z. b. die *Wallinsche* schule in

F. Palmgren, Verhandlungen zur reform des sprachunterrichts etc. 351

Quousque Tandem,
skandinavischer verein für verbesserten sprachunterricht,
aufzufordern.

Ziel des neuen vereins ist, in übereinstimmung mit den forderungen der gegenwärtigen sprachwissenschaft und einer gesunden pädagogik für eine reform des sprachunterrichts auf grund folgender vier thesen zu wirken, deren ersten drei auf der Stockholmer philologenversammlung zum beschluss erhoben wurden:

1) Nicht die schriftsprache, sondern die gesprochene sprache des wirklichen lebens ist dem unterricht zu grunde zu legen. In den sprachen, deren orthographie in höherem grade von der aussprache abweicht, hat man demzufolge mit texten zu beginnen, die in einer, soweit erforderlich, lautgetreuen umschrift abgefasst sind.

2) Der unterricht hat schon von anfang an auszugehen von zusammen-hängenden texten, nicht von abgerissenen sätzen.

3) Insbesondere der unterricht in der grammatik muss sich in der weise an die lectüre anschliessen, dass der schüler angeleitet wird, mit hülfe des lehrers aus dem gelesenen nachträglich die sprachgesetze herauszulösen. Erst später mag ein systematisches lehrbuch in gebrauch genommen werden.

4) Die übersetzung sowohl aus der muttersprache in die fremde, wie aus der fremden in die muttersprache ist einzuschränken und zu ersetzen einerseits durch mündliche und schriftliche reproduction sowie freie production in der fremden sprache unter anschluss an die lectüre, andererseits durch ausgedehntere cursorische lectüre.

Der verein sucht das angestrebte ziel zu erreichen u. a. durch vorträge und debatten, durch druckschriften und mittheilungen, durch herausgabe geeigneter lehr-bücher und durch förderung der herausgabe solcher bzw. ihres gebrauchs.

Der vorstand kann versammlungen des vereins anberaumen, sei es allgemeine, sei es besondere für jedes land.

Zusammengesetzt ist der vorstand aus je einem vertreter der drei skandinavi-schen länder. Diese vertreter werden jährlich von den mitgliedern des betr. landes durch stimmzettel gewählt, welche — unter beifügung des jahresbeitrags von 1 krone — ende februar an den vertreter des voraufgehenden jahres einzusenden sind.

Im januar jeden jahres wird ein rechenschaftsbericht über das vorausgehende jahr veröffentlicht.

Mitglieder haben sich bei den unterzeichneten, welche einstweilen das amt von vertretern versehen, anzumelden.

Für das laufende jahr wird ein beitrag nicht entrichtet.

September 1886.

Otto Jespersen,	*J. A. Lundell,*	*Aug. Western,*
Ole Suhrsgade 18,	*dozent,*	*mag. cand.,*
Kopenhagen.	*Upsala.*	*Fredriksstad.*

Stockholm bereits 69 jungen damen das reifezeugniss ertheilt). Ein theil der künf-tigen neusprachlichen lehrerinnen bildet sich dann entweder sogleich im auslande aus oder betreibt (zuvor) seine studien an den heimischen universitäten. Hiernach ist es begreiflich, dass unsere nordischen fachgenossen, wie aus obigem hervorgeht, gemeinschaftliches zusammenwirken mit den lehrerinnen der töchterschulen als etwas ganz natürliches ansehn, während bei uns die dinge etwas anders liegen.

H. Kl.

457

Nach dem, was ref. von den unterzeichnern des aufrufs in erfahrung gebracht hat, sind dieselben nicht der meinung, dass jeder, der in ihren verein
eintritt, sich damit verpflichtet, die vom verein empfohlene methode auch in der
praxis anzuwenden. Gegen solche anwendung können hindernisse vorliegen, deren
beseitigung nicht in der macht des einzelnen steht. Auch bedeutet der eintritt in
den verein nicht eine bedingungslose zustimmung zu sämmtlichen vier sätzen. Der
verein »Quousque Tandem« — es bedarf für den Deutschen keinen hinweis, dass
der name im anschluss an prof. *Vietor's* pseudonym gewählt ist — will vielmehr
nur ein sammelpunkt sein für alle, welche eine änderung im gegenwärtigen sprachunterricht wünschen, und welche überzeugt sind, dass diese änderung, wenn sie
zum bessern ansschlagen soll, wenigstens theilweise in der durch die vier sätze be-
zeichneten richtung zu erfolgen hat.

Wer noch genaueren aufschluss über den von den gründern des neuen
vereins [1]) eingenommenen standpunkt zu erhalten wünscht, wird denselben finden
in *Franke-Jespersen, Praktisk Tilegnelse af fremmede Sprog, Kopenh. 1884*, und
August Western, Om undervisningen i nyere sprog, Kopenh. 1885 (beides in *C.
Larsen's* verlag erschienen).

UPSALA, september 1886.   F r e d r. P a l m g r e n.

8

OTTO JESPERSEN

How to Teach a Foreign Language

Source: London: Swan Sonnenschein, 1904, translation by Sophia Yhlen-Olsen Bertelsen of *Sprogundervisning*, 1901, Copenhagen: Schuboteske Forlag.

HOW TO TEACH A FOREIGN LANGUAGE

HOW TO TEACH
A FOREIGN LANGUAGE

By

OTTO JESPERSEN, Ph.D.

Professor of English in the University of Copenhagen

TRANSLATED FROM THE DANISH ORIGINAL BY
SOPHIA YHLEN-OLSEN BERTELSEN M.A

"This was sometime a paradox, but now the time gives it proofe."—*Hamlet.*

LONDON
SWAN SONNENSCHEIN & CO. LTD
NEW YORK : THE MACMILLAN CO.
1904

PREFACE

WHEN, in accordance with a wish expressed by English and American friends, I determined to have my *Sprog-undervisning* translated into English, I found it difficult to decide what to retain and what to leave out of the original. So much of what I had written appeared to me to apply more or less exclusively to Danish schools and Danish methods, and I had too little personal experience of the practice of English teachers or of English school-books to be quite sure of the advisability in each case of including or excluding this or that remark. I have, however, made my choice to the best of my ability, and if some parts of my criticism are not altogether applicable to English methods, I hope I may be excused on the plea that what is now the really important thing is less the destruction of bad old methods than a positive indication of the new ways to be followed if we are to have thoroughly efficient teaching in modern languages.

OTTO JESPERSEN.

GENTOFTE,
   Near COPENHAGEN.

5

I

ABOUT twenty years ago, when I began to be interested
in a reformation of the teaching of modern languages,
there were not, as there are now, numerous books and
articles on the subject, but merely scattered hints,
especially in the works of Sweet and Storm. It was not
long, however, before the movement found itself well under
headway, especially in Germany. In Scandinavia it
began at the appearance of the adaptation which I had
made of Felix Franke's capital little pamphlet, "Die
praktische spracherlernung auf grund der psychologie und
der physiologie der sprache." At just about the same
time, Western in Norway and Lundell in Sweden came
forward with similar ideas, and at the Philological Congress
in Stockholm in 1886 we three struck a blow for reform.
We founded a society, of course, and we gave it the name
Quousque tandem (which for the benefit of those not acquainted with Latin may be rendered "Cannot we soon put an end
to this?"), that Ciceronian flourish with which Viëtor had
shortly before heralded his powerful little pamphlet, "Der
sprachunterricht muss umkehren." Our Scandinavian
society published some small pamphlets, and for a time
even a little quarterly paper. But the movement soon
reached that second and more important stage when the

1   B

teachers began to put the reform into practice and when
the editors of school-books began to give it more and more
consideration, until at present it may be said that the
reformed method is well on the way to permanent favour,
at least as far as younger teachers have anything to say in
the matter.

What is the method, then, that I allude to? Well, if
the question means, what is it called, I find myself in some
embarrassment, for the method resembles other pet children in this respect, that it has many names. Though none
of these are quite adequate, yet if I mention them all, I can
perhaps give a little preliminary notion of what the matter
is all about. The method is by some called the " new " or
" newer " ; in England often " die neuere richtung"; by
others the " reform-method," again the " natural," the
" rational," the " correct," or " sensible " (why not praise
one's wares as all dealers do in their advertisements ?) ; the
" direct " comes a little nearer, the " phonetical " indicates
something of its character, but not nearly enough, likewise
the " phonetical transcription method," for phonetics and
phonetical transcription is not all ; the " imitative " again
emphasizes another point ; the " analytical " (as contrasted
with the constructive) could perhaps also be applied to
other methods ; the " concrete " calls attention to something
essential, but so does the German " anschauungsmethode "
too ; " the conversation-method " reminds us perhaps too
much of Berlitz schools ; words with " anti," like the " anti-
classical," " antigrammatical," or " antitranslation " method,
are clumsy and stupidly negative—so there is nothing left
for us but to give up the attempt to find a name, and

recognize that this difficulty is due to the fact that it is not one thing, but many things that we have to reform, and that is of course the reason why the reformers themselves fall into so many sub-parties : the one lays all the stress on one point, the other on another point. However, there is certainly enough to do for any one who wants to get better results out of the teaching of foreign languages than have hitherto been the rule.

It also speaks much in favour of the reform that it is impossible to name the " new " method after some founder, just as in olden days we had Lancaster's, Hamilton's, Jacotot's methods ; later, Robertson's, Ollendorff's, Ahn's, Toussaint-Langenscheidt's, Plötz's, Listov's methods, and as we of later years have Berlitz's and Gouin's methods for the teaching of foreign languages. If in old Norse mythology, the god Heimdall had nine mothers, our reform-method has at least seven wise fathers. In this respect it differs essentially from all the methods just mentioned : each one of them is named after a single man, and he in return is as a rule only remembered as the originator of his method. Our method, on the other hand, owes its origin to men who, for other reasons, may claim a place among the most eminent linguistic scholars of the last decades (Sweet, Storm, Sievers, Sayce, Lundell, and others), and the ideas which they have conceived have been adopted and applied to life with many practical innovations and changes by a large number of educators and schoolmasters (I may mention almost at random Klinghardt, Walter, Kühn, Dörr, Quiehl, Rossmann, Wendt, Widgery, Western, Brekke); on the boundary between both groups stand

especially Viëtor and Paul Passy. That shows that
it is not with theoretical sophistries that we have to do ; it
is not the whim of one man, but the sum of all the best
linguistical and pedagogical ideas of our times, which,
coming from many different sources, have found each other,
and have made a beautiful alliance for the purpose of over-
turning the old routine. Modern languages, which were
formerly treated like Cinderella in our schools and universities, begin to feel of age, and want to have a word
to say, because they cannot put up with various arrangements which may have been more or less satisfactory for the
classical languages, but do not suit modern languages at all.
These want to be treated as *living*, and the method of
teaching them must be as elastic and adaptable as life is
restless and variable.

What is the *object* in the teaching of modern languages ?
Well, why have we our native tongue ? Certainly in order
to get the most out of a life lived in a community of our
fellow-countrymen, in order to exchange thoughts, feelings
and wishes with them, both by receiving something of their
psychical contents and by communicating to them something of what dwells in us. Language is not an end in itself,
just as little as railway tracks ; it is a way of connection
between souls, a means of communication. And it is not
even the only one ; expression of countenance, gesture, etc.,
yes, even a forcible box on the ear can tell me what is
taking place in the mind of one of my fellow-creatures. But
language is the most complete, the richest, the best means
of communication ; it bridges the psychical chasm between
individuals in manifold cases when they otherwise would

wander about isolated and cut off from all intelligent sympathy.

The purpose in learning foreign languages, then, must be in order to get a way of communication with places which our native tongue cannot reach, for there too may be persons with whom I, for some reason or other, desire to exchange thoughts, or at least from whom I wish to receive thoughts. And herein really lies already the answer to the question : which languages shall we give the preference ? Compare the advantage of being able to talk with the inhabitants of the Fiji Islands in their own language with the advantage of being conversant with French or German. If all that we desire or all that we can ever hope to attain in any one language is to receive thoughts, to acquaint ourselves with the works of foreign authors, while we ourselves neither expect nor wish to be able to impart our own thoughts in it, it is always a question if it is not better to use translations than to learn the language itself, especially in the case of the dead languages. A translation is, to be sure, no perfect substitute for the original, but on the other hand one has to know the foreign language pretty well in order to get more out of the original than out of the translation. Then how does the balance stand between the debit-side—the work of learning the language—and the credit-side—the extra profit thus to be got from the authors' works ? It is of course a question which must be decided separately for every individual case, and there are many circumstances which may have to be considered ; but most people will not lose anything if they read Tolstoi or Omar Khayyám in English.

The objection may be raised that there are also other reasons for learning foreign languages. A student of comparative philology, for instance, studies languages for their own sake, without caring if they can serve him as a means of learning anything that he did not know before, or that he could learn much more conveniently in some other way; he may often be very much interested in languages which have no literature at all, or which are spoken by peoples with whom he never comes into contact. But this study, which may be compared to the study of other means of communication for their own sake, locomotive-construction, railway signal-service, etc.—only that it is probably much more interesting—is clearly a special study, which has nothing to do with the reasons why people generally learn languages. Although it undoubtedly is an advantage for every educated person to know something about the life of language, yet I think it will suffice for me merely to touch upon the theoretical study of languages here and there in the following pages, so much the more as it is never with this end in view that any language is placed on the school programme.

Neither were Latin and Greek introduced into our schools for the sake of training the pupils in logic, no matter how much it may occasionally be insisted upon that exactly this is their real value. But it is not necessary to waste many words on this matter, especially since all competent classical scholars—also those who insist upon a privileged position for the classical languages in our schools—have long ago given up as unscholarly the idea that the Latin (or Greek) language should be more logical in construction than, for instance, French or English. And there is no doubt much truth in what Robert Browning says: " Learning Greek teaches Greek, and nothing else; certainly not common sense, if that have failed to precede the teaching !"[1]

But on the other hand it must not be overlooked that everything which is learned with a sensible end in view, and according to a sensible method, tends in itself more or less directly to develop valuable faculties, and that especially the teaching of languages, in addition to the actual results which it gives through the contents of what one reads in foreign languages, is an excellent means of training such important faculties as—

> the faculty of observing (of observing correctly, of observing independently),
>
> the faculty of classifying under different points of view that which has been observed,
>
> the faculty of deducing general laws from the material collected by observation,
>
> the faculty of drawing conclusions and applying them to other cases than the ones hitherto met with,

—all, of course, faculties that are nearly related—also

> the ability to read in general, to read intelligently, and with reflection.

In the construction of our method of teaching, especially if it is to be used in schools, we must also take these things into consideration. Any instruction in languages which merely consisted in a parrot-like repetition of the words of the teacher or the book, if indeed such a method is con-

---

[1] Preface to his translation of the *Agamemnon* of Æschylus.

ceivable, would not be in place in our schools, and besides, no one, so far as I know, has ever tried to introduce such a pure parrot-method there.

The teacher must make the pupils feel interested in the subject; they must have a vivid conception of the reward that their work will bring them, so that it will seem worth while for them to exert themselves. They must feel that their instruction in languages gives them a key, and that there are plenty of treasures that it will open for them; they must see that the literature to which they have gained access contains numerous works which also have messages for them; and they must, to so great an extent as possible in the course of the instruction in a certain language, also have got an interest in the land and people concerned, so that they themselves will make an effort to extend their knowledge about these things. There is thus laid a good foundation for their whole life—and the saying "non scholæ sed vitæ" ought not to be interpreted, as too many (especially parents) do : learn not for the school, but in order to pass a good examination, so that you may prosper in life, and by virtue of your examination get a good position. The school ought to equip its youth in the very best manner for life, and the teacher ought not out of consideration for examination requirements to neglect or hinder anything which otherwise is good. A word about examinations later; here I simply want to warn the teacher against troubling the examination until the examination troubles him. Many of the things which I have to recommend in the following pages, I have time and again heard teachers recognize as really sensible, but they are only afraid of them

on account of the examination for which they have to prepare their pupils. The answer to that is, teach in the right
way, then there will be life and love in it all, and when the
examination comes your pupils will know more than if your
teaching from the very beginning had been fettered by
examination requirements. The pupils really learn most
when they continually have a feeling that it is all something
useful and valuable, and that it is not too far elevated above
that actual life which they either know or are beginning to
get some notion of.

We learn languages, then (our native tongue as well as
others), so as to be enabled to get sensible first-hand communications about the thoughts of others, and so as to have
for ourselves too (if possible) a means of making others
partakers of our own thoughts; and if we consider what
kind of communications we may be more likely to get
through a foreign language than through our own, the
highest purpose in the teaching of languages may perhaps be said to be the access to the best thoughts and
institutions of a foreign nation, its literature, culture—in
short, the spirit of the nation in the widest sense of the
word. But at the same time we must remember that we
cannot reach the goal with one bound, and that there are
many other things on the way which are also worth taking
in. We do not learn our native tongue merely so as to be
able to read Shakespeare and Browning, and neither do we
learn it for the sake of giving orders to the shoemaker or
making out the washerwoman's bill. So likewise in the case
of foreign languages, we ought not exclusively to soar above
the earth, nor on the other hand exclusively to grovel on

the ground ; between those two spheres there are large
fields in manifold shades where it might be of great value
for us to stand in direct communication with other
nations.

II

WE may already from what has been said draw some conclusions as to the method which we ought to use. We ought to learn a language through sensible communications ; there must be (and this as far as possible from the very first day) a certain connection in the thoughts communicated in the new language. Disconnected words are but stones for bread; one cannot say anything sensible with mere lists of words. Indeed not even disconnected sentences ought to be used, at all events, not in such a manner and to such an extent as in most books according to the old method. For there is generally just as little connexion between them as there would be in a newspaper if the same line were read all the way across from column to column. I shall take a few specimens at random from a French reader that is much used : " My aunt is my mother's friend. My dear friend, you are speaking too rapidly. That is a good book. We are too old. This gentleman is quite sad. The boy has drowned many dogs." When people say that instruction in languages ought to be a kind of mental gymnastics, I do not know if one of the things they have in mind is such sudden and violent leaps from one range of ideas to another.

In another French schoolbook we find : " Nous sommes à Paris, vous êtes à Londres. Louise et Amélie, où êtes-vous ? Nous avons trouvé la lettre sur la table. Avez-vous pris le livre ? Avons-nous été à Berlin ? Amélie, vous êtes triste. Louis, avez-vous vu Philippe ? Sommes-nous à Londres ?"

The speakers seem to have a strange sense of locality. First, they say that they themselves are in Paris, but the one (the ones ?) that they are speaking with are in London (conversation by telephone ?) ; then they cannot remember if they themselves have been in Berlin ; and at last they ask if they themselves are in London. Unfortunately, they get no answer, for the next sentence is, " Pierre, vous avez pris la canne."

Or take some of the books which are supposed to help Danes learn English. They are no better. In one (which appeared in 1889) we find : " The joiner has made this chair. What a fine sunshine ! For whom do you make this bed ? Which of you will have this box ? I should like to have it. Of whom have you got this cake ? I am very fond of cakes. I have borrowed a great deal of books from a public library."

From a " practical " primer in English, which appeared in its second edition in 1893, I take the following speci- mens : " Are the king's horses very old ? No ; but the duke's carriage is old. Is it older than your friend's ? . . . Has the nobleman told you the news ? No, sir ; but the lady has told me the news about the business and the wedding. Why do you not give the negro a house ? No, sir ; but I can tell you that the German has given each of the negroes a pretty little house. Has the lady a knife? Yes, the lady has two knives. Why do you not give the ladies the German's keys to the church? The noblemen have the German's keys."

I could give you almost any number of that kind of specimens. The ones I have chosen are not even of the very worst type, since there is (some sort of) meaning in each sentence by itself. But what shall we say when, in a German reader, to the question *Wo seid ihr?* we find the answer, *Wir sind nicht hier*! The author of that book also seems to have had a very vivid imagination when it came to the use of pluperfects. "Your book had not been large. Had you been sensible? Your horse had been old." We ask ourselves in surprise, when did this wonderful horse then cease to be old? But that kind of material information is not given in the book; it stops at the sphinx-like remark: *Dein Pferd war alt gewesen.* Could it really have been that kind of schoolbooks that the Danish writer, Sören Kierkegaard, alluded to when he wrote that language had been given to man, not in order to conceal his thoughts, as Talleyrand asserted, but in order to conceal the fact that he had no thoughts?

Now it must immediately be admitted that there may be a big difference in the schoolbooks made, even according to this single-sentence system. It never seems to have occurred to the authors of some of them that there might be a limit to the amount of rubbish that can be offered children under the pretext of teaching them grammar. Others again try to give sentences which are both sensible and in accordance with a child's natural range of ideas.

479

With respect to the latter principle, there has been steady progress from the times when the sentences either were moral rules of conduct and philosophical profundities, or selections about Greek heroes, etc. But even in the best modern books the exercises are often strangely disjointed (cf., for instance, this exercise from one of the better books : " My brother had not many lessons yesterday. Where had you been ? The weather had been fine for a long time. This boy had only been in our house three or four weeks. Has your uncle had many tulips this year ? How long had you had this frock ? "), and even if they are not so glaringly nonsensical as some others, yet their very disconnectedness makes them bad enough.

It is easy enough, however, to find something to make fun of in all such books. Let us then rather ask the reason why this system has so long been dominant. Its defenders will, of course, refer to the difficulties in all connected reading exercises ; even the simplest stories contain so many grammatical forms, and so many words, that the beginner would be overwhelmed and confused by having them all thrown at him at once. There must be gradual progress in difficulty, that is, the material for instruction must be arranged in stages from very easy to more and more difficult things, and this is supposed to be attainable only by means of disconnected sentences. The principle is sound, but it is unsound to put it into practice in such a manner that other pedagogical principles which are just as sound are neglected. Should pedagogy not also demand some sense in what one treats the children to ? But, as we have seen, it is not always so easy to find the sense.

And should it not also be of some significance to attract the interest of the pupils ? Nothing seems hard to a willing mind. That which is associated with pleasant recollections has a firmer place in the memory than dry stuff. But exercises where it alternates between the Frenchman who has taken the Englishman's hat and the Englishman who has taken the Frenchman's cane, or where either Marie sees Louise's dog or Peter sees Henry's horse—they cannot be anything but boring, even if they give the pupils ever so gradual practice in the use of the genitive. Grown persons can, of course, put up with a little boredom, if they think they can attain anything by it ; but in their heart of hearts they find such things killing, and so they are ; yes, even killing for the linguistic sense. Children can, of course, put up with a good deal, too, when they have a teacher who can win their respect and affection ; they also put up with many things only for the sake of getting good marks, or when they are stimulated by other equally unsound means. But still, it is better to avoid boring them.

I suppose it is also of pedagogical importance for the teaching to be correct. But here we have just one of those points where we see what evil results may come of the system of disconnected sentences : it is so extremely easy for them to become stilted ; indeed, even incorrect. Some examples may be found in the exercise already cited on p. 12, where the sentence, " For whom do you make this bed ? " is not good English, at any rate, and where " a great deal of books " is a bad blunder for "a great many books." It is really easier to write a long connected piece in a foreign language about something that one is interested in than to construct merely eight disconnected sentences for the illustration of a couple of grammatical rules, and without using other words than those the pupils already have had. As impossible, even if not positively incorrect, I consider such sentences as the following, to which any one can find many parallels :—" Tie. Do not tie. Fetch. Do not fetch. . . . Give. Do not give." . . . Judged as thoughts they are unfinished or half-finished ideas. Judged as language, they are also very problematical. Such questions, as " Do I take ? " require the necessary information as to what and when. Such fragments of sentences are never heard in real life.

Finally, sentences of this kind give the pupil quite an erroneous notion of what language is on the whole, and of the relation between different languages. He is too apt to get the impression that language means a collection of words which are isolated and independent, and that there must be a corresponding word in his native tongue for each new foreign word that he learns. These words are then shoved about without any real purpose according to certain given rules, somewhat after the manner of a puzzle that was popular some years ago. The mistake thus made is by Sweet called the arithmetical fallacy, because languages are taken as collections of units where the order of the addends and the factors is immaterial. Everything that is idiomatic in the languages is quite set aside, at all events for the time being, without consideration for the fact that the most indispensable expressions often are those irrational groups which cannot be constructed merely of words and grammatical rules, expressions like "What's the matter? I couldn't help laughing. Serve you right. Ça va sans dire. Ça y est. Voilà qui est drôle. Wie spät haben Sie? Wer ist jetzt an der Reihe? Sie sind dran. Was ist denn los?" Where the Englishman circumstantially says "ring the bell," the Frenchman has the short "sonnez," etc., etc. When the pupil does not get a good deal of that kind of thing as soon as possible, but for years continues translating word-groups of the arithmetical kind until he is well drilled in all the rules of the grammar, the result is that when he is left to his own resources he takes each word of the English phrase that happens to occur to him and translates it literally into the language which he is trying to speak.[1] That is how we come to hear such ridiculous things as "Ich konnte nicht helfen zu lachen."

It is grammar that plays the chief rôle. A characteristic teacher's report is: "In the course of the school-year we have gone through accidence as far as the third class of verbs." The raison d'être of each sentence lies merely in its value for the grammatical exercises, so that by reading schoolbooks one often gets the impression that Frenchmen must be strictly systematical beings, who one day speak merely in futures, another day in passé définis, and who say the most disconnected things only for the sake of being able to use all the persons in the tense which for the time

---

[1] A funny instance of the arithmetical fallacy is the following sign in Copenhagen:

Stövle—og skomager.
Boot—and shoemaker.
Botte—et cordonnier.

C

being happens to be the subject for conversation, while they carefully postpone the use of the subjunctive until next year.

Now, as misfortune will have it, although the whole system is planned for drilling in grammar, this end is by no means attained by these too systematical exercises. The pupils get the scent of what is to be used in a certain exercise, and they use it mechanically there, but they do not learn how to transfer it to other connexions, so if they suddenly have to use a future in an exercise on the pluper-fect the future form is apt to bear a suspicious resemblance to the pluperfect form; when the pupils are being drilled in the endings of the fourth declension, and a word belong-ing to the third declension happens to have crept in, it is very difficult to get it correctly declined without any reminiscence of fourth-class endings, etc. I once read a pedagogical article by a German schoolmaster, I think it was, who had discovered that the reason why there were so many poor Latin exercises written was that the pupils often had to apply several rules of syntax in one and the same sentence; if the sentences were only so made that each one of them contained but one grammatical phenomenon, it would soon be seen how clever the pupils could be. Yes, how pleasant it would be if life too could be so arranged as to have the difficulties come one at a time.

As previously remarked, there is too little attention paid to what is idiomatical, and sentences constructed by non-natives are apt to be of the kind that never would occur to a native, even if it may be difficult enough to find positive " mistakes " in them. Many of the French and German sentences in our schoolbooks must surely have the same air of unreality for a native as not a few of those found in English primers published abroad have for an Englishman.

Very closely connected with the idiomatical elements of a language are its characteristics of style, and in this respect too our schoolbooks are clumsy enough, for words which belong merely to elevated or specially poetical style are bundled together with every-day words in the very beginning of the first primer without any caution to the pupil against using them. A foreigner who wants to learn English has first of all use for words like " grief, sorrow," but he had better postpone acquaintance with " woe," otherwise he is as likely as not to make himself ridiculous by saying " it was a great woe to me." " Unwilling " is more necessary than " loth," " wash " than " lave," " lonely " or " forsaken " than " forlorn," etc. But on one of the very first pages of Listov's English Reader which is written for beginners, we find " I bid him go, which is altogether old-fashioned, stiff and bookish (for : I told him to go, I asked him to go, or I ordered . . .), and in the same book " foe " is preferred to the ordinary, indispensable " enemy." And in several English primers the unnatural " commence " is used all the way through instead of the natural " begin "; likewise the rare " purchase " for the everyday " buy "—the only reason which I can think of is that the ordinary, indispensable words follow irregular declensions and inflexions.

The beginner has only use for the most everyday words; he ought to have nothing to do with the vocabulary of poetry or even of more elevated prose; like everything superfluous,

it is detrimental, because it burdens the memory and
hinders perfect familiarity with that which is most necessary.
It will, moreover, be impossible for him to get a proper conception of the linguistic effectiveness of poetry and elevated
prose, when he is so far advanced as to read the good
writers, because from his very first lesson in the language he
has learned the literary expressions side by side with the
phrases of normal prose and everyday conversation.   But
even among words not belonging to the language of literature, many may without scruple be postponed in order to
make room for the most necessary words, which must be
learned in such a manner that one always may have them
on hand without the slightest hesitation.   In Miss Goldschmidt's picture-method (which is now used a good deal
outside of its native land, Denmark, and also in large
part deserves the popularity and praise which it has
won), I find, for instance, not less than 58 words for
that 'many more or less intimate articles of women's
clothing ; and when I in the same book under the heading
" cuisine " find 46 words, among others, " bouilloire
tamis, passoire, pelle à main, puisoire, lavette, canelle
évier, coquetier, écumoire, entonnoir, pilon, râtelier, râpe,
billot, manne," I cannot help feeling thankful that no one
ever tormented me with learning them ; it seems to me I
have got along pretty well in Paris and elsewhere in French
conversations, just as I have read many French books,
without knowing all these technical words.   But, on the
other hand, I have a strong notion that I should not
have got along so well in conversation, and should not
have been able to read French so well, if my vocabulary

had been limited to the one in Miss Goldschmidt's pictures.

The usual treatment of grammar, too, involves the learning of a number of words that one has no use for. There are few words which even the stupidest pupils in French and English have so pat as "louse," and the reason is that the plural of both " pou " and " louse " happens to be something out of the ordinary. For as soon as a word is declined differently from the usual paradigms, it has to be learned for the sake of so-called completeness. Thus we had to learn in school the rigmarole : " amussis, ravis, sitis, tussis, vis " and usually also " febris, pelvis, puppis, restis, turris, securis," where " vis vim " (perhaps also " sitis sitim ") would have sufficed; the others (with meanings like ruler, hoarseness, rope), I am sure, never occurred in what we read of Latin literature, and as far as the last words are concerned, why it would not have made any difference anyway if we had let the accusative end in " —em," if we had to use the word in a catch exercise. And then there was the " long rigmarole " which it was our pride to be able to run through without winking: " amnis, axis," etc., and which doubtless has cost us all some hours of drudgery before we could quite make it stick. Of the words in it, "scrobis, sentis, torris, vectis," at least, were entirely superfluous for us—aside from the fact that if by some wonderful chance we should come across one of the words in the course of our reading, we were sure enough to remember that the word stood in the long rigmarole, but why it stood there or what the word meant, that was apt to be quite forgotten. Well, it did not make much difference in so far as the chances were a thousand to one that for understanding the passage in question it was absolutely of no consequence if we had remembered that the word was masculine. (It may be of some comfort to add that some of them may also be feminine : the old Romans were not always as big pedants as Latin teachers would like to make them out to be.) Sweet writes : " In the German grammar I began with the word *Hornung*, ' February,' was given as an exception to the rule that nouns in *-ung* are feminine, and for many years no German word was more familiar to me, except perhaps *petschaft*, ' seal,' whose acquaintance I made at the same time and in the same way. But to the present day I cannot remember having met with either of them in any modern German book, still less of ever having heard them in conversation, *Hornung* being now entirely obsolete except in some German dialects. At last, when I began Middle High Grammar, I met with it for the first time in my life in a poem of Walther von der Vogelweide, but by this time I had forgotten all about it." [1]

In most English grammars for foreigners, the word *caiman* plays such an important part that the children never can forget it, and this is just because it is not *caimen* in the plural ; likewise it is carefully inculcated on the pupils that *die* meaning "a stamp used for coining money " has the plural *dies*, but it is scarcely probable that one in a thousand will ever have any use for the word in this sense ; cf. Storm's remark on *travail* quoted below.

Much of that kind of thing has fortunately been removed from the schoolbooks of later years, but there is no doubt still some weeding to be done.

[1] Sweet, *Practical Study of Languages*, p. 110.

III

ON the basis of the above negative criticism, we may perhaps formulate the following positive requirements for those reading selections which are to be the foundation for instruction in languages, namely that as far as possible they must

(1) be connected, with a sensible meaning,
(2) be interesting, lively, varied,
(3) contain the most necessary material of the language first, especially the material of every-day language,
(4) be correct French (German, etc.),
(5) pass gradually from that which is easy to that which is more difficult,
(6) yet without too much consideration for what is merely grammatically easy or difficult.

This order does not indicate the relative importance or value of the requirements, which might be difficult to determine. If there should be any disagreement between them, I suppose it is generally best to try to find some practical compromise. We must now pass on to examine some of these requirements more closely.

The use of *connected* texts in the elementary teaching of

languages has already previously been tried, but it seems as if in the effort to avoid the Scylla of disconnected sentences it has been impossible to escape the Charybdis of such texts as Chateaubriand's *Atala,* Dickens' *Christmas Carol* (Méthode Toussaint-Langenscheidt), the New Testament, or Cæsar's *Gallic War,* etc.   How often after such experiments, when the pupil was overwhelmed and did not learn anything because he was to learn everything at once, has not the teacher returned in despair to the disconnected sentences.

But between the two extremes there is no doubt room for the golden mean of beginning with quite short connected pieces, and then gradually, as each lesson may be lengthened, passing over to longer texts—of course this does not necessarily mean that a whole piece must always be taken for each lesson ; the breaks in the lessons do not need to correspond to the breaks in the text-book.

Anecdotes meet the requirements in so far as they are short connected pieces, and therefore they play such an important part in many readers.   But yet they are not quite the thing, especially when they are used in too great numbers.   A pointed anecdote can only be really funny once ; if it is to be repeated many times, it soon becomes stale and indeed more tiresome than most other things. And just the very quality which makes it amusing makes it less valuable for teaching purposes ; that is, an anecdote must by its very nature contain as few words as possible ; but it is better for beginners to get a little broader colouring, so that the most necessary words and phrases may recur frequently.   If many anecdotes follow one upon the other, it is not easy to avoid frequent jumps between totally different spheres of thought and accordingly between totally different worlds of words ; this increases the difficulty, and the result is apt to be that words and expressions once learned are soon forgotten. Anecdotes depending upon puns cannot be appreciated at all without full familiarity with the words resembling each other, and that can only in a minority of cases be assumed for our pupils. The best way to use anecdotes in teaching languages is to let them serve as spice in or in connection with other pieces, especially descriptive pieces, so that the words used in the anecdotes may there appear in their natural surroundings. This can best be done in short stories about animals ; in my own books for beginners in English, I have taken several such pieces from purely scientific works by Sir John Lubbock, Romanes, Tylor, etc. I mention these as examples of a kind of texts which seem to me to be especially attractive (but which are neither so easy to get hold of nor to concoct), because they give entertaining and sensible information about things which are often neglected in the natural science instruction itself, and at the same time they give an opportunity of learning a good deal of useful language-material without being too difficult. The pieces which are merely descriptive of nature, and which Sweet lays so much stress upon, have the advantage that they in a still greater degree allow of the employment of the most indispensable material of language, and that a number of the sentences may be made self-explanatory (*v.* below). There are, however, but relatively few subjects that can be dealt with in this way—the

most elementary natural phenomena—and when they are
not written in such a masterly manner as in Sweet's
Elementarbuch des gesprochenen Englisch, there are apt to
be so many well-known truths told in these pieces that
the interest flags.

In deciding on what will be of interest as a selection for
reading, differences in age must of course to a great extent
be taken into consideration. But it is an experience which
I myself have had, and in which many teachers bear me
out, that beginners in a foreign language may very well be
interested in certain reading matter even if they are
beyond the age when corresponding things would interest
them in their native language. So one must not be afraid
of childish texts ; but by this I do not mean to recommend
a certain kind of juvenile literature which flourishes in all
countries, and which aunts, especially the unmarried ones,
often think that children appreciate, and so they themselves
also proceed to produce it in large quantities, that is, milk-
and-water stories and verses about the reward of good
children and the frightful punishment of the naughty ones ;
both young and old find such "literature" nauseating, and
it were best to avoid it in text-books in foreign languages.
But there is another class of literature, that collected by
folklorists, which is orally transmitted from generation to
generation, and which shows its vigour by being continually amusing and by continually shooting new shoots.
Much of it can successfully be used in teaching
languages ; and that which amuses a French child of
five or six years may often amuse an English child
of ten or eleven or even more, because in the foreign

language it gets the charm that always is connected with the unknown.

Much of this material—and of other material, which, without belonging to popular tradition, is related to it—is in verse-form, which has the great advantage for our purpose, that rhythm and rhyme naturally rivet the words and expressions fast to each other, so that the memory gets hold of them like an unbreakable chain. It is only with great difficulty and with much repetition that prose sentences can be inculcated in a certain given form ; but to learn verse is like play—it learns itself. If therefore the poetry of art, with its more or less unnatural language, is unsuitable for the beginner, the little witty natural verses of the genuine children's literature are, on the other hand, excellent. But of course not even these are always pure pearls, and there are many of them to be rejected as containing impertinences, nonsense-words, fragments of antiquated language, or words which beginners have no use for ; it seems to me, for instance, that Viëtor and Dörr should not have transferred the nursery rhymes wholesale (even the old forms with —*th* in the third person, and much more) into their otherwise excellent English reader.

With respect to the requirement that the reading must be *easy*—or rather that there must be gradual progress from easy to difficult—it must be recognized that difficulty may depend upon several different things.

In the first place, the subject-matter may be too difficult; it ought never to be beyond the horizon of the pupils. As previously remarked, in the very beginning, one may even take something simpler than what would otherwise be suit-

able for persons of that age.   But later, on the other hand,
the subject-matter ought not to be too light; it is well, as
soon as possible, to use matter which really has a permanent value of its own.   A large part of the reading will no
doubt always be taken from lighter literature, and most of
it will not cause any real difficulty as far as the comprehension of the subject-matter is concerned.   But in addition
to that, there ought surely to be read to a far greater extent
than has hitherto been the case in modern language instruction, matter which cannot be understood without some
serious thinking, articles on natural science and on human
relations in the widest sense of the word, political speeches,
etc.   Many teachers seem to be afraid to read anything
else with their pupils than the most insignificant novel-
literature whose contents furnish starvation food.   A little
friend of mine seven years old once said to his mother :
" I like that best which I can scarcely understand."   He
thereby expressed the same thought as Dante when he said
that man is not happy unless he strains every nerve, or
Stuart Mill in his remark : " A pupil who is never required
to do what he cannot do never does what he can do."
All instruction must spur the pupil on with problems that
are not too easy ; in the first stage of instruction in
languages, there are problems enough in the purely
linguistic difficulties ; later on the contents of the reading,
too, ought to require some independent powers of assimilation.   Sometimes it may even be best to chose selections
where the language is very easy, but the matter rather
weighty—especially in teaching according to the reform-
method, where subject-matter is necessarily assigned a more

important part than hitherto, and where even an easy text can in various ways be advantageously employed as a means of training in purely linguistic skill.

Even linguistic easiness or difficulty may depend upon different things. Difficulties in pronunciation ought not to be piled up, a caution applying especially to selections for the very first beginners. Some teachers try to begin with words which may be almost or wholly pronounced with sounds occurring in the native language of the pupils. Aside from the fact that in most cases it only leads to disappointment to exaggerate the resemblance between the foreign and native sounds, this principle may easily lead to slovenliness at a stage when it might involve the most dangerous consequences. The pupil ought from the very first lesson to have the clearest sensation of being on foreign ground, and he ought to realize that the foreign sounds cannot be learned without work. But the difficult sounds ought not to occur too many in succession or in too difficult combinations. It is perhaps best to begin with words of one syllable, but this need not be strictly carried through. I do not, however, attach so much importance to mere difficulties in pronunciation that I would advise an otherwise suitable opening selection in a French reader for beginners to be discarded because it contained such difficult words as *manger* and *chien*. It cannot be long, anyway, before the pupils must make acquaintance with, and, what is more, master all the sounds in the language they are about to learn. By difficulties in pronunciation here I mean the real ones, and not such apparent difficulties as are due to freaks of orthography; it is equally troublesome for a German to pronounce English *pear* and *pair* ; such difficulties as are found in English *scarce, fatigue, victuals,* French *eut, pupille, pitié, balbutier*, etc., may be overcome by a panacea which I shall come to later, namely, phonetical transcription.

Furthermore linguistic difficulty may be due to the use of too many new words, and in this respect the best principle at all stages is : as few new words as possible. Every one who has read such pages as often occur in Zola or Daudet, where technical expressions are abundantly piled up, will have had the experience that even with the most careful reading or study it did not take long before all the new words were just as unfamiliar as before the selection was read. Likewise, when one sets to work to learn systematic vocabularies like Plötz's *Vocabulaire Systématique,* it requires enormous exertion and a long time to learn them, and it takes an amazingly short time to unlearn them again. But if, in the course of one's reading, the new words turn up occasionally at relatively large intervals, then the mind is able to absorb the one before the next appears ; the intervening passages, which contain only familiar things, manure the soil, as it were, for the new things that are to be sown in it. Ten or twelve new words are more easily and more thoroughly learned when they are scattered over five pages than when they are crowded into ten lines, and then besides there is the benefit to be derived from the recurrence of a number of usual words, to say nothing of sentence-constructions, etc., so that he who has read those five pages has had more opportunity to familiarize himself with the idiosyncrasies of the foreign language than he would have had in ten lines ; the apparent waste of time in reading the longer piece has really been profitable, for the capital which had already been acquired in the language has in that time borne interest and compound interest.

Now since it is also better, as we have said, to learn five absolutely necessary words than twenty-five of less importance, it is of course the duty of the editors of text-books in large part to revise the selections which they reprint, so that that which is of linguistic value for the pupils may be cultivated at the expense of everything that is unusual or odd. Texts whose subject-matter is good, but whose language makes them impossible for our purpose, may often be made pedagogically practicable by means of curtailing, paraphrasing, and adaptation in various ways ; many popular fairy-tales in the collections of folklorists may be used if one only will take the trouble to translate them from the dialect in which they are written. Such a splendid little story as Mrs. Ewing's *Jackanapes*, which is frequently read as it stands in German and Swedish schools, is, according to my judgment, too full of literary expressions and unnecessary words to be easily comprehended by our little pupils. In the passage which I have selected for my own primer, I have therefore in several places made considerable omissions, and the style has throughout been made more colloquial and direct, by means of corrections like these for instance: having *ceased to entertain* (given up) any hopes of his own recovery. | Tony tumbled off *during the first revolution* (before he had gone round once). | And what bright eyes *peeped out of his dark forelock as it was blown by the wind !* (he had !) | told him that he must *be on his very best behaviour* (behave properly) during the visit. If it had been *feasible* (possible) to leave off calling him Jacka-napes and to get used to his *baptismal* (real Christian) name of Theodore before the day after to-morrow *it would have been satisfactory* (she would have done it) | said J., shaking his yellow *mop* (hair), and leaning back in his *one of the two Chippendale* armchair*s in which they sat* (the italicized words left out) | *took their early promenade* (went out for their walk) earlier than usual | His golden hair flew out, *an aureole from which his cheeks shone red and distended with trumpeting* (left out). It is very probable that on comparing the original with the revised text, it will be found that some of the colouring has been lost; I merely maintain that the pupils gain thereby. The more it is insisted upon (as according to the reform-method) that the selections are not only to be read but also to be mastered, so that their language becomes the mental property of the pupil, the more necessary is such revision. It is clear that as the pupil progresses, the texts may become more and more literary, and for various reasons the advisability of such curtailing and adaptation becomes more questionable.

As a sample of such revision, I shall reprint a part of an anecdote, (A) as it ought not to be given in a book for be-ginners (but as it stands in a certain English reader for foreigners) and (B) as it stands in Sweet's excellent edition :—

> (*A*) His table, however, is constantly set out with a dozen covers, and served by suitable attendants. Who, then, are his privileged guests? No less than a dozen of favourite dogs, who daily par-

take of my lord's dinner, seated very gravely in armchairs, each with a napkin round his neck, and a servant behind to attend to his wants. These honourable quadrupeds, as if grateful for such delicate attentions, comport themselves during the repast with a decency which would do more than honour to a party of gentlemen; but if by any chance one of them should, without due consideration, obey his natural instinct, and transgress any of the rules of good manners, his punishment is at hand.

(*B*) Every day he used to have dinner laid for twelve guests besides himself; but no one was ever invited to the house. Who were the twelve covers laid for then, do you think? For twelve dogs. Each dog had a velvet chair to sit up in, and a napkin round his neck, and a footman behind his chair to wait on him. The older dogs always behaved in the most gentlemanly manner, but it sometimes happened that one of the younger dogs forgot his manners, and snatched a chop or a piece of pudding off the plate of the dog that was sitting next to him.

Finally the difficulties may be grammatical. These are the difficulties that teachers have been most afraid of according to the old methods, so that they have even preferred to give up almost all sense and connection in the subject-matter rather than make a break in the systematical progress in grammar. Such a form as *pu* was not allowed to occur before the pupils had learned the whole

D

conjugation of *pouvoir pouvant pu je peux*, etc.; these forms must be learned connectedly, it was said. But the irony of it all is that this "connectedly" means that they are learned out of all connection—and therefore to little profit. When the pupil is required to "understand" the forms which occur in his reader, it will be found on closer examination that this means merely that, for instance, *il a* is understood by the one who knows that it is 3 pers. sing. pres. of *avoir*, or who at least knows the formula *j'ai, tu as*, etc.; that *yeux* is "understood" by the one who has learned that it is an irregular plural belonging to the singular *œil*, etc.; in short, to "understand" means here to know where the form in question belongs in the grammatical system; and the forms must be given in exactly the same order in which they are arranged in the grammar, the present before the past tense, etc. But what has the beginner got to do with all this system? The idea is not carried out consistently either, for when all the exercises on accidence have been gone through, it is generally the rule to pass over to connected (unrevised) texts, where such a form as *puisse* may occur, but the only thing that the pupils get to know about it is that it is subjunctive, for it may easily take a year or two before they learn why the subjunctive is used. Why is syntax less important than accidence? To be quite consistent, it ought no more to be permissible for a syntactical phenomenon than for a form in accidence to occur before the corresponding grammatical section has been learned. But since it seems to be inevitable that we must be inconsistent on some point or other, it is no use beating about the bush; in other words, we must not be afraid of using irregular forms in the very first selection.

Grammatical irregularities, viewed from a pedagogical point of view, fall into two entirely different classes, which are too apt to be treated as if they were co-ordinate. In the first place, all languages contain a number of irregularities which play a most insignificant part both in life and in literature, because they occur so seldom. When the users of the language produce them at long intervals, it is generally with the utmost caution, because they merely have a hazy conception of what the proper form of the expressions ought to be. But they are taken up in the grammars, and as soon as one grammarian has caught sight of one of them, it is carefully copied in all succeeding grammars for the sake of completeness. Foreign grammarians are even more inclined than the natives to pay attention to everything of that kind because they have no instinctive feeling of what is rare and what is common. In some English grammars which are used on the Continent, there may still be found *I catched, I digged, I shined, I writ,* as the preterite forms of *I catch, I dig, I shine, I write*; in one, I find given as two different verbs *I weet, wit* or *wot,* past tense *wot,* and *I wis,* past tense *I wist.* What a big mistake it is, to include such musty and impracticable forms, we can best judge from our own language—but in those French and German grammars which we ourselves write there are things which are just as bad as the above offences in English. When I went to school, I learned the following rule about the plural of *travail,* "*Travail* has *travails* in the plural when it means a report from a minister to the king or from a subordinate official to the minister ; likewise when it means a machine to hold unruly horses, while they are being shoed." This rule is thus criticized by Storm : " Now I must say I have read many hundreds of French books in my day, but so far as I remember, I have never come across *travails* in modern literature ! In the sense of report, it occurs in Mme. de Sévigné. An educated Frenchman, when asked if the word was used with that meaning, answered me that he thought it was no longer used. So one would expect that the word had long ago ceased to have any show in modern grammars, but it seems to be continually creeping in again."

However, it is easy enough to take a position with respect to this first kind of irregularities ; they ought to be removed from the instruction as radically as possible ; they ought to be weeded out root and all to a far greater extent than has yet been done in most text-books, even if it must be admitted that something has been done in this direction of late years. It is quite another matter when we come to the other kind of irregularities, which are found in the very commonest words, in words like German *ist war, kann konnte, geht ging, ich mein, mann männer.* Those irregularities the pupil must learn, and learn thoroughly—there is no doubt about that. The only question is, at what stage ? before or after the regular inflections ? Most teachers will answer, after. That a systematic grammar first gives what is normal, that which can be expressed in general, comprehensive rules, and then afterwards mentions the exceptions, the isolated phenomena, that of course is all right. But it does not necessarily follow that the pupils ought to familiarize themselves with the forms in the same order. What is won thereby? Perhaps some advantage for the theoretical knowledge about the language. But the loss incurred by this method of procedure is undoubtedly far greater. For it will be found to be absolutely impossible to arrange texts which are the least bit suitable without using irregularly inflected words, so indispensable are they. The dread of being unsystematic by taking up exceptions immediately is one of the causes of the prevalence of the disheartening series of detached sentences without any sensible meaning. It is only by freeing ourselves from this principle which requires rules first and exceptions later that we shall be able to get good texts for the teaching of beginners. Furthermore, by beginning with the regular forms, we perhaps run the risk that the pupils will analogically apply the rule even to the exceptional words, whereas the irregular forms generally deviate so much that they preclude the possibility of such mistakes. Those who have learned that the plural in English is formed by adding *s*, may perhaps construct such improper forms as *mans*, *childs*, but the plural forms *men* and *children* are not apt to tempt the pupils to inflect other words after the same pattern. But the moral of this is not that we are to turn the customary method of procedure upside down, and systematically learn the exceptions first. Here, too, nature must be our guide; just as persons talking within a child's hearing never stop to consider if the words they are using are regular or not, so we ought not to be too painfully careful in selecting or arranging the first reading-exercises

in a foreign language; we ought to choose what is otherwise good and take the forms as they come, wasting no
words at this stage to explain their place in the system.
In other words, the deviating forms must be learned as if
they were merely matters of vocabulary. If in one of the
first pieces there stands *Il y avait une fois un roi et une reine,*
it is enough for the time being if the pupil is told that *il y
avait*=there was; the forms for "there is" and "there has
been" he can learn another time when he has use for them,
and then the teacher can refer back to this early piece and
remind the pupil about the related form which he learned
before. For beginners in French, *peux*—"can" is just as
difficult (or easy) as *peu*—"little," and *faire*—"make, do,"
as *fer*—"iron," and it makes no difference if the one is
regular and the other irregular. Indeed, an irregular
plural like *geese* is even easier for Danes than the regular
bees (on account of the z-sound); likewise, it is easier for
an Englishman to learn the German irregular forms ot
comparison *besser best* than regular forms like *süsser süssest.*
Later when the time has come for a more systematic study
of the grammar, it will be rather an advantage that a
number of the "exceptions" already have occurred at so
early a stage that they are not at all felt to be strange and
unusual.[1]

On the other hand, the beginner ought to be spared such
grammatical difficulties as are due to complicated sentence-
structure. All sentences ought from the very beginning to
be constructed as evenly, simply and clearly as possible;

---

[1] It will be noticed that in the whole of this argument I agree with
Sweet.

co-ordinate independent clauses ought to be, if not the only, at least the predominating type of sentence. Not even, for instance, in the second year of Latin instruction, although there are just as many hours devoted to Latin in a year as generally fall to the share of modern languages in the course of two or three years, is it justifiable to let the pupils read the long passages of indirect discourse in Cæsar; they ought not to occur until the pupils are so far advanced that they could easily understand the same matter when directly presented. This is also a point to be kept in mind for any one who undertakes to revise the selections for reading according to the suggestions given above.

IV

So much for the reading selections—now for the way in which they ought to be used in the classroom. I have a very vivid recollection of how most of the language lessons were conducted when I went to school, and I have a suspicion that this method of procedure has not yet quite died out, even if in many places it has more or less felt the influence of the law of change. First the "old lesson" is gone through, and that must take as little time as possible, therefore the pupil is required to be able to translate it fluently without reading it aloud first. Then we come to the "new lesson." A boy stands up and reads a little piece out of the reader—stuttering; the words are separated from each other by pauses and various unaesthetic hm— and er– sounds, and sometimes by the teacher's corrections, or "now hurry," "what a terrible pronunciation!" "how do you pronounce g before e? well, you know that just as well as I do, you blockhead," etc. All that the boy thinks about, whenever he gets an opportunity, is, what in the world can be the meaning of that word I am coming to. Then he translates, interrupted by the teacher's corrections, or "look out," "where is the verb," "but what case is it," etc. Then there are, perhaps, some grammatical questions;

he is to give the principal parts of a verb or two, explain
the use of a subjunctive, etc. ; the questions are not asked
in the foreign language and are not to be answered in that
tongue.   The next boy is called upon to recite in the same
way, and so on until the lesson has been gone through ; if
there is time enough, perhaps we go through it once more,
but that must be in a hurry, so we do not stop to read it first
this time.   The last five or six minutes are devoted to looking through the lesson for next time ; the teacher translates
it while the pupils follow it in their books, and perhaps exert
themselves to write down the meaning of some difficult
word in the margin of the reader or in a note-book.

The most prominent feature of the teaching is haste ;
there is much to be done, especially as examination draws
on.   It seems to be an established custom that the examination marks are determined by the quality of the translation,
and it is in order to get practice in translating that the
reading selections are gone through as many times as
possible.   There is not much time for reading aloud; why,
when ·one has only learned the main principles of pronunciation, one can generally infer the pronunciation of
any word from the spelling, especially in German, but also
in French.   I suppose it is more or less in this confidence
that the· teachers let a piece be translated three or four
times for every time it is read aloud in the original.

How much of the foreign language does the pupil hear
in the course of such a lesson ?   The teacher says a word
now and then—for instance, when a pupil translates incorrectly ; but then the attention is not directed to the
pronunciatiou ; besides, it is generally only one word that

he says, and that word occurs most likely in a sentence in the pupils' own language. Now, it is a matter of fact that even one who pronounces very well cannot get the proper French swing of a French word when it occurs in company with words of another language. The basis of articulation is different in the two languages, and it is not easy to shift from the one to the other in a moment. So it is but little that the pupil hears from his teacher. From his classmates he hears a little more, no doubt; but theirs is not exactly exemplary pronunciation, and besides, it does not interest him to pay attention to it. If he only can manage to keep the place in the book where the others are for the moment, he can very well think about other things while the others are reciting; he can, for instance, review the difficult words in the next piece, if he does not prefer to dream about his stamp collection or his bicycle. Finally, on rare occasions, he is permitted to read a couple of lines aloud in class, but it is considered merely as a sort of introduction to the main business in hand, translation. He never gets an opportunity to say anything himself in the foreign language outside of what stands in the book, and he very seldom hears others say anything that he is not following in print.

So it is no wonder that such instruction scarcely cultivates at all the pupil's ability to understand a foreign language as it is rapidly and naturally spoken by a native. If he should hear the simplest every-day sentence in a foreign language, correctly and naturally pronounced, and he should be asked merely to repeat it, he would in nine cases out of ten betray the strangest perplexity, although he would have had no trouble whatever with a far more difficult piece which he happened to meet with in print.

But that is not all ; this method has other disadvantages. The foreign words gallop past the pupil's eye ; his main object is to be able to recognize them in a vague sort of way so that they may give him the clue to the translation. Oftentimes one word thus vaguely remembered even gives him the clue to the translation of a whole sentence which he knows by heart because there was something special about it. What he gets hold of is the translation, and the whole translation often comes to his mind when he has only looked at the beginning of the sentence in the original—sometimes, however, only on condition that it stands in the same place on the page (at the top to the left, etc.), where he is used to seeing it. There is not the same inducement to remember the forms of the foreign expressions exactly. If you take a clever boy who has been taught according to the usual method and, after he has translated a little piece of his lesson, close his book and ask him to give the original of the last sentence which he has translated, it will in many cases be impossible for him to do it. I reported an example of this at the congress in Stockholm in 1886 ; a clever pupil was translating a piece of Mérimée's *Colomba* at sight, and was doing it very well, when I made the experiment. He apparently remembered the sentence well enough in the translation, but it was slowly and with difficulty that he ventured the French : *Et il pleurait comme le fils de Pietri pleurait.* But in the book there stood : *Et il pleura comme pleurait le fils de Pietri.* It is clear that it is impossible for a pupil to get a correct conception of the radical difference between passé défini and imparfait, or of the effect of the order of words, when he pays so little attention to the French forms that he meets with. One can never get any real appreciation of the idiosyncrasies of a foreign language as long as the translation is the main object.

Let us consider for a moment the workings of a boy's mind when it is his turn to recite and he has to translate such a sentence as, for instance : *cet homme, dont elle ne voyait jamais les enfants. Cet,* this, *homme,* man, *dont,* whose — now he discovers that it will not be English if he continues to take one word after the other in the French order, so he looks ahead, tries every word hurriedly ; finally he finds *les enfants,* the children ; no, I forgot, we must not have the article there in English, so merely children ; back to *elle,* she ; now he sees that *ne jamais* must be taken first . never ; *voyait,* saw. So instead of taking the French words in the natural order, 1, 2, 3, 4, 5, 6, 7, 8, 9, he has to skip backwards and forwards in order to get them in the order 1, 2, 3, (8), 9, 4, 5, 7, 6. In an English text-book for German schools the following sentence [1] is given for translation with numbers indicating the order in which the words are to be taken in English : [1]Würden [2]Sie [3]nicht [6]viel [7]zeit [5]gehabt [4]haben [8]wenn [9]Sie [11]nicht [15]jenen [16]brief [13]zu [14]schreiben [12]gehabt [10]hätten. In other cases, it is the pupils themselves who by means of numbers and letters ("paving letters") smooth the difficulty of translation. Anyone who is accustomed to translate German at sight knows

---

[1] Quoted in *Englische Studien* VIII., 175.

how when he has translated the subject of a dependent clause he silently runs through what follows, often several lines, in order to find the verb, which according to English usage must not be too far separated from its subject, and how in hastily trying each single word his attention is drawn to a number of subordinate thoughts while the main thought stands and waits, as it were. This mental process is made even more complicated by the fact that only in a minority of cases does every word in a sentence (like the simple sentence given above) in any way correspond to an English word ; as a rule the translator also has to think about such questions as, does *sich* here mean him, or her, or himself, or herself, or itself, or oneself ; does *si* mean so, or as, or if ; is *il fait* to be taken as he does, he makes, he has (something done), or it does, or it is, or in still another way, etc., etc. This mental process, which is much more complicated than would generally be supposed, is far beyond the ability of the children. Therefore they often remain contented with the text-book's, the teacher's or the parent's translation, which is learned partly or entirely by heart ; otherwise the translation is apt to swarm with the well-known offences against the mother-tongue, word-formations, phrases, expressions, order of words, etc., which are not English. Since the teacher of course cannot put up with this murdering of the King's English, a large part of every lesson in the foreign language has to be spent in the troublesome task of rooting out these barbarisms.

That is why it is so often said that instruction in foreign languages always is, or ought to be, at the same time instruction in one's native language, or, as the matter is sometimes more pointedly put, that the main object in learning other languages is to get a correct knowledge of one's own.   Of course there is much truth in this last state-ment, if it is the theoretical understanding of languages that we are thinking about; for it is only natural that we cannot appreciate the richness of our mother-tongue, or have any opinion about its structural advantages or disadvantages, or even give a correct description of its structure or understand its historical development, when we have no other lang-uages to compare it with.[1]   Yet all this ought not to close our eyes to the fact that as soon as it is a question of the practical command of the mother-tongue, the assertion is utterly false.   In this respect instruction in foreign languages does not help us, and it is not the people who are most accomplished in other lang-uages who are the best stylists in their own.   On the contrary !   Only compare the language used by the same pupil in his English essays and in his translations from the Latin ; in the latter, you will find a number of offences against good English usage which could not possibly have occurred in the former.   So the errors are in reality not due to a deficient command of the mother-tongue, but solely and alone to the restraining and confusing influence brought to bear upon the pupil's thoughts by the foreign forms of expression ; the strange language lures him in upon linguistic paths where he would never set his foot

---

[1] Wer fremde sprachen nicht kennt, weiss nichts von seiner eignen.
                                                            J. GRIMM.

otherwise, and which only lead him into a mire. It is the school with its translation-method that has sown the dragon's teeth, and it must now reap the consequences. Instruction in foreign languages, according to the prevailing method, is so far from being a help to the pupils in their treatment of English, that, on the contrary, in spite of all the energy which is put in on combating Germanisms, Latinisms, etc., in the translations, it often makes them uncertain and vacillating in their feeling for what is good English.[1]

The acquirement of a certain intuition for good usage in a *foreign* language had best be left out of the discussion here ; a really thorough knowledge of French or German habits of expression is, of course, not to be obtained as long as we are unable to see anything in these languages without straightway turning all our attention to something quite different, namely, the English rendering.[2] We get no further than to a " nodding acquaintance " with the component parts of the foreign language, so that we know them pretty well by sight and can repeat their names, but we do not become quite intimate with them, we do not

[1] Ch. Darwin had the strongest disbelief in the common idea that a classical scholar must write good English ; indeed he thought that the contrary was the case. (*Life and Letters*, i. 155.) See also the strong expressions to the same effect in H. Spencer's *Facts ana Comments*, 1902, p. 70.

[2] Der geist des schülers muss eine ganz wunderliche turnerei treiben, immer hin- und herhüpfen zwischen den beiden sprachen, in keiner recht zur ruhe kommen. Das mag eine treffliche übung sein zu mancherlei anderen verstandesleistungen (? O. J.), nur gerade für die spracherlernung ist der gewinn zweifelhaft.—G. v. d. Gabelentz, *Die Sprachwissenschaft*, 1891, 73.

live together with them, they do not become flesh of our
flesh and blood of our blood. If something difficult is to
be learned, the very first essential is to be much occupied
with it; therefore the first condition for good instruction in
foreign languages would seem to be to give the pupil as
much as possible to do with and in the foreign language;
he must be steeped in it, not only get a sprinkling of it now
and then; he must be ducked down in it and get to feel as
if he were in his own element, so that he may at last
disport himself in it as an able swimmer. But what is most
characteristic for the prevailing methods is that the transla-
lation with its accessories swallows up so much time, that
there is none left for this free disporting in the foreign
element.

Then why does translation play such an important part?
We must first find an answer to this question before we
proceed to ask if it can and ought to be thrust into the
background, and by what means. Now the ability to
translate may either be considered the end of instruction in
foreign languages, or translation may be regarded merely as
a means of instruction (one of several means or perhaps the
only means).

Now is it right to say that the *purpose* of instruction in a
foreign language is that the pupils may learn to *translate*
fluently and exactly (from and into the language)? The
answer must be an emphatic No. The popular opinion
among those who have not thought the matter over, or who
have not given sufficiently careful attention to their own
mental processes, is that a foreign language can be understood only by transposing it into one's mother-tongue; but

this is not so. Those who read foreign authors in the
original with real advantage do not actually first translate
each word, still less each sentence or each period, into
English before they proceed further. Those who are
listening to a French lecture or seeing a play in Paris have
no time to translate to themselves, but it is not necessary
for them to do it either. And finally, it goes without
saying that the Englishman who really speaks French and
German well does not first construct his sentences in
English and then translate them in the same way as a schoolboy translates his exercises. No; in all these mental
processes, English occupies a place in the background and
is just as superfluous as for instance German is for me
while I am reading or talking French. How often are we
not asked the meaning of some foreign word or expression
which we know very well and would neither pay any special
attention to in a book nor hesitate to use in conversation
but yet we cannot give any English equivalent for it without resorting to some vague uncertain circumlocution; then
suddenly, after a good deal of speculation, we hit upon the
correct English expression. Or the questioner may suggest
first one and then another translation of something French
or Latin; we do not feel satisfied, but cannot mention anything better; then he attempts a new suggestion and
instantly it flashes upon us that this is the best. In all these
cases, then, we have clearly and distinctly understood the
foreign expressions without being able to translate them (or
before we could translate them). Of course the German
word *fall* is only one and the same word for me whether it
be used in such a manner as to be best rendered by English

E

case, instance, or by *fall, decline, descent,* or in still another
way (*unglücksfall,* accident ; *schlimmsten falles,* if the worst
come to the worst ; *auf keinen fall,* on no account, etc.).
When I come across the word *gegen,* I do not consciously
stop to decide if it " means " *towards, to, about* or *against* ;
nor in the case of *bleiben,* if it is to be rendered by *remain,
stay, stop, continue, keep,* or *survive. Il a dû se taire; elle a le
cœur serré; il traite le sujet avec la compétence qu'on lui
connaît* —should I really have to hunt for the proper
translation every time such an idiom occurs ?   Should I
stop at every perspicuous German compound until I
had found the cumbersome English circumlocution that is
often needed to render it ?   No ; in all of these cases, I
directly and spontaneously connect the idea with the
language in which it is expressed without going any roundabout way through the words of my native language.   Any
one who introduces a foreign word into his English either
because there is no exact equivalent in English or, at least,
because he cannot recall it for the moment, also thereby
shows that people really can, and very frequently do, learn
words in other languages without getting at their meaning
through their mother-tongue.

"Il trouva la pauvre fille dans un état à faire pitié." "On
a voulu trouver dans ses œuvres un pessimisme de parti
pris." "Pour lui, il y allait de la gloire de cette maison
qu'il servait depuis sa jeunesse." How many a man will
understand without difficulty such sentences as these and a
hundred others, and yet hesitate at once when asked to
translate them !   We must on the whole make a distinction
between the ability to feel at home in a language and skill

in translating from or into it; even if these two accomplishments may be found in one and the same person, yet they are not seldom to be seen separated. If I may be allowed to talk about myself, I may say that my ability to translate quickly and well is so decidedly inferior to my ability to understand and to express my thoughts in those languages which I have studied, that I should scarcely like to have my linguistic attainments judged by my skill in translation.

The lately deceased art-critic, P. G. Hamerton, the author of that interesting book *French and English*, says about himself: "As my wife was a Parisian with a strong taste for the classical literature of her own country, I became her pupil in French and she became mine in English. We made it a rule in our private conversation never to allow a fault in either language to pass uncorrected, and we read aloud to each other a great deal. . . . In the use of languages I have one faculty which seems to be rather uncommon: that of keeping them entirely separated. When speaking or writing French I am, for the time being, like one totally ignorant of English, as English words do not occur to me, and I never translate anything, not even weights and measures, or money, or the thermometer, from one language to the other, but think in each, independently."

When Hamerton here says that this ability is unusual, he no doubt means that it is unusual in so high a degree as he had it. Perhaps it is not all people who get so far that *dix-huit degrés*, for instance, awakens in them just as precise a conception as the corresponding degrees of heat in terms of Fahrenheit; and yet, no doubt, by habit, this too will become quite natural for those who care very much to have the temperature expressed in degrees.   It is just like the foreigner in France who, after a very short time, involuntarily begins to calculate with French money, so that he does not have to transpose *deux francs cinquante* into English shillings and pence before he can judge as to whether the price of an article is high or low.

Though I may admit, however, that this ability to feel at home in a strange language is not altogether common in so high a degree, yet I think it may be said that the same ability only in a less degree is not unusual.   I mean that it is rather the exception than the rule for people who read foreign books to any extent at all to have to translate to themselves in order to understand what they are reading, with the exception, perhaps, of some difficult lines here and there.   And even in the difficult places, where they have to resort to their mother-tongue in order to understand the meaning, it is generally only one or two words which have to be looked up, so they generally do not even pause to translate the whole clause in which those words have occurred; still less frequently do they stop merely to untangle some involved sentence construction.   When a whole population has to make constant use of two languages, the circumstances are no doubt always the same as among the Wends in Lusatia: " They speak both Wendish and German with equal fluency ; yet the common people generally refuse when they are asked to translate something from one language to another: ' he cannot do it,' or, as one of my informants expressed himself, he is afraid to.' He can, however, without difficulty repeat in German a tale which he has heard in Wendish, and *vice versâ*, and likewise he can give the exact translation of single words." [1]

While there are countless persons who have use for the ability to understand a foreign language directly, and while there is at all events a constantly increasing number of people who need to express their thoughts in a foreign language, there are really very few who will ever have any occasion to exercise skill in translation. There are many who write private letters in German, etc., but they do not compose an English text first which they then proceed to translate with exactness. Even those who have foreign business letters to write for someone else are not generally given every word that is to stand in them, but merely a rough draft of the contents, which they are to clothe in a foreign language as best they can. There remain, then, the few translators connected with the law-courts, the providers of translated novels, and finally the very small number of choice spirits who have the courage to grapple with the valuable and charming art of transplanting poetry in a poetical rendering. But they may all find comfort in the fact that skill in translation at the very bottom rests on that same direct command of language that we all need,[2] so

[1] F. Polle, *Wie denkt das volk über die sprache.* Leipzig, 1889, p. 35. The languages are as different from each other as English and Russian.

[2] Only by understanding the connexion in which they occur is it possible to know what is meant by English *light*, or *bow*, French *montre* or *fin*, German *thor* or *lieben*. So the language must be understood before it can be translated.

there is no need for them to feel dissatisfied if we refuse to recognize skill in translation as the end and aim of all instruction in languages.

Our ideal must rather be the nearest possible approach to the native's command of the language, so that the words and sentences may awaken the same ideas in us as in the native—and these ideas, as we well know, are not the same as those called forth by the corresponding words in our own language. The relations between languages are not like the relations between mathematical equivalents ; *cœur, herz, heart* do not all cover the same ground, to say nothing of the difference between *sens, sinn, sense,* etc. Even when the literal meaning may be said to be the same, the suggestions associated with the words vary in the different languages, suggestions arising from related words, from words that are similar in sound or similar in some other way, from frequent combinations in which the words occur, etc. The same animal is in English called *bat,* in French *chauvesouris,* in German *fledermaus,* in Latin *vespertilio,* in Danish *flagermus,* but what a difference in the suggestions ! The French, the German and the Danish words call attention to the animal's resemblance to a mouse, the Danish word besides to its flapping movement (a suggestion which must be lost for the Germans since *flattern* has taken the place of *fledern*), but the French word to its bald appearance ; the Latin word makes us think of the time of day when the animal is abroad, but the English word *bat* is rather an abstract expression without any suggestiveness, and we can understand why Tennyson declared that the provincial word *flittermouse* was far more suitable for poetical use than *bat*. These "undertones" of the words sound more distinctly in puns, rhymes, etc., but still they always lie lurking in the background of our conscience. It is all such things as these, together with the fact that some languages carefully distinguish between certain shades of grammar or meaning which are of no consequence in other languages, where the finesses seem to be extended to totally different points, and furthermore together with different habits as to order of words, etc., etc., which, taken all in all, make it impossible for any translation ever to be a perfect reproduction of the original : *traduttore traditore !*

For all these reasons, it is not translation (or skill in translation) that we are aiming at in teaching foreign languages.

V

But for all that translation might still be a useful and ndispensable *means* in the service of language instruction. In order to judge of this we must have a clear conception of the different ways in which translation can be and really is used :

(*a*)—Translation *into English* is a means of getting the pupil to understand the foreign language, as for instance, when I tell him that *cheval* means "horse," or when I translate a whole sentence for him ;

(*b*)—Translation into English is a means of testing whether the pupil understands, as, for instance, when I ask him what *cheval* means in English, or when I let him translate a whole sentence ;

(*c*)—Translation *from English* is a means of giving the pupil practice in producing something in the foreign language ;

(*d*)—Translation from English is a means of testing whether the pupil can express himself in the foreign language. It is really a subdivision of this when the teacher lets a pupil translate an English sentence in order to see if he understands some grammatical rule in the foreign language.

It is clear that *a* and *b* are right closely connected, likewise *c* and *d*; yet it will be seen later that the one does not necessarily presuppose the other, as is no doubt generally assumed.

Advocates of the routine-method will throw *a*, *b*, *c*, and *d* together indiscriminately and say about them all that translation is an excellent and indeed the only practical means.

But their opponents, now, maintain that in none of these four cases is translation the only means—very far from it !—and that besides it is not equally valuable in all instances.

> (*a*)—There is always danger in translation; but in spite of this there are many who in certain cases will use this means as being the surest and quickest way of getting the pupils to understand, but in other cases will try to do without it ; some teachers even think that in all cases they can find other and better means of getting the pupils to comprehend the meaning of foreign expressions.

> (*b*)—As a means of testing whether the pupil understands the foreign language, it is a tolerably good thing to let him translate, but only tolerably good; it is not always reliable, and ought in many cases to be a last resort.

> (*c*)—Translation from English is, for beginners at least, an extremely poor means in comparison with the many other hitherto generally neglected ways in which the teacher may get a pupil to say (or write) something in the foreign language.

" Das übersetzen in die fremdsprache zum zwecke
der erlernung derselben gehört einfach in das
gebiet pädagogischer sünden und verirrungen "
(Bierbaum, *Die neueren sprachen*, i. 57).

(*d*)—As a test of whether the pupil can express himself in the other language, an oral or written
exercise in translation is either illusory or is at
least suitable only for the most advanced pupils.

These assertions must now be made good, especially by
the suggestion of other means which may be substituted for
translation. I shall not continue strictly to observe the
distinctions between the four categories, *a*, *b*, *c*, *d*. In
order to avoid tedious repetitions of expressions like " the
foreign language in question," I shall in the following pages
say in short " the language " in contrast to English.

Are there other means by which I can get the pupil to
comprehend the meaning of foreign words and sentences?
Yes; in the first place by means of *direct observation* or
immediate perception (what the Germans call anschauung).
This applies to substantives which designate objects, etc.,
to be found in the school-room: fenêtre, porte, banc,
chaise, tableau (noir), craie, livre, plume, crayon, montre,
élève, maître (professeur), etc. All that is necessary is to
point to the objects with such remarks as *c'est* (or *voilà*) *la
craie, on appelle ça le tableau noir*, etc., and the pupil cannot
mistake the meaning of each word. Furthermore, this is
the best way to teach the most necessary words relating to
the human body : tête, cheveux, nez, yeux, bouche, lèvres,
barbe, joue, oreille, bras, main, doigt, etc. But in addition
to the many substantives there are also a number of words

of other classes which can be learned in this manner: voilà une fenêtre, et voilà une *autre* fenêtre ; Pierre est un élève, Paul est un autre élève ; words like *ici, là* ; especially a number of verbs of action : *j'écris* ; Victor écrit. je *prends* la craie ; Jean prend la craie. je me *lève* ; Pierre se lève. *je m'assieds*, je *marche* (vers la porte), *j'ouvre* la porte, je *ferme* la porte ; je *donne* le livre à Pierre, Pierre me donne le livre, etc. At the same time as the teacher or the pupil says something or other, the teacher illustrates the action. In that manner, already in the first stage, before the pupils have any French vocabulary to operate with, a number of words and sentences may be learned without the use of a single English word. Yes, even the various tenses of the verbs can be explained by this method. If, for instance, in the course of their reading, the pupils come across *il a pris* and they do not understand it, the teacher can show what it means—this of course does not apply to the very first lessons—by first taking the chalk and saying : je prends la craie, then a book : je prends le livre de Jean, then his hand : je prends sa main, and then saying : d'abord j'ai pris la craie, puis j'ai pris le livre de Jean, et enfin j'ai pris sa main. With a little ingenuity a good deal can be brought in in this way; some material in French has been well arranged in P. Passy and T. Tostrup, Leçons de choses. I shall later come to the question as to whether and how the pupils are to repeat what the teacher says in this way, as likewise to the objection that the pupils in reality understand these words in English. Here I shall merely caution against taking too much material of this kind at a stretch ; it is best to intersperse it with other things.

525

In the second place, the meaning of the words may be communicated thro ugh *mediate perception*, through pictures. This is what Miss Goldschmidt with so much energy has put into practice in her " picture-words " and in other books on the same plan, which have been edited partly by her and partly by others. Each page contains a collection of pictures representing a series of objects belonging to the same sphere of ideas. Sometimes they are joined together to make a whole scene ; sometimes the objects remain separated, without being brought into connection with each other ; some of the pictures are well put together ; others present several curiosities, as, for instance, a telescope freely hovering in a rainbow. Each object is supplied with a number referring to lists where the corresponding French (English, etc.) words are given. In many German schools, and in several places in Denmark now too, large picture-charts are used to hang upon the schoolroom wall, especially the Hölzel charts, where, for instance, on a winter-picture are collected representations of the most important things belonging to winter. Then the teacher can point to one of these things and at the same time explain it in the language which is being studied. Finally pictures can also be used to illustrate a narrative or descriptive text, as in the English primers published by Sarauw and myself.

There have been several objections raised against the perception-method. Thus Sweet says that the idea is not so sharply defined as in the case of translation. If we see *chapeau* by the side of (the picture of) a silk hat, we do not know if it merely designates that kind of hat or other kinds too, so that the translation " hat " is more apt to suggest the correct idea. Or if the teacher points to his mouth and says *bouche*, the pupils might just as well think that it means lip, etc. The objection comes from a closet philosopher, who has not seen the thing in practice; there is almost no danger except for one who would try to learn a language by himself and exclusively through pictures. In oral instruction, such mistakes are scarcely frequent enough to be worth mentioning, even if it might be a good thing perhaps for teachers to realize that they are possible—they even occur now and then in a child's apprehension of his native language, which in large part follows exactly these same paths. If the teacher understands his business, no mistake at all occurs or else it is soon corrected, for of course he will never stop at merely pointing to the object and giving the word, but he will immediately use it in sentences and connections in which the meaning becomes perfectly clear; for instance, if he only says *tu as une bouche et deux lèvres*, or, after having pointed to his mouth and said *bouche*, he asks one of the boys: *Combien as-tu de bouches?* there will be no danger of such mistakes; indeed all danger is generally precluded from the very beginning, for when the teacher points to his mouth, he is not apt to say merely *bouche*, but *voilà la bouche* or *voilà ma bouche*, where the singular form *la*, *ma* unmistakably indicates the correct meaning. Such misunderstandings as in the case of *chapeau* are no doubt of rare occurrence, but at all events, the teacher may prevent them too by talking about his own and the pupils' hats with the use of the same word.

Another opponent of the perception-method has said that it causes disturbance in the class when the teachers in modern languages now get up, now sit down, open the door, close the door, blow their noses, pull their boots off and on (?) etc.

A third opponent carefully depicts all the asides a pupil will think of when the teacher, in order to teach him the word *gants*, pulls his gloves out of his pocket : " They are pretty bad specimens," or " Oho ! he has brought his best ones along to-day because he knew he was going to use them," etc.   Of course the method can be driven to caricature, and of course the discipline can become lax if the teacher goes through the various actions with too much restlessness, but in general the method does not require very different or more disturbing movements than those which take place in every or every other lesson : a pupil goes to the blackboard or the door or opens a window. And if there is any spirit in the teaching, the pupils indulge in no more irrelevant asides than in other lessons.

There seems to be greater weight in the objection that only apparently is the foreign word directly attached to the idea by means of the perception-method, since either a real hat or a picture of one immediately suggests to the pupil the English word *hat*, so that after all we do not avoid the roundabout way through the native language, as we desire; the hobgoblin moves with us.   Well, if we think it is possible entirely to prevent English words from turning up in the children's consciousness, we certainly deceive ourselves.   But if we are more modest in our demands and simply want the foreign language to be kept as much as possible in the foreground and English in the background, then it cannot be denied that it must make

528

for this end when it is not necessary for either the teacher or the pupil to mention the English word. And the more they both become accustomed to this method of teaching, the more previously learned words there are for the new ones to be associated with, and the more ingenious the teacher is to vary the whole, the more seldom do the English words occur to the pupil.

With the pictures as a basis of suggestion, there can and ought to be conducted talks in the language, at least after the very first lessons are past. It is but seldom necessary to resort to the native language, and the time is almost exclusively occupied in hearing and saying something in the language. But this can best be done when the pictures not only suggest single words but are rich in content. Thus Mrs. Freudenthal, in Finland, has to a large extent in her teaching used reproductions of genre paintings, which give occasion for spinning out whole narratives suggested by the pictures. Perhaps it is still better, as Sarauw and I have done in our book for beginners in English, to supply the tales (or other selections) with little illustrations ; they may occasion conversations which have more or less to do with the text and which can be conducted with essentially the same vocabulary ; and the teacher ought also to return now and then to previously discussed pictures, which may be treated more fully than before on account of the progress made by the pupils in the meanwhile.

Pictures, then, are of undoubted significance in the teaching of languages, even if their scope must not be overrated and they must not be used as the only means

529

of explanation—all one-sidedness is hurtful. But the
pictures ought to be characteristic of the foreign land and
people, especially when they are to be used beyond the
beginner stage. I am not the first one to reproach Miss
Goldschmidt because she gives pictures showing, for
instance, a Danish sitting-room, a Danish postman, etc.,
and lets the pupils use the same pictures in learning all
three foreign languages, something which is not exactly
calculated to win interest but must be pretty monotonous
whereas exactly what should be done is to open the
pupil's eyes to the manifold and characteristic differences
existing between the various nations. Schools ought to be
well supplied with pictures on the walls and illustrated
works which may serve to give the pupils some enlighten-
ment about French and German conditions of life, natural
scenery, buildings, art, institutions. Foreign illustrated
papers will be found to contain much useful material, and
the teacher ought frequently to use 5–10 minutes or more
of the lesson to discuss such a picture in the language with
the pupils. That would be an excellent way in which to
supplement the teaching based on the text-book.

But not only such ready-made pictures may be used in
teaching languages. The teacher can often, by means of
rough chalk-drawings on the blackboard, illustrate various
things in the text which is being read and base his
explanations (in the language) on them. The few times
I have done it, the pupils immediately took to it,
so that I began to deplore my great lack of skill in
drawing. If there was any subject that was neglected
when I went to school, it was drawing. Now people

have, fortunately, begun to get their eyes open to the importance of this branch, first and foremost for teachers of all subjects as a help in their teaching, and, secondly, for the pupils as the good thing it is from an educational point of view for them to learn to see an object correctly and to reproduce what they see in a drawing. And just as in the case of natural history and geography, the drawings of the pupils now are an important feature of the instruction, so they might play a similar part in the teaching of languages. It is a splendid idea that has been put into practice in " Det danske selskabs skole." I shall quote from its " Beretning," 1900:

"Exercises in drawing have also played an important part. Before the lesson begins there is written on the blackboard one subject for each pupil to illustrate by a drawing. Each one has a certain amount of space apportioned to him. The pupil is ordered to draw only such things as he can mention and explain in German. But of course the intention is that much more is to be drawn. For instance, if the subject is a wagon, the pupil naturally draws both wheels, wagon-pole, stud-stave, side pieces, seat, driver with whip, horses, harness, etc. The pupil has to explain his drawing to the class, and of course he gets into a tight place ; the result is that his interest is aroused for what all the things are called, and he pays close attention to the words when the teacher says them. Fourteen boys in a class can finish their drawings in 10 minutes, and it takes 30 minutes to go through the 14 drawings." (C. Lambek.)

Here it looks as if the subject were given in Danish ;

F

and perhaps the words learned in the exercise have been taken up too much in detail. I should think it might be still better to announce the subject orally and rather fully in the language, to say, for instance, to a Danish pupil who is learning English—You draw a picture of a two-storied house with three windows in each story and one door; outside the house a man is to stand smoking his pipe; or, you draw a carriage and pair, inside the carriage is a gentleman, but you see only the tip of his nose; a dog is running fast behind the carriage. If there is—as there always ought to be—blackboard space enough for several pupils to execute their drawings at the same time, so much the better; the rest of the class can be occupied with something else until the drawings are finished; then they are first explained by the drawer, thereupon by one or several of the other pupils; of course both the teacher and the pupils call attention to anything that has been forgotten in the drawing, and new points are brought up, as suggested by Mr. Lambek. Also in connection with little stories, the pupils may be asked to make drawings to show that they have understood what they have been reading. In speaking about the use of pictures, I have wandered a little from my point of departure, namely, the ways in which (aside from translation) the pupil may be taught the meaning of a foreign word.

All of us who are further advanced must confess to ourselves that in reading foreign books we have often omitted to look up an unfamiliar word in the dictionary, because its meaning was perfectly clear from the *context*. And we have all learned thousands of words in our mother-tongue in the same way. Then why not use this experience in the teaching of foreign languages? Because it leads to guess-work, to carelessness in studying, to an approximate and uncertain comprehension, is the answer we get. Granted —as far as some cases are concerned! There are many combinations where the meaning of a word may be "scented" through the context, and where a conscientious teacher cannot remain satisfied without some proof that the pupil really understands the word; and there are cases where the teacher imagines that the pupils cannot help seeing the meaning immediately, and yet their guesses are all wrong. But still the ability to arrive at the meaning of an unfamiliar word through the text is valuable and does not deserve to be neglected, but should, on the contrary, be cultivated—under control, of course. At all events, there can be no danger in using really self-interpreting sentences where the meaning of an unfamiliar word may be assumed with unfailing certainty and without guess-work. In a sentence like "Il y a *douze mois* dans *l'année*," the pupil who is acquainted with any two of the three italicized words will be able to reason out the meaning of the third with as great accuracy as in the equation $a + b = c$ the unknown quantity may be found when the two are given. And if you continue: le premier s'appelle janvier, le second s'appelle février, le troisième s'appelle mars, etc., then it is no guesswork at all if the pupils gather both the ordinal numerals and the names of the months. The same may be said of the following sentences—

Le jour se divise en vingt-quatre heures ; l'heure se divise en soixante minutes, et la minute en soixante secondes.

Soixante secondes font une minute ; soixante minutes font une heure ; vingt-quatre heures font un jour ; sept jours font une semaine ; cinquante-deux semaines et quelques jours font une année ; cent années font un siècle.

Here the pupil can infer the meaning of a number of words without needing the teacher's translation. So it is only a waste of time to let the pupil himself translate such pieces—for he can do that half-asleep without looking very much at the French, and he does not learn much that way. No ; let him repeat them in French until he can say them fluently, then let him isolate the ordinals : le premier, le second . . ., thereupon the names of the months : janvier, février . . . . ; thereupon go through both series backwards, and then finally answer questions at random : Comment s'appelle le troisième mois ? Quel est le dixième mois ? etc. Or in connexion with the second selection, let him go through all the divisions of time, first beginning with the smallest and then with the largest (with the use of the article *un, une*) ; then ask : Comment se divise l'heure ? Comment se divise le jour ? Combien de secondes a une minute ? Trois heures, combien de minutes ? Deux années, combien de mois ? etc., etc. In this way it seems as if a teacher can with complete confidence continue for a long time to keep even those pupils occupied who do not know much French, without needing to mention a single English word.[1]

Now of course there are only few subjects which can thus be talked about in one self-interpreting sentence after

[1] See below about exercises in counting.

the other: Sweet has, in his Elementarbuch, got hold of more of that sort of thing than any other author of similar text-books that I know of; but almost any text will be found to contain sentences where the general sense unmistakably indicates the meaning of the new words; the more of that kind of combinations the pupil commits to memory the better for him. The ability to infer the meaning from the context ought rather to be encouraged and practised than ought the tendency to go by resemblances to words in the mother-tongue or in other languages; even if much may be learned in this way (Eng. *send*, German *senden*; Eng. *ruin*, Ger. French *ruine*, etc.), yet there is still reason to caution against too much confidence in resemblances, for they often lead us astray (even in the case of "etymologically identical words"). Most of the really valuable associations of this kind come of their own accord.

But to continue, the new words may simply be explained in the language to the pupil—this of course really means that the teacher puts the word into a self-interpreting sentence, so it is merely a subdivision of what we have just been speaking about. Anyone who has been accustomed to use the excellent French and English dictionaries, large or small, all the way from Littré and Murray to the little Larousse or Annandale's Concise, knows how often he has been able to find in them quite sufficient explanations of unfamiliar words. Why not use this experience too in the teaching of foreign languages? Thus, for instance, explain *veuf:* Un veuf est un homme dont la femme est morte; une veuve est une femme dont le mari est mort. This explanation, to be sure, contains no more information than is to be got out of the simple translation "widower" ("widow"); but there are cases where an explanation gives better information than a translation. It is not improbable that many Englishmen, when given the translation *primage* or *hat-money* for German *kapplaken*, will remain just as wise as they were before, but they will immediately understand it if it is explained in German: prämiengeld, das früher dem schiffskapitän ausser der fracht gezahlt wurde, ursprünglich freiwilliges geschenk, dann vertragsmässig bestimmt. The English word *dentil* is in English-German dictionaries translated by *kälberzahn*, but I suppose that most Germans would get more out of Annandale's definition: "the name of the little cubes or square blocks often cut for ornament on Greek cornices," or Funk-Wagnalls' definition: "One of a series of small square tooth-like ornamental blocks in the bed-moulding of the cornices of some Ionic and other entablatures" (here even an instructive illustration). Well, such technical words, where we do not even know the English term, we shall scarcely have much use for in school; but sometimes on account of the chance vagaries of language a translation does not give as exact an idea as an explanation. If I say that *stockwerk* means *floor*, I run the risk of getting an exercise with *stockwerk* used where there ought to be *fussboden*; but if I explain it as "eine der horizontalen einteilungen eines hauses," or something like that, there is no danger of any misunderstanding.

On the other hand, it must of course be admitted that there are many words where an English translation gives the information required more quickly and more clearly than it could be given in a long explanation in the foreign language; and the teacher ought to consider in each separate case which of the two ways of helping the pupil is to be preferred. Still he must not let laziness influence him to give the translation, which of course is always easiest for him, but he must remember that an explanation in the language always has the great advantage that the pupil, in addition to the new words, hears a number of others which he thereby reviews, as it were, and that the pupil is for the time being wholly occupied with the foreign language. Besides, these explanations amuse the pupils because they get more intellectual work out of them than out of translations, which are given to them gratis.

However, such explanations ought perhaps not to be used to any great extent in the glossaries of text-books, especially in readers for beginners ; here it is best to weave them into the text itself. In the first place, in such glossaries or notes, the explanations naturally become drier and more like definitions than is necessary; in the second place, the pupil who does not feel inclined to read those few lines through is tempted to get some comrade, a parent, or a sister to tell him in short the meaning of the word : that is, to translate it. To counteract this by *always* requiring the pupil to commit the given explanation to memory is not exactly a wise plan, since it may easily lead to mere thoughtless memory-work. For the glossary ought to play no more important part in really good teaching for beginners than as a help to the forgetful pupil in his home-preparation, where he can look up the meaning (and pro-by heart. The father and mother can teach about 1000 Latin words to the child at the age of 3—5 years!

1828. **George Long**: An introductory lecture delivered in the University of London on Tuesday, November 4th, 1828.

1829. **L. Mühlenfels**: IntroductoryLecture on the Study of German.

1829. **A. Clifford**: Instructions to Parents and Teachers respecting the use of the elementary books for the Latin Language.

1830. **L. P. R. Fenwick** de Porquet: The Fenwickian System of Learning French.

1830. **George Long**: Observations on the Study of the Latin and Greek Languages. An Introductory Lecture delivered in the University of London, November 1, 1830.

1836. **Alexander Allen**: An Etymological Analysis of Latin Verbs. For the use of schools and colleges.

The interesting preface of XLIII. pages affords a good view of philological opinions at the time on roots and crude forms. It is based mainly on Pott's *Etymologische Forschungen* and Dr. Struve's book — *Ueber die Lateinische Declination und Conjugation* (1823).

The author apparently imagines the primitive man as one day making up his mind to have a language, and then glueing it together in this fashion—

Prepo-sition.	Redupli-cation.	Connecting Vowel.	Root.	Flection Syllable.	Tense Vowel.	Plural Sign.	Person Sign.
con	d	i	d	er	u	n	t

1836. **Rev. M. Russell, LL.D.**: Observations on the Advantages of Classical Learning, viewed as the means of cultivating the youthful mind, and more especially as compared with the studies which it has been proposed to substitute in its stead.

1836. **J. Ward**: A short Introduction of Grammar, generally to be used: compiled and set forth for the bringing up of all those, that intend to attain to the knowledge of the Latin Tongue.

1836. **Thomas Wyse, Esq., M.P.**: Education Reform; or, the Necessity of a National System of Education. Vol. I.

1838. **Dr. L. Lersch**: Die Sprachphilosophie der Alten, dargestellt an dem Streite über Analogie und Anomalie der Sprache.

suggestions are necessary for the class to understand immediately.

Finally there are circumlocutions in the language, not straightforward definitions as in the dictionaries, but also other explanations; often it is only necessary to lead the thoughts of the pupils in upon the right track. On coming across German *hauptstadt*, for instance, the teacher can say : London ist die hauptstadt Englands, Paris ist die haupt-stadt Frankreichs, und Kopenhagen ist die hauptstadt Dänemarks—and then ask one of the pupils : Heinrich, weisst du jetzt was hauptstadt bedeutet ? Perhaps he will answer, . " Capital," but then the teacher can say : Ganz richtig, aber kannst du nicht das wort auf deutsch erklären ? The pupil : Ja, die hauptstadt ist die grösste stadt eines landes. The teacher : Ja wohl, es ist die erste stadt, die grösste stadt, die wichtigste oder bedeutendste stadt eines landes. Then he may add : Nun, Johan, kannst du andere hauptstädte Europas anführen, and when he has mentioned a few, the teacher says : Schön, das genügt, and passes on. Even if many words are used, yet they are not superfluous because they are foreign words, and therefore a few minutes' conversation in this manner is about just as useful as if a whole page had been read in the language. And the pupils will ever after remember the meaning of the word *hauptstadt* much better than if the teacher had simply told them the translation and then continued with the reading. In every separate case, the teacher must feel his way to decide where there yet remains something that is not understood, and where further explanation would be superfluous or tiresome ; that is also one of the reasons why such circumlocutions had better be left to the teacher than included in the text-book.

Of course it is necessary to have practice and a good deal of tact in order to give this kind of explanations naturally and well, and carefully adapted to the needs and standpoint of the class ; the teacher must have a pretty good idea of what the class knows beforehand, and thereby which words and expressions he may use with certainty ; the easier and the more colloquial the words are which are used in the circumlocution, and the more concretely it is expressed, the better. It is better to explain too much than too little, and one must not be afraid of using a number of words when they only are in the foreign language. There is some truth in Gabelentz' remark : " Gesprächige leute von engem gedankenkreise sind für den anfang die besten lehrmeister"[1]; the teacher must not exactly make himself stupid, but he must admit that no matter how high he himself stands intellectually, he can very well learn something from the nursery-method of teaching languages: for instance, that taciturnity or conciseness of expression do not lead to the goal. It pays to give some attention to this form of instruction and to find out what kind of explanations are of the greatest linguistic benefit to the pupils. It is not difficult, as a rule—even without direct questions, which, however, the teacher ought not to be sparing of [2]—to feel what is understood and what is not, just as the boys can

[1] *Die Sprachwissenschaft*, 70.

[2] But which, of course, ought not to be asked in the form " Do you understand ? " with the obligatory answer "Yes," which too often means nothing.

easily be trained to say so immediately when there is something that they do not understand. All that is necessary is to make them feel confident that their teacher is always willing and glad to answer their questions, and that they will never be made fun of for asking. Sometimes, of course, he may also make another pupil answer the question if it is an easy one.

The following may serve as a connected specimen of the method of procedure, even if I have, perhaps, explained a word or two which for an English class would need no explanation.

Devant la porte d'une maison forestière [c'est à dire une maison située dans une forêt. Vous ne saver pas ce que c'est qu'une forêt ? Eh, bien, c'est plus grand qu'un bois, une très grande collection d'arbres, ça s'appelle une forêt. Adolphe, peux-tu me nommer une forêt en Angleterre ? La maison dont nous allons parler, était située dans le milieu d'une forêt, et devant la porte] *une jeune femme, les bras nus, cassait du bois à coups de hache sur une pierre.* [Elle avait les bras nus, il n'y avait rien pour couvrir ses bras, elle n'avait pas de manches. Pierre, dis-moi si Jean a les bras nus ? Elle cassait du bois (shown by a gesture) et elle employait pour ça une hache (if the word is not known, and is not understood at once, you may give the translation) ; chaque fois qu'elle fait un coup de hache elle casse un morceau de bois.] *Elle était grande et bien faite, une fille de forêt, fille et femme de forestiers* [son père et son mari étaient des forestiers, ils avaient des

emplois dans la forêt ; et elle avait été élevée dans la forêt de sorte qu'elle appartenait tout à fait à la forêt.   C'est ce qu'on a exprimé en l'appelant fille de forêt.]   *Une voix cria de l'intérieur de la maison :*
Nous sommes seules ce soir, Berthine, il faut rentrer [il faut que tu rentres], *voilà la nuit* [il commence à se faire tard] ; *il y a peut-être des Prussiens* [les Prussiens sont les habitants de la Prusse ; ceci se passe pendant la guerre entre les Allemands et les Français—il y a peut-être des Prussiens] *et des loups qui rôdent* [qui vout çà et là ; le mot rôder s'emploie très souvent en parlant de bêtes féroces].
J'ai fini, maman, répond la jeune femme, n'aie pas peur ; il fait encore jour.   [Elle dit que la nuit n'est pas encore arrivée ; elle y voit encore, et elle n'a pas peur, elle ; mais, du reste, elle a fini son travail ; il n'y a plus de bois à casser.]
Puis elle ferma les volets [les volets, ce sont les pièces de bois qu'on applique sur les fenêtres pour les protéger.   Paul, dis-moi s'il y a des volets sur les fenêtres de cette salle-ci ?   Il y en avait dans la maison   dont   nous   parlons   dans   l'histoire ; Berthine   les   ferma], *rentra, et poussa les lourds verrous de la porte* [un verrou est fait de fer, on le pousse pour empêcher d'ouvrir la porte.]
Sa mère filait auprès du feu.   [To explain *filer*, a gesture and the imitation of the sound of the wheel may be employed, or else the translation supplemented, perhaps, by : filer, ça vient de fil puisqu'en filant on fait des fils.]

*Je ne suis pas tranquille, dit-elle, quand le père est
    dehors.* [Vous voyez que la mère a plus peur, elle,
    que la fille. C'est que son mari n'est pas là.]
    Deux femmes, ça n'est pas fort. [Ce n'est pas
    beaucoup ; c'est si peu de chose que deux
    femmes si les Prussiens viennent.]

La jeune répondit :

Oh ! je tuerais bien un loup ou un Prussien tout de même.

*Et elle montrait du doigt un gros revolver suspendu au-
    dessus de la cheminée.* [La cheminée, c'est là où
    on fait du feu.]

Son mari s'était engagé dans l'armée [il s'était fait
    soldat] *au commencement de la guerre, et les deux
    femmes étaient demeurées seules avec le père, le
    vieux Nicolas Pichon, qui avait refusé de quitter sa
    demeure pour rentrer en ville* [refusé ? Si tu dis
    à Alfred de te prêter son canif, il refuse s'il dit :
    "Non, je ne veux pas te prêter mon canif." On
    avait dit à Pichon d'aller en ville, mais il avait dit :
    "Non, je ne veux pas quitter ma maison" ; donc
    il avait refusé].

La ville prochaine, c'était Rethel. On y était patriote
    [vous savez que celui qui aime sa patrie, est
    nommé patriote] ; *et les bourgeois* [les habitants de
    la ville] *avaient décidé de résister à l'ennemi.
    Tous—boulangers, épiciers, bouchers, menuisiers,
    libraires, pharmaciens, manœuvraient à des heures
    régulières* [Tout le monde s'était fait soldats ; le
    boulanger, c'est celui qui vend du pain ; l'épicier
    vend des épices, du thé, du café, du chocolat, et

mille autres choses ; le menuisier fait des tables
et des chaises ; le libraire vend des livres ; le
pharmacien vend tout ce dont on a besoin
quand on est malade—donc vous voyez que tous
les hommes, de toutes occupations et de toutes
classes, allaient manœuvrer tous les jours à une
heure fixe] *sous les ordres de M. Lavigne, ancien
sous-officier de dragons* [il n'était plus sous-officier,
mais il l'avait été ; c'est ce qui est indiqué par le
mot ancien], etc., etc.

It is best to go through the lesson for the next time in
the beginning of the hour, when both the teacher's and the
pupils' powers are freshest, and when there is sure to be
plenty of time for it ; at the end of the hour the teacher
may be too hurried and nervous in his anxiety to get
through the proper amount before the bell rings.　In going
through it, the teacher may either let the pupils look at
their books or require all books to be closed.　The latter
is the better way, since then the pupils can give more
undivided attention to the teacher ; for they must drink in
all his words and follow his slightest movements.　In that
case it is no doubt always best for him to write down on
the blackboard each new word as he explains it, and after
everything has been explained he may close either by
reading the piece aloud himself (without interpolations)
or by letting one of the pupils read it.　Yet it is not well
to follow one method of procedure all the time ; and if the
piece is easy, so that there are only a few new words, it may
immediately be read aloud by one of the pupils (slowly,
not in a forced way !), who may stop and ask whenever

there is anything that he does not understand. If a sentence contains two or three unfamiliar words or some other difficulty which has given occasion for a question, it must by all means be read again connectedly without interruption as soon as a period has been reached. Finally the teacher can, if it seems necessary, as a further guarantee, let one of the pupils give a free rendering of the contents in his native language; that is a sort of control, at all events until the class has become quite accustomed to having the lesson gone through in this way.

Let me suggest here that, in going through the new lesson, the teacher can also counteract the injury which an unusual order of words or expression occurring in a selection of poetry might do to the pupil's instinct for the natural language, by giving the prose order of words and explaining it. For instance, the lines: " And everybody in the house On tip-toe has to creep" can first be explained as if they ran: " And everybody in the house has to creep on tip-toe "; again, such an expression as *at eve* may be altered to *in the evening*. Then when the pupil sees the changed order of words and the unusual expression in his book, he will understand that they are due to the poetical form. Therefore he will not be tempted to imitate them; if he should do so in later exercises, the teacher must correct him, since there is no earthly reason why the pupil should practise *using* anything else but everyday language. It is, however, a matter of course that whenever I have used verses in my own books for beginners in English, I have tried to find such as contained very few deviations from the usual form of the language.

VI

WE have then come to the following result with respect
to translation as a means of interpreting a foreign
language to the pupils (p. 56 *a*): it is not the only and
the best means ; it ought to be used sparingly ; and at
all events it is not necessary to translate whole connected
pieces, but merely a word or, at the very most, a sentence
now and then.   But this investigation has already thrown
some light upon our next point, namely, translation as *a
means of testing* whether the pupils understand the foreign
language (p. 56 *b*).

Here, too, observation may take the place of translation.
The pupil who obeys the teacher's command, *montre-moi
la fenêtre*, by pointing at the window shows that he understands the word just as well as the one who in answer to
the question : what is the meaning of *fenêtre ?* answers,
window.   Likewise the one who can point to the right
thing when the teacher shows him a picture and says : *où
est le chapeau du garçon ? où sont ses souliers ? vois-tu le toit
de la maison ?* etc., or the one who carries out a command
like *prends la craie, lève-toi, assieds-toi, donne-moi ton livre,
prends le livre de Jean et donne-le à Henri*—especially when
he at the same time says : *voilà la fenêtre, voilà le chapeau du*

garçon, voilà la craie, je me lève, etc., with a correct application of the words desired. Nor can there be any doubt that a boy has understood a French question when he can give a sensible answer in the same language, or that he has understood a narrative which has been told or read to him when he can retell it (in English, or still better in French).

The teacher is no doubt most tempted to let the pupils translate when he wants to make sure that they know the new selection which has been assigned to them for home-study. But even in this case, if the teacher has only gone through the lesson on assigning it (as indicated above) in a detailed and lively way, and with continual appeal to the pupils, so that the whole does not become a mere monologue by the teacher, the translation test is not as necessary as it would have been if the lesson had either not been gone through at all or if the teacher had merely translated it rapidly. He will often find it sufficient to ask a question now and then about some single point in the selection, especially if the selection is used for such exercises as will be described below, which directly and indirectly show whether the pupils have understood it all or not.

But still, let us assume that the teacher insists on having the selection translated—and of course this may always be a good thing once in a while by way of a change, most so perhaps when the teacher has not been quite able to digest and absorb the new methods. Then the best thing for him to do is to require the translation immediately, before the pupil has read the piece aloud. This is the most reliable test as to whether the lesson really has been learned in time, for the pupil has not the chance while he is

G

reading aloud to speculate about how it is to be translated, and, on the other hand, when he comes to read it in the foreign language, he is not disturbed by irrelevant thoughts in his native language. Besides, the teacher must understand that this translation is not the most important event of the hour ; it ought therefore to occupy as little time as possible. The pupil must be required to deliver his translation quickly, and it is not necessary to criticise the English expressions with pedantic exactitude. As soon as it is clear that the pupil understands perfectly, it is better for the teacher himself to give the correct English expression in passing, than to waste time in letting him find it out for himself.

A little turn of expression, a word-formation, or an order of words which is not quite English can very well be allowed to pass unnoticed ; it is just when there is no attention paid to these things that they are less apt to be injurious to the pupil's English than when the translation is treated as if it were the only thing. In case of any unusually awkward expression, the teacher can indulge in a hearty laugh together with the pupils and say : " Well, that is not the very best English you are giving us, but the meaning is clear enough, and all that we are concerned with here is if you understand the French, and that you do. Of course we know that you would never seriously say or write anything like that in your mother-tongue." No more attention than this, it seems to me, ought to be paid to the English in these oral translations—the less we occupy ourselves with our native language during the French or German lessons, the less will it become contaminated ;

good English is not to be learned in *those* lessons, and poor English the teacher must give both himself and his pupils as little occasion as possible to use.

It is a different matter when *advanced pupils* can get both pleasure and benefit out of occasional exercises in translation. Then these must be chosen so that there are considerable deviations between the foreign language and English, which of course does not mean that the selected specimen of the foreign language itself need be difficult to understand. When the pupils are not daily occupied with translation, but move freely in the foreign language, it would just be great sport for them for a change to have a contest as to who could find the best and most exact English equivalents for foreign expressions. Thus there is no little difference between this kind of exercise and those now prevalent sight translations whose chief object seems to be to test the vocabulary of the pupils. The translation exercise that I have in mind should be conducted on about these lines : the selection should be read aloud to the class ; if it contains any unfamiliar words, they should be explained in the manner described above, or, if they are translated instead, there should be given (as in a dictionary) perhaps five or six English equivalents to choose between ; thereupon the pupils (in class under supervision) write their translations, which the teacher afterwards reads aloud and compares, so that the pupils themselves may judge as to whose translation has come nearest to the original and as to whether that rendering is to be preferred where every little element in the original has been taken into account but where the English has thus become a little bit long drawn out, or that rendering which in pith and euphony can stand comparison with the original, but where every detail has not been strictly included, etc. In short, the exercise is not to test the pupils' knowledge in the foreign language, but to give them some idea of the difficulties which the *art* of translation has to contend with ; and for the same reason the pupils might also be asked sometimes to try their skill in a metrical translation of a piece of poetry, but perhaps only in such a way that all participation in the contest is quite voluntary. Such selections might be chosen where we have good poetical translations in our literature, which could then be compared with the efforts of the pupils.[1]

Some few exercises in artistic translation, which the teacher carefully goes through with them, will help to give the more advanced pupils a vivid perception of some of the most delicate shades of variation in the languages as means of expression for human thought—but as the daily bread of language instruction that kind of exercise is not to be recommended, especially not for beginners.

In the daily teaching of languages it is in a number of cases quite superfluous to let the pupils translate. If the reading selections are as easy as is desirable, there will be some sentences in each lesson where neither the vocabulary nor the construction presents the slightest difficulty. In other sentences, the difficulty is simply due to a new word, but if the teacher just devotes a few minutes right away to hearing the new words, it is not necessary to have those

[1] As an introduction to these exercises, the teacher might compare several different translations of a part of Goethe, for instance, with each other, and with the original.

sentences translated either. There are, as we know, many sentences which can be understood without any difficulty at all, but which are still difficult to translate ; if the pupil knows the meaning of *schwören,* he will readily understand "er hat hoch und teuer geschworen," but it will not be so easy for him to find the best way of rendering the adverbs, and it is really purposeless to waste time over them. (See also above, p. 50).

Then finally there remains one or another really complicated sentence, which can be separated out from the rest and translated by the pupils—if the teacher in order to save time does not prefer to translate the whole of it himself. To test the pupil's comprehension of single words by letting him explain them in the language is not very practical except to a limited extent; it might only be useful in dealing with clever advanced pupils where it would not necessarily degenerate into a mere committing of definitions to memory. It is therefore more properly in place in university instruction than in schools.

If any one now says that this method of procedure by which translation as a test of the pupils' comprehension of what they have read is limited to the least possible, and in many lessons even the very last remnant of it is done away with, is far less satisfactory than the old-fashioned translating over and over again of the whole lesson, and that the teacher thus has no means of knowing what the pupils understand and what not, I answer that, in the first place, the pupils' comprehension of a piece which they have even translated several times in the old way is often poor enough ; the most incredible thoughtlessness can thrive under the shelter of rehearsed translations. In the second place (and this is more important) the new method, when applied in the right way, offers such an abundant variety of means by which to sound the pupils and test how deeply they are penetrating into both the language and contents of their reading, that the teacher can easily feel sure of all essentials. This will be made perfectly plain in the following description of the manner in which the lessons ought to be conducted.

The selection must be read aloud. This had best be done—at all events as a rule—by the teacher first; of course he read it yesterday when he went through it for the first time, but he did it more slowly, interrupting himself with explanations, etc., for it was new for the pupils, and it was necessary for them to comprehend the meaning. But now the teacher may read it quickly, fluently, with the proper "expression," in short, in a lively and natural manner. Then the pupil (the pupils) reads the same. At the beginner-stage, the teacher must read each sentence by itself and then get the pupils to repeat it while they have the teacher's pronunciation fresh in mind. Later on the teacher may take larger sections, which may be parceled out to the pupils in not too small portions. And one cannot be too particular with the way in which this reading is done; such stuttering, with pauses between words belonging closely together, and neglect of natural and necessary pauses, which used to be the rule, ought never to be tolerated, not even as an exception. Even the first beginners ought to be required to read each sentence connectedly with natural expression; the teacher will not regret any trouble taken on this account, even if it involves ever so much repetition. The more attention that is paid to this in the first few months, the easier will it be later to require the pupils to read well— that is, intelligibly and intelligently. This reading aloud, besides being an exercise in pronunciation, also has its other advantages for teaching purposes. Milton, already, said that it is easy to hear only from the way in which a piece is read, if the reader understands it or not. A really good reader can in the most delicate manner lay bare his appreciation, and vice versâ it is not difficult for a teacher quick of hearing to detect, through a pupil's uncertainty, false emphasis, etc., what he has not understood (or learned) in the piece he is reading—and then he can pounce on him and get him to disclose the gap in his knowledge. When this is filled up, of course he must read the piece again better than the first time. The reading (or reciting) of dialogues, with the parts assigned to various members of the class, is always amusing, and can easily be used as a means of encouraging natural emphasis and expression.

Reading in unison ought not to be neglected ; it has the advantage of occupying the whole class at once, so that the pupils get more practice in producing the foreign sounds than when each one reads separately. Of course the teacher cannot exercise so sharp a control as when he hears one at a time, but yet he has by no means lost his control ; by practice, he can learn to detect single mistakes through the whole chorus, and can even be tolerably certain as to where they come from, and then he can get the suspected pupil (or pupils) to read the difficult part alone. A help of a similar nature in language-instruction is *singing*. When a teacher knows how to get his pupils to learn to sing some of the verses in the reader, such class-singing will be found to be both beneficial and enlivening; the words are more easily remembered and the pronunciation is improved. Singing in a foreign language as a factor in teaching was already a number of years ago used by Paul Passy; it plays an important part in the well-known "Palmgrenske sam-skola" in Stockholm and in several German schools, and has now of late years also been put into practice by some Danish teachers in a very enjoyable manner; on several occasions, the pupils have even given up a part of their recess in order to sing foreign songs, when the teachers in adjoining classes have looked askance at the singing during the lesson-hours.

The oftener a piece is recited by a pupil, the more firmly are the single words and especially the word-combinations rooted in his memory; indeed it has even been attempted to base a whole system of instruction on this experience, as for instance in v. Pfeil's highly interesting pamphlet: "Wie lernt man eine sprache am leichtesten und besten?" (Breslau, 1884), and in several other works by the same author, especially his "Eins," Beiträge zur erziehung im hause (3rd ed. Leipzig, 1879), which is also valuable for other pedagogical suggestions. His method of procedure is simple: no grammar; no translation from the mother-tongue; only one language at a time, which then is pursued at full speed (as a rule, six or more hours a week) in the following manner. From the very beginning, an author is taken up; the same piece (a couple of lines to begin with) is first read aloud by the teacher, then by the pupil (if necessary, several times), is thereupon translated word by word by the teacher ("to the complete neglect of German sentence-construction; I would not tolerate having turns of expression rendered into good German") and afterwards in the same way by the pupil, is then read aloud by the pupil twice more in the course of the same lesson and once again in the beginning of the next; finally every Monday, the pupil reads aloud all that has been gone through in the preceding week, and, not stopping at that, whole books or large sections of books may be read through connectedly after they have in this manner been studied in instalments. Translation is omitted as soon as there is no danger of miscomprehension, and can soon be quite dispensed with in dealing with easy sentences, which then are only *read* through the stated number of times. During this repeated recitation of the foreign sentences—at least four times after the pupil has understood their meaning—the mother-tongue steps into the background of its own accord, as it were, and the idioms of the foreign language take firm hold upon the memory. So far v. Pfeil, who, as he himself asserts—and why should we not believe the man ?—has had good results in the course of a short time, both in taking and giving instruction according to this method, which, to be sure, he has only employed in private instruction, never having tried it in a class. The impulse to make independent use of the language-material thus learned makes its appearance very early. Thus v. Pfeil tells about a pupil thirty-two years old, who was brought up in a country school and who had never before learned any foreign language, but who after

ten lessons wrote him an Italian letter filling four octavo
pages, which, if not quite correct, was still quite intelligible.

But the method is terribly spiritless and mechanical,
perhaps you will say. Oh, yes—but is it really more spiritless to read something aloud many times in which there is
some meaning—and some meaning which you understand
—than to translate something just as many times in which
there is no meaning at all, to say nothing of all the other
inane things which our old methods bring in their train,
such as grammatical rigmaroles, etc. However, it is by no
means my intention to give the v. Pfeil method an unquali-
fied recommendation, at all events not for school purposes;
it is too monotonous, and a more varied method of instruction may surely have the same or greater advantages.
Already, in the preceding suggestions, it will have been
noticed that there were several deviations from v. Pfeil's
method of procedure; here I shall merely call attention to
some things which we can learn from it: first, that we must
as soon as possible dispense with translation where it is
decidedly superfluous; and secondly, that our most important
object, namely, that the foreign turns of expression shall
make such an impression upon our pupils that they themselves can use them on occasion, cannot be attained
without much repetition.

During the first lessons, it is of so much importance for
the pupils to catch and reproduce the sounds that the repetitions which are necessary for practice in pronunciation
also serve to impress the sentences on their memory; the
teacher must only make sure that the pupils know the
meaning of each sentence before they begin to practise

pronouncing it, and that they do not forget it, so that the words become merely meaningless sounds. Such a selection as the one introducing my French primer (La chèvre)[1] lends itself well to this purpose; it occasions many repetitions of the same sentences, still without becoming tiresome, and the rhythm encourages natural, fluent and non-stuttering recitation.

Later on, of course, there is no necessity for so much repetition merely for the sake of the pronunciation. Then one might require the texts to be committed to memory; but this involves the danger that they might be learned and remembered as lifeless series of words without any regard for their meaning, especially if the teacher makes a routine of it. But it might be quite useful every half-year, for instance, or perhaps a little oftener, for the pupils to be assigned each a piece to commit to memory; they may themselves choose one of the pieces which have been read, and then they must be expected to recite it with a very good pronunciation and correct expression; no parrot-performance! But otherwise the main point is for the pupils to be occupied with the text repeatedly in such a way that they do not lose sight of the meaning, so that they may thus become so familiar with it that at last they know it almost or entirely by heart without having been directly required to commit it to memory. And this can at the same time be done in such a way that the pupils are led to say a number of things without following them in the printed text, so that imperceptibly they are being pre-

---

[1] Somewhat similar to "The House that Jack Built." Biquette veut pas sortir des choux,

pared to be able to say something in the language quite of their own accord.

The teacher can divide the day's lesson into sentences, which he pronounces and the pupils repeat after him. They have all closed their books, and when the teacher says a sentence, no one knows who is to repeat it. By this manner of teaching, which is also practicable in connection with the exercises which I shall suggest later, the teacher makes sure that a pupil's attention cannot wander in the confidence that it is some one else's turn; it is every one's turn all the time. Thus the teacher says, for instance : Les abeilles ressemblent aux mouches ; Pierre, répète.—Peter : L. a. r. a. m.—Teacher : Jean, répète ça encore.—John : L. a. r. a. m.—Teacher : Mais elles ont un aiguillon ; répète, Charles.—Charles : m. e. o. u. ai.— Teacher : Et elles piquent très fort quand elles sont en colère ; répète tout ça, Adolphe, etc. Or, by way of a change, the teacher can let the first one who repeats the sentence mention one of his comrades, who is to repeat it again.

Let me remark in passing that I have always given my pupils French names immediately in one of the first lessons; they are written on the blackboard (in phonetical transcription of course, see below), and are very quickly learned; as a rule, they are simply translations of their first names, occasionally of a nickname, etc. It amuses the pupils, and the teacher has the advantage of being able to use their names in the middle of a French sentence without marring the run of the language.

Other similar methods : pupil A reads aloud ; after

every sentence, either the teacher or he himself appoints someone to repeat.—Or : the teacher reads a sentence aloud, then says : traduis, Jules; and after Julius' translation : répète ça en français, Paul. This is better than to let the same pupil first translate and then say it in French, for thus neither one has to make a sudden change from one basis of articulation to another.—Or : when a piece has been read aloud as a whole, the teacher may render it into English, a sentence at a time, and get the pupils to express the same thought in French. This is, of course, the most difficult of these methods and ought to be employed with caution, for the pupils may easily be tempted to *translate* from English (that is, to construct their French after the English) instead of reproducing the French which has been given, so that we thus risk all the dangers which are commonly associated with the old-fashioned method of translation from the native to the foreign language (cf. below). Therefore it were best that this kind of exercise merely be used occasionally, and only when the selection employed is otherwise so familiar to the pupils that they almost have it by heart in its French form. A variation of all these exercises is, instead of a single pupil, to let the whole class repeat the sentence in unison.

If the pupils should begin to lag, it indicates that the class is not yet sufficiently familiar with the text, and then the best thing to do is to say : Well, now you read the piece through three times in chorus and then we shall begin from the beginning in the same way as before with repetition without the book. It does not take long before the teacher can to advantage enter upon little deviations from

what the pupils know from the book ; thus he secures himself against thoughtless pattering out of what has been committed to memory at home—which of course the attentive
teacher easily can detect through the manner in which the
pupil reads. But too great deviations are scarcely advisable; they easily lead to confusion and to the danger of
wandering too far from the matter in hand, which is of
course to make the pupils thoroughly familiar with the
text. As examples of permissible changes of the sentences
which have just been employed, I shall mention : Une
abeille ressemble à une mouche (L'abeille ressemble à la
mouche) mais elle a un aiguillon | et elle pique très fort
quand elle est en colère—or : Les abeilles ressemblent
beaucoup aux mouches, | mais elles ont un petit aiguillon,
et elles piquent fort. . . . Or one may interpolate : les
mouches ressemblent aux abeilles, | mais elles n'ont pas
d'aiguillon, | et elles ne piquent pas comme les abeilles. It
is best not to enter upon greater deviations, because then
it will too frequently be necessary to let a pupil translate
the sentence constructed by the teacher, since otherwise it
is not certain whether the whole class has understood it or
not.[1] The most important thing in these exercises, as also
in the exercises with questions (see below), is not to let
the pupil get beyond his depth so that he will become
frightened and lose confidence, for then he will never learn
to swim.

We have hitherto assumed that the pupils repeat what

[1] The text-books may sometimes contain a whole piece in two
versions ; perhaps the teacher himself may occasionally undertake to
re-write (on the blackboard) or re-tell a selection.

has been said orally; if the repetition is written, we have *dictation*—an exercise which must not be neglected and which can be conducted in different ways, partly parallel with those just mentioned. The teacher can either say a sentence or one of the boys can read it aloud; once may be enough, but the teacher may also say it twice, or else say it himself first and then let one of the pupils repeat it before it is written down; it may be a sentence taken from the reader (first stage), a sentence taken from the reader but slightly changed (second stage), or an entirely new piece (only for advanced students);[1] the dictation may be written on the blackboard or in copy-books (on slates); one pupil may be occupied in the first way while the rest of the class is occupied in the second way; sometimes the class itself may correct the mistakes; if there is blackboard space enough, several pupils can be writing the same or different things at the same time. The dictation may be required to be written with phonetical transcription (see below) or orthographically, or one pupil may write in one way, another in the other way, the two being afterwards compared.

Finally, dictation may be used in connection with several of the exercises which I shall suggest later. A question is dictated, and the pupils are required to write both the question and the answer; a sentence is dictated in the

---

[1] And even for them only in small measure, since it must be remembered that nothing is learned thereby, but it is merely a test in what has been learned, and that the mistakes made by the pupils, as we know from experience, easily take root in their memory because they have written them, and are not effaced by the teacher's corrections.

first person, which is then to be inflected in all persons, etc. The advantages of dictation are, that it trains the pupils in rapid and sharp comprehension of spoken words, that it gives the teacher an effective means of testing what each pupil has comprehended, and that the pupils generally remember pretty well what they have once written down. But the disadvantage of dictation, as of all written class work, is that it consumes more time than oral exercises. Dictation with " catches " is of course beneath the dignity of a modern language teacher.

VII

I SHALL here deal with various kinds of exercises in which the pupils have to say something in the foreign language which they have not either seen in their books or heard from someone else just a moment before. Some of the first and easiest of these are *arithmetical exercises*. But here I must first stop to make a remark about the numerals in general. It is not so seldom that we find pupils in our schools who have studied French for several years without having become perfectly familiar with the French numerals; they have great difficulty with dates. What is the cause of this phenomenon? Of course the French numerals are difficult, more difficult than the German; but the French verbs are also more difficult than the German, so that alone is not the reason why this class of words troubles the pupils. No; the matter is quite simple. Only imagine a French reader so planned that there is not a single French adjective in the text, while English words like "good," "ugly," "dazzling," "white" are mixed in among the French words. Would the pupils then be able to learn the French adjectives? But is not this exactly what is done in the case of the numerals? It makes no difference if the French text has 1888 or "eighteen hun-

H

dred and eighty-eight," in both cases the pupil has to translate from English to French when he is reading the passage aloud. There are scarcely any exercises at all in translating numerals from French or in understanding French numerals ; as far as this class of words is concerned, the very poorest method of translation is used, the one by which the pupil is himself required to construct expressions in the foreign language according to certain rules, without having previously had sufficient opportunity to see and hear how the foreigners themselves go about it. In the home preparation we may be very sure that only the most conscientious pupils trouble themselves to think about how 1793 ought to be read.

Then here we have a point where reform is necessary and unusually easy to bring about. Let the Arabic numerals disappear from all text-books for beginners in a foreign language, and then if they contain enough of numerals written out in full—and especially if the teacher drills the pupils a good deal in simple arithmetical exercises in the foreign language in the manner now to be suggested—it will be found that when the pupils are so far advanced as to give up text-books and read literary works, they will have no difficulty in reading all the numerals which they happen to come across fluently and correctly.

Already, at a very early stage, after one or two months' instruction, the teacher can begin with arithmetical exercises, because they do not require any great command of language; they not only give the pupils practice in the numerals themselves, but also in catching the foreign words and sounds. The question is directed, as suggested above, to the whole class, and then the teacher points out—by name or merely by a glance—the one who is to answer it ; the answer must include the question. Thus the teacher : Deux fois six, combien, Henri?—Henry : Deux fois six font douze. (Répète, Jean). Trois et neuf font, Alfred? A. : Trois et neuf font onze. T. : C'est faux, n'est-ce pas, Louis?—Louis : Oui, trois et neuf font douze. (Or : Est-ce correct, Louis? or : Est-ce bien ça, Louis?) In addition to this, sums may be set containing concrete numbers, especially such as may familiarize the pupils with the foreign coins : deux francs, combien de sous valent-ils? trois sous, combien de centimes? . . .; or a little rule-of three sum : si une poire coûte trois centimes, combien cinq poires? Or, for instance : deux œufs à deux sous et trois pommes à un sou, combien ça fait-il? The teacher must not be afraid of using several whole lessons for such exercises, and afterwards he can take a few minutes of a lesson now and then in order to keep the pupils in practice. Since of course it is not arithmetic that is being taught, it is best to stick to easy problems, mostly addition and multiplication. Of course, by way of a change, one pupil may be allowed to give a problem to another to solve.

The numerals may also fittingly be brought in when the vocabulary is to be reviewed, the boys being allowed to count with concrete numbers in a certain order, so that each boy in turn has to think of some word which has not previously been used during the lesson; it is often funny to see how eager they are to outdo each other. And it often happens that a pupil who has said Pass, suddenly recalls a whole series of words when one of his comrades mentions a word from a selection which has not been broached before; the one thought suggests another that is associated with it. In French, the pupils must also pay attention to the form of the numeral, which changes according as it precedes a vowel or a consonant.

It very seldom happens that a boy uses a word which is impossible after a numeral, as for instance, *venir* or *bonsoir* or *trot*, which indicates that he is ignorant of the word's signification, but then the whole class laughs of its own accord. But it is the easiest thing in the world to hear from the manner in which the words are said if they are really understood ; and, in case of doubt, the teacher can suddenly ask for a translation ; this is, however, generally superfluous, for the pupils only mention words which they understand, but still of course it is good for them to review them.

One of the most important exercises is to transpose a selection which has been read into *questions* and *answers*. The teacher can begin this rather early, but he must from the very beginning and always strictly require the *pupil's answer to be given in the form of a complete sentence.* We have no use for such an undignified performance in which the pupil gets along bravely if only he is able to answer all his teacher's questions with either Oui, monsieur, or Non, monsieur, or some other equally intelligent answer. As an illustration of the kind of exercise I mean, take for instance the following one based on one of the very first texts in my own French Reader, which runs :

Enfant gâté.

Veux-tu du pâté ?

Non, maman, il est trop salé !

Veux-tu du rôti ?

Non, maman, il est trop cuit !

Veux-tu du jambon ?

Non, maman, il n'est pas bon !

Veux-tu du pain ?

Non, maman, le pain ne vaut rien !

Enfant gâté, tu ne veux rien manger,

Enfant gâté, tu seras fouetté !

The following questions may be based on this piece. The pupils' answers are given in [ ]:—Es-tu un enfant? [Oui, monsieur, je suis un enfant.] Es-tu un enfant gâté? [Non, monsieur, je ne suis pas un enfant gâté.] L'enfant gâté veut-il du pâté? [Non, monsieur, il ne veut pas du paté; or : l'enfant gâté ne . . .] Veut-il du rôti? [Non, monsieur, il ne veut pas du rôti.] Veut-il du pain? [Non, monsieur, il ne veut pas du pain.] Veut-il du jambon? [Non, monsieur, il ne veut pas du jambon.] Pourquoi ne veut-il pas du pâté? [Parce que le pâté est trop salé.] Pourquoi ne veut-il pas du jambon? [Il ne veut pas du jambon parce qu'il n'est pas bon.] Pourquoi ne veut-il pas du rôti? [Parce qu'il est trop cuit.] Pourquoi ne veut-il pas du pain? [Parce que le pain ne vaut rien.] Qu'est-ce qui est trop salé? [C'est le pâté qui est trop salé.] Qu'est-ce qui ne vaut rien ? [C'est le pain qui ne vaut rien.] Qu'est-ce qui est trop cuit ? [Le jambon est trop cuit.] L'enfant gâté sera-t-il fouetté? [Oui, monsieur, il sera fouetté.] Pourquoi sera-t-il fouetté ? [Parce qu'il ne veut rien manger.] Va-t-on chercher le bâton pour taper l'enfant gâté ? [Oui, monsieur, on s'en va chercher le bâton pour venir taper l'enfant.]

Thus it will be seen that a simple little piece can suggest a large number of questions, and it is important, especially in the beginning, for the teachers to ask the pupils *as many questions as possible* in order to accustom them to the exercise, so that they may take part intelligently and fluently.   Anyone who sees all these questions in print may think that they occupy a long time in a monotonous way ; but after a little practice, on the part of both the teacher and the pupils, the exercise really proceeds very rapidly. In dealing with beginners, it were best for the teacher in formulating his questions to *deviate as little as possible from the words of the text*, so that they can be used in the answers almost or entirely without any change.   It is not assumed in this exercise that the pupils have committed the piece to memory, but of course the exercise itself tends to make them thoroughly familiar with it.   In order to give the pupils confidence, and in order not to require too much of them immediately, the teacher can in the first few lessons allow them to keep their books open while the piece is gone through once in question form, so that they can look up their answers when they cannot remember them.   Then they can be told to close their books and answer the same or almost the same questions without referring to the text.   Of course, the first few times when such an exercise is used, it is also well for the teacher to direct the same question to several boys in succession ; and the very first time he can also write a few questions with their corresponding answers on the blackboard, in order to show the class how the exercise is to proceed.

Even if the pupils learn the piece by heart in the course

of the exercise, yet their answering the teacher's questions does not become mechanical, since they have to consider the form of the question, and then reflect over what is to be included in the answer, and how it is to be worded and constructed. Of course, the teacher ought to feel gratified if the pupils of their own accord make slight alterations in the words of the book, substitute a pronoun for a substantive, etc., only it is best not to give too early encouragement to great deviations from the text. The last question of the above examples, which is based on a piece that has been read before in the same book, shows how the teacher already at a very early stage can vary a certain day's exercise by bringing into connection with it something previously learned. The pupils will greet such a question with pleasure, partly the pleasure of recognition, and partly the pleasure of the opportunity thus afforded them to feel at home in the language. As time goes, the teacher may depart more and more from the material of the book. For instance, he may use its words in asking the pupils questions about their own personal affairs, or about things in which they are interested outside of their French lessons. If they are having a selection which contains the word *roi* and the names of various countries, the teacher may say : Comment s'appelle le roi d'Angleterre? (or, notre roi?) Qui est roi d'Espagne? etc.; yes, why not also Comment s'appelle le roi de France?

In the beginning, it is only the teacher that asks questions, but it does not last very long before the teacher by way of a change can allow the *pupils themselves to ask each other questions*; thus they learn to construct sentences in the interrogative form, which, when they come to make practical use of the language, is just as important for them as to be able to answer. In German schools, they have a regular system of exercises on this plan in connection with grammatical categories ; of a given sentence in the book the pupils are to construct first a subject-question, then a verb-question, then an object-question, etc. If, for instance, the sentence is *La mère de Gribouille a cassé sa marmite*, and the teacher wants a subject-question, pupil A asks B : Qui a cassé la marmite ? (or Qui est-ce qui a cassé la marmite ?) ; or a verb-question : Qu'est-ce qu'a fait la mère de Gr. ? ; or an object-question : Qu'est-ce que la mère de Gr. a cassé ? In order to help beginners with the grammatical difficulties, several sentences may be written on the blackboard with their various parts differently underlined. Later on the teacher can tell one of the pupils to change all the sentences in a piece which has been read—of course only in so far as they lend themselves to such a change—into, for instance, object-questions. After each question, the teacher points out the one who is to answer. Then another pupil may change the same sentences (or those in the next paragraph) into subject-questions, etc. Of course the teacher must not put up with a mere mechanical alteration of the text, but must always require the pupils to exercise so much common sense that no questions are made which would not occur in a natural conversation.

When the pupils themselves ask questions, they naturally cannot do anything else but follow the text slavishly as it stands, so therefore it is not advisable always to let *them* ask the question; the teacher must on the whole avoid getting into any rut. He himself must do the asking rather frequently; he may either pounce upon some little point or ask comprehensive questions, including the gist of several sentences. Only he must remember that sentences which are too comprehensive either require too much of the pupils, or are quite empty and meaningless; besides, the result may only be that the exercise shrinks into almost nothing, since then there can only be two or three questions to correspond to a whole page of the text, and thus the text cannot make as strong and detailed an impression as it should. And, above all, the questions must be asked as naturally as possible.

If this question-exercise is used and all its possibilities for variation exhausted in the right way—with liveliness, tact and constant consideration for the pupils' standpoint—it gives ample and abundant opportunities for the teacher not only to talk to, but with, the pupils in the foreign language; and notice that it is not "talking to the pupil in a language which he does not yet understand"—this fear is often expressed by those who have misgivings as to the advisability of conversational exercises at an early stage—but from the very beginning nothing is said which the pupil cannot be required to understand and to answer intelligently in the same language.

Quite imperceptibly the teacher may pass from this exercise to *renarration*; the question has merely to be formulated in such a way that it cannot be answered in a single sentence but only by an account of the contents of at least a few lines or so. Thus longer and longer pieces may be required to be retold, although during the first years it should only be such pieces as have previously been learned and gone through in detail by means of questions and answers. Later on, the teacher can use pieces for renarration which have not been assigned to the class for preparation ; the teacher reads aloud (or may possibly let one of the pupils do it), if necessary, several times, and thereupon requires as much as possible to be retold either orally or in writing, or first orally, then in writing. Or if there is a sufficient number of copies of the book used, the pupils may be given say ten or twenty minutes in which to read the piece through silently to themselves, and then they can use the rest of the hour to write down what they can remember of it. Such exercises are used to a large extent in teaching the mother-tongue, and it is agreed that they are highly beneficial, because they not only sharpen the powers of apprehension, especially the ability to distinguish between the essential and the unessential, but they also develop linguistic technique, that is the formal command of means of expression, since much of the language used in the original creeps into the renarration and thus becomes the possession of the reteller. Of course the pupils are earlier ripe for such exercises in their native language than in foreign languages, but that does not lessen their value in the two respects mentioned, of which the latter is the more important here, while there is perhaps too great a tendency to attach the chief importance to the former in the teaching of the native tongue. Even when the pupils are far advanced, it is highly beneficial for them to give (French, etc.) reports of something which they have read—not merely simple renarrations of bits of fiction or history, but also résumés of the trend of thought in some philosophical or critical essay, etc.

Many pieces also lend themselves to *reshaping* in various ways, whereby grammatical relations may be practised at the same time as the words and sentences of the selection once more pass in review through the minds of the pupils. All the singulars may be changed to plurals, as far as the plurals make sense in the connection. After the piece has been gone through in its printed form, the pupil reads it aloud, remembering in the case of each word to consider whether or not it has to be changed to the plural and what it would be in the plural. Thus, according to circumstances, there are either nouns, adjectives, pronouns or verbs to be changed. Or what is told about a boy may be said about a girl. Changes in time from " now " to " yesterday," from " to-day " to " in a week," occasion many alterations in the forms of the verbs, fewer in the adverbs. The person may also be changed, especially in such a way that the pupil puts himself in the place of that Peter about whom something is told, and thus substitutes *I* for *he*, etc. ; if desirable, those further alterations may be made which make a letter out of the narrative. A change from the first to the third person can easily be combined with the shifting of tense which gives us indirect instead of direct discourse. Thus the following sentence : " Eh bien, Pierre, dit Jean, qu'est-ce que tu vas faire demain ? Je ne sais pas, dit Pierre," may be changed to : " Jean a demandé à Pierre ce qu'il allait faire le lendemain, et Pierre a répondu qu'il ne savait pas (qu'il n'en savait rien)." In German, this kind of transposition involves such complicated changes (person, mood, order of words) that they cannot be required until at a later stage than in French ; but transposition from indirect to direct discourse is not very difficult. Changes from the active to the passive must be undertaken with a good deal of care, since there are comparatively few sentences which can be thus transposed without undergoing a shifting of meaning, which it is not always easy to explain or understand the cause of, and many sentences do not lend themselves to such transposition at all. Likewise there are relatively few connected passages where negative sentences can be made affirmative and vice versâ without giving us sheer nonsense. So these last two kinds of transposition can, as a rule, only be applied to single sentences, which the teacher has to pick out of their connection; but when carefully selected in this way they will be found to be very useful, especially in French, where the correct placing of *ne* and *pas* is so important; they are less useful in German.

Now and then, too, dependent clauses (for instance relative, adverbial clauses, etc.) may be changed to independent clauses and vice versâ, and still more complicated changes may be undertaken by which one may try the different ways in which the thoughts of a passage may be linked together.

Of course it is also possible to have mixed exercises of this kind. For instance, pupil A reads aloud; the teacher interrupts him at the end of a sentence, mentions what kind of change it is to undergo, and thereupon points out one of the other pupils (whose books are closed) who is to make the change. But the teacher must never allow any of these exercises to become something merely mechanical which is turned out according to a certain fixed formula; the pupils must always be trained to consider whether a newly constructed sentence makes sense or not ; thereby both their linguistic intuition and their powers of logic are sharpened at the same time.

VIII

By this time we have fairly encroached upon the question as to the method to be used in training pupils in the *grammar* of a foreign language. I want to introduce my discussion of this subject with the follow quotation from N. M. Petersen (*Sprogkundskab i Norden*, Collected Works, Copenhagen, 1870, ii. 297–8):

"With respect to method, the artificial one must be given up and a more natural one must take its place. According to the artificial method, the first thing done is to hand the boy a grammar and cram it into him piece by piece, for everything is in pieces; he is filled with paradigms which have no connection with each other or with anything else in the world . . . he is filled with words, only half of which occur occasionally, and some never at all in what he reads. How old are not the complaints over this perverted method! how many sighs it has occasioned, how much deformity it has produced! On the other hand, the natural method of learning languages is by practice. That is the way one's native language is acquired. The pupil becomes acquainted with the elements and absorbs them, as it were, into his soul in their entirety before he is conciously able to separate and account for the single parts and their special relations ; he forms whole complete sentences without knowing which is the subject and which the object ; he gradually finds out that he has to give each part of the sentence its correct endings without knowing anything about tense or case. . . . The logical consequence of this, then, is that as a rule one cannot begin with grammar in teaching languages to a child of ten or twelve. His first years at school ought to give him merely materials ; he ought to collect experiences (that is a child's greatest delight), but not speculate over them."

It is now now half a century ago since N. M. Petersen uttered these golden words, and still the old grammar-instruction lives and flourishes with its rigmaroles and rules and exceptions, *that intensely stupid custom, the teaching of grammar to children*, as Herbert Spencer calls it. Only few of the boys in our schools who have studied German for several years, are able to connect for instance *um* with the proper case without hesitation ; but there are certainly still fewer who cannot run through *durch für gegen ohne um* and *wider* like parrots. But strangely enough this ever present phenomenon does not yet seem to have led to a general acknowledgment of the fact that these grammatical rigmaroles as a rule are scarcely worth as much as the counting-out rigmaroles of the children : eeny meeny miny mo.[1]

And, of course, paradigms which are learned by rote also belong to the category of rigmaroles. " Paradigms ought by all means to be given, but should never be learned by

[1] The only thing in the grammar which it might be reasonable to learn by rote is the numerals.

heart in rigmarole-fashion." (N. M. Petersen.) Thoughtlessness and stupidity thrive excellently on this continual repetition of words as words, that is words without any mutual
association, without connection in sentences.   Just think of
the many thousands of boys and girls who time and again
recite : *mourir, mourant, mort, je meurs, je mourus,* and
then ask how many of them, yes even of their teachers,
ever happen to think that the last form in reality is impossible (at all events in conversations in this life).[1]   The per-
centage is scarcely very large.   And when conscientious
philologists like Ayer and Sachs give imperative forms like
nais, naissons, naissez—be born ! let us be born ! ! be ye
born ! ! ! it cannot be denied that we are tempted to use the
exclamation : " die gelehrten, die verkehrten ! " Of course
it is not our aim to get rid of such forms as *je mourus* ;[2]
what is wrong is the system.   I condemn *vivre, vivant,
vécu, je vis, je vécus* just as strongly as *mourir*, etc., even if
none of these forms is really meaningless.   And the reason
why I reject this method of teaching languages is because it
does not and cannot bring us to our desired goal.   The chief
absurdity, the one which it is our business to quarrel with,

---

[1] The story goes that a Swedish dialectologist who was on a tour to investigate how extensively the strong form *dog* (died) was in use, asked
a peasant : do you people here say " jag dog " or " jag döde " ? The
peasant was not a grammarian ; he answered sensibly : well, when we
are dead we generally do not say anything.

[2] Kr. Nyrop informs me that he has found " Mais je mourus hier "
in Mairet, La Silvanire, v. 2,175 ; and I myself have come across it in
a short story by Zola about the sensations felt by a person who has
been buried alive after his apparent death—but that does not make the
form more " living."

is that use of disconnected words for grammatical purposes, which flourishes in all our text-books.

It has often amused me to examine grown-up persons (non-philologists) in what they could remember of the instruction they had received in school in foreign languages. It seems to be extremely common that they have not the slightest idea as to what case for instance a preposition governs, but the rigmarole in which it occurs they generally know by heart. They also know ever so many scraps like *der buchstabe, der friede, der funke* . . . or *das amt, das ass, das bad, das bild, das blatt* . . . but why they have learned these things, and what they were supposed to be good for, to these questions there is generally no answer forthcoming. So those rigmaroles are really of no practical use whatever.

Now, of course, rigmaroles could easily be so arranged— though no one seems to have put it into practice—as to contain an indication of the object in grouping together just those words, for instance by saying *durch das zimmer, für, gegen* . . . or *durch für* . . . *um wider mich*, or *das amt. die ämter, das ass* . . . or *das amt, ämter, bäder, bilder.* . . .

But even in this improved form it seems to me that grammatical rigmaroles are of little value just because they accustom the pupils to learn and say things by rote without *thinking*; they are remnants of the old-fashioned would-be pedagogy where a teacher in any subject was satisfied if the pupil only "knew his lesson," that is, could recite the words of the book, and where no one ever thought about understanding or other such-like modern inventions.

The expressions "living" and "dead" are so often used

I

about languages and words, but those who use them do not always take the trouble to consider in what sense these expressions really have any meaning. A language only lives, and can only live, in a person's mind, and that it lives there means that its component parts are for him associated with certain ideas, which are recalled when he hears the words, and which in turn summon up the corresponding words when he wants to express them, or when he simply wants to make them clear for himself. But ideas do not and cannot exist except in combinations ; an absolutely isolated thought is the same as nothing. It is the same with words ; if they are taken out of their natural surroundings, they suffer atrophy and at last cease to perform the usual function of words, namely to produce ideas. So isolated words, such as are given in rigmaroles and paradigms, are only ghosts or corpses of words. Try to run through the words "jewel, stone, cabbage, knee, owl, toys, louse," and see if a single complete picture has been produced in your mind—but you are no better off when you say the French rigmarole *bijou, caillou, chou, genou, hibou, joujou, pou.* That, as well as *amo, amas, amat, amamus, amatis, amant* and all the others, must by virtue of the fundamental psychical law of the life of language become merely empty jingle and nothing else. Now we see the psychological reason why sensible persons can write such sentences in their books as *je mourus* or the entirely parallel "Wir sind nicht hier." When the mind is occupied with a word as a grammatical phenomenon, the word's normal power of calling forth ideas is of course lessened in a considerable degree.

Furthermore the isolation of words for grammatical purposes may even lead us to make positive mistakes. The pupils are first carefully taught in the grammar that " nobody " in French is *ne personne* and " never " *ne jamais*,[1] and later on it is corrected as a serious mistake when they write *ne personne parlait* or *il ne jamais parle*, mistakes which would never have occurred if the pupils had not been allowed to learn the false formulation. In modern French " nobody " is *personne* and "never" *jamais*, just as "not" is *pas*, etc. *Ne* only exists in connection with a verb, and ought never to be seen or learned by the pupils except in its natural surroundings; out of connection it is no more a word than *un* (in *unfriendly, ungracious*, etc.). The rule for its employment can be thus stated in short, that it is placed in front of the verb, always, if the sentence is wholly negative, also often if it is only half negative (by which I mean the well-known cases after *empêcher, craindre*, comparatives, etc., where *ne* is well on the way to slip out of the living French language, and where we now, after the last ministerial decrees, may allow ourselves a little laxity in teaching these points).[2] Likewise it is only injurious to teach the children that " I " is *je*, " thou " *tu*—as a matter of fact it is *moi, toi*, while of

---

[1] The dots which are given in the printed book between the two words disappear in oral recitation ; so they play no part in the minds of the pupils.

[2] The former " redundant " words are now the most important ones, indeed in reality the only important ones, since *Pas du tout* etc., where there is no verb, is fully recognized, and sentences like *Je veux pas* are becoming more and more common in colloquial language.

course " I go, thou goest," is *je vais, tu vas ;* what usage
has joined together, let no grammar put asunder.

But words, when in their natural connections, show their
vitality in other ways besides in summing up the correct
ideas ; they have another power, which they also lose when
they are isolated, namely the power of breeding new connections in the image of the old ones. If I have often
reproduced a certain type of word-formation or sentence-
construction, then this becomes a part of my mental
mechanism in such a way that I unconsciously make something new (coin a new word, construct a new sentence)
after the same pattern, after the " analogy " of what I
know, whenever I need it, just as the English boy who
has often heard superlatives like *hardest, cleanest, highest,*
etc., does not need any rule to be able to construct forms
like *purest, ugliest, dirtiest,* of his own accord, and who, at
the moment when he says them, would not be able even
by means of the most scrupulous analysis to decide if he
has heard the form often before and is merely reproducing it, or if he himself is creating it without having previously heard it—and, if the latter is the case, if he is
creating something which others also have created, or if it
is the very first time that the word is used in the language
—this is what takes place every minute wherever human
languages are spoken.[1]   An Englishman has so often
heard (and repeated) sentences like " give the man your
hand," " I gave the boy a whipping," " he gave his sister

---

[1] Cf. my remarks on " schaffende und erhaltende analogiebild-
ung," in Techmer's *Internat. Zeitschr. f. allgem. Sprachwissensch.,* iii.
(1887), p. 191 ff.

an apple," that he unconsciously forms his sentences according to a scheme where the indirect object always precedes the direct object, and which even without this grammatical terminology and without any rule would lead him quite naturally to say, for instance, "Will you give your father the money?" A Frenchman would just as instinctively say, "Veux-tu donner cet argent à ton père?" because in all the sentences which he has experienced he has heard the "dative" expressed by *à* after the direct object.

But since this takes place by virtue of inviolable psychical laws, it applies not only to the mother-tongue, but also to the foreign languages which we learn later. We simply cannot avoid thus unconsciously forming types or patterns to go by, in using a foreign language, as soon as the conditions for these typical formations are at hand. If, on learning English, a Dane has frequently heard (read) and (especially) used combinations like *up here, in here, in there, out there,* then he will quite naturally say *down there* when he wants to express this thought; it is not at all necessary for him previously to have learned a rule to the effect that "*here* and *there* in connection with other adverbs of place stand last." As a matter of fact, when we speak or write a foreign language, we employ a number of such rules which we have never seen formulated, and, what is more, also rules which have never at any time been consciously formulated by any grammarian. The reason why we cannot attain the same confidence in all departments of the foreign language that we feel in our native language is of course partly because the conditions are not so favourable, and partly because our mother-tongue acts as a hindrance on account of the tendency it has to intrude on all occasions and mislead us to construct sentences after *its* pattern.

But the conditions become the more favourable for this unconscious mental activity in our pupils the more we know how to make each sentence in the foreign language have its full effect upon them and become their possession, and the more we can keep the mother-tongue in the background. And although we can never bring it about that our pupils come across the forms in the foreign language even approximately as often as that child does who is learning his native language, yet we can to a large extent make amends for this by bringing a better system into our teaching, so that the acquiring of the language will not depend so much upon chance as is the case when babies learn to talk, just as it is also an advantage that our pupils are older and more developed, and that we can get some help from the written and printed language.

Many of the transposition exercises mentioned in the last section are essentially grammatical, but we can easily hit upon still more exercises by which we may in a systematic way encourage the natural tendency toward type- and series-formations. To conjugate a verb all the way through by itself is the sheerest drudgery, but the exercise immediately becomes both more interesting and more beneficial when it is a whole sentence that is to be tackled. For instance, the teacher can write on the blackboard a sentence like " Je donne un sou à Alfred " and get the pupils to conjugate it through all the persons. In the beginning he might also write down all the forms of the verb, one under the other; they are not to be committed to memory, but merely furnish a scheme, which the pupils are to fill out by inserting the correct pronouns before, and *un sou à Alfred* after the verb. Then the next step is to let the pupils use other words instead of *un sou* and *Alfred*, so that pupil A says, for instance, *Je donne un centime à Paul.* B : *tu donnes un franc à Jean.* C : *il donne un livre à papa.* D : *nous donnons des poires à l'épicier*, etc. Then in reality the task which the boys have before them is to hit upon new words to insert (they must make sense!); consequently it becomes a kind of game in which the vocabulary is reviewed like the one mentioned above (p. 99), but at the same time the forms of the verb are practised. If a pupil should happen to say, for instance, *ils donnent deux cerises à le maître*, the teacher must only say the sentence himself with the correct *au* and make him repeat it in this form without scolding him,—yes, even without stopping to give a long explanation of why it should be *au* and not *à le* in this case. This kind of exercise can of course be varied in different ways; such a sentence as *mon père me donne de l argent* is written down, and the pupils are told to inflect it in all the persons, which of course only involves an alteration of *mon* and *me*; or the sentence is to be reconstructed with other tenses, etc. More complicated sentences, too, may be conjugated all the way through, either without changing anything but the pronouns and the forms of the verbs, as for instance, *Je suis allé me promener avec mon père; Das habe ich ihm gestern versprochen, und ich werde es ihm morgen geben*—or in such a way that other things are changed too : *je m'appelle* . . . where the pupil is to insert real names (his own, a comrade's . . . in case it is *vous*, the teacher's) ; *Ich habe meinen vater um etwas brot gebeten. Du hast deinen vater um etwas geld gebeten. Er hat seinen vater um ein stück papier gebeten. Sie hat ihren vater um einen kuchen gebeten*, etc. Of course one can also assign written exercises of a similar kind, as for instance : construct five sentences like *Le père* de *Jean* est allé à la maison de *sa sœur*, using different words in each sentence in place of those here italicized, etc., etc. ; but it were best if these sentences were suggested by, or in some way associated with, sentences in the text-book.

Now some people will say that this is only another way of employing those grammatical isolated sentences which I have declaimed against—and they are right in so far as I admit that the more the exercises are made to resemble the old-fashioned ones, the poorer they are for the purpose, and if they are employed to too great an extent they may easily degenerate into tiresome mechanical routine-work. But if used to moderation they will only be beneficial, and then, besides, they differ from the single sentences of the old method in being associated with a text which has been read, so they are not thus quite isolated from a sensible connection ; they also differ because translation is not used and is not needed (except when the teacher at long intervals has to make sure that pupil A has understood a sentence given by pupil C, who has used an unusual word) ; they differ because, translation being omitted, the whole exercise can proceed at a rapid pace ; they differ because the sentences are constructed by the pupils themselves, who are thus compelled all the time to pay attention both to their form and contents ; and finally they differ because, as a result of all this, they are more interesting and amusing to the pupils. Furthermore such exercises incite the pupils to want to say something of their own accord, and thus they get a desire to extend their knowledge; they will frequently ask what this or that word which they need in a sentence is in French or German—and in that case the teacher must always answer, but then he must always require, too, that they *learn* the word which has been given them (to prevent them from getting into the habit of asking superficially and carelessly just " for the fun of it "). Finally the pupils will thus be brought to appreciate the benefit of learning grammar; their grammatical knowledge is not sheer theory for them, but is continually converted into effective power and thus becomes easier to remember, for there is no doubt that Goethe is right when he says : "Still all that we can remember of our studies in the end is only what we have been able to find practical use for."

Of course, the sentences constructed by the pupils in the course of any one of the exercises recommended in this book may contain mistakes, and the most serious mistakes must be corrected, yet with as little particularity as possible, if they have nothing to do with the phenomenon which is being or just has been carefully considered and practised, and with as few theoretical reasons as possible. Many exercises can be so arranged that it is scarcely possible for the pupils to make any mistake, and this without becoming less valuable ; on the contrary, they will often be the best, for every sentence which a pupil constructs or says correctly confirms good habits of language.   But no matter how much one may favour the theory that " Prevention is better than cure," it is not well to be too anxious to prevent mistakes.   One of the ablest advocates of the reform in Germany, Wendt, says : " It is of more importance for the pupil to talk at all than to talk correctly," and although I know what criticism I have to expect from unsympathetic opponents about my encouraging superficiality and not caring a bit about correctness, yet I cannot deny myself the pleasure of quoting with approbation a Slavic proverb, *Tko zeli dobro govoriti mora natucati* (whoever wants to speak well must murder the language), which Schuchardt has chosen as a motto for his stimulating work about mixed languages,[1] and which he interprets : " Wer aus irgend einem grunde sich scheut eine fremde sprache zu misshandeln, der werd sie nie beherrschen."

In order to reassure people who cannot help feeling anxious, I shall add here three statements from the report of the ninth German " Neuphilologentag " (1901).   Klinghardt (p. 100) confesses that he has been converted to the reform, because, in spite of years of vigorous efforts, he had not succeeded by means of the translation method[2] in training the majority of his pupils to grammatical correctness.   Headmasters of schools where the old method was employed had also told him that there were still serious grammatical mistakes of form in the written exercises which

---

[1] *Slawo-deutsches und Slawo-italienisches,* Graz, 1885.
[2] i.e. Translations from the mother-tongue, beginning with single sentences of the usual kind.

were handed in at the final examinations. But, after he had given up the translation procedure, all of his pupils, even the backward ones, had attained to grammatical correctness. Wendt (p. 101) emphatically denied that anything could be gained in grammatical sureness by translation exercises. And Walter (p. 102) repudiated the accusation which is always on the tongue of many of the opponents of reform, that the reformers entirely do away with grammar, by referring to many of these very gentlemen, who, on visiting his school, had expressed surprise at the grammatical sureness displayed by his pupils.

And since I now seem to be in the mood for quotations, I can also refer to Goethe's words : " Thus I had learned Latin, just like German, French, English, only through practice, without rule and without system. Anyone who knows what the state of school instruction was at that time will not find it strange that I neglected the grammar as well as the rhetoric ; everything seemed to come naturally to me. I retained the words, their formations and transformations in my ear and in my mind, and I employed the language with ease for writing and talking."[1]

In giving the pupil English sentences to translate into the foreign language, we are only artificially creating difficulties. If it is difficult for the pupil to translate into his mother-tongue where at least confirmed habit ought to prevent him from falling into the worst pitfalls, then it must be much more difficult, indeed impossible, to translate into

[1] *Aus meinem leben*, II. vi. Goethes werke, Cotta'sche bibl. d. welt-litteratur. 20. 218.

a foreign language where he is not yet quite at home. We ourselves lead the pupil to make mistakes, and then we have to do all we can to prevent his confronting us with a too overwhelming number of them.   To this end we limit each exercise to illustrating one, or two, or three, paragraphs in the grammar ; we make theoretical rules to serve as a guide in translating, without always remembering how difficult it is to make practical use of such rules ; we bracket the words which are not to be translated ; we try to be helpful by placing alongside of, or underneath, the correct English, some very strange English indeed, which, however, has the advantage that it can be translated literally, etc., etc.   And the result of all this exertion ?   Well, it is a well known fact that they are not always things of beauty that we meet with in the French exercises which are handed in after many years of toil, according to this method.   Experience is sure to teach us that this is not the means to our end.   Joh. Storm is right when he says (*Franske taleövelser*, Preface) : "The worst and most unfruitful torment in the school instruction of the present time is the excessive use of written exercises in foreign languages." As a bright contrast to this "constructive" method of procedure, we have the "imitative" method, which may be so called partly because it is an imitation of the way in which a child learns his native language, partly because it depends upon that invaluable faculty, the natural imitative instinct of the pupils, to give them the proper linguistic feeling, if it only has ample opportunity to come into play.   As a motto for this method, we might perhaps say : Away with lists and rules.   Practise what is right again and again !

IX

" But our pupils must not only know their foreign languages unconsciously and mechanically; they must not
only learn how to express themselves, but they must also
know why." When I think of the instruction in grammar
that has been usual hitherto, I am tempted to say as if in
echo, " Why ? "

In a school in Copenhagen, the story goes that a certain
teacher after having asked about the gender of the French
substantive *mort* and then " Why ? " got the answer,
"Because it comes from Latin *mors*, which is feminine ";
he was not satisfied with that, however, but made the
correction : " No, it is because it is an exception." When
we feel scandalized at this teacher's stupidity, we ought
conscientiously to ask ourselves if many of the answers
given to the question " Why ? " in grammar teaching are in
reality much more valuable than this one; the object in
most cases is merely to classify the sentences or words
under certain given rubrics and to give their names and
the respective rules which have been committed to memory,
something which can in large part be done with very little
real grammatical understanding of the language in question.

The usual superstition that theoretical instruction in

grammar is the best way to teach pupils how to express themselves grammatically is of a piece with the severity with which grammatical mistakes are criticized in comparison with the mildness with which mistakes of vocabulary, etc., are treated.

That grammatical propositions are abstractions, which are often difficult even for experts to understand, and which must therefore be far beyond the horizon of our pupils, we see from the way in which most philologists, on coming across a rule which is the least bit involved, immediately have to resort to the examples to see what the point is ; we also see it from the difficulty which grammarians often find in expressing their rules in such a way as to be really clear. Therefore there is even among persons who have to any extent studied languages theoretically (and perhaps most among them) a great tendency to avoid as much as possible the traditional, grammatical, theoretical method when they want to take up a new language; this feeling has been clearly expressed by the renowned Romance scholar H. Schuchardt.[1] It is true, as has been said, that one really cannot begin to learn the grammar of a language until one knows the language itself.

In contrast to our school-days, when in all subjects a ready-made system was pounded into us, and it was only through the system that we caught sight of some of the facts upon which it was built, so that we indulged in only

[1] Obwohl ich mich seit geraumer zeit mit der theorie der sprachen beschäftige, hege ich noch heutzutage eine abneigung gegen die systematischen sprachlehren.—*Auf anlass des volapüks.* Berlin, 1888, p. 38.

extremely little of anything like independent observation or classification of observations, in contrast to all this, another method of procedure is coming to the front in all teaching, a method which starts out from the things which the child itself can see in its surroundings, a method which trains the child to observe, to classify its observations, to draw its own conclusions, so that finally, when the time is ripe, the scientific system will raise itself, as it were, in a natural way on the foundation of the observations made. The golden rule is : " Never tell the children anything that they can find out for themselves."

Theoretical grammar ought not to be taken up too early, and when it is taken up it is not well to do it in such a way that the pupil is given ready-made paradigms and rules. After the manner of Spencer's " Inventional Geometry," where the pupil is all the way through led to find out the propositions and proofs for himself, we ought to get an *Inventional Grammar.* When a selection in the reader has been read, the pupils may be asked to go through it again (read it aloud), and pay special attention, for instance, to the personal pronouns ; every time one occurs, it is to be written down on the blackboard ; there the forms are finally classified (by the pupils !) according to the natural associations between them, and thus the paradigms are constructed quite naturally ; then, if desired, the pupils can copy them down in special note-books for future reference. For instance, if the French possessive pronoun is found in the two forms *son* and *sa,* in the combinations *sa main, son gant, son épée, son ennemi, sa figure, sa blessure, son opinion,* the object of the pupils must be to discover

the principle of usage. It will not be found difficult
to formulate a rule in these cases; but, if necessary, the
teacher can help the pupils not a little by means of the
emphasis with which he reads the sentences in which the,
forms are found. Then the rule once formulated may be
tested on other forms to see if the same principle of usage
should happen to apply there too, etc.

Of course the teacher must decide beforehand[1] what
points of grammar a certain text is especially fitted to illustrate in this manner. Yet it is not necessary for all the
forms which it is desired to group together to occur in the
piece which is being examined; if there are any empty
spaces in the paradigms, the pupils will of their own accord
desire to get them filled out, and they will thus have an
opportunity to learn something new. It will also frequently
happen that the missing forms are already familiar to the
pupils from previous reading; in that case, if the pupils
themselves do not happen to think of them, the teacher
can easily give them a clue by saying the beginning of the
sentence in which they occur.[2]

[1] If the text-book itself does not recommend certain exercises for
each piece.

[2] On the whole teachers who read connected pieces with their pupils
in the thorough manner which I have suggested, will be surprised at the
strong powers of association produced by successiveness; one word
always recalls the whole context in which it has been learned. In one
of the exercises given by Walter, pupil A mentions one of the words which
the class has had and then the name of pupil B, who is thereupon
expected to give the whole sentence in which the word occurs. Of
course this can be done now and then by way of recreation; as a rule
it is not necessary. This new method of always learning and remembering the words in their natural context may be compared to the newest
methods in natural history teaching, according to which the pupils

594

It follows as a matter of course that only the most elementary things can be so examined in a text of one or two pages that grammatical rules or a tolerably adequate paradigm can be formulated. In dealing with beginners the teacher must not be too ambitious to get, for instance, all the forms of a verb collected in that manner, at all events not all at once; it is not necessary; one tense at a time is quite sufficient. And of course one must not be such a slave of traditional grammatical systems, that one necessarily must go all the way through one class of words before beginning another, etc. There is no reason why these bits of system should not be taken up quite unsystematically, one day a little about pronouns, another day the present tense of verbs, a third day the comparison of adjectives, etc., all according to what comes natural, or what the texts give occasion for.[1] And it will not matter if some time is allowed to pass between these exercises. One of the abominations of the old method of instruction was that the teacher, as a Swedish author has expressed it, considered it his duty on all occasions to feel the grammatical pulse of the pupils.

must see the animals and plants as they are at home in their natural surroundings, acted upon by them and in turn acting upon them.

[1] Each phenomenon which is taken up should, however, be treated to the end with as much thoroughness as is possible at *that* standpoint. Grammar ought not to be taken up during the lesson merely as a matter of secondary importance, subordinated to other exercises, whose object is to help the pupils to understand the text, or to develo their practical skill in the language. If the teacher does not want to devote a whole hour to the grammar, he can at least draw a shar line between these exercises in theory and the other exercises. One thing at a time, and that done well!

K

A teacher in English can, at a rather early stage, set to work in this way to examine and formulate the use of English *do* as an auxiliary verb. A rather long piece which has been read is assigned to the pupils in parts, so that A and B get the first page, C and D the next, etc., and they are to find and note down all the cases which occur. Then the cases found are gone through in the class in such a way that the teacher first requires all those sentences to be read aloud where *do* occurs and there is no negation. After some sentences have been read, he may ask what they have in common ; if no one answers, more sentences may be taken until someone discovers that all the sentences are interrogative, and then this discovery may be tested in the following sentences. Thereupon the negative sentences which were before omitted are gone through. Is it then necessary to have *do* in all questions, and in all negative sentences ? Well, go through the same pages again for next time and note down all the cases of interrogative and negative sentences where *do* does not occur. Then in the next lesson we shall finally be able to formulate the rules. This takes longer than to learn the rule in a grammar. Yes, but then we may also be certain that it will be far better understood and remembered, to say nothing of the pleasure it always gives to discover something oneself ; it has all of it been a little preliminary practice in scientific methods of research and drawing of conclusions. And then—what I always return to—the whole exercise has also been a review of a number of sentences, and there is not much danger that the pupils will forget the words, turns of expression and

596

grammatical relations which they have become intimate with in this manner.

Even if we do not attain to any results that can stand comparison with the rules in our text-books, yet such lessons in grammatical observation and systematization are none the less valuable. For instance, the last three or four days' German lesson may be gone through with special attention given to the gender. One pupil reads aloud; every time he comes to a substantive, he mentions one of his class-mates (or the teacher motions to one of them), who is to give the gender,[1] as well as the reasons for his inference (the form of the article in *in der kirche*, the termination of the adjective in *ein schönes mädchen*, etc.); one of the boys stands at the blackboard, which is divided into three columns, and writes down each word in the right column, after its gender is determined. When the form or the context does not show the gender, the teacher asks if the word is familiar from previous passages, and if the gender could be seen there; otherwise the teacher will have to say what gender it is. At last (toward the end of the lesson, or when the blackboard is full), all the words are repeated together with the article; then, if it seems fit, the teacher may examine one or another pupil, letting him stand with his back to the blackboard. If there are, for instance, two or three words ending in *ung* or *schaft* or some other absolutely certain ending, the pupils may be asked to recall other words with the same ending, and then formulate the

---

[1] Or when a period is reached, he may give all the substantives which he has found one at a time—the rest as above. The advantage of this is that the connexion is kept intact.

rule for themselves.   A few hours employed in this manner will surely bear much more fruit than if all the long rules for gender with their exceptions and exceptions to exceptions were committed to memory ; the attention is roused and the powers of observation are sharpened, so that the pupils will also in the future take note of the gender of new words, when there is anything to indicate it, especially since it is necessary for them to know the gender of the words which they need in the conversation and transposition exercises already described in this book.

Difficult, especially syntactical, phenomena which do not occur very frequently, cannot be treated exactly in this way, but some of them may be taken up in an analogical manner. During the going over of a large section of the French reader, the attention may, for instance, be directed to the subjunctive, so that each subjunctive form is either written down in a notebook or marked in the margin of the reader ; after one or two weeks or so, all these sentences may be collected and arranged in large groups.   During the next week, similar cases are frequently met with, and the pupil is given an opportunity to recall his recent observations, and perhaps supplement them by newly discovered varieties of subjunctive clauses, etc.   But it must be continually borne in mind that much of what is found in grammars is really of no value except to the philological specialist, and should never be learned by schoolboys.

A systematical grammar is not superfluous except in the first stage.   Later on its examples may be used to supplement those collected in the course of the reading ; the teacher can, for instance, read them aloud, make sure that they are understood, and use them to help the pupils to find out the rule. Then, when the pupils have formulated the rule as well as they can, it may be read as rendered in the grammar. To go through the grammar from one end to the other, a section at a time, ought not to be undertaken until most of the phenomena have been treated in connexion with the reading; it will then be both easier and more interesting than if taken up earlier; its chief use will then be to fill out and confirm what has already been learned.[1]

If grammar is taught in this way, the pupils will not get that feeling which they now so frequently have, that they are just learning a series of arbitrarily prescribed instructions as to how they are to avoid making mistakes and getting "poor marks" in their written exercises; they are more apt to conceive of it as something to be compared to the laws of nature, those general comprehensive observations of what takes place under certain conditions; for grammar is made up of observations of the manner in which the natives express themselves. The pupils no longer say to themselves: "We *must* have the subjunctive in purpose clauses for it stands in § 235," but "we find the subjunctive in all purpose clauses." The teacher's chief task is to give the

---

[1] Dr. Sweet tries to throw ridicule on my suggestion as to inventional grammar (*The Practical Study of Languages*, 1899, p. 115–116); he seems to forget the distinction between independent grammatical research and teaching in schools; and when he speaks about the boys having to sort "a hundredweight or so of slips," I think his exaggeration needs no further refutation than the above statements, which are nothing but an amplification of what I wrote in 1886. Fortunately, on p. 117, Dr. Sweet recommends practically the same course as is outlined here, only carried out to a less extent.

pupils insight into the construction of the foreign language, into its peculiarities and the chief points in which it deviates from other languages. As a rule, text-books dwell too much on details, and often neglect very important features, such as for instance the great freedom allowed in English in the use of substantives as verbs and vice-versâ, the different part played by order of words in the different languages, the cause and effect relationship between a fixed order of words and paucity of case-endings, etc.

The usual arrangement of grammatical material is not as shrewd as it might be. The sharp division between accidence and syntax as we find it in most of our text-books is, from a scientific point of view, untenable and impracticable[1]; from a pedagogical point of view it is unfortunate, because it separates form and function, which ought to be learned together, just as well as a word's exterior (its sounds and spelling), and its meaning are learned together.[2] And within each of these two parts of the grammar, the usual order of procedure depends upon a meaningless order of precedence between the classes of words, whereby the adverbs are placed about as far as possible from the adjectives, though if there are any two classes of words which ought to belong together, they are these two, which have comparison in common. In the

---

[1] The French superlative is a purely syntactical, the comparative, a mixed phenomenon.

[2] I have treated accidence and syntax together in my own little English grammar (*Kortfattet engelsk grammatik for tale- og skriftsproget*, Copenhagen, 1st edition 1885, 4th ed. 1903).

case of the verbs, those things are often grouped together which belong together lexically but not grammatically.[1]

The translation-method is injurious here too, because it veils contours which ought to be sharp. For instance, the pupils will not get the proper conception of gender and its relation to expressions for sex, if *er* referring to *der hut* and *sie* referring to *die bank*, and likewise *il* referring to *le chapeau*, and *elle* referring to *la chaise*, are all translated by the English *it*, while the same pronouns, when used about persons, are translated by *he* and *she*.

Comparisons between the languages which the pupils know, for the purpose of showing their differences of economy in the use of linguistic means of expression, will only be a natural outcome of this systematized occupation with the theory of the language, and may often become very interesting, especially for advanced students. (Comparisons between the reflexive pronouns in the different languages ; du ihr Sie sie—toi vous vous ils elles eux— you you you they—il y a, es giebt, there is, etc.). The teacher may call attention to the inconsistency of the languages ; what is distinctly expressed in one case is in another case not designated by any outward sign (haus häuser ; häuschen häuschen—house houses ; sheep sheep —cheval chevaux ; vers vers—yes in reality also maison, maisons, etc. ; mich mir, dich dir, sich sich ; der mann, die frau, das weib ; ein guter mann, eine gute frau, ein gutes weib ; der gute mann, die gute frau, das

---

[1] With reference to grammatical systematization, I may refer to my preliminary remarks in *Progress in Language* (London, Sonnen- schein 894), p. 138 ff.

gute weib; die männer, die frauen, die weiber; die guten m., f., w., etc.). In French and English, there is ample occasion to point out how differently the grammatical relations present themselves in sound and on paper (singular and plural alike in bon bons, beau beaux, hideux hideux, further amer amère, clair claire, révolutionnaire révolutionnaire | church churches, judge judges | sin sinned, fine fined | say said, lay laid, etc.). That this may be a good way to make a beginning in comparative philology scarcely needs further proof; many things belonging to this field of study can be understood by our advanced pupils, and ought to belong to a good general education. Everyone who has received a little more than the most ordinary school education ought to understand what is meant by the relationship and development of languages; he ought to be acquainted with such linguistic phenomena as the loss of sounds, assimilation, analogical formations, differentiations, etc.; he ought to have noticed examples of these phenomena, both in his mother tongue and in the foreign languages which he has learned, just as he ought to realize how these processes continually influence the whole construction of the languages, and, in the course of time, have produced such great differences as those he sees between German and English, or between Latin and French; a valuable point of departure would be to take up the fate of French loan-words in English with the frequent retention of the old French sounds (*ch* in *chase, j* in *journal, n* in *cousin cousine, s* in *beast, feast,* etc.). But however interesting and valuable these things are, it is scarcely advisable to devote too much time to them as long as the living languages have so few hours at their disposal. How much or how little of this sort of thing the teacher takes up will also, to a great extent, depend upon whether the class on the whole is ripe for it, and if the pupils show sufficient interest and desire to ask questions ; very much philology ought not to be *forced* upon them.

Exercises in systematization need not be limited to the field of grammar ; the lexical side of the language may also be taken up in a similar manner, even if to a less extent. Several methods of reviewing vocabulary have been mentioned above, but there are still more ways ; for instance the teacher may give the pupil a certain subject (the human body, war, a railway journey) about which he is to collect all the words and expressions which he can remember—or which occurred in the last narrative read—and he may also arrange them in various subdivisions. This can best be done in the form of a written exercise.

The pupils may also be set to separate a complex event or series of actions, etc., into its single component parts. For instance, they may describe the process of getting dressed in all its details, or the way to school in the morning. The more detailed the pupils can make their descriptions, the better ; they thus get use for a number not only of substantives but especially of verbs in their natural connection, which they see before them in their " mind's eye "—but I scarcely think that Gouin's ideas[1] ought to be used for more than such occasional series.

---

[1] I am tempted here to enlarge upon Gouin's method of teaching languages, but I have neither the space, nor exactly the desire, to do so, since I have never seen it carried out in practice. I can refer to

Advanced students may also be instructed in a systematic collecting of the most important synonyms. Each one should have a special note-book for the purpose, where a whole page is given to each group of synonyms which the teacher wants them to treat ; on this page they write down all those sentences where they come across the word in question. Now and then the teacher and the class together may examine all the sentences which have been collected and try to establish the difference between the synonyms on the basis of the examples found. Of especial value are of course those sentences where several synonyms occur directly after each other (How much of *history* we have in the *story* of Arthur is doubtful. What is not very thrilling as *story* may be of profound interest as *history*. Half a *loaf* is better than no *bread*. A nice little *loaf* of brown *bread*). It will also be of interest occasionally to draw up comparative tabular lists from different languages as for instance—

mensch	man	homme
mann	man	homme
mann	husband	mari

to which remarks may be added about the use of *human being* and *individu* when indication of sex is to be avoided. Furthermore—

| weib | woman | femme |
| weib, frau | wife | femme |

R. Kron's (certainly too enthusiastic) description (*Die neueren sprachen*, III, also published separately), and to Brekke's (for me absolutely convincing) criticism : " Indberetning om en stipendierejse til England for at studere Gouins metode for undervisning i sprog " (Quousque Tandem No. = Norske univ. og skoleannaler, 1894).

frau	lady	dame
frau	Mrs.	madame
dame	lady	dame
baum	tree	arbre
holz	wood	bois
wald	wood, forest	bois, forêt

Such tables will do more than long explanations to illustrate the differences between the languages, and to show how often words are ambiguous and vague in meaning. It is evident, however, that many of the subtle and fanciful indications of shades of meaning found in the dictionaries of synonyms are entirely beyond the grasp of ordinary pupils.

Dr. Walter, in Frankfurt, has still another way of furthering his pupils' familiarity with the resources of the foreign language ; he dictates some of the sentences from what has been read, and lets the pupils themselves find as many different ways as possible of expressing the same thought. I shall reprint one of the sentences from his book, together with the pupils' variants (marked with letters) ; they were written down in the course of 25 minutes : " ohne vorausgegangene besprechung " (in the second year of instruction, with, so far as I know, six hours a week) ; as will be seen, the variations are rather considerable.

The advantage of the English ships lay not in bulk, but in construction.

- a. The English were overwhelming, not by the size of the ships, but their power lay in the construction of the ships.
- b. In construction, not in bulk, lay the advantage of the English ships.

c. The English ships were superior to the Spanish not in bulk, but in construction.

d. The advantage of the English fleet (squadron) consisted not in bulk, but in construction.

e. The advantage of the English was the light construction of their ships.

f. The English had not large ships, but they were better constructed.

g. The power of the vessels of the English was not caused by the extent, but by the construction of the ships.

h. The English men-of-war could do very much against the enemy, because they were well constructed, and not too large.

i. The English vessels were not large, but well constructed.

k. The advantage of the English men-of-war did not consist in size, but in construction.

l. The advantage of the English men-of-war was to be found in their construction.

I have myself, in teaching advanced pupils, in a similar way, let them re-write a half a page or so of a historical work. It has always interested them, and the comparison of the results, which often presented the most varied expressions for the same thought, was always very instructive.

Parallel with the reading of a grammar as a supplement to, and a summary of all the grammatical knowledge which has been gained in the ways suggested, it might seem to be a good plan to go through a systematical collection of the lexical material—of course not an ordinary dictionary, since the alphabetical arrangement is about as unsystematical as possible, but a sensibly arranged vocabulary, something in the line of Roget's *Thesaurus*. But it ought, at any rate, to be much smaller, and only include words and expressions which are actually necessary ; even then, however, the unavoidable dryness of such a book, and the absence of connection between the single words, would make it unfit for use in teaching, even if it were not to be employed in imparting new material, but only to recall words which have already been learned. It would be better worth while for pupils, who have reached a somewhat advanced stage, to go through a little systematic collection of phrases, especially of such turns of expression as play a great part in ordinary daily intercourse, but which are seldom met with in literature. Franke's *Phrases de tous les jours* is the best specimen I know of—but I have it from the very best source that this little book was never intended as a text-book for beginners.

X

HERE, last but not least, comes the treatment of the *pronunciation*, which for several reasons I have not taken up
first, although the questions which are here to be discussed
necessarily play a part already from the very first lesson in
a foreign language.   I have now for many years advocated
the use of phonetics—yes, even of phonetical transcription,
in the teaching of foreign languages, and have to a large
extent put my theories into practice both in dealing with
children of all ages and with grown persons.   New things
always frighten people ; they think with terror that here
the pupils are to be burdened with an entirely new and
difficult science and with a new kind of writing; we had
trouble enough with the old kind, they say, and now we
are to be bothered with this new alphabet with its
barbarous letters !   Every educator must see how objectionable it is ; now we have learned languages for so many
years without such modern inventions, and the old way
ought to be good enough for us still.

That is about the run of the objections raised.   This
the answer : Phonetics is a science, to be sure, and, like all
other sciences, it is not without its difficult and mooted
points.   Yet the fact that large volumes can be written

about botany does not frighten us from teaching our children *some* botany. In mathematics there are many things which are beyond the comprehension of ordinary school-children, but yet they have to learn *some* mathematics. Phonetics is not a new study that we want to add to the school curriculum; we only want to take as much of the science as will really be a positive help in learning something which has to be learned *anyway*. We must remember what science is, and what part it plays. Of course in our days every science collects more and more material and requires more and more specialization, so that parts of it become quite inaccessible for all persons except the specialists themselves; but the whole idea of science is that it shall be *unified knowledge* (Spencer), a summing up of all the numerous details of reality under large, comprehensive points of view, the establishing of great, general laws, which apply to all single cases. That is also why science can be termed "ökonomie des denkens," and that is why science can suggest means of facilitating thought and the acquirement of knowledge. We want to have some phonetics introduced into our schools, because theory has convinced us, and experiment has proved to us, that by means of this science we can, with decidedly greater certainty, and in an essentially easier way, give an absolutely better pronunciation in a much shorter space of time than would be possible without phonetics.

And as for that hobgoblin called phonetical transcription—well, it is no "new alphabet," not even as new as the Gothic (German) letters are, and much less so than the Greek alphabet, with which the pupils are burdened (without their being of the slightest use[1]), to say nothing of the new names for the letters.   In learning Greek the pupils have to operate with thirty odd new symbols ; in our phonetical transcription for school use, we do not need more than from five to eight new symbols for each language ; otherwise it consists of the ordinary letters, and every letter in it retains one of its familiar values, which is used consistently everywhere, the new symbols being mostly modifications of the known letters ; $\int$ reminds us of s, ʒ of z, ε and ə of e, η of n. The whole thingis no worse than that.

If you refer to your experience in opposition to these new ways of teaching, you only invite the answer: Yes, your experience shows how a *poor* pronunciation may be learned !

Why must we learn how to pronounce the foreign languages at all ?   Well, in the first place, it must be because there is the possibility that we may meet natives some time later.   Otherwise we might, perhaps, be satisfied with *reading* the foreign words according to English principles of pronunciation, French *pain* like English "pain," Werther as "worth her," etc.   I have known old parsons who have taught themselves English so as to be able to read novels, and who read English with Danish vowels, pronounced the *k* in *knight*, etc.   For a superficial "getting the gist" of shilling shockers and penny

---

[1] Greek could just as well be read with Latin letters, for they are almost as much like the letters which Demosthenes used as the late black-letters are which we print as Greek.

dreadfuls, this is sufficient perhaps, but I maintain that for a penetrating, delicate comprehension of real works of literature this manner of reading is not enough. Language cannot be separated from sound, and that is the sum of the matter; only he who hears the foreign language within himself in exactly or approximately the same way as a native hears it can really appreciate and enjoy not only poetry, where phonetic effects must needs always play an important part, but also all the higher forms of prose. Then there is the mnemonic benefit of a correct pronunciation. It helps the pupil to keep foreign languages distinct from each other; for instance, he will never be misled to think that *jeune* means "pretty" on account of its resemblance to *schön*, and he will not be apt to confuse French *joli, journée, nouvelle* with English *jolly, journey, novel*. In the second place, Madvig is right—and this applies to the living languages too—when he writes: "Finally there is scarcely any doubt that progress in the dead languages would become more rapid if, so far as possible, for instance, through reading and pronouncing distinctly and through memorizing new expressions, the language came not only through the eye, but more through the ear than it does in most places now."

Our pronunciation according to the old school is extremely poor, indeed, much more frightful than most people imagine. It has among others these two disadvantages, that we do not understand the natives, and that we are not understood by them.

The very first lesson in a foreign language ought to be devoted to initiating the pupils into the world of sounds;

L

if the class has already had such an elementary course in sounds, either in connection with the study of their mother tongue (something we ought to come to in the course of time at any rate), or in connection with another foreign language, it can of course be made briefer ; it is scarcely safe to omit it entirely. The conversation may be formed as simply as the following one, where all scientific terms are avoided ; not even the word " organ " is necessary. (Of course the answers will not always be as prompt and decided as here, and much will need to be repeated several times with different pupils.)

Teacher : John, can you say *papa* ?　Papa.—How do you go about it ?　Say it once more.—*Papa.*　First, I open my mouth, and then I open it once again.—Yes, and in the meantime you must, of course, have closed it.　Look at me, all of you, and see if I too go about it in that way— *Papa.*　What did I do, William ?—First you opened your mouth, then closed it, then opened it again.—What did I close it with ?—With the lips.—Now, when I say *op, ap, ep,* what do I do ?—Close the lips every time, and then open them again.—Then I do that every time I say *p.*　Robert, can you find any other sounds where I also close my lips ? No.—Try the word *mama.*—Yes, in *m.*—Now, say *baby* and *bib.*—Also in *b.*—Good ; then we have three sounds now where the lips are closed, *p, b, m.*　Let us write them in a row on the blackboard.　Is it necessary to close the lips in all sounds?—No.—What is your name?—John Gordon Hunter.—All of you look at him while he says it. John Gordon Hunter.—Did he close his lips at all ? No.— Then all the sounds which are in the whole of his name must be said with other parts of the mouth than the lips. What else have we that we use to speak with?—The tongue.—Now, when we say *n*, for instance, in *John, Anna*, what do we do?—Close with the tongue behind the teeth. —What part of the tongue?—The point.—Now try *t* in *atta*.—There we also close with the point of the tongue behind the teeth.   And *d* in *adda*.—Likewise.—Then we use the point of the tongue for *t, d, n*.   Let us write them down under *p, b,'m*.   Now *k* in *akka* ?—Look into my mouth What do I do?—You close with the tongue farther back in the mouth.—Yes, we call that the back of the tongue. Howard, look into Edward's mouth while he says *akka*. Now *g* in *agga* (the sound *g*, of course, not the name dʒi· of the letter).   Then we can write them down in a third row. *p, b, m* were what kind of sounds?—Lip-sounds.—And *t, d, n*, were what kind?   Point-of-the-tongue sounds.—And the third row?—Back-of-the-tongue sounds.—Yes, we might also say simply point-sounds and back-sounds.   [Here some one will ask]: Why are there not three there?—Yes, there are three sounds there too, but we have no letter for the third.   Say *tinker*, and then *tin-kettle*.   Is there no difference?   Yes, in *tin-kettle* we have a pure *n*, but not in *tinker* ; here we have another sound before *k*.—Now try *finger*.—There we have the same before *g*.—And in *singer*?— The same without a real *g*.—Look into my mouth when I say (s)*inger* [without s].   We can make a letter for this new sound by writing an *n*, with the last stroke lengthened below the line and slightly curled, as in *g*: *ŋ*.—James, come up here and write down the four words as they sound, making use of the new letter.—(He writes first *tin-*

kettle).—No, do you hear more than one *t*? and can you hear any *e* after *l*?—No.—What then? *tinketl*. (It is not worth while at this stage to require greater phonetical exactness than *tinketl, tiŋker, fiŋger, siŋer,* passing over the fact that the final *er* in the words does not really sound like e + r). You see, if you were a Frenchman trying to learn English, you would not know that *n* in *tin-kettle* and in the other words were different sounds, and that the *e* was silent, and you would pronounce the words incorrectly; but if the one were written *tinketl* and the other *tiŋker*, it would be much easier for you to learn how to pronounce them. And then take *fringe*; it looks as if it were simply *finger* with the *r* in another place, and yet it is quite a different sound, so we see that the two letters *ng* may stand for three entirely different sounds. We also write *knight*, and say "nait"; we write *busy* and say "bizi." Can you find any other words which we spell differently from the way in which we pronounce them? [Various examples are found and analyzed.] When we write the words exactly as they sound, we call it *phonetical transcription.* Now, in the beginning, we shall write all French words phonetically, so that you can more easily learn how to pronounce them. But you saw in the case of *tinker* that we occasionally need a new symbol in this transcription, which we do not use otherwise. You will learn a few more of them in the course of time. . . . Then we have seen that in order to say different sounds, we can use the lips and the point of the tongue and the back of the tongue. Is there nothing else that we need to speak with?—The nose? Yes, that is all right in a way, but—can you move your nose? Look at my nose ; do I move it when I speak ?—No.—But is it not possible to use it without moving it ? Now, see if I use my nose when I say a···· [very long drawn out].[1] Now, I suddenly hold my nose with two fingers, and press the nostrils together. Does that make the sound different?— No.—But now I say m in the same way m···· and pinch the nostrils together in the same way. Did anything happen?—Yes, there was no sound.—Now you can try it yourselves. First you, George ; say a···, and then the boy next to you can suddenly pinch your nose together with two fingers. And then say m···, and let Fred pinch your nose again. Can you say m while your nostrils are closed ?—No, at any rate the sound soon disappears. All of you try it ; say a just as long as I do, and pinch the nose together several times with your fingers whenever you see me do it ; and now likewise with m. That is because the air has to escape through the nose in order that the sound m may be made. It is the soft palate that you use in order to open the inner entrance to the nose, so that the air can escape through the nostrils. You can feel the palate behind the teeth, there it is hard ; but if you pass your fingers farther back, you will soon feel that it becomes soft and flexible. See how it can go up and down in my mouth. Look in the mirror[2], and see how your own palate is. First try breathing in and out silently, and then say a ; then you will see how your soft palate suddenly jumps up ;

[1] A dot after the letter and above the line is the best indication of length. a is here taken phonetically, the vowel in *arm*.

[2] A hand-mirror is a useful thing to have in these preliminary phonetical exercises. In several places, the teacher requires each pupil to bring his own along.

that is because it has to close the entrance to the nose, so that no air can get out that way. But when you say m it remains hanging down, so that the air can come out through the nose, the passage through the mouth being closed by the lips. [At this point, you might make a rough sketch on the blackboard, showing a cross-section through the mouth, with the soft palate in the two positions.] In producing n and η, you have the same position of the soft palate as in the case of m. [Try to pinch the nose together.]

Now we have seen how we use the nose and the mouth when we speak, but are they the only things that are necessary in speaking? [If the pupils cannot think of " voice " of their own accord, the teacher may put them on the track by saying : when someone speaks (or sings) very well, we say that he has a good...]—Voice.—Where is the voice ?—In the vocal chords.—And where are they ?—In Adam's apple.—[Here it might be a good thing not to despise the anecdote about the apple which stuck in Adam's throat.] Now we also call that the larynx. In there, there are two vocal chords stretched parallel to each other, and when they vibrate a tone is produced, and that is what we call voice. It is just as when a string of a violin is brought into vibration and gives forth a tone ; or a bell or a wine-glass, which is made to quiver violently. Now do we always use the voice when we speak ? You do not know ; well, then we can experiment. [Whisper a sentence.] Did I use my voice then ?—No.—Now try first to say an a··· quite loudly and forcibly (or sing it), and take firm hold of Adam's apple with your thumb and forefinger ; then you will feel it quiver. Have you never tried to touch a piano with your finger tips while someone was playing on it ? Then you will have felt the same kind of delicate, rapid, quivering movements as you feel on touching the larynx while the voice is in activity. In both cases you can *feel* those movements with your fingers which you *hear* with your ear as a tone. But now whisper an a··· and feel your larynx ; do you feel anything?—No, there are no vibrations.—And try to say s··· [by no means the name of the letter, *es*, but the hissing sound itself.] Is there voice in that ? Do you feel any vibration ?—No.—Then s is a *voiceless* sound, but a is a *voiced* sound. Now, try m··· [not *em !*] Is it voiced ? and n··· ? Notice that you can sing the voiced sounds [test several of them], but not the voiceless sounds. [1] That f··· is voiceless, and that v··· (with strong buzzing !) is voiced, is easily discovered. In the same way, we have for every voiceless sound a corresponding voiced sound. Say s···, and now produce the corresponding voiced sound with the buzzing element. They are the sounds we have in *so* and *zoo*, *seal* and *zebra*. We have also a third corresponding pair ʃ and ʒ ; ʃ is the sound in *shilling, shall*, etc. ; ʒ is the sound in *measure, pleasure*, etc. Then we may write down :

f	s	ʃ	voiceless
v	z	ʒ	voiced.

Now pronounce each sound in chorus as I point to the letter, and continue drawing it out until I take the chalk

---

[1] Here also the experiment in hearing the voice distinctly by holding the hands flat against the ears.

away from the letter.[1]   Thereupon the pupils may be tested singly, the teacher skipping from one sound to the other.   Exercises may also be given with the consonants between two vowels : afffa, avvva, asssa, azzza ; afa, ava, asa, aza.

Now the pupils have already had a little course in elementary phonetics; it interests them and contains nothing that they cannot understand, and nothing that is not useful for them.   Nor does it ever really frighten the children ; but the very thought of it has actually frightened a number of older teachers, who apparently live in holy terror of trespassing beyond the lines laid out for them in their childhood, and who unfailingly think that everything new must be just as useless, dry and pedantical as most of what they learned in their own schooldays, so they are not inclined to have the bother of making themselves familiar with anything new.[2]   In the Danish original of this book, I reprinted as a curiosity a description of the activity of the organs of speech in the production of speech-sounds, which a boy 14 years old, who had never been told anything about the formation of sounds, had written all by himself, without the least instruction or help of any kind (which can easily be seen, among other things, from the fact that he

---

[1] I have often also conducted the exercise in such a way that the class had to voice the sound when I raised my hand, and unvoice it when I lowered my hand ; thus I have made them articulate fffvvvffvvvff, ssszzsss, etc., without any pauses.

[2] That I am not exaggerating (as people certainly will suspect in about ten years from now), I could easily prove by means of a long series of opinions from pedagogical meetings, articles in pedagogical periodicals, newspaper reviews, etc.

sticks to and analyzes the names of the letters); it shows that this dreaded phonetical science is not so terribly far beyond the horizon of ordinary children after all.

The children always "follow" the teacher so well in these phonetical exercises that it is rather necessary to put a damper on their eagerness to try to produce the sounds than to spur them on. Or, in other words, the teacher has but to organize their natural impulse to imitate the sounds by saying to them, when they begin to whistle and hum : " You may say the sounds yourselves directly, just wait a moment," and thereupon, after the explanation has been given, by allowing them ample opportunity to pronounce the sounds, both in chorus and singly. Then, both during recess and at home, they will revel to their hearts' content in the new sounds, and the whole new and amusing world that has been opened to them.

After the introductory course which I have just sketched,[1] I immediately begin with texts in the foreign language. If the teacher will at this point read one or two pages aloud rapidly (or give a little talk) in as characteristically a French or German manner as possible, this is a very good way to give the pupils a preliminary notion of the foreign-ness of the new language. This impression may be further emphasized by means of a little trick which I may recom-mend. The teacher practises an English sentence pro-nounced as a Frenchman (or German respectively) would

---

[1] I have sometimes made the introduction longer, sometimes shorter than here indicated ; some teachers make it more complete, so that they get a whole system of sounds tabulated before they pass on to the reading.

pronounce it, with French vowels, French accent, etc.   He may refer to this sentence now and then in speaking of the single sounds, and it will serve to warn the students against the kind of mistakes that they themselves are to avoid.   Then I take up the new sounds in the more accidental order in which they occur in the selection for reading; I repeat every word, together with its meaning, write it down on the blackboard in phonetical transcription, and explain every symbol as it occurs, at the same time articulating the corresponding sound *isolated* (this is of great importance! also the consonants alone without any vowel, either before or after), and drawing it out very long.[1]

In not a few cases, the pupils will be able to imitate the sound with sufficient exactness, when it has been produced isolated; at all events, they do it far better than when they only hear it among other sounds.   But in many other cases their imitation is not successful, or, at least, it is not sure enough to be quite satisfactory; then it is necessary to resort to phonetics for help, on the basis of the introductory course.

Of course, it is not easy for a Dane to give detailed directions for phonetical instruction, as it is to be conducted when an English teacher is teaching English children French or German.   Therefore, the following section is necessarily shorter than the corresponding section in the

---

[1] But stopped consonants, like *p*, *t*, *k*, are exceptions to these instructions to isolate the sounds—every phonetician knows the reason why.   They should be uttered with a vowel before and one after, e.g. *ata*.

Danish original, where I could treat the subject exhaustively on the basis of my personal experience, as to how good results are to be obtained. But some few remarks may perhaps serve to point out the right way, and any teacher who has thoroughly mastered the first principles of phonetics theoretically, and especially practically, will himself be able to supplement my suggestions.

In the very first French or German sentence in the reader will probably be found one of the sounds [y] (Fr. *sur*, Ger. *über*), or [ø] (Fr. *veut*, Ger. *höhe*). It is best for these two sounds to be practised together, and, in the beginning, in their long form. As experience shows, it is not sufficient for the teacher merely to say these sounds ; they generally cause English people much trouble, and all imitations based on the diphthong in Eng. *few*, etc., ought to be strictly discountenanced from the very first lesson. That it is not impossible to learn the correct sounds was brought home to me in a striking manner a few years ago. These sounds are also found in Danish ; an English lady who had been in Denmark for some years had not been able, in spite of unceasing efforts, to learn them by imitation. Then I made a bet that I could teach her them in less than ten minutes, and I won the bet through five minutes' theoretical explanation of rounded and unrounded vowels, and two minutes' practical exercises. The directions were about as follows : say [uˑ] (or [uw]) in *too* very loudly, and hold it as long as you can without taking breath. Once more : observe in the hand-mirror the position of the lips. Then say *tea* [tiˑ, tij] in the same way ; draw the vowel out until you can hold it no longer ; continue all the time to observe the position of the lips in the mirror.   Now [u⋯] again ; then [i⋯].   The lips are rounded for some vowels, slit-shaped for others.   Try to pout them rather more than you do usually.   Pronounce [u⋯] a couple of times with the lips as rounded and close to each other as possible, and concentrate your attention on the lips.   Then say [i⋯] a couple of times, paying attention to the position of the tongue ; you will feel that the sides of the tongue touch the roof of the mouth or the teeth.   Now look in the mirror ; say [i⋯] again, and now suddenly, taking care to keep the tongue in the same posi-tion, let your lips take the·rounded, pouted position they had before.   It may be that the pupil is still unable to pro-duce any [y], because, despite the teacher's warning, he involuntarily shifts his tongue-position back again to the familiar [u] position.   In that case, however, the teacher must not be discouraged, but pass on to the second part of the experiment, which is surer, and which might therefore have been taken first : place your lips in this pouted [u] position, without producing any sound, look in the mirror, and be very careful that the position of the lips remains unchanged, and then try to say [i⋯].   If the tongue is placed in the correct [i⋯]-position, the result cannot be anything but an [y].   This sound is retained and repeated until the pupil is perfectly sure of both the articulation and acoustic effect.   Then the sound [ø] may be taken up.   It may be produced with [y] as a starting-point, the lower jaw being lowered so that both the underlip and the tongue follow it, while the teacher takes care to stop the downward movement in the right place.   The result may be controlled by starting with [e] and rounding the lips, that is, by going through a process corresponding to the transition from [i⋯] to [y⋯].

One of the most unbecoming mistakes which Englishmen make in their pronunciation of foreign languages is their diphthongizing of long vowels, since long vowels,[1] in ordinary English, are pronounced with an upward glide, so that the jaw and the tongue are raised higher in the last part of the vowels in *see, two, hay, know,* for instance, than in the first part. In vulgar London pronunciation, this English peculiarity is carried further, the beginning of the sound being lowered, at all events in the last two sounds mentioned, so that *lace* sounds like *lice,* and *pay* like *pie.* But even if the best pronunciation does not go to this extreme, yet the glide is there, and this glide is for the native Frenchman or German one of the most striking faults in the Englishman's pronunciation of the respective languages, so the Englishman had best be on his guard in this particular. If the teacher, after a little theoretical explanation, says the English [ei] and the German [e] alternately a number of times, even the dullest pupils cannot help but get their ears trained to detect this difference, but long and patient training is certainly necessary, both with the class in chorus and with the pupils singly, before this deeply rooted tendency to diphthongize can be checked.

Another difficulty is met with in the short (narrow) vowels. French *été* must be pronounced with two short

---

[1] With the exception of the vowels [a·] in *alms,* [ɔ·] in *war,* and [ɘ·] in *sir.*

closed e's; Englishmen have a tendency to pronounce two long or half-long glide-sounds, which begin with a greater distance between the jaws than they ought to, and close with a smaller distance between the jaws than the genuine French sounds have. Anyone who has become accustomed to the undiphthongized long [e], however, can use this as a starting-point for learning the correct short sound, the best way being the frequent repetition of *tétété*··· Likewise the short sounds in *fini, dodo, froufrou*, etc.

Nor do the French nasal vowels occur in English; in phonetical transcription, they are indicated by means of over the vowel-symbol, for instance [õ] in *son*, etc. Here the teacher must immediately make every effort to check the tendency to say [ɔη] as in Eng. *long*, and my experience with Danish pupils has been that it is not sufficient for this purpose merely to let the pupils repeat the sound after me. It is necessary to make it perfectly clear to them wherein the difference consists. First the teacher draws out his õ] and establishes (by means of questions that it is only one sound, the same from first to last. Then one of the pupils is to try to draw out the sound [ɔη], and it thus becomes clear that it is only the last of the two sounds that is prolonged. On the basis of what has been previously learned (p. 149), the teacher shows the difference of effect caused in closing the nostrils with the fingers, and explains that it is due to the fact that in [ɔη] we have first a sound where the air escapes only through the mouth, then another sound where the air only passes out through the nose; but in [õ], both passages are open at the same time. If a pencil is laid in the mouth so that it rests on the tongue (tolerably far back), it will remain lying quietly when [õ] is pronounced, but not in the case of [ɔη]. In connection with [õ], the pupils may practise the [ã] sound in *tant*, [ɛ̃] or, more correctly, [æ̃], the sound in *teint* and the rounded sound in [œ̃], *un*. The sound [ɥ] in *tuer* [tɥe], *lui* [lɥi] is easily learned with sufficient exactness as a [y] which is quickly passed over so that the main stress is allowed to fall on the following sound, the relation between [w] and [u] being brought in by way of comparison.

With respect to the consonants, care must be taken to pronounce [t, d, n] in such a way that the point of the tongue touches the upper teeth ; it must, at all events, not be held as far back as in English ; the same applies to [l], where this difference is still more important ; the hollow sound of the English *l* is also to be avoided by keeping the whole tongue more flat and not hollowing it out like a spoon. The voiceless sounds [r̥] and [l̥] in [fǝnɛˈtr̥] *fenêtre* and [tabl̥] *table* can easily be deduced from what has been learned about the voice (p. 150–151) ; it is necessary to guard against making [r̥] into the vowel found at the end of English words like *mister*, etc. The pupils will easily understand that with the correct unvoiced pronunciation, these sounds are apt to disappear in rapid speech. Finally we take up the sound [ɲ] in [kãpaɲ] *campagne* ; it is explained as lying between [nj] and [η] ; it is best pronounced with the point of the tongue resting in the lower part of the mouth behind the lower teeth, but in using the word "best" I intend to hint that it is not strictly necessary to require this method of formation ; there are

also Frenchmen who (at all events before a vowel) pronounce it like English [nj] in *onion*.

With respect to [p, t, k], it is well known that in French
they have not the aspiration that they have in English;
since the difference is not so great, however, the English
sounds may perhaps be used unchanged in the beginning.
Then if one of the pupils notices the difference, which he
perhaps will express by saying that the teacher pronounces [b]
when there stands [p] in the book, or possibly by merely trying
to imitate the teacher's sound by means of his own English
[b], his attention may be called to the little breath which
there always is between the opening of the English [p] and
the vowel itself; this is not found in French, where the
vowel after [p, t, k] comes exactly at the same moment as
the opening takes place (either by the lips or the tongue),
and therefore they sound to us like [b, d, g] (*capitaine* as if
it were gabidɛn). Try a [p] without a vowel after it, first
with a strong breath (somewhat like when you pooh-pooh
something, but without any voice), then without any breath
like a man puffing at his pipe (about the same sound as
when soap bubbles burst); and then try to place a vowel
after it [1]; it must come immediately, just as quickly as the
movements of a soldier after the drill-master's command.
Then [t] and [k] may be taken up in the same manner.

The French division into syllables (*il a* =i | la, *chaque
écolier* = ʃa | ke | kɔ | lje, | etc.) is best learned by pure imi-
tation, likewise the distribution of stress (accent); by

---

[1] This method of procedure follows in the main the suggestions o
Klinghardt.

reciting or reading connectedly to the pupils and by always requiring them to say *the whole sentence together without any pause*, the teacher can counteract their tendency to pronounce each word separately in that monotone which is intolerable. Thus *il a été ici* is said all together in one with the vowels gliding over into each other, *a* + *é* sounding somewhat similar to [ai] in *lie*, and *é* + *i* to [ei] in *lay*.

German sounds are somewhat easier for Englishmen than French sounds, but yet there are several points to be noticed. In the case of some sounds, any skilled teacher will be able to follow the suggestions given for French, mutatis mutandis; in the case of others, like the two *ch*-sounds, he must in an analogous manner adapt his theoretical knowledge in phonetics to the practical needs of teaching.

Some people have found it inconsistent that I have no partiality for didactic theorizing in questions of grammar, but myself employ theoretical explanations in questions of phonetics. The explanation is not far to seek. Theoretical grammar, as it is generally studied, is more abstract, it is difficult, it is very comprehensive, and still it does not lead to the desired goal, which is grammatical correctness ; the theory of sound which we want introduced is more concrete and it is easy, it is more limited, and it actually leads to the desired goal, which is a good pronunciation. This last assertion is proved by the experiences of numerous teachers in various lands.

Of late years, it has become more and more usual in schools to use a sound-chart in connection with the instruction in languages. On this chart, all the sounds of

M

the language which is being studied are arranged in systematic order, and are indicated with such large letters that they can be seen by the whole class ; various finesses are often used, as for instance to give the voiced and voiceless sounds different colours.[1]   I myself have not used this contrivance, but I have heard from several foreign teachers, and now from a couple of Danish teachers too, that they are very well satisfied with it.   The teacher points to a letter and gets either the whole class or one of the pupils to say the corresponding sound ; or the teacher may let A mention some sound or other, and B, who is standing at the blackboard, shows that he has caught it by repeating it and at the same time pointing at the symbol ; or if C makes a mistake in the pronunciation of a word which he is reading (or saying) D is to point, first to the symbol for the wrong sound, and then to the right one, etc.   In this way, much writing on the blackboard, which would otherwise be necessary, is saved ; and besides, it may be of great benefit for the pupils always to have all the sounds in a connected system before their eyes (even if the teacher of course never intends to examine them in the whole phonetical system of the language as such).

The *elements of phonetical transcription* are learned, as we have seen, together with the corresponding sounds themselves.   Now what is the use of the phonetical transcription itself?   It seems to be commonly supposed that its votaries claim by its help to have " given the pupils a better comprehension of the single

---

[1] If the teacher does not care to prepare such charts himself, he can use Viëtor's Lauttafeln.

sounds and to have taught them more easily to produce them ; " its opponents attack this assertion and strike it down with true Quixotic zeal without stopping to think that it has never been set up by the advocates of phonetical transcription at all. These advocates themselves know as well as anyone what is but natural, namely, that a boy does not of his own accord pronounce a French nasal correctly merely because he has been shown the symbol [ɔ̃]. The pronunciation of the single sounds must be learned in other ways, as has been shown above, and for that purpose alone, all writing could very well be entirely dispensed with without resulting in any essential change in the character of the instruction. When, however, we use phonetical transcription already at the first stage, it is partly on account of the excellent help which it will afford later for quite a different purpose, which I shall come to immediately, partly because it really is of some *help* in the teaching of the sound-formation proper. It saves the teacher a great deal of repetition, since instead of always saying the sound himself, he can point to the symbol and get one of the clever pupils to say it for the others ; it makes the pupils see more clearly how many different sounds there are for them to pay attention to (while in exclusively oral instruction, perhaps one pupil will be inclined to hear [ɑ̃] and [ɛ̃] as one sound, another pupil, [ɑ̃] and [ɔ̃] as one sound) ; finally, the homogeneousness of the symbols will help the pupils more easily to comprehend the nature of the sounds themselves ; when they have learned to pronounce [ɔ̃], they will get the run of all the other nasal vowels more quickly when they see the same

629

flourish over them all ; the double parallelism in the four symbols

$$s \quad \int$$
$$z \quad \mathfrak{z}$$

will aid them in learning the corresponding relations between the sounds themselves.

However, in order to understand the greatest and the proper value of phonetical transcription, it is necessary to have well in mind the fact that there are two essentially different kinds of mistakes in pronunciation—

A. Mistakes in the formation of the sounds, and

B. Mistakes in the employment of the sounds.

We have mistakes belonging to Class A, for instance, when Englishmen use the *ng* combination in place of the French nasals, or when they diphthongize the French long, pure vowels, when they pronounce *∫* or *k* instead of German *ch*, or [z] or [s] for German *z* [ts], [ə·], as in *cur*, instead of [œ·r] in French *cœur*, when they pronounce French *dû* like the English *due*, etc.

Mistakes belonging to Class B arise if you pronounce French *gent* like *gant, peut* like *put,* or vice versâ *eut* like [ø], German *frass* or *fuss* with a short, or *nass* or *nuss* with a long vowel, *bischen* with [∫], etc.

Both kinds of mistakes may occur in the same word, as when *München* is pronounced [minkən] or [mjuŋkən] instead of [mynçen].

The mistakes belonging to class A are not due to the orthography ; those mistakes we can also make in languages whose spelling corresponds to the pronunciation ; they are largely due to our native habits of articulation, and they

are to be counteracted by means of the phonetical training which has been described above. If the foreign
sounds have once been well learned in the introductory course, this kind of mistakes can only occur
through carelessness or through the lack of continued
practice.

Mistakes in the employment of the sounds (class B)
however, are as a rule due to disagreement between the
pronunciation and the orthography of each language ; they
are not caused by our native habits of articulation, and
even those that have learned all the foreign sounds perfectly
(indeed even the natives themselves) are liable to make
them in every new word which they see written, but have
never heard.

*It is this last kind of mistake that phonetical transcrip-
tion helps us to avoid*, it protects us against the mistakes
which the different national orthographies actually seduce
us to make. Phonetical transcription is necessary in the
teaching of all languages, but of course, it may deviate
from the ordinary orthography in greater or less degree in
the different languages. In Finnish and Spanish, the
orthography is so nearly phonetical that only relatively few
changes are necessary in order to indicate the pronunciation ; in Italian, almost all that is needed is to indicate if *e*
and *o* are open or closed, if *s* and *z* are voiced [z, dz] or voiceless [s, ts], and which single consonants are to be pronounced
double (long). In German, the orthography is already
much more capricious, but in languages like French,
Danish, and English, the number of conflicting rules with
all their exceptions is so great that the phonetical trans-

cription necessarily has quite a different appearance from the traditional spelling.

Max Müller once said that the English orthography is a national misfortune, and Viëtor has improved upon this observation by declaring that it is an international misfortune, since it is not only Englishmen but also all educated persons in other lands who have to be bothered with it. Now, by means of phonetical transcription the words of the foreign language are presented to us in a kind of normal or ideal orthography, where every letter always signifies the same sound, and every sound is always indicated in the same manner.

Some persons urge the objection against the use of phonetical transcription that it can never be made so perfect that it can show all the shades of intonation, etc., in the spoken language, so that it cannot take the place of a teacher's oral instruction. But we have never maintained that it could ; aside from private study without a teacher, which must needs always be more or less imperfect, we have always emphasized the exceedingly great importance of the teacher pronouncing the words for the pupils, and we have not recommended phonetical transcription as something to replace, but as something to support, the teacher's oral instruction in pronunciation. Even if it misses some of the very finest shades, it may still be of benefit, just as a table of logarithms can be very useful even if the numbers are not carried out farther than to the fourth decimal place.

Other opponents again have exactly the reverse objection to make, that our system of sound-symbols is too delicately detailed for school use. Even if many people only say this because they confuse the phonetical transcription which is used in scientific works with the far simpler transcription which we want to introduce for school use, and which is by no means beyond the powers of comprehension of an ordinary pupil, still we have an answer right at hand. We are aiming at (and attaining) greater exactness than our predecessors cared for, but this is very necessary too, for the old school pronunciation was too unintelligible to the native. Besides, our system is constructed on such simple principles, that we attain to a higher degree of exactness with less trouble than you do with with far more difficult means. When mathematicians began to designate the value of π in decimal form (3·1416) instead of the fractional form $\frac{22}{7}$, they not only attained greater exactness but also greater ease in using the quantity in long calculations, since the decimal is easier to handle than the fraction. Our phonetical transcription may pride itself on exactly corresponding advantages.

It has already been tried in many old readers (to say nothing of the dictionaries) to counteract the injurious influence of the orthography on the pronunciation by means of different systems of designating the pronunciation, such as numbers over the vowels, strokes denoting length and curves denoting shortness, italicizing of the *s*'s which ought to be voiced, or in other places italicizing of the silent letters, dots and flourishes above and under the letters. All such systems, just because they try to deviate as little as possible from the orthography, necessarily adopt a number of its caprices and thus become too complicated to be of any real benefit to the pupils. But the phoneticians, by starting out from rational principles, have succeeded in creating systems of phonetical transcription which really meet all reasonable demands in the way of exactness and simplicity.[1] That they really are simple and easy to learn has been proved to me more than once in striking ways; in several schools where my books are used but where the teacher has been afraid of the phonetical transcription, the children have resorted to it of their own accord, when they came to a word that they did not know how to pronounce; several parents have also told me that they have familiarized themselves with the phonetical transcription in the books which their children used and they did not find it at all difficult.

Perhaps it is worth while here to consider the four ways in which it is possible to communicate the material of a foreign language to pupils. Either (1) the teacher may not let them use any writing at all, but give them everything orally; or (2) he may give them the orthography alone; or (3) he may give them orthography and phonetical transcription together; or finally (4) he may give them phonetical transcription alone.

(1) The first way obviously has the advantage that there is no sound-symbol whatever to confuse the clear apprehension of the pupils; it resembles the manner in which a child

---

[1] Besides, the different systems of modern phoneticians all resemble each other very much—far more than did the earlier arbitrary methods of designating the pronunciation (for instance, Walker's, Flügel's, Toussaint-Langenscheidt's, Tanger's, etc.). Any one who has learned Sweet's phonetical transcription can easily read Passy's or my own, and vice versâ; the differences are hardly worth speaking of.

learns its mother tongue. It will also be the more in place the more the instruction can be brought to resemble the way in which a child first acquires language, that is, where there is only one pupil, or at least very few ; where the pupil (pupils) is (are) not very old, and especially not yet quite familiar with the secrets of writing ; where the teacher is a native ; and above all, where there is ample time. For we must not shut our eyes to the fact that this exclusively oral instruction in languages takes exceedingly much time ; much repetition is necessary, and the teacher has to have great patience. In schools it is only possible to have purely oral instruction as a short preliminary course of a couple of months at the most, before passing over to the use of writing in some form or other. Walter, who has tried both, is emphatically of the opinion that in class instruction phonetical transcription is much to be preferred to purely oral instruction, because the latter wastes an enormous amount of time, and the teacher cannot feel nearly so sure that the whole class is able to follow.

(2) The pupils are immediately allowed to see the traditional orthography, and the teacher gives them the pronunciation orally. The eternal repetition and the painful small corrections which this method craves make the lessons bothersome for both the teacher and the pupils, who almost always become slovenly out of sheer discouragement over the prodigious task before them. Of course there are some rules for the relations between orthography and pronunciation, but unfortunately there are so few without exceptions that certainty cannot be attained by their means.

(3). The pupils are taught the traditional spelling from the very beginning, but at the same time they are given an antidote in the shape of phonetical transcription, either in the form that every new word is phonetically transcribed in the glossary, or that (in addition) the reading selections themselves are transcribed.   To be sure the advantages of phonetical transcription are made use of by this method ; several teachers have expressed their satisfaction at the results thus obtained, and I have no doubt that they are better than when phonetical transcription is dispensed with. However, I am convinced that by this method it is difficult sometimes to prevent the less intelligent pupils from confusing the two systems of spelling, so that they neither learn the pronunciation nor the orthography very well.

(4) Therefore I have always (like the majority of the advocates of phonetical transcription) preferred to let beginners be employed only with phonetical transcription for some time, so that they may become quite familiar not only with the system of sound-symbols, but also with a good deal of the material of the language before they pass on to seeing the words in their orthographical shape too. The principle to be followed here is that of not allowing the difficulties to pile up, but overcoming them one by one. When the pupils know the symbols after the first few lessons, it causes them no difficulty whatever to read the texts ; these themselves (together with the meaning of the words, the grammatical forms, etc.) are therefore far more easy to learn than if the caprices of the orthography had to be mastered *at the same time.*

For this method, connected texts in phonetical transcription are of course necessary, but such texts are also to be recommended to those who follow method No. 3, since there are many points of pronunciation which cannot come up at all in the transcriptions of the single words in the glossary, such points as appear only in combinations of words, in connected discourse. There is, for instance, French [ə] in *le de, demande, devenir, quatre*, etc., etc., which is sometimes pronounced and sometimes omitted, according to the number of consonants coming immediately before or after the [ə]: *à devenir* [advəni·r], *pour devenir* [purdəvni·r], etc. ; there is the varying treatment of the English *r ;* there are double forms due to the influence of sentence-stress, such as [kæn] and [kən] (= *can*), and many other phenomena of that kind, which it is really necessary to pay attention to, since no sentence can be pronounced naturally without consideration for these points, and since we cannot understand the natives without being familiar with them [1] —for we cannot require the French to make their language stiff and do violence to all their natural habits of speech to suit us. Only by using connected texts in phonetical transcription can the teacher require the pupils from the very beginning to read the foreign language connectedly, intelligently, and with some expression.

In conversations on the subject, I have so often had to answer the question as to whether I also want the pupils to learn to *write* phonetical transcription, that I must devote a

---

[1] I remember a lady's dismay when a Frenchman used the combination [stane] in a sentence ; she could not understand the sentence until I repeated it, inserting [sɛtane]. "O well," she rejoined, "if he had only said [sɛtane] ; we always said it that way in school." (*Cette année.*)

few lines to that question here too. Of course they must write phonetical transcription, but *learn* it—well, that is scarcely necessary, for it will not entail the least bit of extra work or trouble for them. They learn the symbols, and when they know them they can write any word whatever in phonetical transcription, if they only know how to pronounce it ; this is a thing which follows of its own accord from the very nature of phonetical transcription. Dictation, in which the pupils are to write in phonetical transcription what the teacher says to them, presupposes only a correct apprehension of the sounds, and is a very good test as to whether they have heard accurately (cf. p. 95).

How long is a teacher to continue to use exclusively phonetical transcription ? That is one of the most difficult questions, and I cannot venture to give a decided answer. The answer will surely always depend partly upon the age and maturity of the pupils and upon how much time can be spent upon the language on the whole. I myself have even dared to go so far that in teaching a class in English, when I only had two hours a week for two years before the final examination, I spent the whole of the first year on phonetical transcription (Sweet's *Elementarbuch*), and I did not regret it. In French in the lower classes, I once at least used phonetical transcription more than a year, and the only difficulty arose when some boys came in in the course of the year from other schools. At other times, again, I have made the course in phonetical transcription shorter, and on the whole I have experimented in various ways without coming to any certain result—except this:

continue with phonetical transcription as long as possible.
For there is relatively so much more of the language itself
learned in this way, that I have not the slightest doubt
that the pupil who, with the same number of lessons a
week, and at the same age, has read phonetical transcription for two years and orthography for half a year knows
more of the language (not only of the pronunciation !) than
the pupil who has used phonetical transcription for half a
year and thereupon orthography for two and a half years
(in all half a year more than the first boy). And then the
phonetical transcription itself is such a fine means of
training the pupils to minute exactness, because they really
have to be constantly on the lookout in order to read
neither more nor less than each symbol indicates ; therefore I attach great *educational* significance to phonetical
transcription.

But of course we have to begin to learn the orthography
some time ; and I suppose it is this transition more than
anything else that has frightened people away from using
phonetical transcription, because they imagine that it must
be extremely difficult. But now all those who have dared
to try phonetical transcription unanimously declare that
they were surprised at the ease with which the transition
took place ; there was no trouble worth mentioning either
for the teacher or the pupils ; and they were surprised at
the accuracy in orthography displayed by pupils who had
been taught in this way. The psychological reason for
this is probably to be found in the sharper perception
which these pupils necessarily get of the difference between
sound and writing, together with the fact that they are not

compelled like the others to learn many things at a time (spelling, pronunciation, meaning, inflection), but the orthography is separated out as something which is to be learned by itself about words with whose pronunciation and meaning they have already become quite familiar.

The best way of making the transition seems to be in going over some of the selections which have already been read and learned. First, the teacher says a few words about orthography in general, basing his remarks on English spelling; he may call attention to the silent letters in *night*, *know*, the ambiguity of the vowels in *home*, *honest*, etc. Then a French piece the pupils know already is shown to them in orthographical dress; it is gone through word by word in such a way that thep upils themselves may be guided to find out the most important relations between the letters and their sound-values. Here they for the first time have something to do with the accents and the cedilla, whose name they learn.[1]

In the following lessons the comparison between spelling and sound is conducted in the same manner as indicated above for grammatical observations; sometimes starting from a certain sound, the students may point out all the

---

[1] The use of the French or German names of the letters of the alphabet when words are being spelled in English is merely affectation, and deserves only a shrug of the shoulders, especially since, as a rule, it is not consistently carried through, but is applied only to some few letters, *y* being called [igræk] or *ypsilon*, *ch*, [seaʃ] or [tseha], according to circumstances, and this in the midst of other letters which are allowed to retain their English names with diphthongs and everything. It is quite a different thing when the teaching is wholly conducted in the foreign language; then it is necessary to practise the foreign names of the letters, but then it must be carried through consistently.

words in which it occurs on a page or so; sometimes starting from the orthography, they may note and classify all the phonetical values of a certain letter. A few lessons will be sufficient for these preliminaries.

Ought the teacher to require the pupils to learn the orthography from the very beginning, that is, ought he to examine them in spelling or let them write dictation? No—that is not generally the practice according to the non-phonetical method either. First let them become accustomed to seeing the spelling, and in the exercises just suggested let them copy out of the book; later on they may be required to learn how to spell the words in the first line of every lesson, and in the course of a few months the pupils will be just as much at home in their French and German orthography as any pedant could require—and much more at home than they generally are now after a long time.[1]

Phonetical transcription ought by no means to be given up on beginning with the orthography : it is too good an aid to be dispensed with at this point. Not only ought whole pieces to be read, occasionally at least, in phonetical transcription, but it ought to be used in connection with all new words (thus especially in the glossary) in order to prevent all guess-work. Thereby is also obtained another important result

---

[1] Wer jemals in der schule die lautschrift als hilfsmittel zur erzielung einer besseren aussprache benutzt hat, der weiss, welcher nutzen aus ihr entspringt ; der weiss aber auch, dass der schaden, welchen sie bezüglich der orthographie anrichten kann, sich nur auf wenige wochen erstreckt und äusserst gering ist, *jedenfalls viel geringer als der schaden, welchen eine schlechte aussprache in der orthographie anrichtet.* H. P. Junker, *Die neueren sprachen,* v. 99.

at a later stage, namely, the teacher may be *just as strict in requiring the pronunciation to be learned as the meaning*, whereas without phonetical transcription he cannot expect the pronunciation to be prepared at home. By steadily keeping up their practice in transposing phonetical transcription into practical pronunciation the pupils have something of value for their whole life, for, when they no longer have a teacher to ask about the pronunciation of a new word, they can obtain information about it themselves. That which was only a few years ago a possibility reserved for the distant future, namely, that all French and English dictionaries should give the pronunciation accor ding to rational principles, is now, as we know, well under way to become a reality at any time.[1]

The use of phonetics and phonetical transcription in the teaching of modern languages must be considered as one of the most important advances in modern pedagogy, because it ensures both considerable facilitation and an exceedingly large gain in exactness. But these means must be employed immediately from the very beginning ; just as easy as it is to get a good pronunciation in this way, just as difficult is it to root out the bad habits which may become inveterate during a very short period of instruction according to a wrong or antiquated method. Timotheus, an old well-

---

[1] See especially Murray, Bradley, and Craigie's *New English Dictionary*, A. Schröer's edition of Grieb's *Englisch-deutsches wörterbuch*, and Rangel-Nielsen's *Fransk-danske ordbog*. I am myself transcribing the English words in Brynildsen's *Engelsk-dansk-norske ordbog*, two-thirds of which have already appeared. Edgren's French Dictionary should perhaps also be mentioned, but I have never seen it myself.

known music-teacher, used to demand double payment of all those pupils who had taken instruction with other teachers before they came to him ; the reason that he gave was that he had much more trouble in teaching these pupils than those who had not already acquired bad habits for him to break them of. Go ye and do likewise, ye teachers of languages !

I shall add a few words on the use of the phonograph. The apparatus has been very much perfected of late years and renders beautifully most vowels and all the general features of stress, intonation, etc. But the rendering of most consonants is still far from perfect ; you cannot always tell whether you hear a p or an f, etc., and it is impossible to rely on a phonographic record for minute shades of s-sounds and the like. It is clear, too, that even if the apparatus were nearer the ideal than it is now, it could not replace the teacher. But in the hands of an able teacher I have no doubt that it will prove a valuable help : it is patient and will repeat the same sentences scores of times, if required, without tiring or changing a single sound or intonation ; you may also have different records of the same short piece as pronounced by one man from Berlin, another man from Hanover, a third from Munich, and a fourth from Vienna, which may be very useful for comparisons, even if, as a matter of course, in your ordinary teaching you stick to one particular standard of pronunciation—and in various other ways phonographic records may be used to stimulate the pupils. But everything they hear in this way should at the same time be presented to them in phonetic writing—either in their readers

N

or on the blackboard.   Perhaps, at some future day, the
" telegraphone " invented by my countryman V. Poulsen
will supplant Edison's phonograph in this as well as
in other respects.

XI

LIKE most works on pedagogy, this one too has been mostly concerned with the teaching of beginners. But now and then there has been a word about the instruction of advanced pupils, and now I shall add a few more suggestions about it. It is best to continue on the same lines as during the first years, only making those changes which circumstances necessarily demand.

The pupils must *read*—read more and more, read better and better books, books whose contents are of a nature to hold their attention and to give them as much all round information and development as possible—accordingly, as has been previously suggested, not solely works of literature. That sort of reading is especially good which gives the pupils some insight into the foreign nation's peculiarity in the widest sense of the word, and best of all is that reading which is apt to make the pupils love what is best in the foreign people. Tennyson is right when he says, "It is the authors, more than the diplomats, who make nations love one 'another " ;[1] and teachers of modern languages should ever remember that it is their mission to make their countrymen know and understand foreign nations. By

[1] Alfred Lord Tennyson : a Memoir by his Son. (Tauchnitz ed., IV. p. 84).

making their pupils read good literature as well as by capacitating the younger generations of different countries for intelligent intercourse with one another, language-teachers all over the world may ultimately prove more efficacious in establishing good permanent relations between the nations than Peace Congresses at the Hague.

Some reading must be taken thoroughly, some may be *cursory*; it is perhaps best to have several gradations. Whereas in the beginning it is necessary to chew well in order to get all the linguistic nourishment out of the reading, later on it may of course be taken in larger and larger bites. Already rather early in the course of instruction, those pieces may be more lightly passed over whose contents are scarcely fit to be taken too seriously or which contain words which it is not absolutely necessary to remember. The teacher may simply let the pupils read such pieces aloud, explaining every word which they do not understand, but without basing any questions on them, and without requiring them to be studied for the next time. Later on, in the midst of more serious work, a month or two may be taken for reading a light novel through in the same easy manner. The pupils may also have private reading to do at home in addition to what they read in school. The teacher that I had in French and English in the upper classes in Frederiksborg School (H. Mathiesen) had an excellent way of making us desire of our own accord to read novels in the language studied; each one of us was ambitious to give in the longest list of volumes read when the teacher called for the lists at the first lesson in every month, and even if we of course read very rapidly and never looked up any words, yet we learned a good deal, and I consider the habit of reading which I thus acquired to be one of the most valuable acquisitions that I got during my last years in school. In order to test whether we really had read the books as stated, our teacher sometimes talked to us about their contents, but he talked in Danish, sometimes he only made us open the books at random and translate a little piece. It is no doubt better to organize this practice, as it is now done in some parts of Germany, where the whole class reads the same book at home and must have read a certain amount by a certain day (after a fortnight's or a month's interval). Then they must be able to give an account of the contents in the foreign language, must also ask each other questions about the book, and may even occasionally be required to write down the contents as a written exercise; after the teacher has looked through these accounts, the pupils may deliver them orally and more freely, and this will give occasion for further conversation—all in the foreign language.

Most important, however, is the reading which is done *thoroughly*, so thoroughly that the pupils completely master both contents and language, and which therefore in both these respects ought to be as good as possible. In exercises with questions and answers, the contents naturally play an important part, and even if the pupils feel it is one aim, and a very important one, to acquire skill in the language, yet this aim is not always directly kept in view as such; neither does a child talk in order to practise using its mother-tongue, but in order to get some information and in order to communicate itself to others—and thereby it

learns the language.   This feeling of reality becomes more
and more prominent as the pupils become more advanced ;
in the conversations, the pupils show directly, that they
understand the contents, indirectly that they understand
the language.

The pupils must *talk*—about what they have read, and
that the talks are not mere farces with conventional
" parleur " phrases, as our opponents would like to make
out, I hope that I have shown sufficiently well.[1]   When
a certain teacher wrote somewhere that all the conversation
that there is time for consists of the following five questions,
which are asked of the monitor (and only of him) at the
beginning of every lesson : " Who is the monitor?   What
date is it to-day ?   What day of the week is it ?
Who is absent ?   What have you prepared for to-
day ? ", and that he owes it to the truth to confess that it is only the minority of the pupils who at the
end of the year are able to answer these questions correctly
without hesitation, then this deplorable result is primarily
due to the fewness of the questions ; he who only gets the
tip of his finger dipped in the water three times in twenty
weeks will never learn how to swim.   It is secondarily due
to the fact that the questions are stereotyped and have no
connection with what the class is reading.   Furthermore
this same teacher says that he generally cannot spend more
than a few minutes of each lesson on these " elementary

[1] Those who have their doubts may also read the accounts given by
natives who have visited German schools where the instruction was
conducted according to the reformed system, and who have had long
talks with the pupils, in Walter, *Englisch nach dem Frankfurter reform-
plan*, pp. 152–165, and Miss Brebner, *The Method of Teaching*, etc.

exercises," since the reading, translation and grammar requires the rest of the time, in the middle classes, indeed, all the time, so that at this stage there is no time at all for any conversation. But if the talks are used for interpreting the text, two big birds are killed with one stone, and then it will soon be seen that skill in speaking increases like wealth; if you have only reached a certain point, the rest comes of its own accord; the accumulated capital multiplies surprisingly fast and willingly.

The pupils must *write*—original papers in the foreign language, not translations—that is, the form of language used must be as little as possible suggested by English turns of expression. But the subject must be concrete and limited. The chief danger that there may be in such original written exercises, namely that the pupils avoid all the difficulties and only use a slender supply of expressions, which they feel sure of, this danger is greater the vaguer or more comprehensive the subject is. For instance, it is best not to give broad literary subjects, such as "Die romantische schule," etc. A more limited subject is far better, both as an exercise and as a test; for instance, an account of a little anecdote or of the newspaper report of some event, which the teacher has read to the class; a description of what is to be seen on a picture, a renarration of some episode in the novel or in the historical selection which is being read in class, possibly in the form of a letter; [1] a

---

[1] The letter-form is on the whole that form of composition which most persons have most use for, and which therefore ought to be practised most frequently. The international students' letter-exchange, which has just been started a few years ago, will be of great benefit—

summing up of everything relating to one of the characters
in the text read ; a review of the line of thought in (a section
of) some essay which has been read ; a paraphrase of some
poem.   Still more limited are such exercises in which a
certain number of questions have to be answered, or such
exercises in the use of synonymous words and expressions
as have been described on p. 139.

But can such a method of instruction as has here been
described really be carried out under existing circumstances ?   Are there not obstacles to be encountered on
every hand ?   Yes ; unfortunately there are things which
stand in the way and make a good deal of trouble, but
luckily they do not make it quite impossible for the new
system to be used.   As hindrances may be mentioned the
shortness of the time, the apportionment of the time, the
examinations, the teachers.

The *time* which is now set apart for modern languages
is too brief.   Therefore all teachers of modern languages
ought to unite, and, together with all the parents who are
dissatisfied with the arrangements in our grammar schools
(and they are not few), they ought to agitate for the
removal of that burden which weighs heavily on the school
and which prevents the growing generation from getting an
education which can meet the urgent demands of our
times, I mean, the school must be delivered from the
classical languages ; then there will be air and space for all
that is now shoved into the background, among other

for those who happen to get good correspondents and who themselves
are not afraid of taking a little trouble.

things the modern foreign languages.[1]   But—even in the scanty time which is now at disposal, there is much that can be done differently and better than hitherto, and the more the teachers in modern languages show this, and the more they can keep out of the old jogtrot way, the more will their subject be respected, and the more willingness will there be to extend the time when future reforms demand it.

The *apportionment* of the time is poor.   When will people finally realize that everything cannot be learned at once ?   Many subjects, and with so few hours a week for each that the pupils forget what they have learned from one lesson to the next—that is a frightful waste of time.

No, learn a few things or one thing at a time, learn everything well and learn it to the end before passing on to the next.[2]   And especially with respect to languages, there can be no doubt that it is best to take them up one after the other, not side by side ; to every language that is taken up should be devoted many hours a week, and as a rule two years ought to be allowed to pass before commencing a new language ; then the first is so firmly rooted in the minds of the pupils that merely a very few lessons a week will be sufficient for keeping it up and extending it,[3] and then the

[1] But of course the mother-tongue too ; the study of nature, plants, animals, the human race ;, drawing and manual work, out-door life.

[2] An eloquent recommendation of this principle is to be found in v. Pfeil's previously mentioned work " Eins," but the same thought is also gaining ground elsewhere.

[3] Lessons which may be devoted not only to the language itself, but also to the acquisition of useful information in other departments as well ; why not learn the geography and history of France in French during the French lessons, etc.

two languages do not injure each other nearly as much as if they were studied side by side before the pupils have mastered either one of them.   As to the question at what age the children ought to begin to learn foreign languages, I dare not express any decided opinion ; I think I should be afraid to begin too early rather than too late ; first let the mother tongue have time enough to take a firm and lasting hold of the child's mind before other languages are admitted.

The worst canker in our school-system [1] is the *examinations*. Everything is arranged with a view to examinations ; the parents, the children, and unfortunately also a number of the teachers care for nothing but the results attained in the examinations ; the daily instruction is left to shift for itself, but the authorities will take ample care to guard against the least bit of negligence which might be shown by the examiners.

Examinations compel the teachers to lay undue stress on cramming.   " Cram may be defined as the accumulation of undigested facts and second-hand theories to be reproduced on paper, handed in to the examiner, and then forgotten for ever.   A crammed examinee differs from a crammed Strasburg goose in not assimilating his nutriment, and this would be a real advantage were it not that the process leaves him with a nauseated appetite, enfeebled reasoning powers, though abnormally enlarged memory, and a general distaste for disinterested study." [2]

[1] I am here speaking of the Danish school-system, but I have a suspicion that this canker is not unknown in other countries.
[2] A. H. Sayce, *Fortnightly Review*, June 1875.

Examinations cause the mental and physical ruin of many more young men than we can afford. As a test of what a young man is worth in life, an examination is without any value whatever; as a test of how much really valuable knowledge he has, it is not worth much ; and even as a test of how much he knows of what happens to be asked him on such an occasion, an examination is not nearly as reliable as people like to imagine.[1] And then examinations tend in so many ways to impede instruction which would otherwise be really profitable. The question " will that be required for the examination ? " is always, either consciously or unconsciously, present in the schoolroom ; it smothers the teacher's enthusiasm for communicating to his pupils what interests himself most; and it discourages the pupils' natural thirst for knowledge for its own sake. Just before the examinations, the whole school is seized with its yearly attack of its chronic examination-catarrh. In all departments, it is considered necessary to recapitulate for examinations ; for a couple of months, the pupils are transformed into mental ruminants; they receive no new mental sustenance whatever, but have to be satisfied with going through the whole year's work once or twice more at as rapid a pace as possible. The matter which they have been given does not become more savoury on being served again ; all the juice and strength, all that makes it tempting is lost, and nothing remains but what is toughest and dryest.

But even if there is much fault to be found with the

[1] A certificate from the school would be quite sufficient, if the instruction was under good control during the year.

system of examinations, yet it is not necessary to reform that before we can begin to improve the instruction. The examination requirements are not so great that we cannot meet them even if we do not from the very beginning plan all our instruction exactly with them in view. Although the chief stress in the examination may be laid on the translation and not on speaking, yet that is no reason why the latter should be entirely dispensed with. If by a *receptive* command of a foreign language is meant the ability to understand it, and by a *productive* command, the power to express oneself in the language, then I am fully convinced that anyone who merely concerns himself with the receptive side of it injures himself and acquires far less ability to understand it than if he had from the very beginning also aimed at a productive command of the language. Therefore our all round exercises will give our pupils at least just as much receptive knowledge of the language as is attained by the pupils of others ; and even if it is rather provoking for a teacher who has taken a good deal of trouble to teach his pupils to speak to see that this counts for little or nothing at the examination, he can comfort himself with a good conscience at any rate—beside the pleasure which he and his pupils have had in their daily work together.

Nor ought any consideration for examinations to prevent anyone from the best kind of recapitulation, which is, not to wait until the approach of examinations, when much that has been read is forgotten, so that the teacher has to be on the lookout all the time to make sure that the pupils understand everything, but to take it up while the matter is still fresh in the memory, so that it is not necessary to sound the pupils on every little point. Every chapter ought to be revised when it is finished, and every section or book ought to be gone over as a whole. Then the thoughts which were formerly occupied with details may be turned to the connected whole, and since the work can be conducted in the form of almost uninterrupted intelligent reading aloud, the pupils will be enabled to get approximately the same impression and the same enjoyment out of the matter read as a native gets.[1] If the reading has thus been gone over a section at a time at each natural break, it will be seen at the examination that these short revisions distributed throughout the year are more advantageous than a long, tedious recapitulation just before the examination, and besides the pupils have been kept fresh by reading something new up to the very end.

As the last possible impediment in the way of the reform method, I mentioned the *teachers*. Those times are now past when it was considered sufficient for a teacher of modern languages to have taken a degree in law or theology —to have studied Tacitus and Plato, and then by way of amusement to have read by himself a few volumes of *Revue des deux mondes* or some novels by Cherbuliez and Freytag. But even the younger generation of teachers who are better prepared will very often find that it is not so very easy to give good instruction in modern languages. It is a

---

[1] It has been previously suggested that various exercises in linguistic observation and classification may be given in connection with the revision, and that by means of such exercises the revision may be masked, as it were, and thus receive some of the fresh interest that attaches to something new.

shame how little is done to give high-school teachers opportunities for further improvement; they ought to have abundant access to courses in advanced work, but especially to many and liberal travelling scholarships, so that no conscientious teacher in foreign languages need do without a tolerably long stay among the people whose language he (she) teaches.   Poor pay and long hours, too, naturally lead to a teacher's looking merely to examination results.

But still I continue to hope that more and more teachers will avoid the old rut, and they will surely find that it pays to get out of it, even if, especially in the beginning, they have to expend more time and energy on their teaching, and on their preparation for every lesson, in order to meet the greater demands of the new methods. In Germany and the Scandinavian countries, exceedingly great efforts are being made to reform the instruction in languages ; in Norway, much of what has been recommended in this book has even been adopted in the official school-plans issued in 1897 ;[1] and fortunately the movement is also on the way to becoming strong in England.   If this book by a foreigner can contribute ever so little to the encouragement and support of English language-teachers in their zealous and able efforts to introduce newer and better methods, then I am glad to have been enabled in this manner to pay off a little of the debt that I owe to England and to many Englishmen.

In closing let me try to sum up.   The old-fashioned disconnected sentences proved to be a failure

[1] Similarly now in France.

for many reasons, and one reason was because there was nothing else to do with them but to translate them. They could arouse no interest; they could not even be read aloud intelligently; they could not be remembered in that definite form which they happened to have, so they could not be used as patterns for the construction of other sentences; therefore the rules of the grammar, which was committed to memory, came to play such an important part. It all became monotonous and lifeless.

Our method tries to employ many means which mutually support each other. The pronunciation is not learned merely by the teacher's saying the word and the pupils repeating it, or by the pupil's guessing at it through the orthography and the teacher's correcting him. The latter plan we reject entirely; the former, however, we use even to a larger extent than before, and we adopt in addition to it a rational description and indication of sounds. The improved pronunciation thus acquired also helps in a high degree in the acquiring of the other (signification) side of the language. Where formerly there was no other way of communicating the meaning of words but through translation, we have in addition thereto direct and indirect observation, explanations in the foreign language, etc. Where the pupils formerly had to commit to memory paradigms, rigmaroles and rules, which all had to be taken on faith, we let them investigate for themselves and thus get an insight into the construction of the language. And whereas formerly the only exercises were translation from the mother tongue into the foreign language, we now have a whole scale of varying exercises, namely : direct reproduction (repetition of the teacher's words ; answers to questions which are based directly upon the words of the book)—modified reproduction (repetition of sentences with changes of tense, person, etc. ; answers to freer questions ; asking of questions)—free reproduction (renarration) and finally —free production (letters, etc.). And since there is a sensible meaning in all that is read or said or done, the interest is awakened and held, and the instruction becomes not only varied, but what especially beseems living languages, it becomes in the deepest and best sense of the word really *living*